International Courts and Environmental Protection

International environmental law has come of age, yet the global environment continues to deteriorate. The challenge of the twenty-first century is to reverse this process by ensuring that governments comply fully with their obligations, and progressively assume stricter duties to preserve the environment. This book is the first comprehensive examination of international environmental litigation. Analysing the spectrum of adjudicative bodies that are engaged in the resolution of environmental disputes, it offers a reappraisal of their relevance in contemporary contexts. The book critiques the contribution that arbitral awards and judicial decisions have made to the development of environmental law, and considers the looming challenges for international litigation. With its unique combination of scholarly analysis and practical discussion, this work is especially relevant to an era in which environmental matters are increasingly being brought before international jurisdictions, and will be of great interest to students and scholars engaged with this vital field.

TIM STEPHENS is a Senior Lecturer at the Faculty of Law, University of Sydney. He specialises in international environmental law, dispute settlement, and the law of the sea. He holds a doctorate in law from the University of Sydney, and an M.Phil. in geography from the University of Cambridge.

CAMBRIDGE STUDIES IN INTERNATIONAL AND COMPARATIVE LAW

Established in 1946, this series produces high quality scholarship in the fields of public and private international law and comparative law. Although these are distinct legal sub-disciplines, developments since 1946 confirm their interrelation.

Comparative law is increasingly used as a tool in the making of law at national, regional and international levels. Private international law is now often affected by international conventions, and the issues faced by classical conflicts rules are frequently dealt with by substantive harmonisation of law under international auspices. Mixed international arbitrations, especially those involving state economic activity, raise mixed questions of public and private international law, while in many fields (such as the protection of human rights and democratic standards, investment guarantees and international criminal law) international and national systems interact. National constitutional arrangements relating to 'foreign affairs', and to the implementation of international norms, are a focus of attention.

The Board welcomes works of a theoretical or interdisciplinary character, and those focusing on the new approaches to international or comparative law or conflicts of law. Studies of particular institutions or problems are equally welcome, as are translations of the best work published in other languages.

International Courts and Environmental Protection

Tim Stephens
University of Sydney

CAMBRIDGE
UNIVERSITY PRESS

CAMBRIDGE UNIVERSITY PRESS
Cambridge, New York, Melbourne, Madrid, Cape Town, Singapore,
São Paulo, Delhi

Cambridge University Press
The Edinburgh Building, Cambridge CB2 8RU, UK

Published in the United States of America by Cambridge University Press, New York

www.cambridge.org
Information on this title: www.cambridge.org/9780521881227

First published 2009

Printed in the United Kingdom at the University Press, Cambridge

A catalogue record for this publication is available from the British Library

Library of Congress Cataloguing in Publication data
Stephens, Timothy.
International courts and environmental protection / Tim Stephens.
p. cm. — (Cambridge studies in international and comparative law)
Includes bibliographical references and index.
ISBN 978-0-521-88122-7 (hardback)
1. Environmental law, International—Cases. I. Title. II. Series.
K3585.S74 2009
344.04′6—dc22 2008049116

ISBN 978-0-521-88122-7 hardback

Contents

Foreword

Modern legal regimes for the protection and management of the environment have developed rapidly over the past forty years. At the national level, with increasing pressures from development activity and population growth, environmental law became a major preoccupation for developed countries in the 1970s and 1980s and, in the past two decades, for developing countries and countries with economies in transition. Regionally and globally the generation of environmental legal instruments, addressing a vast array of environmental and natural resource issues, has been increasingly motivated by the imperative of environmental, social/cultural, and economic sustainability, with one of the high points being the 1992 United Nations Conference on Environment and Development, and two of its products, Agenda 21 and the Rio Declaration on Environment and Development. States have been encouraged, indeed obliged by necessity, to address by legal means the causes and effects of pollution, resource depletion, climate change, and protection of ecologically significant areas within their jurisdictions, across political boundaries, and beyond national jurisdictions. The increasing complexity of the area is reflected in the number and scope of multilateral environmental agreements and the establishment of associated governance regimes.

There has been an inevitable need to resolve disputes concerning the operation of the growing body of international environmental law and its supporting institutions. This book explores the rich state practice in this area, with a particular focus on the various judicial institutions, tribunals, and related bodies resolving environmental disputes at the international level, the best-known being the International Court of

Justice, the Permanent Court of Arbitration, and the International Tribunal for the Law of the Sea. The substantial case law being built by these tribunals is recorded, with developing principles analysed in considerable detail. While other writers have examined the decisions of these bodies discretely, this book represents the first comprehensive analysis of the jurisprudence through the lens of global environmental governance and the imperative of sustainable ecological development.

The fact that a book on international courts and environmental protection can now be written is an indication that international environmental law, though still fragmented and incomplete, has matured into a distinct and increasingly coherent area of law. It may also be noted that the higher level of litigation activity in recent years means that it is possible for a new generation of lawyers in the field to make the justifiable claim to be practitioners of international environmental law.

While this book brings together a remarkable range of learning in relation to new and established tribunals, it also examines the future of international environmental litigation, giving a realistic assessment of the parameters that hinder international courts from taking a more judicially active approach. It also canvasses the introduction of a broad-based and accessible International Court for the Environment, but leaves that development in the realm of tantalising potential.

Ultimately, the value of this book lies in drawing attention to the fundamental importance of judicial decision-making bodies and their work within the broad landscape of global environmental politics. In doing so, it also provides a challenge for future analysis: how structures for environmental governance can be further strengthened, such as through an overarching global environmental agreement consolidating and extending the current fragmented environmental treaty framework. Such an instrument could in turn form the basis for an international environmental institution to ensure that the obligations under that instrument, and all major multilateral environmental agreements, are complied with and provide a strong global voice for the environment.

A wide range of environmental issues and conflicts over natural resources is likely to arise in the future, as the world's ecosystems and its human communities are further affected by environmental degradation. This may well mean that there will be increasing pressure to establish flexible, approachable, accessible, and informal dispute resolution mechanisms on a regional and international basis (such as an environmental ombudsman). This is especially the case in relation to climate change and innovative mechanisms for the reduction of greenhouse gas emissions, current and emerging conflicts over water allocation and use, and the pressure for larger and more connected protected areas in terrestrial and marine environments. Dealing with conflict in all of these fields is also in large measure a challenge of respecting human rights, especially the right to a clean and healthy environment, and the book makes clear that human rights courts and tribunals are increasingly at the forefront of international environmental dispute settlement.

By coherently bringing together the body of knowledge on the resolution of international disputes concerning environmental protection and the conservation and exploitation of natural resources, this work forms a solid basis for the contemplation and analysis of future dispute resolution possibilities. The work is likely to become a benchmark within this area, and to be a standard reference of use and interest to international legal practitioners, professors, and students of international environmental and natural resources law, legislators, and political advisers around the world.

Ben Boer
Professor in Environmental Law,
University of Sydney
Co-Director, IUCN Academy of Environmental
Law and Visiting Professor,
University of Ottawa

Acknowledgements

I am indebted to many individuals and institutions for their assistance and support during the writing of this book. Primary thanks are extended to my colleagues Professor Donald Rothwell (now at the Australian National University) and Professor Emeritus Ivan Shearer, who offered me guidance from the conception to completion of the work, and to Professor Ben Boer who has greatly inspired my interest in environmental law. I am grateful also for the considerable research assistance provided by Gemma Namey when the book was nearing completion. Thanks are also due to Finola O'Sullivan, Richard Woodham, Paul Stevens, Joanna Breeze and Hilary Scannell at Cambridge University Press for guiding the manuscript through the production process, and to Harry Stephens and Philip Stickler (Cartographer, Department of Geography, University of Cambridge) for drawing the maps that appear in the book.

The decision to embark on this work was made in 2003 when I was a visiting fellow at the Lauterpacht Research Centre for International Law at the University of Cambridge. Thanks are extended to Professor James Crawford and Dr Roger O'Keefe for encouraging my involvement in the life of the Centre. I am grateful also to Dr Alex Mills of the Faculty of Law at the University of Cambridge who later read and commented upon significant parts of the text. My visit to Cambridge would not have been possible without generous financial support from the University of Sydney, through the H. S. Carslaw Memorial Scholarship. When completing the manuscript I was fortunate to receive further support from the University of Sydney through a writing fellowship awarded by the

Research Institute for Humanities and the Social Sciences, and a grant from the Faculty of Law Legal Scholarship Support Fund.

The book draws upon a doctoral dissertation supervised by Professor Rothwell and Professor Shearer and examined by Professor David Freestone, Professor Philippe Sands, and Professor David VanderZwaag. My supervisors and examiners were exceptionally generous in providing detailed and constructive comments that were invaluable in finalising the manuscript for publication. It must also be acknowledged that parts of the book draw upon and develop material that has been published previously. Sections of chapter 4 appeared in Tim Stephens, 'The Limits of Adjudication in International Environmental Law: Another Perspective on the Southern Bluefin Tuna Case' (2004) 19 *IJMCL* 173, parts of chapter 7 in Tim Stephens, 'A Paper Umbrella Which Dissolves in the Rain? Implications of the Southern Bluefin Tuna Case' (2001) 6 *APJEL* 297 and parts of chapter 10 in Tim Stephens, 'Multiple International Courts and the "Fragmentation" of International Environmental Law' (2006) 25 *AustYBIL* 227.

My immediate and extended family have provided immense assistance throughout every step of the research and writing process. My parents, Harry Stephens and Dr Tanya Stephens, first inspired in me a love and respect for the natural world and have extended every encouragement and support throughout my academic career. However, my greatest expression of gratitude is reserved for my wife Anna-Maria, without whom I could never have commenced or completed this book. The book is dedicated to our children, Edward and Matilda.

The law as stated in the text is current as at 1 December 2007.

Tables

Figures

Abbreviations

Aarhus Convention	1998 Convention on Access to Information Public Participation and Decision-Making and Access to Justice in Environmental Matters
ACHR	1969 American Convention on Human Rights
AILJ	*Australian International Law Journal*
AJIL	*American Journal of International Law*
ALJ	*Australian Law Journal*
AnnFDDI	*Annuaire Français de Droit International*
AnnRevEnvRes	*Annual Review of Environment and Resources*
AnnSICL	*Annual Survey of International and Comparative Law*
APJEL	*Asia Pacific Journal of Environmental Law*
ATS	Australian Treaties Series
AustDRJ	*Australian Dispute Resolution Journal*
AustYBIL	*Australian Year Book of International Law*
BCICLR	*Boston College International and Comparative Law Review*
Bevans	*Treaties and Other International Agreements of the United States of America (1776–1949)*
BULR	*Boston University Law Review*
BYBIL	*British Yearbook of International Law*
CACJ	Central American Court of Justice
CalLR	*California Law Review*
CanTS	Canada Treaty Series
CanYBIL	*Canadian Year Book of International Law*

CCAMLR	Convention on the Conservation of Antarctic Marine Living Resources
CCSBT	1993 Convention for the Conservation of Southern Bluefin Tuna
C-CCSBT	Commission for the Conservation of Southern Bluefin Tuna
CEC	Commission for Environmental Cooperation
CFI	Court of First Instance of the Court of Justice of the European Communities
ChiJIL	*Chicago Journal of International Law*
ChineseJIL	*Chinese Journal of International Law*
CITES	1973 Convention on International Trade in Endangered Species of Wild Fauna and Flora
ColoJIELP	*Colorado Journal of International Environmental Law and Policy*
ColumJEL	*Columbia Journal of Environmental Law*
ColumJTL	*Columbia Journal of Transnational Law*
Comp PolStud	*Comparative Political Studies*
ConTS	Consolidated Treaty Series
CornellILJ	*Cornell International Law Journal*
CSD	Commission on Sustainable Development
CTE	Committee on Trade and Environment
CUS	Treaties and Agreements Affecting Canada in force between His Britannic Majesty and the United States of America (1814–1925)
DenJILP	*Denver Journal of International Law and Policy*
DSB	World Trade Organization Dispute Settlement Body
DSU	1994 Understanding on Rules and Procedures Governing the Settlement of Disputes in the World Trade Organization
DukeLJ	*Duke Law Journal*
EC	European Communities
ECHR	1950 Convention for the Protection of Human Rights and Fundamental Freedoms
ECJ	Court of Justice of the European Communities
ECR	European Court Reports
ECtHR	European Court of Human Rights
EELR	*European Environmental Law Review*
EEZ	exclusive economic zone

EFZ	exclusive fishing zone
EHRR	*European Human Rights Reports*
EIA	environmental impact assessment
EJIL	*European Journal of International Law*
ELQ	*Ecology Law Quarterly*
EnvLR	*Environmental Law Reporter*
EPL	*Environmental Policy and Law*
EPLJ	*Environmental and Planning Law Journal*
ETS	European Treaty Series
FAO	United Nations Food and Agriculture Organisation
FinnYBIL	*Finnish Year Book of International Law*
FordhamELJ	*Fordham Environmental Law Journal*
FordhamILJ	*Fordham International Law Journal*
GA	United Nations General Assembly
GaLR	*Georgia Law Review*
GAOR	United Nations General Assembly Official Records
GATT	General Agreement on Tariffs and Trade
GeoIELR	*Georgetown International Environmental Law Review*
GeoWashJIL Econ	*George Washington Journal of International Law and Economics*
GEP	*Global Environmental Politics*
GerYBIL	*German Year Book of International Law*
GESAMP	Joint Group of Experts on the Scientific Aspects of Marine Environmental Protection
GM	genetically modified
GMO	genetically modified organism
Hague Convention	1899 International Convention for the Pacific Settlement of International Disputes
HarvELR	*Harvard Environmental Law Review*
HarvILJ	*Harvard International Law Journal*
HastingsICLR	*Hastings International and Comparative Law Review*
HosfraLR	*Hosfra Law Review*
IAComHR	Inter-American Commission on Human Rights
ICC	International Criminal Court
ICCPR	1966 International Covenant on Civil and Political Rights
ICE	International Court for the Environment (proposed)

ICEF	International Court for the Environment Foundation
ICJ	International Court of Justice
ICJ Pleadings	International Court of Justice Pleadings
ICJ Rep	International Court of Justice Reports
ICLQ	*International and Comparative Law Quarterly*
IELR	*International Environmental Law Reports*
IJC	International Joint Commission
IJMCL	International Journal of Marine and Coastal Law
ILC	International Law Commission
ILM	International Legal Materials
ILR	International Law Reports
IndJGLS	*Indiana Journal of Global Legal Studies*
IntOrg	*International Organization*
IowaLR	*Iowa Law Review*
ItalYBIL	*Italian Year Book of International Law*
ITLOS	International Tribunal for the Law of the Sea
IUU	illegal, unregulated, and unreported
JEL	*Journal of Environmental Law*
JIEconL	*Journal of International Economic Law*
JIWLP	*Journal of International Wildlife Law and Policy*
JLS	*Journal of Legal Studies*
LJIL	*Leiden Journal of International Law*
LNTS	League of Nations Treaty Series
LOS Convention	1982 United Nations Convention on the Law of the Sea
LPICT	*The Law and Practice of International Courts and Tribunals*
MaxPlanckYBUNL	*Max Planck Year Book of United Nations Law*
Madrid Protocol	1991 Protocol on Environmental Protection to the Antarctic Treaty
McGillLJ	*McGill Law Journal*
MichJIL	*Michigan Journal of International Law*
MinnJGT	*Minnesota Journal of Global Trade*
MJIL	*Melbourne Journal of International Law*
MMPA	Marine Mammal Protection Act 1972
Moore	John Bassett Moore, *History and Digest of the International Arbitrations to which the United States has been a Party* (1898) vols. I–VI
MULR	*Melbourne University Law Review*

NAAEC	1993 North American Agreement on Environmental Cooperation
NAFTA	1992 North American Free Trade Agreement
NatResJ	*Natural Resources Journal*
NCP	non-compliance procedure
NethYBIL	*Netherlands Year Book of International Law*
NGO	non-governmental organisation
NILR	*Netherlands International Law Review*
NordicJIL	*Nordic Journal of International Law*
NYUELJ	*New York University Environmental Law Journal*
NYUJILP	*New York University Journal of International Law and Politics*
NZJPIL	*New Zealand Journal of Public International Law*
OAS	Organisation of American States
OAS TS	Organisation of American States Treaty Series
OCM	*Ocean and Coastal Management*
OhioStJDR	*Ohio State Journal on Dispute Resolution*
OJ	Official Journal of the European Communities
OrLR	*Oregon Law Review*
OSPAR Convention	1992 Convention for the Protection of the Marine Environment of the North-East Atlantic
PCA	Permanent Court of Arbitration
PCIJ	Permanent Court of International Justice
PITS	Pacific Islands Treaty Series
PLR	*Public Law Review*
ProcASIL	*Proceedings of the American Society of International Law*
Ramsar Convention	1971 Convention on Wetlands of International Importance, Especially as Waterfowl Habitat
RDC	*Recueil des Cours, Académie de droit international de la Haye*
RECIEL	*Review of European Community and International Environmental Law*
RevAPS	*Review of Asian and Pacific Studies*
RIAA	*United Nations Reports of International Arbitral Awards*
Rio Declaration	1992 United Nations Declaration on Environment and Development
SDL&P	*Sustainable Development Law and Policy*
SICA	Central American Integration System
SingYBIL	*Singapore Year Book of International Law*

SLR	*Sydney Law Review*
SPS Agreement	Sanitary and Phytosanitary Agreement
Stockholm Declaration	1972 Declaration of the United Nations Conference on the Human Environment
SyracuseJIL&Com	*Syracuse Journal of International Law and Commerce*
TAC	total allowable catch
TempleICLJ	*Temple International and Comparative Law Journal*
TexILJ	*Texas International Law Journal*
TIAS	United States Treaties and Other International Acts Series
TouroJTL	*Touro Journal of Transnational Law*
TransL&CP	*Transnational Law and Contemporary Problems*
TulELJ	*Tulane Environmental Law Journal*
UKTS	United Kingdom Treaty Series
UNCED	United Nations Conference on Environment and Development
UNEP	United Nations Environment Programme
UNSCEAR	United Nations Scientific Committee on the Effects of Atomic Radiation
UNSWLJ	University of New South Wales Law Journal
UNTS	United Nations Treaty Series
UPaJIEcon	*University of Pennsylvania Journal of International Economic Law*
UPaLR	*University of Pennsylvania Law Review*
URichLR	*University of Richmond Law Review*
UST	United States Treaties and Other International Agreements
VaELJ	*Virginia Environmental Law Journal*
VaJIL	*Virginia Journal of International Law*
VandJTL	*Vanderbilt Journal of Transnational Law*
VCLT	1969 Vienna Convention on the Law of Treaties
VUWLR	*Victoria University of Wellington Law Review*
WALR	*Western Australia Law Review*
WCED	World Commission on Environment and Development
WisILJ	*Wisconsin International Law Journal*
WisLR	*Wisconsin Law Review*
WTAM	*World Trade and Arbitration Materials*
WTO	World Trade Organization
WTR	*World Trade Review*

YaleHR&DevLJ	*Yale Human Rights and Development Law Journal*
YaleJIL	*Yale Journal of International Law*
YaleLJ	*Yale Law Journal*
YBEuroEL	*Yearbook of European Environmental Law*
YBEuroL	*Yearbook of European Law*
YIEL	*Yearbook of International Environmental Law*

Table of cases

Table of treaties and other international instruments

1783 Definitive Treaty of Peace, opened for signature 3 September 1783, 12 Bevans 8 (entered into force 12 May 1784)

1815 Convention to Regulate the Commerce Between the Territories of the United States and Great Britain, opened for signature 3 July 1815, 12 Bevans 49 (entered into force 3 July 1815)

1866 Additional Act to the Delimitation Treaties Concluded on 2 December 1856, 14 April 1862 and 26 May 1866, opened for signature 26 May 1866, 132 ConTS 359 (entered into force 14 July 1866)

France–Spain Treaty of Delimitation, opened for signature 26 May 1866, 132 ConTS 359 (entered into force 14 July 1866)

1867 Russia–United States Convention Ceding Alaska, opened for signature 29 March 1867, 11 Bevans 1216 (entered into force 20 June 1867)

1892 Great Britain–United States Treaty Submitting to Arbitration the Questions Relating to Seal Fisheries in the Bering Sea, opened for signature 29 February 1892, 12 Bevans 220 (entered into force 7 May 1892)

1899 International Convention for the Pacific Settlement of International Disputes, opened for signature 29 July 1899, 1901 UKTS 9 (entered into force 4 September 1900) (Hague Convention)

1907 International Convention for the Pacific Settlement of International Disputes, opened for signature 18 October 1907, 54 LNTS 435 (entered into force 22 January 1910)

1909 Special Agreement for the Submission of Questions Relating to Fisheries on the North Atlantic Coast, opened for signature 27 January 1909, 12 Bevans 328 (entered into force 5 March 1909)

Treaty Relating to the Boundary Waters and Questions Arising Along the Boundary Between the United States and Canada, opened for signature 11 January 1909, [1909] CUS 312

1911 Convention Respecting Measures for the Preservation and Protection of Fur Seals in the North Pacific Ocean, opened for signature 7 February 1911, 12 Bevans 353 (entered into force 7 July 1911)

1928 General Act for the Pacific Settlement of Disputes, opened for signature 26 September 1928, 93 LNTS 2123 (entered into force 26 September 1928)

1933 Convention Relative to the Preservation of Fauna and Flora in their Natural State, opened for signature 8 November 1933, 172 LNTS 241 (entered into force 14 January 1936)

1935 Convention for the Settlement of Difficulties Arising from the Operation of the Smelter at Trail between Great Britain and the United States, opened for signature 15 April 1935, 162 LNTS 73 (entered into force 15 April 1935)

1946 International Convention for the Regulation of Whaling, opened for signature 2 December 1946, 161 UNTS 72 (entered into force 10 November 1948)

1947 General Agreement on Tariffs and Trade, opened for signature 30 October 1947, 55 UNTS 187 (in force provisionally under the Protocol of Application, 55 UNTS 308)

1948 Universal Declaration of Human Rights, GA Res. 217A(III), UN Doc. A/810 (1948)

1950 Convention for the Protection of Human Rights and Fundamental Freedoms, opened for signature 4 November 1950, 213 UNTS 221 (entered into force 3 September 1953) as amended by Protocol no. 11, opened for signature 11 May 1994, (1994) ETS 155 (entered into force 1 November 1998)

1956 Arbitral Compromis on the Interpretation of the Treaty of Bayonne of 26 May 1866 and Additional Act of the Same Date

Concerning the Utilisation of the Waters of Lake Lanoux, opened for signature 19 May 1956, reprinted in 12 *RIAA* 285 (entered into force 19 November 1956)

1957 Treaty Establishing the European Atomic Energy Authority, opened for signature 25 March 1957, 298 UNTS 167 (entered into force 1 January 1958)

1959 Antarctic Treaty, opened for signature 1 December 1959, 402 UNTS 71 (entered into force 23 June 1961)

1963 Protocol to the Convention for the Protection of Human Rights and Fundamental Freedoms, opened for signature 6 May 1963, 213 UNTS 262 (entered into force 18 May 1954)

Agreement Concerning the International Commission for the Protection of the Rhine Against Pollution, opened for signature 29 April 1963, 994 UNTS 3 (entered into force 1 May 1965)

Treaty Banning Nuclear Weapons Tests in the Atmosphere, in Outer Space and under Water, opened for signature 5 August 1963, 480 UNTS 43 (entered into force 10 October 1963)

1965 Canada – United States, Agreement Concerning the Establishment of an International Arbitral Tribunal to Dispose of United States Claims Relating to the Gut Dam, opened for signature 25 March 1965, [1966] CanTS 22 (entered into force 11 October 1966)

1966 International Covenant on Civil and Political Rights, opened for signature 16 December 1966, 999 UNTS 171 (entered into force 23 March 1976)

1966 Optional Protocol to the International Covenant on Civil and Political Rights, opened for signature 16 December 1966, 999 UNTS 302 (entered into force 23 March 1976)

1968 Canada – United States, Exchange of Notes Concerning the Lake Ontario Claims Tribunal and Lump Sum Settlement of Disputes, 1 October 1968, (1969) VII *CanYBIL* 316, 18 November 1968, 19 UST 7863

1969 American Convention on Human Rights, opened for signature 22 November 1969, 1144 UNTS 123 (entered into force 18 July 1978)

Agreement for Cooperation in Dealing with Pollution of the North Sea by Oil and Other Harmful Substances, opened for signature 9 June 1969, 704 UNTS 3 (entered into force 9 August 1969)

Vienna Convention on the Law of Treaties, opened for signature 23 May 1969, 1155 UNTS 332 (entered into force 27 January 1980)

1971 Convention on Wetlands of International Importance, Especially as Waterfowl Habitat, opened for signature 2 February 1971, 996 UNTS 245 (entered into force 21 December 1975) (Ramsar Convention)

1972 Convention on the Prevention of Marine Pollution by Dumping of Wastes and Other Materials, opened for signature 29 December 1972, 1046 UNTS 120 (entered into force 30 August 1975)

Declaration of the United Nations Conference on the Human Environment, UN Doc. A/CONF.48/14/Rev. 1 (1973), (1972) 11 ILM 1416 (Stockholm Declaration)

1973 Convention on International Trade in Endangered Species of Wild Fauna and Flora, opened for signature 3 March 1973, 993 UNTS 243 (entered into force 1 July 1975) (CITES)

International Convention for the Prevention of Pollution from Ships, opened for signature 2 November 1973, (1973) 12 ILM 1319 (not in force) (as amended and given effect by the Protocol of 1978 Relating to the International Convention for the Prevention of Pollution from Ships, opened for signature 17 February 1978, (1978) 17 ILM 246 (entered into force 2 October 1983))

1974 Nordic Convention on the Protection of the Environment, opened for signature 19 February 1974, (1974) 13 ILM 511 (entered into force 5 October 1976)

1975 Statute of the River Uruguay, opened for signature 26 February 1975, 1295 UNTS 340 (entered into force 18 September 1976)

1976 Convention for the Protection of the Mediterranean Sea Against Pollution, opened for signature 16 February 1976, 1102 UNTS 44 (entered into force 12 February 1978)

Convention on the Protection of the Rhine Against Pollution by Chlorides, opened for signature 3 December 1976, (1977) 16 ILM 265 (entered into force 5 July 1985)

1977 Treaty Concerning the Construction and Operation of the Gabčíkovo-Nagymaros System of Locks, opened for signature 16 September 1977, (1993) 32 ILM 1247 (entered into force 30 June 1978)

1978 Protocol Relating to the 1973 International Convention for the Prevention of Pollution from Ships, opened for signature 17 February 1978, 1340 UNTS 61 (entered into force 2 October 1983)

Convention on Future Multilateral Cooperation in the Northwest Atlantic Fisheries, opened for signature 24 October 1978, 1135 UNTS 369 (entered into force 1 January 1979)

1979 Convention on Long-Range Transboundary Air Pollution, opened for signature 13 November 1979, 1302 UNTS 218 (entered into force 16 March 1983)

Convention on the Conservation of Migratory Species of Wild Animals, opened for signature 23 June 1979, (1980) 19 ILM 15 (entered into force 1 November 1983)

1980 Convention on the Conservation of Antarctic Marine Living Resources, opened for signature 20 May 1980, 1329 UNTS 48 (entered into force 7 April 1982) (CCAMLR)

Convention on the Physical Protection of Nuclear Material, opened for signature 3 March 1980, 1456 UNTS 124 (entered into force 8 February 1987)

1982 African Charter on Human and Peoples' Rights, opened for signature 27 June 1981, (1982) 21 ILM 58 (entered into force 21 October 1986)

Manila Declaration on the Peaceful Settlement of International Disputes, GA Res. 37/10, UN Doc. A/RES/37/10 (1982)

United Nations Convention on the Law of the Sea, opened for signature 10 December 1982, 1833 UNTS 397 (entered into force 16 November 1994) (LOS Convention)

World Charter for Nature, GA Res. 37/7, UN Doc. A/37/51 (1982)

1985 South Pacific Nuclear Free Zone Treaty, opened for signature 6 August 1985, (1985) 24 ILM 1442 (entered into force 11 December 1986)

Vienna Convention for the Protection of the Ozone Layer, opened for signature 22 March 1985, 1513 UNTS 324 (entered into force 22 September 1988)

1986 Protocol I to the South Pacific Nuclear Free Zone Treaty, opened for signature 8 August 1986, [1986] ATS 32 (entered into force 20 September 1996)

1987 Montreal Protocol on Substances that Deplete the Ozone Layer, opened for signature 16 September 1987, 1522 UNTS 29 (entered into force 1 January 1989)

1988 Additional Protocol to the American Convention on Human Rights in the Area of Economic, Social and Cultural Rights, opened for signature 17 November 1988, OAS TS no. 69 (1988) (entered into force 16 November 1999)

Convention on the Regulation of Antarctic Mineral Resource Activities, opened for signature 2 June 1988, (1988) 27 ILM 868 (not in force)

1989 Hague Declaration on the Environment (1989) 28 ILM 1308

Basel Convention on the Control of Transboundary Movements of Hazardous Wastes and Their Disposal, opened for signature 22 March 1989, 1673 UNTS 126 (entered into force 24 May 1992)

Convention on the Rights of the Child, opened for signature 20 November 1989, 1577 UNTS 3 (entered into force 2 November 1990)

1991 Convention on Environmental Impact Assessment in a Transboundary Context, opened for signature 25 February 1991, (1991) 30 ILM 802 (entered into force 10 September 1997)

Protocol on Environmental Protection to the Antarctic Treaty, opened for signature 4 October 1991, (1991) 30 ILM 1461 (entered into force 14 January 1998) (Madrid Protocol)

1992 Agenda 21, UN Doc. A/CONF.151/26/Rev. 1 (1992)

Agreement on the Statute of the Central American Court of Justice, opened for signature 10 December 1992, (1995) 34 ILM 921 (entered into force 2 February 1994)
Convention for the Protection of the Marine Environment of the North-East Atlantic, opened for signature 22 September 1992, (1992) 32 ILM 1069 (entered into force 25 March 1998) (OSPAR Convention)

Convention on Biological Diversity, opened for signature 5 June 1992, 1760 UNTS 143 (entered into force 29 December 1993)

Convention on the Protection and Use of Transboundary Waters and International Lakes, opened for signature 17 March 1992, (1992) 31 ILM 1312 (entered into force 6 October 1996)

Niue Treaty on Cooperation in Fisheries Surveillance and Law Enforcement in the South Pacific Region, opened for signature 9 July 1992, (1993) 32 ILM 136 (entered into force 20 May 1993)

UNECE Convention on the Transboundary Effects of Industrial Accidents, opened for signature 17 March 1992, (1992) 31 ILM 1330 (entered into force 19 April 2000)

United Nations Declaration on Environment and Development, UN Doc. A/CONF.151/5/Rev. 1 (1992) (Rio Declaration)

United Nations Framework Convention on Climate Change, opened for signature 9 May 1992, 1771 UNTS 165 (entered into force 21 March 1994)

North American Free Trade Agreement, opened for signature 17 December 1992, (1993) 32 ILM 289 and (1993) 32 ILM 605 (entered into force 1 January 1994)

1993 Convention for the Conservation of Southern Bluefin Tuna, opened for signature 10 May 1993, 1819 UNTS 359 (entered into force 20 May 1994)

FAO Agreement to Promote Compliance with International Conservation and Management Measures by Fishing Vessels on the High Seas, opened for signature 24 November 1993, (1993) 33 ILM 968 (entered into force 1 October 2004)

North American Agreement on Environmental Cooperation, opened for signature 8 September 1993, (1993) 32 ILM 1480 (entered into force 1 January 1994)

Settlement of the Case in the ICJ Concerning Certain Phosphate Lands in Nauru, opened for signature 10 August 1993, (1993) 32 ILM 1471 (entered into force 10 August 1993)

Special Agreement between the Republic of Hungary and the Slovak Republic for Submission to the International Court of Justice of the Differences between them concerning the Gabčíkovo-Nagymaros Project, opened for signature 7 April 1993, (1993) 32 ILM 1293 (entered into force 28 June 1993)

Convention on Civil Liability for Damage Resulting from Activities Dangerous to the Environment, opened for signature 21 June 1993, (1993) 32 ILM 1228 (not in force)

1994 Convention for the Conservation and Management of Pollock Resources in the Central Bering Sea, opened for signature 16 June 1994, (1994) 34 ILM 67 (entered into force 8 December 1995)

Convention to Combat Desertification in those Countries Experiencing Serious Drought and/or Desertification, Particularly in Africa, opened for signature 14 October 1994, 1954 UNTS 108 (entered into force 26 December 1996)

GATT Ministerial Decision on Trade and Environment (1994), (1994) 33 ILM 1267

General Agreement on Tariffs and Trade (Marrakesh Agreement Establishing the World Trade Organization, opened for signature 15 April 1994, 1869 UNTS 190, annex 1A (entered into force 1 January 1995))

Marrakesh Agreement Establishing the World Trade Organization, opened for signature 15 April 1994, 1869 UNTS 190 (entered into force 1 January 1995)

Protocol to the 1979 Convention on Long Range Transboundary Air Pollution on Further Reduction of Sulphur

Emissions, opened for signature 14 June 1994, (1998) 33 ILM 1540 (entered into force 5 August 1998)

Sanitary and Phytosanitary Agreement (Marrakesh Agreement Establishing the World Trade Organization, opened for signature 15 April 1994, 1869 UNTS 190, annex 1A (entered into force 1 January 1995))

Understanding on Rules and Procedures Governing the Settlement of Disputes in the WTO (Marrakesh Agreement Establishing the World Trade Organisation, opened for signature 15 April 1994, 1869 UNTS 190 annex 2) (entered into force 1 January 1995)

1995 Agreement for the Implementation of the Provisions of the United Nations Convention on the Law of the Sea of 10 December 1982 Relating to the Conservation and Management of Straddling Fish Stocks and Highly Migratory Fish Stocks, opened for signature 4 December 1995, (1995) 34 ILM 1542 (entered into force 11 December 2001)

Agreement on Cooperation for Sustainable Development of the Mekong River Basin, opened for signature 5 April 1995, (1995) 34 ILM 864 (entered into force 5 April 1995)

1996 Convention on Cooperation for the Protection and Sustainable Use of the Danube, opened for signature 29 June 1994, (1996) 19 *International Environment Reporter* 997 (entered into force 22 October 1998)

Protocol to the Convention on the Prevention of Marine Pollution by Dumping of Wastes and Other Matter, opened for signature 7 November 1996, (1997) 36 ILM 1 (not in force)

1997 Kyoto Protocol to the United Nations Framework Convention on Climate Change, opened for signature 11 December 1997, (1998) 37 ILM 22 (entered into force 16 February 2005)

Treaty of Amsterdam Amending the Treaty on European Union, the Treaties Establishing the European Communities and Certain Related Acts, opened for signature 2 October 1997, (1998) 37 ILM 56 (entered into force 1 May 1999)

United Nations Convention on the Law of Non-Navigational Uses of International Watercourses, opened for signature 21 May 1997, (1997) 36 ILM 700 (not in force)

1998 Additional Protocol to the American Convention on Human Rights in the Area of Economic, Social and Cultural Rights, opened for signature 17 November 1998, [1998] OAS TS 69 (entered into force 16 November 1999)

Convention on the Protection of the Environment through Criminal Law, opened for signature 11 April 1998, (1999) 38 ILM 259 (not in force)

Convention on Access to Information, Public Participation and Decision-Making and Access to Justice in Environmental Matters, opened for signature 25 June 1998, (1999) 38 ILM 517 (entered into force 30 October 2001) (Aarhus Convention)

Convention on the Protection of the Rhine, opened for signature 22 January 1998, OJ L289 (entered into force 16 November 2000)

Rome Statute of the International Criminal Court, opened for signature 17 July 1998, 2187 UNTS 90 (entered into force 1 July 2002)

1999 Protocol on Water and Health to the 1992 Convention on the Protection and Use of Transboundary Watercourses and International Lakes, opened for signature 17 June 1999 (1999) 38 ILM 1708 (entered into force 4 August 2005)

2000 Cartegena Protocol on Biosafety to the Convention on Biological Diversity, opened for signature 29 June 2000, (2000) 39 ILM 1027 (entered into force 11 September 2003)

Convention on the Conservation and Management of Highly Migratory Fish Stocks in the Western and Central Pacific Ocean, opened for signature 5 September 2000, (2001) 40 ILM 277 (entered into force June 2004)

2001 Articles on Responsibility of States for Internationally Wrongful Acts, Report of the International Law Commission, 53rd Session, UN Doc. A/56/10 (2001) (noted in GA Res. 56/83, UN Doc. A/RES/56/83 (2001))

Draft Articles on the Prevention of Transboundary Harm from Hazardous Activities, Report of the International Law Commission, 53rd Session, UN Doc. A/56/10 (2001)

Convention on the Conservation and Management of Fishery Resources in the South-East Atlantic Ocean, opened for signature 20 April 2001, (2002) 41 ILM 257 (entered into force 13 April 2003)

2002 ASEAN Agreement on Transboundary Haze Pollution, opened for signature 20 June 2002 (available at www.aseansec.org/pdf/agr_haze.pdf) (entered into force 25 November 2003)

Consolidated Version of the Treaty Establishing the European Community, [2002] OJ C 325, 33

Draft Comprehensive Convention on Terrorism, Report of the Ad Hoc Committee Established by General Assembly Resolution 51/210 of 17 December 1996, UN Doc. A/57/37 (2002)

Draft Protocol on Civil Liability to the 1992 Convention on the Protection and Use of Transboundary Waters and International Lakes, UN Doc. MP.WAT/AC.3/2002/WP3 (2002)

Johannesburg Declaration on Sustainable Development, UN Doc. A/CONF.199/20 (2002)

Plan of Implementation of the World Summit on Sustainable Development, UN Doc. A/CONF.199/20 (2002)

2003 Framework Convention for the Protection of the Marine Environment of the Caspian Sea, opened for signature 11 November 2003, (2005) 44 ILM 1 (not in force)

2004 Draft Principles on the Allocation of Loss in the Case of Transboundary Harm Arising out of Hazardous Activities, Report of the International Law Commission, 56th Session, UN Doc. A/59/10 (2004)

2005 Settlement Agreement in the Case Concerning Land Reclamation by Singapore in and around the Straits of Johor, opened for signature 26 April 2005 (date of entry into force unknown)

1 Introduction

International environmental law has evolved rapidly in recent decades and is now a highly sophisticated and distinctive sub-discipline of public international law that regulates a broad array of human activities affecting natural and built environments.[1] Yet despite the marked increase in the scope and content of this legal field the scale and pace of environmental destruction has also grown. It is estimated that over 60 per cent of all ecosystem services that support life on earth have been degraded or are being used unsustainably, including freshwater resources and natural systems for air and water purification.[2] This is leading to continuing loss of biodiversity and is also preventing effective action against poverty, hunger, and health crises in many parts of the globe.[3]

With the notable exception of climate change, where there is an urgent need to develop and implement an effective regime that builds upon the achievements to date,[4] the main challenge for international environmental law in the twenty-first century is implementing an impressive body of law already in existence.[5] This is a challenge of

[1] For concise histories see Philippe Sands, *Principles of International Environmental Law* (2nd edn 2003) ch. 2; Ben Boer, Ross Ramsay, and Donald R. Rothwell, *International Environmental Law in the Asia Pacific* (1998); Denise K. DeGarno, *International Environmental Treaties and State Behavior: Factors Influencing Cooperation* (2005) ch. 3; Lynton Keith Caldwell, *International Environmental Policy: From the Twentieth to the Twenty-First Century* (3rd edn 1996) chs. 2–8.

[2] Millennium Ecosystem Assessment, *Ecosystems and Human Well-Being: Synthesis* (2005) 1.

[3] *Ibid.* 2.

[4] 1992 United Nations Framework Convention on Climate Change and the 1997 Kyoto Protocol to that convention.

[5] Martti Koskenniemi, 'Breach of Treaty or Non-Compliance? Reflections on the Enforcement of the Montreal Protocol' (1992) 3 *YIEL* 123, 123; Donald R. Rothwell,

environmental governance, requiring the design and operation of institutions that can promote the full and faithful observance by states of their environmental commitments. International adjudication, comprising both arbitration and judicial settlement by international courts and tribunals, is one type of institution gaining increasing prominence in this context. Factors behind this include increasing awareness of international disputation over shared natural resources, and the growth of environmental and other relevant treaties containing dispute settlement mechanisms.[6]

However, there has been considerable ambivalence in state practice and in scholarly commentary concerning the role of international environmental litigation. While some publicists have advocated much greater reliance upon international courts to protect the environment,[7] others have been highly sceptical of the benefits that adjudication can bring to problems of environmental management where cooperation rather than confrontation seems essential.[8] Against the background of such debates, this book seeks to offer a systematic and comprehensive examination of the historical and contemporary role of international courts and tribunals in resolving environmental disputes, promoting compliance with environmental commitments, and developing substantive rules and principles of environmental law. The overarching objective is to assess the extent to which the judicialisation of international environmental policy and practice has contributed to greater levels of global environmental protection and well-being.

1.1 Development of international environmental law

The genesis of international environmental law can be traced to general rules of public international law adapted and applied to address

'Reassessing International Environmental Dispute Resolution' (2001) 6 *APJEL* 201, 214.

6 Cesare P. R. Romano, 'International Dispute Settlement' in Daniel Bodansky, Jutta Brunnée, and Ellen Hey (eds.), *The Oxford Handbook of International Environmental Law* (2007) 1036, 1037.

7 See e.g. Amedeo Postiglione, *The Global Environmental Crisis: The Need for an International Court of the Environment* (1996); Alfred Rest, 'The Indispensability of an International Environmental Court' (1998) 7 *RECIEL* 63.

8 See e.g. Abram Chayes, Antonia Handler Chayes, and Ronald B. Mitchell, 'Managing Compliance: A Comparative Perspective' in Edith Brown Weiss and Harold K. Jacobson (eds.), *Engaging Countries: Strengthening Compliance with International Environmental Accords* (1998) 39.

environmental problems,[9] and to early treaties and conventions dealing with select resource and wildlife issues.[10] However, most aspects of the discipline are of far more recent origin. From the 1960s onwards a range of regional and sectoral regimes were developed to deal with specific environmental issues such as riverine[11] and marine[12] pollution. These regimes frequently emerged in response to major pollution accidents that dramatically raised the global profile of environmental concerns,[13] and as a consequence these initiatives were often piecemeal and ad hoc. It was only in 1972, with the United Nations Conference on the Human Environment at Stockholm, that it became possible to speak of the emergence of a truly distinctive, and increasingly coherent, 'international environmental law'.[14]

The Stockholm Conference adopted the 1972 Declaration of the United Nations Conference on the Human Environment (Stockholm Declaration), a landmark instrument articulating twenty-six fundamental principles to guide the consolidation and evolution of international environmental law.[15] The declaration dealt with several basic issues, such as the responsibility of states for transboundary environmental harm, upon which international consensus had already begun to emerge.[16] However, it went further, emphasising the need for states to protect the environment for its own sake and for the benefit of

[9] Such as the obligation upon states not knowingly to permit their territory to be used in such a way as to result in damage to the territory of other states: *Trail Smelter* case (*Canada/United States of America*) (1938 and 1941) 3 *RIAA* 1911.

[10] See e.g. 1933 Convention Relative to the Preservation of Fauna and Flora in their Natural State.

[11] See e.g. 1963 Agreement Concerning the International Commission for the Protection of the Rhine Against Pollution.

[12] See e.g. 1969 Agreement for Cooperation in Dealing with Pollution of the North Sea by Oil and Other Harmful Substances.

[13] Such as the 1967 *Torrey Canyon* tanker disaster: E. D. Brown, 'The Lessons of the Torrey-Canyon: International Law Aspects' (1968) 21 *Current Legal Problems* 113.

[14] There has been much debate concerning whether 'international environmental law' is in fact a distinctive body of law, or whether it is merely a convenient label for describing the collection of norms that have some relevance to environmental questions: Patricia W. Birnie and Alan E. Boyle, *International Law and the Environment* (2nd edn 2002); Daniel Bodansky, Jutta Brunnée, and Ellen Hey, 'International Environmental Law: Mapping the Field' in Daniel Bodansky, Jutta Brunnée, and Ellen Hey (eds.), *The Oxford Handbook of International Environmental Law* (2007) 1, 5.

[15] See generally Louis B. Sohn, 'The Stockholm Declaration on the Human Environment' (1973) 14 *HarvILJ* 423.

[16] Stockholm Declaration, principle 21.

future generations,[17] and encouraged states to adopt an integrated and coordinated approach to environmental management.[18] In doing so it proved an important catalyst for further efforts to expand the reach of environmental law. This developmental process intensified and accelerated as a raft of new conventions were concluded,[19] soft-law instruments were endorsed,[20] and the World Commission on Environment and Development (WCED) completed its work.[21]

It became evident that despite the importance of these legal and policy initiatives a more comprehensive approach was required to advance global environmental protection. Global environmental challenges, such as climate change, stratospheric ozone depletion, and wide-scale loss of biodiversity, were not addressed within the framework of the Stockholm Declaration, which recognised a fairly limited collection of environmental problems. Awareness of this led to the 1992 United Nations Conference on Environment and Development (UNCED) in Rio. Commemorating the twentieth anniversary of the Stockholm Conference, UNCED ushered in the modern era of international environmental law. It led to the adoption of the 1992 United Nations Declaration on Environment and Development (Rio Declaration) and keystone conventions on biological diversity[22] and climate change.[23] The conference also endorsed Agenda 21, which set out an extensive programme of action to address global environmental challenges in the 1990s and into the twenty-first century.[24]

Since UNCED, international environmental law has developed further apace. This has been achieved principally through an assortment

[17] *Ibid.* principles 2 and 4.

[18] *Ibid.* principles 24 and 25.

[19] See especially 1973 Convention on International Trade in Endangered Species of Wild Fauna and Flora (CITES) and the 1979 Convention on the Conservation of Migratory Species of Wild Animals.

[20] See especially United Nations Environment Programme Principles of Conduct in the Field of the Environment for the Guidance of States in the Conservation and Harmonious Utilisation of Natural Resources Shared by Two or More States (1978) 17 ILM 1097; World Charter for Nature, GA Res. 37/7, UN Doc. A/37/51 (1982); Hague Declaration on the Environment, (1989) 28 ILM 1308.

[21] World Commission on Environment and Development, *Our Common Future* (1987).

[22] 1992 Convention on Biological Diversity (Biodiversity Convention).

[23] The 1992 United Nations Framework Convention on Climate Change was opened for signature prior to UNCED, but its terms were negotiated in the UNCED preparatory process.

[24] UN Doc. A/CONF.151/26/Rev.1 (1992). See Marlene Jahnke, 'UNCED: Rio Conference on Environment and Development' (1992) 22 *EPL* 204, 208.

of multilateral environmental agreements which are characterised by increasing sophistication, both in terms of the standards that are prescribed and the institutional structures established for monitoring implementation and promoting compliance.[25] None the less, the soft- and hard-law instruments concluded at UNCED have continued to provide the main legal and policy direction for international environmental law. They supply the 'practical contours' of mainstream conceptions of sustainable development.[26] Hence, the United Nations Millennium Declaration, which articulated the millennium development goals, spoke of the need to support the principles of sustainable development set out in Agenda 21.[27] The World Summit on Sustainable Development held in Johannesburg in 2002 similarly marked a renewed commitment to achieving the goals set at Rio, albeit with a greater emphasis than UNCED on poverty alleviation.[28] The 2005 World Summit Outcome also referred prominently to the 'Rio principles' in setting out agreed objectives for managing and protecting the global environment.[29]

What emerges from this brief history is that international environmental law has coalesced around a collection of fundamental guiding principles. It is possible to identify at least seven such principles that attract broad acceptance:[30] (1) the principle that states possess permanent sovereignty over their natural resources but also have a responsibility to ensure that they do not cause transboundary damage; (2) the principle of preventive action; (3) the precautionary principle/approach; (4) the principle of cooperation; (5) the principle of sustainable development; (6) the polluter pays principle; and (7) the principle of common but differentiated responsibility.

[25] See especially the Kyoto Protocol.

[26] W. M. Adams, *Green Development: Environment and Sustainability in the Third World* (2nd edn 2001) 99.

[27] UN Doc. A/RES/55/2 (2000).

[28] Johannesburg Declaration on Sustainable Development and Plan of Implementation of the World Summit on Sustainable Development, UN Doc. A/CONF.199/20 (2002).

[29] See e.g. 2005 World Summit Outcome, [48] UN Doc. A/60/L.1 (2005). See generally Joy Hyvarinen, 'The 2005 World Summit: UN Reform, Security, Environment and Development' (2006) 15 *RECIEL* 1.

[30] Sands, above n. 1, 231. See also the nine principles recited in IUCN – World Conservation Union, *Draft International Covenant on Environment and Development* (3rd edn 2004): (1) respect for all life forms (art. 2); (2) common concern for humanity (art. 3); (3) interdependent values (art. 4); (4) intergenerational equity (art. 5); (5) prevention (art. 6); (6) precaution (art. 7); (7) right to development (art. 8); (8) eradication of poverty (art. 9); (9) common but differentiated responsibilities (art. 10).

Environmental principles are an important legacy of the soft-law origins of the discipline.[31] Determining appropriate limits to the exploitation of natural resources, or imposing limitations upon development to preserve species or ecosystems, often involves highly contentious political choices. In this context the notion that states might agree to a non-binding or imprecise standard has obvious attractions as it permits agreement on the goals of environmental protection without appearing to impose absolute fetters on state autonomy.[32] Environmental principles therefore involve some degree of normativity, but do not necessarily bear all the hallmarks of legal rules[33] (although they can acquire such status).[34] Yet regardless of their legal character these principles provide international environmental law with an ethical outlook, a conceptual structure, and a distinctive vocabulary.[35] Among other things they seek to explain why and how the natural environment should be valued, how the objectives of resource conservation and ecosystem protection should be achieved, and how environmental values should be balanced against other objectives pursued by the international community. In all of these respects there remains considerable debate as to precisely what the content of environmental principles are. They remain central sites for contestation in translating broad environmental goals into concrete policies, as seen most clearly

[31] See, generally, Nicolas de Sadeleer, *Environmental Principles: From Political Slogans to Legal Rules* (Susan Leubusher trans. 2002); Geoffrey Palmer, 'New Ways to Make International Environmental Law' (1996) 86 *AJIL* 259; Ranee Khooshie Lal Panjabi, 'From Stockholm to Rio: A Comparison of the Declaratory Principles of International Environmental Law' (1993) 21 *DenJILP* 215.

[32] Patricia W. Birnie, 'International Environmental Law: Its Adequacy for Present and Future Needs' in Andrew Hurrell and Benedict Kingsbury (eds.), *The International Politics of the Environment: Actors, Interests, and Institutions* (1991) 51, 54.

[33] For a discussion of the distinction between 'rules' and 'principles' see Ronald Dworkin, *Taking Rights Seriously* (3rd edn 1981) 26: 'All that is meant, when we say that a particular principle is a principle of law, is that the principle is one which officials must take into account, if it is relevant, as a consideration inclining one way or another.'

[34] The clearest example of this is principle 21 of the Stockholm Declaration (and principle 2 of the Rio Declaration) concerning the responsibility of states to ensure that activities within their jurisdiction and/or control do not lead to damage to other states or to areas beyond national jurisdiction. See *Legality of the Threat or Use of Nuclear Weapons* [1996] ICJ Rep 226, [29] and the *Gabčíkovo-Nagymaros Project* case (*Hungary/Slovakia*) (merits) [1997] ICJ Rep 7, [53].

[35] Duncan French, *International Law and Policy on Sustainable Development* (2005) 52.

in the compendious literature on the precautionary principle.[36] As a growing volume of environmental disputes is brought before international courts and tribunals these institutions are gaining an increasingly prominent role in mediating and influencing this process of conceptual development.

1.2 International environmental governance through courts and tribunals

In parallel with the growth in the substantive content of international environmental law has emerged an awareness of the need for institutions that can promote compliance with international environmental standards.[37] While the question of enforcement has always vexed scholars of international law and international relations,[38] environmental management appears to present a range of particular challenges, especially given the need to manage complex and interconnected ecosystems that are indifferent to territorial and jurisdictional boundaries, and which require high levels of coordination and cooperation between a number of state and non-state actors.

International environmental governance may be described as the way in which rules of environmental law are developed, applied, and enforced.[39] It is an ongoing process in which norms and structures are transformed over time in response to the changing needs of international society.[40] International courts and tribunals constitute one part of this overall governance picture. As with any international

36 Jaye Ellis, 'Overexploitation of a Valuable Resource? New Literature on the Precautionary Principle' (2006) 17 *EJIL* 445. One of the best overviews of the principle in operation is Jacqueline Peel, *The Precautionary Principle in Practice: Environmental Decision-Making and Scientific Uncertainty* (2005).

37 Philippe Roch and Franz Xaver Perrez, 'International Environmental Governance: The Strive Towards a Comprehensive, Coherent, Effective and Efficient International Environmental Regime' (2005) 16 *ColoJIELP* 1, 6.

38 See Benedict Kingsbury, 'The Concept of Compliance as a Function of Competing Conceptions of International Law' (1997–8) 19 *MichJIL* 345.

39 See generally Wayne Sandholtz and Alec Stone Sweet, 'Law, Politics and International Governance' in Christian Reus-Smit (ed.), *The Politics of International Law* (2004) 238, 245; Daniel Bodansky, 'The Legitimacy of International Governance: A Coming Challenge for International Environmental Law?' (1999) 93 *AJIL* 596, 597; Sands, above n. 1, ch. 3.

40 Sandholtz and Stone Sweet, above n. 39, 245. See also Oran R. Young, *International Governance: Protecting the Environment in a Stateless Society* (1994) 15–16.

institution, international courts possess distinctive functional attributes. They are inherently less flexible than other international institutions. The adjudication process is essentially confrontational, adversarial, and will often result in a dichotomous result. It also involves a limited number of parties, and can only deal with a narrow range of issues.[41] However, adjudication also has strengths in being able to resolve environmental disputes in a manner that is to some extent insulated from political processes. International courts involve a third party in the settlement process, are composed of judges who must adhere to high standards of independence and impartiality, must adjudicate claims advanced on the basis of reasoned arguments,[42] and above all are required to render decisions according to accepted legal rules. International adjudication is therefore an inherently rational procedure that can give effect to the wishes of the parties in an amicable settlement while also upholding the environmental or other public values embodied in legal norms applicable to the case at hand.[43] It is also a process productive of decisions that influence the development of environmental norms. All of these attributes make courts unique among other international institutions for giving independent and authoritative recognition to concerns of a community character. Similar benefits have long been recognised in relation to domestic courts with jurisdiction over environmental matters.[44]

Despite these apparent benefits it must be observed that the function performed by each individual court varies considerably, depending upon its place within individual international regimes. Unsurprisingly, the purpose that has been most pronounced has been that of dispute resolution. The obligation upon states to resolve their disputes solely by peaceful means, in such a way that international peace and security and justice are not threatened, is the foundation stone of modern international law.[45] As a consequence, adjudication has often been regarded as simply one among a number of methods for

[41] See generally Lon L. Fuller, 'The Forms and Limits of Adjudication' (1978) 92 *HarvLR* 353.

[42] *Ibid*. 369: 'Adjudication is a process of decision that grants to the affected party a form of participation that consists in the opportunity to present proofs and reasoned arguments.'

[43] Philippe Sands, '"Unilateralism", Values and International Law' (2000) 11 *EJIL* 291, 300–1; A. Neil Craik, 'Recalcitrant Reality and Chosen Ideals: The Public Function of Dispute Settlement in International Environmental Law' (1998) 10 *GeoIELR* 551, 563.

[44] Gerry Bates, *Environmental Law in Australia* (6th edn 2006) 14.

[45] UN Charter, arts. 2 and 33.

alleviating international tensions that might otherwise spill over into armed conflict.[46] However, since the late twentieth century there has been a dramatic proliferation and diversification of international judicial bodies, and international adjudication has been given new functions.[47] Through this judicialisation[48] of some areas of international law the concept of adjudication has shifted from being a device exclusively designed for promoting inter-state peace, to being a means for responding to new governance challenges such as the protection of human rights, the imposition of individual international criminal responsibility, and the resolution of complex commercial disputes.

International environmental law has not been insulated from these developments. There has been a substantial increase in international litigation on environmental questions in courts of general jurisdiction, in courts and tribunals having a specialisation in non-environmental issue areas, and in environment-focused bodies.[49] At the same time, international environmental law has developed a complex bureaucracy in the form of treaty-based institutions such as non-compliance procedures (NCPs) designed to facilitate greater levels of cooperation and coordination among states in responding to environmental problems. These developments appear to be pulling the institutional fabric of international environmental governance in two, quite different, directions. Whereas the reliance on courts and tribunals in some regimes signals a preference for a more confrontational, enforcement-oriented, method

[46] The tradition of thinking about international adjudication in this way can be traced to antiquity and has recurred ever since. See M. N. Tod, *International Arbitration Amongst the Greeks* (1913) 6; David D. Caron, 'War and International Adjudication: Reflections on the 1899 Peace Conference' (2000) 94 *AJIL* 4.

[47] Chester Brown, 'The Proliferation of International Courts and Tribunals: Finding Your Way Through the Maze' (2002) 3 *MJIL* 453; Cesare P. R. Romano, 'The Proliferation of International Judicial Bodies: The Pieces of the Puzzle' (1999) 31 *NYUJILP* 709.

[48] 'Judicialisation' may be described as 'the process through which a [triadic dispute resolution] mechanism appears, stabilizes and develops authority over the normative structure governing exchange in a given community. The judicialization of politics is the process by which triadic lawmaking progressively shapes the strategic behaviour of politics actors engaged in interactions with one another': Alec Stone Sweet, 'Judicialization and the Construction of Governance' (1999) 32 *CompPolStud* 147, 164. Hence while the term 'proliferation' is used to describe the quantitative increase in the number and type of international courts, 'judicialisation' captures the idea that there has been a qualitative expansion in the role of international courts in some areas of international relations and law.

[49] Sands, above n. 1, 65.

of compliance control, the use of NCPs and other treaty bodies indicates a more cooperative and supervisory approach. This raises questions as to whether these trends may be reconciled, and in what particular circumstances courts and tribunals are likely to be most effective in securing tangible improvements in environmental protection.

1.3 Role and relevance of international courts

The three chapters in part I of the book address these questions. Chapter 2 maps the landscape of international environmental adjudication. What becomes evident from this survey is that a wide variety of adjudicative institutions operate in the environmental field. A range of environmental instruments provide for the adjudication of environmental disputes, predominantly in ad hoc arbitral tribunals. Permanent courts and tribunals, most notably the International Tribunal for the Law of the Sea (ITLOS), are also occupying an increasingly important role in some environmental regimes. There has been an effort to improve the capacity of existing institutions to respond to environmental disputes, as is seen in the adoption of specialised environmental procedures by the Permanent Court of Arbitration[50] (PCA) and the establishment in 1993 of a permanent Chamber for Environmental Matters within the International Court of Justice (ICJ). Although these are important developments, some of the most influential forums for environmental dispute settlement are judicial bodies without an environmental specialisation such as the dispute settlement system of the World Trade Organization (WTO). Chapter 2 also offers a critical appraisal of recurring proposals for the establishment of an international court for the environment.

It is evident that the growing patchwork of jurisdictions examined in chapter 2 represents the judicialisation of international environmental law, at least in certain discrete areas such as the law of the sea. However, by comparison with some fields of public international law, particularly those applicable to international trade and foreign investment, international environmental law is not generally reliant upon arbitration and judicial settlement. Indeed it is seen in chapter 3 that the development of environmental governance structures has taken a different path. A key feature of the growing maturity

[50] 2001 Optional Rules for the Arbitration of Disputes Relating to Natural Resources and/or the Environment.

of international environmental law is the emergence of a collection of treaty-based institutions through which the implementation of multilateral environmental agreements can be supervised.[51] Chapter 3 situates international courts and tribunals among these institutions for managing compliance. The argument is made that by comparison with traditional forms of inter-state dispute settlement this supervisory or 'managerial' approach to compliance advanced through flexible institutions offers several advantages in delivering positive environmental outcomes.

However, the adoption of this managerial strategy is not, and need not be, universal. Some environmental agreements rely quite effectively upon adjudicative institutions for resolving disputes and promoting compliance. In light of this practice chapter 4 offers a reassessment of the role of adjudication in international environmental law. It is acknowledged at the outset that it is possible to identify several shortcomings of adjudication, including its generally reactive nature and the limited number of participants who may be involved in the litigation process. However, it also has several strengths, and these are identified and discussed. The variety of institutions examined in chapter 2 underlines that adjudication often performs regime-specific tasks and that it is therefore impossible to generalise the adjudicative function. Hence while the ICJ cannot be said to be at the forefront of the interpretation and application of international environmental law, it can be argued that ITLOS, and the entire dispute settlement system fashioned by the 1982 United Nations Convention on the Law of the Sea (LOS Convention) is vital to the enforcement of, and compliance with, the LOS Convention's regime of marine environmental protection. The fact that the effectiveness of adjudication in international environmental law is intimately tied to its institutional context suggests that the critique of the utility of courts and tribunals in the environmental field by many international relations scholars is overly parsimonious.[52] By reference to an alternative line of

[51] Alan E. Boyle, 'Saving the World? Implementation and Enforcement of International Environmental Law Through International Institutions' (1991) 3 *JEL* 229.

[52] See, especially, Abram Chayes and Antonia Handler Chayes, *The New Sovereignty: Compliance with International Regulatory Agreements* (1995) 205: '[a] century of experience with international adjudication leads to considerable scepticism about its suitability as an international dispute settlement method and, in particular, as a way of securing compliance with treaties.'

international relations scholarship,[53] the case is made that in certain regimes adjudication should be given a more prominent role in resolving disputes and enforcing environmental rules.

1.4 Judicial development of international environmental law

The development of international environmental law has principally occurred as a result of legislative processes.[54] Broad statements of environmental principles, together with increasingly technical environmental standards and regulations, have been articulated in a spectrum of bilateral and multilateral treaties, and in resolutions, declarations and other soft-law instruments. None the less, as in public international law generally, international courts and tribunals have had both a historic and contemporary influence upon the evolution of environmental rules.[55] Judicial exegesis in the course of resolving environmental disputes can greatly assist in the elaboration, clarification, and development both of precise rules of conduct and more general principles of international environmental law. A growing number of international cases have considered questions of law relevant to the protection of the environment. This body of jurisprudence continues to expand as new

[53] See especially Robert O. Keohane, Andrew Moravcsik, and Anne-Marie Slaughter, 'Legalized Dispute Resolution: Interstate and Transnational' (2000) 54 *IntOrg* 457.

[54] Alan E. Boyle, 'Codification of International Environmental Law and the International Law Commission: Injurious Consequences Revisited' in Alan E. Boyle and David Freestone (eds.), *International Law and Sustainable Development: Past Achievements and Future Challenges* (1999) 61, 63; Catherine Redgwell, 'International Environmental Law' in Malcolm D. Evans (ed.), *International Law* (2003) 657, 664.

[55] Allott argues that international courts and tribunals have increasingly relied upon their own, and other courts', previous decisions as a type of judge-made customary law: Philip Allott, *The Health of Nations: Society and Law Beyond the State* (2002) 52. See also Tom Ginsburg, 'Bounded Discretion in International Judicial Lawmaking' (2005) 45 *VaJIL* 631, 632; José E. Alvarez, *International Organizations as Law-Makers* (2005) 460–1. Precisely how this contribution to the content and structure of international environmental law should be characterised remains subject to ongoing debate. A strictly positivist, consent-based, conception of international law regards the judicial process as one involving no more than the application of rules established by states in their relations (see Grigorii I. Tunkin, *Theory of International Law* (1974) 183). However, many commentators have noted that the distinction between the judicial 'application' and 'creation' of law is impossible to sustain: see E. Hambro, 'The Reasons Behind the Decisions of the International Court of Justice' (1954) 7 *Current Legal Problems* 212, 214; Mohamed Shahabuddeen, *Precedent in the World Court* (1996) 67–96; Philippe Sands, 'Turtles and Torturers: The Transformation of International Law' (2000) 33 *NYUJILP* 527, 555; Rosalyn Higgins, *Problems and Process: International Law and How We Use It* (1994) 2.

international courts and tribunals have begun to operate. There has also been a renewed interest in, and appreciation of, the very earliest cases that dealt with questions of natural resources and wildlife conservation. Whereas part I considers the direct functional importance of courts and tribunals in international environmental governance, part II of this book assesses the less immediate, but no less important, contribution made by judicial bodies to the development of international environmental law.

This environmental jurisprudence has emerged in three main issue areas: transboundary environmental harm, international water law, and the protection and preservation of the marine environment. The three chapters in part II examine in turn each of these bodies of case law, which together represent the core texts in the canon of international environmental jurisprudence. These decisions are evaluated within the context in which they were decided, to ascertain whether they responded appropriately to the environmental problems with which they dealt, and whether they might have gone further in addressing environmental issues. An attempt is made to uncover and understand the philosophical underpinnings of these decisions, the conceptual premises concerning the environment, and rationales for its protection expressly adopted in, or implicitly informing, the reasoning. Above all the purpose of part II is to determine the extent to which this jurisprudence has had a positive impact upon the evolution of international environmental law. It is seen that the impact of these decisions has been threefold. Their most obvious normative importance has been in articulating directly applicable rules and principles. A secondary impact has been in illustrating potential environmental problems, and identifying (if not necessarily addressing) the range of legal issues that are implicated. The factual scenarios encountered in some cases therefore provide a template against which the efficacy of subsequent legislative developments can be measured. A third important, yet also indirect, influence has been in highlighting gaps in the international legal framework as it applies to environmental matters, and thereby catalysing further developments to address these deficiencies.

Chapter 5 explores the judicial contribution to the development of rules and principles of environmental law relating to transboundary harm. Norms relating to such damage are the *fons et origo* of international law relating to environmental matters, and the *Trail Smelter* case is almost invariably cited as the first authoritative statement of the principle that states have a responsibility to ensure that activities within their jurisdiction or control do not cause damage to the environment of other states. The point is made, however, that this environmentally significant dictum was fashioned out of more general doctrines of international law regarding sovereignty and territorial integrity. As a consequence, the principle stated in the case, and subsequently elaborated in the Stockholm and Rio Declarations, serves environmental purposes only indirectly. Many of these weaknesses in the decision were made apparent in the *Nuclear Tests* cases, which involved a much more complex scenario of transboundary atmospheric pollution.[56] Although this dispute was never resolved on its merits, the pleadings and oral arguments made by the parties, separate and dissenting opinions, and practice outside the courtroom, all made a contribution to the development of the law, and revealed limitations inherent in approaching environmental problems through the lenses of sovereignty and territorial integrity. Consideration is also given in chapter 5 to the impact of transboundary damage litigation upon treaty practice, and upon the work of the International Law Commission (ILC) in devising general rules for the prevention of transboundary harm, and for imposing state responsibility and non-delictual liability if and when it does in fact occur.

In chapter 6 we turn to a second category of international environmental cases, namely those decisions concerning riverine resources and ecosystems. These cases reveal clearly the development of environmental law from a complete focus upon state sovereignty issues to the contemporary consideration of ecological factors. The contribution of the cases in this area has been vital because it has provided the conceptual underpinnings for a fundamental 'greening' of international water law. Challenging the notions of absolute and limited territorial sovereignty, it has replaced these unworkable and environmentally unsustainable doctrines with the 'community of interest' theory. This doctrine was recognised and endorsed by the ICJ in the *Gabčíkovo-Nagymaros Project* case[57] in which the ICJ placed environmental concerns firmly within the law relating to international watercourses. None the less, there remains much room for further integrating environmental concerns in water resource management, as is seen in the ICJ's response to

[56] *Nuclear Tests* cases: *Australia* v. *France* (interim measures) [1973] ICJ Rep 99, (merits) [1974] ICJ Rep 253; *New Zealand* v. *France* (interim measures) [1973] ICJ Rep 135, (merits) [1974] ICJ Rep 457.

[57] *Gabčíkovo-Nagymaros Project* case [1997] ICJ Rep 7.

Argentina's request for provisional measures in the *Pulp Mills on the River Uruguay* case.[58]

Chapter 7 deals with what is perhaps the most dynamic area of international environmental jurisprudence – that relating to the marine environment. The discussion begins with the *Bering Sea Fur Seals* case,[59] which continues to have relevance for understanding the role of courts in environmental disputes. Although the decision ultimately delivered was of limited compass, the arguments of the parties and individual arbitrators provide many insights into the potential of international law to address environmental problems at an early stage of its development. The long-term value of the case in substantive terms was mainly in highlighting the environmental shortcomings of a rigid adherence to the *mare liberum* doctrine, thereby making clear the need for states to cooperate to achieve conservation objectives in relation to marine wildlife residing beyond, or traversing multiple, political boundaries. The tension between coastal and flag states in relation to the exploitation, management, and conservation of marine wildlife has been a recurring problem, as was seen in the *Fisheries Jurisdiction* cases[60] in which the ICJ attempted to resolve such frictions by developing the controversial notion of 'preferential fishing rights'. This case, and other decisions pre-dating the LOS Convention, are now mainly of historical interest but they do none the less serve to demonstrate how the legal framework has evolved in response to the problems identified in the course of litigation.

Undoubtedly the most important jurisprudence in the marine environmental context has emerged only after the entry into force of the LOS Convention. A number of cases involving environmental issues have now been decided under the compulsory dispute settlement procedures set out in part XV of the LOS Convention. These have brought to life several of the convention's marine environmental provisions, and have revealed the importance of the convention as a comprehensive regime for managing marine environmental challenges. The chapter examines each of the environmentally significant decisions

58 *Pulp Mills on the River Uruguay (Argentina* v. *Uruguay)* (request for provisional measures by Argentina) (2006) 45 ILM 1025.

59 *Bering Sea Fur Seals* case (*Great Britain* v. *United States*) (1893) 1 Moore 755.

60 *Fisheries Jurisdiction* cases: *United Kingdom* v. *Iceland* (jurisdiction) [1973] ICJ Rep 3, (merits) [1974] ICJ Rep 3; *Germany* v. *Iceland* (jurisdiction) [1973] ICJ Rep 49, (merits) [1974] ICJ Rep 175.

of ITLOS and the arbitral tribunals established under annex VII of the LOS Convention. It is observed that despite some degree of timidity in decision-making, there has been increasing recognition of the important interplay between marine living resources issues and broader environmental questions regarding the integrity of marine ecosystems.

1.5 Future challenges for international environmental litigation

Part III of the book assesses several looming challenges facing international environmental litigation, and also offers some reflections on the future prospects for courts and tribunals in international environmental governance.

One particular source of pressure upon existing institutions that may lead to substantial changes in the way environmental disputes are settled is the demand by civil society for a greater role in international adjudicatory procedures. Public interest environmental law is gaining acceptance in many states, and the substantial increase in the use of courts and tribunals for international environmental disputes has raised the prospect of similar environmental litigation in the public interest on the international plane.[61] Chapter 8 considers the extent to which this has occurred, and some of the challenges that it poses. The discussion examines the various ways in which international environmental law has recognised the importance of public participation, and assesses the prospect that international judicial bodies might provide greater opportunities for civil society to initiate proceedings. While it seems unlikely that the participation will be further expanded unless attention is paid to underlying conceptual issues, such as the rights that non-state actors possess in relation to environmental claims, it is none the less essential that the public function of environmental adjudication be enhanced. Suggesting a reconceptualisation of the notion of international public interest proceedings in the context of international environmental law, it is argued that participation falling short of full rights of standing can help ensure that environmental values and interests are appropriately recognised.

Chapter 9 considers the practical consequences flowing from the operation of an uncoordinated patchwork of jurisdictions deciding environmental disputes. Whereas for much of the history of

[61] Linda A. Malone and Scott Pasternack, *Defending the Environment: Civil Society Strategies to Enforce International Environmental Law* (2004).

international law states and other actors had few opportunities for litigating environmental and other grievances, the present situation is characterised by the plethora of judicial bodies that can be turned to. There is little doubt that the existence of multiple judicial organs complicates the processes of international governance generally,[62] and chapter 9 examines these practical problems from the specific perspective of international environmental litigation. Challenges of jurisdictional coordination, including forum shopping, simultaneous, and successive proceedings, have not only increased the duration, cost, and complexity of environmental litigation but have also given rise to substantive problems such as the undermining of some compulsory systems of environmental dispute settlement. The argument is made that in devising strategies to address such problems the international community must have regard not only to considerations such as streamlining the administration of justice, but must also take note of the important role of some dispute settlement bodies in promoting environmental protection. In other words, appopriate consideration must be given to the substantive functions of environmental governance that some international courts and tribunals discharge.

In chapter 10 there is an examination of a further problem deriving from the multiplication in judicial forums examining environmental disputes. Much jurisprudence touching upon environmental matters is now emanating not from dedicated environmental courts and tribunals, but instead is being produced by issue-specific judicial and quasi-judicial bodies. This raises the prospect that such jurisprudence may have a negative influence on international environmental law by developing rules and principles in a way that privileges the non-environmental agendas that these issue-specific regimes are designed to advance. This potential for the 'fragmentation' of international environmental law is tested through a close analysis of the environment-related jurisprudence of human rights courts and complaints bodies and the dispute settlement system of the WTO. It is concluded that, at least to date, the evidence reveals no major or problematic departures from conventional understandings of environmental rules and principles. However, a number of possible problem areas to be kept under continuing watch are identified and discussed.

62 See Yuval Shany, *The Competing Jurisdictions of International Courts and Tribunals* (2003).

PART I • INTERNATIONAL COURTS AND ENVIRONMENTAL GOVERNANCE

2 The patchwork of jurisdictions

Adjudication was used very rarely during the early development of international environmental law, with states preferring other mechanisms for resolving disputes over natural resources or transboundary pollution.[1] This situation has changed substantially in recent decades and environmental matters are now routinely litigated in a growing array of international courts and tribunals.[2] This chapter surveys the diverse and expanding opportunities for international environmental litigation, and assesses the various jurisdictional bases upon which environmental claims can be mounted. It is seen that the defining characteristic of adjudication in contemporary international environmental law is the operation of a largely uncoordinated patchwork of distinctive jurisdictions, several of which operate in competition with one another in addressing environmental disputes.

2.1 Adjudicating international environmental cases

2.1.1 The expanding jurisdictional patchwork

The first judicial engagement with international environmental disputes took place in several well-known arbitrations in the nineteenth and early twentieth centuries. These cases were conducted on an ad hoc basis in relation to specific controversies rather than on the basis of standing treaties dealing with environmental matters. Today the practice is far more varied, and there are four main ways in

[1] Richard B. Bilder, 'The Settlement of Disputes in the Field of the International Law of the Environment' (1975) 144 *RDC* 139, 228.

[2] Ben Boer, Ross Ramsay, and Donald R. Rothwell, *International Environmental Law in the Asia Pacific* (1998) 1–2.

which environmental disputes may be brought before international adjudicative bodies. First, in a continuation of early practice, states may submit specific disputes, on an ad hoc basis, to arbitration or to judicial settlement by permanent courts and tribunals. Second, environmental disputes may be brought before an arbitral panel or court on the basis of a general dispute settlement agreement (such as the 'optional clause' procedure in the ICJ).[3] Third, in a more recent development, many environmental agreements establish procedures for the arbitration or judicial settlement of disputes concerning the interpretation or application of the agreement. Fourth, courts and quasi-judicial bodies with specialisation in non-environmental areas (such as human rights,[4] investment,[5] trade,[6] compensation following armed conflict,[7] or criminal law)[8] may be asked to rule on matters that have some environmental dimensions. The main fault line in this practice is between endogenous systems for the adjudication of environmental disputes stemming from environmental agreements themselves, and exogenous options that are available either through general adjudicative bodies or those with narrower subject matter jurisdiction.[9]

2.1.1.1 Endogenous environmental adjudication

Bilateral, plurilateral, and multilateral treaties supply the vast bulk of the content of international environmental law. General international law remains an important repository of general principle, but it is to more specific treaty arrangements that the international community has looked to address shared environmental challenges, and their number has increased dramatically since the 1970s.[10] While in 1989 the

[3] Statute of the ICJ, art. 36(2).

[4] See e.g. United Nations Human Rights Committee.

[5] See e.g. 1965 Convention on the Settlement of Investment Disputes Between States and Nationals of Other States.

[6] See e.g. 1994 Marrakesh Agreement Establishing the World Trade Organization annex 2 (Understanding on Rules and Procedures Governing the Settlement of Disputes); 1992 North American Free Trade Agreement (NAFTA).

[7] See e.g. the United Nations Compensation Commission, established as a subsidiary organ of the United Nations Security Council in 1991 to process claims for losses and damage suffered as a result of Iraq's unlawful invasion of Kuwait.

[8] See e.g. 1998 Rome Statute of the International Criminal Court, art. 8(2)(b)(iv).

[9] On the endogenous/exogenous distinction see Cesare P.R. Romano, 'International Dispute Settlement' in Daniel Bodansky, Jutta Brunnée, and Ellen Hey (eds.), *The Oxford Handbook of International Environmental Law* (2007) 1036.

[10] R.W. Hahn and K.R. Richards, 'The Internationalization of Environmental Regulation' (1989) 30 *HarvILJ* 421, 423.

United Nations Environment Programme (UNEP) reported that there were 139 multilateral environmental agreements in existence,[11] a recent review found over 750 multilateral and 1,000 bilateral treaties.[12] This growth in treaty law is now beginning to slow, although important developments continue, especially through subsidiary rules, guidelines, and decisions made under existing treaties and protocols.

What is significant for present purposes is that almost all environmental agreements incorporate some form of dispute settlement clause, and that adjudication, whether by arbitration or judicial settlement, is frequently acknowledged as an option for resolving disputes concerning the interpretation or application of the relevant text. Soft-law instruments also regularly refer to the desirability of greater use of existing adjudicative institutions, or the creation of new judicial bodies for this purpose.[13] Around 50 to 60 per cent of environmental agreements include adjudication as a dispute settlement option,[14] roughly double the proportion of treaties generally,[15] suggesting that states are quite favourably inclined towards adjudication in the environmental context.

[11] UNEP, Register of International Treaties and Other Agreements in the Field of the Environment, UN Doc. UNEP/GC 15/Inf.2 (1989).

[12] Ronald B. Mitchell, 'International Environmental Agreements: A Survey of Their Features, Formation, and Effects' (2003) 28 *AnnRevEnvRes* 429, 430. Mitchell (at 432–3) defines an international environmental agreement as 'an intergovernmental document intended as legally binding with a primary stated purpose of preventing or managing human impacts on natural resources' or 'plant and animal species (including in agriculture); the atmosphere; oceans; rivers; lakes, terrestrial habitats; and other elements of the natural world that provide ecosystem services'. Mitchell identifies well over 750 multilateral environmental agreements (including protocols and amendments in addition to head instruments), and over a thousand multilateral treaties: iea.uoregon.edu.

[13] See e.g. the Rio Declaration principle 26, which provides that 'States shall resolve all their environmental disputes peacefully and by appropriate means in accordance with the Charter of the United Nations'. See also Agenda 21, UN Doc. A/CONF.151/26/Rev.1 (1992) ch. 39.10, which provides 'in the area of avoidance and settlement of disputes, States should further study and consider methods to broaden and make more effective the range of techniques available at present'.

[14] Cesare P.R. Romano, *The Peaceful Settlement of International Environmental Disputes: A Pragmatic Approach* (2000) 91–2. Romano identifies at least 150 environmental agreements containing dispute settlement provisions, 85 of which provide for international adjudication as an optional or mandatory means of settling differences. See also Barbara Koremenos, 'If Only Half of International Agreements Have Dispute Resolution Provisions, Which Half Needs Explaining?' (2007) 36 *JLS* 189, 201.

[15] Koremenos, above n. 14, 201.

In environmental texts the most common form of dispute settlement clause comprises a restatement of the customary and UN Charter obligation to resolve disputes peacefully together with a recital of the catalogue of methods set out in article 33 of the UN Charter.[16] Beyond this baseline commonality there is great diversity in terms of the dispute settlement provisions in operation. These range from one-paragraph clauses by which states agree to resolve their dispute by peaceful means of their choosing, to more sophisticated and elaborate procedures that involve multiple stages and a choice of fora (see table 2.1).

While many environmental agreements provide for consensual adjudication, only a select few provide for so-called 'compulsory'[17] adjudication through an obligatory 'compromissory clause'.[18] This is despite recommendations over many years for a strengthened adjudicative system in international environmental law. In 1987, for instance, the Expert Group on Environmental Law of WCED proposed a graduated system of environmental dispute settlement leading to mandatory adjudication. Under this proposal, which supplied a template for a compromissory clause, states would be required to enter into good faith negotiations to settle environmental disputes for a period of eighteen months, and then to conciliation, and finally to arbitration or judicial settlement at the request of any of the parties.[19] Twenty years on, and despite the increase in multilateral environmental agreements during that time, adjudication has not been widely adopted as the preferred dispute settlement strategy by environmental regimes.

2.1.1.2 Exogenous environmental adjudication

The preceding discussion has explained the extent to which states have sought through international environmental agreements to provide for the adjudication of environmental disputes. However, there are a number of important external procedures for activating adjudicative bodies in response to environmental disputes. States may by special

[16] Patricia W. Birnie, 'International Environmental Law: Its Adequacy for Present and Future Needs' in Andrew Hurrell and Benedict Kingsbury (eds.), *The International Politics of the Environment: Actors, Interests, and Institutions* (1991) 51, 69.

[17] Robert Jennings, 'The Judicial Enforcement of International Obligations' (1987) 47 *Zeitschrift für ausländisches öffentliches Recht und Völkerrecht* 3, 3 ('so-called compulsory jurisdiction turns out to be only another form of consensual jurisdiction').

[18] See generally Jonathan I. Charney, 'Compromissory Clauses and the Jurisdiction of the International Court of Justice' (1987) 81 *AJIL* 855.

[19] World Commission on Environment and Development, *Our Common Future* (1987) 395 (Brundtland Report).

Table 2.1 *Types of dispute settlement provisions in multilateral environmental agreements*

	Type of dispute settlement provision	Examples
1	Instruments that include no provision for dispute settlement	1946 International Convention for the Regulation of Whaling 1992 Niue Treaty on Cooperation in Fisheries Surveillance and Law Enforcement in the South Pacific Region
2	Instruments that provide that the parties agree to enter into consultations or negotiations whenever a dispute arises	2003 Framework Convention for the Protection of the Marine Environment of the Caspian Sea
3	Instruments that provide that the parties agree to resolve disputes by a peaceful means of their own choice	1994 Convention for the Conservation and Management of Pollock Resources in the Central Bering Sea
4	Instruments that provide not only that the parties agree to resolve disputes by peaceful means, but also provide a list of available procedures, including arbitration and judicial settlement	1993 Convention for the Conservation of Southern Bluefin Tuna
5	Instruments that provide for the settlement of a dispute by compulsory but non-legal procedures such as mediation or conciliation	1992 Convention on Biological Diversity
6	Instruments that provide for the settlement of a dispute by compulsory and binding adjudication (by arbitration or judicial settlement):	
	(a) by compulsory and binding adjudication where the parties have 'opted in' to the procedure	1985 Convention for the Protection of the Ozone Layer
	(b) by compulsory and binding adjudication (arbitration or judicial settlement) unless the parties have 'opted out' of the procedure	1980 Convention on the Physical Protection of Nuclear Material
	(c) by compulsory and binding adjudication (arbitration or judicial settlement), which is automatically applicable	1982 United Nations Convention on the Law of the Sea

agreement submit a dispute to arbitration or judicial settlement, as in the the *Gabčíkovo-Nagymaros Project* case[20] in which Hungary and Slovakia submitted a dispute raising a range of environmental issues in the context of a shared watercourse to the ICJ.[21] Environmental disputes may also be litigated where the parties have accepted the jurisdiction of a court in advance in relation to a range of international disputes, such as through a general arbitral or other dispute settlement agreement. Such mechanisms have been used in cases with significant environmental dimensions such as the *Nuclear Tests* cases[22] in which Australia and New Zealand relied on the 1928 General Act for the Pacific Settlement of International Disputes in their applications.

The most important general mechanism for establishing the jurisdiction of an international court or tribunal in advance of its exercise is article 36(2) of the Statute of the ICJ, the so-called 'optional clause'. Through this procedure legal disputes touching upon matters of environmental concern can be brought without the need for specific agreement and it was on this basis that the *Certain Phosphate Lands in Nauru* case,[23] which raised issues of responsibility for environmental degradation, was brought by Nauru against Australia.[24] As at 1 December 2007 a total of sixty-five states (around one-third of the UN membership) had deposited declarations recognising the compulsory jurisdiction of the ICJ. As a consequence there are very substantial opportunities for a range of environmental matters to find their way before the Court if states wish to resolve their environmental disputes in this way. However, it must be noted that several states accepting the jurisdiction of the ICJ under article 36(2) have included reservations in relation to environmental matters, and these have limited the jurisdiction of the ICJ in this area.[25] Some states have included broad exclusions in relation to environmental issues, such as Poland's declaration

[20] *Gabčíkovo-Nagymaros Project* case (*Hungary/Slovakia*) [1997] ICJ Rep 7.

[21] See ch. 6.

[22] *Nuclear Tests* cases: *Australia* v. *France* (interim measures) [1973] ICJ Rep 99, (merits) [1974] ICJ Rep 253; *New Zealand* v. *France* (interim measures) [1973] ICJ Rep 135, (merits) [1974] ICJ Rep 457.

[23] *Certain Phosphate Lands in Nauru (Nauru* v. *Australia)* [1992] ICJ Rep 240 (*Nauru* case).

[24] The dispute was ultimately settled: 1993 Settlement of the Case in the ICJ Concerning Certain Phosphate Lands in Nauru. The *Fisheries Jurisdiction* case (*Spain* v. *Canada*) (jurisdiction and admissibility) [1998] ICJ Rep 431 (*Estai* case) was also commenced by Spain on this basis; however the Court found that it had no jurisdiction by operation of Canada's reservation to its optional clause declaration.

[25] Peter H. Sand, *Transnational Environmental Law: Lessons in Global Change* (1999) 45.

that excludes all 'disputes with regard to environmental protection'.[26] More commonly the compulsory jurisdiction is limited on much narrower grounds, such as by excluding the Court's competence over disputes concerning marine pollution or living and non-living resources. Malta's declaration, for instance, excludes disputes in relation to 'the prevention or control of pollution or contamination of the marine environment in marine areas adjacent to the coast of Malta'.[27]

2.2 The proliferation of international adjudicative bodies

The expansion in the number and variety of adjudicative options in international environmental law is in large part a function of the growth of international adjudicative bodies more generally.[28] Various factors explain this growing delegation of governance functions to adjudicative mechanisms, including the fact that states increasingly regard international courts and tribunals as useful for resolving disputes, enforcing international agreements, reviewing the legality of actions and decisions, and providing authoritative interpretation of treaty texts.[29] There has been an associated increase in judicial activity, with almost 13,000 decisions, opinions, and rulings since 1990.[30] Many of the new courts and tribunals have been called upon to resolve

[26] 1996 Declaration of Poland Recognising as Compulsory the Jurisdiction of the ICJ.

[27] 1996 Declaration of Malta Recognising as Compulsory the Jurisdiction of the ICJ. See similar reservations by Barbados, Canada, New Zealand, and the Philippines. Canada's reservation was unsuccessfully challenged by Spain in the *Estai* case [1998] ICJ Rep 431.

[28] The authors of the *Manual on International Courts and Tribunals* arrive at a total of twenty-eight international courts and tribunals, although they include the development banks' inspection panels and non-compliance procedures: Philippe Sands, Ruth Mackenzie, and Yuval Shany, *Manual on International Courts and Tribunals* (1999). See also Chester Brown, 'The Proliferation of International Courts and Tribunals: Finding Your Way Through the Maze' (2002) 3 *MJIL* 453.

[29] Karen J. Alter, 'Delegating to International Courts: Self-Binding vs Other-Binding Delegation' (2007) *Law and Contemporary Problems* (forthcoming 2008). See Yuval Shany, *The Competing Jurisdictions of International Courts and Tribunals* (2003) who offers five reasons for this proliferation (at 3–4):

> (1) the increased density, volume and complexity of international norms… (2) greater commitment to the rule of law in international relations, at the expense of power-oriented diplomacy; (3) the easing of international tensions… (4) the positive experience with some international courts and tribunals… and (5) the unsuitability of the ICJ and other pre-existing courts to address many types of disputes…

[30] Alter, above n. 29. See also Karen J. Alter, 'Do International Courts Enhance Compliance with International Law?' (2003) 25 *RevAPS* 51, 52.

environmental disputes, notwithstanding that relatively few of these institutions have a recognised capacity in the environmental field. The following discussion identifies the main venues for contemporary international environmental litigation.

2.2.1 Ad hoc and institutional arbitration

Although arbitration is the oldest adjudicative institution in international law, it has enjoyed a revival in recent decades, including in the environmental arena. Until the twentieth century arbitration was to a large extent a quasi-diplomatic procedure sharing much in common with mediation or conciliation. Since that time there has been a marked judicialisation of inter-state arbitration, so that in most outward respects it closely resembles judicial settlement.[31] Both now involve essentially the same function of reaching a binding determination of a dispute according to international law.[32] Despite the functional similarity, states have demonstrated a strong preference in environmental treaties for arbitration over judicial settlement. This is true both of early and more recent environmental treaties.[33] Importantly, when it comes to those few systems of compulsory adjudication of environmental disputes, there are far more examples of mandatory arbitration than judicial settlement.[34] Within environmental arbitration practice it is evident that states favour the ad hoc determination of specific

[31] Jonathan I. Charney, 'International Law and Multiple International Tribunals' (1998) 271 *RDC* 115, 119. Hudson noted in 1935, using the term 'adjudication' as a synonym for 'judicial settlement', that 'as it is usually conducted, arbitration is quite as much within the limits of law as adjudication, and the differences between the two processes are to be found chiefly in the constitutional instruments under which the tribunals act': Manley O. Hudson, *By Pacific Means: The Implementation of Article Two of the Pact of Paris* (1935) 9.

[32] Ian Brownlie, *Principles of Public International Law* (6th edn 2003) 675.

[33] Alexandre Kiss, 'Le règlement des différends dans les conventions multilaterals relatives à la protection de l'environnement' in R. J. Dupuy (ed.), *The Settlement of Disputes on the New Natural Resources* (1983) 119, 122–3. For early examples see CITES and the 1979 Convention on the Conservation of Migratory Species of Wild Animals. For an example of a more recent environmental treaty expressing a preference for arbitration see the 1991 Protocol on Environmental Protection to the Antarctic Treaty (Madrid Protocol), arts. 18 and 19 which provide for compulsory arbitration by default if the parties have not selected an alternative mechanism for dispute settlement.

[34] It has been estimated that by the mid-1990s there were around twenty multilateral environmental agreements that provided for compulsory arbitration: Philippe Sands and Ruth Mackenzie, 'Guidelines for Negotiating and Drafting Dispute Settlement Clauses for International Environmental Agreements' in International Bureau of the Permanent Court of Arbitration (ed.), *International Investments and Protection of the Environment* (2001) 305, 316–17.

disputes rather than institutional arbitration, where the procedures are agreed in advance. The most frequently invoked explanation for this preference for arbitration (and its ad hoc variant in particular) is that states have greater confidence in an adjudicative process over which they have a large level of control, by comparison to judicial settlement which is potentially more unpredictable.[35]

Arbitration has been utilised successfully in a number of landmark environmental disputes. The importance of the *Trail Smelter* case[36] between Canada and the United States is often overstated; however, it did greatly assist the development of the law of state responsibility for transboundary environmental harm. Other seminal arbitral decisions include the *Bering Sea Fur Seals* case,[37] between Great Britain and the United States, concerning the latter's attempt to enforce conservancy measures in an area beyond its national jurisdiction, and the *Lake Lanoux* case,[38] between France and Spain, in relation to a French proposal to interfere with the flow of the Carol River for the purposes of a hydroelectricity project. Recent arbitrations of importance include the decisions of arbitral tribunals established under annex VII of the LOS Convention in the *Southern Bluefin Tuna* dispute[39] and the *MOX Plant* dispute.[40] The *Southern Bluefin Tuna* dispute stemmed from a disagreement between Australia and New Zealand on the one hand, and Japan on the other, as to the current state and future prospects for stocks of southern bluefin tuna fished extensively by all three nations. The *MOX Plant* dispute raised quite different environmental issues concerning the development by the United Kingdom of a nuclear reprocessing facility on the shores of the Irish Sea and has given rise to proceedings in the PCA under the LOS Convention and the OSPAR Convention.[41] However, as with the *Southern Bluefin Tuna* dispute, in the *MOX Plant* dispute the

[35] J. G. Merrills, *International Dispute Settlement* (3rd edn 1998) 116.

[36] *Trail Smelter* case (*Canada/United States of America*) (1938 and 1941) 3 *RIAA* 1911.

[37] *Bering Sea Fur Seals* case (*Great Britain/United States of America*) (1893) 1 Moore 827.

[38] *Lake Lanoux* case (*France/Spain*) (1957) 12 *RIAA* 285.

[39] *Southern Bluefin Tuna* cases: *New Zealand* v. *Japan*; *Australia* v. *Japan* (provisional measures) (1999) 38 ILM 1624 (*Southern Bluefin Tuna* order); *Australia and New Zealand* v. *Japan* (award on jurisdiction and admissibility) (2000) 39 ILM 1359 (*Southern Bluefin Tuna* award).

[40] *MOX Plant* cases: *Ireland* v. *United Kingdom* (provisional measures) (2002) 41 ILM 405 (*MOX Plant* order); *Ireland* v. *United Kingdom* (suspension on jurisdiction and merits and request for further provisional measures) (order 3, of 24 June 2003) (2003) 42 ILM 1187 (order 4, of 14 November 2003) (order 5, of 22 January 2007) (*MOX Plant* award).

[41] *OSPAR Arbitration (Ireland* v. *United Kingdom)* (final award) (2003) 42 ILM 1118. See Ted L. McDorman 'Access to Information under Article 9 of the OSPAR Convention (Ireland v. United Kingdom)' (2004) 98 *AJIL* 330.

arbitration under the rubric of the LOS Convention stalled as a result of jurisdictional complications.[42]

2.2.1.1 PCA

One of the apparent reasons for increasing resort to arbitration in the environmental context is the availability of established procedures, the most significant of which is the PCA. When established by the 1899 International Convention for the Pacific Settlement of International Disputes (Hague Convention) the PCA marked the first step towards the creation of a permanent international judicial body. The PCA was created 'for the maintenance of the general peace'[43] through the resolution of major international disturbances.[44] Despite its name it was not a standing court with compulsory jurisdiction, as many proponents had hoped it would be.[45] None the less, the PCA does have a permanent institutional basis as it operates through an intergovernmental organisation, the PCA secretariat (known as the International Bureau), which receives requests for arbitration, assists in the selection of arbitrators, facilitates the conduct of arbitrations, and promotes the services offered by the court to potential litigants.[46]

Although the PCA has not been utilised as regularly as initially expected, it has had a respectable caseload for most of its history. Fifty cases have been brought before the PCA since 1902, leading to forty-three awards.[47] The Court has also overseen five commissions of inquiry and conducted three international conciliation commissions.[48] It was most active immediately after its establishment (seventeen cases were submitted prior to the First World War), and was then infrequently used until the 1980s when it attracted renewed interest (with twenty-four new cases).[49] Arguably the highlight in its history was the Iran–USA claims tribunal, a mixed claim tribunal supported by the International Bureau to resolve disputes arising

[42] See ch. 9. [43] 1899 Hague Convention, preamble.

[44] David Caron, 'War and International Adjudication: Reflections on the 1899 Peace Conference' (2000) 94 *AJIL* 4.

[45] Merrills, above n. 35, 90.

[46] See generally Sands, Mackenzie, and Shany, above n. 28, 23–38. Reference is also occasionally made to the International Bureau to appoint arbitrators for ad hoc arbitral tribunals where the parties (or appointed arbitrators) are unable to agree: e.g. the 1935 Convention for the Settlement of Difficulties Arising from the Operation of the Smelter at Trail between Great Britain and the United States, art. 2.

[47] Permanent Court of Arbitration, *106th Annual Report* (2006).

[48] *Ibid.* [49] *Ibid.*

from the detention of nationals of the United States at its embassy in Tehran in 1979, and the subsequent freezing of Iranian assets by the United States.

As the PCA was established to address international disputes generally it is unsurprising that only five environmental disputes have been brought before it. The first case with environmental elements was the *North Atlantic Coast Fisheries* case,[50] which concerned the rights of Great Britain, pursuant to a treaty with the United States, to regulate fishing by United States vessels in Canadian waters. Over ninety years later the dispute between Ireland and the United Kingdom over the MOX plant at Sellafield gave rise to two arbitrations before PCA panels.[51] A fourth arbitration involved a dispute between France and the Netherlands concerning the 1976 Convention on the Protection of the Rhine Against Pollution by Chlorides.[52] In the fifth and most recent case, the Arbitration Regarding the Iron Rhine Railway,[53] a PCA panel sought to balance Belgium's wish to exercise a long-standing international right of transit across Holland with the legitimate interests of the Netherlands government in safeguarding the natural environment along the transit corridor.

2.2.1.2 Optional Rules for the Arbitration of Environmental Disputes

In view of its light environmental caseload the International Bureau has taken several steps to promote the court as a forum for environmental litigation. Chief among these has been the 2001 Optional Rules for the Arbitration of Disputes Relating to Natural Resources and/or the Environment (Environmental Rules) adopted by consensus by PCA member states in 2001 to address certain special characteristics of international environmental litigation. The Environmental Rules are optional in that they can only be used when specific disputes arise, unless they have been incorporated by reference in an arbitration

[50] *North Atlantic Coast Fisheries* case (*Great Britain/United States of America*) (1910) 11 *RIAA* 167.

[51] *MOX Plant* award (2003) 42 ILM 1187, *OSPAR Arbitration* (2003) 42 ILM 1118.

[52] *Protection of the Rhine Against Pollution by Chlorides* arbitration in application of the convention of 3 December 1976 and the Additional Protocol of 25 September 1991 (12 March 2004) (pt I available at www.pca_cpa.org/ENGLISH/RPC/PBF/Sentence%20I.pdf and pt II available at www.pca_cpa.org/ENGLISH/RPC/PBF/Sentence%20II.pdf).

[53] *Iron Rhine (Ijzeren Rijn) Railway (Belgium/Netherlands)*, arbitration (24 May 2005) (available at www.pca-cpa.org/showfile.asp?fil_id=377).

clause in an environmental agreement.[54] As at the time of writing the rules have not been used in any arbitration by the PCA, or any other arbitral tribunal.

The Environmental Rules have potentially wide and flexible application. They do not seek to define 'disputes relating to natural resources/ and or the environment' as a precondition to their operation, and article 1(1) reinforces this in stating that '[t]he characterisation of the dispute as relating to the environment or natural resources is not necessary for jurisdiction'. It is therefore for the parties themselves to determine whether the rules should apply to a dispute, and it is not open to a tribunal to find that it has no jurisdiction because a case is not sufficiently connected to an environmental issue. Further enhancing the flexibility of the Environmental Rules is their applicability beyond inter-state environmental disputes to litigation involving international organisations of states, non-governmental organisations (NGOs) and corporations.[55] This provision for multiparty environmental litigation is an important acknowledgement that a number of states and non-state actors may have a legitimate interest in participating in complex environmental litigation.

Other aspects of the Environmental Rules are similarly responsive to the realities of environmental litigation. Recognising that environmental disputes often involve complex scientific issues, article 27 allows an arbitral tribunal to appoint one or more experts to report on specific issues as determined by the tribunal. To assist the tribunal, an indicative list of experts with expertise in scientific and technical matters is provided by the Secretary-General of the PCA (and contained in annex II to the Environmental Rules).[56] As the arbitral tribunal has significant control in appointing experts, both in relation to the issue areas in which assistance is sought and in respect of the identity of the appointee(s), the procedure set out in article 27 may be helpful where there is fundamental disagreement between the expert scientific evidence adduced by the parties.

[54] The first and only example of the adoption of the rules in this way is in art. 14 of the 2003 Protocol on Civil Liability and Compensation for Damage Caused by the Transboundary Effects of Industrial Accidents on Transboundary Waters to the 1992 Convention on the Protection and Use of Transboundary Waters and International Lakes.

[55] Environmental Rules, introduction and art. 1(1).

[56] *Ibid.* art. 27(5).

Provisional measures have proved to be important in international environmental litigation and reflecting this article 26 of the Environmental Rules empowers an arbitral tribunal to make, at the request of the parties, such interim orders as 'it deems necessary to preserve the rights of any party or to prevent serious harm to the environment falling within the subject-matter of the dispute'.[57] This formulation is designed to prevent a tribunal from restraining actions involving minor or transitory harm, or potentially serious damage unconnected with a dispute before the Court. In so doing it imposes on applicants a significant legal and evidentiary burden to establish the seriousness of injury and its relationship with the issues in dispute. Arguably this jurisdictional hurdle is inappropriate at an interlocutory stage in proceedings, particularly in the context of environmental disputes where a preventative and precautionary approach is to be preferred. An additional feature of concern is article 26(2) that goes further than other provisional measures procedures in allowing the arbitral tribunal to require security for costs in the event that the merits are ultimately decided against an applicant.[58]

In terms of costs more generally, an arbitral tribunal operating under the Environmental Rules has the discretion to 'apportion each of such costs between the parties if it determines that apportionment is reasonable, taking into account the circumstances of the case'.[59] This approach differs from most international adjudicative procedures, in which the parties ordinarily bear their own costs,[60] and may operate as a disincentive to international environmental litigation in the public interest by creating uncertainty as to where the financial burden will ultimately lie. Also sitting uncomfortably with the public interest character of international environmental litigation is the presumption in the Environmental Rules that any arbitral award will be confidential, unless the parties agree otherwise.[61] This provision runs against the prevailing trend in environmental law, both domestic and international, which has been to open environmental decision-making

[57] *Ibid.* art. 26(1).

[58] There exists no such provision in relation to the ICJ or ITLOS. See Hugh Thirlway, 'The Indication of Provisional Measures by the International Court of Justice' in R. Bernhardt (ed.), *Interim Measures Indicated by International Courts* (1994) 1.

[59] Environmental Rules, art. 40(1).

[60] See e.g. Statute of the ICJ, art. 64; ICJ Rules, art. 97.

[61] *Ibid.* art. 32(6).

processes to public scrutiny and participation.[62] Such transparency is essential for ensuring that arbitrators are accountable to the international community at large in achieving a settlement of the dispute in accordance with prevailing environmental standards and values.

2.2.1.3 Arbitration and judicial settlement compared

There is little doubt that arbitration has been critical to the peaceful resolution of a number of environmental disputes. On occasion arbitral panels have even laid the groundwork for subsequent legislative developments by articulating regimes for environmental protection and resource conservation.[63] The main reason for the success of arbitration in bringing some environmental disputes to an effective conclusion is that most arbitrations have taken place on an ad hoc basis in which the parties have jointly committed to the process and agreed to respect any award delivered.[64] The record of cooperation and compliance is far more mixed when environmental litigation is commenced unilaterally on the basis of compulsory procedures.[65]

However, the very attributes of arbitration that enhance its effectiveness as a dispute settlement technique also reduce its utility as an institution for giving effect to the public values of international environmental law. Arbitration is highly adaptable, allowing the parties to agree on a process that matches their needs in resolving disputes as they arise.[66] Among other things the parties will need to agree upon the composition of the arbitral tribunal, the rules for making submissions on law and fact, the applicable law, and modalities for implementing

[62] See e.g. Rio Declaration, principle 10: 'Environmental issues are best handled with participation of all concerned citizens, at the relevant level.' See also the 1998 Convention on Access to Information, Public Participation and Decision-Making and Access to Justice in Environmental Matters (Aarhus Convention).

[63] See e.g. *Bering Sea Fur Seals* case (1893) 1 Moore 755; *Trail Smelter* case (1938 and 1941) 3 RIAA 1911.

[64] Romano, above n. 14, 324–8.

[65] See e.g. *Fisheries Jurisdiction* cases; *United Kingdom* v. *Iceland* (merits) [1974] ICJ Rep 3; *Germany* v. *Iceland* (merits) [1974] ICJ Rep 175. Iceland declined to recognise the Court's jurisdiction or play any part in the proceedings. In the *Nuclear Tests* cases (*Australia* v. *France* (interim measures) [1973] ICJ Rep 99, (merits) [1974] ICJ Rep 253; *New Zealand* v. *France* (interim measures) [1973] ICJ Rep 135, (merits) [1974] ICJ Rep 457) France similarly refused to participate in the proceedings, and initially continued with its atmospheric nuclear testing programme in defiance of provisional measures indicated by the Court.

[66] Christine Gray and Benedict Kingsbury, 'Inter-State Arbitration since 1945: Overview and Evaluation' in Mark W. Janis (ed.), *International Courts for the Twenty-First Century* (1992) 55, 63.

the award. On the one hand, this means that states can adjust arbitral rules to respond to the some of the particular features of environmental litigation (as seen in the PCA's Environmental Rules).[67] However, the flexibility also means that states may set procedures that will achieve the most rapid and acceptable result for the parties, rather than a process that will allow an arbitral tribunal to evaluate environmental issues (which are likely to be of public concern) in a comprehensive manner. Adding further pressure for a truncated, settlement-oriented, process are the heavy organisational and financial burdens faced by states when using arbitration, as compared with judicial settlement where litigation costs are shared to some extent with the broader international community.[68]

A more fundamental deficiency in environmental arbitration reflects its origins as an extension of diplomatic modes of dispute settlement. Arbitration is much closer today to judicial settlement than it has ever been, but there remains a continuing emphasis on arbitration as a private process concerned first and foremost with achieving justice as between the parties.[69] The propensity for arbitration to promote a private settlement may be further amplified if the parties do not accept the involvement of other interested parties, either as intervenors or as *amici curiae*, or if they agree that the proceedings and any award should remain confidential.[70] Environmental disputes seldom fit comfortably within a solely *inter partes* process, given that they almost always involve matters of concern to other states and non-state actors. Moreover the decisions produced by arbitration focused on the parties,

[67] Bilder, above n. 1, 228.

[68] Romano, above n. 14, 103. Although not a case involving environmental questions, the *M/V Saiga* case (*no. 2*) (*St Vincent and the Grenadines* v. *Guinea*) (prompt release) (1997) 110 ILR 736, (provisional measures) 1998 117 ILR 111, (admissibility and merits (1999) 120 ILR 143) illustrates some of the difficulties that may be encountered in this respect. This dispute was originally to be resolved by arbitration under annex VII of the LOS Convention; however, the parties subsequently agreed to transfer the case to ITLOS apparently because of the costs and other burdens imposed upon the parties by ad hoc arbitration: Tullio Treves, 'Conflicts Between the International Tribunal for the Law of the Sea and the International Court of Justice' (1999) 31 *NYUJILP* 809, 821.

[69] A. Neil Craik, 'Recalcitrant Reality and Chosen Ideals: The Public Function of Dispute Settlement in International Environmental Law' (1998) 10 *GeoIELR* 551, 562–5; Elihu Lauterpacht, *Aspects of the Administration of International Justice* (1991) 86.

[70] The conduct of arbitral proceedings, or parts of proceedings, in closed session is not uncommon, even in relation to environmental disputes that raise issues beyond those of immediate concern to the parties. See 1907 Hague Convention, art. 78.

and not the environmental problem in its true context, may prove to be an obstacle to normative development in this field.[71]

In contrast, permanent courts and tribunals have the capacity to adopt a more independent stance, oriented towards public interest considerations. International courts have acquired substantial autonomy as international actors in their own right,[72] and are composed of independent and impartial judges appointed for lengthy terms. These features mean that international courts may develop a more self-directed approach to the settlement of environmental disputes, consider interests beyond those of the disputants, and render decisions that contribute to the principled development of international environmental law.[73]

2.2.2 ICJ

In practice international courts have not always seized the opportunities that have been afforded to them by their more independent positioning in the international legal order. This observation applies, at least to some extent, to the ICJ, the principal judicial organ of the United Nations and the pre-eminent international court.

2.2.2.1 Origins of the World Court

The Permanent Court of International Justice (PCIJ), and its successor the ICJ, are the only two international courts to have been established with general subject matter jurisdiction and global reach.[74] Both founded in the aftermath of internecine conflict, the progenitor of these institutions was the same popular belief that inspired and animated the 1899 and 1907 Hague Peace Conferences which successively established and reformed the PCA, namely the conviction that the creation of a permanent mechanism for the pacific settlement of inter-state disputes was an essential step towards international peace and security. However, in securing peace these institutions have played only a subsidiary and indirect function. Instead, in times of amity, they have performed an

[71] Marcel T. A. Brus, *Third Party Dispute Settlement in an Interdependent World: Developing a Theoretical Framework* (1995) 191 (ad hoc procedures may be demanded by pragmatism, but should be avoided as they may be inadequate for the further development of a 'community of principle').

[72] Lauterpacht, above n. 69.

[73] See Laurence R. Helfer and Anne-Marie Slaughter, 'Why States Create International Tribunals: A Response to Professors Posner and Yoo' (2005) 93 *CalLR* 901, 938–9.

[74] Statute of the PCIJ, arts. 34 and 36; Statute of the ICJ, arts. 34 and 36.

instrumental role in clarifying, refining, and developing international law, including in the environmental field.

2.2.2.2 Environmental cases in the World Court

The PCIJ was established in 1920 when the statute of the Court was adopted by the League of Nations.[75] Although the PCIJ was not a core institution in the League system that emerged out of the Paris Peace Conference, it proved to be an important body. Sixty-six cases were submitted to the Court[76] and it handed down fifty-nine judgments[77] during its brief existence in the inter-war period. From an environmental perspective the most significant decision of the PCIJ was the *Territorial Jurisdiction of the International Commission of the River Oder* case.[78] Although the litigation did not raise environmental issues directly, the case enunciated the 'community of interest' theory for shared access to international rivers which has major ramifications for sustainable and equitable watercourse management.[79]

In large part the PCIJ model was retained in the ICJ that emerged out of the United Nations Conference on International Organisation in San Francisco in 1945. However, unlike the PCIJ's arm's length relationship with the League of Nations, the ICJ was established as a principal organ of the United Nations.[80] Reflecting this, the Statute of the ICJ 'forms an integral part'[81] of the UN Charter. Environmental disputes have been far more prominent in the docket of the ICJ than they were in its predecessor. Environmental cases may be brought before the ICJ in several ways, and it has already been noted that the ICJ only has general and obligatory jurisdiction in contentious matters to the extent that jurisdiction has been conferred upon it by states in accordance with article 36(2) of the Statute of the ICJ. In addition to its contentious jurisdiction, the ICJ also has competence to render advisory opinions 'on any legal question at the request of whatever body may be authorized by

[75] Pursuant to the 1919 Covenant of the League of Nations, art. 14.

[76] Thirty-eight of these cases were contentious, the remaining twenty-eight in the PCIJ's advisory jurisdiction.

[77] Thirty-two of these were judgments in contentious cases, the remaining twenty-seven advisory opinions.

[78] *Territorial Jurisdiction of the International Commission of the River Oder (Czechoslovakia, Denmark, France, Germany, Great Britain, Sweden/Poland)* [1929] PCIJ (ser. A) no. 23, 5.

[79] See ch. 6. [80] UN Charter, art. 92.

[81] *Ibid*. In addition all members of the UN are *ipso facto* parties to the Statute of the ICJ: UN Charter art. 93(1).

or in accordance' with the UN Charter to make a request.[82] The Court rendered an advisory opinion with implications for environmental protection during wartime in the *Legality of the Threat or Use of Nuclear Weapons*[83] in which it concluded that treaty prohibitions on methods of warfare causing widespread, severe, and permanent damage to the natural environment had entered into customary international law.

The ICJ's broad jurisdiction, and its position as the pre-eminent international judicial organ, mean that it is well suited to considering major inter-state disputes concerning environmental issues. As Judge Weeramantry noted in the *Request for an Examination of the Situation in Accordance with Paragraph 63 of the Court's Judgment of 20 December 1974 in the Nuclear Tests (New Zealand v. France)* case,[84] 'the [ICJ], situated at the apex of international tribunals, necessarily enjoys a position of special trust and responsibility in relation to the principles of environmental law especially those relating to what is described in environmental law as the Global Commons'.[85] The Court is also a reasonably adaptable institution, capable of forming chambers to deal with individual disputes or classes of disputes,[86] and can call upon the assistance of technical or scientific assessors.[87]

2.2.2.3 Chamber for Environmental Matters

None the less, there has been a widespread view that the ICJ, as with the PCA, has major functional limitations that prevent it from effectively addressing environmental cases. In 1993, in response to this perceived concern, the ICJ sought to enhance its environmental credentials by establishing a permanent seven-member Chamber for Environmental Matters (Environmental Chamber).[88] After referring to the Nauru case

[82] Statute of the ICJ, art. 65(1).

[83] *Legality of the Threat or Use of Nuclear Weapons* [1996] ICJ Rep 226 (*Nuclear Weapons* advisory opinion).

[84] *Request for an Examination of the Situation in Accordance with Paragraph 63 of the Court's Judgment of 20 December 1974 in the Nuclear Tests (New Zealand v. France)* case [1995] ICJ Rep 288.

[85] *Ibid.*, dissenting opinion of Judge Weeramantry, 345.

[86] Statute of the ICJ, art. 26.

[87] *Ibid.* arts 50 and 34(1). See Philip C. Jessup, 'Do New Problems Need New Courts?' (1971) 65 *ProcASIL* 261, 262–3.

[88] See generally Phoebe N. Okowa, 'Environmental Dispute Settlement: Some Reflections on Recent Developments' in Malcolm D. Evans (eds.), *Remedies in International Law: The Institutional Dilemma* (1998) 157, 168–9; John Collier and A. Vaughan Lowe, *The Settlement of Disputes in International Law: Institutions and Procedures* (1999) 127–9. Sands notes that the decision to establish the Chamber 'may... have

and the *Gabčíkovo-Nagymaros Project* case, the communiqué issued by the Court stated that the Chamber would allow it to be 'prepared to the fullest extent possible to deal with any environmental case falling within its jurisdiction'.[89]

The Environmental Chamber was established under article 26(1) of the Statute of the ICJ, which allows the Court to form one or more chambers composed of three or more of the ICJ's fifteen judges to deal with particular categories of case. In appointing judges to a chamber the Court should 'have regard to any special knowledge, expertise or previous experience which any of the Members of the Court may have in relation to the category of case the chamber is being formed to deal with'.[90] This first and only permanent[91] chamber to be formed by the ICJ has been celebrated by a number of commentators. Fitzmaurice has observed that the creation of the Environmental Chamber 'may well be regarded as the most important development in the ICJ concerning the environment, rendering it fully prepared to deal with all kinds of environmental matters which may come before it'.[92] Merrills notes that it has strengthened the role of the Court in developing and clarifying international environmental law.[93] Yet despite such upbeat assessments the Chamber suffers from essentially the same limitations as the ICJ sitting in plenary, including the restrictive standing rules.[94] Moreover doubts have been expressed concerning the willingness of states to resort to the chamber, given the difficulty of defining any dispute as

been motivated by the desire to pre-empt the establishment of a specialized international environmental court': Philippe Sands, 'International Environmental Litigation and its Future' (1999) 32 *URichLR* 1619, 1626.

89 ICJ, Communiqué 93/20 on the Establishment of a Permanent Chamber for Environmental Matters (19 July 1993).

90 Rules of the ICJ, art. 16(2).

91 The Court had previously established a number of ad hoc chambers under art. 26(2) of the Statute of the ICJ. See generally Stephen M. Schwebel, 'Ad Hoc Chambers of the International Court of Justice' (1987) 81 *AJIL* 831.

92 Malgosia A. Fitzmaurice, 'Environmental Protection and the International Court of Justice' in A. Vaughan Lowe and Malgosia A. Fitzmaurice (eds.), *Fifty Years of the International Court of Justice: Essays in Honour of Sir Robert Jennings* (1996) 293, 305. Fitzmaurice has also suggested that the Court's initiative 'evidences that environmental law has come of age': Malgosia A. Fitzmaurice, 'International Protection of the Environment' (2001) 293 *RDC* 9, 364.

93 Merrills, above n. 35, 306. See also Raymond Ranjeva, 'Jurisdiction International Arbitrage. L'énvironnement, Le Court International de la Justice et sa Chamber spéciale pour les questions d'environnement' (1994) *XL AnnFDDI* 433.

94 Okowa, above n. 88, 169.

wholly or predominantly environmental in character.[95] These factors may partly explain why no cases have been submitted to the Chamber, including the recent and ongoing *Pulp Mills on the River Uruguay* case,[96] and why the Court decided in 2006 to cease the usual practice of holding annual elections for the Chamber's membership.

2.2.3 *ITLOS and part XV of the LOS Convention*

While the ICJ's efforts to tailor its procedures to suit the demands of environmental litigation have not paid dividends in terms of caseload, other tribunals with an expertise in environmental dispute settlement have been more successful in attracting cases. The systems of adjudication created by the LOS Convention stand as the best example of this.

2.2.3.1 Significance of the LOS Convention

The LOS Convention is a landmark multilateral environmental agreement, providing a global framework both for sustainable development of ocean resources and the protection of the marine environment generally. The provisions relating to environmental matters were more detailed and comprehensive than existing multilateral environmental agreements,[97] and as a result the convention has been an important model for the development of international environmental law in other areas.[98]

The central provisions of the LOS Convention giving effect to its stated objective of promoting 'the protection and preservation of the marine environment'[99] are found in part XII.[100] Among other things, these seek to limit pollution of the marine environment,[101] encourage cooperation on a global and regional basis to protect and preserve the marine environment,[102] promote the technical and scientific capacity of developing states for marine environmental protection,[103] and require

[95] Alan E. Boyle, 'The *Gabčíkovo-Nagymaros* Case: New Law in Old Bottles' (1997) 8 *YIEL* 13.

[96] *Pulp Mills on the River Uruguay* (*Argentina* v. *Uruguay*) (request for provisional measures by Argentina) (2006) 45 ILM 1025 (request for provisional measures by Uruguay) (2007) (available at www.icj-cij.org/docket/files/135/13615.pdf).

[97] Jonathan I. Charney, 'The Marine Environment and the 1982 United Nations Convention on the Law of the Sea' (1994) 28 *International Lawyer* 879, 882.

[98] Patricia W. Birnie and Alan E. Boyle, *International Law and the Environment* (2nd edn 2002) 348.

[99] LOS Convention, preamble, 3rd recital.

[100] *Ibid*. art. 192.

[101] *Ibid*. arts. 194, 195, 199, 204–6, 207–22 and 223–33.

[102] *Ibid*. arts. 197–201.

[103] *Ibid*. arts. 202–3.

states to undertake monitoring and environmental assessment.[104] In addition, the conservation and management of 'marine living resources' is a major focus of the convention and several articles deal with the rights and responsibilities of coastal and flag states in this regard,[105] and establish a framework for more specific implementing agreements.

2.2.3.2 Overview of dispute settlement provisions

In addition to its substantive innovations in marine environmental protection, the LOS Convention incorporates a sophisticated dispute settlement system. Elaborated in part XV of the convention this system is highly distinctive in international environmental law by virtue of its comprehensive coverage and its compulsory character.[106] With limited exceptions, part XV makes disputes concerning the interpretation and application of the convention the subject of compulsory and binding third-party settlement. This was considered essential to hold the 'package deal' convention together and to guarantee the authoritative and consistent interpretation of its provisions.[107] Part XV also carries a potentially broader significance as evidence of a trend towards greater reliance on the rule of law in international relations.[108]

The three sections that make up part XV seek both to utilise existing courts and to establish new institutions. Section 1 sets out jurisdictional prerequisites, section 2 contains the core compulsory dispute settlement provisions, and section 3 provides for several exceptions to the part XV system. The pivotal provision in section 2 of part XV is article 287, which outlines the various compulsory dispute settlement procedures available.[109] At any time states are free to declare a preference for one or more of four procedures, namely ITLOS, the ICJ, an annex VII arbitral tribunal, or an annex VIII special arbitral tribunal. Article 287 further provides that annex VII arbitration is the default procedure where no declaration has been made by a party to a dispute[110] or where

104 *Ibid.* arts. 204–6. 105 *Ibid.* arts. 61–73, 116–20.

106 Tullio Treves, 'Dispute Settlement Clauses in the Law of the Sea Convention and their Impact on the Protection of the Marine Environment: Some Observations' (1999) 8 *RECIEL* 6.

107 Christine M. Chinkin, 'Dispute Resolution and the Law of the Sea: Regional Problems and Prospects' in James Crawford and Donald R. Rothwell (eds.), *The Law of the Sea in the Asian Pacific Region: Developments and Prospects* (1995) 237, 245.

108 Natalie Klein, *Dispute Settlement in the UN Convention on the Law of the Sea* (2005) 24.

109 See Robin R. Churchill and A. Vaughan Lowe, *The Law of the Sea* (3rd edn 1999) 455–9.

110 LOS Convention, art. 287(3).

Table 2.2 *Summary of declarations under article 287 of the LOS Convention indicating party preference(s) for method of dispute settlement*

State party	Preferred fora, in order of preference
Argentina	(a) ITLOS (b) annex VIII special arbitration
Australia	(a) ITLOS/ICJ[a]
Austria	(a) ITLOS (b) annex VIII special arbitration (c) ICJ
Belarus	(a) annex VII arbitration (b) annex VIII special arbitration
Belgium	(a) ITLOS/ICJ
Canada	(a) ITLOS/annex VII arbitration
Cape Verde	(a) ITLOS (b) ICJ
Chile	(a) ITLOS (b) annex VIII special arbitration
Croatia	(a) ITLOS (b) ICJ
Denmark	(a) ICJ
Egypt	(a) annex VII arbitration
Estonia	(a) ICJ/ITLOS
Finland	(a) ICJ/ITLOS
Germany	(a) ITLOS (b) annex VII arbitration (c) ICJ
Greece	(a) ITLOS
Honduras	(a) ICJ
Hungary	(a) ITLOS (b) ICJ (c) annex VIII special arbitration
Italy	(a) ITLOS/ICJ
Latvia	(a) ITLOS (b) ICJ
Lithuania	(a) ITLOS (b) ICJ
Mexico	(a) ITLOS/ICJ/annex VIII special arbitration
Netherlands	(a) ICJ
Nicaragua	(a) ICJ
Norway	(a) ICJ
Oman	(a) ITLOS/ICJ
Portugal[b]	(a) ITLOS (b) ICJ (c) annex VII arbitration (d) annex VIII special arbitration
Russian Federation	(a) annex VII arbitration/annex VIII special arbitration
Slovenia	(a) annex VII arbitration
Spain	(a) ITLOS/ICJ
Sweden	(a) ICJ
Tanzania	(a) ITLOS
Trinidad and Tobago	(a) ITLOS (b) ICJ
Tunisia	(a) ITLOS (b) annex VII arbitration
Ukraine	(a) annex VII arbitration/annex VIII special arbitration
United Kingdom	(a) ICJ

Table 2.2 *(cont.)*

State party	Preferred fora, in order of preference
United Republic of Tanzania	(a) ITLOS
Uruguay	(a) ITLOS

[a] This indicates that ITLOS and ICJ have both been chosen, and no preference has been expressed for one forum over the other.
[b] Portugal's declaration does not appear to express any order of preference for these procedures, notwithstanding that they are listed in this order.
Source: www.un.org/Depts/los/settlement_of_disputes/choice_procedure.

the parties have accepted different procedures.[111] There are now 155 parties to the LOS Convention, with thirty-seven of these indicating a preferred procedure pursuant to article 287 (see Table 2.2). Twenty-five of these states have expressed confidence in ITLOS by selecting the tribunal as their preferred (or equally preferred) body for dealing with convention disputes.

Each of the four courts or tribunals referred to in article 287 is given broad jurisdiction under article 288 to address any dispute under the LOS Convention, and any dispute concerning the interpretation or application of an international agreement related to the purposes of the convention submitted consistently with that agreement. The jurisdiction of the four bodies extends to most of the convention's environmental provisions and accordingly there are significant opportunities for environmental issues to be the subject of compulsory dispute settlement.[112] Importantly, 'special arbitration' under annex VIII is designed specifically to deal with a range of disputes concerning the protection and preservation of the marine environment including fisheries cases, and disputes relating to vessel sourced pollution and ocean dumping.[113]

However, there are some limitations to the jurisdiction of these bodies over cases that may involve environmental issues. In the first place

[111] *Ibid.* art. 287(5).

[112] H. S. Schiffman, 'UNCLOS and Marine Wildlife Disputes: Big Splash or Barely a Ripple?' (2001) 4 *JIWLP* 257. For an overview of various environmental disputes that may arise under the LOS Convention see Thomas A. Mensah, 'The International Tribunal for the Law of the Sea and the Protection and Preservation of the Marine Environment' (1999) 8 *RECIEL* 1.

[113] LOS Convention, annex VIII, art. 1.

states may declare that they do not accept the compulsory dispute settlement procedures for certain disputes including (a) maritime boundary delimitations or disputes involving historic bays or titles; (b) disputes over military activities; and (c) disputes in respect of which the United Nations Security Council is exercising its functions under the UN Charter.[114] Twenty-seven states have made declarations under article 298 indicating that they do not accept one or more of the four procedures in relation to one or more of these three types of dispute. Secondly, article 297 sets out some non-optional limitations on the adjudication of disputes involving coastal marine scientific research and fisheries. The only major, non-optional, limitation on jurisdiction over environmental matters is found in article 297(3)(a) which provides that a coastal state is not obliged to submit disputes 'relating to its sovereign rights with respect to the living resources in the exclusive economic zone or their exercise, including its discretionary capacity, the allocation of surpluses to other States and the terms and conditions established in its conservation management laws and regulations'. These disputes may, however, be the subject of compulsory conciliation.[115]

In relation to disputes concerning the exploration and exploitation of the seabed and ocean floor and subsoil beyond the limits of national jurisdiction ('the area')[116] there is a special regime that refers such disputes to a Sea-Bed Disputes Chamber of ITLOS, a special chamber of ITLOS, an ad hoc chamber of the Sea-Bed Disputes Chamber, or binding commercial arbitration.[117] The parties to disputes before the Sea-Bed Disputes Chamber of ITLOS or binding commercial arbitration may include not only states parties to the LOS Convention, but also the Sea-Bed Authority,[118] the enterprise,[119] state enterprises, natural or juridical persons, and prospective contractors.

2.2.3.3 Provisional measures jurisdiction

One feature of part XV that is critical for a timely response to environmental disputes is its machinery for provisional measures.[120] Article 290 allows for the prescription of interim orders either by an agreed court or tribunal or, failing agreement, by ITLOS in order 'to preserve

[114] *Ibid.* art. 298. [115] LOS Convention, art. 297(3)(b). [116] *Ibid.* art. 1(1).
[117] *Ibid.* arts. 186–91. [118] *Ibid.* arts. 156–8. [119] *Ibid.* art. 170.
[120] See generally Klein, above n. 108, 59–87. See also Chester Brown, *A Common Law of International Adjudication* (2007) ch. 4.

the respective rights of the parties to the dispute *or to prevent serious harm to the marine environment*, pending the final decision'.[121] This has proved to be an important source of jurisdiction for ITLOS, which has now issued provisional measures on four occasions, with three of these applications raising environmental issues.[122]

The reference in article 290 of the LOS Convention to the avoidance of 'serious harm to the marine environment' indicates the specific design of the mechanism to respond effectively to situations of potential environmental damage, and not only to preserve the rights of the parties.[123] The requirement of seriousness could limit the availability of provisional measures, although in practice this may not prove to be a significant limitation as lower standards of proof are likely to be accepted in an interlocutory setting. Indeed it may be noted more generally that as jurisdiction need only be established on a prima facie basis, and the court in deciding on interim measures must be cautious of definite findings that may prejudice a later determination on the merits, there is an obvious conceptual affinity between the precautionary principle and the LOS Convention's provisional measures procedure.[124]

2.2.3.4 Pre-eminence of ITLOS

Although there is no formal hierarchy among article 287 courts and tribunals, ITLOS as a new permanent and dedicated institution is at the fulcrum of the part XV dispute resolution system.[125] ITLOS has sought to stamp its authority on this system in several environmental

[121] Emphasis added.

[122] *Southern Bluefin Tuna* order (1999) 38 ILM 1624; *MOX Plant* order (2002) 41 ILM 405; *Land Reclamation by Singapore in and around the Straits of Johor (Malaysia* v. *Singapore)* (provisional measures) (8 October 2003) (available at www.itlos.org).

[123] Tullio Treves, 'The Role of Dispute Settlement Mechanisms in the Protection of the Marine Environment in Cases Concerning Economic Activities in the Sea and Seabed' in International Bureau of the Permanent Court of Arbitration (ed.), *International Investments and Protection of the Environment* (2001) 113.

[124] As Judge Treves noted in his separate opinion in the *Southern Bluetin Tuna* order (1999) 38 ILM 1624 'a precautionary approach seems ... inherent in the very notions of provisional measures' (at [9]).

[125] Tullio Treves, *Le Controversie Internazionali. Nuovi Tendenze, Nuovi Tribunali* (1999) 102 (ITLOS 'esso è parte integrante del complesso sistema di regole sulla soluzione pacifica delle controversie relative all'interpretazione e all'applicazione della Convenzione previsto nella parte XV di essa').

cases,[126] and it occupies a central role in the judicial development of international law relating to the marine environment.[127]

Environmental issues have figured prominently in cases before ITLOS and annex VII arbitral tribunals. Since it commenced operation in 1996, ITLOS has dealt with fourteen distinct cases, delivered seven judgments and made several dozen orders both of a substantive and procedural nature. Although nine of these cases have raised significant issues of environmental concern, none of these proceeded to a full hearing on the merits by ITLOS or another article 287 institution. Three of the decisions have been in exercise of the tribunal's provisional measures jurisdiction, while the remaining cases have involved cases of prompt release of vessels and crew. The two cases that were subject to annex VII arbitration (the *Southern Bluefin Tuna* dispute and *MOX Plant* dispute) have led to essentially procedural decisions deferring the settlement of those disputes to other fora. Notwithstanding this, in dealing with provisional measures and prompt release applications the tribunal has had an opportunity to consider a range of important environmental matters involving fisheries management and the protection of the marine environment.

2.2.3.5 ITLOS Chamber for Marine Environmental Disputes

ITLOS has imitated the ICJ in establishing a Chamber for Marine Environmental Disputes under the special chambers mechanism of annex VI to the LOS Convention.[128] Former ITLOS president Thomas Mensah noted that in so doing 'the Tribunal has taken cognisance of the special role it is expected to play in the implementation of the Convention's provisions on the protection and preservation of the marine environment'.[129] Under the resolution adopting the initiative, it was said that the chamber would be available to deal with disputes relating to the marine environmental provisions of the LOS Convention, disputes arising out of special conventions and agreements concerning the marine environment referred to in article 237 of

[126] See in particular the discussion by ITLOS of jurisdictional issues in the *MOX Plant* order (2002) 41 ILM 405. See also A. Vaughan Lowe, 'Advocating Judicial Activism: The ITLOS Opinions of Judge Ivan Shearer' (2005) 24 *AustYBIL* 145, 152.

[127] The environmental jurisprudence of ITLOS is considered in ch. 7.

[128] International Tribunal for the Law of the Sea, *Resolution on the Chamber for Marine Environment Disputes* (2002).

[129] Mensah, above n. 112, 4.

the LOS Convention, and disputes under any other relevant agreement which conferred jurisdiction on the tribunal. However, as with the ICJ Environmental Chamber, parties are not required to use the chamber in preference to ITLOS in plenary even if the case at hand involves exclusively environmental issues.

In sum, the dispute settlement system in the LOS Convention is a model for dispute settlement mechanisms in multilateral environmental treaties more generally.[130] It is comprehensive, and generally compulsory, while also allowing a degree of flexibility in permitting states a choice of institution for resolving their disputes. At the same time, by ensuring that ITLOS possesses residual jurisdiction to prescribe provisional measures, it allows the tribunal to intervene promptly in marine environmental disputes to safeguard the interests of the parties and the marine environment itself.

2.2.4 WTO

The discussion to this point has examined systems of arbitration and judicial settlement that are either of a general character (in allowing any type of dispute to be brought before them, including environmental matters) or which have some more targeted environmental competence (such as ITLOS). However, other judicial bodies with a far more specific and non-environmental jurisdiction are also encountering a growing number of environmental disputes. The dispute settlement system of the WTO is without question the most important example of this phenomenon.

2.2.4.1 Environment/trade interface

The vexed relationship between international economic law and international environmental law remains the subject of extensive public and scholarly debate. The central tension in the interaction between the two fields is the extent to which the imposition of trade restrictions on environmental grounds is compatible with general rules that seek to promote the liberalisation of international trade. This conflict between economy and ecology arises from two competing policy objectives: the protection of the environment on the one hand and the promotion of 'world economic welfare', through free trade, on the

[130] See J. W. Kindt, 'Dispute Settlement in International Environmental Issues: The Model Provided by the 1982 Convention on the Law of the Sea' (1989) 22 *VandJTL* 1097.

other.[131] The interaction between trade liberalisation and environmental protection agendas has been played out in several international adjudicative bodies, the most prominent among them being the WTO dispute settlement system.

2.2.4.2 WTO dispute settlement understanding

The WTO is the pre-eminent multilateral trade organisation, and now has 151 members. Established in 1995,[132] the WTO is an international organisation responsible for administering the trade rules found in the 1947 General Agreement on Tariffs and Trade[133] (GATT) and related instruments. One of the most important features of the WTO is its dispute settlement system, established by the 1994 Understanding on Rules and Procedures Governing the Settlement of Disputes[134] (DSU). Three core institutions make up the WTO dispute settlement system: the Dispute Settlement Body (DSB), ad hoc panels and the standing Appellate Body. Membership of the DSB, the WTO's political body, comprises all WTO members, and it has ultimate responsibility for the administration of the dispute settlement system.

Disputes between WTO members are referred first to consultations[135] and, where no settlement is reached, a state may request adjudication by an ad hoc panel.[136] The possibility of a review on legal grounds then lies to an Appellate Body, which is made up of seven permanent members, three of whom will be appointed to hear the case.[137] Although panel and Appellate Body reports are themselves non-binding, they must be complied with if they are adopted by the DSB. However, as adoption is automatic (reports can only be rejected by a unanimous decision of the DSB) the DSU therefore effectively establishes a compulsory system of adjudication. This is a major development from the GATT system in which panel recommendations only acquired binding force when there was consensus among GATT members in favour of adoption.

The jurisdiction of the panels and the Appellate Body is restricted to matters arising from the 'covered agreements',[138] all of which are concerned exclusively with trade issues. None the less, there are several

[131] John H. Jackson, *The Jurisprudence of GATT and the WTO* (2000) 414.

[132] 1994 Marrakesh Agreement Establishing the World Trade Organization (Marrakesh Agreement).

[133] See now the Marrakesh Agreement, annex 1A GATT 1994.

[134] Marrakesh Agreement, annex 2. [135] *Ibid.* art. 4.

[136] *Ibid.* art. 6. [137] *Ibid.* art. 17. [138] *Ibid.* appendix 1.

ways in which environmental questions and norms of environmental law may be considered by panels and the Appellate Body. For instance, by operation of article 3.2 of the DSU, GATT and other covered agreements are to be construed 'in accordance with customary rules of interpretation of public international law'. In *United States – Standards for Reformulated and Conventional Gasoline*[139] the Appellate Body held that the '*General Agreement* [was] not to be read in clinical isolation from public international law',[140] and this included the rules and principles of international environmental law.

On account of its sophistication and frequent use, the WTO is regarded as possessing one of the most highly judicialised international regimes.[141] Because of its record of effectiveness it has also been suggested as a possible model for compliance systems in international environmental law.[142] Regardless of whether this happens it is evident that given the widespread reach of international trade law, and the compulsory jurisdiction of the WTO's dispute settlement system, WTO panels and the Appellate Body are likely to have a major impact upon the evolution of international environmental law. In the decisions to date it would appear that WTO panels and the Appellate Body have recognised the relevance of international environmental law to global trade issues, and are relatively conversant with issues of environmental law and policy.[143]

2.2.4.3 NAFTA and other trade regimes

The settlement of disputes under bilateral and plurilateral trade regimes also has the potential to influence the development of international environmental law. Among the most important such regional trade regimes is NAFTA, which is modelled in general terms upon GATT. In the ordinary course of events the three NAFTA parties (Canada, Mexico, and the United States) may pursue a settlement of their trade disputes under either NAFTA or in the WTO system.[144] However, disputes involving certain health or environmental concerns may be

[139] *United States – Standards for Reformulated and Conventional Gasoline*, WTO Doc. WT/DS2/AB/R (1996) (report of the Appellate Body).

[140] *Ibid.* 16.

[141] Martin Shapiro and Alec Stone Sweet, *On Law, Politics and Judicialization* (2002) 72–8.

[142] Steve Charnovitz, 'WTO Dispute Settlement as a Model for International Governance' in Alexandre Kiss, Dinah Shelton and Kanami Ishibashi (eds.), *Economic Globalization and Compliance with International Environmental Agreements* (2003) 245, 253.

[143] For a discussion of these cases see ch. 10.

[144] NAFTA, art. 2005.1.

required by a NAFTA party to be brought exclusively under the NAFTA dispute settlement regime.[145]

A growing number of environmental disputes have arisen under chapter 11 of NAFTA, which sets out protections for investment and allows investors to challenge measures taken by NAFTA states in arbitral tribunals. By early 2007 a total of thirteen environmental cases had been commenced under NAFTA auspices, and several of these are currently underway. These cases have concerned matters such as restrictions on gasoline additives, moratoria on exports of bulk water, bans on pesticides containing persistent organic pollutants, prohibitions of deep sea disposal of nuclear wastes, and regulations imposed upon waste disposal facilities. A central question confronted by NAFTA arbitral panels in many of these cases has been whether certain environmental regulations have constituted an indirect expropriation of an investment. In *Metalclad Corp.* v. *United Mexican States*[146] a NAFTA arbitral tribunal found that Mexico had violated NAFTA by failing to overrule a local government's refusal to grant a permit for a waste landfill. In reaching this conclusion the tribunal adopted an exceptionally broad interpretation of the NAFTA prohibition on measures that are 'tantamount to nationalisation or expropriation'.[147]

The handling by NAFTA tribunals of environmental cases has been highly controversial, and raises broader questions concerning the appropriateness of temporary arbitral panels deciding disputes centred not only on issues of investment, but also on issues of environmental protection, human rights, and labour standards.[148] In the NAFTA context these concerns have been tempered to some extent by the 1993 North American Agreement on Environmental Cooperation (NAAEC), which also incorporates a dispute settlement procedure. The NAAEC was negotiated as a side agreement to NAFTA in order to allay anxieties that greater freedom of trade and investment would lead to poor enforcement of environmental standards. Under the NAAEC, natural and legal persons, and NGOs, may lodge a complaint with the Commission on Environmental Cooperation (CEC) that one of the parties 'is failing to effectively enforce its environmental law'.[149] Although limited in scope, this procedure is an important

[145] *Ibid.* arts. 2005.3 and 2005.4.

[146] *Metalclad Corp.* v. *United Mexican States* (2001) 401 ILM 36.

[147] NAFTA, art. 1110.

[148] Philippe Sands, *Lawless World* (2005) 142.

[149] NAAEC, art. 14. See generally Kal Raustiala, 'Citizen Review and Treaty Review in the NAAEC' in David L. Markell and John H. Knox (eds.), *Greening NAFTA: The North*

development in international environmental law, representing a form of 'supranational' adjudication that exists within a broader, supervisory, regime.[150]

2.2.5 Court of Justice of the European Communities

2.2.5.1 European Community (EC) environmental law

Following the conclusion of the 1997 Treaty of Amsterdam Amending the Treaty on European Union, the Treaties Establishing the European Communities and Certain Related Acts, environmental considerations were placed at the forefront of EC law. Article 6 of the Treaty Establishing the European Community (EC Treaty) now requires the integration of environmental protection in all Community policies and activities 'with a view to promoting sustainable development'.[151] Even without this express mandate, environmental protection had been recognised several decades ago by the Court of Justice of the European Communities (ECJ) as one of the Community's 'essential objectives'.[152] The ECJ, the principal judicial organ of the EC, has been responsible for creating a strong 'community of law',[153] including in the environmental field, by taking an expansive view of its function to ensure 'that in the interpretation and application of this Treaty the law is observed'.[154] Since 1988 the ECJ has been assisted in its Community-building efforts by the Court of First Instance (CFI).

American Commission for Environmental Cooperation (2003) 256.

[150] John H. Knox 'A New Approach to Compliance with International Environmental Law: The Submissions Procedure of the NAFTA Environmental Commission' (2001) 28 *ELQ* 1, 12. In this context 'supranational' means that the international judicial process directly involves private actors as litigants. As Grieves has explained, 'supranational' in a more general sense means that

> states have transferred to an international institution certain limited decision-making powers normally exercised only by the governmental organs of a sovereign state, powers which include the capability of issuing, under certain specified conditions, binding norms to the states or to their inhabitants…

Forest L. Grieves, *Supranationalism and International Adjudication* (1969) 14.

[151] In relation to the environmental provisions of the draft Constitution for Europe see Peter Beyer *et al.*, 'The Draft Constitution for Europe and the Environment' (2004) 13 *EELR* 218.

[152] *Procureur de la République* v. *Association de Défense des Brûleurs d'Huiles Usagées* (C-240/83) [1985] ECR 531.

[153] Laurence R. Helfer and Anne-Marie Slaughter, 'Toward a Theory of Effective Supranational Adjudication' (1997) 107 *YaleLJ* 273.

[154] EC Treaty, art. 220.

2.2.5.2 The environmental jurisdiction of the ECJ

The ECJ has jurisdiction over cases brought by the Commission against member states for breaches of Community law (the 'infringement procedure'),[155] claims brought against Community institutions (the Council, Commission, Parliament, and the European Central Bank),[156] and in relation to requests by domestic courts of member states for preliminary ruling on questions of Community law (the 'preliminary reference' procedure).[157] The CFI has coterminous jurisdiction, with the exception of preliminary rulings. Environmental cases have been brought before the ECJ under all three heads of jurisdiction. Importantly, natural and juridical persons may bring claims concerning environmental questions against Community institutions.[158]

In several hundred cases the European Commission has commenced proceedings against member states for breaching environmental obligations under Community law.[159] In this way the Commission has been able to call upon the assistance of the judicial organ of the Community in order to ensure compliance with the environmental protection provisions of Community law.[160] The ECJ has also reviewed the legality of acts of Community institutions in relation to environmental matters. In addition, under its jurisdiction to issue preliminary rulings on the interpretation and application of Community law, the ECJ has issued decisions construing environmental provisions of EC law.[161]

The ECJ is perhaps the most effective among international courts and tribunals by virtue of its high degree of integration in the European legal system and the acceptance of its expanding role by member states. It has been a driving force behind the development of European

[155] *Ibid.* arts. 226 and 227. [156] *Ibid.* art. 230.

[157] *Ibid.* art. 234.

[158] *Ibid.* arts. 230 and 232.

[159] See for example *Commission of the European Communities* v. *French Republic* (C-182/89) [1990] ECR I-4337 (action against France in relation to import permits for skins of a species of wildcat listed under CITES). See generally Peter G. G. Davies, *European Union Environmental Law* (2004) 83–91.

[160] It should be noted that while international environmental agreements to which the Community is a party form an integral part of EC law, the Commission has adopted a policy of not monitoring the implementation by member states of these agreements: Ellen Hey, 'The European Community's Courts and International Environmental Agreements' (1998) 7 *RECIEL* 4, 7.

[161] *Etablissements Armand Mondiet SA* v. *Armement Islais SARL* (C-405/92) [1993] ECR I-6133 (concerning effect of EC ban on import of driftnet fishing nets on contractual obligations).

environmental law[162] and in many respects is a model for efficacious adjudication of environmental and other international disputes. It has placed environmental considerations at the centre of the EC's legal order, and has recognised objectives of European environmental protection as carrying equal (and sometimes greater) weight than the founding objectives of economic union.[163]

2.2.6 *Human rights courts and other bodies*

Sometimes overlooked in international environmental law is the contribution made by regional human rights tribunals and international human rights bodies. Although most international environmental instruments avoid the use of rights-based language, and the notion of environmental rights is generally underdeveloped, environmental concerns have increasingly been pursued through international human rights law and institutions. By using the vocabulary of rights, both procedural and substantive, litigants have been able to bring essentially environmental claims before established human rights complaints procedures.[164]

Notwithstanding legitimate concerns as to the appropriateness of transforming issues of environmental protection into the inherently anthropocentric terminology of human rights,[165] safeguarding human rights and preserving ecosystems are in most cases complementary objectives. Moreover, in the absence of mechanisms that provide access for natural persons to claim satisfaction for environmental harm suffered directly by them,[166] human rights courts and other quasi-judicial bodies present opportunities that otherwise do not exist for pursuing

[162] Sands, above n. 88, 1626; Alec Stone Sweet and Markus Gehring, 'Environmental Protection' in Alec Stone Sweet, *The Judicial Construction of Europe* (2004) 199.

[163] Philippe Sands, 'The International Court of Justice and the European Court of Justice' in Jacob Werksman (ed.), *Greening International Institutions* (1996) 227.

[164] Dinah Shelton, 'The Environmental Jurisprudence of International Human Rights Tribunals' in Romina Picolotti and Jorge Daniel Taillant (eds.), *Linking Human Rights and the Environment* (2003) 1, 1.

[165] Catherine Redgwell, 'Life, the Universe and Everything: A Critique of Anthropocentric Rights' in Alan E. Boyle and Michael R. Anderson (eds.), *Human Rights Approaches to Environmental Protection* (1996) 72. See also more generally Alexander Gillespie, *International Environmental Law Policy and Ethics* (1997).

[166] The United Nations Human Rights Committee has confirmed that there exists no *actio popularis* under the 1966 Optional Protocol to the International Covenant on Civil and Political Rights to complain about rights infringements involving environmental harm: *Brun* v. *France* [2006] UNHRC 72.

environmental claims on the international plane.[167] The growing body of human rights case law addressing environmental concerns also offers a potentially rich vein of jurisprudence for the development of international environmental law, although the distinctiveness of human rights discourse makes difficult the extrapolation of rules generally applicable in the environmental context.[168]

2.2.7 International Criminal Court (ICC)

As with human rights courts and complaints procedures, international criminal courts and tribunals challenge the essentially statist orientation of international law by drawing individuals within their frame of reference. Whereas human rights bodies allow individuals to hold states accountable for breaches of rights standards relating to environmental harm, criminal tribunals allow individuals themselves to be held responsible for deliberate environmental degradation.

Individuals and corporations causing environmental damage have long been subject to criminal sanctions under domestic legal systems, and there have been efforts in some regional contexts to adopt international instruments that strengthen and harmonise domestic laws applicable to environmental crimes.[169] By contrast there have been only tentative steps towards an international legal and institutional framework for the criminalisation and prosecution of offences against the environment,[170] even though this could well enhance the capacity of domestic authorities themselves to take action.[171] The expansion

[167] Shelton, above n. 164, 2; Romina Picolotti and Sofia Bordenave, 'The Enforcement of Environmental Law from a Human Rights Perspective' (2003) 3 *SDL&P* 11, 11; C. Miller, 'The European Convention on Human Rights: Another Weapon in the Environmentalist's Armory' (1999) 11 *JEL* 157.

[168] See further ch. 10.

[169] 1998 Convention for the Protection of the Environment Through Criminal Law.

[170] Note, however, art. 2(1)(b) of the Draft Comprehensive Convention on Terrorism which provides that a general offence of terrorism will be committed where a person causes 'serious damage' to 'the environment', 'when the purpose of the conduct ... is to intimidate a population, or to compel a Government or an international organization to do or abstain from doing any act': Report of the Ad Hoc Committee Established by General Assembly Resolution 51/210 of 17 December 1996, UN Doc. A/57/37 (2002). See Tim Stephens, 'International Criminal Law and the Response to International Terrorism' (2004) 27 *UNSWLJ* 454, 462–6.

[171] Brownlie notes that if relevant environmental crimes attracted universal jurisdiction it would be possible to regulate, in domestic legal systems, many problems involving extraterritorial environmental degradation: Ian Brownlie,

with Amedeo Postiglione,[181] judge of the *Corte Suprema di Cassazione* and founder of the International Court for the Environment Foundation (ICEF).[182]

The first detailed blueprint for an ICE was drawn up in 1989 at a congress sponsored by ICEF and convened at the National Academy of Lincei in Rome. The assembly recommended, among other things, that an international environmental court accessible to states, organs of the United Nations, and private citizens be established and have jurisdiction over disputes relating to breaches of a proposed covenant on the environment.[183] Subsequently in 1992 a Draft Convention for the Establishment of an International Court for the Environment was prepared by Judge Postiglione and presented to UNCED.[184] However, the proposal was ultimately removed from the UNCED agenda,[185] and the notion of a dedicated environmental court was the subject of criticism by Sir Robert Jennings, then president of the ICJ, in an address to the conference.[186] A revised draft treaty for an ICE was published in 1999.[187]

Subsequent to UNCED there has been no strong support among states for the ICE project, and no proposal for such a body was considered by the 2002 World Summit on Sustainable Development at Johannesburg. Undeterred by the lukewarm response, ICE proponents have suggested that pending the ICE's establishment the PCA should become the main forum for the resolution of international environmental disputes.[188] ICE enthusiasts have also sought to establish a

organisation having the full status as an organ of the United Nations would probably perform.

181 See Amedeo Postiglione, *The Global Environmental Crisis: The Need for an International Court of the Environment* (1996).

182 Since 1991 the *Corte Suprema di Cassazione* has provided support to ICEF via a dedicated secretariat established in Rome for this purpose.

183 Amedeo Postiglione, 'A More Efficient International Law on the Environment and Setting Up an International Court for the Environment Within the United Nations' (1990) 20 *Environmental Law* 321, 327.

184 See www.icef-court.org/icef/presentation/statute.htm.

185 Jeffrey L. Dunoff, 'Institutional Misfits: The GATT, the ICJ and Trade-Environment Disputes' (1994) 15 *MichJIL* 1043, 1107.

186 Robert Jennings, 'Need for an Environmental Court?' (1992) 20 *EPL* 312.

187 For a summary of the statute see Peggy Rogers Kalas, 'International Environmental Dispute Resolution and the Need for Access by Non-State Entities' (2001) 12 *ColoJIELP* 191, 235–41.

188 Alfred Rest, 'The Indispensability of an International Environmental Court' (1998) 7 *RECIEL* 63, 65–6; M. Vespa, 'An Alternative to an International Environmental

private forum for international environmental dispute settlement,[189] but this body has had virtually no influence on the environmental problems raised in 'cases' before it.

2.3.1 ICE project

There is some lack of clarity as to the objectives that an ICE would serve. However, the chief assumption appears to be that the ICE would play an enforcement role, holding states and other actors to account for breaches of international environmental law. It would be open to all non-state actors and would allow individuals to file complaints regarding alleged violations of their environmental rights.[190] Additionally, some advocates of an ICE contend that the court could possess criminal jurisdiction to prosecute individuals for grave crimes against the environment.[191]

In addition to having a role in enforcement, it is also suggested by some proponents that an ICE should be the primary forum for resolving international environmental disputes.[192] On the premise that environmental disputes possess a distinctive character it is contended that a dedicated environmental court with appropriately qualified judges, and the capacity to evaluate complex matters of environmental law, policy, and science, would offer significant advantages over existing tribunals. With such specialised capabilities, and with expansive personal and subject matter jurisdiction, ICE advocates anticipate that the court would be in a unique position to contribute to the development of an ecologically sensitive jurisprudence. Rest suggests that this contribution could be made directly by the court resolving environmental disputes, and also through a procedure akin to the

Court? The PCA's Optional Arbitration Rules for Natural Resources and/or the Environment' (2003) 2 *LPICT* 295.

189 The International 'Court' of Environmental Arbitration and Conciliation, established in Mexico in 1994, is an NGO that seeks to assist in the resolution of environmental disputes submitted by states and natural or legal persons. See Eckard Rehbinder and Demetrio Loperena, 'Legal Protection of Environmental Rights: The Role and Experience of the International Court of Environmental Arbitration and Conciliation' (2001) 31 *EPL* 282.

190 Kenneth F. McCallion and H. Rajan Sharma, 'Environmental Justice Without Borders: The Need for an International Court of the Environment To Protect Fundamental Human Rights' (2000) 32 *GeoWashJILEcon* 351.

191 Kenneth F. McCallion, 'International Environmental Justice: Rights and Remedies' (2002–3) 26 *HastingsICLR* 427, 436; Alfred Rest, 'Need for an International Court for the Environment?' (1994) 24 *EPL* 173–4.

192 Rest, above n. 188, 64.

preliminary ruling mechanism by which national courts in Europe may turn to the ECJ for an authoritative interpretation upon issues of EC law.[193]

The ICE could conceivably be established either within, or outside, the United Nations system.[194] As regards its relationship to other dispute settlement procedures, some suggest that much like the ICC in relation to criminal matters, an ICE would have only residual or complementary jurisdiction in relation to environmental disputes. Others suggest that it should be at the forefront of enforcement, available even where domestic remedies have not been exhausted, and situated at the apex of all courts operating in the field of international environmental law.[195]

2.3.2 *Critique of the ICE project*

There appears much to recommend an ICE, if it could achieve only some of the objectives set for it by its proponents, particularly if it raised public awareness of the central importance of environmental matters to international governance.[196] However, this is unlikely, as existing proposals for an ICE are intrinsically problematic and overly ambitious. They imagine that an ICE would be central to guarantees of an environmental 'rule of law', and for developing international environmental law to meet changing needs.[197] It is also suggested that a permanent environmental court could be endowed with contentious, criminal, and appellate jurisdiction, and entertain cases brought by states and individuals or by itself on its own motion.[198] In several

[193] Alfred Rest, 'Enhanced Implementation of the Biological Diversity Convention by Judicial Control' (1999) 29 *EPL* 32, 37.

[194] Audra E. Dehan, 'An International Environmental Court: Should There Be One?' (1992) 3 *TouroJTL* 31, 54.

[195] Rest, above n. 193.

[196] Justice Stein argues that this has been an important consequence of the establishment of specialist environmental courts in some Australian jurisdictions: Stein, above n. 179, 263.

[197] Rest, above n. 191, 173–84. See also McCallion and Sharma, above n. 190, who make the bold claim (at 365) that

> [o]nly an [International Environmental Court] can effectively address global issues and disputes relating to the degradation of the planet's environmental resources, such as depletion of the ozone layer, the greenhouse effect, the dumping of hazardous wastes at sea, nuclear power and chemical hazards, deforestation, desertification, irresponsible genetic manipulation, and ocean and atmospheric pollution.

[198] Rest, above n. 193, 37.

respects the ICE project is therefore quixotic, proposing a court that bears little resemblance to any judicial institution operating internationally or domestically. It seeks to transpose, and radically extrapolate from, the successful domestic experience of environmental adjudication to the international plane without accounting for the significant differences between these two systems of law or the character of international relations. Accordingly it represents, to borrow remarks from Allott made in another context, a 'naïve constitutional extrapolation (institutions which are effective nationally can surely be effective internationally)'.[199]

It is certainly the case that existing arrangements suffer from several weaknesses. However, it is by no means clear that some or all of these failings could be overcome in an ICE.[200] The jurisdictional limitations, and the restrictions on rights of participation, are arguably better addressed through progressive reform or adaption of existing bodies that already command support from states,[201] rather than through the establishment of a fresh institution in relation to which states have not yet expressed confidence. An additional difficulty is that proposals for an ICE rest on the questionable assumption that environmental disputes possess a quality or character that allows them to be clearly delimited from other types of dispute, and that they are therefore best dealt with in a specialised body.[202] In reality, environmental disputes are almost always closely intertwined with other issues, and with other sub-disciplines of international law.[203] They are 'likely to be part of more complex disputes involving questions of trade, production, investment, rights of the individual, policy of international organisations and other matters that are inseparable from the general body of international law'.[204]

[199] Philip Allott, *The Health of Nations: Society and Law Beyond the State* (2002) 59.

[200] Sean D. Murphy, 'Does the World Need a New International Environmental Court?' (2000) 32 *GeoWashJILEcon* 333, 333; Okowa, above n. 88, 170–1.

[201] Judge Jessup made several suggestions in this respect, including that the services and facilities of the ICJ could be lent to an ad hoc environmental tribunal in much the same way as the Internal Bureau of the PCA assists in the conduct of arbitrations outside the PCA system: Jessup, above n. 87, 266. But note that Boer argues that opening the ICJ to allow standing for non-state parties 'may well be insurmountable': Ben Boer, 'The Globalisation of Environmental Law: The Role of the United Nations' (1995) 20 *MULR* 101, 121.

[202] Okowa, above n. 88, 158. On the definition of an 'international environmental dispute' see Romano, above n. 14, 4–33.

[203] Ellen Hey, *Reflections on an International Environmental Court* (2000) 4–9.

[204] Francisco Orrego Vicuña, *International Dispute Settlement in an Evolving Global Society* (2004) 83–4.

Consequently, an international tribunal comprising only experts in international environmental law may attract little business.[205]

The value of any proposed ICE must also be questioned on the grounds that it could add a further layer of institutional complexity to the patchwork of jurisdictions already operating in the environmental field, with all the implications this carries both for increased jurisdictional competition and conflict,[206] and for the possible fragmentation of international law.[207] It therefore may be more practicable, and more consistent with the notion of integration (which emphasises the need to incorporate sustainable development policies in all aspects and levels of governance),[208] for the capacity of existing courts to deal with environmental disputes to be improved wherever possible.

2.4 Conclusion

Since the Brundtland Report and the 1989 Hague Declaration made the first pointed calls for more widespread use of binding dispute settlement mechanisms to promote the implementation of environmental treaties, there has been a significant expansion in the architecture of adjudication in international environmental law, driven both by the inclusion of adjudication as a dispute settlement option in environmental agreements and by the proliferation of international courts and tribunals more generally. Whereas once the only international judicial bodies competent to determine environmental disputes were arbitral panels established on an ad hoc basis, a variety of courts and tribunals now exist with jurisdiction extending to environmental controversies. These bodies include courts and tribunals with general competence, and also institutions with more focused subject matter jurisdiction.

[205] Sands, above n. 88, 1638 (given the almost inevitable intertwining of environmental and other issues 'an international tribunal composed solely of experts in international environmental law might not fare well in attracting cases … what is needed is a body of judges with a mix of general and specialized expertise'). Boyle has argued in the same vein in relation to the *Gabčíkovo-Nagymaros Project* case ([1997] ICJ Rep 7) that given the interaction of international environmental law, the law of international watercourses, and the law of treaties in that case, a prudent legal adviser would have been compelled to recommend resort to the ICJ in plenary rather than to the specialist environmental chamber which may not be capable of dealing with these intersections in the law: Boyle, above n. 95.

[206] Susan M. Hinde, 'The International Environmental Court: Its Broad Jurisdiction as a Possible Flaw' (2003) 32 *HosfraLR* 727. See also ch. 9.

[207] Hey, above n. 203, 4–9. See also ch. 10.

[208] See especially Rio Declaration, principle 4.

In relation to some courts, including the ICJ and the PCA, considerable efforts have also been expended in enhancing their capacity to resolve environmental cases. This is in recognition of the particular challenges faced in resolving environmental cases involving multiple parties and complex scientific evidence. Despite these very substantial developments there has been relatively little progress towards the creation of comprehensive mechanisms with broad and compulsory jurisdiction over environmental disputes. Although proponents of an ICE suggest that such a body would address this perceived problem, there appears little appetite in the international community for adding yet another element to the patchwork of judicial and quasi-judicial bodies operating in the environmental arena.

3 Institutions of international environmental governance

Compliance is now widely seen as the overriding governance objective in international environmental law.[1] This priority rests on the premise that environmental law is now in a post-ontological era in which an extensive body of law requires immediate and effective implementation to halt the continuing global environmental decline. This enthusiasm for norm enforcement over norm generation is sometimes misplaced, because in some situations compliance with environmental regimes does not equate with regime effectiveness. Many environmental regimes set such modest goals that full compliance cannot address the underlying environmental problem,[2] whereas partial compliance with more ambitious regimes can produce better than expected outcomes. A related complication is that the structure of environmental problems varies substantially and this differentiation is a key variable in the effectiveness of environmental regimes.[3] Despite these caveats, which go to meta-questions of institutional design, compliance remains

[1] See in particular the work of UNEP on compliance and enforcement: UNEP, *Comparative Analysis of Compliance Mechanisms under Selected Multilateral Agreements* (2005); *UNEP Manual on Compliance with and Enforcement of MEAs* (2006); UNEP Guidelines on Compliance and Enforcement of Multilateral Environmental Agreements, Decision 21/27 (2001) UN Doc. A/56/25(SUPP).

[2] The most obvious example is the emission reduction and limitation targets for the first commitment period under the Kyoto Protocol which would deliver only around a 1 per cent reduction in total greenhouse gas emissions: David G. Victor 'Toward Effective International Cooperation on Climate Change: Numbers, Interests and Institutions' (2006) 6 *GEP* 90, 91; David G. Victor, Joshua C. House, and Sarah Joy, 'A Madisonian Approach to Climate Policy' (2005) 309 *Science* 1820, 1821. See also George Monbiot, *Heat: How to Stop the Planet Burning* (2006) 16.

[3] Ronald B. Mitchell, 'Problem Structure, Institutional Design, and the Relative Effectiveness of International Environmental Agreements' (2006) 6 *GEP* 72.

an important objective not only because it often correlates with better levels of environmental protection, but also because it improves environmental governance by maintaining the credibility of environmental regimes, which in turn can be a catalyst for deeper international cooperation.[4]

Accepting the compliance imperative, the question of which institutions are best able to achieve it remains. In this respect international environmental law has been a field for substantial institutional experimentation and innovation. When public international law first acquired norms of an environmental character, these were enforceable (as with other rules of international law) through the traditional mechanisms of state responsibility and dispute settlement. However, the advent of sophisticated multilateral environmental agreements saw the development of new treaty-based institutions that could more actively manage compliance with environmental regimes.[5] This chapter traces this transition from bilateral dispute settlement systems to multilateral structures of international supervision through reporting, monitoring, and inspection systems, meetings of treaty parties, treaty secretariats and, most importantly, NCPs. As a consequence of these developments, enforcement and compliance in international environmental law is increasingly controlled by the relevant environmental regimes themselves, leaving little room for the general machinery of international law, including adjudicative bodies such as the ICJ. International courts have also been sidelined within environmental regimes, with relatively few environmental agreements relying on their own adjudicative systems for managing compliance issues.[6] None the less it is also significant that some NCPs, which are ostensibly non-adjudicative institutions, have begun to take on some judicial features, a fact which suggests some convergence of supervisory and adjudicative approaches to dealing with compliance challenges.

[4] Nicholas Stern, *The Economics of Climate Change: The Stern Review* (2007) 524.

[5] Martti Koskenniemi, 'New Institutions and Procedures for Implementation Control and Reaction' in Jacob Werksman (ed.), *Greening International Institutions* (1996) 236, 237.

[6] The current emphasis on non-adjudicative means of compliance control is reflected in the UNEP Guidelines on Compliance with and Enforcement of Multilateral Environmental Agreements, above n. 1, which give priority to non-compliance procedures (see [14]) over 'arbitration and other possible judicial arrangements' ([17]), with the latter consigned largely to a dispute settlement rather than enforcement or compliance role.

3.1 Traditional approaches to compliance control

3.1.1 State responsibility

The most elementary mechanism for managing compliance with international law is provided by the collection of customary norms relating to state responsibility. These secondary or subsidiary rules of international law set out the consequences of unlawful action, including the situations in which states may invoke a breach of international law and pursue a remedy. Principles of state responsibility constituted the baseline enforcement system when public international law began to engage with environmental concerns by applying general rules to situations involving environmental harm (such as the obligation to ensure that activities within one state do not damage the territory or nationals of other states).[7] As the purview of international environmental law expanded, and specialised environmental regimes emerged, state responsibility became less useful for dealing with compliance problems in the environmental field.[8] None the less, it remains central to the fabric of the international legal system and, as such, an important residual means for addressing the consequences of wrongful acts by states that have an impact upon the environment. Moreover, there have been significant efforts expended in improving the responsiveness of state responsibility principles to circumstances of environmental harm.

3.1.1.1 Principles of state responsibility

Article 1 of the ILC Articles on Responsibility of States for Internationally Wrongful Acts[9] (Articles on State Responsibility) expresses the basic principle that an internationally wrongful act by a state entails the international responsibility of that state. In relation to any international claim concerning environmental matters it is therefore essential first to identify the relevant international obligation that has been

[7] See further ch. 5.

[8] Patricia W. Birnie and Alan E. Boyle, *International Law and the Environment* (2nd edn 2002) 181–200; Markus Ehrmann, 'Procedures of Compliance Control in International Environmental Treaties' (2002) 13 *ColoJELP* 377, 379–87; Malgosia A. Fitzmaurice, 'International Protection of the Environment' (2001) 293 *RDC* 9, 220–32; Martti Koskenniemi, 'Breach of Treaty or Non-Compliance? Reflections on the Enforcement of the Montreal Protocol' (1992) 3 *YIEL* 123, 125–8.

[9] Articles on Responsibility of States for Internationally Wrongful Acts, Report of the International Law Commission, 53rd Session, UN Doc. A/56/10 (2001), 43–59 (noted in GA Res. 56/83, 12 December 2001, UN Doc. A/RES/56/83 (2001)).

breached. Discussion of state responsibility for environmental harm often revolves around examples such as the *Trail Smelter* case[10] scenario where industrial activities in Canada caused damage to the environment across the border in the United States. However, the law of state responsibility is of much broader application, and will operate whenever there has been a breach of an international obligation whatever its source.[11] It functions as a type of international civil liability for wrongful action and as such has both corrective functions (by establishing a system of remedies, including compensation) and preventative objectives (by deterring wrongful behaviour).[12]

3.1.1.2 Standing

The mere fact that a wrongful act has been identified does not necessarily mean that there is a remedy, because only 'injured' states possess standing to invoke the responsibility of a state that has violated international law. A state will be injured in the relevant sense if the obligation infringed was owed to that state individually.[13] There will also be an injury if the obligation breached was owed to a group of states, or the international community as a whole, and the breach specially affected the injured state.[14] These principles apply reasonably well to situations such as the *Trail Smelter* case involving transboundary damage to the environment of another state, or to damage to global commons areas that also involves discernible impact upon one or more states. An example given by the ILC in this regard is pollution on the high seas, in violation of article 194 of the LOS Convention, which specially affects one or more coastal states by damaging coastal environments.[15]

Historically, a more problematic scenario for the law of state responsibility is damage to global commons areas not directly affecting the legal rights or interests of any state.[16] The Articles on State Responsibility

[10] *Trail Smelter* case (*Canada/United States of America*) (1938 and 1941) 3 *RIAA* 1911.

[11] Articles on State Responsibility, above n. 9, art. 12.

[12] René Lefeber, *Transboundary Environmental Interference and the Origin of State Liability* (1996) 1. See also Kathy Leigh, 'Liability for Damage to the Global Commons' (1992) 14 *AustYBIL* 129, 148–9.

[13] *Ibid*. art. 42(a). [14] *Ibid*. art. 42(b).

[15] This is an example given in the ILC's commentary to art. 42(b)(i) of the Articles on State Responsibility, above n. 9.

[16] See generally Alan E. Boyle, 'Remedying Harm to International Common Spaces and Resources: Compensation and Other Approaches' in Peter Wetterstein (ed.), *Harm to the Environment: The Right to Compensation and the Assessment of Damages* (1997) 83 and Tullio Scovazzi, 'State Responsibility for Environmental Harm' (2001) 12 *YIEL* 43.

seek to deal with this in article 48, under which a state that is not injured may none the less invoke the responsibility of another state if the obligation breached is owed to a group of states, including that state, and is established for the protection of a collective interest, or the obligation is owed to the international community as a whole. To the extent that there are applicable *erga omnes* obligations[17] relating to an environmental matter there therefore exists the potential for any state to initiate a complaint (a type of *actio popularis*).[18] In such circumstances the invoking state can be seen to be acting not only in its own capacity but also as an agent on behalf of a group of states (such as all parties to a multilateral environmental agreement) or the international community as a whole (so as to uphold a customary obligation relating to the global environment).[19]

While the ILC's acceptance, in principle, of public interest international environmental claims is to be welcomed, there is limited evidence to suggest that it has been accepted by states as part of customary international law.[20] Even if it is ultimately recognised as part of customary

[17] The ICJ in the *Barcelona Traction, Light and Power Company Limited* case (*Belgium* v. *Spain*) (second phase) [1970] ICJ Rep 3, [33] recognised the existence of obligations which '[i]n view of the importance of the rights involved, all States can be held to have a legal interest in their protection'. The Court included among such obligations the prohibition on acts of aggression, genocide, slavery, and racial discrimination. No mention was made by the Court of environmental obligations, which may be explained by the relatively inchoate nature of the discipline at the time of the Court's decision. On the concept of responsibility to the international community as a whole see James Crawford, *International Law as an Open System* (2002) 341–59.

[18] It has been suggested that the term *actio pro societate* may be more appropriate to describe such an action: Rüdiger Wolfrum, 'Means of Ensuring Compliance With and Enforcement of International Environmental Law' (1998) 272 *RDC* 9, 99:

> [I]n multilateral environmental treaties the State parties of the respective regimes have established a community with the intention to collectively achieve the objective of the said regime. Non-compliance with these commitments endangers the very existence of this community. A State party invoking non-compliance of another member of that community hence defends its own rights in the preservation of the said community and thus indirectly the community itself.

[19] Julio Barboza, 'The ILC and Environmental Damage' in Peter Wetterstein (ed.), *Harm to the Environment: The Right to Compensation and the Assessment of Damages* (1997) 76.

[20] See François Voeffray, *L'actio popularis, ou la défense de l'intérêt collectif devant les jurisdictions internationals* (2004) 55–88. Catherine Redgwell, 'International Environmental Law' in Malcolm D. Evans (ed.), *International Law* (2003) 657, 666; Shabtai Rosenne, 'Some Reflections *Erga Omnes*' in Antony Anghie and Garry Sturgess (eds.), *Legal Visions of the 21st Century: Essays in Honour of Judge Christopher Weeramantry* (1998) 509, 519: 'In current … practice … there is a sharp dichotomy

international law a host of subsidiary issues will need to be addressed in order to ensure that the *actio popularis* is responsive to challenges of environmental compliance. For instance, a state not directly affected by environmental harm would be permitted under current rules to seek only very limited remedies (namely cessation and satisfaction) and pure environmental harm would attract no obligation of restitution or compensation.[21] In such circumstances a claim would be largely without object in an enforcement and compliance sense as it would impose no real sanction for wrongful behaviour. In addition there is the unresolved question of whether standing should be limited to states alone, or whether the general law of state responsibility should be developed to reflect practice in some specific contexts, most notably human rights regimes, which permits non-state actors to invoke state responsibility.[22] The ILC was not prepared to accord non-actors such rights in article 48, which substantially weakens the capacity of the Articles on State Responsibility to deal with major environmental problems of global concern.

3.1.1.3 General deficiencies

Beyond the limitations deriving from standing rules more general problems are encountered in deploying the law of state responsibility to promote compliance with international environmental law. As with all systems of liability it is inherently reactive, relying upon states to take action where there has been a breach of an international obligation, by which time permanent damage may already have been caused to the environment. And where damage is relied upon to make out a claim, it will need to be established both that the invoking state has been injured in the relevant sense and that the injury was caused by the delinquent state. This may be exceptionally difficult to prove to the requisite legal standard in many situations.[23] These difficulties are

between the enunciation of rules of law in *erga omnes* form, and the employment of procedural, and especially judicial, remedies for disputes …'.

[21] Boyle, above n. 16, 98.

[22] See Edith Brown Weiss, 'Invoking State Responsibility in the Twenty-First Century' (2002) 96 *AJIL* 798.

[23] Brownlie has noted in this regard that

> [t]he process of contamination is often … incremental and may involve complex causal mechanisms [and] the requirement of damage as a necessary condition of claim bears an uneasy relation to the scientific proof of a certain threshold of damage caused by an overall rise in radiation or other forms of pollution and problems of multiple causation then arise…

Ian Brownlie, *Principles of Public International Law* (6th edn 2003) 274.

further compounded for complex global environmental problems such as climate change, in relation to which it is next to impossible to identify a causal linkage between the actions of a particular state in failing to restrain greenhouse gas emissions, and damage caused to the environment of other nations.[24]

Perhaps the most fundamental obstacle to utilising state responsibility to address compliance problems is that these secondary rules are not supported by an institutional system capable of responding promptly and effectively to breaches.[25] Mere public assertion of a claim may highlight the violation by a state of its international obligations, and identify its secondary obligations to make reparation. However, unless subject to compulsory dispute settlement, there is no mechanism by which such claims could be subject to authoritative determination. Even with such a system the pursuit of a claim would remain voluntary and discretionary, and states have historically shown great reluctance to initiate proceedings even where the environmental damage is very severe.[26] The decision of European governments not to invoke the responsibility of the former Soviet Union in relation to the Chernobyl disaster is the most frequently cited instance of such reluctance. There were a variety of reasons why affected states did not pursue claims against the Soviet Union, including a desire not to impede the thawing of East–West relations.[27]

[24] But see Roda Verheyen, *Climate Change Damage and International Law: Prevention Duties and State Responsibility* (2005).

[25] Boyle, above n. 16, 91.

[26] Birnie and Boyle, above n. 8, 199. Examining the role of Indonesia in failing to prevent poor forestry and agricultural practices that gave rise to severe forest fires in the late 1990s, Tan has argued that Indonesia was responsible for the transboundary injury to neighbouring states: Alan Khee-Jin Tan, 'Forest Fires in Indonesia: State Responsibility and International Liability' (1999) 48 *ICLQ* 826. None the less, Indonesia was not subject to any inter-state claim, and instead, in conformity with the non-interventionist 'ASEAN way', the members of ASEAN responded by concluding a specific agreement to deal with the growing phenomenon of transboundary haze: 2002 ASEAN Agreement on Transboundary Haze Pollution. Similarly in relation to the Sandoz spill in 1986, riparian states on the Rhine downstream of Switzerland waived their right to invoke the responsibility of Switzerland: Astrid Boos-Hersberger, 'Transboundary Water Pollution and State Responsibility: The Sandoz Spill' (1997) 4 *AnnSICL* 103, 130.

[27] See generally Philippe Sands, *Chernobyl: Law and Communication* (1988) 26–30; Mary Ellen O'Connell, 'Enforcing the New International Law of the Environment' (1992) 35 *GerYBIL* 293, 315–16.

3.1.2 *Breach of treaty*

Many environmental agreements, or more general regimes that include in their coverage environmental matters, specify procedures through which parties may respond to breaches of the regime. NCPs established by several environmental agreements, and discussed below, are an example of this phenomenon, as is EC law under which member states may bring complaints regarding the performance of environmental obligations before the ECJ. However, where there is no such procedure, or where treaty-specific machinery proves ineffective, states may turn to general options presented under the law of treaties, as codified by the 1969 Vienna Convention on the Law of Treaties (VCLT), to enforce obligations applicable under environmental treaties.

Under the VCLT a party to a multilateral treaty specially affected by a breach may suspend the treaty's operation as between itself and the violating party.[28] Additionally, all parties to an environmental agreement may, by unanimous agreement, effectively exclude the defaulting state by suspending or terminating the operation of the treaty in whole or in part.[29] Both of these enforcement strategies rely on there having been a 'material breach', that is repudiation of the treaty or violation of a provision of the treaty essential to the accomplishment of its object or purpose.[30] These are onerous criteria to meet, as illustrated in the *Gabčíkovo-Nagymaros Project* case,[31] where the ICJ held that a joint development treaty continued to operate notwithstanding several significant breaches of its provisions by both parties. In any event it is highly questionable whether excluding a state from an environmental treaty will serve its long-term interests. By way of example, the expulsion of Japan from the 1946 International Convention for the Regulation of Whaling for violating the commercial whaling moratorium by its thinly disguised 'scientific' whaling programmes would probably leave its activities almost wholly unregulated on the international plane. Suspending or terminating treaty membership is therefore unlikely to be an appropriate response in many environmental regimes where the widest participation, and the greatest degree of cooperation, is required to achieve an environmental objective.

[28] VCLT, art. 60(2)(b). [29] *Ibid.* art. 60(2)(a). [30] *Ibid.* art. 60(3).

[31] *Gabčíkovo-Nagymaros Project* case (*Hungary/Slovakia*) [1997] ICJ Rep 7.

3.1.3 Inter-state dispute settlement

A breach of an environmental norm, treaty based or customary, will allow states to pursue a claim through available dispute settlement procedures. With the UN Charter prohibition on the use of force, and limited circumstances in which countermeasures may be deployed, these procedures now comprise the classical mechanism of enforcement in public international law. Article 33 of the UN Charter catalogues the main methods of settlement, namely negotiation, inquiry, mediation, conciliation, arbitration, judicial settlement, and 'resort to regional agencies or arrangements'.[32] Each of these has had some role to play in environmental dispute settlement.

Although it is supposed that the existence and operation of inter-state dispute settlement mechanisms are essential for promoting compliance, in reality such procedures have often proved to be of limited effectiveness. Drawing on the work of Abram and Antonia Handler Chayes,[33] Edith Brown Weiss has argued that traditional dispute settlement procedures, including courts, are inherently confrontational, are rarely invoked by states, and do not address underlying reasons for non-compliance such as ambiguities with the applicable law or the incapacity of the defaulting state to meet its commitments.[34] States seldom deem it to be in their interests to pursue a claim because of the political costs involved, even where their nationals are seriously affected.[35] An additional reason for doubting the effectiveness of general dispute settlement procedures of international law (as opposed to those nested within an environmental regime itself) is their organising rationale which is (as expressed in the UN Charter) to maintain peace, even at the cost of justice.

There is therefore a fundamental strain in the international system between, on the one hand, private ordering of public values through dispute settlement procedures and, on the other hand, upholding the

[32] See also the Declaration on Principles of International Law concerning Friendly Relations and Cooperation among States in accordance with the Charter of the United Nations, GA Res. 2625 (XXV), UN Doc. A/RES/2625 (XXV) (1970); Manila Declaration on the Peaceful Settlement of International Disputes, GA Res. 37/10, UN Doc. A/RES/37/10 (1982).

[33] Abram Chayes and Antonia Handler Chayes, *The New Sovereignty: Compliance with International Regulatory Agreements* (1995).

[34] Edith Brown Weiss, 'Understanding Compliance with International Environmental Agreements: The Baker's Dozen Myths' (1999) 32 *URichLR* 1555, 1582.

[35] Rosalyn Higgins, *Problems and Process: International Law and How We Use It* (1994) 52.

interests of the general international community in faithful adherence to environmental treaties.[36] In such a system there is a danger that the environment will be 'sold out'[37] in negotiation between private litigants. Although this tension is most pronounced in diplomatic procedures of settlement such as negotiation and mediation,[38] the strain is also visible in legal dispute settlement processes including international adjudication. When controversies do arise these mechanisms may help facilitate an amicable solution to a fractious dispute without addressing directly the issue of the environmental disturbance or threat that gave rise to those tensions. In other words, inter-state dispute settlement systems tend to be process oriented, in promoting peaceful relations regardless of the outcome, rather than goal oriented, in seeking to achieve a substantive improvement in compliance. With these general limitations in mind, we turn to examine more specifically how the available dispute settlement mechanisms function in the international environmental legal context.

3.1.3.1 Consultation and negotiation

Discussion between states at a diplomatic level is normally the first and last resort in resolving disputes over compliance with international obligations.[39] Consultation and negotiation may occur directly between states, or may take place through the good offices of a third party, conferences of treaty parties, or international organisations. Given that international cooperation is required to address many environmental threats, there is a general interest in encouraging such dialogue.

The term consultation is generally used to describe discussions between states prior to an activity that may generate a dispute.[40] Where there is a likelihood of significant interference with shared natural resources it appears that states are under a positive obligation

[36] Christine M. Chinkin, 'Alternative Dispute Resolution under International Law' in Malcolm D. Evans (ed.), *Remedies in International Law: The Institutional Dilemma* (1998) 123, 127–8.

[37] Christopher D. Stone, *Should Trees Have Standing? And Other Essays on Law, Morals, and the Environment* (1996) 25. Stone suggests that one way of avoiding this situation is to accord ecosystems and their components legal status so that they cannot be ignored by the parties or by a court. See also Thomas Gehring, 'International Environmental Regimes: Dynamic Sectoral Legal Systems' (1990) 1 *YIEL* 35, 51.

[38] Chinkin, above n. 36, 130.

[39] Hilary Charlesworth and Christine Chinkin, *The Boundaries of International Law: A Feminist Analysis* (2000) 288.

[40] J. G. Merrills, *International Dispute Settlement* (3rd edn 1998) 3.

to engage in preliminary consultations before implementing a project that will have this effect. This was seen in the *Lake Lanoux* case[41] where the tribunal held that France was required to consult with Spain in relation to a hydroelectricity project that affected Spain as a downstream river user.[42] The importance of consultations was also seen in the *Fisheries Jurisdiction* cases[43] in which it was held that all states with an interest in fisheries surrounding Iceland were under an obligation to keep under constant review the marine living resources of the waters and to work together to adopt agreed measures for conservation and equitable allocation.[44]

Where consultations have not taken place, or are unsuccessful, and a dispute does arise, then the parties may seek to reach a negotiated settlement. As with consultation, negotiation may take a variety of forms, and be carried out in many different fora. In almost all environmental instruments negotiation or consultation is presented as the initial method of dispute settlement.[45] While it is generally preferable to begin to resolve environmental disputes through such procedures, they are not normally required to be exhausted before other dispute settlement mechanisms can be invoked.[46] Moreover negotiations may be employed concurrently with other procedures invoked to resolve a dispute.

3.1.3.2 Mediation

Whereas the disputants themselves are generally the only participants in negotiatory or consultative dispute settlement, in the process of mediation a third party takes an active role in the settlement process. Mediation none the less remains firmly under the control of

[41] *Lake Lanoux* case (*France/Spain*) (1957) 12 *RIAA* 285. [42] *Ibid*. 371.

[43] *Fisheries Jurisdiction* cases: *United Kingdom* v. *Iceland* [1974] ICJ Rep 3; *Germany* v. *Iceland* [1974] ICJ Rep 175.

[44] *Ibid*. [72]. The ICJ stated that in relation to the dispute before it 'the most appropriate method for the solution of the dispute is clearly that of negotiation' (at [73]).

[45] Cesare P. R. Romano, *The Peaceful Settlement of International Environmental Disputes: A Pragmatic Approach* (2000) 48.

[46] *Land and Maritime Boundary between Cameroon and Nigeria* (*Cameroon* v. *Nigeria*) (preliminary objections) [1998] ICJ Rep 275, [56] ('Neither in the Charter nor otherwise in international law is any general rule to be found that the exhaustion of diplomatic negotiations constitutes a precondition for a matter to be referred to the Court'). See also *Southern Bluefin Tuna* cases (*New Zealand* v. *Japan; Australia* v. *Japan*) (provisional measures) (1999) 38 ILM 1624, [60]; *MOX Plant* case (*Ireland* v. *United Kingdom*) (provisional measures) (2002) 41 ILM 405, [60]. See also John Collier and A. Vaughan Lowe, *The Settlement of Disputes in International Law: Institutions and Procedures* (1999) 21–2.

the parties, and is therefore a diplomatic procedure that does not lead to a binding determination by a mediator according to legal criteria. Although many environmental treaties present mediation as an option for dispute settlement,[47] it does not appear to have been used in dealing with any environmental dispute.[48]

3.1.3.3 Conciliation

Conciliation procedures depart from the purely diplomatic dispute settlement options of consultation, negotiation, and mediation. While conciliation bears many similarities to mediation, the third party is expected to take a more active, formal, and neutral role. Much like mediation, it does not normally lead to a determination that is binding on the parties;[49] however, some environmental instruments require that parties must consider the conciliation report 'in good faith'.[50] In addition, conciliation usually proceeds according to somewhat flexible criteria rather than involving the application of exclusively legal standards to the dispute.

A range of environmental treaties refer to conciliation as a dispute settlement option.[51] In several of these regimes conciliation is made compulsory in certain situations, as in the Desertification Convention which requires disputes to be submitted to conciliation if the parties have not accepted arbitration or judicial settlement by the ICJ.[52] In most environmental instruments, however, conciliation is simply one option, among several that the parties may select to resolve their differences.[53] It may be carried out by a single conciliator, a panel of

[47] 1985 Vienna Convention for the Protection of the Ozone Layer, art. 11(2); Biodiversity Convention art. 27(2); 1997 United Nations Convention on the Law of the Non-Navigational Uses of International Watercourses (UN Watercourses Convention), art. 33(2).

[48] Laura Horn, 'The Role of the Mediator in International Environmental Law' (1993) 4 *AustDRJ* 16, 30.

[49] See e.g. LOS Convention, annex V, art. 7(2).

[50] See e.g. 1985 Vienna Convention for the Protection of the Ozone Layer, art. 11(5).

[51] See e.g. *ibid*. art. 11(4); 1992 Climate Change Convention, art. 14(5); OSPAR Convention, art. 32(1); 1994 Convention to Combat Desertification in Countries Experiencing Serious Drought and/or Desertification, Particularly in Africa (Desertification Convention), art. 28(6).

[52] Desertification Convention, art. 28(6). See also LOS Convention, art. 297(3)(b), which establishes a compulsory conciliation procedure in relation to certain types of dispute that are not subject to mandatory adjudication under art. 286.

[53] See e.g. 1980 Convention on the Conservation of Antarctic Marine Living Resources (CCAMLR), art. XXV.

conciliators, or an international body such as a permanent commission established by an environmental agreement.[54] Bodies that principally operate as arbitral tribunals may also have the capacity to engage in environmental conciliation.[55]

An advantage of conciliation over mediation in the environmental context is the greater independence of the conciliator, which may lead to a report that serves not only to provide guidance to the parties but which also highlights publicly the environmental problem giving rise to the dispute. This may, in turn, prompt pressure from other states, international organisations, and domestic constituencies to ensure that the relevant state addresses the environmental threat giving rise to a dispute. However, despite its evident potential, conciliation does not appear to have been used in an environmental case. The closest a state has come to utilising conciliation was in 1995 when New Zealand reportedly considered invoking the conciliation procedure in the Biodiversity Convention in response to a fresh round of French nuclear tests in the Pacific.[56]

3.1.3.4 Commissions of inquiry and fact-finding

Inquiry and fact-finding are interchangeable terms to describe a process of independent investigation of disputed facts and issues. This may involve a variety of activities including site visits, the examination of witnesses, and the evaluation of written and oral submissions made by the parties themselves. Several examples of inspection procedures are found in environmental agreements such as the NCP established by the 1987 Montreal Protocol on Substances that Deplete the Ozone Layer[57] which empowers the implementing committee (with the consent of the

[54] See e.g. the OSPAR Convention, art. 32(1) which provides that in the first instance disputes should be settled by means of inquiry or conciliation 'within the Commission' established by art. 10 and made up of representatives of each of the contracting parties.

[55] See e.g. the PCA's 2002 Optional Rules for Conciliation of Disputes Relating to Natural Resources and/or the Environment.

[56] Philippe Sands and Ruth MacKenzie, 'Guidelines for Negotiating and Drafting Dispute Settlement Clauses for International Environmental Agreements' in International Bureau of the Permanent Court of Arbitration (ed.), *International Investments and Protection of the Environment* (2001) 305, 314.

[57] Decision IV/5, Report of the Fourth Meeting of the Parties to the Montreal Protocol on Substances that Deplete the Ozone Layer, UN Doc. UNEP/Oz.L.Pro.4/15 (1992) (as revised by Decision X/10, Report of the Tenth Meeting of the Parties to the Montreal Protocol on Substances that Deplete the Ozone Layer, UN Doc. UNEP/OzL.Pro.10/9 (1998)) (Montreal Protocol NCP).

party involved) to undertake information-gathering. Another example is the system of inspection established by the Madrid Protocol which provides in article 14 for inspections of stations and other facilities by designated observers 'in order to promote the protection of the Antarctic environment and dependent and associated ecosystems, and to ensure compliance with this Protocol'.[58]

These two instruments present fact-finding as a way to improve compliance. By revealing to the international community at large the extent to which one or more states are responsible for bringing about environmental harm it may bring these states back to compliance. Several other environmental instruments treat inspection procedures primarily as a method for solving differences. Under the UN Watercourses Convention, for instance, impartial fact-finding is compulsory unless the parties have agreed to another procedure or have declared acceptance of judicial settlement by the ICJ or arbitration by an arbitral tribunal.[59] Fact-finding commissions are to be composed of members nominated by the parties, who are in turn responsible for selecting a chairperson. Such commissions may adopt reports by majority vote, rather than consensus, in which findings and recommendations are made 'for an equitable solution of the dispute'.[60] A similar system is found in the ILC's Draft Articles on Prevention of Transboundary Harm from Hazardous Activities.[61] Where a dispute over transboundary harm cannot be resolved through consultation or negotiation within a period of six months, the articles provide that a party to a dispute may invoke compulsory fact-finding procedures to be carried out by an impartial commission.[62]

As with all procedures that involve the independent and impartial examination of evidence and the finding of facts, commissions of

[58] See also the inspection mechanism under the 1959 Antarctic Treaty, art. VII. See generally Tim Stephens and Ben Boer, 'Enforcement and Compliance in the Australian Antarctic Territory: Legal and Policy Dilemmas' in Lorne K. Kriwoken, Julia Jabour and Alan D. Hemmings (eds.), *Looking South: Australia's Antarctic Agenda* (2007) 54.

[59] Art. 33(3). [60] *Ibid.* art. 33(8).

[61] Report of the International Law Commission, 53rd Session, 366, UN Doc. A/56/10 (2001). See Bruno Simma, 'The Work of the International Law Commission at Its Fifty-Third Session' (2002) 71 *NordicJIL* 123, 137.

[62] *Ibid.* art. 19. The ILC's commentary notes that '[t]his compulsory procedure is useful and necessary to help States resolve their disputes expeditiously on the basis of an objective identification and evaluation of the facts. Lack of proper appreciation of the correct and relevant facts is often at the root of differences or disputes among States.'

inquiry can help verify the true dimensions of an environmental threat and thereby contribute to attempts to avert, lessen, or remedy damage to ecosystems. Inquiry can be of particular assistance where there are complex and disputed scientific considerations requiring independent verification. This is recognised in the procedure for special arbitration under annex VIII of the LOS Convention, which may only be utilised for certain matters including disputes concerning the protection and preservation of the marine environment.[63] Under annex VIII, a special arbitral tribunal may be requested to carry out an inquiry and establish the facts giving rise to a dispute.[64] Unless the parties agree otherwise, any findings of fact made in this process are binding.[65]

3.1.3.5 Arbitration and judicial settlement

International adjudication by arbitration or judicial settlement is distinguished from the other dispute settlement mechanisms already described by several important characteristics. The critical differences are found in the role of the third party (judges or arbitrators who sit 'above' rather than 'between' the parties), the process of decision-making (according solely to legal, and not political, criteria) and the result and effect of decisions (binding upon the parties, and having a potential influence on the development of the law).

It was seen in chapter 2 that various adjudicative procedures now resolve environmental disputes. Some of these are embedded within environmental regimes (such as ITLOS), while others exist outside and remain part of the general dispute settlement machinery of international law (such as the ICJ). It is clear that states have preferred to utilise these judicial mechanisms over other traditional systems of inter-state dispute settlement such as mediation or conciliation, and the engagement by a range of courts with environmental questions suggests that adjudication is a popular option for dealing with such disputes. However, when a broader view is taken it becomes apparent that there is a strong trend away from inter-state dispute settlement systems altogether in favour of treaty-based institutions such as NCPs which are more administrative than judicial. The effect of this is to introduce a degree of imbalance in international governance arrangements for environmental matters. While there is a range of limitations

[63] Special arbitration panels are to comprise both legal and scientific experts: LOS Convention, annex VIII, art. 3.

[64] *Ibid.* annex VIII, art. 5(1). [65] *Ibid.* annex VIII, art. 5(2).

to any court (national or international) engaging with environmental issues, courts provide a modality for disinterested dispute settlement where public interest in environmental matters can be given appropriate recognition. This fact is recognised the world over in domestic settings, where courts are increasingly charged with upholding environmental laws and regulations. This means that for all the virtues of new approaches to managerial types of dispute settlement, there remains a role for judicial determinations of international environmental questions. This theme is taken up in chapter 4 which considers the valuable functions that courts and tribunals can and do play in systems of international environmental governance.

3.2 New approaches to compliance control

The widely cited deficiencies of inter-state dispute settlement in dealing with compliance have been the main reason for investigating other options for ensuring that states meet their international environmental commitments. This has led to developments at two quite different scales. First, there have been new efforts to involve national legal institutions in the task of day-to-day compliance management such as through environmental regimes that confer jurisdiction on domestic courts to hear complaints by or against foreign nationals and companies for causing environmental damage. Second, on the international plane, a new approach has been taken when crafting environmental regimes (or updating existing agreements)[66] to involve new treaty-based institutions in a process of active treaty management, a development exemplified by the emergence of NCPs.

3.2.1 Domestic courts

Principles 10 and 13 of the Rio Declaration[67] emphasise the important function of domestic courts in the context of environmental protec-

[66] See for instance the new compliance mechanism devised for CITES: Res. 14.3 ('CITES Compliance Procedure') adopted 15 June 2007 (available at www.cites.org/eng/res/all/14/E14–03.pdf).

[67] Principle 10 provides that '[e]nvironmental issues are best handled with the participation of all concerned citizens, at the relevant level … Effective access to judicial administrative proceedings, including redress and remedy, shall be provided.' Principle 13 provides that '[s]tates shall develop national law regarding liability and compensation for the victims of pollution and other environmental damage'.

tion.[68] Their most important role is in enforcing national (and subnational) environmental laws and regulations, including those that implement environmental treaty obligations.[69] A secondary role, and the one most relevant in this context, is their growing involvement in dealing with transboundary environmental disputes, chiefly through civil liability regimes. A third important function is in influencing the development of international environmental law by articulating new, or developing existing, rules and principles.[70]

The desirability of turning to domestic mechanisms for enforcing rules of international environmental law receives substantial theoretical support from recent liberal theories of international law. In developing her liberal conception of international law and relations Slaughter argues that domestic courts can provide a coercive means of enforcement absent in traditional inter-state dispute settlement, and as a consequence that they can be just as effective in upholding agreements between states as they are in safeguarding contracts between individuals.[71] At the same time, however, there is a recognition that domestic courts may be assisted in their efforts to develop a consistent approach to the enforcement of environmental and other international standards through a dialogue with relevant international courts. Put simply, while the task of enforcement is performed most effectively at the local level, the work of domestic courts can be enhanced when they can turn to an international court for an authoritative interpretation of the treaty provisions in dispute. Eckersley has made a similar point when arguing against excessive devolution of responsibility for environmental management to local polities.[72]

[68] See also the IUCN – World Conservation Union, *Draft International Covenant on Environment and Development* (3rd edn 2004) art. 54(1) which provides that states 'shall ensure the availability of effective civil remedies that provide for cessation of harmful activities as well as for compensation to victims of environmental harm *irrespective of the nationality or the domicile of the victims*' (emphasis added).

[69] Mary Ellen O'Connell, 'Enforcement and the Success of International Environmental Law' (1995–6) 3 *IndJGLS* 47, 58.

[70] Daniel Bodansky and Jutta Brunnée, 'The Role of National Courts in the Field of International Environmental Law' (1998) 7 *RECIEL* 11, 13.

[71] Anne-Marie Slaughter, 'International Law in a World of Liberal States' (1995) 6 *EJIL* 503–32. See also Alex Mills and Tim Stephens, 'Challenging the Role of Judges in Slaughter's Liberal Theory of International Law' (2005) 18 *LJIL* 1.

[72] Robyn Eckersley, *Environmentalism and Political Theory: Toward an Ecocentric Approach* (1992) 174 ('bodies such as the International Court of Justice and the World Heritage Committee are salutary reminders of the ways in which institutions created by

Ultimately the effectiveness of domestic courts in the context of international enforcement and compliance depends on the extent to which governments agree to submit their activities to the scrutiny of the courts of other states. No foreign government has in fact ever been brought before a domestic court for failing to fulfil its environmental obligations, despite the narrowing of the doctrine of foreign state immunity. There has, however, been much more success in actions against private enterprises through jurisdictional arrangements such as the United States Alien Tort Claims Act 1789, even though this unilateral assertion of civil jurisdiction has been controversial. The establishment of internationally agreed rules to address jurisdictional issues in environmental cases avoids this problem. To this end a range of civil liability regimes have been developed, most notably in Europe, which give domestic courts a specific role in deciding transboundary pollution cases.[73]

Civil liability treaties concluded to date follow a broadly similar approach of providing for strict liability, a compulsory insurance system, restricted choice of forum for litigation, and recognition and enforcement of judgments in the courts of all parties. One of the principal benefits of such regimes is the directness of the claim by individuals harmed against those natural or legal persons responsible for the environmental damage.[74] With states being reluctant to take up the claims of their nationals, or to assume responsibility for environmental damage caused by their citizens,[75] civil liability regimes afford an opportunity for dealing with environmental harm by allowing the nationals of one state affected by environmental harm emanating from another state to sue the polluter directly in the courts of the latter.[76] They thereby recognise the reality that most environmental problems are caused by private conduct rather than state activities.

international treaties can serve to protect both human rights and threatened species and ecosystems from the "excesses" of *local* political elites' (emphasis added)).

73 See in particular the 1974 Nordic Convention on the Protection of the Environment.

74 Peter H. Sand, *Transnational Environmental Law: Lessons in Global Change* (1999) 97; Stephen C. McCaffrey, *The Law of International Watercourses: Non-Navigational Uses* (2001) 435.

75 Benedetto Conforti, 'Do States Really Accept Responsibility for Environmental Damage?' in Francisco Francioni and Tullio Scovazzi (eds.), *International Responsibility for Environmental Harm* (1991) 179, 179–80.

76 Such systems therefore give concrete effect to the polluter-pays principle – by providing private rights of enforcement to affected individuals they force polluters to internalise the environmental costs of their activities. The principle was first articulated in an international instrument in the Rio Declaration, principle 16.

3.2.2 *Compliance procedures*

Civil liability regimes plug an important gap in compliance arrangements. However, they deal only with the specific issue of transboundary harm and not the full panoply of international environmental issues. There is therefore a continuing need for systems of compliance control operating on the international plane. Boyle has used the term 'supervision' to describe the approach taken in many multilateral environmental agreements in establishing procedures and institutions for monitoring and managing compliance.[77] Increasing the flow of information concerning performance through reporting obligations[78] and observer or inspection schemes[79] improves the transparency of environmental regimes and enhances voluntary compliance by the parties.[80] Often superadded to these obligations is supervisory machinery such as regular conferences of parties, subsidiary committees, scientific and technical commissions, treaty secretariats, monitoring bodies, and intergovernmental commissions.[81] These provide fora, both of experts and of governmental representatives, for the ongoing and active management of the compliance challenges that inevitably arise.

3.2.2.1 From Montreal to Aarhus

A more formalised approach to managing compliance in a growing number of agreements is found in NCPs. These bodies are mandated to address compliance problems in a more targeted way than other treaty-based institutions, and in a more responsive and non-confrontational

[77] Alan E. Boyle, 'Saving the World? Implementation and Enforcement of International Environmental Law Through International Institutions' (1991) 3 *JEL* 229, 229.

[78] See e.g. CITES, art. 8.

[79] See e.g. Madrid Protocol, art. 14 which provides for an inspection system 'in order to promote the protection of the Antarctic environment…and to ensure compliance with this Protocol'.

[80] Abram Chayes, Antonia Handler Chayes, and Ronald B. Mitchell, 'Managing Compliance: A Comparative Perspective' in Edith Brown Weiss and Harold K. Jacobson (eds.), *Engaging Countries: Strengthening Compliance with International Environmental Accords* (1998) 39, 81. See also Kamen Sachariew, 'Promoting Compliance with International Environmental Standards: Reflections on Monitoring and Reporting Mechanisms' (1991) 2 *YIEL* 31.

[81] Patrick Széll, 'The Development of Multilateral Mechanisms for Monitoring Compliance' in Winfried Lang (ed.), *Sustainable Development and International Law* (1995) 97, 98.

manner than traditional dispute settlement systems.[82] The first NCP was ushered into existence in 1992 under the Montreal Protocol[83] and since that time similar systems have been established under a host of other environmental agreements.[84] There is considerable variation among these systems, which range from 'softer' managerial institutions to 'harder' quasi-judicial bodies more focused on enforcement.[85] An overview of the procedures found in the Montreal Protocol, the Kyoto Protocol[86] and the Aarhus Convention[87] highlights the main types of NCPs currently in existence.

Montreal Protocol NCP

The objective of the Montreal Protocol, one of the most successful environmental regimes,[88] is to reduce and ultimately to eliminate global emissions of ozone-depleting substances[89] and to this end the protocol

[82] Geir Ulfstein, 'Dispute Resolution, Compliance Control and Enforcement in International Environmental Law' in Geir Ulfstein (ed.), *Making Treaties Work: Human Rights, Environment and Arms Control* (2007) 115, 132.

[83] Montreal Protocol NCP, above n. 57.

[84] See e.g. Decision V/16, Report of the Fifth Meeting of the Conference of the Parties to the Basel Convention, UN Doc. UNEP/CH.5/29 (1999); Decision 1997/2, Report of the Fifteenth Session of the Executive Body for the Convention on Long-Range Transboundary Air Pollution, UN Doc. ECE/EB.AIR/53 (1998).

[85] Jan Klabbers, 'Compliance Procedures' in Daniel Bodansky, Jutta Brunneé, and Ellen Hey (eds.), *The Oxford Handbook of International Environmental Law* (2007) 995, 999 (noting that some NCPs constitute 'an elaborate, complex structure, which gives the impression of a judicial organ dressed in political (or bureaucratic) garb').

[86] Decision 24/CP.7, Report of the Conference of the Parties on its Seventh Session, UN Doc. FCCC/CP/2001/13/Add.3 (2002) (Kyoto Protocol NCP). See generally Massimiliano Montini, 'Improving Compliance with Multilateral Environmental Agreements through Positive Measures: The Case of the Kyoto Protocol on Climate Change' in Alexandre Kiss, Dinah Shelton, and Kanami Ishibashi (eds.), *Economic Globalization and Compliance with International Environmental Agreements* (2003) 157. For an analysis of compliance issues prior to the adoption, or during the negotiation, of the Kyoto Protocol NCP see Gregory Rose, 'A Compliance System for the Kyoto Protocol' (2001) 24 *UNSWLJ* 588; Peggy Rodgers Kalas and Alexia Herwig, 'Dispute Resolution Under the Kyoto Protocol' (2000) 27 *ELQ* 53.

[87] Decision 1/7, Report of the First Meeting of the Parties to the Convention on Access to Information, Public Participation in Decision-Making and Access to Justice in Environmental Matters, UN Doc. ECE/MP.PP/2/Add.8 (2002) (Aarhus NCP).

[88] Edward A. Parson, 'Protecting the Ozone Layer' in Peter M. Haas, Robert O. Keohane, and Marc A. Levy (eds.), *Institutions for the Earth: Sources of Effective International Environmental Protection* (1993) 27; Jørgen Wettestad, 'The Vienna Convention and the Montreal Protocol on Ozone-Layer Depletion' in Edward L. Miles *et al.* (eds.), *Environmental Regime Effectiveness: Confronting Theory with Evidence* (2002) 149.

[89] Montreal Protocol, preamble, fifth recital.

sets specific limitations in relation to the production, distribution, and consumption of such substances. Negotiations on the modalities of an NCP began at the first meeting of the parties in 1989, as required by article 8 of the Montreal Protocol, and the NCP was adopted in 1992.[90] It is intended to be non-complex, non-confrontational, non-judicial, transparent, and subject to the supreme authority of the meeting of the parties.[91]

The Montreal Protocol NCP may be activated in three ways. In the first place, any party may address concerns relating to implementation to the secretariat.[92] Second, the secretariat may itself initiate the procedure when it becomes aware of possible non-compliance.[93] Third, a party that is unable to comply with its obligations may itself invoke the procedure. The procedure is designed so that it can be invoked wherever there are concerns about actual or potential non-compliance, notwithstanding that there has been no injury to a state party. It can therefore be utilised in the collective interest, an important feature for a regime designed to protect a vital commons resource.[94] Once invoked, the implementation committee, a standing body elected by the meeting of the parties, considers non-compliance situations.[95] This committee meets biannually and considers the submissions, information, and observations provided by the parties and the secretariat in relation to non-compliance 'with a view to securing an amicable solution of the matter on the basis of respect for the provisions of the Protocol'.[96] The implementation committee reports to the meeting of the parties, making any recommendations as to decisions which it considers appropriate, and the parties must then decide upon, and call for steps to bring about, full compliance with the protocol, including any measures to assist a non-compliant state.[97] A number of measures may be taken in response to non-compliance including providing appropriate assistance, issuing cautions and, in extreme situations, suspending rights and privileges under the protocol. Although the procedure has been frequently used since it was first activated in 1995,[98] no suspension

[90] See Ehrmann, above n. 8, 391–5; Romano, above n. 45, 69–72.

[91] Report of the First Meeting of the Ad Hoc Working Group of Legal Experts on Non-Compliance with the Montreal Protocol, UN Doc. UNEP/OzL.Pro.LG 1/3 (1989).

[92] Montreal Protocol NCP, above n. 57, [1]. [93] *Ibid.* [2].

[94] Ehrmann, above n. 8, 396. [95] Montreal Protocol NCP, above n. 57 [5].

[96] *Ibid.* [8]. [97] *Ibid.* [9].

[98] Report of the Eleventh Meeting of the Implementation Committee Under the Non-Compliance Procedure for the Montreal Protocol, UN Doc. UNEP/OzL.Pro/ImpCom/11/1 (1995).

action has been recommended or taken, with the implementation Committee and the meeting of parties more focused on assisting parties to meet their commitments.

Kyoto Protocol NCP

A more complex and detailed NCP was established for the Kyoto Protocol. It will commence operation in 2008, simultaneously with the commencement of the first commitment period for the reduction or limitation of greenhouse gas emissions. Under the Kyoto Protocol NCP, which is more detailed and comprehensive than the Montreal Protocol NCP, compliance is monitored and acted upon by the compliance committee. The committee functions through a plenary session, a bureau and two branches: the facilitative branch and the enforcement branch.[99] The committee is constituted by independent experts, operates according to highly structured procedures, and can make essentially self-executing decisions. As a consequence it is more judicial in character than the Montreal NCP.

The facilitative branch provides 'advice and facilitation to Parties' in implementing the protocol, promoting compliance having regard to the principle of common but differentiated responsibilities.[100] The enforcement branch is responsible for determining whether a party is complying with provisions of the Kyoto Protocol, including quantified limitation or reduction commitments,[101] and for applying the consequences set out in the NCP in cases of non-compliance.[102] In applying such measures, the enforcement branch is required to aim 'at the restoration of compliance to ensure environmental integrity, and shall provide for an incentive to comply'.[103] By comparison with the Montreal Protocol NCP this procedure is therefore more clearly directed at remedying defaulting behaviour rather than resolving disputes.

Situations of non-compliance, described somewhat obliquely in the Kyoto Protocol NCP as 'questions of implementation', may be raised by expert review teams, any party with respect to itself, or any party with respect to another party.[104] The bureau is responsible for allocating questions of implementation to the appropriate branch, which then undertakes a preliminary examination of the situation in order to determine whether the matter should proceed.[105] If the matter does

[99] Kyoto Protocol NCP, above n. 86, s. II. [100] *Ibid.* s. IV [4].
[101] *Ibid.* s. V [4], [5]. [102] *Ibid.* s. V [5]. [103] *Ibid.* s. V [6].
[104] *Ibid.* s. VI [1]. [105] *Ibid.* s. VII.

proceed, then the party concerned may designate persons to represent it during the consideration of the question of implementation by the relevant branch.[106] Deliberations by the relevant branch are to be based, *inter alia*, on reports of any expert review team, the party concerned, or the party that raised the question of implementation.[107] Importantly, competent intergovernmental organisations and NGOs may submit relevant factual and technical information to the relevant branch,[108] and the branch itself may seek expert advice.[109]

Many aspects of the procedure for the enforcement branch are judicial in character. Decisions must include conclusions and reasons, the party concerned may request the holding of a hearing (which will ordinarily be public) by the enforcement branch at which it will have an opportunity to present its views,[110] and final decisions by the enforcement branch as to non-compliance are to be made available to the other parties and to the public.[111] Decisions by each branch within their respective competencies are also self-executing. Unlike the Montreal Protocol NCP, there is no need for adoption of the decisions by the meeting of the parties. However, there does exist a system of review, by which a party may appeal to the conference of the parties serving as the meeting of the parties against a decision of the enforcement branch if the party believes that it has been denied due process.[112]

The enforcement branch has at its disposal a host of possible measures that can be applied in the event of non-compliance. When the requirements for developing systems for estimating and reporting emission levels have not been met, the enforcement branch is to make a declaration of non-compliance and develop a plan in collaboration with the party concerned in order to bring the party back into compliance.[113] The enforcement branch may suspend the eligibility of a party to transfer emission reduction units in relation to sinks of greenhouse gases, to participate in the clean development mechanism, or to engage in emissions trading when it determines that the party does not meet the eligibility requirements for these mechanisms.[114]

When the enforcement branch determines that a party has failed to meet its emission target, then it is required to declare that the party is not in compliance with its commitments. The defaulting party must then make up for any excess emissions during the second commitment

[106] *Ibid.* s. VIII [2]. [107] *Ibid.* s. VIII [3]. [108] *Ibid.* s. VIII [4].
[109] *Ibid.* s. VIII [5]. [110] *Ibid.* s. IX [2]. [111] *Ibid.* s. IX [10].
[112] *Ibid.* s. XI. [113] *Ibid.* s. XV [1], [2]. [114] *Ibid.* s. XV [4].

period, and the new target will include a further 30 per cent reduction by way of penalty for non-compliance. The enforcement branch must also suspend the eligibility of the party to participate in emissions trading, and develop a compliance action plan to ensure that the party meets its quantified emission limitation or reduction commitment in the subsequent commitment period.[115]

Aarhus Convention NCP

The Aarhus Convention seeks to protect the right of civil society to participate in environmental decision-making by governments. To this end it requires states parties to protect rights of access to information, participation in making decisions, and access to justice. The Aarhus Convention NCP was adopted at the first meeting of the parties in 2002 and while it shares many features with other NCPs it also takes NCP practice in new and important directions.[116] Its distinctive features are reflective of the organising rationale of the Aarhus Convention, which is to open up decision-making to public scrutiny and involvement.

As with the Kyoto NCP, the compliance committee operating in the Aarhus NCP is composed of independent experts, and this means that the committee has the advantages of stable composition (rather than a revolving membership of government representatives) and independence in its deliberations and decision-making. What is unique about the Aarhus NCP is that NGOs may nominate candidates for election to the compliance committee. Although the election remains a matter for parties to the convention, the opening of the nomination process has allowed meaningful participation by civil society in shaping the membership of the committee.[117] A further entitlement accorded to NGOs by the Aarhus NCP is the right to submit communications concerning non-compliance. Indeed any member of the public of a party to the convention may submit a case to the compliance committee. This unique feature of the Aarhus NCP was controversial, and consequently an opt-out procedure was included which allows parties to declare that they will not accept such complaints for up to four years (no such declarations have in fact been made).[118] The thresholds for

[115] *Ibid.* s. XV [5].

[116] Svitlana Kravchenko, 'The Aarhus Convention and Innovations in Compliance with MEAs' (2007) 18 *ColoJIELP* 1.

[117] *Ibid.* 10. [118] *Ibid.* 17.

citizen submissions, which include the exhaustion of local remedies, share much in common with human rights complaints procedures. By the end of 2007, twenty-one complaints had been initiated in the Aarhus NCP and all but one of these were commenced by NGOs or individual citizens. Through its findings and recommendations the compliance committee is now building a body of jurisprudence on important issues concerning the public participation rights safeguarded by the convention.[119] It would also appear that the recommendations of the committee are being implemented by the parties.

Innovations of NCPs

There are many areas of distinction between NCPs and traditional dispute settlement procedures for enforcing environmental obligations. They have a capacity to act as preventive mechanisms, dealing with compliance issues when they first arise and assisting parties to discharge their obligations before serious problems of non-compliance or environmental damage arise. The general standing approach adopted by NCPs means that they can be activated more readily than dispute settlement procedures in order to deal with interests of a community character that might otherwise be ignored.[120] Not only may NCPs be invoked by any party, by treaty bodies, and in some situations even civil society, but there is also no threshold requirement that the instigator of a complaint has been injured. NCPs are also non-confrontational and non-adversarial, meaning that they involve much lower political costs for parties to disputes, and the focus is less on ascribing fault than in determining a way forward to assist all parties to meet their obligations. This is reflected in the prominence of assistance measures in the tools available to NCPs, including assistance in the collection and reporting of data, other technical assistance including the transfer of technology, and financial assistance. In certain situations a non-compliant party may be suspended from a treaty regime, although termination is not normally among the range of enforcement options, as complete exclusion of a party is likely to be counterproductive in terms of achieving a regime's objects and purposes.

In contrast with traditional methods of enforcement activated on the breach of an obligation, NCPs ascertain compliance and

[119] See also Veit Koester, 'The Compliance Committee of the Aarhus Convention: An Overview of Procedures and Jurisprudence' (2007) 37 *EPL* 83.

[120] Sand, above n. 74, 50.

non-compliance according to much more flexible criteria. Under NCPs there is a blending of both negotiatory and adjudicative powers,[121] and they can provide positive encouragement to states to comply with an environmental regime rather than punitive sanctions. In this regard NCPs have been described as 'a form of conciliation between a state and the international community in which a non-compliant state is, initially, not condemned, but given a helping hand'.[122] This has advantages given that environmentally deleterious activities often fall short of the breach of a treaty-based or customary environmental obligation.

However, these features have attracted some criticism, with some commentators concerned that this 'softer' form of enforcement may, over time, devalue the provisions of the environmental regimes they are designed to uphold.[123] Klabbers argues that the soft character of NCPs is indicative of a 'disappointment with the law'[124] and that as 'anything seems negotiable … including compliance', it is only 'a small step to suggest that the binding force of law is negotiable'.[125] Such criticisms are not necessarily well founded as there may be value in a precise environmental rule that is enforced somewhat flexibly. Because NCPs offer greater prospects of a cooperative rather than confrontational approach to compliance problems, states may be more willing to agree to more extensive and better defined environmental obligations. Not only can NCPs take a range of measures to ensure that states comply with such clear rules, but action outside an environmental regime is also more likely to be possible as clearly expressed rules permit NGOs and other actors to bring greater political pressure to bear on defaulting governments. In addition, the critique falsely presupposes that formal processes of dispute settlement are necessarily 'harder'. In practice there is a great reluctance by international courts to conclude that a state has breached international law.

It is none the less the case that NCPs are quite different institutions from the traditional methods of inter-state claim and dispute settlement that they are designed to complement, rather than replace. As a consequence, the interaction between NCPs and general international

[121] Chinkin, above n. 36, 129.

[122] Marcel T. A. Brus, *Third Party Dispute Settlement in an Interdependent World: Developing a Theoretical Framework* (1995) 40.

[123] Martti Koskenniemi, 'Comment on the Paper by Antonia Handler Chayes, Abram Chayes and Ronald B. Mitchell' in Winfried Lang (ed.), *Sustainable Development and International Law* (1995) 91, 94; Klabbers, above n. 85, 997.

[124] Klabbers, above n. 85, 1000. [125] *Ibid.*

law relating to breach of treaty and state responsibility raises several issues.[126] These include foundational questions about the relationship between the concepts of non-compliance and breach of obligation, and more practical concerns about the potential competition between NCPs and dispute settlement procedures. While of considerable academic interest, there are several reasons why the relationship between these two different models of environmental governance is less problematic than it might initially appear.[127] In the first place, most non-compliance situations will fall far short of a technical breach of treaty and thereby other parties would not in any event be in a position to complain of such violations in parallel dispute settlement procedures. Second, even if non-compliance does involve a breach of a treaty obligation entailing state responsibility, it may be difficult to identify situations in which another state has suffered the requisite injury to be able to invoke the responsibility of the delinquent state. In this regard NCPs fulfil a need that has to date been served inadequately by traditional procedures.

3.3 Conclusion

International environmental law initially developed as a collection of aspirational and soft-law instruments but these broad, frequently non-binding, texts have since been supplemented by a growing body of hard treaty law. It might therefore have been expected that compliance and enforcement in this area would follow the model of judicialisation and legalisation found in other areas of international law, such as international trade law, where there is a high degree of normative precision coupled with mandatory dispute settlement procedures readily initiated by members. However, the movement to law and legal institutions has to date been different in the international environmental field. There has been a marked increase in the use of dispute settlement procedures, including courts and tribunals. Yet in terms of addressing the specific challenge of compliance, the tendency has been towards the establishment of detailed and binding environmental standards that

126 For a discussion of these issues in relation to the Kyoto Protocol see Malgosia A. Fitzmaurice, 'The Kyoto Protocol Compliance Regime and Treaty Law' (2004) 8 *SingYBIL* 23.

127 See Nout van Woudenberg, 'Compliance Mechanisms: A Useful Instrument' (2004) 34 *EPL* 185, 185–6 (noting that the differences between NCPs and dispute settlement procedures 'are substantial and fundamental, and a procedure under [a] compliance mechanisms ... does not prejudice any dispute settlement procedure').

are combined with NCPs and other supervisory institutions to promote a much 'softer' form of dispute settlement. This development appears, at least in part, to constitute recognition of the limitations of traditional methods of inter-state dispute settlement. However, the picture is a complex one, as seen in some NCPs which possess adjudicative and enforcement characteristics.

This chapter has endeavoured to situate international courts and tribunals among the institutions that have been established to address issues of compliance, enforcement, and dispute settlement in international environmental law. It was seen that the basic system of inter-state claims, made under the rubric of state responsibility and the law of treaties and leading to the invocation of dispute settlement methods, provides only rudimentary tools for inducing compliance. Several reasons were advanced for this conclusion, the most important being that dispute settlement bodies can be constrained by their central purpose or rationale, which is to resolve controversies peacefully rather than to uphold community values. By being responsive to the dynamics of the compliance problem, supervisory bodies established under multilateral regulatory agreements appear to present a vital part of institutional frameworks for ensuring that states meet their international environmental obligations. Such treaty-based institutions, including NCPs, secretariats, permanent commissions, and other bodies, may perform multiple tasks across the life of an environmental regime, and through various stages from the identification of a potential non-compliance situation to the resolution of a dispute between the parties. These include the collection of information, reviewing reports from states on treaty implementation, assessing the performance of states of their obligations, deciding upon measures to be taken in response to non-compliance, and the negotiation and adoption of additional regulations applicable under the treaty regime. A major strength of such international regulatory institutions is that they may maintain a resolute focus on the critical question of the performance of a regime against set environmental criteria and less on questions of breach, responsibility, or liability.

4 International courts and environmental governance

Ever since environmental matters emerged as a subject of international concern, debate has surrounded the value of arbitration and judicial settlement in addressing environmental disputes.[1] This debate has often appeared one sided, with an array of arguments mounted against the capacity of international courts to resolve complex environmental controversies or hold states to their environmental obligations. It was seen in the previous chapter that states increasingly prefer supervisory institutions to perform these functions,[2] a trend which appears to vindicate many criticisms of international environmental litigation. However, the adoption of a managerial approach to dispute settlement and compliance control has not been universal within or across environmental agreements.[3] Not only do several judicial mechanisms exist alongside treaty bodies in environmental regimes, but adjudicative elements have also been incorporated within newer and softer enforcement institutions. This chapter assesses this diversity of practice and identifies the value that adjudication can bring to international environmental governance. Drawing on international relations scholarship

[1] Phoebe N. Okowa, 'Environmental Dispute Settlement: Some Reflections on Recent Developments' in Malcolm D. Evans (ed.), *Remedies in International Law: The Institutional Dilemma* (1998) 157; Richard B. Bilder, 'The Settlement of Disputes in the Field of the International Law of the Environment' (1975) 144 *RDC* 139; Christine Gray, *Judicial Remedies in International Law* (1987).

[2] Andreas L. Paulus, 'Dispute Resolution' in Geir Ulfstein (ed.), *Making Treaties Work: Human Rights, Environment and Arms Control* (2007) 351, 365: 'For all the impact of dispute settlement on environmental questions … the dynamics is clearly in favour of informal mechanisms instead of judicial settlement.'

[3] Christian J. Tams, 'Enforcement' in Geir Ulfstein (ed.), *Making Treaties Work: Human Rights, Environment and Arms Control* (2007) 391, 399: 'Contrary to the firmly held views of many writers, many of the more recent agreements rely on hard enforcement as well, and seem to do so increasingly.'

it is argued that the constraints upon judicial bodies assuming a more prominent role stem less from inherent limitations with the adjudicative process than from the positioning of international courts within environmental regimes.

4.1 International courts and environmental governance

There has been an increasing use of the concept of 'governance' to explore the ways in which environmental issues can be managed in a more integrated, coordinated, and effective manner.[4] At its crux, international governance refers to the manner by which international norms and institutions are established and come to exert an influence on the behaviour of states. International environmental governance therefore embraces all of the processes through which states and other actors address environmental issues that transcend national borders.[5] Given the complexity of environmental challenges, and the difficulties in coordinating the behaviour of multiple states, this is no easy task. The turn to international environmental law is a response to this problem and the most formal manifestation of the environmental governance process. But while it lends the discourse of public international law and its supporting institutions to the task of supranational environmental management, international environmental law differs from many other fields of international law in the way in which normativity is used to regulate state behaviour. Public international law has always contained a degree of normative hierarchy, from the hardest and most stringent of rules (*ius cogens* norms) to softer and less demanding standards. However, international environmental law is characterised by its combination of hard- and soft-law standards, as seen most obviously in the body of generalised environmental principles which guide the operation of more precise rules, but which themselves impose few if any binding obligations. The complex nature of international environmental problems, and the

[4] See e.g. Norichika Kanie and Peter M. Haas (eds.), *Emerging Forces in Environmental Governance* (2004). For a critique of the use of the concept see Martti Koskenniemi, 'International Legislation Today: Limits and Possibilities' (2005) 23 *WisILJ* 61, 74: 'Instead of international legislation, commentators today speak of global "governance" indicating that the idea of a formal international government under law may have become unworkable, pointless or perhaps old-fashioned.'

[5] Daniel Bodansky, 'The Legitimacy of International Governance: A Coming Challenge for International Environmental Law?' (1999) 93 *AJIL* 596, 597.

informal character of some aspects of international environmental law, raise the question as to where the outer limits lie in using the formalised process of international adjudication to address environmental disputes.

4.2 Adjudication as a method of dispute settlement

In many environmental treaties, particularly early agreements, arbitration and judicial settlement were regarded as methods of dispute settlement with equal standing alongside other peaceful means for resolving differences. This is evident in regimes such as CITES and the 1979 Convention on the Conservation of Migratory Species of Wild Animals, which encourage parties to resolve their disputes by negotiation and to turn to arbitration, by mutual agreement, if such negotiation is unsuccessful. While this attitude towards adjudication of environmental matters is retained in some more recently concluded agreements including the 1994 Desertification Convention,[6] other regimes locate adjudication in a more central dispute settlement role, as seen in the Madrid Protocol[7] and, most notably, the LOS Convention.[8]

4.2.1 Challenges of multiparty litigation

This use of adjudication as a central forum for dispute settlement in some environmental regimes has invoked the criticism that courts are essentially bilateral institutions that cannot embrace the multilateral character of international environmental disputation. The reality is that the scale of many environmental problems implicates multiple (and sometimes all) states, as is evident in attempts to protect the great global commons – the oceans, the atmosphere, and the planet's biological diversity. A dispute that demonstrates this 'parties problem' in international environmental adjudication is the *Bering Sea Fur Seals* case[9] between the United States and Great Britain, which concerned excessive harvesting by Canadian sealers of Alaskan fur seals. The tribunal devised regulations to prevent the species from being driven to extinction, but they were not effective as they could not bind other

[6] Art. 28. [7] Art. 19.

[8] Part XV. Alan E. Boyle, 'Dispute Settlement and the Law of the Sea Convention: Problems of Fragmentation and Jurisdiction' (1997) 46 *ICLQ* 37, 46.

[9] *Bering Sea Fur Seals* case (*Great Britain* v. *United States*) (1893) 1 Moore 945. See further ch. 7.

sealing states who were not parties to the proceedings, namely Japan and Russia, which thereafter lent flags of convenience to Canadian vessels so that they could continue sealing. It was only after all the main players were brought together in a 1911 treaty that pelagic sealing was brought under control.[10]

It is certainly the case that most international courts are limited in the parties that may be involved in proceedings. For the most part this is a consequence of the consensual character of international jurisdiction, and in this respect a clear distinction must be drawn between the emergence of environmental rules and other norms of a community character, and consent to jurisdiction that confers competence upon international courts.[11] None the less, considerable efforts have been made by some courts to expand participation in environmental cases, as seen in the multiparty procedures in the PCA's 2001 Optional Rules for the Arbitration of Disputes Concerning the Environment and/or Natural Resources, and the willingness of the WTO Appellate Body to accept *amicus curiae* briefs from environmental NGOs in several cases touching on environmental questions.[12] And it has been noted that whereas the contentious jurisdiction of the ICJ has not been able to involve more than a few states, the ICJ's advisory proceedings can quite effectively bring multiple parties together to address issues of interest and concern to the international community as a whole.[13] In addition, international courts, including the ICJ, generally possess wide fact-finding powers to consider the full circumstances surrounding cases touching on the public interest, such as environmental disputes.

Despite these developments, the fact remains that courts, whether national or international, cannot be entirely open to participation without losing their attributes as settlers of concrete disputes according to law between parties with a defined interest in proceedings. Judicial settlement is highly formalised and necessarily focused on specific questions cast in legal terms.[14] Almost inevitably a number of states and

[10] 1911 Convention Respecting Measures for the Preservation and Protection of Fur Seals in the North Pacific Ocean.

[11] See *East Timor (Portugal* v. *Australia)* [1995] ICJ Rep 90, [29].

[12] See especially United States – Import Prohibition of Certain Shrimp and Shrimp Products, WTO Doc. WT/DS58/AB/R (report of the Appellate Body).

[13] Alan E. Boyle, 'The *Gabčíkovo-Nagymaros* Case: New Law in Old Bottles' (1997) 8 *YIEL* 13, 20.

[14] José E. Alvarez, 'The New Dispute Settlers: (Half) Truths and Consequences' (2003) 38 *TexILJ* 405, 407 (noting that 'international adjudication, like its domestic

other actors will be excluded from the adjudicative process. But this does not mean that courts cannot make a meaningful contribution to addressing environmental disputes within the particular limits in which they operate. In this context the *Bering Sea Fur Seals* case emerges in a more positive light. While it did not (and could not) constrain non-parties to the litigation, the award did contribute profoundly to the ultimate resolution of a regional dispute by laying down innovative management regulations that formed the basis for a subsequent binding agreement and national laws. Similar observations may be made with respect to domestic courts that have grappled with problems of global environmental management such as climate change and articulated principles of general applicability.[15]

4.2.2 Polycentricity of environmental disputes

A further argument against turning to adjudication in international environmental law is that it cannot address the full panoply of issues implicated in most environmental disputes.[16] It must be noted that this critique goes beyond the argument that environmental disputes frequently turn on complex scientific questions. Rather, it stems from the argument, made particularly forcefully by Fuller, that environmental problems are intrinsically 'polycentric' in involving a 'web' of competing values and interests.[17] Fuller argued that polycentric environmental disputes can be successfully addressed by 'managerial direction' from multilateral institutions, but that formalised adjudication

counterpart, is routinely seen as involving four basic elements: (1) independent judges apply (2) relatively precise and pre-existing legal norms after (3) adversary proceedings in order to achieve (4) dichotomous decisions in which one of the parties clearly wins'). See also Philip Allott, 'The International Court and the Voice of Justice' in A. Vaughan Lowe and Malgosia A. Fitzmaurice (eds.), *Fifty Years of the International Court of Justice* (1996) 17, 24 (observing that the distinctiveness of adjudication stems from the physical, symbolic, and systematic isolation of courts from other international decision-making processes); J. G. Merrills, 'The Role and Limits of International Adjudication' (1987) 24 *Coexistence* 169, 171–4.

15 See e.g. *Massachusetts* v. *Environmental Protection Authority* (no. 05–1120) 415 F. 3d 50 (US Supreme Court) (noting, at 23, that '[a] reduction in domestic emissions would slow the pace of global emissions increases, no matter what happens elsewhere').

16 L. D. M. Nelson, 'The Development of the Legal Regime of High Seas Fisheries' in Alan E. Boyle and David Freestone (eds.), *International Law and Sustainable Development: Past Achievements and Future Challenges* (1999) 113, 132–3; A. Vaughan Lowe, 'Sustainable Development and Unsustainable Arguments' in Alan E. Boyle and David Freestone (eds.), *International Law and Sustainable Development: Past Achievements and Future Challenges* (1999) 19, 29.

17 Lon L. Fuller, 'The Forms and Limits of Adjudication' (1978) 92 *HarvLR* 353, 401.

is likely to lead to one of three undesirable results. First, there may be a complete failure to resolve the dispute because the questions posed are simply not reducible to a form that can be resolved by a court. Second, if a court does attempt to resolve the dispute, it may step well beyond its proper sphere. Third, the court or tribunal may recognise the impossibility of dealing with the dispute on its own terms, and instead seek to reformulate the problem more narrowly to be suitable for judicial decision.

The history of international environmental dispute settlement lends some support to Fuller's thesis, but his argument presents a somewhat incomplete portrait of the ways in which courts can contribute to environmental dispute settlement. In relation to the first likely outcome suggested by Fuller, an apparent example is the *Southern Bluefin Tuna* dispute[18] decided under the aegis of part XV of the LOS Convention. In that case, the legal questions before ITLOS, and a subsequent arbitral tribunal, appeared fairly limited. They related to the legality of a unilateral experimental fishing programme undertaken by Japan, and whether the part XV compulsory dispute settlement system should take precedence over the consensual system of the 1993 Convention for the Conservation of Southern Bluefin Tuna. However, these specific legal issues were embedded in a more fundamental disagreement concerning sustainable fishing limits, a dispute that involved competing conceptions of the meaning and place of conservation values in fisheries management.[19] As a consequence, neither ITLOS nor the annex VII tribunal were invited to address the full range of issues between the parties, and the parties were therefore forced to return to seemingly intractable negotiations over catch allocations in the Commission for the Conservation of Southern Bluefin Tuna (C-CCSBT). On its face this outcome would suggest that the *Southern Bluefin Tuna* dispute delivered very little in terms of promoting a durable and complete settlement of a multifaceted dispute over a migratory fishery. However, an alternative assessment is that the litigation was helpful in bringing the parties together and catalysing greater levels of cooperation within a

[18] *Southern Bluefin Tuna* cases: *New Zealand* v. *Japan*; *Australia* v. *Japan* (provisional measures) (1999) 38 ILM 1624 (*Southern Bluefin Tuna* order); *Australia and New Zealand* v. *Japan* (award on jurisdiction and admissibility) (2000) 39 ILM 1359 (*Southern Bluefin Tuna* award).

[19] Tim Stephens, 'The Limits of International Adjudication in International Environmental Law: Another Perspective on the Southern Bluefin Tuna Case' (2004) 19 *IJMCL* 173.

fisheries commission that was dysfunctional.[20] Mansfield has argued in this regard that both tribunals helped to move the parties from a position of deadlock to one of renewed cooperation, and as a result the *Southern Bluefin Tuna* award is more significant for revitalising the C-CCSBT than it is for its formal outcome.[21]

There are also cases which appear to support concerns about the second consequence identified by Fuller, namely that a court attempting to resolve a polycentric environmental dispute could overreach its mandate and thereby compromise the legitimacy and authority of the court in the eyes of the parties, and the international community more generally. Arguably this occurred in the *Fisheries Jurisdiction* cases[22] where the ICJ sought to develop the problematic doctrine of preferential fishing rights to address concerns over unsustainable harvesting of cod in the North Sea.[23] The articulation of this doctrine was a creative and bona fide attempt to resolve a complex dispute, but it was not supported by the parties to the case, or by states more generally, which preferred to address the matter through the Third United Nations Conference of the Law of the Sea. However, this mismatch between the decision and the expectations of the parties and other states might well have been avoided if the Court had recognised the pace of developments in the law of the sea, and sought to work within the existing constraints of state practice in reaching its decision. Indeed, the ICJ's discussion of the importance of cooperation as an underlying environmental obligation[24] may be cited as just such an acknowledgement of the practical realities of environmental dispute settlement involving multiple parties and multiple issues, and the decision on this point stands in good stead today.

The third possible outcome identified by Fuller is that a court will be intimidated by the political consequences of resolving the dispute as framed by the parties, and instead seek to reformulate the matters in

[20] *Ibid.*

[21] Bill Mansfield, 'Compulsory Dispute Settlement after the Southern Bluefin Tuna Award' in Alex G. Oude Elferink and Donald R. Rothwell (eds.), *Oceans Management in the 21st Century: Institutional Frameworks and Responses* (2004) 255.

[22] *Fisheries Jurisdiction* case (*United Kingdom* v. *Iceland*) (merits) [1974] ICJ Rep 3 (*Germany* v. *Iceland*) (merits) [1974] ICJ Rep 175.

[23] See further ch. 7.

[24] The Court noted that the '[p]arties have the obligation to keep under review the fishery resources … and to examine together, in the light of scientific information … the measures required for the conservation and development … of those resources': *Fisheries Jurisdiction* case [1974] ICJ Rep 3, 32.

dispute in less controversial terms. This may mean that the question ultimately decided is highly qualified and bears little relationship to the environmental concerns at the root of the dispute. An instance of this process of framing in international environmental litigation was seen in the *Nuclear Tests* cases[25] where the ICJ avoided the environmental implications of French nuclear testing by recasting the dispute from one concerning international environmental law to one relating to the legal effects of unilateral statements. There are competing views as to whether this was an appropriate course for the Court to take,[26] and it needs to be noted that the case was made particularly controversial by France's refusal to participate even though the ICJ's jurisdiction had been regularly invoked. Had France been a willing interlocutor with Australia and New Zealand it would have been a relatively straightforward matter for the ICJ to address the issues of international environmental law raised by the applicants, notwithstanding that their submissions pressed at the then boundaries of international environmental law.

Koskenniemi has offered an analysis of international environmental adjudication that shares much in common with Fuller's third critique. He has pointed to the propensity of international courts to seek an outcome in environmental matters that is broadly acceptable to the parties, rather than one that involves a clear determination of breach and responsibility for wrongdoing. Koskenniemi contends that this is a consequence of the 'proceduralisation'[27] inherent in many environmental regimes, which are ambivalent and defer difficult political choices for resolution by diplomatic or legal dispute settlement procedures.[28] Environmental regimes almost inevitably engage with some

[25] *Nuclear Tests* cases: *Australia* v. *France* (interim measures) [1973] ICJ Rep 99, (merits) [1974] ICJ Rep 253; *New Zealand* v. *France* (interim measures) [1973] ICJ Rep 135, (merits) [1974] ICJ Rep 457.

[26] Compare Edward McWhinney, 'International Law-Making and the Judicial Process: The World Court and the French Nuclear Tests Case' (1975) 3 *SyracuseJIL&Com* 9 with Lyndel V. Prott, 'Avoiding a Decision on the Merits in the International Court of Justice' (1976) 7 *SLR* 433.

[27] Martti Koskenniemi, 'Peaceful Settlement of Environmental Disputes' (1991) 60 *NordicJIL* 73. An important distinction must be drawn between the strategy of 'proceduralisation' and the use of procedural obligations in multilateral agreements requiring states, *inter alia*, to identify and assess environmental risks, or notify of possible environmental impacts. See Phoebe N. Okowa, 'Procedural Obligations in International Environmental Agreements' (1996) 67 *BYBIL* 275.

[28] As an example see the 2000 Convention on the Conservation and Management of Highly Migratory Fish Stocks in the Western and Central Pacific Ocean which

of the most complex and controversial issues confronting humanity. In such circumstances it is clear that '[a]greement on substantive law requires more of a consensus about political value than agreeing upon procedure'.[29] So rather than crafting an environmental regime to deal with the issue area that is clear in its provisions, and far-reaching in the behavioural modifications required of parties, the environmental conflict is instead postponed by

> referring its normative regulation elsewhere; into further cooperation between the parties, into unilateral measures or into cooperation within international organisations. The matter is thereby proceduralised in order to make it amenable for diplomatic treatment.[30]

This tendency to proceduralise may lead to the impression that international environmental law has acquired more content and institutional sophistication than in reality it has.[31] This is because it is easier to agree on broadly defined environmental objectives than it is to reach consensus on the precise modalities for achieving them. Proceduralisation can thereby obscure fundamental conflict, deferring at the stage of regime formation questions that must then be confronted when dispute settlement procedures are invoked.[32] As a further consequence, a judicial forum seised of a dispute will be given very uncertain guidance as to how to resolve controversies arising out of the environmental regime.[33] If an environmental treaty incorporates no

established 'principles' rather than confronting the substantive 'conflicts of interest' which were left for resolution by the Commission established by the convention: Are K. Sydnes, 'Establishing a Regional Fisheries Management Organisation for the Western and Central Pacific Tuna Fisheries' (2001) 44 *OCM* 787, 797.

29 Koskenniemi, above n. 27, 74. Koskenniemi has argued elsewhere (Martti Koskenniemi, *From Apology to Utopia: The Structure of International Legal Argument* (reissue, 2005)) that an attraction to procedural over substantive solutions is a characteristic of international law generally.

30 Koskenniemi, above n. 27, 78.

31 Christine M. Chinkin, 'Alternative Dispute Resolution under International Law' in Malcolm D. Evans (ed.), *Remedies in International Law: The Institutional Dilemma* (1998) 123, 139. See also Christine M. Chinkin, 'The Peaceful Settlement of Disputes: New Grounds for Optimism?' in Ronald St John Macdonald (ed.), *Essays in Honour of Wang Tieya* (1993) 165, 178.

32 Martti Koskenniemi, 'The Future of Statehood' (1991) 32 *HarvILJ* 397, 403.

33 Philippe Sands, 'International Environmental Litigation and its Future' (1999) 32 *URichLR* 1619, 1637: 'Called upon to interpret vague norms, an international court faces a situation of real difficulty when asked to apply the law to the particular facts of a case.'

strong consensus on substantive questions, a court presented with an unresolved issue must look beyond the text in order to find an acceptable solution. As this can involve a court entering into unchartered and controversial territory it may wish to make a pragmatic attempt to facilitate an amicable resolution of the dispute, rather then render a decision that could potentially be viewed as not being appropriately grounded in law.

This facilitative strategy has attracted some support in the literature. Writing in relation to the *Southern Bluefin Tuna* dispute, Johnston has argued that the willingness of ITLOS in the *Southern Bluefin Tuna* order to assist the parties in reaching an amicable settlement 'should be applauded' and that the '*facilitative* function of modern international adjudication should in no way be relegated to a lower position than the more traditional *resolutive* and *declaratory* functions'.[34] Another commentator has similarly suggested that were courts generally to seek to moderate agreed outcomes, they would be more effective in resolving environmental disputes.[35] And this approach has been tethered to the view that the international community has an overriding need to preserve the maintenance of minimum order against dark tendencies towards violent conflict, especially over natural resources.[36]

Koskenniemi's critique undoubtedly has purchase in relation to environmental regimes that can be described as shallow – those that set only broad principles and then leave it to institutions, both political and legal, to supply additional content so that the regimes can fulfil their stated objects and purposes. However, not all environmental regimes are of this character: some framework environmental agreements have been dragged from the shallows of general commitment to the depths of detailed prescription through formal processes of amendment, the addition of protocols and implementing agreements, or through decisions of conferences and meetings of parties. This means that facilitation should not be celebrated as a virtue in all circumstances.

There are two fundamental difficulties with a positive appraisal of the notion of adjudication as facilitation. The first objection is that

[34] Douglas M. Johnston, 'Fishery Diplomacy and Science and the Judicial Function' (1999) 10 *YIEL* 33, 38.

[35] Francis N. Botchway, 'The International Adjudicatory Process and Trans-Boundary Resource Disputes' [2001] *AILJ* 143, 151.

[36] See e.g. Elli Louka, 'Cutting the Gordian Knot: Why International Environmental Law is Not Only About the Protection of the Environment' (1996) 10 *TempICLJ* 80.

although promoting a joint settlement can help broker a temporary or permanent compromise, it may not necessarily resolve the underlying political disagreement over such issues as the allocation of scarce environmental resources. Second, although removing discord, a facilitative solution may suggest that the environmental regime is functioning successfully, while in reality there is no net improvement in environmental outcomes. Encouraging the parties to a dispute to reach a compromise may well produce more harmonious international relations but it will not necessarily advance the objects and purposes of a given environmental regime.

The tendency towards a facilitative approach, even as regards factual findings, can be discerned in several cases. The decision of the ICJ in the *Gabčíkovo-Nagymaros Project* case[37] can be seen as one in which the Court studiously avoided the determination of any breach of international environmental law, and instead sought to encourage the parties to work together to reach consensus on a regime to protect the environment of the Danube, while simultaneously continuing work on the joint dams project.[38] The ICJ also made no definitive factual findings regarding the extent of environmental damage threatened by the project, preferring to leave these matters to the parties to resolve between themselves.

The decisions of ITLOS in relation to marine environmental matters also signal a tendency to shy away from definitive conclusions regarding compliance with environmental obligations. It can be argued that this is a consequence of the proceduralisation strategy adopted in the negotiation of the LOS Convention. Lowe has noted in this respect that 'the states parties were prepared to sign off the Convention text without dotting every i and crossing every t because the details in critical areas would be worked out either by state practice or, if all else failed, by recourse to adjudication'.[39] ITLOS has without question contributed significantly to the evolution of the LOS Convention, however, the Tribunal has been reticent in identifying clear situations of breach, and has instead been inclined to encourage the parties to settle their

37 *Gabčíkovo-Nagymaros Project* case (*Hungary/Slovakia*) [1997] ICJ Rep 7.

38 Attila Tanzi and Cesare Pitea, 'Emerging Trends in the Role of Non-State Actors in International Water Disputes' in International Bureau of the Permanent Court of Arbitration (ed.), *Resolution of International Water Disputes* (2003) 259, 262.

39 A. Vaughan Lowe, 'Advocating Judicial Activism: The ITLOS Opinions of Judge Ivan Shearer' (2005) 24 *AustYBIL* 145, 150.

differences.[40] It has also displayed some caution in engaging with the relevant principles of international environmental law, again for reasons that appear connected to its desire to promote a friendly settlement. For instance, in its provisional measures orders in environmental cases, ITLOS has been careful to avoid taking a position in the debate concerning the legal status of the concept of 'precaution'. Rather than identifying precaution as a customary 'principle' of law, or indeed merely a guiding 'approach', the Tribunal has favoured the more neutral notion of 'prudence and caution'.[41] This reticence seems particularly inappropriate in the context of the LOS Convention, a deep regime in many respects, which specifically established a dispute settlement system to hold parties to the package-deal consensus and supply authoritative interpretations of its terms. As with any international agreement there are inevitably ambiguities, but the task of ITLOS and arbitral tribunals is not to avoid these by promoting settlements at all costs, but rather to engage with them so as to serve the interests of all parties to the regime, including those who happen to be disputants in any particular case.

4.3 Adjudication as a method of compliance control

That courts are not simply facilitative bodies confirms that they have a further function beyond dispute settlement: eliciting compliance from states with their environmental obligations. While the initial rationale for international courts was to promote peaceful settlement,[42] the objective of compliance has been regarded as increasingly important as the gap between the stated objectives of environmental regimes and their performance in preventing environmental decline appears

[40] This tendency provoked Judge ad hoc Shearer to remark in the *Southern Bluefin Tuna* order (1999) 38 ILM 1624 at [14] that

> the Tribunal, in its prescription of provisional measures in this case, has behaved less as a court of law and more as an agency of diplomacy. While diplomacy, and a disposition to assist the parties in resolving their dispute amicably, have their proper place in the judicial settlement of international disputes, the Tribunal should not shrink from the consequences of proven facts.

[41] *Southern Bluefin Tuna* order (1999) 38 ILM 1624 [77]; *MOX Plant* case (*Ireland* v. *United Kingdom*) (provisional measures) (2002) 41 ILM 405, [84]; *Land Reclamation by Singapore in and around the Straits of Johor* (*Malaysia* v. *Singapore*) (provisional measures) (8 October 2003) (available at www.itlos.org) [99]. See Jacqueline Peel, 'Precaution: A Matter of Principle, Approach or Process?' (2004) 5 *MJIL* 483, 493–5.

[42] See the discussion in ch. 2.

to widen. However, a large body of international relations scholarship has questioned whether the compliance objective can be advanced by the turn to international judicial institutions.

4.3.1 *Managerialist critique*

The most long-standing divide in international relations scholarship is between realism and institutionalism. Realist theorists view international courts as just as ineffective as international law itself, at least as regards critical issues of national interest.[43] As many environmental issues, including access to natural resources,[44] fall into this category this means that international environmental law and its supporting institutions, including courts, will do little to influence state behaviour. At the other end of the spectrum of international relations theory lies institutionalism, which takes a far more positive view of international cooperation, particularly in areas such as environmental management where the fact of global ecological interdependence means that there are powerful incentives for action to be coordinated through legal norms and institutions.[45]

Institutionalist (or 'regime') theorists argue that international legal regimes can shape international relations in important ways.[46] Most variants of institutionalist theory share with realism the view that states are the primary international actors, and that they act in an essentially rational manner in seeking to maximise their interests. However, whereas for realists international law is a chimera, or at most epiphenomenal of power relations,[47] institutionalists argue that states rationally pursuing their interests will agree to be bound by international legal commitments, compliance with which they take

[43] Hans Morgenthau, *Politics Among Nations: The Struggle for Power and Peace* (1951) 224: '[I]nternational adjudication is unable to impose effective restraints upon the struggle for power on the international scene.'

[44] Cass R. Sunstein, 'Of Montreal and Kyoto: A Tale of Two Protocols' (2007) 31 *HarvELR* 1.

[45] Denise K. DeGarno, *International Environmental Treaties and State Behavior: Factors Influencing Cooperation* (2005) 9.

[46] 'Institutions' or 'regimes' are defined by regime theorists as 'persistent and connected sets of rules and practices that prescribe behavioural roles, constrain activity, and shape expectations': Robert O. Keohane, Peter M. Haas, and Marc A. Levy, 'The Effectiveness of International Environmental Institutions' in Robert O. Keohane, Peter M. Haas, and Marc A. Levy (eds.), *Institutions for the Earth: Sources of Effective International Environmental Protection* (1993) 3, 4–5.

[47] Benedict Kingsbury, 'The Concept of Compliance as a Function of Competing Conceptions of International Law' (1997–8) 19 *MichJIL* 345, 350–1.

seriously.[48] They do this for the reason that collective action can achieve positive outcomes that would otherwise be beyond their reach.

A sizeable body of institutionalist scholarship now exists which seeks to explain the reasons for the success or failure of environmental regimes.[49] The managerialist theory presented by Abram and Antonia Handler Chayes,[50] which represents the mainstream view,[51] holds that adjudication is fundamentally unsuited to the task of achieving treaty compliance, because it is 'costly, contentious, cumbersome, and slow' and has the tendency of 'raising the political visibility of the problem and failing to be subject to party control'.[52] This critique points to real-world experience to support this conclusion: states have shown no great enthusiasm for adjudicative procedures in international environmental law, and have instead preferred a regulatory approach to resolving disputes and promoting compliance. A particular weakness attached by this criticism to adjudication is that it is inherently reactive, and can only be activated when a litigant commences proceedings in respect of a discrete legal matter.[53] The only exception to the otherwise reactive character of most international adjudicative proce-

[48] Beth A. Simmons, 'Compliance with International Agreements' in Charlotte Ku and Paul F. Diehl (eds.), *International Law: Classic and Contemporary Readings* (2003) 181, 186.

[49] See in particular Edward L. Miles *et al.* (eds.), *Environmental Regime Effectiveness: Confronting Theory With Evidence* (2002); Oran R. Young (ed.), *The Effectiveness of International Environmental Regimes* (1999); Edith Brown Weiss and Harold K. Jacobson (eds.), *Engaging Countries: Strengthening Compliance with International Environmental Accords* (1998); David G. Victor, Kal Raustiala, and Eugene B. Skolnikoff (eds.), *The Implementation and Effectiveness of International Environmental Commitments: Theory and Practice* (1998); Peter M. Haas, Robert O. Keohane, and Marc A. Levy (eds.), *Institutions for Earth: Sources of Effective International Environmental Protection* (1993).

[50] Abram Chayes and Antonia Handler Chayes, *The New Sovereignty: Compliance with International Regulatory Agreements* (1995) 205: '[a] century of experience with international adjudication leads to considerable scepticism about its suitability as an international dispute settlement method and, in particular, as a way of securing compliance with treaties.

[51] For concise summaries of the literature see George W. Downs, Jyle W. Danish, and Peter N. Barsoom, 'The Transformational Model of International Regime Design: Triumph of Hope or Experience?' (2000) 38 *ColumJTL* 465, 482–8; Edith Brown Weiss, 'Understanding Compliance with International Environmental Agreements: The Baker's Dozen Myths' (1999) 32 *URichLR* 1555.

[52] Abram Chayes, Antonia Handler Chayes, and Ronald B. Mitchell, 'Managing Compliance: A Comparative Perspective' in Edith Brown Weiss and Harold K. Jacobson (eds.), *Engaging Countries: Strengthening Compliance with International Environmental Accords* (1998) 39, 54.

[53] Merrills, above n. 14, 170: the function of international courts 'is not to head off disagreements before they become serious, nor to alleviate situations of amorphous tension, but to intervene only when called upon to resolve a particular crisis in the parties' relations'.

dures is the availability of provisional measures[54] in some jurisdictions which can allow action to be taken to prevent irreversible environmental harm until an environmental dispute is considered on its merits.[55]

By contrast, a managerialist approach involves building institutions that complement regimes and pull states to compliance through enhancing transparency, accountability, and cooperation among regime participants. They may adopt a proactive stance, relying on compliance 'information systems', and any inherent powers of inspection and inquiry, to monitor the compliance by states with their obligations. Some non-compliance response systems may actively manage the spectrum of state behaviour between full compliance and non-compliance, continually measuring the performance of member states against the provisions of a treaty, and its aims and objectives. Treaty bodies, secretariats, or mechanisms such as NCPs, can all provide ongoing management of compliance issues in this way.

4.3.2 *New institutionalist perspectives*

Although this remains the prevailing attitude of international relations scholarship to international environmental adjudication, an alternative and more positive perspective has recently emerged from one branch of institutionalist theory. Scholarship on the 'legalisation' of international relations (by which is meant increased reliance upon formal legal institutions) maintains that international courts and tribunals can perform many of the functions successfully discharged by judicial bodies in domestic legal systems,[56] especially in terms of deterring violations of the law and enforcing environmental obligations in situations of breach.[57] The very threat of judicial proceedings can cast

54 The main function of provisional measures in international law is to preserve the integrity of a court or tribunal's final judgment, although the historical rationale for the institution was to prevent resort to self-help: L. Collins, 'Provisional and Protective Measures in International Litigation' (1992) 234 *RDC* 9, 23.

55 See in particular Statute of the ICJ, art. 41; LOS Convention, art. 290.

56 See especially Robert O. Keohane, Andrew Moravcsik, and Anne-Marie Slaughter, 'Legalized Dispute Resolution: Interstate and Transnational' (2000) 54 *IntOrg* 457.

57 Anne-Marie Slaughter, 'International Law in a World of Liberal States' (1995) 6 *EJIL* 503, 532:

> Enforcement through the mechanism of a neutral tribunal backed by coercive force is an optimal way to ensure compliance with any agreement, whether between individuals or States. It is the mode of dispute resolution established where possible by societies the world over. A system of horizontal counter-measures, by contrast, inevitably entails each party being judge in its own cause, with the attendant illegitimacy of the resulting determination.

a shadow over the political relations of states, encouraging a resolution of disputes in conformity with a regime. When an adjudicatory procedure is invoked, it involves an impartial and independent examination of the performance of actors measured against defined legal commitments. It results in binding decisions that are ordinarily complied with not because of any threat of punitive sanctions (which are almost always absent) but rather because decisions may carry the persuasive weight of authority and legitimacy,[58] thereby allowing other international actors, and domestic constituencies,[59] to impose pressure on a principled basis. Perhaps most importantly it can assist in clarifying legal principles, thus ensuring that actors know precisely what is expected of them by an environmental regime.[60]

However, much depends on the nature of the regime in question, with deeper obligations more suited to adjudication than their shallower counterparts.[61] Early agreements often emphasised the importance of environmental protection, but often in general and non-binding language, and did not contain detailed prescriptions to regulate state behaviour.[62] Moreover they often went no further than requiring environmental standards already met by the willing

[58] Thomas M. Franck, *The Power of Legitimacy Among Nations* (1990) 24 and 316–17: legitimacy, that is the general belief that rules are articulated and applied according to 'accepted principles of right process' is essential for ensuring compliance. While unable to enforce its decisions directly, through principled reasoning an international court can 'pull states to compliance with its opinions [because of] the general perception of the legitimacy and fairness of its opinion-forming process'. See also Thomas M. Franck, 'Fairness and the General Assembly Advisory Opinion' in Laurence Boisson de Chazournes and Philippe Sands (eds.), *International Law, The International Court of Justice and Nuclear Weapons* (1999) 511, 512. Oran R. Young, *The Institutional Dimensions of Environmental Change: Fit, Interplay and Scale* (2002) 40 (compliance can follow effectively from the 'logic of appropriateness rather than the logic of countermeasures').

[59] Robert O. Keohane *et al.*, above n. 56, 467.

[60] John H. Knox, 'A New Approach to Compliance with International Environmental Law: The Submissions Procedure of the NAFTA Environmental Commission' (2001) 28 *ELQ* 1, 5. Ginsburg notes that a ruling can affect state behaviour in future cases even if not initially complied with by a party to a particular dispute: Tom Ginsburg, 'Bounded Discretion in International Judicial Lawmaking' (2005) 45 *VaJIL* 631, 647.

[61] Presciently, O'Connell predicted well over a decade ago that 'the need for enforcement will increase as environmental law develops more concrete, detailed, and wide-reaching rules'. Mary Ellen O'Connell, 'Enforcement and the Success of International Environmental Law' (1995–6) 3 *IndJGLS* 47, 57.

[62] See for instance the 1971 Convention on Wetlands of International Importance, Especially as Waterfowl Habitat (Ramsar Convention). The Ramsar Convention includes no provision for dispute settlement.

signatories. Downs, Danish, and Barsoom have contended that for such shallow environmental agreements, enforcement is unnecessary to promote compliance.[63] Alter has similarly argued that agreements with broad aims such as 'addressing poverty, improving education, providing rural health etc. are unlikely to be enhanced by creating an international court to enforce the agreement'.[64] Hence adjudication is unlikely to be of a great deal of value to environmental capacity-building obligations found in treaties such as the 1999 Protocol on Water and Health to the 1992 Convention on the Protection and Use of Transboundary Watercourses and International Lakes.[65] On the other hand, more detailed and demanding environmental agreements benefit from correspondingly more exacting procedures for enforcement. An example is the OSPAR Convention, which seeks to prevent and eliminate pollution in a specific maritime region and combines detailed obligations with a compliance machinery that includes compulsory arbitration.[66]

While international adjudication may, in some settings, deliver similar ultimate governance results as domestic courts, the process by which this occurs is, in structural terms, radically different. In this respect Helfer and Slaughter contend that international courts are created and conferred with jurisdiction by states in some multilateral settings as a way of enhancing the credibility of the obligations entered into.[67] This is because the availability of adjudication 'rais[es] the probability that violations of those commitments will be detected and accurately labelled as noncompliance', thereby creating 'material and reputational costs for the state in default'.[68] The fact that violations can be detected and exposed has the effect of encouraging ongoing compliance, which ensures that the agreement functions to the benefit of all states, even for a party that may be in breach in any particular dispute.[69] In this way courts have the characteristics of a trustee of obligations, and can be activated by litigants to test whether a party is in default, thereby providing 'monitoring' and 'evaluation' functions which parties themselves cannot supply.[70] This describes the

[63] Downs *et al.*, above n. 51.

[64] Karen J. Alter, 'Do International Courts Enhance Compliance with International Law?' (2003) 25 *RevAPS* 51, 66.

[65] See e.g. art. 8(1)(c). [66] OSPAR Convention art. 32.

[67] Laurence R. Helfer and Anne-Marie Slaughter, 'Why States Create International Tribunals: A Response to Professors Posner and Yoo' (2005) 93 *CalLR* 901.

[68] *Ibid.* 904. [69] *Ibid.* 904. [70] *Ibid.* 933.

international dynamics at play in some specific multilateral settings, but there is also a two-level game in operation here, with adjudicative procedures having implications for domestic political constituencies. Helfer and Slaughter argue that decisions of international courts can have implications for domestic politics, because by making findings on matters of fact, law, responsibility, and culpability 'tribunal rulings can mobilize compliance constituencies to press governments to adhere to their treaty obligations'.[71]

In this analysis Helfer and Slaughter allude to several features of effective adjudicatory systems which they explored in more detail in landmark research into the supranational judicial institutions of the European legal order, institutions that have been critical to the success of regional legal community.[72] Their central thesis was that the ECJ and the European Court of Human Rights (ECtHR) have been especially effective in eliciting compliance with European law because their decisions are able to penetrate the boundary of the state, to be directly enforceable in domestic courts.[73] And they argued that it should be possible to isolate and replicate those factors which underlie the performance of this supranational judicial system. To this end Helfer and Slaughter compiled a list of factors that appeared to correlate with effective supranational adjudication, and which could be used as a template for judicial bodies in other contexts. These included: (1) factors within the control of states (such as the organisation of the court); (2) factors within the control of the supranational court (such as its style of decision-making); and (3) factors which were outside the control of states or judges (such as whether the states that established the court possessed liberal democratic institutions).[74]

Building upon this work, Keohane *et al.* have conceptualised the various forms of adjudicative settlement, from ad hoc arbitration through to judicial settlement by a permanent body, as lying on a continuum between 'inter-state' dispute settlement and 'transnational' or 'supranational' dispute settlement.[75] They explain that where a particular

[71] *Ibid.* 935.

[72] Laurence R. Helfer and Anne-Marie Slaughter, 'Toward a Theory of Effective Supranational Adjudication' (1997) 107 *YaleLJ* 273.

[73] *Ibid.* 290 ('effectiveness' ought to be defined 'in terms of [a tribunal's] ability to compel compliance with its judgments by convincing domestic government institutions, directly and through pressure from private litigants, to use their power on its behalf').

[74] Helfer and Slaughter, above n. 72, 336.

[75] Keohane *et al.*, above n. 56.

court falls on this scale depends on three variables: independence, which refers to the extent to which a dispute resolution body can make impartial decisions independent of state interests; access, which describes the extent to which non-state actors have standing; and embeddedness, which refers to the extent to which decisions can be enforced without specific action by governments. While all international courts share one common feature – the task of interpreting and applying international law – they differ substantially according to these three criteria.

In inter-state dispute resolution, the task entrusted to a third party is no more than the resolution of disputes between governments. States are the parties to the dispute, control access to the settlement mechanism, and are also responsible for the implementation of any decision. States therefore 'act as gatekeepers both to the international legal process and from that process back to the domestic level'.[76] The contrasting ideal type in the dialectic is transnational dispute resolution in which states play a minor gatekeeping role. While states are initially responsible for the creation of such mechanisms, access to such courts and tribunals is more open to individuals and groups, and states are unable to (in the ideal), or constrained from (in practice), controlling access and the enforcement of decisions.[77]

Keohane *et al.* explain that increased levels of independence, access, and embeddedness all correlate with an improved likelihood that the institution may be effectively and routinely used to promote compliance. But how do dispute settlement procedures operating in international environmental law measure against these parameters?

4.3.2.1 Independence

In terms of independence, real question marks hang over many judicial and quasi-judicial procedures operating in international environmental law. It was noted in chapter 2 that there has been a marked preference for arbitration over other forms of adjudication. While arbitration shares many of the same features of judicial settlement, one major distinction is the independence of arbitral panels. Arbitration is more

[76] *Ibid.* 457. See also Robert Y. Jennings, 'The Judicial Enforcement of International Obligations' (1987) 47 *Zeitschrift für ausländisches öffentliches Recht und Völkerrecht* 3, 4 (noting that in relation to intergovernmental adjudication there is no infrastructure in general international law for the decisions of international courts to be effectively implemented at the domestic level).

[77] Keohane *et al.*, above n. 56, 458.

closely controlled by the parties, and for this reason is not necessarily able to deal appropriately with concerns of a public order.[78] Being more 'dependent', arbitral panels are susceptible to pressure to reach a conclusion acceptable to the parties, not a result which is optimal from the perspective of environmental governance.[79] By contrast, there are some examples of highly independent judicial regimes in environmental regimes such as the judicial system established by the LOS Convention. The LOS Convention was greeted with glowing reviews and high expectations not only as regards its substantive provisions on marine environmental protection, but also for its dispute settlement machinery. Charney described part XV of the LOS Convention as containing the 'strongest [dispute settlement provisions] of any environmental treaty to date', and argued that the compulsory system was 'the best guarantee possible' that parties would be 'compelled' to adhere to the terms of the regime.[80] The template provided by the LOS Convention has subsequently been followed in several key fisheries agreements, including the Straddling Stocks Agreement.[81] Adjudication is given a pivotal role in supervising the implementation of the regime and exists alongside only a limited number of other treaty-based structures for compliance.[82]

[78] Helfer and Slaughter, above n. 67, 938 ('Independent tribunals are also more likely to help states resolve cooperation problems arising from treaties that regulate public goods or the global commons').

[79] *Ibid.* 939.

[80] Jonathan I. Charney, 'The Marine Environment and the 1982 United Nations Convention on the Law of the Sea' (1994) 28 *International Lawyer* 879, 894–5. For a sceptical analysis of the utility of adjudication in marine environmental governance see Ted L. McDorman, 'Global Ocean Governance and International Adjudicative Dispute Resolution' (2000) 43 *OCM* 255, 257 ('despite a multitude of processes for settlement of oceans disputes, states have been reluctant to make use of these processes with the result that third-party adjudication has contributed little to existing governing ocean structures').

[81] 1995 Agreement for the Implementation of the Provisions of the United Nations Convention on the Law of the Sea of 10 December 1982 Relating to the Conservation and Management of Straddling Fish Stocks and Highly Migratory Fish Stocks, part VIII. See also the 2000 Convention on the Conservation and Management of Highly Migratory Fish Stocks in the Western and Central Pacific Ocean, pt IX and the 2001 Convention on the Conservation and Management of Fishery Resources in the South-East Atlantic Ocean, art. 24.

[82] Natalie Klein, *Dispute Settlement in the UN Convention on the Law of the Sea* (2005) 146:

> UNCLOS does not follow [a] cooperative, institutional approach but instead requires mandatory third-party review. Clearly, the regulatory and compliance regimes formulated in other areas of international environmental law were not perceived as workable, or perhaps inadequate, for the protection and preservation of the marine environment within the context of UNCLOS.

A further distinctive feature of the LOS Convention is that there are very few exceptions to the use of the adjudicative procedures, particularly in relation to marine environmental disputes. The general intent of the LOS Convention is to ensure that law of the sea disputes are resolved in an authoritative and binding manner. Unlike other environmental instruments providing for compulsory adjudication, the LOS Convention is also notable for its reliance upon a permanent judicial institution, ITLOS. In relation to most disputes under the LOS Convention the parties have four adjudicative bodies to select from, including annex VII arbitration, 'special arbitration' under annex VIII, or judicial settlement by the ICJ or by ITLOS.[83] While annex VII arbitration applies by default, ITLOS has residual jurisdiction in relation to matters that can involve important marine environmental issues, namely prompt release cases[84] and applications for provisional measures pending the determination of a hearing of a dispute on the merits.[85] Both heads of jurisdiction have been frequently invoked.[86] Moreover, the provisional measures jurisdiction specifically recognises the importance of marine environmental protection,[87] and can be used to uphold, at least on an interim basis, the environmental obligations of the LOS Convention.

4.3.2.2 Access

Turning to the issue of access, Keohane *et al.* have argued that permitting high levels of public participation in international dispute settlement creates a political dynamic that amplifies regime effectiveness.[88] Whereas in traditional inter-state adjudication governments are responsible for invoking proceedings, and abiding by and implementing judgments, in supranational adjudicatory systems individuals may commence litigation directly against governments, and have any judgment in their favour enforced by domestic courts. Keohane *et al.* explain that such 'transnational dispute resolution opens up an additional source of political pressure for compliance, namely favourable judgments in domestic courts'.[89] As a consequence the international court or tribunal possesses 'additional means to pressure or influence domestic government institutions in ways that enhance the likelihood of compliance with their judgments' because governments will not be able to override their domestic legal system.[90]

[83] LOS Convention, art. 287. [84] *Ibid.* art. 292. [85] *Ibid.* art. 290. [86] See ch. 7.

[87] LOS Convention, art. 290(1) (provisional measures may be issued 'to prevent serious harm to the marine environment').

[88] Keohane *et al.*, above n. 56. [89] *Ibid.* 477. [90] *Ibid.*

These factors can be seen in operation in environmental litigation in the European legal system. Private actors have a range of options for gaining access to judicial procedures to ensure that European environmental law is faithfully implemented and enforced by member states. Natural and legal persons involved in domestic litigation may prompt the relevant municipal court to seek a preliminary ruling from the ECJ, and in those proceedings make submissions to the Court.[91] Civil society can also commence proceedings to contest the legality of actions of Community institutions under EC law.[92] Finally, it should be noted that while individuals may not bring claims in the ECJ against member states in order to ensure compliance with EC law, these proceedings may be commenced by the European Commission, and the Commission has been actively involved in such enforcement efforts, often at the prompting of environmental groups.[93]

The right conditions have yet to be set for widespread supranational adjudication in the environmental context outside of Europe. With the exception of the PCA's 2001 Optional Rules for the Arbitration of Disputes Concerning the Environment and/or Natural Resources, which have never been used, environmental arbitration is a process reserved exclusively for governments. The main permanent courts engaged in environmental dispute settlement are also generally open only to states. Although the ICJ has decided several cases involving environmental issues in the exercise of its contentious jurisdiction, in none of these could private actors be involved in the process as litigants given the statutory restriction on non-state participation.[94] The ICJ's advisory jurisdiction is somewhat more open in permitting authorised organs and agencies of the UN to seek opinions, but it is far from providing open access to civil society to contest the compliance of governments with environmental norms. Standing before ITLOS is also limited to states for most marine environmental disputes.[95]

[91] EC Treaty, art. 234.

[92] But only if the decision is addressed to that person, and is of 'direct and individual concern' to them: EC Treaty, art. 230.

[93] See Richard C. Visek, 'Implementation and Enforcement of EC Environmental Law' (1995) 7 *GeoIELR* 377, 406.

[94] Statute of the ICJ, art. 34(1) ('[o]nly states may be parties in cases before the Court').

[95] The only possible exception is in relation to environmental disputes involving the deep seabed regime. In such circumstances the Seabed Disputes Chamber may adjudicate disputes which involve a limited number of private entities. See LOS Convention, annex VI (Statute of ITLOS) art. 37.

However, there are some indications that elements of the supranational approach to adjudication may be translated to environmentally focused regimes. In this respect one of the more remarkable recent innovations in environmental dispute settlement is the citizen submissions procedure of the NAAEC,[96] which was agreed alongside NAFTA. The NAAEC was designed to allay concerns that trade liberalisation between Canada, Mexico, and the United States would lead to a 'race to the bottom', with polluting industries taking advantage of jurisdictions where environmental standards were not enforced. The NAAEC addresses this problem through two primary obligations. First, each party is required to enforce its environmental laws 'effectively'.[97] Second, the parties are required to maintain their environmental laws at sufficiently high standards, and work to improve them further.[98]

The NAAEC establishes several institutions and procedures for ensuring that these obligations are discharged. In overall terms the NAAEC appears to adopt a managerial approach.[99] However, two of its institutions for compliance control adopt a more coercive strategy. One of these is the convoluted procedure for establishing an arbitral tribunal where one NAAEC party considers that another has systematically failed to enforce its environmental laws effectively.[100] However, the more important mechanism is the citizen submissions system through the CEC which seeks public involvement to hold parties to account for any violations of their domestic environmental laws.[101] Under this procedure private parties may claim that any NAAEC party is failing effectively to enforce its environmental laws.[102] The NAAEC secretariat may, in response, decide to author a factual record on the matter submitted.[103] In deciding whether to commence such an investigation the secretariat must consider the extent to which an applicant has an interest in the complaint, whether addressing the submission would advance the goals of the NAAEC, and whether available domestic

[96] See generally Kal Raustiala, 'Citizen Submissions and Treaty Review in the NAAEC' in David L. Markell and John H. Knox (eds.), *Greening NAFTA: The North American Commission for Environmental Cooperation* (2003) 256.

[97] NAAEC art. 5(1). [98] *Ibid.* art. 3. [99] Knox, above n. 60, 56.

[100] *Ibid.* 59 (describing this procedure as 'a dead letter…because the parties will be extremely averse to invoking it against one another, for all the reasons that states are generally reluctant to invoke adjudication to resolve international environmental disputes').

[101] R. McCallum, 'Evaluating the Citizens Submissions Procedure Under the North American Agreement on Environmental Cooperation' (1997) 8 *ColoJELP* 395, 400.

[102] NAAEC, art. 14 (1). [103] *Ibid.* art. 15.

remedies have been pursued.[104] If these preconditions are met, then the secretariat may inform the NAAEC council that a factual record should be prepared. If the council considers that it should, then the secretariat will be asked to draw up the report on the alleged infringement.[105]

The NAAEC secretariat has received a sizeable number of submissions since it commenced operation in 1994, with around five citizen submissions made to the CEC each year.[106] The NAAEC process falls short of a truly compulsory adjudicative procedure in that it cannot be automatically invoked, and does not lead to binding determinations, characteristics which have led one commentator to describe the CEC as a 'cosmetic organisation'.[107] Additionally it only measures the performance of NAAEC parties against their domestic environmental standards, and not international environmental commitments more broadly. None the less it bears many of the hallmarks of successful supranational adjudication in other contexts, including that of the European legal system, in granting access to private individuals to make complaints regarding state compliance with environmental standards, in allowing these claims to be reviewed by independent experts, and in providing for the possibility of adverse reports based upon findings of fact and determinations of law.[108] Moreover in practice the secretariat has adopted a quasi-judicial approach, issuing carefully reasoned reports based upon a close reading of NAAEC provisions.[109]

4.3.2.3 Embeddedness

Finally, in relation to the embeddedness of adjudicative procedures in international environmental law, states have generally retained primary responsibility for enforcing environmental arbitral awards and court rulings (with the European legal order again being the exception). By way of examples, the Biodiversity Convention and the LOS Convention establish inter-state enforcement mechanisms and rely

[104] *Ibid.* art. 14(2). [105] *Ibid.* art. 15.

[106] Fifty-eight citizen submissions had been made as of December 2006: David L. Markell, 'Citizen-Friendly Approaches to Environmental Governance' (2007) 37 *EnvLR* 10362, 10368. For an analysis of the submissions from 1994 to 2003 see also David L. Markell, 'The CEC Citizen Submissions Process: On or Off Course?' in David L. Markell and John H. Knox (eds.), *Greening NAFTA: The North American Commission for Environmental Cooperation* (2003) 274, 289–93.

[107] Malgosia A. Fitzmaurice, 'Public Participation in the North American Agreement on Environmental Cooperation' (2003) 52 *ICLQ* 333, 366.

[108] Knox, above n. 60, 121. [109] *Ibid.*

upon governments to utilise these compulsory conciliation and adjudication procedures in order to enforce the substantive environmental protection obligations. Given the reluctance of states to bring such claims,[110] the practical result has been the instigation of no conciliation proceedings under the Biodiversity Convention for alleged breaches, and a relatively modest number of cases commenced under the LOS Convention. This state control over the implementation process means that some environmental decisions have simply not been given effect. To adapt Henkin's famous aphorism, while it may be true that most states obey the decisions of most courts most of the time,[111] there have been some notable examples of delinquency in the environmental field such as the *Fisheries Jurisdiction* case[112] and *Nuclear Tests* cases.[113]

It is therefore with respect to embeddedness rather than independence and access that international environmental adjudication is most clearly distinguished from the conditions of effective supranational adjudication identified by liberal institutionalist theory as the basis for effectiveness. However, it was noted above that low levels of embeddedness are not fatal to an international tribunal's capacity to promote compliance with a regime because even a decision of a purely interstate court can serve to mobilise domestic political actors who can use formal and informal channels to pressure governments to meet their environmental obligations.[114]

4.4 Conclusion

While proposals for an international environmental court attract fair criticism for being overly ambitious, the managerialist critique is also open to challenge for its overly stylised and dismissive account of adjudication as an institution for environmental governance. There can be no doubt that adjudication has not been extensively used in the environmental field, but this fact alone cannot prove that it has no utility.

110 See David A. Wirth, 'Re-examining Decision-Making Processes in International Environmental Law' (1994) 79 *IowaLR* 769, 779 (noting the political and strategic costs often involved in the bringing of third-party dispute settlement procedures).

111 L. Henkin, *How Nations Behave* (1961) 47 ('almost all nations observe almost all principles of international law almost all of the time').

112 *Fisheries Jurisdiction* case [1974] ICJ Rep 175.

113 *Nuclear Tests* cases [1973] ICJ Rep 99, 106; [1973] ICJ Rep 135, 142. See Constanze Shulte, *Compliance with Decisions of the International Court of Justice* (2004) 308–10.

114 *Ibid.* 935.

Instead regime context is (almost) everything. By paying attention to the character of an environmental agreement, and the structure of international courts and tribunals operating within the regime, it appears possible to explain the limited utility of courts to date in alternative terms. This more nuanced analysis also supports the conjecture that adjudicative structures could be utilised more extensively and effectively in ensuring that international environmental law is more widely and faithfully observed.

Given the tide of developments in international environmental law, which have been towards bureaucratisation rather than judicialisation, it is perhaps unrealistic to expect a rapid and wholesale embracing of supranational forms of environmental adjudication. However, it would appear that complaints procedures in the environmental context modelled loosely on those existing in the arena of international human rights protection could provide a valuable forum for individuals to contest governmental acts or omissions that are contrary to environmental standards. The NAAEC provides just such a mechanism, and its success or otherwise will provide many lessons as to the feasibility of its use in other regimes. Despite several apparent limits, adjudication possesses particular strengths in the environmental context, including the capacity to address environmental disputes through a process that is to a considerable extent divorced from political disputation. The institution of adjudication (in its independence), the process of argumentation (according to criteria of rationality), and the decision-making process (according to law) means that courts, international and national,[115] are uniquely placed to speak beyond the confines of the dispute at hand and confront the major environmental challenges of our time. These are to be contrasted with softer forms of dispute settlement, the value of which may have been overstated. As Koskenniemi has noted, turning to NCPs can have the effect of diluting regimes, giving the impression that everything remains negotiable

[115] Gerry Bates, *Environmental Law in Australia* (6th edn 2006) 14:

> Despite the problems, the advantages of courts and tribunals as forums for evaluating arguments and balancing conflicting interests should not be overlooked. They are politically unbiased and free of such influences; independent of the administration, whose job it is to translate policy into action; staffed by judges who are experienced in evaluating conflicting arguments and whose decisions are respected; and above all such forums should enable citizens to be heard and ensure that their views are taken into account in the ultimate decision-making processes.

for an indeterminate period.[116] Whereas courts comprise independent judges hearing arguments made in public and rendering decisions made public and accountable, NCPs effect a 'transfer in power from public officials to technical experts and private actors including stakeholder groups, and erodes the international rule of law'.[117]

[116] Koskenniemi, above n. 4, 80. [117] *Ibid.*

PART II • JUDICIAL DEVELOPMENT

5 Transboundary environmental damage

Rapid and extensive industrialisation in many states in the nineteenth century generated serious atmospheric, terrestrial, riverine, and marine pollution highly damaging to human health and the natural environment. In the early twentieth century these problems took on transboundary dimensions as pollutants crossed borders and damaged the environment of other states and global commons areas,[1] and this proved an important catalyst for developments in international environmental law. It was atmospheric pollution originating in Canada, and damaging to agricultural interests in the United States, that led to the seminal *Trail Smelter* case[2] in which an arbitral tribunal concluded that no state has the right to use, or permit the use of, its territory in such a way as to cause serious injury by pollution in the territory of another state. There is no more elemental stipulation of customary international law relating to environmental questions.[3]

This chapter examines the critical contribution that arbitral awards and judicial decisions have made to the evolution of legal principles relating to transboundary environmental damage. It is seen that this field of law did not spring from environmental concerns *per se*, but rather from a more general and protean notion that states should be protected from unreasonable interference. Despite the substantial evolution of this area of law since the *Trail Smelter* case, especially through the work of the ILC, it remains tied to some of its problematic conceptual origins as a body of principle concerned primarily with the

[1] Phoebe N. Okowa, *State Responsibility for Transboundary Air Pollution in International Law* (2000) 6–23.

[2] *Trail Smelter* case (*Canada/United States of America*) (1938 and 1941) 3 *RIAA* 1911.

[3] *Legality of the Threat or Use of Nuclear Weapons* [1996] ICJ Rep 226, [26] (*Nuclear Weapons* advisory opinion).

limits of state sovereignty rather than positive duties of environmental protection.

5.1 Jurisprudence

5.1.1 *Origins*

The notion that states should not permit the use of their territory to damage the environment of others was a logical extension of the concept of state sovereignty.[4] Whether expressed in the notion of relative as opposed to absolute sovereignty,[5] the principle *sic utere tuo ut alienum non laedas*,[6] the notion of good neighbourliness,[7] or the doctrine of abuse of rights,[8] the idea is essentially one of balancing the sovereign rights and interests of states engaged in polluting activities against the interests of states affected by such pollution.[9] Sovereignty acts as a brake upon outside interference with the local environment, and gives affected or potentially affected states important rights. As the United States Supreme Court put it in an early case concerning pollution in Georgia from neighbouring Tennessee, states affected by transboundary pollution should have 'the last word as to whether [their] mountains shall be stripped of their forests and [their] inhabitants shall breathe pure air'.[10] This dictum also reveals that sovereignty is a double-edged

[4] The term 'sovereignty' as used in international legal discourse is usually traced to the writings of Bodin who, in 1583, defined the concept as 'the absolute and perpetual power of a commonwealth': Jean Bodin, *On Sovereignty* (1583, reprinted 1992) 46. See generally Stéphane Beaulac, 'The Social Power of Bodin's "Sovereignty" and International Law' (2003) 4 *MJIL* 1.

[5] The doctrine of 'absolute sovereignty' is often referred to as the Harmon doctrine, in reference to the opinion of United States Attorney-General Judson Harmon concerning the supposed rights of the United States to divert water from the Rio Grande: see Tuomas Kuokkanen, *International Law and the Environment: Variations on a Theme* (2002) 9–24.

[6] 'Use your own property so as not to harm that of another.' This principle is of ancient origin. See *Nuclear Tests* case (*Australia* v. *France*) (merits) [1974] ICJ Rep 253, dissenting opinion of Judge de Castro, 388–9 (referring to principles of Roman law and contemporary civil law prohibiting *immissio* (of water, smoke, or objects) into neighbouring property).

[7] The idea of international 'good neighbourliness' is found in several instruments, including art. 74 of the UN Charter in relation to the duties of administering authorities.

[8] Michael Byers, 'Abuse of Rights: An Old Principle, A New Age' (2002) 47 *McGillLJ* 389.

[9] René Lefeber, *Transboundary Environmental Interference and the Origin of State Liability* (1996) 20.

[10] *Georgia* v. *Tennessee Copper Co.* 206 US 230, 237 (1907).

concept. As Stone has observed, so long as it does not damage the environment of other states, sovereignty gives '[e]ach nation ... the right to pull up its forests, bulldoze habitats, wipe out species, fish, farm, and mine' and it is not required 'to answer to any "outside" authority for any repercussions on its own environment'.[11]

In international law these two components of the sovereignty concept were articulated clearly by Judge Huber in the *Island of Palmas* case[12] where it was said that sovereignty 'involves the exclusive right to display the activities of a State' while at the same time involving 'the obligation to protect ... the rights of other States, in particular their right to integrity'.[13] This decision, and the much later *Corfu Channel* case[14] in which the ICJ affirmed 'every State's obligation not to allow knowingly its territory to be used for acts contrary to the rights of other States',[15] are frequently said to have articulated rules having environmental significance.[16] However, Lammers notes that although these decisions 'enjoined States not to allow their territory to be used for acts contrary to the *rights* of other States', they 'did not indicate what substantive rights or duties States possessed in respect of transfrontier water pollution or other forms of transfrontier nuisance'.[17]

5.1.2 Trail Smelter *case*

The *Trail Smelter* case by contrast involved an opportunity to elaborate and adapt the basic sovereignty rights in the context of transboundary harm. The case epitomises the method by which international law relating to environmental matters first came in to being: namely through the extension of general principles rather than the articulation of dedicated environmental rules.[18]

[11] Christopher D. Stone, 'Defending the Global Commons' in Philippe Sands (ed.), *Greening International Law* (1994) 34, 35.

[12] *Island of Palmas* case (*Netherlands/US*) (1928) 2 *RIAA* 829. [13] *Ibid*. 838.

[14] *Corfu Channel* case (*United Kingdom* v. *Albania*) (merits) [1949] ICJ Rep 4. [15] *Ibid*. 22.

[16] See e.g. Judge Weeramantry in his dissenting opinion in *Request for an Examination of the Situation in Accordance with Paragraph 63 of the Court's Judgment of 20 December 1974 in the Nuclear Tests* case (*New Zealand* v. *France*) [1995] ICJ Rep 288 (*Nuclear Tests* case), who observed that '[t]he *Corfu Channel* case laid down the environmentally important principle that, if a nation knows that harmful effects may occur to other nations from facts within its knowledge and fails to disclose them, it will be liable to the nation that suffers damage' (at 362).

[17] Johan G. Lammers, *Pollution of International Watercourses: A Search for Substantive Rules and Principles of Law* (1984) 528 (original emphasis).

[18] Lynton K. Caldwell, 'Concepts in Development of International Environmental Policies' (1973) 13 *NatResJ* 190, 190.

5.1.2.1 Contextual considerations

The *Trail Smelter* case has attracted extensive scholarly attention[19] and has frequently been cited by parties before international courts and tribunals, by these bodies themselves in their awards and judgments,[20] and by states in relation to transboundary pollution disputes not leading to litigation.[21] However, the importance of the decision to contemporary international environmental law is often overstated.[22] Moreover, frequent reference to the case conveys a misleading impression that transboundary pollution cases are routinely and effectively resolved by inter-state dispute settlement.[23]

The tendency to exaggerate the significance of the *Trail Smelter* case reinforces the symbolic power of international judicial decisions in the environmental field. While not always achieving by themselves a major development in the law, they may none the less carry significant influence by articulating the kernel of an idea that is modified and amplified in future decisions and in state practice. However, this lasting legacy may also include the retention of early and problematic understandings of the environment that do not lend themselves today to an appropriate and effective environmental law. The *Trail Smelter* case is such a decision, given the limited consideration it gave to a range of environmental issues that would today be considered pivotal in resolving a similar pollution dispute. This does not render the decision irrelevant or of no lasting value, but does mean that an appreciation of its place in the canon of international environmental jurisprudence must

[19] See in particular Rebecca M. Bratspies and Russell A. Miller, *Transboundary Harm in International Law: Lessons from the Smelter Arbitration* (2006).

[20] See in particular *Nuclear Tests* case (*Australia* v. *France*) (merits) [1974] ICJ Rep 253, dissenting opinion of Judge de Castro, 388–9; *1995 Nuclear Tests* case [1995] ICJ Rep 288, dissenting opinion of Judge Weeramantry, 346 and 362 and dissenting opinion of Judge Palmer, 408; *Gabčíkovo-Nagymaros Project* case (*Hungary/Slovakia*) [1997] ICJ Rep 7 separate opinion of Judge Weeramantry, 111–12.

[21] See e.g. in relation to the Cherry Point oil spill, the statement of the Canadian External Affairs Secretary (1973) 11 *CanYBIL* 333, 334.

[22] Günther Handl, 'Balancing of Interests and International Liability for the Pollution of International Watercourses: Customary Principles of Law Revisited' (1975) 3 *CanYBIL* 156, 167–8; Ian Brownlie, 'A Survey of International Customary Rules of Environmental Protection' in L. A. Teclaff and A. E. Utton (eds.), *International Environmental Law* (1974) 1, 2 (the decision 'is actually a rather modest contribution to the jurisprudence – as it was bound to be in view of the restricted terms of reference').

[23] Peter H. Sand, *Transnational Environmental Law: Lessons in Global Change* (1999) 43.

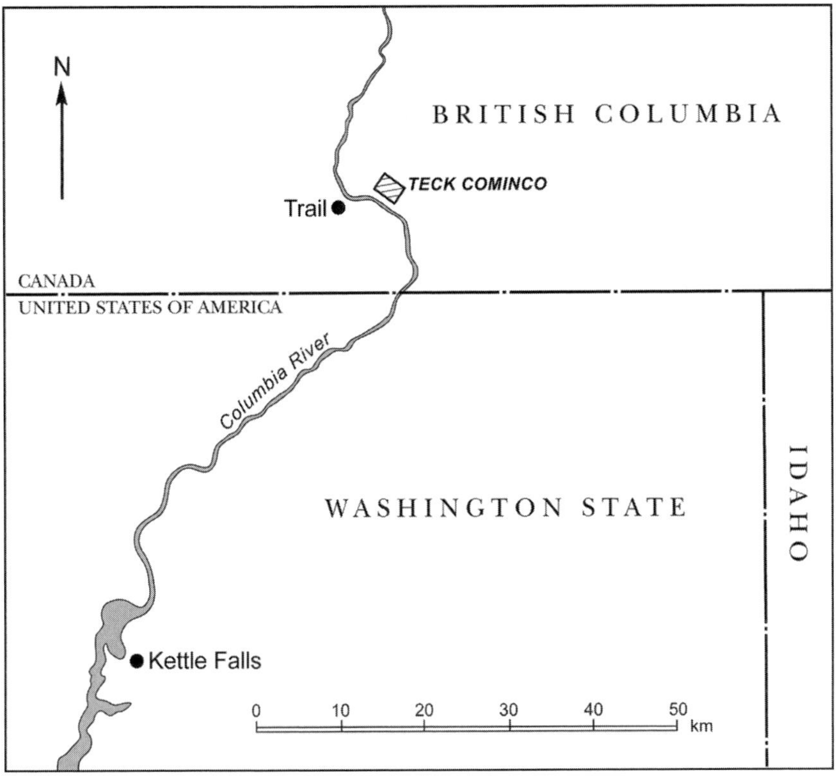

Figure 5.1 The Columbia River and the smelter at Trail

acknowledge the social, political, and economic context in which the litigation took place.[24]

5.1.2.2 Background

The dispute in the case arose out of the operation of a zinc and lead smelter in British Columbia near the town of Trail on the Columbia River, seven miles from the United States border. By the early twentieth century the natural resources of the Columbia River valley had been heavily exploited. Intensive forestry and agricultural activities caused significant deforestation, and had stripped large parts of the landscape of biodiversity. Mining and smelting operations also

[24] Karin Mickelson, 'Rereading *Trail Smelter*' (1993) 31 *CanYBIL* 219, 229; John D. Wirth, *Smelter Smoke in North America: The Politics of Transborder Pollution* (2000) 80.

contributed to the environmental decline. Following a series of claims in domestic courts, smelting operations ceased on the United States side of the boundary. In contrast the smelter at Trail thrived. Under its Canadian owners, the Consolidated Mining and Smelting Company Ltd, which acquired the smelter from its original American founders, the plant became one of the world's largest and best equipped lead and zinc smelters, and was a key driver in the economic growth of the region.[25]

The operations of the Trail smelter greatly affected the surrounding natural environment. Atmospheric emissions included lead dust and other metallic compounds, and substantial quantities of sulphur. By 1916 sulphur emissions had reached 160 tons per day, and by 1930 they peaked at around 300–350 tons per day.[26] Forming sulphur dioxide and sulphuric acid in the atmosphere, two compounds highly toxic to plant tissues, the sulphur emissions caused substantial and widespread damage to local vegetation. As a consequence Canadian farmers raised a series of complaints regarding the smelter and these were mostly resolved by Consolidated Mining by means of compensatory payments or the purchase of smoke easements. However, the emissions also began to affect United States users south of the boundary and these pollution victims were not readily placated.

In 1925, in an effort to improve the dispersal of sulphur emissions, Consolidated Mining increased the height of the smelter stacks.[27] The new arrangements improved the conditions in Canada, but further concentrated emissions drifting south. As a result the town of Northport in Stevens County, Washington, and surrounding farms, were subjected to heavy clouds of sulphur dioxide, often lasting for several days. United States farmers and other landowners, who did not share in the economic benefits that the smelter brought to the town of Trail and British Columbia more generally, vigorously pursued claims

[25] D. H. Dinwoodie, 'The Politics of International Pollution Control: The Trail Smelter Case' (1971–2) 27 *International Journal* 219, 219. The Trail smelter is now owned and operated by Teck Cominco Metals Ltd, the corporate successor to Consolidated Mining. The smelting complex at Trail is one of the world's largest zinc and lead smelting and refining complexes, producing approximately 290,000 tonnes of zinc and 120,000 tonnes of lead per annum. See www.teckcominco.com.

[26] *Trail Smelter* case (1938 and 1941) 3 *RIAA* 1911, 1917. Despite its increased capacity, the Trail smelter now emits between 3 and 10 tons of sulphur dioxide per day: Golder Associates Ltd, *Analysis of the Effects of Smelter Emissions on Vegetation within the Trail Regional Area* (2004) 3.

[27] Dinwoodie, above n. 25, 220.

against the company.[28] While some of these were resolved, Consolidated Mining denied most as exorbitant.[29] Modest compensation was offered by the company, but an increasingly well-organised group of Stevens County residents encouraged affected farmers to refuse the individual settlements, and they petitioned the United States government to pursue their grievances directly with Canada.

The *Trail Smelter* case arose in large part because the United States residents affected by the transboundary pollution did not possess admissible claims in the British Columbia courts. Following the House of Lord's decision in *British South Africa Company* v. *Companhia de Moçambique*,[30] those courts could not assume jurisdiction in cases involving trespass to foreign land. Hence it was because of this domestic legal limitation that an otherwise unremarkable occurrence of pollution by a private company affecting individuals was elevated to an international dispute.[31]

5.1.2.3 International Joint Commission

The United States and Canada agreed in August 1928 that the matter should be referred to the International Joint Commission (IJC)[32] established under the 1909 Treaty Relating to the Boundary Waters and Questions Arising Along the Boundary Between the United States and Canada.[33] In 1931 the IJC issued a unanimous report,[34] recommending an award of US$350,000 for injury to private interests up to

28 *Ibid.* 29 *Trail Smelter* case (1938 and 1941) 3 *RIAA* 1911, 1917.

30 [1893] AC 602. On the '*Moçambique* rule' see generally Pete E. Nygh and Martin Davies, *Conflict of Laws in Australia* (7th edn 2002) 136.

31 John E. Read, 'The Trail Smelter Dispute' (1963) 1 *CanYBIL* 213, 213–14. See also John H. Knox, 'The Flawed Trail Smelter Procedure: The Wrong Tribunal, the Wrong Parties, and the Wrong Law' in Rebecca M. Bratspies and Russell A. Miller (eds.), *Transboundary Harms in International Law: Lessons from the Trail Smelter Arbitration* (2006) 66.

32 *Trail Smelter* case (1938 and 1941) 3 RIAA 1911, 1918.

33 Boundary Waters Treaty, art. VII. The IJC continues to operate today (see www.ijc.org). An independent body, it is mandated to prevent and resolve disputes relating to the use and quality of boundary waters between Canada and the United States, and to advise both governments on related questions (Boundary Waters Treaty, preamble, 1st recital). The IJC is conferred investigative powers by the Boundary Waters Treaty, art. IX.

34 Report of the International Joint Commission in the Trail Smelter Reference (1931) (available at www.ijc.org). Although the compromise report attracted the support of all six commissioners, the proceedings were fractious, and the commission split along national lines. In addition, the scientific evidence presented by each government was in almost complete opposition: see Dinwoodie, above n. 25, 225–6.

1 January 1932, by which stage the Commission considered that the damage was likely to be eliminated by the installation of 'sulphuric acid units' to capture and convert emissions.[35] In relation to any damage suffered after 1 January 1932 the IJC recommended that if appropriate compensation was not forthcoming, the two governments should jointly determine an amount payable by Consolidated Mining.

5.1.2.4 Ad hoc arbitration

Although satisfactory to Canada,[36] the IJC's recommendations were not acceptable to the United States, as they provided inadequate past, and uncertain future, indemnification for damage.[37] Hence after further negotiations the two governments concluded a special agreement submitting their dispute to arbitration.[38]

Several features of the Trail Smelter Arbitral Agreement are noteworthy. Under article I, Canada effectively accepted liability in relation to past damage caused by the smelter's operations. That provision required the Canadian government to pay US$350,000 by way of compensation for all damage sustained in the United States prior to 1932. In determining the United States' claims in relation to damage after that date, article IV required the tribunal to apply 'the law and practice followed in dealing with cognate questions in the United States of America as well as international law and practice'. This reference to United States, rather than Canadian law, was supported by Canada, partly because decisions of its courts regarding industrial nuisance were considerably less favourable to industry.[39] Any assessment of the precedential value of the decision must acknowledge this proper law clause which clearly allowed the tribunal to look beyond applicable principles of public international law.[40]

Article IV also provided that the tribunal 'shall give consideration to the desire of the high contracting parties to reach a solution *just* to all parties concerned'.[41] As a result the tribunal, though deciding an essentially intergovernmental dispute, was none the less empowered

[35] *Ibid.* 1. [36] Read, above n. 31, 214. [37] Dinwoodie, above n. 25, 228.

[38] 1935 Convention for the Settlement of Difficulties Arising from the Operation of the Smelter at Trail between Great Britain and the United States (Trail Smelter Arbitral Agreement).

[39] Read, above n. 31, 227.

[40] Günther Handl, 'Territorial Sovereignty and the Problem of Transnational Pollution' (1975) 69 *AJIL* 50, 60.

[41] Emphasis added.

to take into consideration the interests of the private parties involved, including the residents of the Columbia River valley and Consolidated Mining. It is therefore an early model of international environmental adjudication in which a specific effort was made to consider the public interest, albeit somewhat indirectly.

The key provision of the Trail Smelter Arbitral Agreement was article III, in which the parties agreed upon the four questions to be resolved by the tribunal:

(1) Whether damage caused by the Trail Smelter in the State of Washington has occurred since the first day of January, 1932, and, if so, what indemnity should be paid therefor?
(2) In the event of the answer to the first part of the preceding Question being in the affirmative, whether the Trail Smelter should be required to refrain from causing damage to the State of Washington in the future and, if so, to what extent?
(3) In the light of the answer to the preceding Question, what measures or regime, if any, should be adopted or maintained by the Trail Smelter?
(4) What indemnity or compensation, if any, should be paid on account of any decision or decisions rendered by the Tribunal pursuant to the next two preceding Questions?

In responding to these questions, the tribunal delivered its award in two phases. In its initial decision in 1938 the tribunal decided the first question for the period from 1932 to 1937 and prescribed a temporary regime for controlling emissions in response to the remaining three questions.

Interim decision

On the first issue, namely the indemnity to be paid for any damage sustained in the State of Washington after 1 January 1932, the tribunal rejected most of the United States' claims in the seven categories to which they related.[42]

In assessing the United States' allegations of damage, the tribunal undertook an extensive review of the topography and climatic

[42] The United States claimed damages of US$2,100,011.17 divided into seven categories, in respect of (1) cleared land and improvements, (2) uncleared land and improvements, (3) livestock, (4) property in the town of Northport, (5) wrong done to the United States in violation of sovereignty, measured by cost of investigation, (6) interest on US$350,000 accepted in satisfaction of damage to 1 January 1932, but not paid on that date, and (7) business enterprises: *Trail Smelter* case (1938 and 1941) 3 *RIAA* 1911, 1940.

conditions in the Columbia River valley south of Trail. With respect to cleared land used for crops, there was evidence of damage by sulphur fumigation from 1932 to 1936, and the tribunal ordered that there be recompense for the reduced value of this land.[43] As for land used as pasture and for forestry industries, the tribunal found that although there was little evidence of damage to pasture, the sulphur dioxide fumes had damaged harvestable trees. This damage varied from year to year, and from species to species, and the tribunal's assessment was complicated by the heavy deforestation that had already occurred as a result of logging, forest fires, and by smelters that had operated in Northport.[44] Further confirming the focus of the parties and the tribunal upon commercial rather than ecological interests, the tribunal rejected compensation for damage to timber found in inaccessible areas.

For the compensable losses the tribunal awarded a total of US$78,000 for the period from 1932 until 1937. All other categories of claimed losses were rejected, including damages for discharges of smelter wastes into the Columbia River. This was arguably the only category of loss sought by the United States that related to pure environmental harm.[45] The tribunal found that even if such injury came within the term 'damage' as used in article III of the Trail Smelter Arbitral Agreement, the United States had presented no evidence to support its claim.

Finally, in respect of the United States' claim for 'damages in respect of the wrong done the United States in violation of sovereignty', the tribunal concluded that it was unnecessary to decide whether such a violation had occurred. This was because the damages claimed related only to expenditure for investigation of the 'problems caused by the Trail Smelter' and these could not, according to the tribunal, constitute 'damage caused by the Trail Smelter' as those words were used in article III of the Trail Smelter Arbitral Agreement.[46]

The tribunal refrained from deciding questions (2), (3) or (4), on the grounds that there was insufficient information. However, pending the final award, temporary arrangements were made to undertake further assessments of the impact of the smelter fumes, and to limit sulphur emissions during specified periods.

[43] *Ibid.* 1925. [44] *Ibid.* 1928.

[45] Philippe Sands, 'International Environmental Litigation and Its Future' (1999) 32 *URichLR* 1619, 1622.

[46] *Trail Smelter* case (1938 and 1941) 3 *RIAA* 1911, 1932.

Final award

Whereas the interim award was mostly concerned to ascertain the quantum of damages payable by Canada for damage from 1932 onwards, in the final award the tribunal had to consider Canada's ongoing obligations to prevent emissions being carried into the United States. The tribunal was also asked to devise a regime that could ensure that no further damage occurred.

However, some remaining issues in relation to past injury were first addressed. The tribunal concluded that the evidence did not sustain the United States' claim in relation to damage from 1937 onwards. The United States also sought to recontest the issue of compensation for the costs of its investigation of the circumstances giving rise to the claim. After lengthy consideration, the tribunal also rejected this petition. In relation to expenditures incurred up to the first award, the tribunal concluded that its disposition of the issue in the interim decision constituted a *res judicata*.[47] Costs incurred for scientific and other investigations subsequent to that award were also disallowed.

The tribunal's reasoning here principally revolved around its interpretation of article III of the Trail Smelter Arbitral Agreement. It was concluded that the expenses were directed to the presentation of the case, and were not traceable to 'damage' caused by the Trail smelter in the state of Washington. Interestingly the tribunal drew a distinction between 'expenditure incurred in mending the damageable consequences of an injury and monies spent in ascertaining the existence, the cause and the extent of the latter'.[48] This dictum implies that damages for repair and remediation, had they been claimed, may well have been recovered and therefore suggests that the litigation might have embraced additional environmental concerns had the United States developed more wide-ranging submissions.

The tribunal then turned to question (2) ('whether the Trail Smelter should be required to refrain from causing damage in the State of Washington in the future, and to what extent'), the core issue to be resolved in its final award. As a preliminary matter the tribunal observed that whether the question was determined on the basis of domestic or international law the same principles were applicable because both systems of law adopted the same approach.[49] The tribunal acknowledged the frequent statement by publicists of a general duty to respect other states and their territory.[50] However, the difficulty here

[47] *Ibid.* 1948–58. [48] *Ibid.* 1959. [49] *Ibid.* 1963. [50] *Ibid.*

was resolving 'what, *pro subjecta materiae*, is deemed to constitute an injurious act'.[51] On this point the tribunal noted that although there was no previous decision of an international tribunal concerning air pollution, there were decisions of the United States Supreme Court on cognate questions of pollution across federal boundaries.[52] Having regard to this jurisprudence, and to scientific and technical developments in the control of air pollutants, the tribunal reached its landmark conclusion that:

> [U]nder the principles of international law, as well as of the law of the United States, no state has the right to use or permit the use of its territory in such a manner as to cause injury by fumes in or to the territory of another or the properties or persons therein when the case is of serious consequence and the injury is established by clear and convincing evidence.[53]

Applying the principle to the facts before it, the tribunal concluded that Canada was responsible in international law for the operation of the Trail smelter, and was under a duty to ensure that its future operation was in conformity with its obligations as stated by the tribunal.[54] In this respect the tribunal was evidently concerned not with previous conduct (as Canada had accepted responsibility for past damage),[55] but rather with Canada's obligations in relation to the ongoing operation of the Trail smelter.

As a result of its conclusion on question (2), the tribunal was required to respond to question (3), by which the parties requested that the tribunal develop a regime for the future conduct of smelting operations at Trail. Drawing upon what the tribunal acknowledged was 'probably the most thorough study ever made of any area subject to atmospheric pollution by industrial smoke',[56] and expressly seeking to adopt an equitable approach that did not unduly hinder the smelter's operation, the tribunal devised a comprehensive regime to be adopted and maintained at the Trail smelter. The objective of the regime was self-evidently not to protect the natural environment in the immediate vicinity of the smelter, but rather to reduce diurnal fumigations to the point where agriculture was not affected.[57]

[51] *Ibid.* [52] *Ibid.* 1963–4. [53] *Ibid.* 1965. [54] *Ibid.* 1965–6.

[55] Lammers, above n. 17, 520: '[Nowhere] in the Tribunal's Interim Award do we find any indication that in the absence of the explicit obligation assumed by Canada under the Convention the Tribunal would have held Canada responsible for such damage on account of a breach of a substantive obligation of general international law in respect of transfrontier air pollution.'

[56] *Trail Smelter* case (1938 and 1941) 3 *RIAA* 1911, 1973. [57] *Ibid.* 1974.

Finally, the tribunal considered the fourth question, namely whether compensation should be paid on account of its decisions on questions (2) and (3). The tribunal was of the view that the prescribed regime would probably remove the cause of the dispute.[58] However, it also indicated that Canada would be liable to indemnify the United States for any substantial damage taking place in the future 'whether through failure on the part of the Smelter to comply with the regulations herein prescribed or notwithstanding the maintenance of the regime'.[59]

5.1.2.5 Legacy

The *Trail Smelter* case is best remembered for the statement that states must not permit their territory to be used in such a way as to cause damage to the territory of other states by atmospheric pollution. The influence of the case was ensured because even though it considered only airborne pollutants as required by the Trail Smelter Arbitral Agreement[60] it had adapted a general principle regarding sovereignty and territorial integrity that could extend to other forms of transboundary damage. For this reason the tribunal's statement ultimately found expression in principle 21 of the Stockholm Declaration which was substantially repeated in principle 2 of the Rio Declaration.

The longevity of the dictum is a consequence of the flexible and negotiable standard articulated by the tribunal. It is implicit in the tribunal's reasoning that the duty to prevent transboundary harm is not a strict or absolute one, but rather applies only to harm that is foreseeable and preventable.[61] Moreover, the tribunal found that states would only be required to prevent transboundary harm of 'serious consequence' and that any injury be 'established by clear and convincing evidence'. The imposition of a more demanding threshold of damage would clearly have been desirable from an environmental viewpoint.[62] However, given the strong interest of both parties in continued

[58] *Ibid.* 1980. [59] *Ibid.*

[60] And on this basis the tribunal did not consider the United States' claims that the Columbia River had been damaged by the discharge of slag containing sulphates, chlorides, arsenic, zinc, and lead. The tribunal found that such alleged harm did not constitute 'damage' for the purposes of art. III of the Trail Smelter Arbitral Agreement. The river pollution was in many senses as serious as the atmospheric, resulting in the decline of fishstocks and birdlife dependent upon the river system: Wirth, above n. 24, 101.

[61] But see *contra* L. F. E. Goldie, 'Liability for Damage and the Progressive Development of International Law' (1965) 14 *ICLQ* 1189, 1226–31.

[62] Alfred P. Rubin, 'Pollution by Analogy: the Trail Smelter Arbitration' (1971) 50 *OrLR* 259, 272–4.

regional economic expansion, and the scope of the United States cases on which the tribunal relied,[63] it is perhaps unrealistic to have expected the adoption of a different approach. The tribunal was aware of these dynamics, noting that 'while the United States' interests may now be claimed to be injured by the operations of a Canadian corporation, it is equally possible that at some time in the future Canadian interests might be claimed to be injured by an American corporation'.[64] Subsequent state practice has confirmed that a threshold should be maintained.[65] However, it has gradually been lowered as is seen in the recent efforts of the ILC to codify and develop the basic primary rules of international law relating to transboundary harm. The ILC's Draft Articles on Prevention of Transboundary Harm from Hazardous Activities (Draft Articles on Prevention)[66] and Draft Principles on the Allocation of Loss in the Case of Transboundary Harm Arising out of Hazardous Activities (Draft Principles on Liability)[67] apply in respect of any 'significant' damage, that is harm which is more than 'detectable', but not necessarily 'serious' or 'substantial'.

Other aspects of the *Trail Smelter* case have been decisively abandoned, including the requirement that a complaining state provide 'clear and convincing evidence' of harm. Such an approach runs against the precautionary trend in environmental management at national and international levels. Indeed had this antiquated evidentiary hurdle remained, it would effectively render nugatory a general duty to prevent transboundary harm as many longer-term or complex causes of environmental harm would escape regulation. This was one of the reasons why the *Trail Smelter* case was not helpful for the applicants in the *Nuclear Tests* cases[68] where there were great difficulties in clearly

[63] These did not permit recovery for bare trespass: Alan E. Boyle, 'Reparation for Environmental Damage in International Law: Some Preliminary Problems' in Michael Bowman and Alan E. Boyle (eds.), *Environmental Damage in International and Comparative Law* (2002) 17, 19.

[64] *Trail Smelter* case (1938 and 1941) 3 *RIAA* 1911, 1938–9.

[65] Johan G. Lammers, 'The Present State of Research Carried out by the English-Speaking Section of the Centre for Studies and Research' in Académie de Droit International de la Haye, *La Pollution Transfrontière* (1985) 90, 94.

[66] Report of the International Law Commission, 53rd Session, 366, UN Doc. A/56/10 (2001).

[67] Report of the International Law Commission, 56th Session, 153–6, UN Doc. A/59/10 (2004).

[68] *Nuclear Tests* cases: *Australia* v. *France* (interim measures) [1973] ICJ Rep 99; *New Zealand* v. *France* (interim measures) [1973] ICJ Rep 135; *Australia* v. *France* (merits) [1974] ICJ Rep 253; *New Zealand* v. *France* (merits) [1974] ICJ Rep 457.

establishing environmental effects in Australia and New Zealand caused by atmospheric nuclear tests carried out by France thousands of kilometres away.

Also separating the tribunal's approach from contemporary environmental law and policy is the exclusion of injury to the environment itself from the range of compensable interests.[69] Given the extensive scientific investigation of the Columbia River valley undertaken for the litigation, it is remarkable that no attention was paid by the litigants, or the tribunal itself, to the impact of the smelter upon native animal and plant life (except as regards harvestable areas of forest).[70] Nor was the question of human health raised, even though evidence of these matters had been presented to the IJC.[71] These exclusions have provoked strong criticism;[72] however, the tribunal's omission to consider them must be viewed in its proper context. The limited environmental consciousness of the time, and the primary concern of the parties with addressing economic losses in the United States, largely explain the tribunal's narrow focus.

Other aspects of the decision must also be regarded as being largely confined to their particular context. Importantly, the case does not stand for the proposition that disputes over transboundary environmental harm are to be resolved by equitable rather than legal criteria. While considerations of equity certainly played a role in the tribunal's decision,[73] this is because it was specifically mandated by the Trail

[69] Boyle, above n. 63, 18–19 (while material injury of some kind is necessary, this may extend to the intrinsic worth of natural ecosystems, including biological diversity and areas of wilderness or aesthetic significance).

[70] The area surrounding the Trail smelter is rich in faunal diversity. Species of mammals found in the area include the black bear, Columbian ground squirrel, coyote, deer mouse, dusky shrew, river otter, red squirrel, southern red-backed vole, white-tailed deer and Townsend's big eared bat. The Trail ecological risk assessment, required under British Columbia's Environment Management Act 1996 (BC) RSBC c 118 in relation to contaminated sites, identified the dusky shrew and river otter as mammalian species potentially at risk due to smelter emissions: Teck Cominco Metals Ltd, *Living Summary: Trail Ecological Risk Assessment* (2004).

[71] Stevens County residents developed severe respiratory problems after the height of the smelter stacks was increased in 1925 and 1927: Wirth, above n. 24, 99.

[72] See in particular Rubin, above n. 62, 273.

[73] McCaffrey suggests that the 'tribunal endeavoured to achieve a "just solution" to the controversy by striking a balance between the industrial and agricultural interests involved' and that 'the solution arrived at by the tribunal may thus be said to reflect an equitable allocation of the capacity of the airshed to accommodate pollution from the smelter': Stephen C. McCaffrey, *The Law of International Watercourses: Non-Navigational Uses* (2001) 207.

Smelter Arbitral Agreement to reach a just and equitable solution in devising a regime for the future operation of the plant.[74] Admittedly the statement of principle articulated by the tribunal itself enshrines a degree of balance by tolerating a certain level of transboundary emissions; however, the case does not suggest that in determining conformity with this standard reference may be had to equitable considerations.

Turning, finally, to the implications of the decision for institutional structures to address transboundary harm, the legacy of the *Trail Smelter* case must similarly be subject to contextual appraisal. It is certainly the case that benefits flowed to the parties from the litigation. It brought to a conclusion a lengthy and difficult chapter in relations between Canada and the United States, and resulted in the establishment of a comprehensive regime for ongoing monitoring and control of the Trail smelter.[75] However, the use of inter-state dispute settlement procedures was an indirect and cumbersome means to deal with an environmental problem involving damage to private interests by a private company. The international litigation took well over a decade and a half to complete, by which time the original complainants had either moved, or were deceased. Despite these limitations (which are cited as a reason why states have seldom gone down this path in dealing with such disputes)[76] the *Trail Smelter* case illustrates the importance of inter-state settlement as a last resort method for dealing with otherwise intractable environmental controversies. Indeed it has been argued that a new round of international litigation concerning the Trail smelter is needed to address uncompensated claims by Native American tribes for environmental damage caused by wastes dumped into the Columbia River from the 1900s until the mid-1990s.[77]

[74] The tribunal observed that 'the phraseology of the questions submitted to the Tribunal clearly evinces a desire and an intention that, to some extent, in making its answers to the questions, the Tribunal should endeavour to adjust the conflicting interests by some "just solution" which would allow the continuance of the Trail Smelter': *Trail Smelter* case (1938 and 1941) 3 *RIAA* 1911, 1939.

[75] However, it resolved these issues in only one region, while the problem of transboundary air pollution was then, and remains today, a much wider one across the North American continent: John E. Carroll, 'The Acid Rain Issue in Canadian-American Relations: A Commentary' in John E. Carroll (ed.), *International Environmental Diplomacy: The Management and Resolution of Transfrontier Environmental Problems* (1988) 141.

[76] Lynton Keith Caldwell, *International Environmental Policy: From the Twentieth to the Twenty-First Century* (3rd edn 1996) 151.

[77] Austen L. Parrish, '*Trail Smelter* Déjà Vu: Extraterritoriality, International Environmental Law, and the Search for Solutions to Canadian-US Transboundary

5.1.3 *Nuclear Tests litigation*

The *Trail Smelter* case left unresolved a host of issues relating to the obligations of states to prevent transboundary harm. The litigation concerned damage suffered by another state and did consider or speculate on the legal consequences of damage to the atmospheric commons *per se*.[78] Nor had the tribunal given consideration to the standard of care expected of states in discharging their obligation to prevent extraterritorial environmental harm, or how the seriousness of damage threshold might apply in situations where the transboundary pollution was more complex than the sulphur wastes discharged by the Trail smelter.

Several of these issues were of central importance in the *Nuclear Tests* cases brought by Australia and New Zealand in response to atmospheric nuclear tests conducted by France in the South Pacific from 1966 onwards. Closely following the conclusion of the 1972 United Nations Conference on the Human Environment at Stockholm, the litigation presented an opportunity for the ICJ to consider the applicability of rapidly developing principles of international environmental law to the most serious of environmental hazards. As a result of a complex interplay of political and jurisdictional issues the Court never pronounced upon the merits of the dispute. Instead the litigation is best known for the important contribution made to explaining the international legal effects of unilateral acts.[79] None the less, the submissions of the parties, aspects of the Court's interim orders and the judgment on jurisdiction, and the separate and dissenting opinions, provide much valuable discussion and practice concerning the development of the *Trail Smelter* case dictum.[80]

5.1.3.1 Background

In 1963 the French government announced that it intended to relocate its nuclear tests centre from Algeria to French Polynesia. The main firing site was to be Mururoa atoll, and nearby Fangataufa island, two

Water Pollution Disputes' (2005) 85 *BULR* 363, 429: 'Domestic litigation is not a viable solution, either practically or conceptually ... the United States should explore utilizing international legal mechanisms ... modelled after the famous *Trail Smelter Arbitration*.'

[78] Kathy Leigh, 'Liability for Damage to the Global Commons' (1992) 14 *AustYBIL* 129, 141.

[79] In this respect Franck has observed that 'cases need not have monumental outcomes to make monumental law': Thomas M. Franck, 'Word Made Law: The Decision of the ICJ in the Nuclear Tests Cases' (1975) 69 *AJIL* 612, 612.

[80] Philippe Sands, *Principles of International Environmental Law* (2nd edn 2003) 320.

remote and uninhabited atolls. France subsequently conducted its first atmospheric test in the Pacific in 1966, and exploded an average of four devices per annum until 1973 when Australia and New Zealand simultaneously instituted proceedings against France in the ICJ.

The French testing programme was not unique: nuclear weapons tests had been conducted in the Pacific region since the 1950s, including on Australian soil.[81] However, from 1963 onwards, and reflecting widespread public concern at the potentially serious, but uncertain, human and environmental impacts of these tests, Australia and New Zealand, together with other South Pacific nations, expressed strong opposition to French nuclear testing in the Pacific. For its part France entertained only limited consultations, and contended that its testing programme was not only consistent with international law but had negligible environmental impact.[82]

Australia and New Zealand's opposition to the tests was part of a broader regional and global movement against the development, testing, and proliferation of nuclear arms. The conclusion of the 1963 Treaty Banning Nuclear Weapons Tests in the Atmosphere, in Outer Space and under Water, had ended atmospheric testing for all nuclear nations except France and China.[83] Moreover in a series of resolutions the United Nations General Assembly urged all states to become parties to the treaty, emphasised the harmful environmental effects of nuclear tests, and condemned nuclear testing.[84] The testing and deployment of nuclear weapons had also been a key concern of the Stockholm Conference with principle 26 of the Stockholm Declaration calling for the 'elimination and complete destruction of such weapons'. These legal and political developments were accompanied by increased

[81] See generally Ben Boer, Ross Ramsay, and Donald R. Rothwell, *International Environmental Law in the Asia Pacific* (1998) 64–8. In relation to United States nuclear tests on the Marshall Islands see *In the Matter of the People of Enewetak* (2000) 39 ILM 1214.

[82] République Française, Ministère des Affaires étrangères, *Livre Blanc sur les experiences nucléares* (1973) 8–9.

[83] The third recital of the preamble to the treaty expresses the parties' desire 'to put an end to the contamination of man's environment by radioactive substances'. It prohibits nuclear tests in the atmosphere, in outer space, under water, or in any other environment 'if such explosion causes radioactive debris to be present outside the territorial limits of the State under whose jurisdiction or control such explosion is conducted' (art. 1(1)).

[84] See in particular GA Res. 1762 A (XVII), UN Doc. A/RES/1762A(XVII) (1962) (which condemned all nuclear tests) and GA Res. 2934 (XXVII), UN Doc. A/RES/2934(XXVII) (1972) (which referred specifically to nuclear tests in the Pacific).

scientific understanding of the perilous effects of radioactive materials on the natural environment and human health.[85]

5.1.3.2 Applications to the ICJ

Anticipating a new round of tests in 1973, Australia and New Zealand instituted proceedings in the ICJ by invoking the compulsory compromissory clause in the 1928 General Act for the Pacific Settlement of Disputes. The applicants also requested that the Court indicate provisional measures requiring France to refrain from testing giving rise to radioactive fall-out pending the judgment of the Court on the merits.

Australia and New Zealand sought the same ultimate objective, namely an end to French nuclear testing in the Pacific causing the deposit of nuclear materials on Australian and New Zealand territory and on the high seas. Both states also shared broadly the same concerns regarding environmental damage and impacts upon the health of present and future generations caused by tropospheric and stratospheric nuclear fall-out.[86] However, the two applications differed in several critical respects. In particular, while the Australian position emphasised the illegality of atmospheric tests, New Zealand objected more generally to all methods of nuclear testing causing radioactive pollution.[87]

Australia contended that the conduct of the tests violated its rights individually, and in common with other states, to be free from atmospheric nuclear tests. Australia also argued that the interference with ships and aircraft on the high seas (by the tests themselves and the enforcement of exclusion zones), and high seas pollution through radioactive fall-out, constituted infringements of high seas freedoms. In these submissions Australia sought to assert an *actio popularis*, invoking the responsibility of France notwithstanding that Australia's interests were no more seriously affected than those of several other states.

[85] Particularly as a result of the work of the UN Scientific Committee on the Effects of Atomic Radiation (UNSCEAR) established by GA Res. 913 (X) UN Doc. A/RES913(X) (1955).

[86] *Nuclear Tests* cases: *Australia* v. *France* [1973] 1 ICJ pleadings 3, 8–11; *New Zealand* v. *France* [1973] 1 ICJ pleadings 3, 5–7.

[87] J. S. Kós, 'Interim Relief in the International Court: New Zealand and the Nuclear Tests Cases' (1984) 14 *VUWLR* 357, 370–5; Malgosia A. Fitzmaurice, 'Environmental Protection and the International Court of Justice' in A. Vaughan Lowe and Malgosia A. Fitzmaurice (eds.), *Fifty Years of the International Court of Justice: Essays in Honour of Sir Robert Jennings* (1996) 293, 297–9.

Anticipating difficulties in sustaining the common interest claim in the wake of the *South West Africa* case,[88] Australia also made two inventive claims regarding transboundary pollution. In the first place it was said that the deposit of any radioactive material within Australian territory violated Australian territorial sovereignty. Second, it was argued that the testing interfered with Australian 'decisional sovereignty' by '[impairing] Australia's independent right to determine what acts shall take place within its territory and in particular whether Australia and its people shall be exposed to radiation from artificial sources'.[89] Rather than relying upon the *Trail Smelter* case, Australia therefore sought to downplay any requirement for actual damage. Establishing serious injury to the satisfaction of a court was a difficult task given the complex chain of causation between the nuclear tests and eventual effects, potentially many years later, upon human health and environmental systems. In relying upon the fact of interference alone, regardless of its scale or immediacy, Australia impelled the doctrine of sovereignty underpinning the *Trail Smelter* case much further than it had previously been advanced. Australia's assertion essentially amounted to a claim of international trespass, in which a wrongful act flowed from mere proof of the deposit of radioactive particles on Australian soil, even though it could not be established that this material had yet (or would ever) cause environmental or other harm.[90]

New Zealand's application addressed a broader range of infringed interests, and did not refer specifically to the atmospheric nature of the tests. As with the Australian application, New Zealand contended that the nuclear tests giving rise to fall-out constituted a violation of the rights of all members of the international community. New Zealand also asserted France's interference with the freedom of the high seas, and similarly complained that the testing violated its rights to prevent the entry of radioactive material into its territory, including New Zealand

[88] *South West Africa* case (second phase) (*Ethiopia* v. *South Africa; Liberia* v. *South Africa*) [1966] ICJ Rep 6, 47: 'although a right of this kind may be known to certain municipal systems of law, it is not known to international law as it stands at present'. See François Voeffray, *L'actio popularis, ou la défense de l'intérêt collectif devant les jurisdictions internationals* (2004) 65–73.

[89] *Nuclear Tests* cases (*Australia* v. *France*), Australian application [1973] 1 ICJ pleadings 3, 14.

[90] Handl, above n. 40, 53; Ian Brownlie, *Principles of Public International Law* (6th edn 2003) 275. In relation to the development of common law trespass which is actionable *per se*, without proof of material damage, see John G. Fleming, *The Law of Torts* (9th edn 1998) 3–5, 21–40.

air space and territorial waters. The New Zealand application also strongly emphasised what it argued was a violation of an obligation by France to protect 'all members of the international community, including New Zealand ... from unjustified artificial radioactive contamination of the terrestrial, maritime and aerial environment'.[91]

A striking feature of the Australian and New Zealand submissions is the way in which they range beyond concerns with human health and also discuss in detail the effects of the nuclear testing on marine and terrestrial ecosystems. The statement in Australia's application that nuclear testing fall-out settles on the sea and is absorbed into the water and 'the life-chains which comprise the marine environment' is the first reference in international litigation to the importance of ecosystem protection.[92] Indeed the imbuing of both submissions with references to the natural environment suggests a major departure from the *Trail Smelter* case, which was concerned with environmental damage only insofar as it affected human interests. In addition to foreshadowing the ecosystem approach in international environmental law, the submissions also hint at an application of a precautionary approach by adverting to the need to prevent potential effects upon human health and ecosystems even though they are not clearly established.[93]

5.1.3.3 Interim orders

Although the ICJ acceded to Australia and New Zealand's request for provisional measures, the Court engaged in no substantive analysis of the factual or legal claims.[94] The Court was satisfied on a prima

[91] *Nuclear Tests* cases (*New Zealand* v. *France*), New Zealand application [1973] 2 ICJ pleadings 3, 8.

[92] *Nuclear Tests* cases (*Australia* v. *France*), Australian application [1973] 1 ICJ pleadings 3, 11. The term 'ecosystem' may be defined as 'a community of organisms interacting with one another and with the environment in which they live' (*Macquarie Dictionary* (3rd edn 2001) 600). For one of the first discussions of the concept see A. G. Tansley, 'The Use and Abuse of Vegetational Concepts and Terms' (1935) 16 *Ecology* 284, 299. A convenient definition in an international environmental text is found in the Biodiversity Convention, art. 2 ('[A] dynamic complex of plant, animal and micro-organism communities and their non-living environment interacting as a functional unit').

[93] Nathalie L. J. T. Horbach and Pieter H. F. Bekker, 'State Responsibility for Injurious Transboundary Activity in Retrospect' (2003) 50 *NILR* 327, 344.

[94] Although France did not appear before the Court, it indicated several objections to the Court's jurisdiction in a letter to the Registry. For a discussion see Jerome B. Elkind, 'French Nuclear Testing and Article 41: Another Blow to the Authority of the Court?' (1974) 8 *VandJTL* 39, 43–4.

facie basis as to jurisdiction and admissibility and observed that the information before it did 'not exclude the possibility that damage to [Australia and New Zealand] might be shown to be caused by the deposit on [Australian and New Zealand] territory of radio-active fall-out resulting from such tests and to be irreparable'.[95] The basis of the Court's orders was to preserve the claimed rights of Australia and New Zealand to prevent the deposit of nuclear materials in their territory,[96] and the Court expressly indicated that the circumstances of the case did not require the indication of interim measures in respect of other claimed rights.[97] This aspect of the Court's order was questioned by several dissenting judges, three of whom suggested that the Court's order had gone too far in effectively recognising principle 21 of the Stockholm Declaration as a rule of customary international law.[98]

The applicants' victory in the provisional phase of the proceedings appeared initially to confirm the value of interim orders for dealing with threatened environmental damage, especially as the Court affirmed that its powers could be mobilised on a finding of mere prima facie (and not clearly manifest) jurisdiction. However, the optimism was short lived as France undertook a planned test, in open defiance of the Court, shortly after the order was issued. This illustrated the political difficulties in using judicial procedures to protect the environment from the activities of a respondent state that had consistently objected to the proceedings. Ultimately the interim orders had no direct effect, and were only helpful for Australia and New Zealand because the French refusal to comply further catalysed international opposition to the testing programme.[99]

95 *Nuclear Tests* cases: *Australia* v. *France* (interim measures) [1973] ICJ Rep 99, [29]; *New Zealand* v. *France* (interim measures) [1973] ICJ Rep 135, [30]. See generally Kathie D. Frankel, 'The Nuclear Tests Cases' (1974) 7 *NYUJILP* 163.

96 *Nuclear Tests* cases: *Australia* v. *France* (interim measures) [1973] ICJ Rep 99, [30]; *New Zealand* v. *France* (interim measures) [1973] ICJ Rep 135, [31].

97 *Nuclear Tests* cases: *Australia* v. *France* (interim measures) [1973] ICJ Rep 99, [31]; *New Zealand* v. *France* (interim measures) [1973] ICJ Rep 135, [32].

98 *Nuclear Tests* case: *Australia* v. *France* (interim measures) [1973] ICJ Rep 99, dissenting opinion of Judge Ignacio-Pinto (at 131), dissenting opinion of Judge Gros (at 288), and the dissenting opinion of Judge Petrén (at 303–6). But note the joint dissenting opinion of Judges Onyeanma, Dilard, Jiminez de Arechega, and Waldock (at 367–8). In addition Judge de Castro (at 389) referred to the general 'right to demand prohibition of the emission by neighbouring properties of noxious fumes'. See also Philippe Sands, 'Pleadings and the Pursuit of International Law: Nuclear Tests II (New Zealand v. France)' in Antony Anghie and Garry Sturgess (eds.), *Legal Visions of the 21st Century: Essays in Honour of Judge Weeramantry* (1998) 601, 614.

99 Constanze Shulte, *Compliance with Decisions of the International Court of Justice* (2004) 309.

5.1.3.4 1974 judgment

Before delivering its judgment in the subsequent phase of the proceedings there was an important development which presented the Court with an opportunity to avoid considering the merits of what had now become a highly charged and fractious *cause célèbre*. The French government made a general announcement in June 1974 that 'in view of the stage reached in carrying out the French nuclear defence program France will be in a position to pass on to the stage of underground explosions as soon as the series planned for this summer is completed'.[100]

Relying on the doctrine of unilateral acts the Court concluded that the announcement amounted to an assumption of a binding obligation to cease all atmospheric tests in the South Pacific.[101] This was despite the fact that the statement was made to the world at large, and not to Australia and New Zealand specifically, and France did not express any intention to be bound by its announcement. None the less the Court concluded that the dispute had become moot: 'the Court having found that the Respondent has assumed an obligation as to conduct, concerning the effective cessation of nuclear tests, no further judicial action is required'.[102]

This conclusion depended on a strained interpretation of the Australian and New Zealand claims, particularly those of New Zealand which complained against all French nuclear tests, not only atmospheric testing. Contending that it was for the Court to determine the substance of the applications,[103] the ICJ interpreted the 'true' objective of the Australian and New Zealand applications as being the cessation of atmospheric testing and not compensation for any injury suffered.[104] While it was certainly the case that neither Australia nor New Zealand had made damages claims, they had requested a declaration that the

[100] *Nuclear Tests* cases: *Australia* v. *France* (merits) [1974] ICJ Rep 253, [34]; *New Zealand* v. *France* (merits) [1974] ICJ Rep 457, [35]. In violation of the Court's provisional measures order, France conducted tests in July and August 1973, and from June to September in 1974, causing some radioactive fall-out on Australian and New Zealand territories.

[101] *Nuclear Tests* cases: *Australia* v. *France* (merits) [1974] ICJ Rep 253, [52]; *New Zealand* v. *France* (merits) [1974] ICJ Rep 457, [55].

[102] *Nuclear Tests* cases: *Australia* v. *France* (merits) [1974] ICJ Rep 253, [56]; *New Zealand* v. *France* (merits) [1974] ICJ Rep 457, [59].

[103] *Nuclear Tests* cases: *Australia* v. *France* (merits) [1974] ICJ Rep 253, [30]; *New Zealand* v. *France* (merits) [1974] ICJ Rep 457, [31].

[104] *Nuclear Tests* cases: *Australia* v. *France* (merits) [1974] ICJ Rep 253, [30]; *New Zealand* v. *France* (merits) [1974] ICJ Rep 457, [31].

French testing was illegal *per se*. Unfortunately the Court did not give the applicants an opportunity to be heard on this issue, or on the question of the unilateral acts doctrine.[105]

By adopting the conclusion it did on the effect of the French declaration, the Court found an ingenious, if not wholly convincing, way of avoiding an assessment of Australia's and New Zealand's factual and legal claims. There is little discussion in the decision of the serious environmental questions at issue in the proceedings. Indeed even in reciting the facts underlying the dispute the Court steered clear of any substantive description of the environmental dangers of nuclear testing, and merely noted the existence of a disagreement between the parties about the effects of radioactive materials dispersed by the French testing.[106] Although several of the separate and dissenting opinions similarly downplayed or ignored the environmental dimensions of the case,[107] several others did grapple to some extent with the novel issues of international environmental law and policy raised in the litigation.

Dissenting opinions

There was some disagreement among the dissenting judges as to which claims by the applicants should be determined on the merits. In their joint dissenting opinion, Judges Onyeama, Dillard, Jiménez de Aréchaga, and Waldock concluded that both Australia and New Zealand had made claims concerning individual and collective legal interests that the Court could evaluate. Judge de Castro in his dissenting opinion categorically dismissed the entitlement of the applicants to bring an *actio popularis*, arguing that in respect of the high seas they possessed 'no legal title authorising [them] to act as [spokespersons] for the international community'.[108] He was more receptive to Australia's and New Zealand's claims regarding infringement of their sovereignty by radioactive fall-out. The only judge to refer to the *Trail Smelter* case, Judge de Castro undertook a general discussion of the principle stated

[105] Lyndel V. Prott, 'Avoiding a Decision on the Merits in the International Court of Justice' (1976) 7 *SLR* 433, 451.

[106] *Nuclear Tests* cases: *Australia* v. *France* (merits) [1974] ICJ Rep 253, [18]; *New Zealand* v. *France* (merits) [1974] ICJ Rep 457, [18].

[107] It is somewhat surprising that Judge Petrén, who had been president of the arbitral tribunal in the *Lake Lanoux* case (1957) 12 *RIAA* 285, was not one of the judges to consider the applicability of developing principles of international environmental law to this case.

[108] *Nuclear Tests* case (*Australia* v. *France*) (merits) [1974] ICJ Rep 253, dissenting opinion of Judge de Castro, 390.

in the case, noting that it was well-known in civil law systems derived from Roman law. Judge ad hoc Barwick's dissenting opinion also analysed closely the nature of each applicant's asserted interests, but as with the other dissenting judges he refrained from evaluating their merits. Judge Barwick noted that the dispute turned on whether 'actual and demonstrable damage is the "gist" of the right to territorial integrity or is the intrusion of radio-active nuclides into the environment *per se* a breach of that right'[109], and this was a genuine and admissible legal question to be decided.

5.1.3.5 1995 *Nuclear Tests* case

France ceased atmospheric nuclear testing in 1974, but continued with its nuclear programme, carrying out over a hundred underground tests in the South Pacific until 1992, when a moratorium was announced in the lead-up to UNCED.[110] Just three years later, in June 1995, France declared that the moratorium would be lifted, and that a final series of eight underground tests would be conducted to obtain data for future computer-based simulations.

The French decision to resume tests coincided with renewed international efforts to end nuclear weapons testing which had gained considerable momentum after the 1986 Chernobyl disaster.[111] Within the Pacific region, the South Pacific Forum states reaffirmed their opposition to nuclear testing with the conclusion of the 1985 South Pacific Nuclear Free Zone Treaty which prohibited the manufacture or acquisition,[112] stationing,[113] and testing[114] of nuclear weapons, and the dumping of any radioactive materials.[115] The politics of South Pacific nuclear testing became even more highly charged following the bombing of the Greenpeace vessel the *Rainbow Warrior* in Auckland harbour by two agents of the French secret service.[116]

[109] *Nuclear Tests* case (*Australia* v. *France*) (merits) [1974] ICJ Rep 253, dissenting opinion of Judge ad hoc Barwick, 433.

[110] See Donald K. Anton *et al.*, 'Memorandum on the Legality of the Planned Resumption of Nuclear Testing by France' (1995) 12 *EPLJ* 300.

[111] Alan E. Boyle, 'Nuclear Energy and International Law: An Environmental Perspective' (1989) 60 *BYBIL* 257, 259–60.

[112] 1985 South Pacific Nuclear Free Zone Treaty, art. 3.

[113] *Ibid.* art. 5.

[114] *Ibid.* art. 6.

[115] *Ibid.* art. 7.

[116] The dispute between New Zealand and France over the actions of the French agents, and their arrest by New Zealand authorities, was referred to the United Nations Secretary-General for a ruling: *Ruling on the Rainbow Warrior Affair between France and New Zealand* (1987) 26 ILM 1346. After France breached the

It was against this background that New Zealand sought to reactivate the proceedings commenced in 1973 by invoking paragraph 63 of the Court's 1974 judgment[117] in which the Court had indicated that its decision was based on France's undertaking to refrain from further tests, and that 'if the basis of this Judgment were to be affected, the Applicant could request an examination of the situation in accordance with the provisions of the Statute'.[118] New Zealand asked the Court to adjudge and declare that the new tests would violate the rights of New Zealand and other states under international law, and alternatively that it was unlawful for France to undertake the tests without first conducting an environmental impact assessment.[119] On the basis that the New Zealand application to revive its 1973 case had a better chance of success than a similar attempt by Australia to reopen the original decision, Australia decided to refrain from joining New Zealand's application and instead sought to intervene in the proceedings.[120]

New Zealand argued that the basis of the Court's initial judgment was directly affected because underground nuclear testing would result in the same or similar environmental impacts as the original atmospheric tests. It asked the Court to recognise

> those rights that would be adversely affected by entry into the marine environment of radioactive material as a result of the further tests to be carried out at Mururoa or Fangataufa ... and of its entitlement to the protection and benefit of a properly conducted Environmental Impact Assessment.[121]

It was argued in particular that the French tests posed the risk of weakening the structure of Mururoa and Fangataufa atolls to such an

Secretary-General's ruling by releasing both agents from imprisonment in French Polynesia, the parties agreed to submit the dispute to ad hoc arbitration: *Rainbow Warrior Arbitration* (*New Zealand/France*) (1990) 82 ILR 499.

117 See generally Matthew Craven, 'New Zealand's Request for an Examination of the Situation in Accordance with Paragraph 63 of the Court's Judgment of 20 December 1974 in the Nuclear Tests Case' (1996) 45 *ICLQ* 725. New Zealand was not able to commence fresh proceedings in the ICJ as France withdrew its acceptance of the Court's compulsory jurisdiction following the original litigation.

118 *Nuclear Tests* case (*New Zealand* v. *France*) (merits) [1974] ICJ Rep 457, [63].

119 1995 *Nuclear Tests* case [1995] ICJ Rep 288, [6].

120 Statement by Senator the Hon. Gareth Evans QC, Minister for Foreign Affairs, 8 August 1995, reprinted in (1996) 17 *AustYBIL* 684. Minister Evans noted that there was a key difference in the way Australia and New Zealand had framed their 1973 applications: 'Australia's 1973 case was entirely concerned with atmospheric testing, whereas New Zealand's was more broadly drafted, relating to contamination from nuclear testing generally.'

121 *Ibid*.

extent that massive discharges of accumulated nuclear materials were possible if either atoll were to split or disintegrate.[122] In so arguing New Zealand sought to engage France in a debate about the environmental implications of its tests which France had up to that point refused to join.[123] New Zealand also specifically argued that the principle stated by the tribunal in the *Trail Smelter* case now constituted a clear norm of customary international law.[124]

However, in yet another controversial judgment, the Court found it unnecessary to consider New Zealand's substantive claims, or the request by Australia and other states to intervene in the proceedings.[125] On this occasion the Court concluded that because France was now engaged in underground nuclear testing the basis of the original judgment was unaffected.[126] According to the Court, the 1974 judgment dealt exclusively with atmospheric nuclear tests, and consequently it was not now possible to take into consideration questions relating to alternative testing methods.[127] This was an exceptionally narrow reading of the Court's original judgment, and a highly problematic one given the nature of New Zealand's original application.[128] While it was certainly the case that in 1974 New Zealand was specifically concerned to halt atmospheric nuclear testing, this reflected the fact that such tests were the only type used by France at the time in the Pacific. Moreover, as has already been noted, New Zealand's original application to the Court referred generically to the environmental dangers inherent in all nuclear tests.

The Court's judgment therefore did not consider the developments in international law since its 1974 decision, including emerging rules

[122] *Ibid.* [21]–[55]; Catherine Giraud, 'French Nuclear Testing in the Pacific and the 1995 International Court of Justice Decision' (1996) 1 *APJEL* 125, 129–30.

[123] Don MacKay, 'Nuclear Testing: New Zealand and France in the International Court of Justice' (1995–6) 19 *FordhamILJ* 1857, 1881.

[124] 1995 *Nuclear Tests* case [1995] ICJ Rep 288, request by New Zealand, [98].

[125] In its application for permission to intervene Australia argued that because the obligations invoked by New Zealand were of an *erga omnes* character all states had a right to make arguments before the Court. Because of its narrow jurisdictional conclusion the Court did not have an opportunity to consider this application: Phoebe N. Okowa, 'Environmental Dispute Settlement: Some Reflections on Recent Developments' in Malcolm D. Evans (ed.), *Remedies in International Law: The Institutional Dilemma* (1998) 157, 165.

[126] 1995 *Nuclear Tests* case [1995] ICJ Rep 288, request by New Zealand, [62].

[127] *Ibid.* [63].

[128] Malgosia A. Fitzmaurice, 'International Protection of the Environment' (2001) 293 *RDC* 9, 376.

relating to environmental impact assessment and the precautionary principle. None the less it did at least recognise the existence of this growing body of law, by reminding the parties that its order was 'without prejudice to the obligations … to respect and protect the natural environment'.[129] While its precise meaning is unclear, the statement does suggest that France was not at liberty to pursue underground testing in defiance of international environmental rules. Indeed, although contesting the application in this case, France accepted that it was bound by environmental duties and did not challenge New Zealand's argument that principle 21 of the Stockholm Declaration and principle 2 of the Rio Declaration were reflective of a 'well established proposition of customary international law'.[130]

Dissenting opinions

The Court's 1995 judgment offered little new as regards international environmental law. By contrast the three dissenting opinions of Judges Weeramantry, Koroma, and Judge ad hoc Palmer engaged with some of the environmental issues raised by the case in considerable depth. Judge Weeramantry analysed a range of existing and developing principles of international environmental law, including the precautionary principle, the requirement to undertake environmental impact assessment, and the illegality of introducing nuclear materials into the marine environment. Judge Weeramantry also referred to the *Trail Smelter* case and principle 21 of the Stockholm Declaration, observing that 'no nation is entitled by its own activities to cause damage to the environment of any other nation'.[131] According to Judge Weeramantry, principle 21 represented 'a deeply entrenched principle, grounded in common sense, case law, international conventions and customary international law'.[132]

Judge Koroma and Judge ad Hoc Palmer also considered the environmental arguments made by New Zealand in order to evaluate whether the Court's 1974 judgment should be reopened. For Judge Koroma, international environmental law had developed to such a stage that '[u]nder contemporary international law, there is probably a duty not to cause gross or serious damage which can reasonably be avoided, together

[129] 1995 *Nuclear Tests* case [1995] ICJ Rep 288 [64].
[130] *Ibid.* [98]. See Sands, above n. 98, 606.
[131] 1995 *Nuclear Tests* case [1995] ICJ Rep 288, dissenting opinion of Judge Weeramantry, 347.
[132] *Ibid.*

with a duty not to permit the escape of dangerous substances'.[133] Judge ad hoc Palmer's dissenting opinion offered a detailed excursus of developments in international environmental law since 1974. He referred to the *Trail Smelter* case and the obligation, discussed in the *Lake Lanoux* case,[134] that states should give notice when engaging in actions that might impair the environment of another state. However, Judge Palmer's attention was mainly focused upon specific principles relating to hazardous radioactive materials, the emerging international law on environmental impact assessment, and the precautionary principle.

5.1.3.6 Legacy

The *Nuclear Tests* litigation provided an opportunity for the ICJ to consider the importance of newly developed principles of international environmental law. As Judge Weeramantry observed in 1995, the Court had for too long been silent upon these issues.[135] International environmental law had developed rapidly in the years leading up to the Court's 1974 judgment, and by the time of New Zealand's 1995 request included a range of rules and principles having a bearing on the case, including the precautionary principle, requirements for environmental impact assessment, and clear obligations to protect the marine environment set out in the LOS Convention.

However, in these proceedings these issues of international environmental law and policy were inseparable from a highly political dispute that carried implications for civil and military use of nuclear technologies globally. On this basis it has been argued that the Court was correct to avoid pronouncing on the controversial issues before it, including those concerning questions of international environmental law.[136] However, the contrary, and better view, is that the jurisdiction of the ICJ was regularly invoked and as a consequence the Court was

[133] 1995 *Nuclear Tests* case [1995] ICJ Rep 288, dissenting opinion of Judge Koroma, 378.

[134] *Lake Lanoux* case (*France/Spain*) (1957) 12 *RIAA* 285.

[135] 1995 *Nuclear Tests* case [1995] ICJ Rep 288, dissenting opinion of Judge Weeramantry, 362.

[136] Edward McWhinney, 'International Law-Making and the Judicial Process: The World Court and the French Nuclear Tests Case' (1975) 3 *SyracuseJIL&Com* 9, 36. Similar doubts have been expressed by Koskenniemi in relation to the *Nuclear Weapons* advisory opinion [1996] ICJ Rep 226: Martti Koskenniemi, 'The Silence of Law/The Voice of Justice' in Laurence Boisson de Chazournes and Philippe Sands (eds.), *International Law, The International Court of Justice and Nuclear Weapons* (1999) 488, 489.

under a duty to decide the legal issues clearly defined by the applicants in accordance with international law.[137]

Notwithstanding the formal outcome, Australia, New Zealand, and other South Pacific nations gained considerable international support for their campaign against nuclear testing as a result of the litigation.[138] In addition, the *Nuclear Tests* case helped set the agenda for further elaboration of international environmental law both in relation to transboundary damage and nuclear pollution. The factual scenario confronted in the case, and the arguments advanced by the parties, simultaneously highlighted not only how far international environmental law had progressed, but also how much additional development was required. This included the need for the principle stated in the *Trail Smelter* case to be refashioned to encompass situations where the extent and cause of transboundary damage was unclear, and where the damage involved the impairment of global commons areas. The 1995 *Nuclear Tests* case, and particularly the dissenting opinions, also helped bring into focus the range of procedural obligations such as the requirement to undertake consultations and environmental impact assessments to ensure that the basic obligation stated in the *Trail Smelter* case to prevent transboundary harm can operate effectively.

5.1.4 *Transboundary harm and international watercourses*

Thus far the discussion has been concerned with landmark litigation that has directly involved questions of transboundary harm. However, these questions have also arisen incidentally in other cases, particularly in the context of shared watercourses.

5.1.4.1 *Lake Lanoux* case

In the context of international rivers, the *Lake Lanoux* case confirmed the existence of the principle stated in the *Trail Smelter* case but offered no significant analysis of its application. The dispute in the *Lake Lanoux* case concerned a French scheme to generate electricity by diverting waters from Lake Lanoux, a large alpine lake in the French Pyrenees, to the Ariège River, which would have resulted in reduced flows into the Carol River which flowed into Spain. Following Spanish protests

[137] Prott, above n. 105, 444.

[138] MacKay, above n. 123, 1886–7. This ultimately contributed to France, along with the United States and the United Kingdom, joining a protocol to the 1985 South Pacific Nuclear Free Zone Treaty which required states to desist from further nuclear tests in the region: 1986 Protocol I to the South Pacific Nuclear Free Zone Treaty.

France agreed to return from another source the exact quantity of water extracted. The case therefore did not turn on any allegation as to downstream transboundary damage.[139] In *obiter dicta* the tribunal none the less accepted that 'there [was] a principle which prohibits the upstream State from altering the waters of a river in such a fashion as seriously to prejudice the downstream State'.[140]

5.1.4.2 *Gabčíkovo-Nagymaros Project* case

Questions of transboundary damage featured more prominently in the *Gabčíkovo-Nagymaros Project* case.[141] In this case concerning a joint project between Slovakia and Hungary to construct extensive dam and other works on a stretch of the Danube, several arguments were made by Hungary regarding the potential impact of the project upon the downstream environment, and on supplies of drinking water in Hungary. As the Court ultimately concluded that all the environmental matters could be addressed by ongoing cooperation between the parties within the terms of a bilateral agreement, it did not proffer any view as to any breach by Slovakia of an obligation to prevent transboundary harm. However, it was accepted that the *Trail Smelter* case principle had acquired customary status, and the ICJ repeated its clear statement in the *Nuclear Weapons* advisory opinion that 'the existence of the general obligation of States to ensure that activities within their jurisdiction and control respect the environment of other States or areas beyond national control is now part of the corpus of international law relating to the environment'.[142]

5.2 Impact of the case law

5.2.1 *Principle 21 of the Stockholm Declaration*

The most visible impact of the *Trail Smelter* case upon international law is to be found in principle 21 of the Stockholm Declaration. However, in that principle the duty to prevent damage to other states was given a clearly environmental dimension not evident in the *Trail Smelter* case. Principle 21 provides that

> States have, in accordance with the Charter of the United Nations and the principles of international law, the sovereign right to exploit their own

[139] This reflected the way in which the case was argued, as it was possible (indeed likely) that the arrangement would have had transboundary environmental effects. See ch. 6.

[140] *Lake Lanoux* case (1957) 12 *RIAA* 285, 308. See ch. 6.

[141] *Gabčíkovo-Nagymaros Project* case [1997] ICJ Rep 7. See ch. 6.

[142] *Ibid.* [53].

resources pursuant to their own environmental policies, and the responsibility to ensure that activities within their jurisdiction or control do not cause damage to the environment of other States or of areas beyond the limits of national jurisdiction.[143]

This obligation has been described as the 'cornerstone of international environmental law',[144] and was substantially repeated in principle 2 of the Rio Declaration.[145] The policy of principle 21/2 is 'to balance the right of a state to control matters within its territory with its responsibility to ensure that what is done within that territory does not cause damage outside'.[146] Accordingly it does not express an absolute environmental objective. The first part of the principle expressly permits development within a state's jurisdiction, and the obligation to protect the environment in the second part applies only to the environment of other states, and areas beyond national jurisdiction.[147] Principle 21/2 was recognised as a norm of customary international law in the environmental field in the *Nuclear Weapons* advisory opinion,[148] and this conclusion was reaffirmed in the *Gabčíkovo-Nagymaros Project* case.[149]

143 This principle emerged after considerable debate, and several proposals, and ultimately resembled the formulation suggested by the Australian delegation to the Conference: see UN Doc. A/CONF.48/PC/WG.I(II)/CRP.9 (1972) 2.

144 Sands, above n. 80, 236.

145

> States have, in accordance with the Charter of the United Nations and the principles of international law, the sovereign right to exploit their own resources pursuant to their own environmental and developmental policies, and the responsibility to ensure that activities within their jurisdiction or control do not cause damage to the environment of other States or of areas beyond the limits of national jurisdiction.

On the significance of the inclusion of the words 'and developmental policies' in principle 2 and the Rio Declaration's emphasis on development see David A. Wirth, 'The Rio Declaration on Environment and Development: Two Steps Forward and One Back or Vice Versa?' (1995) 29 *GaLR* 599; Marc Pallemaerts, 'International Environmental Law from Stockholm to Rio: Back to the Future' (1992) 1 *RECIEL* 254, 256.

146 Louis B. Sohn, 'The Stockholm Declaration on the Human Environment' (1973) 14 *HarvILJ* 423.

147 Klaus Bosselmann, 'Environmental Governance: A New Approach to Territorial Sovereignty' in Robert J. Goldstein (ed.), *Environmental Ethics and Law* (2004) 293, 301.

148 *Nuclear Weapons* advisory opinion [1996] ICJ Rep 226, [29]. On the difference between the language adopted by the Court and principle 21 of the Stockholm Declaration see Edith Brown Weiss, 'Opening the Door to the Environment and to Future Generations' in Laurence Boisson de Chazournes and Philippe Sands (eds.), *International Law, The International Court of Justice and Nuclear Weapons* (1999) 338, 340 (observing that the Court's use of the word 'respect' imposes a broader obligation than the requirement of principle 21 merely to prevent 'damage').

149 *Gabčíkovo-Nagymaros Project* case [1997] ICJ Rep 7, [53].

Although widely referred to, or incorporated, in environmental instruments, principle 21/2 provides little practical guidance to states in their activities, and requires further elucidation and elaboration.[150] Relevant issues not addressed include the type and degree of environmental harm to be prevented, the procedural obligations (such as notification, consultation, and cooperation) that are necessary to ensure that harm does not occur or is minimised, and whether the obligation of prevention is one of strict liability or due diligence, and the relevant remedies applicable in the event of any breach.[151]

Several of these were addressed to varying degrees of specificity in other principles incorporated in the Rio Declaration. Principle 18 refers to the requirement that states notify others of emergencies likely to affect their environment, and principle 19 states that prior notification should be provided, and consultation undertaken, before activities that may have serious effects on the environment of other states or common spaces are permitted. These principles now reflect customary international law and augment the basic preventive principle in principle 21/2.[152] Somewhat controversial from a customary perspective, but no less important to the practical functioning of principle 21/2, is principle 17 which concerns environmental impact assessment and principle 15 which sets out the precautionary approach.

5.2.2 *Treaty transformation*

The transformation of principle 21/2 into environmental treaties has taken differing forms reflecting the particular objects and purposes of the relevant instrument, and the limitations of the principle as a tool of environmental management. In treaties such as the 1991 Convention on Environmental Impact Assessment in a Transboundary Context which specifically aim to prevent or limit adverse transboundary effects, principle 21/2 can be given direct application.[153] However,

[150] One commentator has argued that principle 21 belongs to a 'mythology' of international environmental law, with the principle having acquired great symbolism, when in reality it is a modest, and vague, legal standard: John H. Knox, 'The Myth and Reality of Transboundary Environmental Impact Assessment' (2002) 96 *AJIL* 291, 293–5. See also Daniel Bodansky, 'Customary (and Not so Customary) International Environmental Law' (1995) 3 *IndJGLS* 105.

[151] Sands, above n. 80, 241.

[152] Patricia W. Birnie and Alan E. Boyle, *International Law and the Environment* (2nd edn 2002) 126.

[153] Art. 2(1) provides that '[t]he Parties shall, individually or jointly, take all appropriate and effective measures to prevent, reduce and control significant

in some other formulations of the principle the underlying implication that the rule exists to protect the environment of a receiving state is subordinated to a more general obligation to protect the environment *per se*.[154] This is particularly evident in treaty law addressing damage to common spaces such as the provisions of the LOS Convention relating to the protection of the marine environment of the high seas.[155] A similar approach animates other regimes. For instance, both the 1985 Vienna Convention for the Protection of the Ozone Layer[156] and the 1992 United Nations Framework Convention on Climate Change[157] recognise principle 21/2 in their respective preambles but go on to provide for regimes which of necessity require a global approach.[158] The Biodiversity Convention in article 3 also repeats principle 21/2 verbatim. This trend to expand the principle beyond its connection with transboundary disputes was recognised in the *Iron Rhine Railway* arbitration[159] where it was said that the duty to prevent significant harm to the environment (and not only the environment of other states) constituted 'a principle of general international law'.[160]

adverse transboundary environmental impact from proposed activities'. See also the 1992 UNECE Convention on the Transboundary Effects of Industrial Accidents, preamble, 8th recital and art. 3.

154 See e.g. the 1992 Convention on the Protection and Use of Transboundary Watercourses and International Lakes, arts. 2(1) and 2(2)(b).

155 Art. 193: 'States have the sovereign right to exploit their natural resources pursuant to their environmental policies and in accordance with their duty to protect and preserve the marine environment.'

156 Preamble, 2nd recital. 157 Preamble, 8th recital.

158 See also the 1972 Convention on the Prevention of Marine Pollution by Dumping of Wastes and Other Materials (1972 London Convention), preamble, 3rd recital (but see also art. 1) and the 1996 Protocol to the Convention on the Prevention of Marine Pollution by Dumping of Wastes and Other Matter which will replace the 1972 London Convention and contains no reference to principle 21/2. Instead art. 2 provides simply that states 'shall individually and collectively protect and preserve the marine environment from all sources of pollution'. Other environmental treaties that do not refer to or incorporate the principle include several instruments that seek to protect the global commons: 1978 Protocol Relating to the International Convention for the Prevention of Pollution from Ships 1973; 1976 Convention for the Protection of the Mediterranean Sea Against Pollution; OSPAR Convention; Madrid Protocol. In acknowledgement of its limited application to environmental problems having global dimensions, principle 21/2 is also not referenced in the 1987 Montreal Protocol on Substances that Deplete the Ozone Layer or the 1997 Kyoto Protocol.

159 *Iron Rhine (Ijzeren Rijn) Railway* arbitration (*Belgium/Netherlands*) (24 May 2005) (available at www.pca-cpa.org/showfile.asp?fil_id=377).

160 *Ibid.* [59].

5.2.3 *Work of the ILC*

Beyond specific treaties dealing with transboundary harm issues, the international community has recognised the need for more generalised rules and principles. The ILC has been given the task of formulating the residual legal framework applicable to transboundary damage, building upon the decision in the *Trail Smelter* case and principle 21/2. The ILC's examination of the questions of responsibility, prevention, and liability illustrate how far this area of law has come from its origins and how the litigation in the *Nuclear Tests* cases has influenced its development. It also shows how some problematic aspects of the *Trail Smelter* case have been retained in contemporary practice.

Turning first to the topic of responsibility, it must be observed that the ILC's Articles on Responsibility of States for Internationally Wrongful Acts[161] apply to violations of principle 21/2 as a customary rule as much as they apply to the breach of any international legal obligation. This reflects the intention of the Articles on State Responsibility to provide secondary rules applicable in the event of the violation of primary obligations. Rather than dealing with the nature and extent of the obligation to prevent transboundary harm in any detail in the Articles on State Responsibility, the ILC has sought to achieve this in two additional texts.

The first of these is the Draft Articles on Prevention which were adopted and submitted to the United Nations General Assembly in 2001 with the recommendation that they form the basis of a convention. The second is the Draft Principles on Liability which were adopted on first reading by the ILC in 2004.[162] Both of these documents emerged out of a long and contentious programme of work initiated in 1978 to examine the topic of 'international liability for injurious consequences arising out of acts not prohibited by international law'. Progress within the ILC on the topic was slow for many years as a result of

[161] Articles on Responsibility of States for Internationally Wrongful Acts, Report of the International Law Commission, 53rd Session, 43–59, UN Doc. A/56/10 (2001) (noted by the General Assembly in GA Res. 56/83, UN Doc. A/RES/56/83 (2001)) (Articles on State Responsibility).

[162] The ILC explains that the term 'draft principles' was to be preferred in this context over that of 'draft articles' because the instrument is 'inevitably general and residual in character' and designed to be adapted when applied to particular situations involving the risk of hazardous activities causing significant transboundary harm: Report of the International Law Commission, 56th Session, 153–6, UN Doc. A/59/10 (2004) at 160.

ongoing debate over the scope of the inquiry. In order to separate the 'international liability' project from the more general topic of state responsibility, the ILC had initially adhered to a distinction between 'lawful' and 'wrongful' activities resulting in transboundary harm. This approach was widely criticised[163] as most activities causing transboundary harm, such as the industrial air pollution in the *Trail Smelter* case, are not themselves prohibited, and it is only the failure to prevent significant damage to the environment of other states which constitutes a wrongful act. As Boyle has noted, the Commission based its work on the erroneous assumption 'that there could be responsibility for harmful activities only if these were prohibited, whereas liability could only arise in respect of non-prohibited or "lawful" activities'.[164]

In 1996 the Commission abandoned its earlier approach and placed the topic on a more realistic and conceptually defensible footing.[165] The topic was essentially divided into two core questions (which, from 1997, formed the basis of two entirely separate programmes of work).[166] First, what is the nature and scope of the obligation to prevent transboundary environmental damage? In other words, what are the primary rules relating to the prevention of transboundary damage the breach of which allows secondary rules of state responsibility to be invoked? A secondary question, and one distinct from that of responsibility, is what should happen if transboundary environmental harm is not caused by an internationally wrongful act? If states discharge their prevention obligations but transboundary harm nevertheless eventuates, who should bear the costs of the damaging consequences, the polluting state or victim state?

163 See in particular Alan E. Boyle, 'State Responsibility and International Liability for Injurious Consequences of Acts Not Prohibited by International Law: A Necessary Distinction?' (1990) 39 *ICLQ* 1, 12–14; Ian Brownlie, *State Responsibility (Pt I)* (1983) 50; Michael Akehurst, 'International Liability for Injurious Consequences Arising out of Acts Not Prohibited by International Law' (1985) 16 *NethYBIL* 3. See also Fitzmaurice, above n. 128, 233–44.

164 Alan E. Boyle, 'Codification of International Environmental Law and the International Law Commission: Injurious Consequences Revisited' in Alan E. Boyle and David Freestone (eds.), *International Law and Sustainable Development: Past Achievements and Future Challenges* (1999) 61, 73.

165 *Ibid.* 76.

166 Report of the International Law Commission, 48th Session, UN Doc. A/51/10 (1996).

5.2.3.1 ILC Draft Articles on Prevention

The Draft Articles on Prevention deal with the first question and articulate a regime of primary rules for the prevention and control of activities not prohibited by international law, but which none the less involve a risk of significant transboundary harm.[167] The articles rely considerably upon the *Trail Smelter* case and principle 21/2, and encompass all activities at risk of causing transboundary damage.[168]

They apply both to hazardous activities of the type encountered in the *Trail Smelter* case and ultra-hazardous activities of the kind involved in the *Nuclear Tests* cases and the *1995 Nuclear Tests* case. Regrettably they deal only with transboundary damage to other states, and not to damage to global commons areas. Consequently they operationalise only part of principle 21/2 and carry the original focus of this area of law on sovereignty, rather than the environment *per se*, into contemporary practice. Significantly, the Draft Articles on Prevention also define 'harm' broadly to include damage to persons, property, or the environment. It is clear therefore that the Draft Articles on Prevention do not codify or develop principle 21/2 by embracing an overt environmental focus.

The Draft Articles on Prevention only operate when the combined probability of occurrence and the potential extent of harm is 'significant'. The Commission considered this threshold essential because the reality of the 'ecological unity of the planet which does not correspond to political boundaries'[169] means that it is inevitable that activities within states will have some impact upon others. The ILC has therefore maintained much the same approach as that adopted in the *Trail Smelter* case, and similarly leaves unregulated many environmentally damaging activities. However, the requirement of 'significant' damage is considerably lower than damage of 'serious consequence' as required in the *Trail Smelter* case.

Where the Draft Articles on Prevention advance the law considerably is in relation to the procedural duties largely ignored in the *Trail*

[167] Draft Articles on Prevention, above n. 66, art. 1. See also IUCN – World Conservation Union, *Draft International Covenant on Environment and Development* (3rd edn, 2004) art. 50: 'A State Party is liable for significant harm to the environment of other States or of areas beyond the limits of national jurisdiction, as well as for injury or loss to persons resulting therefrom, caused by acts or omissions attributable to them or to activities under their jurisdiction or control.'

[168] Report of the International Law Commission, 53rd Session, 149, UN Doc. A/56/10 (2001).

[169] *Ibid*. 152.

Smelter case and in the *Nuclear Tests* cases. Article 3 provides that states 'shall take all appropriate measures to prevent significant transboundary harm or at any rate to minimise the risk thereof'. This obligation is then elaborated upon through an ensemble of supporting duties. States must cooperate in good faith and, if necessary, seek the assistance of competent international organisations.[170] This effectively codifies the *Lake Lanoux* case which stipulated that states must undertake negotiations and consultations in respect of potentially damaging transboundary activities.[171] Further, to maintain control over potentially harmful activities, systems of prior authorisation must be established,[172] and these must be based upon comprehensive environmental impact assessment.[173] Such assessments should include consideration of the potential impacts upon the environment of other states, independently of any impairment of human health or damage to property.[174] In essence these provisions incorporate the duties identified by New Zealand in the 1995 *Nuclear Tests* case as *sine quibus non* for France to resume its nuclear tests.

The obligation to take preventative measures is one of due diligence, not an absolute guarantee against the occurrence of harm. According to the commentary to the Draft Articles on Prevention, 'due diligence is manifested in reasonable efforts by a State to inform itself of factual or legal components that relate foreseeably to a contemplated procedure and to take appropriate measures in timely fashion, to address them'.[175] This reflects state practice generally, in which there has been great reluctance to accept a stricter standard.[176] Indeed in the *Trail Smelter* case it was accepted that a due diligence standard was to apply having regard to the capacity of Canada, via improving emissions control technologies, to limit transboundary damage.

[170] Draft Articles on Prevention, above n. 66, art. 4.

[171] It was held in the *Lake Lanoux* case that 'the upstream State has ... a right of initiative ... If, in the course of discussions, the downstream State submits schemes to it, the upstream State must examine them, but it has the right to give preference to the solution contained in its own scheme provided that it takes into consideration in a reasonable manner the interests of the downstream State': *Lake Lanoux* case (1957) 12 *RIAA* 285, 316.

[172] *Ibid.* art. 6. [173] *Ibid.* art. 7.

[174] Report of the International Law Commission, 53rd Session, 159, UN Doc. A/56/10 (2001).

[175] *Ibid.* 393.

[176] Patricia Birnie, 'The Role of International Law in Solving Certain Environmental Conflicts' in John E. Carroll (ed.), *International Environmental Diplomacy: The Management and Resolution of Transfrontier Environmental Problems* (1988) 95, 111.

In so far as the foregoing issues are concerned, the Commission's approach is firmly founded on state practice and judicial decisions. However, a highly contentious aspect of the Draft Articles on Prevention is the combined operation of articles 9 and 10 relating to consultations between states to achieve an 'equitable' balancing of interests. Article 9(1) sets out the generally accepted obligation that originating and potentially affected states should enter into consultations in order to reach agreement upon measures to prevent or minimise significant transboundary harm. Far more controversial is the stipulation in article 9(2) that the consultations should be directed at achieving a solution 'based on an equitable balance of interests' in light of the criteria contained in article 10. The ILC appears here to have misinterpreted the legacy of the *Trail Smelter* case.

The difficulty with the ILC's approach is that the tribunal did not in fact engage in any such equitable balancing because general international law demanded it, but rather because the Trail Smelter Arbitral Agreement provided in article IV that the tribunal 'shall give consideration to the desire of the high contracting parties to reach a solution *just* to all parties concerned'.[177] The ILC's approach is also manifestly problematic in principle because it permits states to reach an agreement that pays little, or no, regard to environmental considerations when reaching an 'equitable' agreement.[178] In one sense, therefore, the ILC's incorporation of equitable standards tends to confirm that the law in this area continues to be influenced by its conceptual origins in the notion of a 'balancing' of sovereign interests and is only concerned, in a derivative sense, with absolute standards for the protection and preservation of the environment.

5.2.3.2 Draft Principles on Liability

The second question, namely the extent of liability in the event of complete discharge of a state's obligations of prevention, has also been addressed by the ILC. Whereas the Draft Articles on Prevention mostly codify customary international law, the Commission's Draft Principles on Liability are more in the nature of progressive development and, unusually for the ILC, are expressed as soft-law principles rather than as rules that are or may eventually be binding. The principles draw on domestic law and liability conventions and offer a model for liability

[177] Emphasis added. [178] Birnie and Boyle, above n. 152, 107.

that states may wish to adopt to give victims of pollution clear rights of redress.[179]

In this topic the ILC has sought to address a major lacuna in pre-existing law relating to transboundary harm: a system of liability for damage that does not result from the breach of an international obligation.[180] The Draft Principles on Liability are of a framework character, and encourage states to develop specific liability regimes on a global, regional, or bilateral basis[181] to implement the polluter pays principle.[182] They are designed to stand alongside the Draft Articles on Prevention and likewise apply to activities not prohibited by international law involving a risk of causing significant physical harm beyond territorial boundaries. As with the Draft Articles on Prevention, the Draft Principles on Liability do not apply to damage to the global commons, with the Commission expressing the view that this question requires separate treatment.[183]

The primary aim of the Draft Principles on Liability is to ensure prompt and adequate compensation for individuals and states suffering transboundary damage, including environmental degradation.[184] They therefore deal with questions not addressed in the *Trail Smelter* case, or subsequent international litigation. They rest on the premise that even if states comply with their international legal obligations to prevent transboundary harm, such damage may none the less occur accidentally or otherwise in circumstances beyond the control of the originating state, and in such cases those who suffer loss or harm as a result should be compensated. Consistent with existing bilateral, regional, and sectoral liability regimes the Draft Principles on Liability seek to make the operators of hazardous or risk-bearing activities liable for adverse transboundary effects. This is to be achieved by states establishing procedures allowing victims to obtain effective remedies, including compensation. To this end, the principles require that administrative and judicial mechanisms of the originating state treat nationals and non-nationals alike.[185]

[179] Alan E. Boyle, 'Globalising Environmental Liability: The Interplay of National and International Law' (2005) 17 *JEL* 3, 25.

[180] Boyle, above n. 164, 73.

[181] Draft Principles on Liability, above n. 67, principle 7.

[182] For a definition of the principle see Rio Declaration, principle 16.

[183] Report of the International Law Commission, 56th Session, 158, UN Doc. A/59/10 (2004).

[184] Draft Principles on Liability, above n. 67, principle 3.

[185] *Ibid.* principles 4 and 6.

5.3 Conclusion

Each of the cases examined in this chapter assisted, to varying degrees, in successfully resolving contentious disputes involving transboundary damage.[186] Yet, in terms of addressing the underlying pollution problem, or other environmental issue giving rise to these controversies, the achievements of the litigation have been more limited. The *Trail Smelter* case led to the establishment of a detailed regime to reduce the damaging effects of sulphur dioxide emitted from the smelter at Trail but did not, and could not, resolve the broader problem of aerial pollution and acid rain in North America. This was left to domestic laws and regional agreements. The litigation in relation to French nuclear testing in the South Pacific contributed to the end of the atmospheric and underground nuclear testing, but it was never accepted by France that its programmes violated rules of international law regarding environmental protection. In the *Lake Lanoux* case and *Gabčíkovo-Nagymaros Project* case the proposed projects, the credentials of which were impugned by Spain and Hungary respectively, were ultimately given judicial approval, although in modified form.

The normative contribution of the cases has been more important and enduring, as they have supplied general principles that have been given practical effect through detailed treaty regimes.[187] The *Trail Smelter* case involved the first application of the principle of respect for the territorial integrity of other states to a situation involving environmental damage. The decision signalled the abandonment of the notion of absolute sovereignty and therefore set the stage for a new era of international law which respected the environmental interests of all states.[188] The *Trail Smelter* case also exposed the many questions that must be addressed in devising any comprehensive international legal regime for regulating transboundary environmental harm, including the standard of care to be expected of originating states, the level of harm necessary to give rise to state responsibility, and the range of commercial and environmental interests that may be protected.

[186] For an assessment of the success or otherwise of this litigation in achieving a lasting settlement of all of these disputes see Cesare P. R. Romano, *The Peaceful Settlement of International Environmental Disputes: A Pragmatic Approach* (2000) 219–32 (in relation to the *Lake Lanoux* case), 246–60 (in relation to the *Gabčíkovo-Nagymaros Project* case) 261–78 (in relation to the *Trail Smelter* case) and 279–306 (in relation to the *Nuclear Tests* cases).

[187] For a discussion of the key regimes see Okowa, above n. 1, 24–59.

[188] Kuokkanen, above n. 5, 93.

In the *Nuclear Tests* cases, some thirty-five years later, an attempt was made by Australia and New Zealand to take the concept of sovereignty lying at the heart of the principle articulated in the *Trail Smelter* case to its logical conclusion, by arguing that any interference with another state's environment, however slight, may gave rise to state responsibility. It was also sought to adapt these basic principles to a dispute involving damage to the environment of commons areas. By studiously avoiding a decision on the merits in 1974, and again in 1995, the ICJ did not consider this question, or issues concerning the extent to which the prevention principle operates in conjunction with a range of other environmental rules, including those relating to environmental impact assessment or the precautionary principle. New Zealand addressed these issues in detail in its submissions in the 1995 *Nuclear Tests* case, and several judges supported the cogency of New Zealand's arguments in dissenting opinions. In addition, in the *Nuclear Weapons* advisory opinion the ICJ finally recognised that the principle enunciated in the *Trail Smelter* case had acquired customary status.

The cases discussed in this chapter therefore reveal the early origins of international environmental law and the character of its development by analogy from more general concepts of sovereignty and territorial integrity. Although it has undergone significant evolution, general international environmental law in the context of transboundary harm remains heavily influenced by these foundations which are inherently statist and, as a consequence, anthropocentric. Indeed to label the principles that these cases have developed as rules of 'international environmental law' is perhaps to ascribe to them too great a significance. They have a much more general genesis, and retain a general application, as confirmed in the ILC's Draft Articles on Prevention, and Draft Principles on Liability which are applicable to all types of injury, not merely ecological damage. These instruments do not have a strong environmental focus; they expressly resile from regulating transboundary damage to the global commons, and are concerned, as was the *Trail Smelter* case, in reconciling two competing sovereign rights.

6 Freshwater resources and ecosystems

The overuse and pollution of water basins throughout the world has caused severe environmental damage and resulted in worsening crises of water scarcity.[1] As the world's population increases the per capita share of freshwater diminishes, and around 33 per cent of the world's population experience moderate to high water stress.[2] Reversing the decline of freshwater ecosystems and addressing the challenge of scarcity requires a high level of international cooperation, as around one-third of the world's river basins are shared by two or more riparian states.[3] In this context international environmental law has a role to play in addressing water security, improving water quality, maintaining freshwater ecosystems, promoting cooperative management, and preventing conflict through the peaceful settlement of disputes.[4] This

1 Agenda 21, ch. 8, [18.1]–[18.4], UN Doc. A/CONF.151/26/Rev.1 (1992).

2 Nicolas Stern, *The Economics of Climate Change: The Stern Review* (2007) 76. As compared to 6 per cent in 1990: Commission on Sustainable Development, Freshwater Resources: Report of the Secretary-General, UN Doc. E/CN.17/1994/4 (1994); Stephen C. McCaffrey, 'Water, Water Everywhere, But Too Few Drops to Drink: The Coming Freshwater Crisis and International Environmental Law' (2000) 28 *DenJILP* 325, 330. To remedy this a key United Nations Millennium Development Goal is to halve the proportion of the world's population who do not have access to safe drinking water: UN GA Res. 55/2, [19], UN Doc. A/RES/55/2 (2000). See also 2005 World Summit Outcome, [56(h)], UN Doc. A/60/L.1 (2005).

3 Elli Louka, International Environmental Law: Fairness, Effectiveness and World Order (2006) 171. See the 1997 United Nations Convention on the Law of Non-Navigational Uses of International Watercourses (UN Watercourses Convention), art. 2 which defines an international watercourse as 'a system of surface waters and groundwaters constituting by virtue of their physical relationship a unitary whole and normally flowing into a common terminus'.

4 Stephen C. McCaffrey, 'Water Scarcity: Institutional and Legal Responses' in Edward H. P. Brans *et al.* (eds.), *The Scarcity of Water: Emerging Legal and Policy Responses* (1997)

chapter considers the specific and important contribution that arbitral awards and judicial decisions have made to this field of international environmental law. It is seen that although this case law has traditionally been concerned with the equitable utilisation of freshwater resources, more recent decisions suggest an important (though far from complete) movement towards an ecologically oriented jurisprudence.

6.1 Jurisprudence

Relatively few disputes concerning international watercourses have to date proceeded to adjudication,[5] with riparian states instead preferring diplomatic methods of settlement, often through joint river commissions.[6] Indeed there has been significant debate as to the utility of adjudication in dealing with watercourse disputes. Some early commentators, concerned with the absence of clear principles, argued that 'water disputes are generally agreed to constitute a classic example of disputes which cannot be satisfactorily resolved by judicial decision'.[7] Others have taken the view that adjudication can assist in developing a more secure legal basis for resolving disputes over water rights.[8]

There are now several important regional instruments establishing compulsory adjudicative procedures,[9] and the two leading multilateral instruments also provide for adjudication as a dispute settlement

52; J. Starr, 'Water Wars' (1991) 82 *Foreign Policy* 17; H. L. F. Saeijs and M. V. van Berkel, 'The Global Water Crisis: The Major Issue of the 21st Century' in Edward H. P. Brans *et al.* (eds.), *The Scarcity of Water: Emerging Legal and Policy Responses* (1997) 3.

[5] Stephen C. McCaffrey, *The Law of International Watercourses: Non-Navigational Uses* (2001), 177. See generally B. R. Chauhan, *Settlement of International Water Law Disputes in International Drainage Basins* (1981).

[6] L. Caflisch, 'Judicial Means for Settling Water Disputes' in International Bureau of the Permanent Court of Arbitration (ed.), *Permanent Court of Arbitration Peace Palace Papers: Resolution of International Water Disputes* (2003) 235, 240. See e.g. the 1995 Agreement on the Cooperation for Sustainable Development of the Mekong River Basin, art. 34: '[w]henever any difference or dispute may arise ... the Commission shall first make every effort to resolve the issue'.

[7] F. J. Berber, *Rivers in International Law* (1959) 263. But see W. W. Van Alstyne, 'The Justiciability of International River Disputes: A Study in the Case Method' [1964] *DukeLJ* 307.

[8] J. G. Laylin and R. L. Biancho, 'The Role of Adjudication in International River Disputes' (1959) 53 *AJIL* 30, 49.

[9] See e.g. 1996 Convention on Cooperation for the Protection and Sustainable Use of the Danube, art. 24; 1998 Convention on the Protection of the Rhine, art. 16.

option.[10] Moreover the cases that have been decided have had a significant impact upon the evolution of international water law and cognate rules and principles of international environmental law. These cases can be separated into two main categories: disputes over access to water resources, and disputes over pollution or other environmental damage caused to shared watercourses.

The first type of dispute has most commonly arisen when a downstream state has asserted that an upstream user has diverted excessive volumes of water, such as through the construction of a dam as part of a power generation or irrigation project. These projects often have profound environmental impacts on rivers, and dependent tributaries and floodplains,[11] and on local and distant communities.[12] Several disputes between riparians concerning the manipulation of rivers and other shared water resources have been the subject of international adjudication, beginning as early as 1872.[13] Only rarely, however, have environmental concerns been explicitly at the centre of these disputes. Indeed the protection of the riparian environment, as distinct from preserving the interests of riparian states, has not traditionally been regarded as a concern of the law of international watercourses.[14] Instead, environmental issues have been subsumed within disputes over matters such as sufficiency of downstream water flows for agricultural uses or possible physical damage to the territory of one riparian state as a result of hydrological works carried out by another riparian.[15] There has

[10] UN Watercourses Convention, art. 33; 1992 Convention on the Protection and Use of Transboundary Waters and International Lakes (1992 Watercourses Convention), art. 22.

[11] The World Dam Commission has reported that large dams have several, mostly negative, impacts on riverine and dependent ecosystems including damage to terrestrial ecosystems and biodiversity. Large dams often cause the fragmentation of river basin ecosystems, and around 60 per cent of all large river basins are highly or moderately fragmented: World Commission on Dams, *Dams and Development: A New Framework for Decision-Making* (2000) ch. 3.

[12] See e.g. Chile – Petition 4617/02 – Mercedes Julia Huenaeo Beroiza – Report no. 30/04 (Inter-American Commisssion on Human Rights) [2004] IACommHR 26 (concerning effects of hydroelectricity project on environment and livelihoods of indigenous group).

[13] *Helmand River* cases *(Afghanistan/Persia)* (1872) 5 Moore 4706.

[14] Malgosia A. Fitzmaurice, 'International Protection of the Environment' (2001) 293 *RDC* 9, 445.

[15] That dam construction could lead to transboundary environmental damage was seen following Canada's construction of the Gut dam in 1903 on the St Lawrence River, which contributed to flooding in United States territory on the shores of Lake Ontario and the St Lawrence River. Although the United States and Canada agreed

been only one international decision on the second group of disputes, those relating to riverine pollution, even though pollution remains an endemic problem in many shared water systems. Although similar cases have been considered in domestic courts of federal states,[16] the one case that has so far been the subject of international adjudication involved environmental issues only tangentially.[17]

6.1.1 Lake Lanoux *case*

The *Lake Lanoux*[18] case falls within the first category of decision, and has been cited frequently to support several environmentally significant rules, most notably the obligation upon states to cooperate in good faith when managing shared water resources.

6.1.1.1 Background

The dispute concerned a French scheme to generate electricity by diverting waters from Lake Lanoux, a large alpine lake in the French Pyrenees, to the Ariège River. As originally planned the scheme would have led to the permanent removal of a large quantity of water from the Carol River, a tributary of Lake Lanoux, which flowed into Spain where it supported a range of agricultural interests. After Spain opposed the original project, and rejected an offer of monetary compensation,

to submit the dispute to ad hoc arbitration (1965 Canada – United States Agreement Concerning the Establishment of an International Arbitral Tribunal to Dispose of United States Claims Relating to Gut Dam) the matter was later discontinued when the United States accepted Canada's offer of a lump-sum settlement (1968 Agreement on the Settlement of Claims Relating to the Gut Dam).

16 Note in particular the involvement by the United States Supreme Court in resolving disputes between states of the union concerning the pollution of interstate watercourses. See *Missouri* v. *Illinois and the Sanitary District of Chicago*, 180 US 208 (1901); 200 US 496 (1905) (in which Missouri sought an injunction to restrain Illinois from discharging sewage into the Des Plaines River) and *New York* v. *New Jersey* 256, US 296 (1920) (in which New York sought an injunction to restrain New Jersey from discharging sewage into New York Bay).

17 *Protection of the Rhine Against Pollution by Chlorides* Arbitration in Application of the Convention of 3 December 1976 and the Additional Protocol of 25 September 1991 (12 March 2004) (Pt I available at www.pca_cpa.org/ENGLISH/RPC/PBF/Sentence%20I.pdf and Pt II available at www.pca_cpa.org/ENGLISH/RPC/PBF/Sentence%20II.pdf) related primarily to a technical issue concerning the financing by France of measures undertaken in conjunction with the Netherlands and the other states parties to control the discharge of chlorides into the Rhine. However, the tribunal did note (at [103]) that the 'polluter pays' principle was not part of general international law, and therefore was not relevant to an interpretation of the Convention.

18 *Lake Lanoux* case (*France/Spain*) (1957) 12 *RIAA* 285.

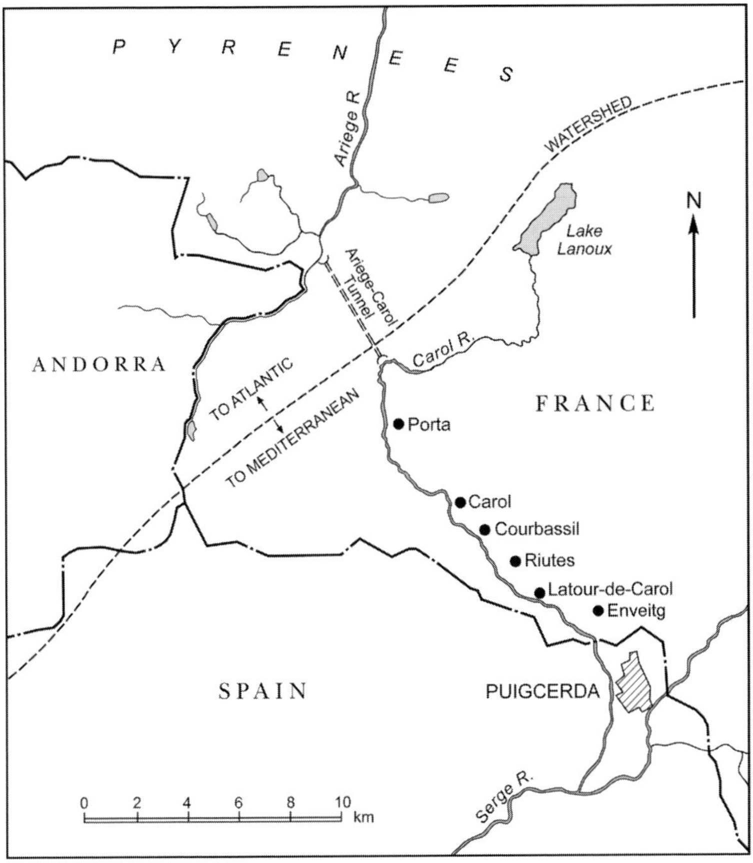

Figure 6.1 Lake Lanoux and the Carol and Ariège rivers

France proposed an alternative arrangement which would return to the Carol, via an underground tunnel, the same quantity of water removed from its headwaters. However, Spain also rejected this scheme, essentially because France would thereby assume control over continued flows of the Carol.

The parties agreed to submit the dispute to arbitration,[19] and the question posed for the tribunal was a narrow one: whether the French government could commence the modified project without Spain's

[19] 1956 Arbitral Compromis on the Interpretation of the Treaty of Bayonne of 26 May 1866 and Additional Act of the Same Date Concerning the Utilisation of the Waters of Lake Lanoux.

consent consistent with the provisions of the 1866 France–Spain Treaty of Delimitation (1866 Treaty of Bayonne)[20] and the 1866 Additional Act to the Delimitation Treaties Concluded on 2 December 1856, 14 April 1862 and 26 May 1866. The tribunal divided this question into two sub-questions: whether the proposed scheme would itself infringe Spain's rights or, if not, whether Spain's consent was required before work on the project could commence.[21]

Spain had not argued that the French works would pollute the waters of the Carol, or that the water to be returned would differ in chemical composition or temperature.[22] Instead the Spanish argument was simply that the French proposal would lead to the '*de facto* preponderance of one Party in place of the equality of the two parties as provided' in the 1866 Treaty of Bayonne and the Additional Act[23] by making the restoration of the Carol's waters dependent on French government action. The tribunal considered that Spain was here making a twofold submission which related:

> on the one hand, to the prohibition, in the absence of the consent of the other Party, of compensation between two basins, despite the equivalence of what is diverted and what is restored, and, on the other hand, the prohibition, without the consent of the other Party, of all acts which may create by a *de facto* inequality the physical possibility of a violation of rights.[24]

6.1.1.2 Award

The essence of Spain's first argument was that the hydrographic basins of the Ariège and Carol River systems should remain in their natural state. The tribunal's response to this contention was unequivocal – nature must bend to the law:

> [T]he unity of a basin is sanctioned at the juridical level only to the extent that it corresponds to human realities. The water which by nature constitutes a fungible item may be the object of a restitution which does not change its qualities in regard to human needs. A diversion with restitution, such as that envisaged by the French project, does not change a state of affairs organised for the working of the requirements of social life.[25]

It is clear therefore that the tribunal conceived of water resources as constituting in law an interchangeable commodity, existing solely for the

[20] The 1866 Treaty of Bayonne was one of three treaties settling the border between France and Spain.
[21] *Lake Lanoux* case (1957) 12 *RIAA* 285, 301. [22] *Ibid.* 303. [23] *Ibid.* [24] *Ibid.* 304.
[25] *Ibid.*

satisfaction of human needs. The key issue was therefore ensuring the return of an equivalent amount of water to the watercourse, not how that return was effected and certainly not whether an upstream project would result in the permanent alteration of the watercourse environment. In this conceptual framework there was little or no room for a consideration of the ecological impacts that the French scheme might have upon either the Carol or the Ariège, even had they been raised by Spain.

In relation to the control that France would assume over future flows into the Carol, the tribunal rejected Spain's argument that this was illegal. France had given an assurance that it would not impair Spain's rights, and bad faith was not to be presumed:[26]

> [T]he growing ascendancy of man over the forces and the secrets of nature has put into his hands instruments which he can use to violate his pledges just as much as for the common good of all; the risk of an evil use has so far not led to subjecting the possession of these means of action to the authorisation of the States which may possibly be threatened.[27]

Having disposed of the first main issue, the tribunal then considered the second, namely whether France could carry out the project without Spain's consent. The tribunal concluded that there was no right of veto, but instead

> international practice prefers to resort to less extreme solutions by confining itself to obliging the States to seek, by preliminary negotiations, terms for an agreement, without subordinating the exercise of their competences to the conclusion of such an agreement.[28]

It was acknowledged by the tribunal that even if there did exist a principle which prevented upstream states from altering the waters of a river so as to 'prejudice the downstream State' such a rule was not relevant here because the French scheme 'will not alter the waters of the Carol'.[29]

The final issue addressed by the tribunal was French adherence to a series of obligations contained in the 1866 Treaty of Bayonne and the Additional Act concerning prior notice and the establishment of 'machinery for dealing with compensation claims and safeguards for all interests involved on either side'.[30] There was no doubt as to French compliance with its notice obligations. As to the second set of obligations, those concerning adequate consideration of downstream interests, the Tribunal noted that a strict interpretation of the relevant provision,

[26] *Ibid.* 305. [27] *Ibid.* 305–6. [28] *Ibid.* 306. [29] *Ibid.* 308. [30] *Ibid.* 314–15.

article 11 of the Additional Act, would lead to the inclusion of only those interests which related to riparian rights. Interestingly, the tribunal instead preferred what it called 'a more liberal interpretation',[31] so that '*account must be taken of all interests, of whatsoever nature*, which are liable to be affected by the works undertaken, even if they do not correspond to a right'.[32] However, while extolling the need to consider all interests of 'whatsoever nature', the tribunal did not include 'nature' itself among these. None the less it is perhaps conceivable that had Spain invoked such environmental concerns France would have been required to pay due regard to them.

6.1.1.3 Legacy

One commentator has noted that the *Lake Lanoux* case illustrated the constructive role of adjudication in resolving a 'venomous dispute',[33] and in enunciating foundational principles of international environmental law.[34] However, the litigation was clearly not directly concerned with issues of an environmental character. Even though the subject matter of the case related to the substantial alteration of natural flows in the headwaters of a shared watercourse, there was a striking absence of any recognition of environmental issues in the pleadings or the decision. The tribunal simply assumed that returning the same quantity of water would lead to Spain being placed in exactly the same situation as it was before construction of the French scheme. It was, of course, not obvious that the ecology of the Carol or the Ariège would have remained unaltered, although this question was never before the tribunal as it was not raised by Spain. None the less, and despite these limitations, the decision does illustrate that litigation argued on the basis of the rights of states *qua* states can serve important environmental objectives. A downstream state successful in arguing that an upstream user should not interfere with a shared basin serves not only to protect its agricultural or other industries dependent on an international river, but it can also effectively serve to protect the equilibrium of ecosystems that would otherwise be disturbed.

As the tribunal ventured beyond the precise terms of its remit and considered general principles of international law, the *Lake Lanoux* case made an important contribution to the development of international

[31] *Ibid.* [32] *Ibid.* (emphasis added).

[33] Cesare P. R. Romano, *The Peaceful Settlement of International Environmental Disputes: A Pragmatic Approach* (2000) 219.

[34] *Ibid.*

water law. The tribunal clearly recognised the right of upper riparians to develop an international watercourse without having to seek the prior agreement of any lower riparian. However, the tribunal also articulated two environmentally important limitations. In the first place it was emphasised that states should cooperate wherever possible to reach a shared solution, that the upper riparian should engage in negotiations to this end when proposing works, and above all should seek in good faith to accommodate all interests concerned. Although the tribunal did not refer to environmental considerations as among these interests, the emphasis placed upon cooperation can be seen to be the foundation of modern international law relating to the utilisation of shared watercourses.[35] Second, while inapplicable in the case before it, the tribunal also noted that 'there [was] a principle which prohibits the upstream State from altering the waters of a river in such a fashion as seriously to prejudice the downstream State'.[36] While expressed narrowly, this essentially reaffirms the principle adopted in the *Trail Smelter* case.[37]

6.1.2 River Oder *case*

Although the case was not concerned with environmental matters, or indeed with issues relating to the non-navigational uses of international watercourses more generally, the decision of the PCIJ in the *Territorial Jurisdiction of the International Commission of the River Oder*[38] case is frequently cited in the environmental context. This is chiefly because the PCIJ provided a simple and elegant statement of the 'community of

35 Alan E. Boyle, 'Codification of International Environmental Law and the International Law Commission: Injurious Consequences Revisited' in Alan E. Boyle and David Freestone (eds.), *International Law and Sustainable Development: Past Achievements and Future Challenges* (1999) 61, 80; Alan E. Boyle, 'The Principle of Co-operation: The Environment' in A. Vaughan Lowe and Colin Warbrick (eds.), *The United Nations and the Principles of International Law: Essays in Honour of Michael Akehurst* (1994) 120, 122.

36 *Lake Lanoux* case (1957) 12 *RIAA* 285, 308. See also the *San Juan River* case (*Costa Rica/Nicaragua*) (1888) 2 Moore 1964, 1964–5 in which President Cleveland, as arbitrator of the dispute, held that 'Costa Rica cannot prevent the Republic of Nicaragua from executing ... within her own territory ... works of improvement, provided such works ... do not result in the occupation or flooding or damage of Costa Rica territory'.

37 *Trail Smelter* case (*Canada/United States*) (1938 and 1941) 3 *RIAA* 1911.

38 *Territorial Jurisdiction of the International Commission of the River Oder (Czechoslovakia, Denmark, France, Germany, Great Britain, Sweden/Poland)* [1929] PCIJ (ser. A) no. 23 (*River Oder* case).

interests' theory, which asserts that a natural resource shared by two or more states is common property and must be subject to equitable use by all interested states.[39] In this respect the case is discussed here as an important precursor to the ICJ's judgment in the *Gabčíkovo-Nagymaros Project* case[40] in which this early decision was expressly affirmed, and its reasoning extended.

6.1.2.1 Background

The dispute in the *River Oder* case concerned the competence of the International Commission of the Oder, a body established by part XII of the 1919 Treaty of Peace Between the Allied and Associated Powers and Germany (Treaty of Versailles), to manage the use of the river.[41] Article 331 of the Treaty of Versailles provided that sections of the Elbe, the Vltava, the Niemen, and the Danube 'and all navigable parts of these river systems which naturally provide more than one State with access to the sea' were 'declared international'. Under article 343, the Oder Commission was tasked with defining the sections of the Oder and its tributaries to which the international regime applied.

The Oder Commission became deadlocked when discharging this function. The Polish representative insisted that the Warthe and Netze tributaries beyond the Polish frontier were excluded from the Oder Commission's jurisdiction.[42] However, the other members of the commission (Czechoslovakia, Denmark, France, Germany, Great Britain, and Sweden) took the opposite position, and sought the greatest possible access to the entire river system.[43] By special agreement the parties submitted a two-part question to the PCIJ, namely whether the jurisdiction of the Commission extended to the Polish sections of the Warthe

[39] The *River Oder* case stands in contrast to the other decision of the PCIJ touching upon water law issues, the *Diversion of Water from the River Meuse* (*Netherlands* v. *Belgium*) [1937] PCIJ (ser. A/B) no. 70. That case, which similarly did not raise environmental questions, is of far more limited significance because the PCIJ insisted that the dispute was to be determined solely by reference to bilateral arrangements between the Netherlands and Belgium concerning the diversion of water from the Meuse.

[40] *Gabčíkovo-Nagymaros Project* case (*Hungary/Slovakia*) (merits) [1997] ICJ Rep 7.

[41] The Oder (or Odra) River begins in what is now the Czech Republic, passes through western Poland, later forming the border between Poland and Germany and ultimately emptying into the Baltic Sea.

[42] *River Oder* case [1929] PCIJ (ser. A) no. 23, 14. These tributaries rose in Poland and passed across the border into Germany before converging and joining the Oder.

[43] *Ibid.*

and Netze and, if so, what principle was to guide the Commission in determining the upstream limits of its jurisdiction.[44]

6.1.2.2 PCIJ decision

Although the issue at the centre of the dispute was primarily one concerning navigation rights, the PCIJ enunciated a general principle that has been influential in the broader context of non-navigational watercourse issues. In aid of its interpretation of article 331 of the Treaty of Versailles, the Court considered that it must 'go back to the principles governing international fluvial law in general',[45] and in a critical passage set out the 'community of interest' concept:

> [W]hen consideration is given to the manner in which States have regarded the concrete situations arising out of the fact that a single waterway traverses or separates the territory of more than one State, and the possibility of fulfilling the requirements of justice and the considerations of utility which this fact places in relief, it is at once seen that a solution of the problem has been sought not in the idea of right of passage in favour of upstream States, but in that of a community of interest of riparian States. *This community of interest in a navigable river becomes the basis of a common legal right, the essential features of which are the perfect equality of all riparian States in the user of the whole course of the river and the exclusion of any preferential privilege of any one riparian State in relation to the others…*[46]

The Court held that the common right of navigation extended throughout the navigable course of the river irrespective of political boundaries,[47] and concluded that the Treaty of Versailles adopted the position of 'complete internationalization'.[48] Accordingly, the Commission possessed jurisdiction over the navigable portions of the Warthe and the Netze in Polish territory.

6.1.3 Gabčíkovo-Nagymaros Project *case*

The community of interest theory also arose in the *Gabčíkovo-Nagymaros Project* case, in which an environmental controversy concerning the development of the Danube was nested within in a broader dispute involving the law of treaties, state responsibility and the succession of states.[49] Indeed, in many ways the dispute involved a clash between

[44] *Ibid.* 6. [45] *Ibid.* 26. [46] *Ibid.* 27 (emphasis added).
[47] *Ibid.* 27–8. [48] *Ibid.*
[49] Stephen M. Schwebel, 'The Judgment of the International Court of Justice in the *case concerning the Gabčíkovo-Nagymaros Project (Hungary/Slovakia)*' in International Bureau

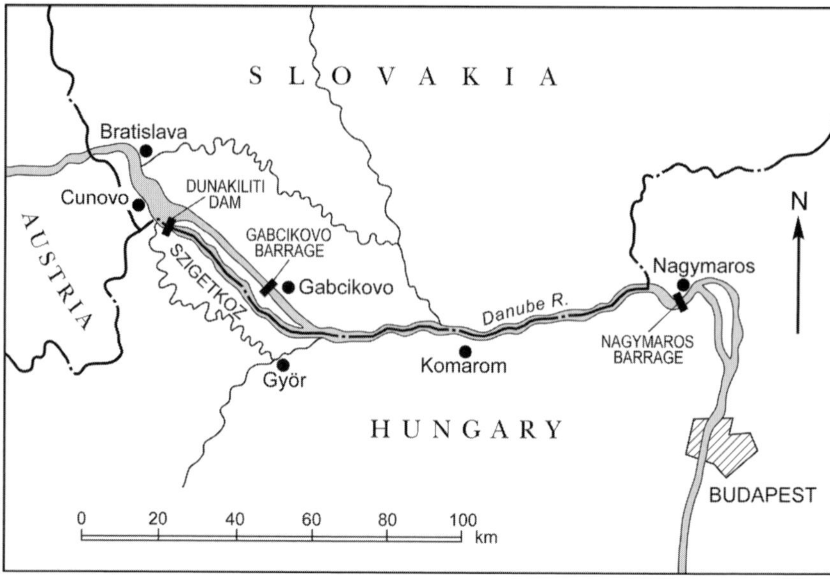

Figure 6.2 The original Gabčíkovo-Nagymaros project[50]

established principles of public international law concerning treaty performance and state responsibility and evolving principles of international environmental law.[51]

6.1.3.1 Background

The dispute concerned a joint project between Hungary and Czechoslovakia to construct a series of locks and dams along a shared stretch of the Danube. The Danube is the second longest river in Europe, and drains an area of 817,000 square kilometres, including all or part of Austria, Germany, Hungary, Czech Republic, Slovakia, Slovenia, Croatia, Bosnia and Herzegovina, Serbia, Montenegro, Bulgaria, Romania, Moldova, and Ukraine before discharging into the Black Sea.

of the Permanent Court of Arbitration (ed.), *Resolution of International Water Disputes* (2003) 247, 258.

[50] Adapted from 'Sketch-Map no. 2: The Original Project' in *Gabčíkovo-Nagymaros Project* case [1997] ICJ Rep 7, 21.

[51] Rosalyn Higgins, 'Natural Resources in the Case Law of the International Court' in Alan E. Boyle and David Freestone (eds.), *International Law and Sustainable Development: Past Achievements and Future Challenges* (1999) 87, 105.

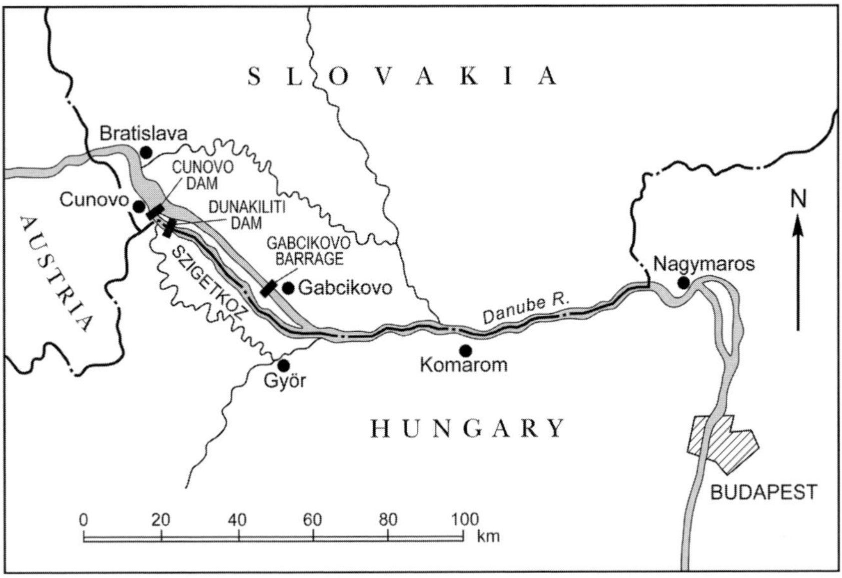

Figure 6.3 Variant C to the Gabčíkovo-Nagymaros project[52]

The details of the joint project, which was designed to produce hydroelectricity, improve navigation, and to improve flood protection, were set out in a bilateral agreement, the 1977 Treaty Concerning the Construction and Operation of the Gabčíkovo-Nagymaros System of Locks. Article 1(1) of that instrument provided for the construction of two systems of locks, one at Gabčíkovo (in what was then Czechoslovakia) and a second at Nagymaros (in Hungary), which were to form 'a single and indivisible' operational system. The treaty also included provisions addressing the environmental impacts of the project, by which the parties undertook to maintain high standards of water quality in the Danube.[53] Hungary and Slovakia also committed themselves to 'compliance with the obligations [imposed by general international law] for the protection of nature arising in connection with the construction and operation of the System of Locks'.[54] More detailed measures to protect the ecology of the Danube were to be incorporated in a 'joint contractual plan'.

[52] Adapted from 'Sketch-Map no. 3: "Variant C"' in *Gabčíkovo-Nagymaros Project* case [1997] ICJ Rep 7, 26.

[53] 1977 Treaty, art. 15.

[54] *Ibid.* art. 19.

The terms of the joint project required the construction of a dam and reservoir at Dunakiliti together with a series of locks at Nagymaros, which was within Hungarian territory. By early 1989 the project along the shared stretches of the Danube was well advanced, with the Dunakiliti dam 90 per cent complete.[55] The Gabčíkovo dam, wholly inside Czechoslovak territory, was also 85 per cent finished.[56] However, in the Nagymaros sector only minor preparatory works had been completed, and in May 1989, following strong domestic opposition on environmental grounds, Hungary decided to suspend further work. It was argued that there was inadequate knowledge of the environmental risks both in terms of ecological and water quality impacts.[57] Subsequently, in October 1989, Hungary abandoned the project at Nagymaros altogether,[58] while retaining the partially completed Dunakiliti complex.[59] Although the Czechoslovak president at one stage described the entire dam scheme as a 'totalitarian, gigomaniac monument which is against nature', the Czechoslovak government insisted that the project should be completed and to this end investigated alternative plans.[60] In November 1991 it began construction of 'variant C' which involved the unilateral diversion of the Danube and the construction of a dam at Cunovo.[61]

6.1.3.2 Three questions

In May 1992 the Hungarian government formally notified Czechoslovakia that the 1977 Treaty was terminated.[62] In 1993, shortly after Czechoslovakia was dissolved and Slovakia attained independence, Hungary and Slovakia then agreed to submit the dispute to the ICJ.[63] This decision to refer the dispute to the Court came after considerable efforts were expended by the European Commission to promote a negotiated settlement.[64] The Court was requested to decide three main questions, namely whether Hungary was entitled to suspend and abandon the works, whether Slovakia was entitled to proceed with variant C, and the legal effects of Hungary's purported termination

[55] *Gabčíkovo-Nagymaros Project* case [1997] ICJ Rep 7, [31].
[56] *Ibid.* [57] *Ibid.* [34]. [58] *Ibid.* [37]. [59] *Ibid.* [38].
[60] *Ibid.* [61] *Ibid.* [23]. [62] *Ibid.* [23].
[63] 1993 Special Agreement between the Republic of Hungary and the Slovak Republic for Submission to the International Court of Justice of the Differences between them concerning the Gabčíkovo-Nagymaros Project.
[64] Paul R. Williams, *International Law and the Resolution of Central and East Asian Transboundary Environmental Disputes* (2000) 68–73.

of the treaty.[65] In relation to all three questions, which will now be considered in turn, Hungary expressly based its arguments on environmental concerns.[66]

Suspension and abandonment of works

In order to justify its conduct in suspending and abandoning work on the joint project, Hungary relied first on a 'state of ecological necessity'.[67] In this respect several environmental dangers were identified. First, the scale of the Dunakiliti reservoir and the use of the Gabčíkovo dynamo in peak mode twice a day would reduce flows along the Danube river bed to a 'trickle', thereby 'condem[ning] to extinction'[68] the fauna and flora of the river and the Szigetköz alluvial plains. Second, in relation to the Nagymaros locks, Hungary argued that they would lead to vast quantities of silt accumulating in the river, thereby lowering water quality and threatening aquatic habitats. For its part Slovakia argued that international law did not permit a 'state of ecological necessity' to be invoked either to suspend treaty obligations, or as a defence for an otherwise internationally wrongful act.[69] Slovakia also contested the factual basis for Hungary's claim, arguing that it was overly pessimistic and that while environmental problems were significant, they could be addressed.[70]

The Court assessed Hungary's ecological necessity argument on the basis of what was then article 33 of the Draft Articles on Responsibility of States for Internationally Wrongful Acts,[71] which the parties and the

[65] 1993 Special Agreement, art. 2(1).

[66] For a comprehensive appraisal of Hungary's environmental concerns see Williams, above n. 62, 55–7.

[67] *Gabčíkovo-Nagymaros Project* case [1997] ICJ Rep 7, [40]. Necessity has been raised in several situations involving environmental damage. In the Russian fur seals controversy of 1892 the Russian government issued a decree prohibiting sealing in an area of the high seas in the Bering Sea and explained that this action was taken because of 'absolute necessity' in light of the imminent opening of the hunting season. In the *Torrey Canyon* incident of March 1967, the British government in bombing the Liberian oil tanker that had run aground off the coast of Cornwall beyond the British territorial sea justified its actions on the basis of necessity. In the *Fisheries Jurisdiction* case (*Spain* v. *Canada*) (jurisdiction and admissibility) [1998] ICJ Rep 431 necessity was an issue as Canada claimed that it was entitled to exercise legislative and enforcement jurisdiction over a Spanish fishing vessel on the high seas in order to prevent the extinction of Greenland halibut. See James Crawford, *The International Law Commission's Articles on State Responsibility* (2002) 180–2.

[68] *Gabčíkovo-Nagymaros Project* case [1997] ICJ Rep 7, [40]. [69] *Ibid.* [44]. [70] *Ibid.*

[71] Art. 33 was finally adopted, with some amendments, as art. 25 of the Articles on Responsibility of States for Internationally Wrongful Acts, art. 2, Report of

Court accepted as reflecting customary international law. The Court noted that the environment could constitute an 'essential interest' for the purposes of the necessity defence, and pointed out that in the *Legality of the Threat or Use of Nuclear Weapons*[72] it had stressed the 'great significance that it attaches to respect for the environment'.[73] However, the Court concluded that the perils invoked by Hungary 'were not sufficiently established in 1989', were not imminent and, in any event, that Hungary could implement mitigation measures rather than abandoning the works.[74]

Several aspects of the Court's reasoning here are open to criticism. Although the Court stated that it was not necessary to reach a view as to which party's scientific evidence was better founded,[75] the Court did in fact engage in a relatively detailed assessment of the gravity and imminence of the ecological risks asserted by Hungary. Moreover, in evaluating the evidence the Court effectively required Hungary to establish the alleged risks to a very high degree of scientific certainty, an approach which effectively precluded the operation of the precautionary principle.[76] While this may well have been justified given the exceptional character of the necessity defence, the Court made no attempt to explain the relationship between the law of state responsibility and developing rules of international environmental law.

Variant C

Slovakia's unilateral commencement of variant C involved the construction of a dam and reservoir at Cunovo, and the diversion of 80 to 90 per cent of the waters of the Danube to a bypass canal for hydroelectric power generation at Gabčíkovo. The environmental concerns in

the International Law Commission, 53rd Session, UN Doc A/56/10 (2001). The commentary to art. 25 observes that necessity 'has been invoked to protect a wide variety of interests, including safeguarding the environment, preserving the very existence of the State and its people in time of public emergency, or ensuring the safety of a civilian population' (at 83).

72 *Legality of the Threat or Use of Nuclear Weapons* [1996] ICJ Rep 226 (*Nuclear Weapons* advisory opinion).

73 *Gabčíkovo-Nagymaros Project* case [1997] ICJ Rep 7, [53]. 74 *Ibid.* [57]. 75 *Ibid.* [54].

76 Afshin A-Khavari and Donald R. Rothwell, 'The ICJ and the Danube Dam Case: A Missed Opportunity for International Environmental Law?' (1998) 22 *MULR* 507, 514. See also Stephen Stec and Gabriel E. Eckstein, 'Of Solemn Oaths and Obligations: The Environmental Impact of the ICJ's Decision in the *Case Concerning the Gabcikovo-Nagymaros Project*' (1997) 8 *YIEL* 41, 49; Daniel Dobos, 'The Necessity of Precaution: The Future of Ecological Necessity and the Precautionary Principle' (2002) 13 *FordhamELJ* 375.

relation to variant C were essentially the same as those for the original project as it involved an almost complete diversion of water from the Danube.

Slovakia justified the legality of variant C on two main grounds. First, it was said that Hungary's abandonment of the Dunakiliti works meant that Slovakia was entitled to proceed with a solution that 'closely approximated' the original project. Second, Slovakia argued that even if prima facie unlawful, variant C could none the less be justified as a legitimate countermeasure. In relation to the first argument, the Court did not determine whether there was a principle of 'approximate application' but found that even if such a principle did exist it would only allow an alternative scheme within the limits of the treaty. Variant C was not within those limits because it was a unilateral measure whereas the 1977 Treaty provided for joint ownership and management of the project as a coordinated single unit.[77]

It was in responding to Slovakia's countermeasures argument that the ICJ sought to draw most extensively upon general principles of international water law. The Court noted that Hungary's refusal to participate in the project 'could not mean that Hungary forfeited its basic right to *an equitable and reasonable sharing of the resources of an international watercourse*'.[78] In support of this principle the Court cited the dictum in the *River Oder* case that the 'community of interest in a navigable river becomes the basis of a common legal right'.[79] The Court also referred to the UN Watercourses Convention as evidencing acceptance of the community of interest theory, despite the fact that the Convention had not yet entered into force.[80]

The ICJ's strong approval of the community of interest theory was highly significant. At a conceptual level the theory has obvious affinities with the general notion, derived from Roman law,[81] that natural systems which cross or are beyond borders (i.e. international rivers, the atmosphere, and the oceans) are common property requiring cooperative management by all members of the relevant community.[82] There

[77] *Gabčíkovo-Nagymaros Project* case [1997] ICJ Rep 7, [78]. [78] *Ibid.* (emphasis added).

[79] *River Oder* case [1929] PCIJ (ser. A) no. 23, 27.

[80] *Gabčíkovo-Nagymaros Project* case [1997] ICJ Rep 7, [147].

[81] See e.g. Justinian, *Institutiones* (Peter Birks and Grant McLeod trans. 1987) II.1.1: 'The things which are naturally everybody's are: air, flowing water, the sea, and the sea-shore.'

[82] One commentator has even suggested that the 'community of interest' theory could be developed further in line with conceptions of 'common heritage': McCaffrey, above n. 5, 172–3: 'The international community has devised a system for sharing

are also important intersections between the community of interest notion and the 'ecosystem approach' to environmental management adopted in recent environmental agreements.[83] The theory emphasises the need to view an international watercourse as a whole, having regard to the entire 'community' of interested states dependent upon it. It also implies that states sharing an international river should be concerned not only with an equitable distribution of water resources, but also with the protection of the whole riverine ecosystem from a river's headwaters to its terminus.

These aspects of the theory were not expressly considered by the ICJ. The Court simply concluded that Slovakia had deprived Hungary 'of its right to an equitable and reasonable share of the natural resources of the Danube – with the continuing effects of the diversion of these waters on the ecology of the riparian area of the Szigetköz'.[84] The absence of any elaboration on this cursory reference to ecological issues appeared on its face to constitute a major opportunity missed, as the relationship between environmental concerns and rules relating to equitable use of watercourses has been a source of ongoing uncertainty in international water law. Boyle has none the less argued that, if the judgment is viewed as a whole, the Court did appear to have set the notion of equitable utilisation in the broader context of 'environmentally *sustainable* utilisation' and therefore the judgment represents 'the most radical re-writing of the law relating to international watercourses since the *River Oder* case'.[85]

Purported treaty termination

Hungary proffered five arguments to justify its purported termination of the 1977 treaty, four of which raised environmental concerns. The first of these, that a state of ecological necessity existed which allowed Hungary to terminate the treaty, was promptly rejected on

the resources of the sea with developing and geographically disadvantaged states. It would seem equally important that it begin the elaboration of a system for the sharing of the world's freshwater resources equitably among all states, especially those that are *hydrologically* disadvantaged' (emphasis in original).

[83] See e.g. Biodiversity Convention, art. 8. The ecosystem approach has been particularly prominent in the Antarctic context: see the Madrid Protocol and the 1980 Convention on the Conservation of Antarctic Marine Living Resources, art. I(3).

[84] *Gabčíkovo-Nagymaros Project* case [1997] ICJ Rep 7, [85].

[85] Alan E. Boyle, 'The *Gabcikovo-Nagymaros Case:* New Law in Old Bottles' (1997) 8 *YIEL* 17.

the grounds that necessity might exonerate a state of responsibility, but could not justify termination of a treaty. Second, Hungary sought to rely on the principle of impossibility of performance,[86] arguing that an essential object of the treaty (a joint investment arrangement consistent with norms of environmental protection) had disappeared. The Court dismissed this argument, holding that '[t]he 1977 Treaty – and in particular its Articles 15, 19 and 20 – actually made available to the parties the necessary means to proceed at any time, by negotiation, to the required readjustments between economic imperatives and ecological imperatives'.[87] Third, Hungary submitted that there had been a fundamental change of circumstances including 'the progress of environmental knowledge and the development of new norms and prescriptions of international environmental law'.[88] Applying article 62 of the VCLT, the Court stated that developments in environmental knowledge and international environmental law were not 'completely unforeseen' and in any event 'the formulation of Articles 15, 19 and 20, which were designed to accommodate change, made it possible for the parties to take account of such developments and to apply them when implementing those treaty provisions'.[89]

The fourth and final environment related treaty law argument made by Hungary was the most ambitious. Hungary contended that it could terminate the 1977 Treaty on the basis that 'new requirements of international law for the protection of the environment precluded performance of the Treaty'. The Court again rejected this submission, holding that there was no conflict between the treaty and emerging principles of international environmental law. This was because such new norms could be incorporated through articles 15, 19 and 20 which were not 'specific obligations of performance' but instead required the parties to take environmental considerations, including developing principles, into account on an ongoing basis. The 1977 Treaty, it was concluded, was 'not static, and [was] open to adapt to emerging norms of international law'.[90]

The Court emphasised the importance of discharging this joint responsibility because, as it had held in its *Nuclear Weapons* advisory opinion, 'the environment is not an abstraction but represents the living space, the quality of life and the very health of human beings,

[86] As reflected in art. 61 of the VCLT.
[87] *Gabčíkovo-Nagymaros Project* case [1997] ICJ Rep 7, [103].
[88] *Ibid.* [104]. [89] *Ibid.* [104]. [90] *Ibid.* [111].

including generations unborn'.[91] The repetition of this statement in two places in the judgment in the *Gabčíkovo-Nagymaros Project* case communicated a clear recognition by the Court of the growing importance of environmental concerns within international law. None the less it should be noted that in reciting this passage the Court also reaffirmed a rationale for environmental protection that was wholly anthropocentric (the preservation of nature as a human life support system) rather than one which acknowledged the intrinsic value of the environment.

Moreover, the Court did not identify the relevant principles of international environmental law which could assist the parties in adapting the 1977 Treaty to meet the growing international awareness of environmental vulnerability. It was suggested instead that the parties should continue to work together, and possibly seek the assistance of a third party, in responding to the environmental challenges that the project posed.[92] Significantly the Court did not adopt a consistent explanation as to why the parties were required to take into account evolving norms of international environmental law.[93] While in this part of the judgment the Court suggested that such norms were incorporated by reference in the 1977 Treaty, later in its reasons the Court appears to conclude that new principles of international environmental law have a general applicability to existing treaty regimes.[94] The latter, more expansive approach is clearly to be preferred and environmental norms crystallising in customary international law after the conclusion of a treaty should be applied in the interpretation and application of the treaty unless it specifically excludes their operation.[95]

6.1.3.3 Future conduct of the parties

When it came to prescribing the future conduct of the parties, the Court held that the parties should negotiate an agreement for the operation of the joint project consistent with the 1977 Treaty, and with developing principles of international environmental law. The Court also took note of several facts on the ground, including that the Gabčíkovo power plant had operated for seven years fed by a smaller reservoir

[91] *Ibid.* [112] (citing *Nuclear Weapons* advisory opinion [1996] ICJ Rep 226, [29]).

[92] *Ibid.* [93] Boyle, above n. 85, 15.

[94] *Gabčíkovo-Nagymaros Project* case [1997] ICJ Rep 7, [140].

[95] Boyle, above n. 85, 15–16. See also Fragmentation of International Law: Difficulties Arising from the Diversification and Expansion of International Law: Report of the Study Group of the International Law Commission, Finalised by Chairman M. Koskenniemi ILC, UN Doc. A/CN.4/L.682 [475]–[480].

than originally planned. Environmental concerns were 'of necessity a key issue'[96] and had to be accommodated within the framework of the 1977 Treaty. In what is undoubtedly the most environmentally significant passage to be found in any of its decisions, the Court made implicit reference to the precautionary principle, identified the development of international environmental law in tandem with growing scientific awareness of environmental risks, expressly referred to the concept of sustainable development, and sought to apply the principle to the dispute at hand:

> The Court is mindful that, in the field of environmental protection, vigilance and prevention are required on account of the often irreversible character of damage to the environment and of the limitations inherent in the very mechanism of reparation of this type of damage.
>
> Throughout the ages, mankind has, for economic and other reasons, constantly interfered with nature. In the past, this was often done without consideration of the effects upon the environment. Owing to new scientific insights and to a growing awareness of the risks for mankind – for present and future generations – of pursuit of such interventions at an unconsidered and unabated pace, new norms and standards have been developed, set forth in a great number of instruments during the last two decades. Such new norms have to be taken into consideration, and such new standards given proper weight, not only when States contemplate new activities but also when continuing with activities begun in the past. This need to reconcile economic development with protection of the environment is aptly expressed in the concept of sustainable development. For the purposes of the present case, this means that the Parties together should look afresh at the effects on the environment of the Gabčíkovo power plant. In particular they must find a satisfactory solution for the volume of water to be released into the old bed of the Danube and into the side-arms on both sides of the river.[97]

Judge Weeramantry in his separate opinion explored the principle of sustainable development in far greater detail. He stopped short of recognising the notion as a binding norm, and he did not conclude that the original project and variant C were 'unsustainable'. However, for Judge Weeramantry sustainable development was 'more than a mere *concept*' and was 'a *principle* with normative value which is crucial to the determination of this case'.[98] Drawing on diverse practice from various legal traditions, Judge Weeramantry concluded that sustainable development

[96] *Gabčíkovo-Nagymaros Project* case [1997] ICJ Rep 7, [140]. [97] *Ibid.*

[98] *Gabčíkovo-Nagymaros Project* case [1997] ICJ Rep 7, separate opinion of Vice-President Weeramantry, 88 (emphasis added).

was 'one of the most ancient of ideas in the human heritage'.[99] For Judge Weeramantry it reconciled what he considered to be two human rights: the right to environment and the right to development.

Applying 'sustainable development'

Even though the Court (and indeed Judge Weeramantry) stopped short of recognising sustainable development as a binding rule of law, the concept was used by the Court in a meaningful way of integrating developmental and environmental considerations.[100] Lowe has argued in this respect that the Court correctly refrained from accepting sustainable development as a customary rule of law, on the grounds that the notion is intrinsically multidimensional and does not possess a fundamentally norm creating character.[101] At best sustainable development 'is a convenient, if imprecise, label for a general policy which may be adopted by states unilaterally, bilaterally, or multilaterally'.[102]

Although not recognised as a positive rule of conduct, the concept of sustainable development was important for the Court's decision, in two important respects. First, the principle was deployed both by the Court and by Judge Weeramantry to reconcile two norms of international law that were openly in conflict in this case – the right to development and the obligation to protect the environment. In this sense sustainable development was used by the Court as a 'meta-principle, acting upon other legal rules and principles – a legal concept exercising a kind of interstitial normativity, pushing and pulling the boundaries of true primary norms when they threaten to overlap or conflict with each other'.[103] The second, related way in which the Court implicitly supported the importance of sustainable development was through its emphasis upon the procedural aspects of the concept.[104] Boyle has

[99] *Ibid.* 110.

[100] Duncan French, *International Law and Policy on Sustainable Development* (2005) 47–51; Philippe Sands, 'International Courts and the Application of the Concept of "Sustainable Development"' (1999) 3 *MaxPlanckYBUNL* 404.

[101] A. Vaughan Lowe, 'Sustainable Development and Unsustainable Arguments' in Alan E. Boyle and David Freestone (eds.), *International Law and Sustainable Development: Past Achievements and Future Challenges* (1999) 19, 30 (referring to the ICJ's use of the term 'fundamentally norm-creating character' in the *North Sea Continental Shelf* cases (*Federal Republic of Germany* v. *Denmark*; *Federal Republic of Germany* v. *Netherlands*) [1969] ICJ Rep 3 to describe those rules of treaty law susceptible to crystallisation as customary rules).

[102] *Ibid.* 30–1. [103] *Ibid.* 31.

[104] Patricia W. Birnie and Alan E. Boyle, *International Law and the Environment* (2nd edn 2002) 96. See generally Phoebe N. Okowa, 'Procedural Obligations in International Environmental Agreements' (1996) 72 *BYBIL* 276.

argued that the case 'was not about the public interest in sustainable development. It was about the public interest in cooperation and in the processes that serve the interests of sustainable development.'[105] The Court required the parties to reconsider the environmental consequences of the project and undertake monitoring and protective measures consistent with contemporary international environmental law.[106] Such an approach allowed the Court to further the objective of sustainable development while at the same time 'relieving [it] of the impossible task of deciding what is and what is not sustainable'.[107] The apparent attraction of this procedural approach to sustainable development is that it allows account to be taken of differing, dispute-specific, views as to where the balance between environmental protection and economic development should lie, while establishing a principled basis upon which an accommodation between these imperatives can be achieved.[108] It is none the less to be regretted that the Court did not elaborate the nature and content of the procedural obligations that appear critically relevant here, namely environmental impact assessment and continuous environmental monitoring.[109]

6.1.3.4 Future of the project

The *Gabčíkovo-Nagymaros Project* case did not lead to a comprehensive resolution of the dispute between Hungary and Slovakia, although it did encourage the parties to continue joint environmental monitoring of the river,[110] and established a legal framework for ongoing negotiations. These discussions have proved difficult and have been punctuated by long periods of abeyance, and arguably have not met the requirement for comprehensive negotiations in good faith required by

[105] Boyle, above n. 85, at 20. [106] Birnie and Boyle, above n. 104, 96.

[107] *Ibid.* [108] French, above n. 100, 72.

[109] These issues were canvassed by Judge Weeramantry in his separate opinion. Judge Weeramantry argued that a continuing obligation to carry out environmental impact assessment was imported into the 1977 Treaty by arts. 15 and 19. He held that the obligation was a principle of international environmental law, namely a specific application of the more general principle of caution which must be read into treaties which have a significant impact upon the environment: *Gabčíkovo-Nagymaros Project* case [1997] ICJ Rep 7, separate opinion of Vice-President Weeramantry, 112.

[110] For a detailed analysis of the joint environmental monitoring of the stretch of the Danube affected by the Gabčíkovo-Nagymaros project, before and after the *Gabčíkovo-Nagymaros Project* case [1997] ICJ Rep 7, see Libor Jansky, Masahiro Murakami, and Nevelina I. Pachova, *The Danube: Environmental Monitoring of an International River* (2004).

the Court.[111] Shortly after the judgment was delivered, Slovakia sought an additional judgment of the Court on the grounds that Hungary had not implemented the 1997 judgment. However, this request was not pressed, and as the parties continue to work together to monitor and mitigate environmental problems stemming from the project it is doubtful whether further involvement by the ICJ would helpfully resolve the dispute.[112]

In broad terms there appear to be two continuing points of disagreement remaining between the parties, the first being the upstream diversion of water for hydropower generation and second Slovakia's insistence that a downstream dam be constructed by Hungary so as to improve navigation and facilitate peak mode operation of the Gabčíkovo dynamo. These raise sensitive questions of environmental policy and science, and the parties have continued to negotiate a resolution to the dispute within the terms of the Court's judgment and the 1977 Treaty. In addition, the environmental concerns that have been raised consistently by Hungary since its initial abandonment of works in 1989 must now be addressed in the context of the European Union's Water Framework Directive, which applies to existing and new dams.[113]

6.1.3.5 Legacy

The judgment of the ICJ in the *Gabčíkovo-Nagymaros Project* case did not produce a comprehensive resolution of the dispute between the parties, and did not involve a clear application of the principle of sustainable development. It was none the less of critical importance for the development of international environmental law.[114] The Court affirmed the community of interest theory which, as has been seen, can be adapted to serve environmental objectives. Most important, however, were the Court's pronouncements on the impact of recent environmental norms upon an existing treaty regime. The judgment asserts the legitimacy

[111] Colter Paulson, 'Compliance with Final Judgments of the International Court of Justice Since 1987' (2004) 98 *AJIL* 434–61, 449.

[112] Constanze Schulte, *Compliance With Decisions of the International Court of Justice* (2004) 249.

[113] Directive of the European Parliament and of the Council Establishing a Framework for Community Action in the Field of Water Policy, 2000/60/EC [2000] OJ L 327.

[114] But see *contra* Johan G. Lammers, 'The Gabcikovo-Nagymaros Case Seen in Particular from the Perspective of the Law of International Watercourses and the Protection of the Environment' (1998) 11 *LJIL* 287, 318 (arguing that the Court's judgment brought few innovations on these topics).

of environmental concerns influencing the operation of a treaty concluded in the late 1970s, which did not have a strong focus on environmental protection. The Court effectively held that the parties could and should update this treaty framework in order to bring the joint dam project into conformity with contemporary international environmental standards.[115]

In addition, although the Court did not enter into a detailed analysis of the content and legal consequences of the concept of sustainable development, the *Gabčíkovo-Nagymaros Project* case does suggest that the ICJ is willing to look beyond the narrow ambit of the dispute to examine general principles and norms that may assist the court in the resolution of a case. However, it would have been preferable for the Court to have explained in express terms the relevance of sustainable development to its reasons, and why other equally important concepts, such as that of environmental impact assessment, and the principles of prevention and precaution, were not considered and given effect.

The Danube is today suffering serious effects from the joint dams project. The construction of the Gabčíkovo dam means that around 8,000 hectares of floodplain forest that was once a thriving wetland must be artificially irrigated. Flows in the main river have also seriously declined as a result of the dam, with only 10 to 20 per cent of original volumes. These radical changes to the hydrology of the basin have led to falls in surface and groundwater levels of up to 4 metres, with serious effects on dependent ecosystems. It may well be the case that a clearer and more expansive decision from the ICJ which ruled on specifics of the project, including the dam at Gabčíkovo, could have helped to prevent and lessened these environmental impacts.

6.1.4 Pulp Mills *case*

The ongoing litigation in the ICJ between Argentina and Uruguay concerning the construction of two paper pulp mills on the River Uruguay near Fray Bentos holds the potential to be the most significant international judicial decision on watercourse law since the *Gabčíkovo-Nagymaros*

[115] Sands observes that this conclusion is 'potentially of great significance, possibly even radical significance': Philippe Sands, 'International Environmental Litigation and its Future' (1999) 32 *URichLR* 1619, 1632. For a discussion of this aspect of this case see also *OSPAR Arbitration (Ireland* v. *United Kingdom)* (final award) (2003) 42 ILM 1118 [101]–[103].

Project case.[116] However, this is not immediately apparent from the two decisions that have been handed down to date on provisional measures requests by the parties.

Argentina instituted proceedings in 2006 under article 60 of the 1975 Statute of the River Uruguay by which the parties agreed to submit disputes arising under the agreement to the ICJ. The 1975 Statute established a joint machinery for the parties to manage the use of River Uruguay, and deals with matters including pollution of the river. In its application Argentina contended that when fully operational the pulp mills would discharge pollutants that would seriously damage the environment of the River Uruguay and have flow on effects for fishery and tourism industries and human health. In terms of the legal consequences of this damage, Argentina submitted that several provisions of the 1975 Statute had been infringed, including obligations to notify the Commission of the River Uruguay and Argentina, to prepare a full environmental impact study, to preserve the aquatic environment and prevent pollution, to protect biodiversity and fisheries, and to cooperate in the prevention of pollution and the projection of biodiversity.

It is unlikely that the Court will adjudicate upon the merits of these matters for some time. However, there have been two decisions on provisional measures applications that give some insights both as to the Court's attitude towards the environmental threats apparently posed by the pulp mills and, more broadly, when it is appropriate to invoke the Court's interim measures jurisdiction in environmental cases. In July 2006 the ICJ ruled on Argentina's request for provisional measures made with its application, while in January 2007 a decision was handed down on a subsequent petition by Uruguay for interim orders. Only Argentina's request concerned environmental issues, with Uruguay's request relating to a blockade by Argentine civil society groups of the international bridge at Fray Brentos in protest against the pulp mill projects.

The measures requested by Argentina were that Uruguay suspend authorisations for the construction of the mills, halt ongoing and proposed building works for the mills, and cooperate with Argentina to implement the 1975 Statute and thereby protect and preserve the riverine environment. For its part Uruguay argued that it had complied fully

[116] *Pulp Mills on the River Uruguay* case (*Argentina* v. *Uruguay*) (request for provisional measures by Argentina) (2006) 45 ILM 1025 (request for provisional measures by Uruguay) (2007) (available at www.icj-cij.org).

with the 1975 Statute, and that there was no current or imminent threat of prejudice to any rights pertaining to Argentina under the agreement. Uruguay also submitted that environmental impact assessments had been carried out, and that the pulp mills would meet stringent environmental controls, including the latest European standards.

As the parties were broadly in agreement on the issue of jurisdiction, the Court readily found that the requirement for prima facie jurisdiction in provisional measures proceedings had been met. However, the ICJ went on to dismiss Argentina's request for interim measures, concluding that the circumstances did not require them. The Court recognised the concerns expressed over the River Uruguay environment and affirmed 'the great significance it attaches to respect for the environment'.[117] However, it found 'nothing in the record to demonstrate that the very decision of Uruguay to authorize the construction of the mills poses an imminent threat of irreparable damage to the aquatic environment of the River Uruguay or to the economic and social interests of the riparian inhabitants'.[118] It noted in this respect that the threat of pollution was not imminent because the two mills were not expected to be operational until August 2007 and June 2008 respectively. However, the Court also went on to find that Argentina had not presented any evidence that pollution from the operation of the mills 'would be of a character to cause irreparable damage'.[119] No reasons were provided for this conclusion, notwithstanding the copious submissions made by Argentina on the environmental impacts. As noted by Judge ad hoc Vineusa in his dissenting opinion, in adopting this approach the Court resiled from applying the precautionary principle and shifted the onus of proof on Argentina to establish environmental damage, rather than requiring Uruguay, as the project proponent, to establish that the mills would be environmentally benign.

In essence Argentina's application was unsuccessful because the Court considered it to be premature: construction of the mills had not been completed, and they were several months from commencing operation. As a consequence there were no interests of the parties currently in issue to protect through a provisional measures order. In terms of a bilateral settlement of a dispute this result was unremarkable. However, there are passages in the order that suggest that the

[117] *Pulp Mills* case (request for provisional measures by Argentina) (2006) 45 ILM 1025, [72].
[118] *Ibid.* [73]. [119] *Ibid.* [75].

Court has backed away from its strong statements in the *Gabčíkovo-Nagymaros Project* case concerning the importance of sustainable development in water resource management. Indeed the Court made no mention of the concept in the *Pulp Mills* case, and devised instead a new formulation ('sustainable *economic* development')[120] that appeared to give preference to developmental considerations over those of ecological protection. Also separating the *Pulp Mills* case from the judgment in the *Gabčíkovo-Nagymaros Project* case was the absence of any reference to the relevance of international environmental law to the case. Whereas in the *Gabčíkovo-Nagymaros Project* case it in was said that Hungary and Slovakia must implement their joint project taking into account recent developments in international environmental law, in the *Pulp Mills* case the Court referred in the *Pulp Mills* case only to the need to meet the requirements of the 1975 Statute.

Admittedly in this interlocutory stage in the *Pulp Mills* case the Court could not have dealt with all matters raised before it in any detail. None the less, in a case having clear parallels with the *Gabčíkovo-Nagymaros Project* case, and coming after several interim orders by ITLOS have expressly referred to the concept of precaution and environmental protection, it would have been desirable for the Court to have reaffirmed the centrality of environmental concerns to contemporary international watercourse law.

6.2 Impact of the case law

The decisions examined in this chapter have played an important role in the development of international water law, principally by focusing attention on underlying theoretical considerations. Four theories have influenced the evolution of this area of international law, namely those of 'absolute territorial sovereignty', 'absolute territorial integrity', 'limited territorial sovereignty', and 'community of interest'.[121] The absolute territorial sovereignty theory is associated with the Harmon doctrine, and asserts that upstream riparians have complete freedom of use of a watercourse. It is an extreme position that has enjoyed no support in judicial decisions. Also rejected has been the similarly extreme doc-

[120] *Ibid.* [80] (emphasis added).

[121] Malgosia A. Fitzmaurice, 'Water Management in the 21st Century' in Antony Anghie and Gary Sturgess (eds.), *Legal Visions of the 21st Century: Essays in Honour of Judge Christopher Weeramantry* (1998) 425, 427.

trine of absolute territorial integrity which holds that downstream riparians have a right to use the watercourse free from any interference by upstream riparians.[122]

The approaches that have found more favour have been the 'limited territorial sovereignty' and 'community of interest' doctrines.[123] The *Lake Lanoux* case essentially approved the limited territorial sovereignty approach in concluding that France's rights to exploit the headwaters of the River Carol were limited by an obligation to have regard to the downstream interests of Spain. In many respects this approach can be said to be 'the prevailing theory of international watercourse rights and obligations'[124] as it forms the conceptual basis for the principle of equitable utilisation.[125] The 'community of interest' theory adopted first in the navigational context by the PCIJ in the *River Oder* case was affirmed and expanded in the *Gabčíkovo-Nagymaros Project* case. It looks beyond issues of sovereignty and instead asserts that all riparian states have equal and common legal rights in the shared watercourse. Arguably it is also the only theory through which environmental considerations may be given appropriate recognition, especially as it supports the notion of freshwater management at the watershed rather than stream-level scale, which is a precondition for effective stewardship of river environments.

Beyond this contribution to the conceptual foundations of international water law, the influence of judicial decisions upon the emergence of environmental rules in the context of shared watercourses has been far more modest. In the *Lake Lanoux* case this was because of the overt focus on freshwater as a resource, rather than as being vital to the health of a complex aquatic ecosystem. None the less, the

122 The absolute territorial integrity approach has affinities with the position taken by some states with respect to transboundary pollution. Note for instance the arguments by Australia in the *Nuclear Tests* case (*Australia* v. *France*) (interim measures) [1973] ICJ Rep 99, (merits) [1974] ICJ Rep 253 that the deposit of any radionuclides on Australian territory as a result of French nuclear testing in the South Pacific would constitute a violation of Australian territorial sovereignty.

123 Alistair Rieu-Clarke, *International Law and Sustainable Development: Lessons From the Law of International Watercourses* (2005) 101.

124 McCaffrey, above n. 5, 137.

125 For a convenient encapsulation of the equitable utilisation principle see the UN Watercourses Convention, art. 5. See also the Helsinki Rules on the Use of the Waters of International Rivers, art. IV in International Law Association, Report of the 52nd Conference (1966) 484: 'Each basin State is entitled, within its territory, to a reasonable and equitable share in the beneficial uses of the waters in an international drainage basin.'

decision did emphasise the importance of consultation and cooperation among riparians, and developed a framework which could encompass environmental considerations. The award also recognised the no-harm principle that had been articulated in more general terms in the *Trail Smelter* case. In contrast the *Gabčíkovo-Nagymaros Project* case had a more overtly environmental focus, reflecting the arguments made to this end by Hungary. The Court affirmed the community of interest theory, and emphasised the necessity for the parties to have regard to environmental considerations when carrying out their joint project. However, the Court did not explain how developing rules of international environmental law intersected and interacted with traditional rules of international water law which have generally focused on questions of resource allocation. And although the *Pulp Mills* case has yet to be decided on the merits, there are indications from the interlocutory rulings that the Court may be prepared to backtrack to some extent from its key holdings in the *Gabčíkovo-Nagymaros Project* case.

One is left with the conclusion, therefore, that the contribution of the case law has been momentous in terms of international water law, but somewhat limited in relation to international environmental law. The integration of environmental concerns into this area of law has therefore largely been left to legislative efforts, the most notable being the ILC's Articles on the Law of the Non-Navigational Uses of International Watercourses[126] which were subsequently codified in the UN Watercourses Convention. Although this convention is yet to enter into force, it draws upon extensive state practice relating to riverine ecosystem protection[127] and was referred to by the ICJ in the *Gabčíkovo-Nagymaros Project* case. It now establishes the international legal benchmark not only for the equitable utilisation of international watercourses but also for maintaining the equilibrium of freshwater ecosystems, and marks a decisive shift away from an exclusive focus upon issues of resource exploitation and transboundary harm.[128]

[126] Report of the International Law Commission, 46th Session, 195 ff., UN Doc. A/49/10 (1994).

[127] For a review of this practice see McCaffrey, above n. 5, 388–93 (McCaffrey concludes (at 392) that 'there is now at least an emerging obligation to protect international watercourse systems and their ecosystems against degradation').

[128] See for instance the emphasis upon issues of transboundary harm rather than ecosystem protection in the UN Watercourses Convention, art. 2(1): 'The Parties shall take all appropriate measures to prevent, control and reduce any transboundary impact.'

The key environmental protection provisions of the UN Watercourses Convention are found in part IV. Article 20, which is modelled on article 192 of the LOS convention,[129] provides that watercourse states must 'individually and, where appropriate, jointly protect and preserve the ecosystems of international watercourses'. Recognising that pollution constitutes one of the most serious threats to freshwater ecosystems, article 21 sets out a series of obligations upon watercourse states to prevent and mitigate 'any detrimental alteration in the composition or quality of an international watercourse which results directly or indirectly from human conduct'.[130] Under article 22, watercourse states are also obliged to take all measures necessary to prevent the introduction of alien species that might have a detrimental effect upon watercourse ecosystems. In its commentary the ILC explained the obligation to protect freshwater environments:

> In essence ... [it] requires that watercourse States shield the ecosystems of international watercourses from harm or damage. It thus includes the duty to protect those ecosystems from a significant threat of harm. The obligation to 'preserve' the ecosystems of international watercourses, while similar to that of protection, applies in particular to freshwater ecosystems that are in a pristine or unspoiled condition... Together, protection and preservation of aquatic ecosystems help to ensure their continued viability as life support systems, thus providing an essential basis for sustainable development.[131]

Environmental disputes concerning shared watercourses must now be viewed through the prism of the UN Watercourses Convention. The principles relating to environmental protection included in the Convention mark a paradigm shift from the mere equitable balancing of riparian interests[132] toward a recognition of the independent importance of environmental interests. Article 20 in particular imposes an absolute obligation, requiring a state to protect and preserve the ecosystems of international watercourses even if there is no threat of transboundary harm[133] and accordingly the protection of freshwater ecosystems has become more than simply one factor to be considered

[129] Art. 192 provides that 'States have the obligation to protect and preserve the marine environment.'

[130] UN Watercourses Convention, art. 21(1).

[131] Report of the International Law Commission, 46th Session, 282, UN Doc. A/49/10 (1994).

[132] See for example the Helsinki Rules on the Use of the Waters of International Rivers, above n. 125, ch. 3.

[133] McCaffrey, above n. 5, 394.

in achieving an equitable and reasonable balance of interests between riparian states.[134]

6.3 Conclusion

This chapter has examined the judicial development of international environmental law as it relates to freshwater resources and ecosystems, and offered some critical observations concerning the place of environmental concepts and concerns within these decisions. It has been seen that for the most part environmental issues have not featured prominently in the case law. This is not to suggest that this jurisprudence has been of no relevance to environmental law. Quite to the contrary, in articulating the community of interest theory the PCIJ in the *River Oder* case expressed the kernel of a concept that would come to have profound implications for the sustainable and equitable management of freshwater resources. In addition, the tribunal in the *Lake Lanoux* case enunciated the no-harm principle and emphasised the importance of cooperation in relation to the exploitation of a shared natural resource. By stressing the breadth of considerations that an upstream state may be called upon to address in negotiations with downstream users, the decision also opened the door for environmental concerns to be given a prominent place in the resolution of watercourse disputes.

The *Gabčíkovo-Nagymaros Project* case is widely regarded as the most significant international judicial decision on environmental matters, and marks a fundamental shift in perceptions from the *Lake Lanoux* case. Whereas earlier cases might be said to be 'disputes about concessions and control of natural resources', the *Gabčíkovo-Nagymaros Project* case signalled a new focus on 'sustainability and the limits of resource use'.[135] Admittedly the ICJ avoided many of the opportunities with which it was presented to develop the law, and thereby 'sent a clear message of its conservatism'.[136] None the less, the Court recognised the importance of the principle of sustainable development and sought to fashion an approach to the dispute that would give the concept life and meaning. This was achieved not through a black-and-white

[134] Rieu-Clarke, above n. 123, 130. [135] Higgins, above n. 50, 111.

[136] Stec and Eckstein, above n. 76, 42–3. See also Adriana Koe, 'Damming the Danube: The International Court of Justice and the Gabcikovo-Nagymaros Project (Hungary v. Slovakia)' (1998) 20 *SLR* 612, 628–9.

judgment[137] as to the 'sustainability' of the original project, or of Slovakia's variant C, but instead was a result of the Court's conclusion that the parties must implement the terms of the 1977 Treaty having regard to developments in international environmental law. Ultimately the most important legacy of the *Gabčíkovo-Nagymaros Project* case may be this emphasis upon the procedural dimensions of the principle of sustainable development. The concept of sustainability assisted the court in facilitating the resolution of the dispute in a way that was consistent with international environmental law, without testing the bounds of justiciability by applying in a prescriptive way environmental concepts that do not possess clear and uncontroversial content.

[137] Peter H. F. Bekker, '*Gabcikovo-Nagymaros Project*' (1998) 92 *AJIL* 273, 277 (that the case is 'a good example of how the ICJ gives and takes with a view to achieving a result that is acceptable to both litigants and that, consequently, stands the best chance of being complied with').

7 Marine wildlife and ecosystems

Disputes concerning the marine environment, which supports the vast majority of the planet's biological diversity,[1] have been the subject of ongoing international judicial attention since the *Bering Sea Fur Seals* case[2] was decided in the late nineteenth century. This litigation has intensified as the marine environment has faced increasing pressures.[3] Among the most serious threats include climate change, pollution from terrestrial, marine, and atmospheric sources, and the unsustainable exploitation of marine living organisms.[4] Disputes relating to several of these threats have found their way before international courts and tribunals, including the ITLOS which has come to play a prominent role in global efforts to protect ocean ecosystems.[5]

This chapter examines this dynamic area of international environmental jurisprudence, from the earliest fisheries cases through to recent litigation under the compulsory procedures established by

[1] For example thirty-three of the thirty-four major categories of animals (*phyla*) are found in the oceans compared to only fifteen found on land: Joint Group of Experts on the Scientific Aspects of Marine Environmental Protection, *A Sea of Troubles*, Report No. 70 (2001) 12. The marine environment is also an essential source of resources, including food for the planet's growing population, with fish now accounting for more than 15 per cent of the total world supply of animal protein: United Nations Food and Agriculture Organisation, *The State of the World Fisheries and Aquaculture* (2006) 36.

[2] *Bering Sea Fur Seals* case (*Great Britain* v. *United States*) (1893) 1 Moore 755.

[3] See generally Independent World Commission on the Oceans, *The Ocean Our Future* (1998) 97–118.

[4] United Nations Environment Programme, *Global Environment Outlook 3* (2002) 180.

[5] Tullio Treves, 'Dispute-Settlement Clauses in the Law of the Sea Convention and their Impact on the Protection of the Marine Environment: Some Observations' (1999) 8 *RECIEL* 6.

the LOS Convention.[6] The first section of the chapter examines the plentiful case law relating to the exploitation and conservation of ocean resources.[7] This section is in turn divided into two sub-sections, with one dealing with disputes relating to the limits of the jurisdiction of littoral states over fisheries and other marine wildlife in adjacent waters, and the other discussing cases concerning the exploitation of straddling and high seas fisheries. The second section of the chapter discusses the more limited collection of cases dealing with issues of marine pollution. Together these two sections trace the development of marine environmental law from an early and exclusive focus upon marine resources to contemporary decisions that recognise the importance of international legal measures to protect the integrity of marine and coastal ecosystems.

7.1 Marine wildlife and ecosystems

Whereas once marine fish stocks were regarded as an inexhaustible resource to be exploited free from regulation,[8] it is now apparent that appropriate international legal measures and institutions are essential

[6] As was recognised in Agenda 21, UN Doc. A/CONF.151/26/Rev.1 (1992), the LOS Convention represents the most important effort to date to provide a global legal framework for the protection of marine ecosystems, constituting the 'basis upon which to pursue the protection and sustainable development of the marine and coastal environment and its resources' (ch. 17.1).

[7] Adopting terminology used in treaty-based and customary law more generally, such cases are conventionally described as those relating to 'marine living resources' (see for example Shigeru Oda, *International Control of Sea Resources* (2nd edn 1988) xx–xxvi). The use of this terminology is resisted in this book as it unhelpfully concentrates on the commercial value of marine wildlife as a harvestable commodity to the exclusion of a more complete conception that acknowledges the intrinsic value of marine wildlife as an aspect of biological diversity and as an essential component of marine ecosystems. See generally Simon Lyster, *International Wildlife Law* (1985); Lynton K. Caldwell, 'Concepts in Development of International Environmental Policies' (1973) 13 *NatResJ* 190, 194: the concept of ' "natural resources" ... is primarily an economic concept categorizing the various elements of the natural world according to their usefulness to man'.

[8] Believing that fisheries were practically inexhaustible, Grotius argued that there could be no limits on nations seeking to exploit them – hence the oceans and its fruits, as *res communis*, could be used by all without restriction: Hugo Grotius, *The Freedom of the Seas: or the Right Which Belongs to the Dutch to Take Part in the East Indian Trade* [1609] (Ralph van Deman Magoffin trans. 1916) 57. For a discussion of changing perceptions of oceans resources from Grotius to the Third United Nations Conference on the Law of the Sea see Lawrence Juda, *International Law and Ocean Use Management: The Evolution of Ocean Governance* (1996).

to address the crisis in global fisheries.[9] This is seen most clearly in global assessments of ocean fisheries, which have found that 77 per cent of fish stocks have been fished up to or beyond their sustainable limits.[10]

Disputes over marine wildlife have typically emerged out of the competing interests of flag states in the freedom of fishing on the oceans on the one hand, and the interests of coastal states in their adjacent fisheries on the other. The law of the sea has developed in response to this conflict, and the LOS Convention is the most comprehensive result to date of this process.[11] It establishes an entirely new maritime zone, the 200 nautical miles exclusive economic zone (EEZ),[12] in which coastal states have primary responsibility for the management of fisheries,[13] and it also provides a framework for promoting the sustainable utilisation of high seas fisheries.[14] Importantly, the LOS Convention extends the compulsory jurisdiction of its dispute settlement procedures over high seas fishing, and in so doing circumscribes the right of flag states to insist that their vessels be free from any restrictions on unsustainable fishing practices.[15]

[9] Report of the Secretary-General on Oceans and Seas, [14], UN Doc. E/CN.17/1999/4 (1999).

[10] Food and Agriculture Organisation, above n. 1, 29. This figure comprised of fisheries that are fully exploited, overexploited, or depleted: 52 per cent of the main stocks or species groups are fully exploited; a further 17 per cent of stocks or species groups are overexploited; 8 per cent of stocks have become significantly depleted or are recovering from depletion. Accordingly, only 23 per cent of major marine fish stocks or species groups are underexploited or moderately exploited.

[11] Ellen Hey, 'The Fisheries Provisions of the LOS Convention' in Ellen Hey (ed.), *Developments in International Fisheries Law* (1999) 13. See also Shigeru Oda, 'Fisheries under the United Nations Convention on the Law of the Sea' (1983) 77 *AJIL* 739.

[12] LOS Convention, art. 56.

[13] As 90 per cent of harvestable fish stocks are found within this area, coastal states possess the primary responsibility for ensuring the sustainable utilisation of the majority of the world's fisheries: Robin R. Churchill and A. Vaughan Lowe, *The Law of the Sea* (3rd edn 1999) 162.

[14] LOS Convention, arts. 116–20. See Francisco Orrego Vicuña, 'The International Law of High Seas Fisheries: From Freedom of Fishing to Sustainable Use' in Olav Schram Stokke (ed.), *Governing High Seas Fisheries: The Interplay of Global and Regional Regimes* (2001) 23. In relation to high seas fisheries see now the 1993 FAO Agreement to Promote Compliance with International Conservation and Management Measures by Fishing Vessels on the High Seas and the Food and Agriculture Organisation of the United Nations, Code of Conduct for Responsible Fisheries (1995).

[15] Bernard H. Oxman, 'Complementary Agreements and Compulsory Jurisdiction' (2001) 95 *AJIL* 277, 288.

The compromise between coastal and distant-water fishing states found in the LOS Convention, and adjusted by the Straddling Stocks Agreement,[16] was only struck following several major disputes between states, some of which have been subject to adjudication. These cases have served as litmus tests of the efficacy of existing rules and institutions governing fisheries, and by highlighting serious omissions and inefficiencies in the legal framework they have provided the impetus for international legal reform. Although these cases have arisen under a variety of distinct regimes, almost all disputes have revolved around two common issues, namely the limits of coastal state jurisdiction to protect and conserve adjacent fisheries and the necessary features of effective regimes for high seas fisheries conservation.[17] Accordingly these disputes generally involve both a complex balancing of the rights and interests of coastal and distant-water fishing states and a consideration of the broader interests of the international community in the sustainable exploitation of marine wildlife and the protection of marine ecosystems.

[16] 1995 Agreement for the Implementation of the Provisions of the United Nations Convention on the Law of the Sea of 10 December 1982 Relating to the Conservation and Management of Straddling Fish Stocks and Highly Migratory Fish Stocks.

[17] Marine wildlife issues have also arisen less directly in the context of maritime boundary cases. In the *Delimitation of the Maritime Boundary in the Gulf of Maine Area (Canada/United States of America)* case [1984] ICJ Rep 246 the United States submitted that ecological considerations were relevant in defining a single maritime boundary dividing the continental shelf and EFZ of Canada and the United States in the Gulf of Maine. When it came to fixing a boundary, the ICJ noted that 'essentially ecological' or other natural criteria could not be determinative in identifying a single maritime boundary line for both the EFZ and the continental shelf. On subsequent developments in marine environmental management in the region see A. Chircop, D. VanderZwaag, and P. Mushkat, 'The Gulf of Maine Agreement and Action Plan: A Novel but Nascent Approach to Transboundary Marine Environmental Protection' (1995) 19 *Marine Policy* 317. In the *Maritime Delimitation in the Area Between Greenland and Jan Mayen (Denmark* v. *Norway)* case [1993] ICJ Rep 38 the ICJ was also presented with an opportunity to incorporate ecological considerations in delimiting the boundaries of the opposing continental shelves and EFZs claimed by Denmark (from Greenland) and Norway (from Jan Mayen). However, notwithstanding that the near extinction of a particular species of fish (capelin, *Mallotus villosus*) was one of the reasons for the emergence of the dispute, the ICJ made no mention of environmental considerations in its judgment. In his separate opinion, Judge Weeramantry argued that among the relevant equitable considerations in the process of delimitation was 'the sacrosanct nature of earth's resources, harmony of human activity with the environment, respect for the rights of future generations, and the custody of earth's resources with the standard of due diligence expected of a trustee' (at 276–7).

7.1.1 *Limits of coastal state jurisdiction*

7.1.1.1 *Bering Sea Fur Seals* case

The decision handed down in the *Bering Sea Fur Seals* case, together with the views of individual arbitrators and the submissions by the parties, provide many insights into the environmental awareness of the international community in the late nineteenth century. The dispute giving rise to the case arose in 1886 following the arrest by the United States of British-flagged Canadian sealing schooners engaged in pelagic sealing for Alaskan fur seals (*Callorhinus alascanus*) near the Pribilof Islands, part of United States territory.[18] United States authorities had seized the vessels on the high seas pursuant to domestic legislation prohibiting the taking of wildlife from Alaskan territory 'or the waters thereof',[19]

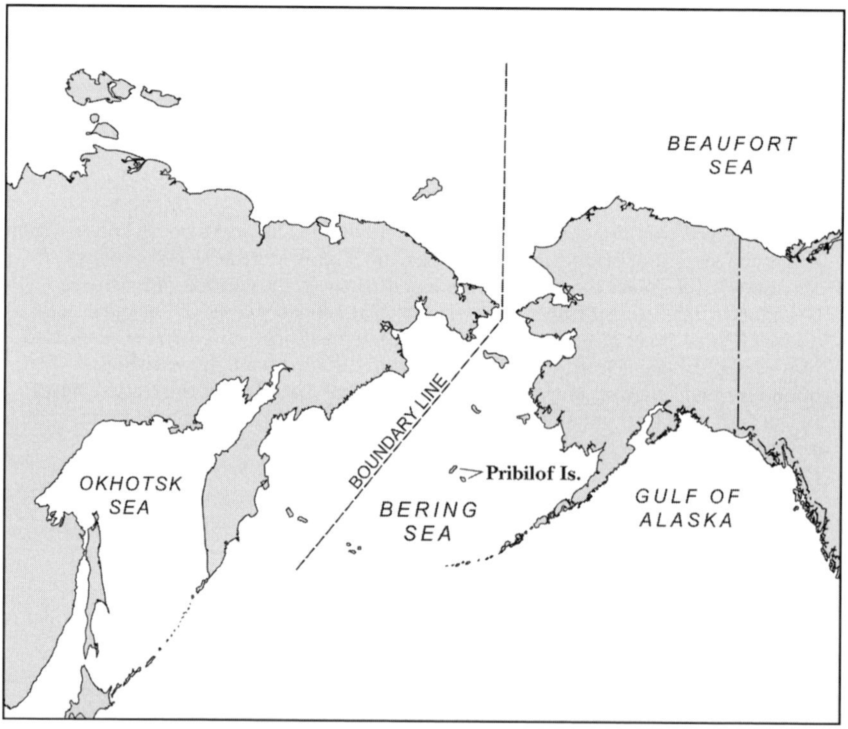

Figure 7.1 The Bering Sea and Pribilof Islands

[18] For a detailed history of sealing in the North Pacific up to 1942, see Jozo Tomasevich, *International Agreements on Conservation of Marine Resources* (1943, reprinted 1971) 65–122.

[19] *Bering Sea Fur Seals* case (1893) 1 Moore 755, 763.

and it was claimed that the sealing threatened the existence of seal colonies that frequented the Pribilof Islands for five months each year.[20] Pelagic sealing had a particularly negative effect on the overall fur seals population as it involved killing a disproportionate number of female seals (up to 90 per cent of catches).[21]

The legal arguments presented by both parties were relatively straightforward. Justifying its actions the United States asserted that it possessed jurisdiction over the seas where the British vessels were arrested under a treaty of cession concluded with Russia.[22] It also claimed that the killing of fur seals at sea was an offence *contra bonos mores* and a violation of the property rights of the United States in the seal herds.[23] For its part, Britain insisted that the vessels enjoyed complete freedom on the high seas and had therefore been improperly seized. The British government also argued that any questions regarding the management of the species should be referred to a commission of experts.[24]

Following unsuccessful attempts to resolve the dispute by diplomatic means,[25] the parties agreed to submit the dispute to arbitration.[26] The tribunal was presented with five questions,[27] the first four of which concerned United States jurisdiction over the seas where the British vessels were arrested. The fifth, and more interesting, question was whether, assuming there was no such jurisdiction, the United States possessed rights of protection or property in the fur seals on the high seas. Additionally the tribunal was asked, should it conclude that the United States did not have jurisdiction or a right of protection or property in the seals, to determine what 'concurrent regulations outside the jurisdictional limits of the respective Governments [were] necessary for the proper protection and preservation of the Fur Seals'.[28] By this procedure the tribunal was effectively requested to legislate a joint regulatory regime for sustainable sealing in the Bering Sea.[29]

In its submissions the United States relied heavily on the evidence that Alaskan fur seals were begotten, born, and reared on Alaskan

[20] William Williams, 'Reminiscences of the Bering Sea Arbitration' (1943) 37 *AJIL* 562, 569.

[21] *Ibid.* [22] 1867 Russia–United States Convention Ceding Alaska.

[23] *Bering Sea Fur Seals* case (1893) 1 Moore 755, 793–4. [24] *Ibid.*

[25] For an overview of these attempts see Cesare P. R. Romano, *The Peaceful Settlement of International Environmental Disputes: A Pragmatic Approach* (2000) 137–8.

[26] 1892 Great Britain–United States Treaty Submitting to Arbitration the Questions Relating to Seal Fisheries in the Bering Sea.

[27] *Ibid.* art. VI. [28] *Ibid.* art. VII. [29] Romano, above n. 25, 143.

territory and always returned to the Pribilof Islands, and that the herd was on the verge of extinction due to the inappropriate and wasteful method of sealing employed by British sealers. The United States made a threefold legal argument: first that it had property in the fur seals; second, that irrespective of its property rights it had an interest in harvesting the seal herd which it was entitled to protect; and third that it was the trustee for 'preserving and cherishing this valuable interest'.[30]

The United States' arguments in relation to the third submission are remarkable for their conceptualisation of the environment. Although fundamentally anthropocentric in outlook, being reliant on the notion of custodianship of nature and natural 'resources', it was argued that the obligation to protect marine wildlife derived from the importance of marine wildlife as elements of a 'natural trust' held for the benefit of future generations. Counsel for the United States went on to describe the earth and its natural resources as a 'gift in common' to mankind, which could only be the subject of usufructuary possession and not absolute beneficial ownership, and which had to be protected for the interests of 'succeeding tenants'.[31] This was an early and important expression of the idea of intergenerational rights – the idea that as 'members of the present generation, we hold the earth in trust for future generations'[32] – which forms an integral part of the broader notion of sustainable development. There was no engagement with these concepts by the British submissions, which were far more prosaic. The United Kingdom relied primarily on the freedom of the high seas doctrine, and the argument that the United States case must fail for want of any precedent in international law. Hence, although the case arose out of an environmental dispute, from the British perspective the case was a vehicle for resolving a broader question of legal principle regarding high seas freedoms which carried global implications for its empire.

The tribunal delivered a brief award, characteristic of many arbitral decisions of the period, in which it did not evaluate the parties'

[30] *Bering Sea Fur Seals* case (1893) 1 Moore 755, 812–14.

[31] Written argument by Mr Carter, Counsel for the United States. Reproduced in *Bering Sea Fur Seals* case (1893) 1 Moore 755, 833–4.

[32] Edith Brown Weiss, 'Our Rights and Obligations to Future Generations for the Environment' (1990) 84 *AJIL* 198, 199. See also Edith Brown Weiss, *In Fairness to Future Generations: International Law, Common Patrimony and Intergenerational Equity* (1989).

arguments. It simply issued the epigrammatic statement that the United States 'has not any right of protection or property in the Fur Seals frequenting the islands of the United States in Behring Sea, when such seals are found outside the ordinary three mile-limit'.[33] Having found against the United States on all substantive points, the tribunal turned to devise recommendations for a regulatory scheme for the protection and preservation of the fur seals herd. These regulations, to apply to the United States and to Britain on the high seas only, were set out in nine detailed articles, and provide a basic model for conservation measures adopted by regional fisheries management organisations to this day.[34] The regulations incorporated several important features. They provided for a closed area for sealing around the Pribilof Islands, a closed season in an adjacent area of high seas, limitations on the type of vessels to be used, a vessel licensing scheme, a requirement that catch records be kept by masters, limitations on the gear to be used, and exceptions from the regulations for indigenous peoples. Not only did the tribunal recommend that these regulations be agreed to by the United States and Britain but also declared that they should be implemented in their respective national legal systems.[35]

Conceptual constraints

Although the tribunal resolved the case by rigid adherence to the freedom of the seas doctrine, individual statements by members of the tribunal acknowledged that the dispute raised issues relating to environmentally sustainable ocean management. The president of the tribunal, Baron de Courcel, observed that the award of the tribunal was 'a first attempt at a sharing of the products of the ocean, which has hitherto been undivided'.[36] The president also alluded to the tragedy of the commons, noting the overexploitation of the 'fruits' of the seas by 'men, who, like the hero Alexander ... feel confined in a world too narrow'.[37]

The arbitrators appointed by the United States thought that the tribunal had taken an inflexible approach not justified under the terms of the arbitration treaty, which afforded the tribunal considerable latitude

[33] *Ibid.* 949.

[34] Patricia W. Birnie and Alan E. Boyle, *International Law and the Environment* (2nd edn 2002) 650.

[35] *Bering Sea Fur Seals* case (1893) 1 Moore 755. Both states enacted domestic legislation in 1894.

[36] *Ibid.* 945. [37] *Ibid.*

in resolving the dispute according to equitable considerations.[38] Justice Harlan observed that the twin claims that the United States possessed property in the seals and could assert a right of protection of the seals on the high seas had to be rejected if precedent were required, as there was no such precedent.[39] However, he argued, the question of whether public international law supported the United States' claim had to be examined by respect to 'the law of nature; that is, by the principles of justice, sound reason, morality, and equity, as recognized and approved by civilized peoples'.[40] A particularly interesting feature of Justice Harlan's dissenting decision concerned the question of property in the Alaskan fur seals herd, in relation to which the United States was able to draw upon principles of Roman law concerning rights over animals evincing an *animus revertendi* ('intention to return home').[41] Justice Harlan suggested that wild animals could not ordinarily become property unless

> by care, watchfulness, self-denial, and industry, [a person] induces or causes them to abide, for stated periods in each year, upon his premises, so that he, and he only, is in a position to deal with the race as a whole, taking its increase regularly for commercial purposes without impairing the stock.[42]

To a considerable extent the tribunal overlooked the essence of these arguments which were based on a special and historic claim on behalf of humankind generally, rather than a specific jurisdictional claim over areas of the high seas. The United States was effectively asserting an entitlement to be the primary guardian or steward of a particular species and this can be seen as an important and indirect reference, if not to the ecosystem approach in exact terms, then to a related notion that a species should be regulated according to predominant geographical occurrence. There are obvious practical difficulties with the approach to environmental management advocated by the United States in comparison with a scheme that draws clear jurisdictional

[38] *Ibid.* [39] *Ibid.* 914. [40] *Ibid.*

[41] See for instance Justinian, *Institutiones* (Peter Birks and Grant McLeod trans. 1987) II.1.12–15:

> Wild animals, birds and fish... become the property of the taker as soon as they are caught. However wild animals may be to some extent domesticated so that they go back and forth from the wilderness. Such animals remain in the ownership of the person to whose property they habitually return for 'so long as they keep their homing instinct'.

See also Henry Sumner Maine, *International Law: A Series of Lectures Delivered Before the University of Cambridge 1887* (1888) 95.

[42] *Bering Sea Fur Seals* case (1893) 1 Moore 755, 914.

boundaries. None the less, the notion that a state possessing a substantial connection with migratory marine wildlife should be entitled to protect the species in adjacent high seas if threatened with extinction appears preferable to an approach that asserts absolute high seas freedoms. At the very least a cogent argument could be made that the United States was legitimately protesting against the abuse of rights of other states in the exploitation of a shared resource.[43]

Given the inchoate state of the law of the sea, and the broad ambit of the arbitral agreement conferring jurisdiction upon the tribunal, it appears to have been open to the tribunal in 1893 to have accepted the United States' submissions.[44] Indeed it should be noted that in the *Fisheries Jurisdiction* cases,[45] which will shortly be discussed, the ICJ suggested a somewhat similar concept of 'preferential rights', under which coastal states are said to have a special, but not exclusive, entitlement to adopt conservation measures in relation to adjacent fisheries on the high seas when they can demonstrate a long-standing interest in the fisheries in question. However, rather than accepting the invitation of the United States, the tribunal chose to avoid a consideration of the fundamental issue - whether, and in what circumstances, it is appropriate for a state to act unilaterally in order to protect an interest of the international community as a whole.[46]

The deficiencies with the tribunal's *mare liberum* approach, and with the bilateral regulations which it developed, were made apparent not long after the case was decided. The tribunal's regulations permitted enforcement by United States and Britain in relation to each other's vessels; however, neither Japan nor Russia, whose sealers were also heavily engaged in pelagic sealing in the Bering Sea, agreed to similar regulations and Canadian vessels began to fly Japanese and Russian

[43] See Michael Byers, 'Abuse of Rights: An Old Principle, A New Age' (2002) 47 *McGillLJ* 389, 428 (arguing that the principle of abuse of rights offers a way of protecting common spaces in the absence of more precise treaty-based or customary rules).

[44] But see *contra* Douglas M. Johnston, *The International Law of Fisheries: A Framework for Policy-Oriented Inquiries* (1985) 111 (arguing that the tribunal was confronted with a difficulty commonly faced by international courts dealing with environmental problems, namely the lack of prior coherent and authoritative decisions).

[45] *Fisheries Jurisdiction* cases: *United Kingdom* v. *Iceland* (jurisdiction) [1973] ICJ Rep 3 (merits) [1974] ICJ Rep 3; *Germany* v. *Iceland* (jurisdiction) [1973] ICJ Rep 49 (merits) [1974] ICJ Rep 175. Unless otherwise indicated all references are to the United Kingdom case.

[46] On the role of unilateral measures in the environmental context see generally Daniel Bodansky, 'What's So Bad about Unilateral Action to Protect the Environment?' (2000) 11 *EJIL* 339.

flags of convenience. Eventually, in the face of imminent extinction of the Alaskan fur seals, all four states agreed to a treaty in 1911 suspending pelagic sealing in the North Pacific Ocean.[47]

7.1.1.2 *North Atlantic Coast Fisheries* case

The *North Atlantic Coast Fisheries* case[48] is an important counterpoint to the *Bering Sea Fur Seals* case. Whereas the latter award made clear that the United States could not seek to protect Alaskan fur seals in areas beyond its jurisdiction through the exercise of enforcement jurisdiction over foreign vessels, the *North Atlantic Coast Fisheries* case was concerned with the rights and duties of coastal states over marine wildlife that fell clearly within their jurisdictional reach.

The case concerned a dispute between Britain and the United States over the interpretation and application of provisions of the 1783 Definitive Treaty of Peace and the 1815 Convention to Regulate the Commerce Between the Territories of the United States and Great Britain under which United States residents continued to enjoy fishing privileges along the North Atlantic coast, including parts of the coast of Newfoundland. The dispute was provoked by restrictive fisheries legislation introduced by Newfoundland and the subsequent seizure of American fishing vessels. By special agreement concluded in 1909 the parties agreed to submit the dispute to the PCA.[49]

The first and primary question for the PCA was whether Britain could, in the absence of United States consent, impose reasonable regulations upon fishing operations conducted by United States residents.[50] The PCA, in its first case involving environmental questions, held that requiring such consent would make the fishery 'unregulatable'[51] and that Britain was the local sovereign and was 'not only entitled, *but obliged*, to provide for the protection and preservation of the fisheries'.[52] Therefore, although emerging out of a specific regime for the exploitation of a fishery by two neighbouring states pursuant to long-standing

47 1911 Convention Respecting Measures for the Preservation and Protection of Fur Seals in the North Pacific Ocean. For a discussion of this and subsequent developments in relation to the management of northern fur seals see Lyster, above n. 7, 40–8.

48 *North Atlantic Coast Fisheries* case (*Great Britain/United States of America*) (1910) 11 *RIAA* 167.

49 1909 Special Agreement for the Submission of Questions Relating to Fisheries on the North Atlantic Coast.

50 *Ibid.* art. I.

51 *North Atlantic Coast Fisheries* case (1910) 11 *RIAA* 167, 186.

52 *Ibid.* 187 (emphasis added).

agreement, the PCA's decision does helpfully emphasise the primary responsibility of a coastal state to protect and conserve the marine environment within its jurisdiction.[53] However, it must also be recognised that the decision was not framed in environmental terms, and the chief concern was to ensure the rational exploitation of fisheries to protect human industry.

7.1.1.3 *Fisheries Jurisdiction* case

This case arose out of the so-called 'cod war' between Iceland and several other North Atlantic fishing states that was precipitated by Iceland's progressive extension of an Exclusive Fishing Zone (EFZ). With increased interest by distant-water fishing fleets in fully exploited fisheries on the Icelandic continental shelf, Iceland extended its claims to an EFZ so as to conserve demersal fisheries and thereby ensure the survival and expansion of its fishing industry.[54] However, Iceland's extension of its fisheries jurisdiction and its arrest of foreign fishing vessels attracted the strong opposition of a number of states with an interest in the fisheries.

Pursuant to a 1948 law that permitted the establishment of conservation zones within Iceland's continental shelf,[55] Iceland extended its EFZ in progressive stages: from 3 to 4 nautical miles (in 1952) to 12 nautical miles (in 1958) and eventually to 50 nautical miles (in 1971). The United Kingdom and Germany objected to these claims, and in 1972 both states commenced proceedings against Iceland in the ICJ pursuant to respective exchanges of notes agreed with Iceland in 1961.[56] Iceland, however, refused to take any part in any stage of either proceeding.

[53] See now LOS Convention, art. 61.

[54] Robin R. Churchill, 'The Fisheries Jurisdiction Cases: The Contribution of the International Court of Justice to the Debate on Coastal States' Fishing Rights' (1975) 24 *ICLQ* 82, 84. At the time Iceland's economy was more dependent on fishing than any other nation in the world, with its fishing industry generating 20 per cent of its gross national product: Richard B. Bilder, 'The Anglo-Icelandic Fisheries Dispute' (1973) 37 *WisLR* 37, 43.

[55] Law Concerning the Scientific Conservation of the Continental Shelf Fisheries (1948), art. 1. Reproduced in the *Fisheries Jurisdiction* case (jurisdiction) [1973] ICJ Rep 3, 10.

[56] The relevant provisions of these two instruments are reproduced in the *Fisheries Jurisdiction* case (jurisdiction) [1973] ICJ Rep 3; [1973] ICJ Rep 45. Under these notes Germany and the United Kingdom withdrew their objection to Iceland's 12 nautical mile fishing zone and, in return, Iceland permitted German and British vessels to fish between 6 and 12 nautical miles off its coast within specified areas to be phased out over a period of three years. In addition, and providing the jurisdictional basis for the subsequent case in the ICJ it was provided that

> [t]he Icelandic Government will continue to work for the implementation of the Althing Resolution of May 5, 1959 [which declared that 'Iceland has an

As with the *Bering Sea Fur Seals* case, this case raised the difficult question as to the permissibility of unilateral assumption of prescriptive and enforcement jurisdiction by a coastal state over adjacent high seas areas in order to protect its economic and environmental interests. Three main issues were posed for the Court: whether Iceland's claim to a 50 nautical mile EFZ was consistent with international law, whether Iceland's claim to the EFZ could be asserted against the United Kingdom, and whether Iceland could unilaterally impose conservation measures in high seas areas adjacent to its coast.

The ICJ issued interim orders in 1972 calling upon the parties to refrain from actions which would aggravate the dispute, requiring Iceland to suspend enforcement of its new regulations and stipulating that Germany and the United Kingdom limit their annual catches in the area claimed by Iceland.[57] The ICJ subsequently handed down its judgment on the merits in 1974, at an important stage both for the development of the law of the sea and international environmental law more generally.[58] In what is widely regarded as a highly unsatisfactory decision,[59] the Court avoided answering directly the central question posed for decision – the legality of Iceland's 50 nautical mile claim. Instead the Court found that the claim was not opposable to the applicants. In relation to the question of Iceland's conservation measures the Court developed the problematic doctrine of 'preferential rights'. However, the Court did find that coastal states could assert a claim to a 12 nautical mile EFZ consistent with customary international law and this conclusion, coupled with the court's preferential fisheries doctrine, which is inherently incompatible with the notion of exclusivity, suggests an implicit rejection of Iceland's 50 nautical mile EFZ.[60]

The reasoning of the Court in relation to the customary status of a 12 nautical mile EFZ revealed little awareness of, or concern for, the environment of the North Atlantic or the more general problem of

unequivocal right to the entire continental shelf'], regarding the extension of the fisheries jurisdiction around Iceland, but shall give to the [German and United Kingdom] Government[s] six months' notice of such extension and, in case of a dispute in relation to such extension, the matter shall, at the request of either party, be referred to the International Court of Justice.

[57] *Fisheries Jurisdiction* case (interim measures) [1972] ICJ Rep 12, 17; [1972] ICJ Rep 30, 35.

[58] The judgment was handed down midway through the first session of the Third United Nations Conference on the Law of the Sea and three years after the Stockholm Declaration recognised in principle 4 the need 'to safeguard and wisely manage the heritage of wildlife and its habitat'.

[59] Churchill, above n. 54. [60] *Ibid.* 90.

unsustainable exploitation of high seas fisheries. The Court described the EFZ claimed by Iceland and other states as 'a *tertium genus* between the territorial sea and the high seas'.[61] However, beyond this the Court did not evaluate the purpose of such a zone, or the respective rights and duties of coastal states and flag states within this 'third type' of ocean space. Significantly the Court did not identify the implications of the EFZ for the exploitation and conservation of marine wildlife.

Separate and dissenting opinions did address some of these issues. The joint separate opinion of Judges Forster, Bengzon, Jiménez de Aréchaga, Singh, and Ruda recognised that a coastal state's claim to an EFZ could help prevent the serious depletion of fisheries resources, as coastal states generally have the greatest interest in ensuring that their adjacent fisheries are not overexploited. These judges acknowledged the reality of the tragedy of the commons, observing that unrestricted access to coastal waters 'inevitably results in physical and economic waste, since there is no incentive for restraint in the interest of future returns: anything left in adjacent waters for tomorrow may be taken by others today'.[62] In his separate opinion Judge Dillard also explored the concept of the EFZ in detail, and was the only judge to discuss some of the scientific realities of fisheries conservation. Fish, Judge Dillard wryly observed, 'are no respecters of national jurisdictions'.[63] Accordingly, while not disavowing the notion of the EFZ, Judge Dillard suggested that a flexible approach should be taken depending on the fishery concerned.[64]

By contrast to the Court's brief treatment of the concept of the EFZ, the majority judgment considered the notion of 'preferential fishing rights' in depth. The Court explained that such rights of a coastal state arise only 'when the intensification in the exploitation of fishery resources makes it imperative to introduce some system of catch-limitation and sharing of those resources' so as 'to preserve *the interests of their rational and economic exploitation*'.[65] However, these preferential rights are by definition not exclusive, and hence the coastal state and other states with an interest in the fisheries must seek an accommodation of their competing claims through negotiation and cooperation.[66]

Judicial activism and environmental protection

There are several questionable features of the doctrine of preferential fishing rights as expounded by the Court. Not only was the issue not

[61] *Fisheries Jurisdiction* case (merits) [1974] ICJ Rep 3, 24. [62] *Ibid.* 48–9. [63] *Ibid.* 61. [64] *Ibid.* [65] *Ibid.* 27 (emphasis added). [66] *Ibid.* 27–8.

raised by the parties (indeed Iceland had never claimed such rights),[67] but there is little evidence to support the Court's conclusion that it constituted a part of customary law.[68] According to Churchill, the concept was a 'sheer invention',[69] and a clear example of 'judicial creativity'.[70]

Although this reveals the willingness, and indeed the capacity, of the ICJ to develop the law in a situation of perceived need, it also confirms the importance for judicial innovation to be based on a sound appreciation of relevant issues of environmental and economic policy. At a conceptual level the doctrine of preferential rights appears to disregard environmental considerations, and is instead concerned with reconciling the competing economic interests of coastal and distant-water fishing states. Hence when the Court speaks of the requirement for the preferential fishing rights of coastal states to be limited having regard to '*the needs of conservation*',[71] the term 'conservation' is understood only in terms of ensuring maximum sustainable yield, not as an objective to preserve the ecosystem of which the fishery forms part.[72]

Furthermore, the Court failed to foresee the harmful consequences of its preferential rights doctrine for some fisheries yet to be fully exploited. It effectively established a perverse incentive to coastal states to overexploit fisheries so that they would be able to prove a historic dependence in any future negotiations with distant-water fishing nations.[73] This is unfortunate as the notion of preferential fishing rights might have been developed by the Court in such a way as to recognise the special interest of coastal states in managing and conserving adjacent fisheries on the high seas and thereby go some way to resolving the substantive question posed, but not satisfactorily answered, in the *Bering Sea Fur Seals* case.[74]

[67] Churchill, above n. 54, 93.

[68] *Ibid.* 93–6. Churchill and Lowe note that the rule is imprecise and that no state before or since the ICJ's judgment has sought to claim such preferential fishing rights: Churchill and Lowe, above n. 13, 285. However, it must be noted that the development of the EEZ rendered the preferential fishing rights doctrine otiose.

[69] Churchill, above n. 54, 104. [70] *Ibid.*

[71] *Fisheries Jurisdiction* case (merits) [1974] ICJ Rep 3, 31 (emphasis added).

[72] For a general analysis of the influence of economic rationales for ecosystem protection and resource conservation in environmental law see Alexander Gillespie, *International Environmental Law Policy and Ethics* (1997) 28–61.

[73] Churchill, above n. 54, 103.

[74] Indeed Iceland's representatives had argued publicly that coastal fisheries should be considered part of the natural resources of the coastal state: see Juda, above n. 8, 178.

By contrast, one of the more helpful aspects of the decision is the Court's discussion of the need for negotiation and cooperation in order to promote the equitable and rational exploitation of high seas fisheries. In an important passage the Court remarked that:

> It is one of the advances in maritime international law resulting from the intensification of fishing, that the former *laissez-faire* treatment of the living resources of the sea in the high seas has been replaced by a recognition of a duty to have due regard to the rights of other States *and the needs of conservation for the benefit of all.* Consequently, both Parties have the obligation to keep under review the fishery resources in the disputed waters and to examine together, in the light of scientific and other available information, the measures required for the conservation and development, and equitable exploitation, of those resources, taking into account any international agreement in force between them.[75]

The Court therefore emphasised the necessity for states to have regard to the interests of others and to seek on a continuous basis to manage and conserve fisheries in a cooperative and equitable manner.[76] Although tentative, and reliant on an economic conception of conservation, the Court's statement is an important presage of future developments in international environmental law relating to the marine environment.[77] The LOS Convention repeatedly emphasises the need for states to cooperate to the greatest extent possible to adopt policies of management and conservation of marine living resources based on the best available scientific data.[78]

This part of the judgment can also be seen to illustrate the practical limitations of utilising an essentially bilateral and adjudicative process to resolve a dispute involving multiple states and concerning complex questions of resource allocation and management. The Court appears to have recognised these constraints. When it came to the actual disposition of the case, the ICJ observed that the most appropriate method for resolving the dispute was negotiation, and that as the parties were in possession of the relevant scientific information and expertise it

[75] *Fisheries Jurisdiction* case (merits) [1974] ICJ Rep 3, 32 (emphasis added).

[76] Ellen Hey, *The Regime for the Exploitation of Transboundary Marine Fisheries Resources* (1989) 34–5.

[77] Indeed this passage has even been interpreted as an early articulation of aspects of the precautionary approach in oceans governance: *Southern Bluefin Tuna* cases (*New Zealand* v. *Japan*; *Australia* v. *Japan*) (provisional measures) (1999) 38 ILM 1624, separate opinion of Judge Laing, [20].

[78] See e.g. LOS Convention, art. 118: 'States shall cooperate with each other in the conservation and management of living resources in the areas of the high seas.'

was not desirable for the Court to set out a precise scheme.[79] None the less it was expected that the Court's articulation of guiding principles would encourage the parties towards a satisfactory resolution of the 'cod wars'. This expectation proved to be misplaced.[80] From the outset Iceland refused to take any part in any aspect of the proceedings, and the Court's judgment provided uncertain guidance to the parties on the applicable law. Legal developments outside the courtroom soon made redundant the Court's statements regarding the 12 nautical mile EFZ and the doctrine of preferential rights. In 1976 the United Kingdom claimed a 200 nautical mile EFZ, and in 1977 this became the European Community limit.[81] Subsequently the LOS Convention established the 200 nautical mile EEZ regime which accorded coastal states jurisdiction and sovereign rights over marine wildlife within this area.

7.1.1.4 *Estai* case

The persistent question as to the limits of coastal state competence to manage adjacent high seas fisheries arose once again in the *Estai* case,[82] which concerned another piscatorial conflict – this time the 'turbot war'.[83] The dispute arose against the background of severe overfishing in the north-west Atlantic, and a European Union quota for the catch of turbot (*Reinharditus hippoglossoides*)[84] over five times above the catch levels recommended by the Northwest Atlantic Fisheries Organization.[85] Canada seized a Spanish fishing vessel, the *Estai*, on the high seas pursuant to the Coastal Fisheries Protection Act 1994 (Can.) which enabled Canadian authorities to take urgent action necessary to protect endangered straddling stocks on the Grand Banks. As Iceland had done twenty years earlier in the context of the *Icelandic Fisheries* case, Canada invoked the doctrine of necessity to defend its actions, asserting that

79 *Fisheries Jurisdiction* case (merits) [1974] ICJ Rep 3, 32.

80 Romano, above n. 25, 152.

81 Fisheries Limits Act 1976 (UK).

82 *Fisheries Jurisdiction* case (*Spain* v. *Canada*) (jurisdiction and admissibility) [1998] ICJ Rep 431.

83 Christopher C. Joyner, 'On the Borderline? Canadian Activism in the Grand Banks' in Olav Schram Stokke (ed.), *Governing High Seas Fisheries: The Interplay of Global and Regional Regimes* (2001) 207. See also Andrew Schaefer, 'Canada–Spain Fishing Dispute (The Turbot War)' (1996–7) 8 *GeoIELR* 437.

84 A species of deepwater flatfish also known as 'Greenland halibut' and 'Greenland turbot'.

85 Established by the 1978 Convention on Future Multilateral Cooperation in the Northwest Atlantic Fisheries.

an essential interest of Canada was threatened by a grave and imminent peril.[86]

The arrest prompted Spain to commence proceedings against Canada in the ICJ. Although the Court did not consider the dispute on the merits, in an important decision on jurisdiction and admissibility[87] it was held that Canada's optional clause declaration[88] excluded the Court's jurisdiction.[89] Clearly this case posed profound questions concerning the adequacy of international fisheries law to protect highly endangered fish stocks, and had it proceeded to the merits stage the ICJ would have had an opportunity to evaluate the legality of Canada's attempts to protect a threatened fishery in the light of significant developments in international environmental law since the *Fisheries Jurisdiction* case.[90]

Although aborted at an early stage, the *Estai* case none the less had a significant impact on the development of the law of the sea relating to the conservation of straddling fisheries. Disputes over straddling stocks had been described as the 'greatest threat'[91] to the law of the sea since the conclusion of the LOS Convention and Canada's arrest of the *Estai* while the United Nations Straddling Stocks Conference was underway

[86] Glen Plant, 'The EC/Canadian Fisheries Dispute in the Northwest Atlantic' (1995) 44 *ICLQ* 927, 936. See also the commentary to art. 25 of the ILC's Articles on Responsibility of States for Internationally Wrongful Acts, Report of the International Law Commission 53rd Session, UN Doc. A/56/10 (2001).

[87] See Louise De La Fayette, 'The Fisheries Jurisdiction Case (*Spain* v. *Canada*), Judgment on Jurisdiction of 4 December 1998' (1999) 48 *ICLQ* 664; Malgosia A. Fitzmaurice, 'The Optional Clause System and the Law of Treaties: Issues of Interpretation in Recent Jurisprudence of the International Court of Justice' (1999) 20 *AustYBIL* 127, 148–50.

[88] In its art. 36(2) declaration, made 10 May 1994, Canada accepted the jurisdiction of the Court with respect to all disputes excluding

> disputes arising out of or concerning conservation and management measures taken by Canada with respect to vessels fishing in the NAFO Regulatory Area, as defined in the Convention on Future Multilateral Cooperation in the Northwest Atlantic Fisheries, 1978, and the enforcement of such measures:

1994 Declaration of Canada Recognising as Compulsory the Jurisdiction of the ICJ.

[89] *Estai* case [1998] ICJ Rep 431, [87]. Significantly, had both Canada and Spain been parties to the LOS Convention at the time of the arrest of the *Estai*, Spain could have pursued the case under the compulsory procedures established by part XV of the LOS Convention.

[90] Romano, above n. 25, 194. Although it seems probable that the Court would have found in favour of Spain: Robin Churchill, 'Fisheries Jurisdiction Case (*Spain* v. *Canada*)' (1999) 12 *LJIL* 597, 609.

[91] Bernard H. Oxman, 'Complementary Agreements and Compulsory Jurisdiction' (2001) 95 *AJIL* 277, 304.

highlighted the deficiencies in the rudimentary regime for conserving high seas fisheries contained in the LOS Convention. As a result it was a catalyst for the conclusion of the Straddling Stocks Agreement which substantially addressed Canada's concerns.[92]

7.1.2 Disputes under the LOS Convention

The dispute settlement system established by part XV of the LOS Convention represents one of the most significant developments in the mosaic of adjudicative institutions for the settlement of international environmental disputes.[93] Under part XV most disputes over marine environmental issues may be subject to judicial settlement by ITLOS, by the ICJ, or by arbitral panels established pursuant to annexes VII or VIII of the LOS Convention. Since the entry into force of the LOS Convention, both ITLOS and annex VII arbitral tribunals have considered significant disputes involving questions as to the exploitation and conservation of marine wildlife. The following discussion examines the decisions of ITLOS relating to the prompt release of foreign vessels arrested by coastal states on suspicion of illegal, unregulated, and unreported (IUU) fishing, before turning to consider the decisions of ITLOS and an annex VII arbitral tribunal in the *Southern Bluefin Tuna* dispute.

7.1.2.1 Prompt release decisions

While the LOS Convention conferred significant jurisdictional capacity upon coastal states to protect the marine environment within their EEZs, there was an appreciation by the convention's drafters of the potential for enforcement processes to be abused when coastal states arrested flag state fishing vessels for breaches of fishing regulations.

Article 73 of the LOS Convention seeks to reconcile these competing interests. Article 73(1) provides that coastal states may, in the exercise of their sovereign rights to explore, exploit, conserve, and manage the living resources in the EEZ, take such enforcement action against vessels as is necessary to ensure conformity with its fishing

[92] Christopher C. Joyner and Alejandro Alvarez von Gustedt, 'The Turbot War of 1995: Lessons for the Law of the Sea' (1996) 11 *IJMCL* 425, 451. For discussion of recent Canadian practice see Rosemary Rayfuse, 'Canada and Regional Fisheries Organizations: Implementing the UN Fish Stocks Agreement' (2003) 34 *ODIL* 209. Canada became a party to the Straddling Stocks Agreement on 3 August 1999.

[93] See further Donald R. Rothwell and Tim Stephens, 'Dispute Resolution and the Law of the Sea: Reconciling the Interaction Between the LOS Convention and Other Environmental Instruments' in Alex G. Oude Elferink and Donald R. Rothwell (eds.), *Oceans Management in the 21st Century: Institutional Frameworks and Responses* (2004) 209.

Table 7.1 *Cases brought before ITLOS and/or arbitral tribunals established under annex VII of the* LOS Convention *(an asterisk denotes that the case involved environmental issues)*

Cases in the ITLOS

1 *M/V Saiga (Saint Vincent and the Grenadines* v. *Guinea)* (prompt release) (1997)
2 *M/V Saiga (no. 2) (Saint Vincent and the Grenadines* v. *Guinea)* (provisional measures) (1998) (admissibility and merits) (1999)
3 and 4 **Southern Bluefin Tuna (New Zealand* v. *Japan; Australia* v. *Japan)* (provisional measures) (1999)
5 **Camouco (Panama* v. *France)* (prompt release) (2000)
6 **Monte Confurco (Seychelles* v. *France)* (prompt release) (2000)
7 **Conservation and Sustainable Exploitation of Swordfish Stocks in the South-Eastern Pacific Ocean (Chile/European Community)* proceedings suspended
8 *Grand Prince (Belize* v. *France)* (prompt release) (2001)
9 *Chaisiri Reefer 2 (Panama* v. *Yemen)* (prompt release) proceedings discontinued
10 **MOX Plant (Ireland* v. *United Kingdom)* (provisional measures) (2002)
11 **Volga (Russian Federation* v. *Australia)* (prompt release) (2003)
12 **Land Reclamation by Singapore in and Around the Straits of Johor (Malaysia* v. *Singapore)* (provisional measures) (2003)
13 **Juno Trader (St Vincent and the Grenadines* v. *Bissau)* (prompt release) (2004)
14 *Hoshinmaru (Japan* v. *Russian Federation)* (prompt release) (2007)
15 *Tomimaru (Japan* v. *Russian Federation)* (prompt release) (2007)

ARBITRATIONS UNDER THE LOS CONVENTION, ANNEX VII

Southern Bluefin Tuna Case (Australia & New Zealand v. *Japan)* (jurisdiction and admissibility) (2000)
**MOX Plant (Ireland* v. *United Kingdom)* (suspension of proceedings on jurisdiction and merits and request for further provisional measures) (order 3, of 24 June 2003) (order 4, of 14 November 2003)
**Land Reclamation by Singapore in and Around the Straits of Johor (Malaysia* v. *Singapore)* (Case settled 2005)
Barbados and the Republic of Trinidad and Tobago Concerning Maritime Delimitation (2006)
Guyana and Suriname Concerning Maritime Delimitation (2007)

regulations. However, the *quid pro quo* for flag states is the requirement in article 73(2) that arrested vessels and their crews be 'promptly released upon the posting of reasonable bond or other security'. In addition, article 292 establishes a procedure by which coastal states may seek the resolution of any dispute concerning such arrests by either an agreed tribunal or, in all other situations, by ITLOS. Article 292 therefore confers compulsory jurisdiction on ITLOS in relation to prompt release cases.[94]

Prompt release cases have dominated the Tribunal's docket.[95] Nine such applications have been made to the Tribunal, although two of these were not heard on their merits.[96] What is significant from the perspective of international environmental law is that three prompt release cases (the *Camouco* case,[97] *Monte Confurco* case,[98] and the *Volga* case[99]) have raised significant issues relating to the conservation and management of 'marine living resources'. In addition, an underlying question in these cases was the interaction between the LOS Convention and another environmental instrument: the 1980 Convention on the Conservation of Antarctic Marine Living Resources (CCAMLR).[100]

The *Camouco* case, *Monte Confurco* case, *Grand Prince* case, and *Volga* case all arose out of arrests by coastal states of foreign fishing vessels engaged in IUU fishing for Patagonian toothfish (*Dissostichus eleginoides*)[101] in the EEZs around sub-Antarctic islands, within the area covered by

[94] R. Lagoni, H. Heinrich-Noll, and H. Vogel, 'The International Tribunal for the Law of the Sea: Establishment and "Prompt Release" Procedures' (1996) 11 *IJMCL* 137.

[95] See table 7.1. For an overview of the tribunal's prompt release jurisprudence see Yoshifumi Tanaka, 'Prompt Release in the United Nations Convention on the Law of the Sea: Some Reflections on the ITLOS Jurisprudence' (2004) 51 *NILR* 237; Andrew Serdy and Michael Bliss, 'Prompt Release of Fishing Vessels: State Practice in the Light of the Cases Before the International Tribunal for the Law of the Sea' in Alex G. Oude Elferink and Donald R. Rothwell (eds.), *Oceans Management in the 21st Century: Institutional Frameworks and Responses* (2004) 273.

[96] In the *Grand Prince* case (*Belize* v. *France*) (prompt release) (2001) 125 ILR 251, ITLOS found that it did not have jurisdiction to consider the application while in the *Chaisiri Reefer 2* case (*Panama* v. *Yemen*) (prompt release) (available at www.itlos.org) the dispute was settled prior to hearing.

[97] *Camouco* case (*Panama* v. *France*) (prompt release) (2000) 125 ILR 151, (2000) 39 ILM 666.

[98] *Monte Confurco* case (*Seychelles* v. *France*) (prompt release) (2000) 125 ILR 203.

[99] *Volga* case (*Russian Federation* v. *Australia*) (prompt release) (2003) 42 ILM 159.

[100] For an overview of the CCAMLR regime see Steinar Anderson, 'The Convention for the Conservation of Antarctic Marine Living Resources: Improving Procedures but Lacking Results' in Edward L. Miles *et al.* (eds.), *Environmental Regime Effectiveness: Confronting Theory with Evidence* (2002) 405.

[101] Also known as 'Chilean sea bass'. See generally Richard Herr, 'The International Regulation of Patagonian Toothfish: CCAMLR and High Seas Fisheries Management' in Olav Schram Stokke (ed.), *Governing High Seas Fisheries: The Interplay of Global and Regional Regimes* (2001) 303. For a popular account of IUU fishing practices in relation to Patagonian toothfish see G. Bruce Knecht, *Hooked: A True Story of Pirates, Poaching and the Perfect Fish* (2006).

CCAMLR.[102] The *Camouco, Monte Confurco*, and *Grand Prince* were seized by French authorities for violating fishing regulations in force in the EEZs around the French islands of Crozet and Kerguelen. Similar issues arose in the *Volga* case in which Australia arrested a Russian-flagged vessel for illegal fishing in the Australian EEZ adjacent to Heard and McDonald Islands.[103]

In the *Camouco, Monte Confurco*, and *Volga* cases, the Tribunal was required to consider whether the bond set by the arresting state for the release of the vessels was a 'reasonable bond or other security' for the purposes of articles 73 and 292 of the LOS Convention. In undertaking this task the Tribunal has held that it must have regard to a supposed balance established in the LOS Convention between coastal and flag state interests.[104] Striking an acceptable balance has proved to be problematic for the Tribunal, and it has in all three cases left unresolved the tension in the LOS Convention between the responsibility of coastal states for conserving marine wildlife and the interests of flag states in having their vessels promptly released following arrest.[105]

While article 61 of the LOS Convention requires coastal states to 'ensure through proper conservation and management measures that the maintenance of the living resources in the exclusive economic zone is not endangered by over-exploitation', that obligation must be appreciated in light of article 73. The latter provision seeks to reconcile the interests of coastal states in ensuring compliance with their laws adopted 'in the exercise of its sovereign rights to explore, exploit, conserve and manage the living resources in the exclusive economic zone'[106] with the interests of flag states in having their '[a]rrested vessels and their crews … promptly released upon the posting of reasonable bond

[102] See generally Dean Bialek, 'Sink or Swim: Measures Under International Law for the Conservation of the Patagonian Toothfish in the Southern Ocean' (2003) 34 *ODIL* 105.

[103] Australia has arrested a number of vessels for IUU fishing in Australia's EEZ near the Heard and McDonald islands. One such arrest (that of the *Viarsa 1*) involved the longest hot pursuit in maritime history. See Tim Stephens, 'Enforcing Australian Fisheries Laws: Testing the Limits of Hot Pursuit in Domestic and International Law' (2004) 15 *PLR* 12; Erik Jaap Molenaar, 'Multilateral Hot Pursuit and Illegal Fishing in the Southern Ocean: The Pursuits of the *Viarsa 1* and the *South Tomi*' (2004) 19 *IJMCL* 19; Knecht, above n. 101.

[104] *Monte Confurco* case (2000) 125 ILR 203, [71]–[72].

[105] Donald R. Rothwell and Tim Stephens, 'Illegal Southern Ocean Fishing and Prompt Release: Balancing Coastal and Flag State Rights and Interests' (2004) 53 *ICLQ* 171, 186.

[106] LOS Convention, art. 73(1).

or other security'.[107] Although article 61 appears highly relevant to a determination of the reasonableness of a bond,[108] the Tribunal has not ventured into environmental issues in any substantial way in its prompt release jurisprudence.[109] The reticence of the Court as a whole is clearly confirmed in the *Volga* case, the most recent prompt release decision to raise major issues relating to marine environmental protection.[110]

In its judgment in the *Volga* case the Tribunal recalled its brief statement, in the *Camouco* case, of some factors relevant to assessing the reasonableness of a bond, including the gravity of alleged offences, possible penalties under the domestic law of the detaining state, the value of the vessel detained and the cargo seized, and the amount and form of bond imposed by the detaining state.[111] The Tribunal also noted that in the *Monte Confurco* case it had held that articles 292 and 73 sought to 'balance' the interests of flag states in having their vessels and crews released promptly with the interests of coastal states detaining such vessels in securing the appearance of the master in their court and the payment of fines.[112]

When it came to perform this process in the *Volga* case, the Tribunal took a restrictive approach. It held that no direct weight was to be placed on the serious problem of IUU fishing in the CCAMLR area.[113]

107 *Ibid.* art. 73(2).

108 *Camouco* case (2000) 125 ILR 151, dissenting opinion of Judge Anderson.

109 Although several judges in separate opinions have made reference to the environmental impact of IUU fishing. See in particular the separate opinions of Judge Anderson in the *Camouco* case (2000) 125 ILR 151, and *Monte Confurco* case (2000) 125 ILR 203, and the dissenting opinion of Judge Wolfrum in the *Camouco* case (2000) 125 ILR 151 (noting that CCAMLR represents 'one of the most important structural principles of the [LOS] Convention namely that conservation and management of marine living resources is a task in which all States involved shall cooperate').

110 See generally Robin Churchill and A. Vaughan Lowe, 'The International Tribunal for the Law of the Sea: Survey for 2002' (2003) 18 *IJMCL* 447; Tim Stephens and Donald R. Rothwell, 'The "Volga" Case (*Russian Federation* v. *Australia*)' (2004) 35 *JMLC* 283; Chester Brown, '"Reasonableness" in the Law of the Sea: The Prompt Release of the *Volga*' (2003) 16 *LJIL* 621; Philippe Gautier, 'The International Tribunal for the Law of the Sea: Activities in 2002' (2003) 2 *ChineseJIL* 341. In the *Juno Trader* case (*St Vincent and the Grenadines* v. *Bissau*) (prompt release) (2004) (available at www.itlos.org) environmental concerns were raised but were not discussed in the majority order, or in separate declarations and opinions.

111 *Volga* case (2003) 42 ILM 159, [63]; *Camouco* case (2000) 125 ILR 151, [67].

112 *Volga* case (2003) 42 ILM 159, [65]; *Monte Confurco* case (2000) 125 ILR 203, [72].

113 CCAMLR applies 'to the Antarctic marine living resources of the area south of 60° South latitude and to the Antarctic marine living resources of the area between that latitude and the Antarctic Convergence which form part of the Antarctic

Australia had argued that international concern over IUU fishing for toothfish was highly relevant to the assessment of the bond[114] and pointed out that IUU fishing threatened the viability of toothfish and by-catch species such as albatross that were snared on the long-lines set by IUU vessels.[115] While ITLOS stated that it 'understands the international concerns about [IUU] fishing and appreciates the objectives behind the measures taken by States, including the States Parties to *CCAMLR*'[116] it noted that the task set for the Tribunal under article 292 was to decide whether the bond set by Australia was reasonable and that it was only by reference to the possible penalties for the alleged offences that ITLOS could determine their gravity.[117]

In his dissenting judgment, Judge Anderson noted that the Tribunal's appreciation of international concern over IUU fishing in the CCAMLR area was a significant and positive development in its jurisprudence.[118] However, he also argued that coastal state duties to conserve the marine living resources of its EEZ under article 61, and the complementary obligations imposed by CCAMLR to protect and preserve the Antarctic environment, were relevant factors for determining the reasonableness of a bond. Judge ad hoc Shearer went further in his dissenting opinion, holding that the question of reasonableness in the *Volga* case could not be assessed in isolation from the 'grave allegations of illegal fishing in a context of the protection of endangered fish stocks in a remote and inhospitable part of the seas'.[119]

Clearly the Tribunal has taken a narrow view of its task in prompt release cases, an approach that might be considered appropriate given the summary nature of its jurisdiction in this context. On the other hand the LOS Convention bestows upon coastal states significant responsibility for conserving marine living resources and protecting the marine environment within the EEZ, and arguably this should have been given greater recognition in the balancing process undertaken by ITLOS. Additionally it can also be questioned whether the notion of balancing coastal and flag state interests is appropriate in prompt release cases. Not only is the concept of a balance of these

marine ecosystem': art. I(1). See Donald R. Rothwell, *The Polar Regions and the Development of International Law* (1996) 124–8.

114 *Volga* case (2003) 42 ILM 159, Australian statement in response, [22], [26], [42] and [54] (available at www.itlos.org).

115 *Ibid.* [45]. 116 *Volga* case (2003) 42 ILM 159, [68]. 117 *Ibid.* [69].

118 *Volga* case (2003) 42 ILM 159, dissenting opinion of Judge Anderson, [2].

119 *Volga* case (2003) 42 ILM 159, dissenting opinion of Judge ad hoc Shearer, 194.

rights not expressly referred to in article 292, there can also be no effective balance in cases such as the *Volga* case where the real competing interests involved were those of the well-funded IUU fishers on the one hand and the coastal state on the other.[120] A better approach to the question of reasonableness may lie not in the artificial evaluation preferred by the Tribunal, but instead in the concept of proportionality.[121] Determining the reasonableness of a bond by reference to whether it is appropriate and adapted to the environmental interest to be protected appears to offer a preferable framework for analysis, not least because it could allow the integration of environmental concepts, including the precautionary principle, in the reasoning process.[122]

7.1.2.2 *Southern Bluefin Tuna* dispute

Whereas in its prompt release jurisprudence ITLOS has not sought to engage with fisheries management issues in any significant depth, ITLOS did consider these questions in the first phase of the *Southern Bluefin Tuna* dispute.[123]

Background

The *Southern Bluefin Tuna* dispute arose out of a breakdown in cooperation among the founding members of the 1993 Convention for the Conservation of Southern Bluefin Tuna (CCSBT) which was concluded to 'ensure, through appropriate management, the conservation and optimum utilisation of Southern Bluefin Tuna'.[124] Among other things, the CCSBT established the Commission for the Conservation of Southern Bluefin Tuna (C-CCSBT) to manage catches by member states by setting, by consensus, the total allowable catch (TAC) for southern bluefin tuna and individual national allocations.

The issue at the heart of the disagreement between Australia and New Zealand on the one hand, and Japan on the other, was the current state, and future prospects for recovery, of stocks of southern bluefin

120 *Volga* case (2003) 42 ILM 159, dissenting opinion of Judge ad hoc Shearer, [19].

121 Brown, above n. 110, 630. 122 *Ibid.*

123 *Southern Bluefin Tuna* (*New Zealand* v. *Japan*; *Australia* v. *Japan*) (provisional measures) (1999) 38 ILM 1624 (*Southern Bluefin Tuna* order); (*Australia and New Zealand* v. *Japan*) (award on jurisdiction and admissibility) (2000) 39 ILM 1359 (*Southern Bluefin Tuna* award). See Tim Stephens, 'A Paper Umbrella Which Dissolves in the Rain? Implications of the *Southern Bluefin Tuna* case for the Compulsory Resolution of Disputes Concerning the Marine Environment Under the 1982 LOS Convention' (2001) 6 *APJEL* 297.

124 Art. 3.

tuna (*Thunnus maccoyii*). This is a highly migratory species[125] of pelagic fish that spawn in the waters south of Indonesia and traverse the high seas, EEZs and territorial seas of various states, including Australia and New Zealand.[126] They are long-living, late breeding, and are mostly fished on the high seas.[127] Mature and juvenile southern bluefin tuna have a high market value, particularly on the Japanese *sashimi* market, and have been fished heavily since the 1950s with the catch peaking at 81,605 tonnes in 1961.[128]

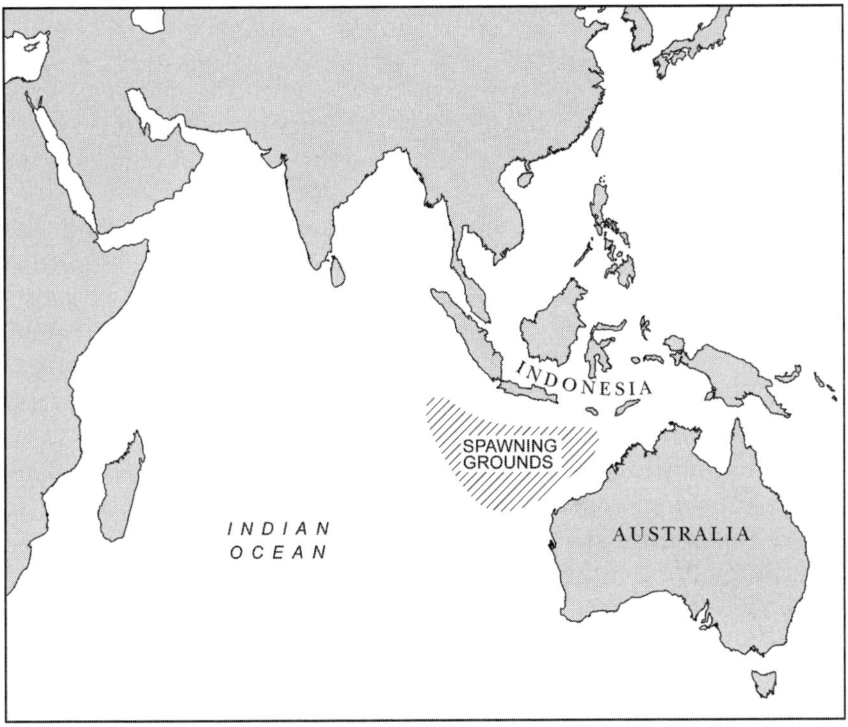

Figure 7.2 Southern bluefin tuna spawning grounds[129]

[125] Southern bluefin tuna are included on the list of highly migratory species in annex I of the LOS Convention.

[126] *Southern Bluefin Tuna* award (2000) 39 ILM 1359, [21].

[127] Anthony Bergin and Marcus Haward, 'Southern Bluefin Tuna Fishery: Recent Developments in International Management' (1994) 18 *Marine Policy* 263, 271.

[128] Of which Japan's catch was 77,927 tonnes and Australia's 3,678 tonnes: *ibid.* 266 (table 1).

[129] After figure 1 ('Distribution of Bluefin Tuna Catch off the Australian Coast') included in David Campbell, 'Change in Fleet Capacity and Ownership of Harvesting Rights in the Australian Bluefin Tuna Fishery' (available at www.fao.org/DOCREP/_005/Y249E/y2498e0d.htm).

By virtue of its high market value, and late breeding cycle, this is a species highly vulnerable to overfishing. By the early 1980s parental southern bluefin tuna stock had declined to less than 30 per cent of its 1960 levels[130] and since 1996 the species has been listed as critically endangered on the IUCN – World Conservation Union's Red List of Threatened Species.[131] In order to manage the exploitation of southern bluefin tuna, and to protect the fishery, Australia, New Zealand, and Japan informally agreed in 1989 to a TAC of 11,750 tonnes.[132] In 1994, at the first meeting of the C-CCSBT, it was agreed that the TAC should be maintained at the 1989 level.[133] The same TAC was set at the annual meeting of the Commission each subsequent year up to 1997. After that time there was no agreement on TAC until the meeting of the Commission in October 2003.[134] In the absence of consensus on catch limits, the parties in practice maintained their national catches at the 1994 levels.[135]

From 1994 onwards Japan sought an increased TAC maintaining that, although they were at historically low levels, southern bluefin tuna stocks had begun to recover. Australia and New Zealand consistently opposed such proposals, taking the view that the species remained under threat. Beginning in 1995 Japan began to urge the C-CCSBT to approve a joint experimental fishing programme to assess the recovery of the stock. As with Japan's request for additional TAC, this was opposed by Australia and New Zealand, which maintained that Japan's proposed fishing programme could endanger the species.[136] Unable to secure the Commission's support for the plan, Japan began its own pilot programme in June 1998 followed by the commencement of a much more substantial programme a year later.[137]

[130] *Southern Bluefin Tuna* award (2000) 39 ILM 1359, [22].

[131] IUCN – World Conservation Union, Red List of Threatened Species (available at www.iucnredlist.org/search/details.php?species=21858).

[132] *Southern Bluefin Tuna* award (2000) 39 ILM 1359, [22].

[133] 6,065 tonnes to Japan, 5,265 tonnes to Australia and 420 tonnes to New Zealand: *ibid.* [24].

[134] *Ibid.* The Commission must meet at least annually (CCSBT, art. 6(3)). Agreement was finally reached on a provisional global catch at C-CCSBT8 in October 2001.

[135] *Southern Bluefin Tuna* award (2000) 39 ILM 1359, [24].

[136] *Southern Bluefin Tuna* order (1999) 38 ILM 1624, [74].

[137] *Southern Bluefin Tuna* award (2000) 39 ILM 1359, [25]. The estimated catch from the pilot programme was 1,464 tonnes. See also Julia Baldock, 'Determining the Fate of Southern Bluefin Tuna – International Tribunal for the Law of the Sea (1999) *New Zealand* v. *Japan; Australia* v. *Japan*' (2000) 17 *EPLJ* 157.

Although the essence of the disagreement between the parties was a fundamental divergence of views as to the status of the southern bluefin tuna stock, Japan's unilateral programme proved to be the catalyst for, and the subject of, the litigation. Australia and New Zealand objected to Japan's programme and consultations under the rubric of the CCSBT in Canberra and Tokyo in late 1998 aimed at resolving the dispute failed. Australia informed Japan that the dispute concerned not only the CCSBT but also the parties' rights and obligations under the LOS Convention.[138] Japan expressed its willingness to submit the dispute to mediation; however, the offer was refused on the grounds that Japan had not undertaken to suspend its programme pending the results of the mediation.[139] Japan also suggested arbitration pursuant to article 16(2) of the CCSBT but again declined to halt its programme.[140] Accordingly Australia and New Zealand rejected the offer to have the matter referred to third party settlement under the CCSBT and instead announced their intention to pursue settlement of the dispute under part XV of the LOS Convention.

On 15 July 1999, Australia and New Zealand requested the establishment of an arbitral tribunal under annex VII of the LOS Convention to hear the merits of the dispute.[141] Both Australia and New Zealand maintained that Japan, by unilaterally designing and undertaking an experimental fishing programme, had breached several provisions of the LOS Convention relating to the conservation and management of highly migratory species within the EEZ and high seas fisheries. It was argued *inter alia* that Japan had violated the duty under article 118 of the LOS Convention 'to co-operate ... in the conservation and management of living resources in the areas of the high seas' and the requirement in article 117 that in relation to their nationals all states should take such conservation measures 'as may be necessary for the conservation of the living resources of the high seas'.[142]

[138] *Southern Bluefin Tuna* award (2000) 39 ILM 1359, [27]. Australia, New Zealand and Japan became parties to the LOS Convention on 16 November 1994, 18 August 1996, and 20 July 1996 respectively.

[139] *Southern Bluefin Tuna* award (2000) 39 ILM 1359, [28].

[140] *Ibid.*

[141] As none of the parties had at that stage made a declaration selecting a procedure, annex VII arbitration applied by default (LOS Convention, art. 287).

[142] The applicants also alleged that Japan's programme breached art. 64(1) of the LOS Convention which provides that

> [t]he coastal State and other States whose nationals fish in the region for ... highly migratory species ... shall cooperate directly or through

Southern Bluefin Tuna *order*

Pending the establishment of the annex VII tribunal, Australia and New Zealand sought provisional measures in ITLOS to halt Japan's unilateral programme. In August 1999, ITLOS unanimously found that the annex VII tribunal to be established would prima facie have jurisdiction over the dispute.[143] ITLOS went on to order, by eighteen votes to four, that catches be maintained at 11,750 tonnes and by twenty votes to two ordered that none of the parties engage in an experimental fishing programme.[144]

As many commentators have noted, this was an important decision for international environmental law, principally because ITLOS applied a precautionary approach even though it did not refer expressly to the concept in its decision.[145] Although brief, the *Southern Bluefin Tuna* order contains significant conclusions on several issues of marine environmental law and is therefore deserving of close analysis.

ITLOS began the substantive part of its reasons by noting that although Japan maintained that the dispute was scientific rather than legal, the differences between the parties did involve points of law.[146] The Tribunal observed that under the LOS Convention, states had the duty to cooperate directly or through appropriate international organisations in order to conserve and promote the objective of optimum utilisation of highly migratory species. Emphasising the primacy of the LOS Convention as an overarching framework agreement for the protection of the marine environment, the Tribunal considered that breaches of the convention could be invoked notwithstanding that they related to conduct also regulated by a regional fisheries agreement such as the CCSBT.[147] ITLOS found that the arbitral tribunal to be established would prima facie have jurisdiction over the dispute, rejecting Japan's arguments that the non-binding dispute settlement

> appropriate international organizations with a view to ensuring conservation and promoting the objective of optimum utilization of such species throughout the region...

Articles 116 to 119 are found in s. 2 of pt VII of the LOS Convention and relate to the conservation and management of marine wildlife on the high seas.

143 *Southern Bluefin Tuna* order (1999) 38 ILM 1624, [62]. 144 *Ibid.* [90(c), (d)].

145 See Adrianna Fabra, 'The LOSC and the Implementation of the Precautionary Principle' (1999) 10 *YIEL* 15; David Freestone, 'Caution or Precaution: "A Rose By Any Other Name...?"' (1999) 10 *YIEL* 15; Simon Marr, 'The Southern Bluefin Tuna Cases: The Precautionary Approach and Conservation and Management of Fish Resources' (2000) 11 *EJIL* 815.

146 *Southern Bluefin Tuna* order (1999) 38 ILM 1624, [42]–[43]. 147 *Ibid.* [51].

mechanisms of the CCSBT applied in lieu of the compulsory procedures under part XV of the LOS Convention.[148]

Satisfied as to its jurisdiction, ITLOS turned to the question of provisional measures and noted that under article 290 of the LOS Convention provisional measures may be prescribed to preserve the respective rights of the parties or to prevent serious harm to the marine environment, where the urgency of the situation so requires. Identifying an important linkage between the provisions of the LOS Convention relating to the conservation and management of marine wildlife, and the more general obligations under the convention to protect and preserve the marine environment, ITLOS expressly observed that 'the conservation of the living resources of the sea is an element in the protection and preservation of the marine environment'.[149]

Article 290 was enlivened, ITLOS went on to suggest, as it was clear that the stock of southern bluefin tuna were seriously depleted and that conservation measures were necessary in order to prevent the disappearance of the species. On this basis not only did the tribunal encourage the parties to 'act with *prudence and caution* in order to ensure that effective conservation measures are taken'[150] but it went on to apply a precautionary approach in prescribing detailed provisional measures. The precautionary principle or approach was therefore relevant in the *Southern Bluefin Tuna* order in two senses: first as a specific rule or norm regulating the conduct of the parties, and second as an organising principle to guide the Tribunal's assessment of Australia and New Zealand's request for interim orders.

Therefore, even though ITLOS did not expressly refer to or endorse the precautionary 'principle', its decision revealed a classic 'precautionary approach'. Indeed it is notable as the first international judicial decision to use the notion to structure its analysis,[151] albeit in qualified terms.[152] ITLOS noted that there was scientific uncertainty regarding the measures necessary to conserve stocks of the tuna, but that the tribunal was not in a position to assess this evidence conclusively and that the urgency of the situation demanded measures to preserve the rights

[148] *Ibid.* [52]–[62]. [149] *Ibid.* [70]. [150] *Ibid.* [77] (emphasis added).

[151] Freestone, above n. 145, 29.

[152] It is noteworthy that the majority opinion did not venture an opinion as to whether the precautionary concept was to be regarded as a legal 'principle' or as a policy 'approach': Jacqueline Peel, 'Precaution: A Matter of Principle, Approach or Process?' (2004) 5 *MJIL* 483, 494.

of the parties and to avoid further deterioration of the tuna stock.[153] Freestone has suggested that in so doing ITLOS appeared to have given effect to the obligation to apply the precautionary approach to straddling and highly migratory species under article 6 of the Straddling Stocks Agreement, notwithstanding that the instrument was not then in force,[154] and despite the controversy surrounding its applicability to fisheries management.[155]

This treatment of the precautionary principle tends to suggest that ITLOS is more aware of, and more favourably disposed to, environmental considerations and environmental principles than other international courts.[156] Several judges in separate opinions also considered both the environmental dimensions of the dispute and the precautionary principle in significant detail,[157] although they stopped short of recognising the notion as a rule of custom.[158] Judge Laing expressed a clear preference for the term precautionary 'approach' rather than 'principle', if the latter is understood as a precise norm of conduct.[159] Judge Treves's separate opinion exemplified the potential for general principles of international environmental law to influence judicial decision-making. He argued that it was unnecessary for the precautionary approach to be considered a principle of customary international law in order to have an application in the case, as 'the precautionary approach seems ... inherent in the very notion of provisional measures'.[160]

Judge ad hoc Shearer delivered the most comprehensive separate opinion. Judge Shearer was critical of the order for not being expressed in stronger terms, particularly for failing to find Japan prima facie in breach of its obligations under the LOS Convention, and for not concluding that the jurisdiction of the annex VII tribunal was clearly manifest.[161] In his view, the tribunal 'behaved less as a court of law and

[153] *Southern Bluefin Tuna* order (1999) 38 ILM 1624, [80].

[154] Freestone, above n. 145, 31. See also *Southern Bluefin Tuna* order (1999) 38 ILM 1624, separate opinion of Judge Treves and separate opinion of Judge ad hoc Shearer.

[155] For an outline of this controversy see Grant J. Hewison, 'The Precautionary Approach to Fisheries Management: An Environmental Perspective' (1996) 11 *IJMCL* 301.

[156] Nicolas de Sadeleer, *Environmental Principles: From Political Slogans to Legal Rules* (Susan Leubusher trans. 2002) 108.

[157] *Southern Bluefin Tuna* order (1999) 38 ILM 1624, separate opinion of Judge Laing, [12]–[21].

[158] *Ibid.* [16]. [159] *Ibid.* [20].

[160] *Southern Bluefin Tuna* order (1999) 38 ILM 1624, separate opinion of Judge Treves, [9].

[161] For criticism of this view see A. Vaughan Lowe, 'Advocating Judicial Activism: The ITLOS Opinions of Judge Ivan Shearer' (2005) 24 *AustYBIL* 145, 149–53.

more as an agency of diplomacy'[162] and while 'a disposition to assist the parties in resolving their disputes amicably' was an appropriate function of judicial settlement, the tribunal 'should not shrink from the consequences of proven facts'.[163]

Southern Bluefin Tuna *award*

The *Southern Bluefin Tuna* order is one of the most important judicial decisions in international environmental law, demonstrating a sensitivity both to the gravity of the problem of overfishing and the interplay between 'living resources' issues and marine environmental questions more generally. As Judge Wolfrum has noted in statements made *ex curia*, 'the effect fisheries have on species and marine ecosystems due to ecological inter-dependency is considerable; stock depletion affects *inter alia* coral reefs, mangroves, estuaries as well as mammal species and turtles'.[164] Most notably the order recognises the importance and applicability of the precautionary principle/approach both to the conduct of states and to the process of judicial decision-making more generally.[165]

In stark contrast the *Southern Bluefin Tuna* award is a largely procedural decision, which evinces apparent ambivalence to the seriousness of the environmental issues underlying the dispute. In August 2000 the annex VII tribunal, the first arbitral tribunal to be established under annex VII of the LOS Convention, handed down the award in which it reached the opposite conclusion to ITLOS on jurisdiction and therefore declined to consider the merits of the case. It found, by four votes to one, that it did not have jurisdiction and unanimously discharged the provisional measures prescribed by ITLOS. The controversial conclusion in the award was that by operation of article 281 of the LOS Convention the non-compulsory dispute resolution provisions of the CCSBT contained in article 16 excluded the operation of the obligatory dispute settlement procedures established by part XV of the LOS Convention.[166] What is noteworthy in the context of the present discussion is that the

162 *Southern Bluefin Tuna* order (1999) 38 ILM 1624, separate opinion of Judge ad hoc Shearer, 1649.

163 *Ibid.*

164 Rüdiger Wolfrum, 'The Role of the International Tribunal for the Law of the Sea' in Myron H. Nordquist and John N. Moore (eds.), *Current Fisheries Issues and the Food and Agriculture Organization of the United Nations* (2000) 369, 371.

165 Judge Wolfrum has described the precautionary principle as 'a matter of inherent logic' in such cases: *ibid.* 380.

166 This aspect of the decision is considered in detail in ch. 9.

annex VII tribunal did not acknowledge the relevance of the part XV machinery for protecting the marine environment, and therefore did not consider the implications of its narrow approach to jurisdiction to international marine environmental management. The practical effect of the *Southern Bluefin Tuna* award is to allow unsustainable high seas fishing to continue while precluding direct enforcement of the duty of all states to conserve and manage living resources.

7.1.2.3 *Swordfish Stocks* case

The *Conservation and Sustainable Exploitation of Swordfish Stocks in the South-Eastern Pacific Ocean* case[167] raised the same types of issues concerning the rights of coastal states to manage adjacent marine resources that had been confronted in the *Bering Sea Fur Seals* case, the *Icelandic Fisheries* case and the *Estai* case. On this occasion the litigation was brought under the LOS Convention, which substantially improved the existing legal framework applicable to straddling, migratory and high seas fisheries.

In order to conserve stocks of swordfish (*Xiphias gladius*) found in the high seas adjacent to the Chilean coast from collapse, Chile imposed a port ban on the landing of swordfish caught in these waters by Spanish vessels. This measure provoked litigation under two distinct dispute settlement systems. In September 2000 the EC requested consultations with Chile under article 4 of the WTO Understanding on Rules and Procedures Governing the Settlement of Disputes[168] and subsequently, in November 2000, requested the establishment of a WTO panel. Effectively by way of counterclaim, in September 2000 Chile commenced proceedings against the EC under part XV of the LOS Convention, contending that the EC had not discharged its duty to cooperate with Chile under articles 64 and 117 to 119 of the LOS Convention in order to conserve stocks of swordfish. In addition to challenging the jurisdiction of the special chamber of ITLOS that

[167] *Conservation and Sustainable Exploitation of Swordfish Stocks in the South-Eastern Pacific Ocean (Chile/European Community)* (proceedings suspended) (15 March 2001 and 16 December 2003) (available at www.itlos.org). See generally Andrew Serdy, 'See You in Port: Australia and New Zealand as Third Parties in the Dispute Between Chile and the European Community Over Chile's Denial of Port Access to Spanish Vessels Fishing for Swordfish on the High Seas' (2002) 3 *MJIL* 79; John Shamsey, 'ITLOS vs Goliath: The International Tribunal for the Law of the Sea Stands Tall with the Appellate Body in the Chilean-EU Swordfish Dispute' (2002) 12 *TransL&CP* 513; Marcos A. Orellana, 'The Swordfish Dispute between the EU and Chile at the ITLOS and the WTO' (2002) 71 *NordicJIL* 55.

[168] 1994 Marrakesh Agreement Establishing the World Trade Organization, annex 2.

was formed at the request of the parties, the EC argued that Chile's domestic conservation measures violated the freedom of the high seas as enshrined in article 87 of the LOS Convention.

These legal proceedings therefore raised a familiar type of dispute between a coastal state and flag state over attempts to protect adjacent fisheries, although unlike the *Fisheries Jurisdiction* case and the *Estai* case the impugned activities clearly took place within Chilean territorial jurisdiction. Given the limited range of enforcement options available to coastal states in relation to unsustainable fishing activities on the high seas that adversely affect their adjacent fisheries, Chile and other coastal states would probably have welcomed clarification of their legal rights by the ITLOS special chamber.[169] This is now unlikely, as the parties have effectively resolved the dispute, and proceedings under both the LOS Convention and the WTO have been suspended indefinitely.[170]

7.2 Pollution or alteration of marine environments

The discussion now turns to the second main category of marine environmental dispute that has been the subject of adjudication in international courts and tribunals – cases relating to marine pollution.

The international legal regime for the protection of the marine environment from pollution is highly developed, with the LOS Convention,[171] and a coterie of complementary global and regional agreements, providing an expansive framework for the control of marine pollution.[172] Although the comprehensiveness and clarity of this area of marine environmental law may partly explain why relatively few disputes have arisen, there have been several important cases including the recent *Land Reclamation by Singapore in and Around the Straits of Johor* case[173] which related to coastal engineering works

[169] Serdy, above n. 167, 108.

[170] For a discussion of the terms of the settlement see Shamsey, above n. 167, 538.

[171] See pt XII of the LOS Convention, in particular arts. 194, 195, 198, 199 and 202–22.

[172] None the less there remain some weaknesses in the regulatory scheme, the most significant of which is the relatively few and ineffective international controls of land-based sources of marine pollution (which account for over 80 per cent of pollutants entering the oceans): Thomas A. Mensah, 'The International Legal Regime for the Protection and Preservation of the Marine Environment from Land-Based Sources of Pollution' in Alan E. Boyle and David Freestone (eds.), *International Law and Sustainable Development: Past Achievements and Future Challenges* (1999) 297.

[173] *Land Reclamation by Singapore in and Around the Straits of Johor* (*Malaysia* v. *Singapore*) (provisional measures) (8 October 2003) (available at www.itlos.org).

affecting estuarine and marine ecosystems. The possibility for future litigation on pollution and other issues concerning the alteration of the marine environment remains high, particularly having regard to the capacity of coastal states to prescribe and enforce pollution standards applicable to foreign vessels within coastal state maritime zones.[174]

7.2.1 French nuclear testing in the Pacific

The conduct by France of atmospheric and underground nuclear tests in the Pacific has generated several disputes leading to litigation in the ICJ, and in other fora, and these cases have raised important issues concerning the principles of international environmental law applicable to transboundary pollution.[175] These cases also raised marine pollution issues. Australia and New Zealand both contended in the *Nuclear Tests* cases[176] that French atmospheric nuclear testing generating radioactive fall-out constituted an infringement of high seas freedoms by interfering with the freedom of navigation and overflight and interfering with the freedom to explore and exploit the resources of the sea and the seabed.[177] To this end Australia and New Zealand sought interim orders in relation not only to potential pollution on each respective metropolitan land mass, but also ocean space. However, the Court did not consider the issue of marine pollution and ordered France to refrain from nuclear tests causing the deposit of radioactive fall-out on Australian or New Zealand territory.[178] The arguments relating to marine pollution were also not considered on the merits, with the Court finding that the dispute had become moot following France's public undertaking to cease atmospheric testing.[179]

[174] LOS Convention, art. 220. [175] See the discussion in ch. 5.

[176] *Nuclear Tests* cases: *Australia* v. *France* (interim measures) [1973] ICJ Rep 99, 103; *New Zealand* v. *France* (interim measures) [1973] ICJ Rep 135, 139–40.

[177] The Australian written submissions focused on what was said to be French infringement of Australian territorial sovereignty and its rights to enjoy the freedom of the high seas and exploit its resources. In its oral submissions environmental issues were stressed more forcefully. The New Zealand government included an entire chapter in its request for interim measures concerning the environmental consequences of the tests. See Malgosia A. Fitzmaurice, 'Environmental Protection and the International Court of Justice' in A. Vaughan Lowe and Malgosia A. Fitzmaurice (eds.), *Fifty Years of the International Court of Justice* (1996) 293, 297–9.

[178] *Nuclear Tests* cases: *Australia* v. *France* (interim measures) [1973] ICJ Rep 99, 106; *New Zealand* v. *France* (interim measures) [1973] ICJ Rep 135, 142.

[179] *Nuclear Tests* cases: *Australia* v. *France* (merits) [1974] ICJ Rep 253, 270–1; *New Zealand* v. *France* (merits) [1974] ICJ Rep 457, 474–6.

In its 1995 request for an examination of the situation in accordance with paragraph 63 of the Court's 1974 judgment,[180] New Zealand sought recognition 'of those rights that would be adversely affected by entry into the *marine environment* of radioactive material' as a consequence of the underground tests to be carried out at Mururoa or Fangataufa atolls and 'of its entitlement to the protection and benefit of a properly conducted Environmental Impact Assessment'.[181] New Zealand also sought provisional measures requiring France to undertake an environmental impact assessment in relation to its underground tests and required France to refrain from the tests unless the assessment revealed that the tests would not give rise to radioactive contamination of the marine environment.

However, in a narrow reading of its original judgment,[182] the Court again found it unnecessary to consider New Zealand's argument concerning marine environmental impacts, on this occasion because, as France was now engaged in underground nuclear testing, the basis of the original judgment, which related to atmospheric testing, was unaffected.[183] The Court therefore did not consider developments in the law of the sea since its 1974 decision, including the emergent principles of environmental impact assessment and precaution. None the less, it did recognise the existence of this growing body of law, by reminding the parties that its order was 'without prejudice to the obligations of [New Zealand and France] to respect and protect the natural environment'.[184]

The three dissenting judges addressed a host of issues not canvassed in the majority decision, including questions relating to the marine environment. They considered that developments in international environmental law did affect the basis of the 1974 judgment, thus justifying the Court's consideration of the permissibility of France's underground tests.[185] Judge Weeramantry analysed these issues in depth,[186] and devoted considerable attention to the concepts of intergenerational

180 *Request for an Examination of the Situation in Accordance with Paragraph 63 of the Court's Judgment of 20 December 1974 in the Nuclear Tests (New Zealand* v. *France)* case (*New Zealand* v. *France)* [1995] ICJ Rep 288 (1995 *Nuclear Tests* case).

181 *Ibid.* [6].

182 Malgosia A. Fitzmaurice, 'International Protection of the Environment' (2001) 293 *RDC* 9, 376.

183 1995 *Nuclear Tests* case [1995] ICJ Rep 288, [63].

184 *Ibid.* [64].

185 1995 *Nuclear Tests* case [1995] ICJ Rep 288, dissenting opinions of Judge Weeramantry, 339–41; Judge Palmer, 412; Judge Koroma, 379.

186 1995 *Nuclear Tests* case [1995] ICJ Rep 288, dissenting opinion of Judge Weeramantry, 317.

equity, the precautionary principle, and environmental impact assessment (which he described as ancillary to the principle of precaution).[187] Importantly, Judge Weeramantry held that New Zealand had made out a prima facie case that France's underground tests would violate international law by introducing radioactive waste into the marine environment.[188] The illegality of polluting the environment through the discharge of radioactive waste was described by Judge Weeramantry as a principle 'too well established to need discussion'.[189] The other dissentients, Judge ad hoc Palmer and Judge Koroma, stopped short of endorsing Judge Weeramantry's view regarding the customary status of the precautionary principle and environmental impact assessment, but did concur that international law prohibited nuclear testing where the practice led to the introduction of nuclear material into the marine environment.[190]

7.2.2 MOX Plant *dispute*

This other major dispute relating to marine pollution culminating in international litigation also concerned nuclear materials. The dispute between Ireland and the United Kingdom relates to the establishment of a mixed oxide fuel (MOX) plant at the Sellafield nuclear processing facility located on the Irish Sea in north-west England.[191] As no nuclear facilities in the United Kingdom currently use the mixed uranium and plutonium fuel to generate electricity, MOX fuel is intended for export, via the Irish Sea. Ireland is particularly concerned that the operation of the plant will lead to radioactive discharges into the Irish Sea both from the operation of the plant and from increased shipments of nuclear material.

Following public consultation and feasibility studies, the operation of the MOX plant was authorised by the United Kingdom in October 2001 with a view to commissioning of the plant in December 2001. Throughout this process Ireland strongly objected to the plant on health and environmental grounds, and ultimately commenced proceedings against the United Kingdom under both the LOS Convention (the

[187] *Ibid.* 341–5. [188] *Ibid.* 345–6. [189] *Ibid.* 345.

[190] 1995 *Nuclear Tests* case [1995] ICJ Rep 288, dissenting opinions of Judge Koroma, 379; Judge Palmer, 413.

[191] For a comprehensive overview see Maki Tanaka, 'Lessons From the Protracted Mox Plant Dispute: A Proposed Protocol on Marine Environmental Impact Assessment to the United Nations Convention on the Law of the Sea' (2004) 25 *MichJIL* 337.

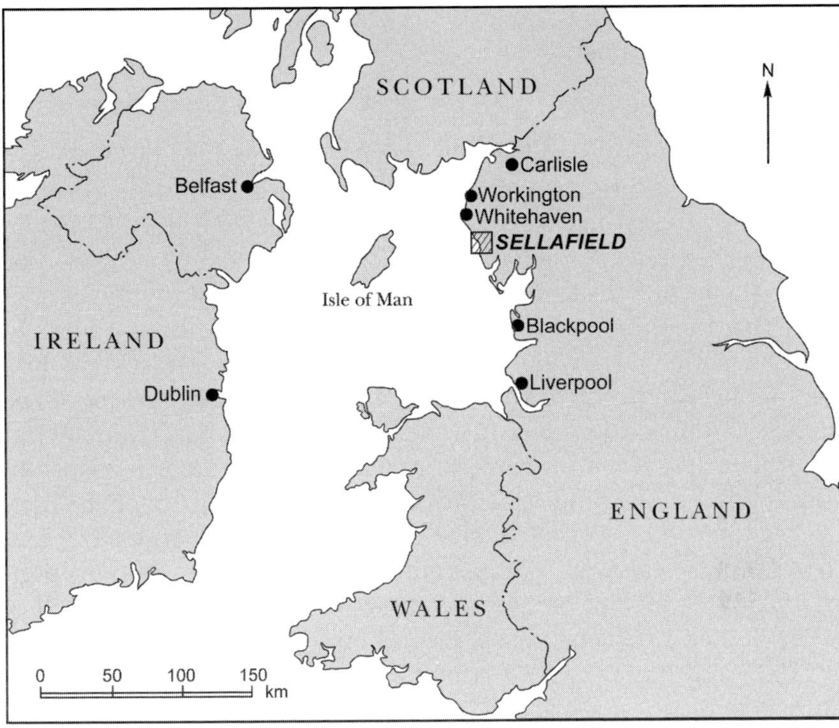

Figure 7.3 Sellafield nuclear processing facility, north-west England

MOX Plant dispute[192]) and the OSPAR Convention.[193] Subsequently, the European Commission was successful in proceedings brought against Ireland in the ECJ.[194] The ECJ held that by bringing the case to ITLOS and to an annex VII tribunal under the LOS Convention, Ireland had violated the exclusive jurisdiction of the ECJ enshrined in article 292

[192] *MOX Plant* case (*Ireland* v. *United Kingdom*) (provisional measures) (2002) 41 ILM 405 (*MOX Plant* order); *MOX Plant* case (*Ireland* v. *United Kingdom*) (suspension of proceedings on jurisdiction and merits and request for further provisional measures) (order 3, of 24 June 2003) (2003) 42 ILM 1187 (order 4, of 14 November 2003) (order 5, of 22 January 2007) (*MOX Plant* award) (available at www.pca-cpa.org).

[193] *OSPAR Arbitration* (*Ireland* v. *United Kingdom*) (final award) (2003) 42 ILM 1118. See Ted L. McDorman 'Access to Information under Article 9 of the OSPAR Convention (*Ireland* v. *United Kingdom*) (2004) 98 *AJIL* 330; Malgosia A. Fitzmaurice, 'Dispute Concerning Access to Information Under Article 9 of the OSPAR Convention (*Ireland* v. *United Kingdom*)' (2003) 18 *IJMCL* 541.

[194] *Commission of the European Communities* v. *Ireland* (2006) 45 ILM 1051.

of the EC Treaty[195] and article 193 of the 1957 Treaty Establishing the European Atomic Energy Authority.

7.2.2.1 *MOX Plant* order

In November 2001 Ireland sought provisional measures in ITLOS suspending the authorisation of the plant pending the constitution of an annex VII tribunal to determine its claims that the United Kingdom had breached several obligations under the LOS Convention in relation to the plant.[196] Ireland asserted in its notification and statement of claim that the United Kingdom had breached its obligations under the LOS Convention[197] (1) by failing to take the necessary measures to prevent, reduce, and control pollution of the marine environment of the Irish Sea from accidental or intended releases of radioactive material or releases as a result of terrorist attack;[198] (2) by failing to cooperate with Ireland in the protection of the marine environment of the Irish Sea by, *inter alia*, refusing to share information with Ireland;[199] and (3) by failing to carry out a proper environmental impact assessment in relation to the marine environmental impacts of the MOX plant.[200]

The United Kingdom raised several objections to the jurisdiction of ITLOS and the annex VII tribunal to be established. These objections were made on the grounds that several other dispute settlement regimes were applicable, and therefore that the prerequisites for jurisdiction under part XV of the LOS Convention were not met. Although the Tribunal was ultimately satisfied as to its jurisdiction, the Tribunal declined to make the orders requested by Ireland, concluding that there was insufficient urgency to justify their prescription.[201]

Ireland had in essence sought two provisional measures: the suspension of the commissioning of the MOX plant and the prohibition of any transportation of radioactive materials associated with the MOX plant

[195] 2002 Consolidated Version of the Treaty Establishing the European Community.

[196] See generally Barbara Kwiatkowska 'The *Ireland* v. *United Kingdom (MOX Plant)* Case: Applying the Doctrine of Treaty Parallelism' (2003) 18 *IJMCL* 1; Malcolm Forster, 'The *Mox Plant* Case: Provisional Measures in the International Tribunal for the Law of the Sea' (2003) 16 *LJIL* 611; Chester Brown, 'Provisional Measures Before the ITLOS: The MOX Plant Case' (2002) 17 *IJMCL* 267; Victoria Hallum 'International Tribunal for the Law of the Sea: The MOX Nuclear Plant Case' (2002) 11 *RECIEL* 372; Ted L. McDorman, 'International Tribunal for the Law of the Sea' (2001) 12 *YIEL* 589.

[197] *MOX Plant* order (2002) 41 ILM 405, [26].

[198] Ireland relied on the LOS Convention, arts. 192, 193, 194, 207, 211 and 213.

[199] *Ibid.* arts. 123 and 197. [200] *Ibid.* art. 206.

[201] *MOX Plant* order (2002) 41 ILM 405, [81].

through Irish coastal zones. Rather than acceding to this request, ITLOS arrived at its own formulation for interim relief requiring Ireland and the United Kingdom to cooperate and to enter into consultations in order to (1) exchange further information with regard to possible consequences for the Irish Sea arising out of the commissioning of the MOX plant; (2) monitor risks or effects of the operation of the MOX plant for the Irish Sea; and (3) devise, as appropriate, measures to prevent pollution of the marine environment which might result from the operation of the MOX plant.[202] These orders were clearly designed to facilitate a solution to the dispute by encouraging the parties to cooperate to the greatest extent possible. In this respect the operative orders appear to have been informed by the statement, found in the body of the decision, that

> the duty to cooperate is a fundamental principle in the prevention of pollution of the marine environment under Part XII of the [LOS Convention] and general international law and that rights arise therefrom which the Tribunal may consider appropriate to preserve under Article 290 of the Convention.[203]

The Tribunal did not explain in detail the reasons for concluding that the situation was not sufficiently urgent to justify the imposition of the provisional measures requested by Ireland. However, ITLOS appears to have been influenced in particular by assurances given to the Tribunal by the United Kingdom that there would be no additional marine transports of radioactive material to or from Sellafield as a result of the commissioning of the MOX plant,[204] and that there would be no imports to, or from, Sellafield in relation to the operation of the MOX plant until October 2002.[205]

Significantly, and by contrast with the *Southern Bluefin Tuna* order, ITLOS did not implicitly apply the precautionary principle in the *MOX Plant* order. Apparently in support of its provisional measures orders, the Tribunal stated that 'prudence and caution' required Ireland and the United Kingdom to cooperate in exchanging information concerning risks or effects of the operation of the MOX plant and in devising ways to deal with them.[206] However, in finding that there was no

[202] *Ibid.* [89].

[203] *Ibid.* [82]. In his separate opinion Judge Wolfrum described the obligation to cooperate as 'a *Grundnorm* of part XII of the Convention as of the customary international law for the protection of the environment' (at [16]).

[204] *MOX Plant* order (2002) 41 ILM 405, [78]. [205] *Ibid.* [79]. [206] *Ibid.* [84].

urgency[207] and, accordingly, refusing Ireland's requested measures, the Tribunal appears to have rejected Ireland's argument that the precautionary principle was applicable to the dispute. Ireland had contended that the principle placed the burden on the United Kingdom to establish that no harm would arise from the operation of the MOX plant and that the precautionary principle 'might usefully inform the assessment by the Tribunal of the urgency of the measures it is required to take in respect of the operation of the MOX plant'.[208]

Given the existence of scientific uncertainty as to the marine environmental impacts of the MOX plant, together with the highly dangerous nature of the radioactive materials involved, it is surprising that the Tribunal made no reference to the precautionary approach or principle.[209] Such characteristics of the dispute suggest that it is a 'textbook example'[210] of a situation that would ordinarily demand the invocation of the precautionary approach. Ultimately, however, it appears to have been determinative that there was no evidence of any likelihood of an increase in radioactivity in the Irish Sea during the few months before the annex VII tribunal would become seised of the merits of the dispute and could indicate provisional measures on its own terms.[211] None the less, the *MOX Plant* order suggests that ITLOS may have retreated to some extent from its previous favourable stance towards the precautionary principle in the *Southern Bluefin Tuna* order.[212]

[207] Given the Tribunal's assessment that the situation was not in fact urgent there are doubts whether the Tribunal had jurisdiction to order interim measures at all: Brown, above n. 196.

[208] *MOX Plant* order (2002) 41 ILM 405, [71].

[209] See David VanderZwaag, 'The Precautionary Principle and Marine Environmental Protection: Slippery Shores, Rough Seas, and Rising Normative Tides' (2002) 33 *ODIL* 165, 177–8 (noting that the central argument made by Ireland was essentially that the precautionary principle imposed a burden on the United Kingdom to show that no harm would eventuate from discharges from the plant, or other consequences of its operation).

[210] McDorman, above n. 196, 596.

[211] *MOX Plant* order (2002) 41 ILM 405, separate opinion of Judge Tullio Treves, [8].

[212] Note also the separate opinion of Judge Wolfrum in which he was strongly critical of the invocation of the precautionary approach. He noted that it was still a matter for contention whether the 'precautionary principle/approach has become part of customary international law': *MOX Plant* order (2002) 41 ILM 405, 428. He also suggested that if it was followed in the context of provisional measures then not only would there be a danger of ITLOS anticipating the judgment on the merits, but also it would make the granting of provisional measures automatic. This is a curious argument, and one that appears to misunderstand the operation of the

7.2.2.2 *MOX Plant* award

In June 2003 the annex VII tribunal established to determine the merits of the dispute decided to suspend proceedings in the case pending the finalisation of pending litigation in the ECJ.[213] None the less, the annex VII tribunal maintained that it was satisfied as to its prima facie jurisdiction and on this basis considered Ireland's fresh request for revised provisional measures. Ireland's proposed orders were far more extensive than its initial request to ITLOS. Ireland sought interim orders (1) restraining any discharge from the MOX plant into the Irish Sea; (2) requiring the United Kingdom to cooperate fully with Ireland by providing information concerning the operation of the plant and any movements of materials; and (3) requiring the parties not to engage in any action which might prejudice any environmental impact assessment required of the United Kingdom under article 206 of the LOS Convention.[214]

After a much more detailed assessment of the competing claims of the parties than that undertaken by ITLOS, the annex VII tribunal refused Ireland's request and fashioned orders in its own terms. Importantly the tribunal provided an analysis of the terms of article 290(1) that permit the prescription of provisional measures 'to prevent *serious harm* to the marine environment'.[215] The importance of the criterion of seriousness was strongly emphasised by the tribunal, and it was concluded that Ireland had not satisfactorily established that any potential harm which would meet this threshold could be caused to the marine environment pending the determination of the case on the merits.[216] On one view it might appear that the tribunal has thereby reversed

precautionary principle which, as expressed in principle 15 of the Rio Declaration, does not mandate positive action but instead seeks to ensure that lack of scientific certainty is not used as a justification for a potentially environmentally harmful activity.

213 *MOX Plant* award (order 3, of 24 June 2003) (2003) 42 ILM 1117. See the discussion of this aspect of the decision in ch. 9. See also Volker Röben, 'The Order of the UNCLOS Annex VII Arbitral Tribunal to Suspend Proceedings in the Case of the MOX Plant at Sellafield: How Much Jurisdictional Subsidiarity?' (2004) 73 *NordicJIL* 223; Robin Churchill and Joanne Scott, 'The MOX Plant Litigation: The First Half-life' (2004) 53 *ICLQ* 643.

214 LOS Convention, art. 206 requires states having reasonable grounds for believing that planned activities under their jurisdiction or control may cause damage to the marine environment to undertake an assessment of the potential impacts of those activities and make public the results of such assessments.

215 Emphasis added.

216 *MOX Plant* award (order 3, of 24 June 2003) (2003) 42 ILM 1187, [55].

the conventional wisdom, expressed by Judge Tullio Treves in the *Southern Bluefin Tuna* order, that provisional measures under article 290 of the LOS Convention have a natural affinity with the precautionary approach.[217] However, rather than altering radically the operation of article 290, the *MOX Plant* award simply suggests that the requirement of seriousness cannot be ignored. Although the burden is upon the applicant for interim orders to establish the significance of the potential harm, once that threshold is met there remains room for the precautionary approach to inform the reasoning of the court's analysis as to the risk of the harm eventuating.

In addition to rejecting Ireland's environmental arguments, the tribunal also concluded that provisional measures in the terms sought by Ireland were not necessary to protect its rights under the LOS Convention pending an award on the merits. Environmental issues intruded in this context also, with Ireland asserting that the rights that would be damaged included irreversible injury to the Irish Sea caused by liquid discharges from the Sellafield plant. However, the tribunal was not satisfied that there was any indication of the possibility of additional discharges, and therefore there was no urgent and serious risk of irreparable harm to Ireland's claimed rights.[218]

In concluding, the tribunal reaffirmed the original ITLOS provisional measures and sought to take a proactive role in supervising the parties in complying with these orders and with its recommendation that the parties engage in meaningful cooperation and consultation at a suitable intergovernmental level.[219] To this end the tribunal required that the parties submit to the tribunal reports on their compliance with the provisional measures. This 'hands-on' approach to a dispute is unusual, but clearly desirable from the perspective of the expeditious resolution of a case that has been characterised by a lack of cooperation and consultation. Such supervision also ensures that ongoing judicial attention is focused on any environmental damage between the date of the order and any eventual decision on the merits.

In January 2007 the tribunal suspended until further notice the requirement to submit periodic reports and information,[220] following the ruling of the ECJ in May 2006 that Ireland had violated article

[217] *Southern Bluefin Tuna* order (1999) 38 ILM 1624, separate opinion of Judge Treves, [9].
[218] *MOX Plant* award (order 3, of 24 June 2003) (2003) 42 ILM 1187 [61]–[62].
[219] *Ibid.* [67].
[220] *MOX Plant* award (order 5, of 22 January 2007) (available at www.pca-cpa.org).

292 of the EC Treaty which confers exclusive jurisdiction on the ECJ over matters of EC law.[221] Significantly, the ECJ decision did not engage in any way with any of the environmental matters raised by Ireland. The prospects of a judicial determination of Ireland's complaints now appears remote, although it would be open for Ireland or the European Commission to commence proceedings in the ECJ against the United Kingdom over the latter's compliance with marine environmental standards in relation to the MOX plant.

7.2.2.3 OSPAR arbitration

In parallel with the litigation under the LOS Convention, Ireland commenced proceedings against the United Kingdom in June 2001 under article 32 of the OSPAR Convention, seeking access to the full contents of two reports commissioned by the United Kingdom to examine the economic justifications for the MOX plant.[222] In this case, in which the PCA acted as registry, Ireland asserted that the disclosure would place it in a better position to consider the impacts which the MOX plant might have on the environment, and to assess the extent of the United Kingdom's compliance with the OSPAR Convention and the LOS Convention.[223] The United Kingdom refused to release this information, contending that it was not information within the meaning of article 9 of the OSPAR Convention.[224] The essence of the dispute was that while Ireland was seeking all information as to the environmental impacts of the operation of the plant, the United Kingdom insisted that the only information it was required to release related specifically to the discharging of radioactive materials into the Irish Sea.

In its July 2002 award, a majority of the arbitral panel (with Gavan Griffith dissenting)[225] concluded that the information requested by Ireland did not come within article 9(2). It was held that article 9 was

[221] *Commission of the European Communities* v. *Ireland* (2006) 45 ILM 1051.

[222] *OSPAR Arbitration* (2003) 42 ILM 1118. [223] *Ibid.* [41].

[224] OSPAR Convention, art. 9(1) provides that '[t]he Contracting Parties shall ensure that their competent authorities are required to make available the information described in paragraph 2', while art. 9(2) provides that '[t]he information referred to in paragraph 1 ... is any available information in written, visual, aural or database form on the state of the maritime area, on activities or measures adversely affecting or likely to affect it'.

[225] Gavan Griffith was the only member of the tribunal to refer to the precautionary principle, finding that its application shifted the burden of proof to the United Kingdom: *OSPAR Arbitration* (2003) 42 ILM 1118, dissenting opinion of Gavan Griffith [90].

not a general freedom of information provision,[226] and that none of the categories of information requested by Ireland could be characterised as material concerning the state of the maritime area within the meaning of article 9(2).[227] Indeed the tribunal went further, observing that even if article 9(2) covered the same information as 'environmental information' within the meaning of article 2(3) of the 1998 Convention on Access to Information, Public Participation and Decision-Making and Access to Justice in Environmental Matters it was far from clear whether Ireland's request could be accepted.[228]

McDorman has suggested that criticism of the decision for not taking into account environmental considerations, including international legal developments since the 1980s, is unfounded as the tribunal was bound to adhere to the precise terms of the OSPAR Convention.[229] He argues that in 'international environmental litigation, hard law and international legal obligations matter more than environmental aspirations and atmospherics'.[230] However, McDorman's defence of the majority appears misplaced, as the choice for the tribunal was not between the polar opposites of 'hard law' and 'environmental aspirations', but rather reaching a conclusion as to the United Kingdom's legal obligations under the OSPAR Convention which gave appropriate recognition to the environmental context of the dispute. Indeed Sands has argued in this regard that the PCA's 'textual and "acontextual" approach' confirms that environmental considerations have 'not yet fully permeated the reasoning processes of some classical international lawyers'.[231]

7.2.3 Straits of Johor *case*

This case, which was settled in 2005,[232] concerned land reclamation work being carried out by Singapore in and adjacent to the Straits of Johor, a narrow international strait separating the island of Singapore from the Malay peninsula. In July 2003 Malaysia instituted arbitral proceedings against Singapore, requesting that an annex VII tribunal be established to: (1) delimit a maritime boundary between the territorial waters of the two states in the Straits of Johor; (2) declare Singapore had breached its obligations under the LOS Convention by commencing

[226] *OSPAR Arbitration* (2003) 42 ILM 1118 [170].
[227] *Ibid.* [179]. [228] *Ibid.* [178], [181]. [229] McDorman, above n. 193. [230] *Ibid.* 338.
[231] Philippe Sands, *Principles of International Environmental Law* (2nd edn 2003), 857–8.
[232] 2005 Settlement Agreement in the Case Concerning Land Reclamation by Singapore in and Around the Straits of Johor.

land reclamation without adequate notification and consultation; and (3) decide that as a consequence of these breaches Singapore should cease land reclamation activities until it had undertaken an adequate environmental impact assessment.[233]

Pending the constitution and decision of the annex VII tribunal, Malaysia sought provisional measures in ITLOS. Specifically Malaysia asked ITLOS to order: (1) that Singapore suspend all current land reclamation activities in the vicinity of the maritime boundary; (2) that Malaysia be provided with full information on the current and projected works; (3) that Malaysia be afforded an opportunity to comment on the works and their potential impacts; and (4) that Singapore agree to negotiate with Malaysia on unresolved issues.[234]

ITLOS considered that the annex VII tribunal to be established would prima facie have jurisdiction, rejecting among other arguments Singapore's claim that neither ITLOS nor the annex VII tribunal were competent to hear the dispute until negotiations between the parties had been exhausted.[235] Malaysia's essential claim was that provisional measures were necessary to protect and preserve the marine environment in the straits, and to ensure continued maritime access to its coastline.[236]

The precautionary principle emerged in the arguments of the parties, with the Tribunal observing that Malaysia had contended that the concept of precaution must direct the application and implementation of obligations under the LOS Convention.[237] However, the Tribunal did not consider these submissions directly, instead focusing on the need for cooperation between the parties to resolve the dispute and to avoid potential marine environmental damage. The Tribunal observed that it could not be excluded that Singapore's land reclamation works might have adverse effects on the marine environment.[238] Repeating what has now become a well-worn phrase in its jurisprudence, ITLOS further held that given these possible implications '*prudence and caution* require that Malaysia and Singapore establish mechanisms for exchanging information and assessing the risks or effects of land reclamation works and devising ways to deal with them'.[239] But while suggesting that the parties themselves must adhere to the precautionary approach, the Tribunal itself declined to make the orders requested

[233] *Straits of Johor* case (8 October 2003) (available at www.itlos.org) [22].
[234] *Ibid.* [24]. [235] *Ibid.* [48]. [236] *Ibid.* [61]. [237] *Ibid.* [74]. [238] *Ibid.* [96].
[239] *Ibid.* [99] (emphasis added).

by Malaysia, and instead sought to establish a regime that would draw upon the expertise of a group of independent experts.

ITLOS unanimously ordered the parties to cooperate and, for this purpose, enter into consultations to establish an independent group of experts to conduct a study into the effects of Singapore's land reclamation activities.[240] Significantly, although stopping short of ordering the cessation of the land reclamation, the Tribunal also directed Singapore not to conduct its land reclamation in a way that might cause irreparable prejudice to the rights of Malaysia or serious harm to the marine environment, having regard to the reports of the group of independent experts to be established.[241] The Tribunal also ordered that the parties submit a report on compliance with its orders.[242]

The *Straits of Johor* case indicates ITLOS's continued awareness of environmental considerations. Environmental questions occupied a central position in the arguments of the parties and in the reasoning of the Tribunal, and the need for environmental protection and the importance of cooperation to achieve this goal were also recognised in several declarations and separate opinions.[243] As explained by Judge Anderson in his declaration, the Tribunal's orders were 'intended to be constructive guidance to the parties, designed to preserve the marine environment'.[244] In aid of this objective, the Tribunal in its provisional measures attempted both to encourage the resolution of the dispute and also to ensure that the environment was protected by reference to independent, expert, advice. Similar orders were made by ITLOS in the *Southern Bluefin Tuna* order and *MOX Plant* order, but in the *Straits of Johor* case, ITLOS showed greater willingness to become involved in the detailed modalities of environmental dispute resolution through a high degree of curial supervision of the settlement process. This appears to have been successful in inducing the parties to establish cooperative, science-based, arrangements to assess the extent of the environmental risks involved, and to devise jointly agreed solutions.

[240] *Ibid.* [106]. The report of the group of independent experts proved critical to the ultimate resolution of the dispute, and the parties in the 2005 settlement agreement committed to carrying out the various mitigating measures recommended by the group of independent experts.

[241] *Straits of Johor* case (8 October 2003) (available at www.itlos.org) [106].

[242] *Ibid.*

[243] *Ibid.* declaration of President Nelson, [7]; declaration of Judge Anderson [1], [5]; joint declaration of Judges ad hoc Hussain and Oxman, [1].

[244] *Ibid.* declaration of Judge Anderson, [5].

7.3 Conclusion

The discussion in this chapter began with an examination of two cases, the *Bering Sea Fur Seals* case, and the ICJ's decision in the *Icelandic Fisheries* case, which revealed the deficiencies in the international legal framework for marine environmental protection. As was seen, both decisions relied on problematic understandings and assumptions about the marine environment, and stated a broad right to exploit marine wildlife subject only to a limited obligation of rational use. Although the *Bering Sea Fur Seals* case is often viewed positively as having contributed to the evolution of international environmental law, the case can also be seen as having failed to adapt the law at a critical juncture when existing principles were amenable to development to recognise the needs of nature conservation. The *Fisheries Jurisdiction* case is a clear example of judicial creativity, but one that was not grounded in a satisfactory appreciation of the science and policy factors at play in fisheries management. Ultimately, both decisions share a conceptualisation of the marine environment as a domain of exploitation rather than one of protection.

These decisions therefore assisted in the development of marine environmental law principally by uncovering weaknesses in the legal framework. The problems revealed were ultimately addressed in the LOS Convention, which sought to establish a new basis for the sustainable and cooperative management of coastal and other fisheries. However, it did not comprehensively address coastal state responsibility for straddling and migratory fisheries. In the *Estai* case and the *Swordfish Stocks* case these questions concerning coastal state management of adjacent fisheries arose once again. Although neither of these cases proceeded to judgment, the controversy underlying the *Estai* case may be credited with encouraging states to conclude the Straddling Stocks Agreement to provide a more effective management regime for fisheries lying beyond the limits of coastal state EEZ jurisdiction.

The jurisprudence emerging out of the dispute settlement system of the LOS Convention has been considerably more promising from an environmental perspective than earlier case law generated by other adjudicative bodies, including the ICJ. This is despite the fact that ITLOS operates at the interface between the 'traditional logic' of the law of the sea and the more 'progressive ethic' of international environmental law.[245] Most importantly, and consistent with its broad

[245] Douglas M. Johnston, 'Fishery Diplomacy and Science and the Judicial Function' (1999) 10 *YIEL* 33, 35.

mandate over marine environmental cases, ITLOS has issued provisional measures on three occasions to protect marine environmental interests. In all these cases there has been at least implicit reliance upon the precautionary principle.

It must none the less be asked whether ITLOS and annex VII tribunals have been overly timid in applying the innovative provisions of the LOS Convention, principally found in part XII, regarding marine resource and ecosystem protection. It cannot be doubted that the jurisprudence emerging out of the part XV dispute settlement system evinces greater cognisance of environmental questions than any of the earlier cases. However, there has also been some resistance, particularly in the prompt release cases, in recognising the significance of the LOS Convention as an environmental instrument. The compulsory dispute settlement system of the LOS Convention is arguably the most important environment-focused adjudicative arrangement currently in existence, and it remains to be seen whether ITLOS judges and ad hoc arbitrators appointed to annex VII arbitral tribunals will seek to realise its full potential in this respect.

PART III • CONTEMPORARY CHALLENGES

8 Public interest proceedings

One of the consequences of the increased use of adjudicative procedures to resolve environmental disputes is that it has raised the expectations of international civil society[1] that states can now be more effectively compelled to observe their environmental commitments. Much as public interest environmental litigation has been pursued in some domestic jurisdictions,[2] it is contended that international courts may be used by environmental NGOs and other private actors to 'defend the environment'.[3] Against the background of such expectations, the three sections of this chapter consider whether it is indeed possible

[1] The term 'international civil society' refers here to the range of private actors, principally environmental NGOs, involved in advocating environmental causes in international fora: Tullio Treves, 'Introduction' in Tullio Treves *et al.* (eds.), *Civil Society, International Courts and Compliance Bodies* (2005) 1, 2; Pierre-Marie Dupuy, 'Le concept de société civil internationale, identification et genèse' in H. Gherari and S. Szurek (eds.), *L' émergence de la société civile internationale vers la privatisation du droit international?* (2003) 5.

[2] See Joseph L. Sax, *Defending the Environment: A Handbook for Citizen Action* (1970), ch. 4 ('A Role for the Courts'). Preston identifies eleven benefits yielded by domestic public interest environmental litigation: (1) it can help to realise a truly democratic process; (2) it can enforce legality in governance, maintain institutional integrity and ensure executive accountability; (3) it can assist in the progressive and principled development of environmental law and policy; (4) it can improve the quality of executive decision-making; (5) it can explicate and give force to environmental values; (6) it promotes environmental values by putting a price on them; (7) it can ensure rational discourse on environmental issues and disputes; (8) it can encourage society to debate public values, national identity, and sense of place; (9) it can have positive social effects; (10) it can foster environmentalism and environmental consciousness in society; (11) it can promote achievements in other areas of endeavour: Brian Preston, 'The Role of Public Interest Environmental Litigation' (2006) 23 *EPLJ* 337.

[3] See Linda A. Malone and Scott Pasternack, *Defending the Environment: Civil Society Strategies to Enforce International Environmental Law* (2004).

and appropriate to speak of public interest environmental litigation on the international plane.[4] The first section surveys the changes in international environmental law through which private actors have come to assume important roles in the formation and operation of environmental regimes. In the second section the chapter examines the extent to which civil society has been granted access to adjudicatory bodies resolving environmental disputes. It is contended in the third section that the character of public participation in most judicial and quasi-judicial bodies deciding environmental disputes bears only limited resemblance to domestic public interest environmental litigation. None the less, through the reception by some courts of *amicus curiae* briefs it is increasingly possible for international adjudication to be responsive to interests of community concern that lie at the heart of much international environmental disputation.[5]

8.1 Public participation in international environmental law

Two main normative and institutional developments are behind the imperative for increased public participation in the institutions of international environmental law.[6] The first is the international legal recognition of the importance of civil society involvement in domestic environmental governance, and the attempt to extrapolate these principles to address the 'democratic deficit' in international environmental regimes.[7] The second development of significance has been the growing engagement by NGOs, both formally and informally, in the

[4] Domestically, public interest environmental litigation involves proceedings commenced by an individual or community organisation against individuals, corporations, or governments to protect the environment for the benefit of the community.

[5] Markus Benzing, 'Community Interests in the Procedure of International Courts and Tribunals' (2006) 5 *LPICT* 369, 371 (community interests are 'those which transcend the interests of individual states and protect public goods of the international community as a whole or a group of states').

[6] For a concise distillation of international relations perspectives on the role of NGOs in international environmental law see Peter J. Spiro, 'Non-Governmental Organisations' in Daniel Bodansky, Jutta Brunneé, and Ellen Hey (eds.), *The Oxford Handbook of International Environmental Law* (2007) 771.

[7] Philippe Sands, 'Turtles and Torturers: The Transformation of International Law' (2000) 33 *NYUJILP* 527, 540: 'If participatory democracy is relevant to the national levels of governance then it is equally applicable at the international level, particularly since so many important decisions are now being taken outside national jurisdictions.'

identification of environmental issue areas, and in the formation, operation, implementation, and enforcement of environmental regimes. This reality sits in stark contrast to the limits faced by civil society in its involvement in international environmental litigation.

8.1.1 *Domestic environmental governance*

The concept of public participation in international environmental law is most closely associated with the idea that citizens should be afforded an opportunity to participate in governmental decision-making on environmental matters. Hence principle 10 of the Rio Declaration proclaimed that '[e]nvironmental issues are best handled with the participation of all concerned citizens, at the relevant level', and to this end encouraged states to provide '[e]ffective access to judicial and administrative proceedings, including redress and remedy'.[8] Agenda 21 also stressed the importance of public participation for sustainable development, particularly in environmental impact assessments and environmental decision-making,[9] and spoke of NGOs as 'play[ing] a vital role in the shaping and implementation of participatory democracy'.[10] These texts therefore establish a linkage between democratic governance and sound environmental management, a connection that was to be further emphasised in the Plan of Implementation of the World Summit on Sustainable Development.[11]

The concept of democratic environmental governance through citizen participation that these non-binding texts espouse has now been given concrete recognition in the Aarhus Convention. Described by former United Nations Secretary-General Kofi Annan as 'the most ambitious venture in environmental democracy undertaken under the auspices of the United Nations',[12] the Aarhus Convention rests on three main pillars which give legal force to the language of principle 10

[8] See also IUCN–World Conservation Union, *Draft International Covenant on Environment and Development* (3rd edn 2004) art. 12(4): 'The Parties shall ensure that all concerned persons have the right to participate effectively during decision-making processes at the local, national and international levels regarding activities, measures, plans, programmes and policies that may have a significant effect on the environment.'

[9] UN Doc. A/CONF.151/26/Rev.1 (1992), ch. 23. [10] *Ibid.* ch. 27.

[11] UN Doc. A/CONF.199/20 (2002), [138]: 'Good governance is essential for sustainable development. Sound economic policies, solid democratic institutions responsive to the needs of the people and improved infrastructure are the basis for sustained economic growth, poverty eradication, and employment creation.'

[12] Jeremy Wates, 'NGOs and the Aarhus Convention' in Tullio Treves *et al.* (eds.), *Civil Society, International Courts and Compliance Bodies* (2005) 167, 167.

of the Rio Declaration. The first of these is access to environmental information,[13] the provision of which allows citizens to take advantage of the second and third participatory rights – public participation in environmental decision-making,[14] and access to justice in environmental matters.[15]

In addition to speaking to questions of domestic environmental governance, the Aarhus Convention is also noteworthy for the way in which it highlights the importance of civil society engagement with international environmental diplomacy and law. This was witnessed in the very negotiation of the convention text, with environmental NGOs admitted on the basis that a regime addressing public interest environmental concerns necessarily required input from civil society.[16] The role of NGOs is also formalised in the operation of the Aarhus Convention itself. They are entitled to participate in meetings of the parties, and can trigger the NCP established under article 15 (which mandated the development of an NCP that would 'allow for appropriate public involvement').[17] In addition, article 3(7) requires the parties 'to promote the application of the principles of [the] Convention in international environmental decision-making processes and within the framework of international organisations in matters relating to the environment'. Although the extent of this obligation ('to promote') is somewhat open ended, its inclusion buttresses arguments that international environmental organisations should be opened to appropriate civil society involvement.[18] Specifically, it suggests that the provisions of the Aarhus Convention regarding the importance of open-standing rules for environmental NGOs in domestic justice mechanisms should also be given effect in international courts and tribunals.[19]

[13] Aarhus Convention, arts. 4 and 5.

[14] *Ibid.* arts. 6 (public participation in decisions on specific activities), 7 (public participation concerning environmental plans and policies) and 8 (public participation during the legislative and administrative process).

[15] *Ibid.* art. 9. [16] Wates, above n. 12, 177–9.

[17] Decision 1/7, Report of the First Meeting of the Parties to the Convention on Access to Information, Public Participation in Decision-Making and Access to Justice in Environmental Matters, UN Doc. ECE/MP.PP/2/Add.8 (2002). See [18]: 'communications may be brought before the Committee by one or more members of the public concerning a Party's compliance with the Convention'.

[18] See also the Almaty Guidelines on Public Participation in International Forums, UN Doc. ECE/MP.PP/WG.1/2005/8/Add.1 (2004); Elisa Morgera, 'An Update on the Aarhus Convention' (2005) 14(2) *RECIEL* 138.

[19] See arts. 9(2) and 2(5).

8.1.2 *International environmental governance*

Well before the Aarhus Convention sought to transpose the notion of public participation from the domestic plane to international institutions, many environmental regimes had recognised civil society groups as legitimate observers and participants. The 1987 Montreal Protocol on Substances that Deplete the Ozone Layer opened meetings of parties to '[a]ny body or agency, whether national or international, governmental or non-governmental, qualified in fields relating to the protection of the ozone layer'.[20] This formula has been replicated in other global and regional environmental agreements including the 1992 United Nations Framework Convention on Climate Change,[21] the Kyoto Protocol[22] and the Biodiversity Convention.[23] Even in earlier regimes, most of which do not provide for civil society participation,[24] NGOs have over time been granted observer status and have taken an active role in their operation. For instance, the 1946 International Convention for the Regulation of Whaling makes no reference to participation by any actor other than the parties themselves,[25] yet from 1977 onwards NGOs began to be accredited as observers and have made a significant contribution to the functioning of the International Whaling Commission.[26]

The almost universal experience has been that NGOs have taken advantage of even the most restricted rights of access and, in so doing, they have brought a range of benefits to environmental regimes. These include raising the public profile of environmental issues, increasing the transparency of negotiations and decisions, providing policy and technical guidance, and applying pressure to states to hold to their commitments.[27] As Yamin explains, in discharging these functions NGOs act out a host of roles including as 'agenda-setters', 'conscience keepers', 'partners' with states and intergovernmental organisations, 'experts', 'lobbyists' and, finally, as 'enforcers'.[28]

[20] Art. 11(5). [21] Art. 7(6). [22] Art. 13(8). [23] Art. 23(5).

[24] One striking exception is CITES, art. 11. CITES is also unusual in providing that observers who are admitted have a 'right' to participate.

[25] Although see art. 4 (providing that the Commission may collaborate with 'public or private organisations' to gather information and conduct studies in relation to whales and whaling).

[26] Kal Raustiala, 'The "Participatory Revolution" in International Environmental Law' (1997) 21 *HarvELR* 537, 545.

[27] *Ibid.* 558–65.

[28] Farhana Yamin, 'NGOs and International Environmental Law: A Critical Evaluation of their Roles and Responsibilities' (2001) 10 *RECIEL* 149.

8.2 Public participation in international environmental litigation

8.2.1 Civil society in international environmental litigation

Reflecting the statist character of international law, traditionally only states have enjoyed standing to pursue claims in international courts and tribunals, notwithstanding the fact that international judicial decision-making impacts upon the lives of individual citizens and other subjects of international law.[29] Non-state actors, including natural persons, corporations, and NGOs have, for the most part, been excluded as claimants or as respondents. Similarly, international organisations of states have rarely been permitted to initiate or intervene in arbitral or judicial proceedings. A major implication of these exclusions is that the opportunities for international litigation in the public interest have been impeded even though international law has recognised a number of environmental *erga omnes* obligations (in both treaties, and in custom) which require such proceedings if they are to be given effect.[30]

None the less, there has been considerable movement from the earliest dispute settlement practice, which was wholly exclusionary as regards non-state actors. While Chinkin and Sadurska observed in 1991 that 'dispute resolution processes, in their goals, participants, procedures, and outcomes, remain geared towards excluding individuals and downgrading their claims as against those of the relevant states',[31] there are many indications that this situation is now changing, and that previously impenetrable institutions are becoming more amenable to public participation. Romano has argued that, as a consequence, the 'international judicial process has changed from a device concocted by states to serve their own interests into a tool available to all entities ... to obtain justice and further the rule of law'.[32] This conclusion may be somewhat premature in the environmental context

[29] Christine M. Chinkin, 'Alternative Dispute Resolution under International Law' in Malcolm D. Evans (ed.), *Remedies in International Law: The Institutional Dilemma* (1998) 123, 139.

[30] See Benzing, above n. 5.

[31] Christine M. Chinkin and Romana Sadurska, 'The Anatomy of International Dispute Resolution' (1991) 7 *OhioStJDR* 39, 78.

[32] Cesare P. R. Romano, 'The Proliferation of International Judicial Bodies: The Pieces of the Puzzle' (1999) 31 *NYUJILP* 709, 739. See also Francisco Orrego Vicuña, *International Dispute Settlement in an Evolving Global Society* (2004) 31: there is 'a new trend in dispute settlement under international law, one where access of individuals and corporations to international claims and remedies is gradually being recognised as a right inherent in their possession of international personality'.

(even though it is apposite in other areas, such as in relation to investment arbitration),[33] but it none the less highlights the general trend in developments.

8.2.2 Existing opportunities for public interest proceedings

8.2.2.1 Courts of general jurisdiction

Courts and tribunals with general subject matter jurisdiction currently present the most limited opportunities for civil society instigation of international judicial or arbitral proceedings.

ICJ

Only states may be parties to, or intervene in, contentious cases before the ICJ[34] and no exceptions have been made for disputes involving environmental, or other community, interests. Hence the dedicated Environmental Chamber of the Court, established in 1993, can only admit states as parties. The chamber has not been used, which tends to support the widely held view that the ICJ is unlikely to play a major role in environmental dispute settlement unless it is open to broader participation. In this respect Judge Jessup argued in 1971 that 'it would be folly' for environmental treaties to allow disputes to be settled in the ICJ without reform to the ICJ to admit non-state entities 'which will be as much concerned with enforcement of the new standards as will governments of states'.[35]

Although they may not appear as parties, in some circumstances non-state actors may have some involvement in environmental litigation in the ICJ. Under article 34(2) of the Statute of the ICJ, the Court may request of public international organisations information relevant to cases before it, and may receive relevant information provided by such international organisations on their own initiative. The Court and the Registrar have made it clear, however, that article 34(2) encompasses only international organisations of states, and not NGOs.[36] In addition,

[33] Elihu Lauterpacht, *Aspects of the Administration of International Justice* (1991) 60–75.

[34] Statute of the ICJ, arts. 34(1), 62, 63.

[35] Philip C. Jessup, 'Do New Problems Need New Courts?' (1971) 65 *ProcASIL* 261, 265.

[36] Christine M. Chinkin and Ruth Mackenzie, 'Intergovernmental Organizations as "Friends of the Court"' in Laurence Boisson de Chazournes, Cesare P. R. Romano, and Ruth Mackenzie (eds.), *International Organizations and International Dispute Settlement: Trends and Prospects* (2002) 135, 140–1. The Court declined to accept an NGO submission in the *Gabčíkovo-Nagymaros Project* case (*Hungary/Slovakia*) [1997] ICJ Rep 7: see Alan E. Boyle, 'The *Gabcikovo-Nagymaros* case: New Law in Old Bottles'

the ICJ has authority, under article 50, to seek expert advice from any individual, body, bureau, commission, or other organisation. Although this procedure would appear to allow the Court to seek information from any body, including an environmental organisation such as the IUCN–World Conservation Union, to date the Court has not sought to do so.

In the exercise of its advisory jurisdiction, which may only be initiated by a competent agency of the United Nations, the ICJ is more open to participation by non-state actors.[37] This is appropriate given that, as Rosenne has observed, '[t]he advisory competence of the International Court supplies a true *erga omnes* procedure'.[38] In advisory proceedings the agency invoking the procedure is afforded an opportunity to present oral statements in support of its position, and states entitled to appear before the Court may also present written and oral arguments.[39] Additionally, international organisations considered likely to be able to furnish information on the question before the Court may be permitted to make written and oral submissions.[40] It would appear that in advisory proceedings the Court may receive submissions from NGOs, which could therefore act, at least in a limited sense, as *amici curiae*.[41] However, the involvement by civil society in advisory cases has

(1997) 8 *YIEL* 13, 20. Similarly in the *Asylum* case (*Colombia/Peru*) [1950] ICJ Rep 266 a submission by the International League for the Rights of Man was rejected on the grounds that the organisation was not a public international organisation within the meaning of the Statute of the ICJ, art. 34.

37 Statute of the ICJ, art. 65(1).

38 Shabtai Rosenne, 'Some Reflections *Erga Omnes*' in Antony Anghie and Garry Sturgess (eds.), *Legal Visions of the 21st Century: Essays in Honour of Judge Christopher Weeramantry* (1998) 509, 522.

39 Statute of the ICJ, art. 66(2).

40 *Ibid.*

41 In Practice Direction XII (adopted 30 July 2004) the ICJ has clarified the procedure for the submission of *amicus* briefs and other material. It provides:

1. Where an international non-governmental organization submits a written statement and/or document in an advisory opinion case on its own initiative, such statement and/or document is not to be considered as part of the case file.
2. Such statements and/or documents shall be treated as publications readily available and may accordingly be referred to by States and intergovernmental organizations presenting written and oral statements in the case in the same manner as publications in the public domain.
3. Written statements and/or documents submitted by international non-governmental organizations will be placed in a designated location in the Peace Palace. All States as well as intergovernmental organizations presenting written or oral statements under Article 66 of the Statute

not universally been welcomed. In his separate opinion in the *Legality of the Use or Threat of Nuclear Weapons*,[42] Judge Guillaume was critical of the role of NGOs in bringing pressure to bear on the World Health Organisation and General Assembly to request advisory opinions of the Court.[43]

PCA

On its face, the PCA appears substantially more accessible than the ICJ. Under the 2001 Optional Rules for the Arbitration of Disputes Relating to Natural Resources and/or the Environment (Environmental Rules), disputes may involve parties other than states, including international organisations, NGOs, and corporations.[44] However, these innovative arrangements have never been used despite the growing number of environmental cases brought before the PCA, a fact which suggests that, in practical terms, only states are likely to be regular parties to PCA proceedings. None the less, the Environmental Rules remain a helpful and innovative template for the possible organisation of environmental dispute resolution involving civil society groups and other non-state participants.

ITLOS

Although the subject matter jurisdiction of ITLOS does not reach as far as that of the ICJ or the PCA, its broad competence in marine environmental matters justifies a consideration of its rules relating to standing alongside these two bodies. It is principally in relation to deep seabed disputes, which may well implicate environmental matters, that non-state parties enjoy standing to commence proceedings in ITLOS. In such proceedings, not only states but also the Seabed Authority, the enterprise, and natural or juridical persons parties to a contract relating to the area, may appear before the ITLOS Seabed Disputes Chamber.[45]

In relation to environmental disputes arising under the LOS Convention more generally, natural persons and other non-state entities may not invoke the compulsory dispute settlement provisions. However, it should be noted that international organisations

will be informed as to the location where statements and/or documents submitted by international non-governmental organizations may be consulted.

42 *Legality of the Threat or Use of Nuclear Weapons* [1996] ICJ Rep 226.

43 *Ibid*. 287.

44 Environmental Rules, introduction and art. 1(1).

45 LOS Convention, annex VI, art. 20(2).

of states satisfying certain specific criteria may be parties to the LOS Convention.[46] As such they may participate in contentious cases under part XV, including as applicants or respondents in disputes heard by ITLOS, annex VII, or annex VIII arbitral panels. One case has been brought on this basis, although it was subsequently suspended indefinitely when the parties reached an apparent settlement.[47] Finally, ITLOS is open to entities other than states parties in any cases submitted pursuant to an agreement conferring jurisdiction on ITLOS that is accepted by all parties to a dispute.[48]

To date no environmental or other NGO has sought to participate in ITLOS proceedings as an *amicus curiae*.[49] However, it would appear possible for ITLOS to call upon NGO submissions in exercising the powers granted to it under the ITLOS Rules of Court to seek and receive expert opinion.[50]

8.2.2.2 Regional economic courts free trade regimes

In contrast to international courts with general subject matter and geographic jurisdiction, courts and other dispute settlement bodies at the centre of regional integration or free trade regimes tend to be far more open to participation by non-state actors.

Central American Court of Justice

The most accessible institution in this respect is the Central American Court of Justice (CACJ), the principal judicial organ of the Central American Integration System (SICA), in which any interested party, including natural and legal persons, may commence proceedings

[46] *Ibid.* art. 305(1)(f) and annex IX ('Participation by International Organizations'). The EC appears to be the only international organisation to meet the strict requirements of this provision.

[47] *Conservation and Sustainable Exploitation of Swordfish Stocks in the South-Eastern Pacific Ocean (Chile/European Community)* (proceedings suspended) (15 March 2001 and 16 December 2003) (available at www.itlos.org).

[48] LOS Convention, annex VI, art. 20(2).

[49] However, the positions of intergovernmental environmental organisations have sometimes been made known to the tribunal by parties to cases. See in particular the reference made by Australia to the practice of the Commission for the Conservation of Antarctic Marine Living Resources in the *Volga* case (*Russian Federation* v. *Australia*) (prompt release) (2003) 42 ILM 159.

[50] ITLOS Rules of Court, art. 82. See also art. 84 under which intergovernmental organisations may furnish information to ITLOS at the request of the tribunal or upon its own initiative. See generally Philippe Gautier, 'NGOs and Law of the Sea Disputes' in Tullio Treves *et al.* (eds.), *Civil Society, International Courts and Compliance Bodies* (2005) 233.

against a state party that has enacted laws inconsistent with SICA law.[51] Similarly, where they are directly affected, non-state entities may bring proceedings against SICA organs on the grounds that they have failed to fulfil a requirement of SICA law.[52]

ECJ

Access to the ECJ is somewhat more limited than access to the CACJ. Natural and legal persons involved in domestic court proceedings in which a preliminary ruling is requested of the ECJ may make submissions.[53] In addition, individuals may initiate proceedings to contest the legality of actions of EC institutions under EC law, but only if the decision is addressed to that person, and is of 'direct and individual concern' to them.[54] The latter condition has been interpreted fairly narrowly by the ECJ, so that purely public interest proceedings are inadmissible.[55] The impugned decision must affect complainants 'by reason of certain attributes which are peculiar to them or by reason of circumstances in which they are differentiated from all other persons and by virtue of these factors distinguishes them individually just as in the case of the person addressed'.[56]

Individuals may not bring claims in the ECJ against member states in order to ensure compliance with EC law – such proceedings may only be commenced by other member states, or by the Commission. However, the Commission has been highly active in this respect, and has been encouraged by NGOs and other non-state actors to take action against

[51] 1992 Agreement on the Statute of the Central American Court of Justice, art. 22(c).

[52] *Ibid.* art. 22(g).

[53] EC Treaty, art. 234; 1957 Protocol on the Statute of the Court of Justice of the European Economic Community; Statute of the ECJ, art. 20.

[54] EC Treaty, art. 230.

[55] Ludwig Krämer, 'Public Interest Litigation in Environmental Matters Before European Courts' (1996) 8 *JEL* 1, 11–12.

[56] *Plaumann & Co* v. *Commission* (C-25/62) [1963] ECR 95, 107. This test is of remarkable longevity, and was applied in *Stichting Greenpeace Council (Greenpeace International)* v. *Commission* (C-321/95) [1998] ECR I-1651 to deny standing to an environmental NGO which challenged a decision by the Commission to provide financial support to Spain for the construction of power stations. See Jacqueline Peel, 'Giving the Public a Voice in the Protection of the Global Environment: Avenues for Participation by NGOs in Dispute Resolution at the European Court of Justice and World Trade Organization' (2001) 12 *ColoJELP* 47, 50; Diana L. Torrens, '*Locus Standi* for Environmental Associations under EC Law – *Greenpeace* – A Missed Opportunity for the ECJ' (1999) 8 *RECIEL* 336, 343 (arguing that '[s]ituations do arise in which it is the Commission which needs to be monitored and … environmental associations … have a positive role to play in the enhanced enforcement of environmental rules).

members for breaches of Community environmental laws.[57] In doing so the Commission has cooperated with civil society and assumed a guardianship role in relation to European environmental legality.

In terms of *amicus curiae* participation, no right to submit *amicus* briefs is expressly recognised in relation to the ECJ. However, arguably the public interest function of the system is adequately served through the unique role given to advocates-general before the Court.[58] Finally, it must be noted that civil society possesses an indirect method of enforcing EC environmental law via the preliminary reference procedure under article 234 of the EC Treaty. Under this mechanism national courts may submit a request for a preliminary ruling to the ECJ on an issue concerning the interpretation or validity of a provision of EC environmental law.[59]

NAFTA and NAAEC

NAFTA does not itself provide an avenue for public interest environmental litigation, although it does allow non-state actors to commence proceedings in relation to investment matters that may well involve environmental issues. In a world first NAFTA has also elaborated procedures permitting environmental groups to submit *amicus* briefs.

Under chapter 11 of NAFTA, private investors are entitled to institute arbitral proceedings where there has been an interference with a foreign investment contrary to NAFTA rules. There have now been several cases on this basis, with private investors seeking determinations that environmental laws of member states are inconsistent with NAFTA. This has been a source of significant contention given that the process may lead to the effective overriding of domestic environmental standards.[60] However, these concerns have been tempered to some

[57] Peel, above n. 56, 50. For a discussion of the problems faced by the Commission in enforcing member state compliance see R. Williams, 'The European Commission and the Enforcement of Environmental Law: An Invidious Position' (1995) 14 *YBEuroL* 351.

[58] Jessica Maria Almqvist, 'The Accessibility of European Integration Courts from an NGO Perspective' in Tullio Treves *et al.* (eds.), *Civil Society, International Courts and Compliance Bodies* (2005) 271, 276.

[59] See generally Han Somsen, 'The Private Enforcement of Member State Compliance with EC Environmental Law: An Unfulfilled Promise?' (2000) 1 *YBEuroEL* 311.

[60] See generally Joseph Freedman, 'Implications of the NAFTA Investment chapter for Environmental Regulation' in Alexandre Kiss, Dinah Shelton, and Kanami Ishibashi (eds.), *Economic Globalization and Compliance with International Environmental Agreements* (2003) 89.

extent by the decision of the NAFTA Free Trade Commission,[61] and the arbitral tribunal in *Methanex Corp.* v. *United States*,[62] to accept *amicus* submissions from environmental NGOs. This important development has had spill-over effects, with model Canadian and United States bilateral investment treaties now including provision for involvement by civil society as a quasi-third party in investment disputes through *amicus* procedures.[63]

The Statement of the NAFTA Free Trade Commission on Non-Disputing Party (NDP) Participation represents the most serious effort to date by an international organisation to set out detailed procedures governing the acceptance of *amicus curiae* briefs, including those submitted by environmental NGOs raising public interest concerns regarding environmental issues. The NAFTA NDP Statement, which confirms a decision to allow *amici* briefs by a NAFTA panel, acknowledges that no provision of NAFTA limits a tribunal's discretion to accepted written submissions from a person or entity that is not a disputing party. Under the procedure, NDPs are required to seek leave from the tribunal to file a submission. In determining whether to grant leave to file such a submission, the tribunal must consider, among other things, the extent to which the submission would assist the tribunal in determining a factual or legal issue in dispute, whether the non-disputing party has a significant interest in the arbitration, and also whether there is public interest in the subject matter of the arbitration. Even if leave is granted there are strict limits to *amicus* participation. Only a written brief may be submitted, and the tribunal has no power to authorise access to materials or to allow an *amicus* to participate in, let alone attend, hearings.[64]

Additionally, NAFTA is accompanied by the NAAEC under which NAFTA parties undertake to enforce their environmental laws. Knox notes that the NAAEC 'provides unprecedented opportunities for

[61] 'Statement of the Free Trade Commission on Non-Disputing Party Participation' (2004) 16 *WTAM* 167.

[62] *Methanex Corp.* v. *United States*, Decision on Petitions from Third Persons to Intervene as 'Amicus Curiae' (2001) (available at www.state.gov/documents/organization/6039.pdf); 'Tribunal Announcement on Procedures for Amicus Submissions' (2004) (available at www.worldbank.org/icsid/methanex.htm). See Howard Mann, 'Opening the Doors, At Least a Little: Comment on the Amicus Decision in Methanex v. United States' (2002) 10 *RECIEL* 241.

[63] Kyla Tienhaara, 'Third Party Participation in Investment-Environment Disputes: Recent Developments' (2007) 16 *RECIEL* 230, 233.

[64] *Ibid.* 231.

participation by civil society at the international level'.[65] Part five of the NAAEC establishes a public complaints procedure under which any citizen of the three NAFTA parties, Canada, Mexico, and the United States, may make a submission to the NAAEC alleging that a party to NAFTA is failing to implement its environmental laws.[66] The NAAEC secretariat may, in response, decide to author a factual record on the matter submitted.[67] The NAAEC also incorporates a procedure for binding arbitration where there is a 'persistent pattern of failure by [a] Party to enforce its environmental law',[68] although this mechanism has not yet been utilised. However, it is the citizen submission procedure that has attracted the most detailed scrutiny, as the first and only example outside the European context where individuals may bring claims regarding environmental matters directly to a quasi-judicial supranational body.

WTO

The WTO dispute settlement system is designed to resolve inter-state disputes regarding compliance with WTO rules and non-state entities have no rights of standing.[69] However, in the face of growing demands for greater accessibility and accountability in the WTO's engagement with issues concerning environmental and human rights standards civil society has been given an increased voice in WTO proceedings. This has come principally as a result of the decision of the Appellate Body in *United States – Import Prohibition of Certain Shrimp and Shrimp Products*[70] (*Shrimp–Turtle I*). Significantly, therefore, it is the judicial

[65] John H. Knox and David L. Markell, 'The Innovative North American Commission for Environmental Cooperation' in David L. Markell and John H. Knox (eds.), *Greening NAFTA: The North American Commission for Environmental Cooperation* (2003) 1, 2.

[66] Kal Raustiala, 'Citizen Submissions and Treaty Review in the NAAEC' in David L. Markell and John H. Knox (eds.), *Greening NAFTA: The North American Commission for Environmental Cooperation* (2003) 257.

[67] NAAEC, art. 15. [68] *Ibid.* arts. 22–36.

[69] Initially it was thought that the dispute settlement process was entirely closed so that not even the private representatives of governments could take part. However, a panel decision to this effect was reversed by the Appellate Body: *European Communities – Regime for the Importation, Sale and Distribution of Bananas*, WTO Doc. WT/DS27/R (1997) (Report of the Appellate Body). For an overview of early practice in the WTO in relation to NGO participation see Steve Charnovitz, 'Participation of Nongovernmental Organizations in the World Trade Organization' (1996) 17 *UPaJIEconL* 331.

[70] *United States – Import Prohibition of Certain Shrimp and Shrimp Products*, WTO Doc. WT/DS58/R (1998) (report of the panel), WTO Doc. WT/DS58/AB/R (1998) (report of the Appellate Body) (*Shrimp–Turtle I* Appellate Body Report).

rather than the political organs of the WTO that have been responsible for opening WTO dispute settlement to involvement by non-state actors.

The WTO DSU[71] does not provide for the submission of *amicus curiae* briefs, but in *Shrimp–Turtle I* the Appellate Body held none the less that under articles 12 and 13 of the DSU a WTO panel 'has the discretionary authority either to accept and consider or to reject information submitted to it, whether requested by a panel or not'.[72] The Appellate Body also upheld the panel's earlier finding that it could consider NGO submissions when they were incorporated with those of a party to the proceedings.[73] *Amicus* briefs by environmental NGOs may therefore find their way before WTO dispute settlement bodies via two routes – directly when submitted by the NGO, or indirectly as part of a brief submitted by a disputing party.[74]

Although some degree of public participation in WTO dispute settlement proceedings is now possible, the extent of non-state actor involvement remains a contentious and unresolved issue with the General Council, the WTO's plenary body, opposing efforts by the WTO's judicial bodies to allow *amicus* submissions.[75] In response to concerns of WTO members (principally developing states),[76] in *European Communities – Measures Affecting Asbestos and Asbestos-Containing Products*[77] the Appellate Body adopted, under article 16(1) of its working procedures, guidelines for the submission of *amicus* briefs.[78] Notwithstanding the significant issues of public interest in this dispute, the Appellate Body rejected all seventeen applications to submit *amicus* briefs on the grounds that they

71 1994 Marrakesh Agreement Establishing the World Trade Organization, annex 2.

72 *Shrimp–Turtle I* Appellate Body report, WTO Doc. WT/DS58/AB/R (1998) 38. See generally Georg C. Umbricht, 'An "Amicus Curiae Brief" on Amicus Curiae Briefs at the WTO' (2001) *JIEconL* 773.

73 *Shrimp–Turtle I* Appellate Body report, WTO Doc. WT/DS58/AB/R (1998) 39.

74 For a discussion of the decision and its implications for dispute settlement under the WTO see Peel, above n. 56, 64–70.

75 John H. Knox, 'The Judicial Resolution of Conflicts Between Trade and the Environment' (2004) 28 *HarvELR* 1, 46.

76 See generally Maki Tanaka, 'Bridging the Gap Between Northern NGOs and Southern Sovereigns in the Trade-Environment Debate: The Pursuit of Democratic Dispute Settlements in the WTO Under the Rio Principles' (2003) 30 *ELQ* 113.

77 *European Communities – Measures Affecting Asbestos and Asbestos-Containing Products*, WTO Doc. WT/DS135/AB/R (2001) (Report of the Appellate Body).

78 *European Communities – Measures Affecting Asbestos and Asbestos-Containing Products* (communication from the Appellate Body), 2000 WTO Doc. AB-2000–11 (2000); additional procedure adopted under rule 16(1) of the working procedures for appellate review, WTO Doc. WT/DS135/9.

did not comply with the guidelines it had articulated.[79] It has been speculated that this outright rejection (with few reasons) was partly motivated by an awareness of the controversy surrounding the reception of *amicus* briefs.[80] In addition, in *United States – Import Prohibition of Certain Shrimp and Shrimp Products; Recourse to article 21.5*[81] (*Shrimp–Turtle II*) the Appellate Body refused, without giving reasons, to consider the one *amicus* brief it received.[82] In the recent *European Communities – Measures Affecting the Approval and Marketing of Biotech Products*[83] the panel accepted *amicus* briefs from scientists, academics, and NGOs but went on to find that it was unnecessary to take them into account.[84] In light of this pattern, McDonald has argued that the WTO has achieved little in practice in involving civil society, and that its much-trumpeted interpretation of the DSU constitutes 'little more than an indulgence of civil society's contribution'.[85]

As matters currently stand, the admission of *amicus* briefs in the WTO depends upon procedures of an essentially improvised and discretionary character. There is a need to formalise these procedures in a way that not only gives meaningful opportunities for participation, but also deals with the fundamental question as to qualifications for admitting civil society groups. *Amici curiae* can serve a number of important functions in WTO dispute settlement, including by providing evidence, legal, and factual analysis and above all by bringing a trade dispute into its broader social, political, and environmental focus.[86] If the interface between trade and environment agendas is to be satisfactorily resolved, it seems essential that this contribution is recognised through detailed procedures for *amicus* participation that apply generally, rather than to specific disputes when they arise.

79 Mary Footer and Salman Zia-Zarifi, 'European Communities – Measures Affecting Asbestos and Asbestos-Containing Products: The World Trade Organization on Trial for its Handling of Occupational Health and Safety Issues' (2002) 3 *MJIL* 120, 131–3.

80 Lise Johnson and Elisabeth Tuerk, 'CIEL's Experience in WTO Dispute Settlement: Challenges and Complexities from a Practical Point of View' in Tullio Treves *et al.* (eds.), *Civil Society, International Courts and Compliance Bodies* (2005) 243, 246.

81 *United States – Import Prohibition of Certain Shrimp and Shrimp Products; Recourse to article 21.5*, WTO Doc. WT/DS58/AB/RW (2001) (report of the Appellate Body).

82 *Ibid.* [78].

83 *European Communities – Measures Affecting the Approval and Marketing of Biotech Products* WTO Docs WT/DS291/R, WT/DS292/R, WT/DS293/R (2006) (report of the panel).

84 *Ibid.* [7.11].

85 Jan McDonald, 'Look While you Leap: The WTO Biotech Dispute Panel Report' (2006) 23 *EPLJ* 417, 423.

86 Johnson and Tuerk, above n. 80, 249.

8.2.2.3 Human rights bodies

Human rights courts and complaints procedures are among the most accessible international judicial and quasi-judicial mechanisms in existence. Once local remedies have been exhausted,[87] and a claim raising environmental concerns is framed in terms of a human rights violation, then individuals may turn to such bodies to seek a remedy.[88]

The most important global institution in this respect is the Human Rights Committee.[89] However, it is the ECtHR that has been the most active in the environmental field.[90] Under the amended 1950 Convention for the Protection of Human Rights and Fundamental Freedoms,[91] individuals, NGOs, and groups may bring a case in the Court against a state party alleged to have committed a human rights violation.[92] They must, however, establish that they have been a 'victim', a term which the court has construed narrowly, and to the exclusion of public interest proceedings.[93]

Development bank inspection panels

Several development banks have established an inspection panel process under which individuals may, in relation to a particular project funding by these banks, seek review of the compliance by the bank with its operational policies and procedures. Accordingly, complaints regarding compliance with international environmental standards are therefore only possible to the extent that these have been incorporated in the relevant bank's internal policies and lending guidelines.

In the World Bank, affected persons from the borrowing state may make a request for inspection to an inspection panel composed of three members.[94] Individual complainants may not seek review on

87 See Dinah Shelton, *Remedies in International Human Rights Law* (2nd edn 2005) chs. 5 and 6.

88 Malone and Pasternack, above n. 3, 9; Caroline Dommen, 'Claiming Environmental Rights: Some Possibilities Offered by the United Nations' Human Rights Mechanisms' (1998) 11 *GeoIELR* 1.

89 Established under the 1966 Optional Protocol to the International Covenant on Civil and Political Rights, art. 2.

90 For a review of this jurisprudence see ch. 10.

91 See the 1994 Protocol No. 11 to the European Convention on Human Rights.

92 European Convention on Human Rights, art. 34.

93 *Klass* v. *Germany* (1978) 2 EHRR 214. Much the same approach has been taken by the Human Rights Committee: *Brun* v. *France* [2006] UNHRC 72.

94 International Bank for Reconstruction and Development Resolution 93–10 and International Development Association Resolution 93–6, 22 September 1993, (1993) 34 ILM 520 (IBRD and IDA Inspection Panel Resolutions). See also Operating

their own behalf, but only via a 'community of persons', such as a citizens' organisation or other group.[95] Additionally, the rights or interests of the complaining party must have been seriously affected in some way as a result of an act or omission of the Bank as a consequence of a failure to follow its own operational policies and procedures.

8.3 Reconceptualising international public interest litigation

Raustiala has described the prolific growth in the opportunities for civil society to participate in international environmental governance as a 'participatory revolution'.[96] However, as has been seen, this revolution has not swept away the statist orientation of international adjudication in the environmental field. Before this is possible it is essential that attention be paid to underlying conceptual issues.[97] As Fitzmaurice has explained, there is presently no 'coherent overall doctrine' to account for the legal status of individuals and other non-state actors in international environmental law as bearers of rights or as subjects of responsibilities.[98] Similarly uncertain is on what basis civil society groups and other non-state actors could be recognised as litigants in international environmental proceedings.

One purpose that may currently be discounted is that of vindicating individual interests and rights. Unlike international human rights law, international environmental law seldom speaks to non-state actors as rights-bearers even though they may have a direct interest in global environmental problems.[99] It is therefore unsurprising that there is no international mechanism for individuals to complain

Procedures, Inspection Panel for the International Bank for Reconstruction and Development and the International Development Association (1995) 34 ILM 510.

[95] IBRD and IDA Inspection Panel Resolutions, above n. 94, [12].

[96] Raustiala, above n. 26.

[97] Ellen Hey, *Reflections on an International Environmental Court* (2000) 14–16; Peggy Rodgers Kalas, 'International Environmental Dispute Settlement and the Need for Access by Non-State Entities' (2001) 12 *ColoJELP* 191.

[98] Malgosia A. Fitzmaurice, 'International Environmental Law as a Special Field' in L. A. N. M. Barnhoorn and K. C. Wellens (eds.), *Diversity in Secondary Rules and the Unity of International Law* (1995) 181, 222.

[99] See generally John H. Knox, 'A New Approach to Compliance with International Environmental Law: The Submissions Procedure of the NAFTA Environmental Commission' (2001) 28 *ELQ* 1; David A. Wirth, 'Reexamining Decision-Making Processes in International Environmental Law' (1994) 79 *IowaLR* 769.

directly of breaches of international environmental norms.[100] Instead, international law seeks to address environmental problems of direct concern to individuals, such as environmental damage or poor administrative decision-making, by promoting more effective environmental justice mechanisms at the domestic level and, in the specific context of transboundary pollution, through civil liability schemes.

A rationale for relaxing standing rules that is more compatible with international environmental law as presently configured is that it would allow non-state actors to function as guardians of global environmental values. Whereas governments have been unwilling to incur the diplomatic costs involved in taking action against states in breach of their environmental obligations, a procedure for non-state actors to institute claims could allow environmental commitments to be more regularly and effectively enforced. Elihu Lauterpacht has argued along these lines that:

> the international community should certainly contemplate the day when the enforcement of obligations under, say, conventions for the prevention of aerial pollution, or the protection of the ozone layer, will take the form of proceedings initiated before the ICJ at the instance of the United Nations Environment Programme or some other agency ...[101]

This rationale essentially reflects the experience in some domestic jurisdictions where citizen suit procedures allow individuals and community groups to bring proceedings directly against those in breach of environmental standards.[102] Stone has sought to advance this idea

[100] But see Jason N. E. Varuhas, 'One Person Can Make a Difference: An Individual Petition System for International Environmental Law' (2005) 3 *NZJPIL* 329, 330–1 (arguing for a petition system, similar to those operating in the human rights context, under which 'private individuals would be afforded the right to file petitions with a supranational body alleging that their state of nationality was breaching its international environmental obligations').

[101] Lauterpacht, above n. 33, 63–4. For a discussion of the proposal by Malta to the Preparatory Committee of the United Nations Conference on Environment and Development to institute an official guardian for generations as yet unborn see Stone, below n. 103, 65–80.

[102] See e.g. in the Australian context the New South Wales Land and Environment Court in which any person may bring proceedings to enforce the provisions of the Environmental Planning and Assessment Act 1979 (NSW), even where that person has no special interest in the proceedings. See also the provision in Australian federal legislation for any 'interested person' to apply for an injunction to restrain certain environmentally damaging activities: Environment Protection and Biodiversity Conservation Act 1999 (Cth). 'Interested person' is defined (in s. 475) as a person or organisation whose interests have been, are, or would be affected

somewhat further, arguing that effective protection of the natural environment depends not only on extending the class of litigants, but also upon a new conception of the environment as an independent holder of rights.[103] In developing this view, Stone points to the progressive expansion of human rights through the occidental legal tradition, and argues that, at least for some purposes, rights should also be conferred on animals, plants, and 'natural objects'. Through the familiar legal institution of guardianship it is then possible to allow these rights to be enforced through legal processes and institutions, including international courts. To this end Stone has argued that environmental treaties should endow non-state actors 'with standing to initiate legal and diplomatic action on the ocean ecosystem's behalf in appropriate cases; to sue at least in those cases where, if the ocean were a sovereign State, the law would afford it some prospect of relief'.[104]

The issue that inevitably arises is which actors should be admitted to perform a global environmental guardianship role. Lauterpacht refers to intergovernmental environmental organisations as being suitable candidates,[105] and this is reflective of the established personality of international organisations in public international law.[106] However, with the exception of the ECJ, in which the Commission enjoys standing, no international court or tribunal currently permits an international organisation to perform a guardianship function, even though there are analogous roles performed by treaty institutions in environmental NCPs.[107] More controversial are proposals to afford access to

by the conduct or proposed conduct or who has been engaged in activities for the protection or conservation of, or research into, the environment: s. 475(6). See generally Paul Stein, 'A Specialist Environmental Court: An Australian Experience' in David Robinson and John Dunkley (eds.), *Public Interest Perspectives in Environmental Law* (1995) 256, 271.

[103] Christopher D. Stone, *Should Trees Have Standing? And Other Essays on Law, Morals and the Environment* (1996) 32–3. Note, however, the debate as to whether the recognition of individual animals or plants as possessors of rights and interests is conducive to systematic and ecosystem-based environmental management: Mark Sagoff, *The Economy of the Earth* (1988) 156–7.

[104] Christopher D. Stone, 'Defending the Global Commons' in Philippe Sands (ed.), *Greening International Law* (1994) 34, 41.

[105] Lauterpacht, above n. 33, 63–4.

[106] See *Reparation for Injuries Suffered in the Service of the United Nations* case [1948] ICJ Rep 174.

[107] Such as the NCP under the Montreal Protocol which can be activated by the Ozone Secretariat: decision IV/5, Report of the Fourth Meeting of the Parties to the Montreal Protocol on Substances that Deplete the Ozone Layer, UN Doc. UNEP/Oz.L.Pro.4/15 (1992) (as revised by decision X/10, Report of the Tenth Meeting of the

civil society groups to institute proceedings.[108] While such rights are granted in the context of the Aarhus Convention NCP, this makes sense in a regime designed to protect individual rights to environmental information and justice. In other situations it is highly unlikely that states would welcome civil society actors as litigants, even though in many respects they are more appropriate representatives of global environmental interests than governments.[109]

Beyond questions surrounding the identity of public interest litigants there are other hurdles to community enforcement of international environmental law. The extent of environmental obligations *erga omnes* remains limited and unsettled,[110] and even the right of governments themselves to initiate an *actio popularis*, or to intervene as third parties representing the public interest,[111] is not universally accepted. The principles by which states may enforce rules for the protection of the environment on behalf of the international community as a whole are therefore incomplete and imperfect,[112] and international adjudication continues to be structured around a bilateral system that involves the vindication of the private legal rights of states.[113]

Unless and until international environmental law develops a clearer and more accepting attitude to civil society, and marries this with legal rules and principles that recognise public interest environmental litigation, increased public participation will need to take forms other than full standing rights. One obvious avenue is to expand the entitlement of non-state actors to participate as *amici curiae*. It has been seen that such procedures have begun to be developed and utilised in

Parties to the Montreal Protocol on Substances that Deplete the Ozone Layer, UN Doc. UNEP/OzL.Pro.10/9 (1998)) [2].

108 Philippe Sands, 'The Environment, Community and International Law' (1989) 30 *HarvILJ* 393, 394.

109 Peel, above n. 56, 70–2; Raustiala, above n. 26, 558–71.

110 In *obiter dicta* in the *Barcelona Traction* case the ICJ confirmed the existence of *erga omnes* obligations designed to protect humanitarian interests, but made no reference, in its admittedly non-exhaustive list, to possible *erga omnes* obligations serving environmental objectives: *Barcelona Traction, Light and Power Company Limited (Belgium v. Spain)* case (second phase) [1970] ICJ Rep 3, [34].

111 See Christine M. Chinkin, *Third Parties in International Law* (1993) 282, 284: the 'notion of intervention by a third party on behalf of the entire world community would cut across the bilateralism of international adjudication, and constitute major intrusion upon state autonomy'.

112 Sands, above n. 108, 397. See Boyle, above n. 36, 19–20.

113 Phoebe N. Okowa, 'Environmental Dispute Settlement: Some Reflections on Recent Developments' in Malcolm D. Evans (ed.), *Remedies in International Law: The Institutional Dilemma* (1998) 157, 158.

various courts and tribunals. Although they do not afford non-state actors a right to litigate in the public interest, they do allow broader interests to be acknowledged and considered in the course of inter-state environmental litigation. This is important, as the judicial settlement of international environmental disputes involves not only a private function of *inter partes* dispute settlement, but also an intrinsically public purpose.[114] This public function is beginning to be given recognition in some judicial procedures with an environmental focus. For instance, under the LOS Convention ITLOS has competence to issue provisional measures not only to protect the rights of the parties, but also to prevent damage to the environment,[115] and a similar provision was subsequently incorporated in the Straddling Stocks Agreement.[116] Noyes has argued that, given these provisions, 'ITLOS should bear in mind that the goal of standard-setting in such a case is to help implement important community rights or interests'.[117]

Allowing private actors to participate in international environmental adjudication in the capacity of *amici curiae* can also improve the quality of judicial analysis and reduce judicial error,[118] enhance the legitimacy and authority of international judicial decision-making,[119] and thereby strengthen the influence of these decisions on the behaviour of governments and other actors. Granting access to environmental NGOs in some proceedings such as those under the WTO dispute settlement

[114] *Ibid.* ('most environmental disputes, even in the form of the most straightforward case of transboundary pollution, always affect the interests of other States, say in a clean environment, and a bilateral resolution of such a dispute will invariably marginalise the wider community concerns').

[115] LOS Convention, art. 290(1).

[116] 1995 Agreement for the Implementation of the Provisions of the United Nations Convention on the Law of the Sea of 10 December 1982 Relating to the Conservation and Management of Straddling Fish Stocks and Highly Migratory Fish Stocks, art. 31(2).

[117] John E. Noyes, 'The International Tribunal for the Law of the Sea' (1998) 32 *CornellILJ* 109, 162.

[118] Dinah Shelton, 'The Participation of Non-Governmental Organizations in International Judicial Proceedings' (1994) 88 *AJIL* 611, 616.

[119] See generally Daniel Bodansky, 'The Legitimacy of International Governance: A Coming Challenge for International Environmental Law?' (1999) 93 *AJIL* 596. See also ICSID Case no. ARB/03/17, *Suez, Sociedad General de Aguas de Barcelona SA and InterAguas Integrales del Agua SA* v. *Argentina*, order in response to a petition for participation as *amicus curiae* (17 March 2006) (available at www.worldbank.org/icsid/cases/ARB0317-AC-en.pdf) at [22]: 'Public acceptance of the legitimacy of international arbitral processes, particularly when they involve … matters of public interest, is strengthened by increased openness and increased knowledge as to how these processes function.'

system may be an important counterbalance to the influence of corporate interests, for which states may effectively be acting as proxies.[120] None the less, several cautionary notes must be sounded in relation to any expansion of *amicus curiae* rights in international environmental litigation.[121] Courts may find themselves inundated with requests, and unable to decide upon those persons or organisations most appropriately admitted to participate. If, for instance, an environmental group is admitted as an *amicus* it may be difficult to resist demands from a representative industry body that it be permitted to offer a countervailing view.[122] There are few established procedures for determining access to *amici*, and some commentators have suggested that expanding such access on an ad hoc basis would only result in the creation of opportunities for 'well-monied special interest groups',[123] not for input by groups truly representative of the public interest. Moreover, allowing unfettered access by NGOs may make states increasingly reluctant to utilise international adjudicative mechanisms to resolve environmental disputes.[124]

8.4 Conclusion

States face a host of political impediments in commencing environmental litigation in the community interest, or in raising public interest considerations in inter-state environmental disputes. Where governments have feared to tread, environmental NGOs and other civil society groups have demonstrated a willingness to speak for the

[120] Jeffrey L. Dunoff, 'The Misguided Debate over NGO Participation at the WTO' (1998) *JIEconL* 433, 434.

[121] See generally D. B. Hollis, 'Private Actors in Public International Law: *Amicus Curiae* and the Case for the Retention of State Sovereignty' (2002) 25 *BCICLR* 235 (arguing that the outer limits of expanding private actor participation are to be found in maintaining the legitimacy of dispute settlement systems in the eyes of states who remain the primary international actors).

[122] Robert O. Keohane, Andrew Moravcsik and Anne-Marie Slaughter, 'Legalized Dispute Resolution: Interstate and Transnational' (2000) 54 *IntOrg* 457, 463. Note also the request by a business association (the National Mining Association) to submit an amicus brief in a NAFTA ch. 11 arbitration: *Clamis Gold Ltd* v. *United States of America* (available at www.naftaclaims.com).

[123] Phillip M. Nicols, 'Extension of Standing in the World Trade Organization Disputes to Nongovernmental Parties' (1996) 17 *UPaJIEconL* 295, 327.

[124] Brownlie makes similar observations in relation to more relaxed rights of intervention for third states: Ian Brownlie, 'Arbitration and Judicial Settlement: Comments on a Paper by Judge Lachs' in Alfred H. A. Soons (ed.), *International Arbitration: Past and Prospects* (1990) 60.

environment. International civil society groups have sought access to international adjudicative procedures to advance public interest environmental claims and concerns. These efforts have begun to yield results in international environmental litigation, although these have been relatively modest in comparison with gains in environmental diplomacy generally, where civil society groups have become active and valued participants.

Despite growing recognition of the importance of public participation in international environmental governance, and the ongoing convergence of many features of international judicial procedure,[125] no uniform rules have emerged to regulate matters of standing, intervention, or *amicus curiae* participation.[126] Such a standardised approach would require further recognition and consensus on the fundamental question as to the interests that non-state actors may prosecute in international environmental litigation. As matters stand, the extent to which a particular international judicial or quasi-judicial body may be used to defend the environment in the public interest will vary considerably. In general, however, public interest environmental litigation is far less developed than such proceedings in some domestic jurisdictions. Despite these limitations, international judicial bodies engaged in environmental decision-making are discharging an inherently public function. As such, a high level of public participation, consonant with the community character of environmental disputes, is desirable both as a matter of principle and for the practical reason that it can assist international courts in more effectively adjudicating complex matters of environmental law, policy and science.

[125] See Chester Brown, *A Common Law of International Adjudication* (2007).

[126] Ruth Mackenzie, 'The *Amicus Curiae* in International Courts: Towards Common Procedural Approaches?' in Tullio Treves *et al.* (eds.), *Civil Society, International Courts and Compliance Bodies* (2005) 296, 311.

9 Jurisdictional coordination

The heterogeneous collection of adjudicative procedures currently engaged in resolving environmental disputes has been described in this book as a jurisdictional patchwork because of the absence of any systematic organisation. The patchwork is characterised by substantial gaps, as proponents of an international court for the environment have been quick to point out.[1] However, there are also overlaps, and these give rise to several practical challenges of jurisdictional competition and coordination including forum shopping, simultaneous litigation in multiple fora, and successive proceedings. This chapter examines the ways in which such practical difficulties can compromise the effective operation of international courts and tribunals in the environmental field. It is seen that these ostensibly procedural or technical problems have confounded clear resolution, and have produced substantive effects by preventing environmental cases from being resolved promptly and effectively. The first section identifies the types of jurisdictional competition that can arise between dispute settlement mechanisms operating in international environmental law. By reference to several recent disputes, the second section considers the ways in which such overlaps or conflicts may lead to practical difficulties. The third section assesses the efficacy of existing jurisdiction-regulating norms, and considers prospects for overcoming the growing problem of fragmentation in the governance of international environmental disputes.

[1] See ch. 2.

9.1 Gaps and overlaps

9.1.1 Jurisdictional competition

The growing collection of bilateral agreements and multilateral environmental agreements have largely been developed in isolation from one another. As a consequence, the phenomenon of environmental 'treaty congestion'[2] has given rise to several overlaps both in terms of substantive rules and institutional arrangements.[3] Much of the normative replication is benign, with two or more instruments applying similar standards to the same issues.[4] However, some overlaps can generate difficulties if they involve differing normative standards and prescriptions.[5] Institutional difficulties have also been confronted, including in relation to competing adjudicative procedures that operate under a growing number of international environmental agreements.[6] Although in most environmental regimes adjudication is presented as simply one option among several for the resolution of disputes, several treaties go further and allow[7] or positively require compulsory judicial settlement or arbitration.[8]

In parallel with these developments in environmental regimes have been efforts to enhance the environmental capacity and expertise of

[2] Bethany Lukitsch Hicks, 'Treaty Congestion in International Environmental Law: The Need for Greater International Coordination' (1999) 32 *URichLR* 1643.

[3] See Rüdiger Wolfrum and Nele Matz, *Conflicts in International Environmental Law* (2003).

[4] *Ibid*. 3.

[5] See e.g. problems arising in the Antarctic context from overlapping regimes: Donald R. Rothwell, 'A Maritime Analysis of the Conflicting International Law Regimes in the Antarctic and the Southern Ocean' (1994) 15 *AustYBIL* 155.

[6] Cesare P. R. Romano, *The Peaceful Settlement of International Environmental Disputes: A Pragmatic Approach* (2000) 91–2.

[7] See e.g. 1985 Vienna Convention for the Protection of the Ozone Layer, art. 11(3); 1992 United Nations Framework Convention on Climate Change, art. 14; Biodiversity Convention, art. 27; 1992 UNECE Convention on the Transboundary Effects of Industrial Accidents, art. 21; 1994 Protocol to the 1979 Convention on Long Range Transboundary Air Pollution on Further Reduction of Sulphur Emissions, art. 9.

[8] See e.g. Convention on the Physical Production of Nuclear Material, Art. 17(2); OSPAR Convention, art. 32; 1973 International Convention for the Prevention of Pollution from Ships (as amended and given effect by the Protocol of 1978 Relating to the International Convention for the Prevention of Pollution from Ships), art. 10; Madrid Protocol, arts. 18–20; LOS Convention, pt XV; 1995 Agreement for the Implementation of the Provisions of the United Nations Convention on the Law of the Sea of 10 December 1982 Relating to the Conservation and Management of Straddling Fish Stocks and Highly Migratory Fish Stocks (Straddling Stocks Agreement), part VIII; 2000 Convention on the Conservation and Management of Highly Migratory Fish Stocks in the Western and Central Pacific Ocean, art. 31. See also Convention on the Regulation of Antarctic Mineral Resource Activities, arts. 55–9.

existing judicial bodies through initiatives such as the establishment of an Environmental Chamber of the ICJ and the elaboration of special arbitral procedures for environmental dispute settlement by the PCA.[9] More broadly, the proliferation of international courts and tribunals has also resulted in the establishment of a variety of specialised adjudicative bodies, several of which have been involved in deciding disputes involving questions of environmental law and policy.

9.1.2 *Typology of competition*

The consequence of these three trends has been growing levels of competition between dispute settlement mechanisms resolving environmental cases. Before examining the implications of this phenomenon it is necessary to clarify the main types of jurisdictional intersection that may arise.[10]

One type of competition may arise between two or more dispute settlement systems with similarly broad subject matter jurisdiction. In such circumstances the jurisdictional overlap is total, in the sense that both bodies possess concurrent and identical subject matter jurisdiction. One example of this is found in the relationship between the ICJ and the PCA, both of which may be assigned general jurisdiction over environmental and other disputes. This has not yet occurred, although such competition is possible having regard to the efforts of both institutions to increase their capacity to deal with environmental controversies.

A second type of jurisdictional competition may emerge in circumstances where two dispute settlement systems possess jurisdiction that only partly overlaps. This includes situations where one dispute settlement mechanism has general subject matter jurisdiction, while a second procedure operates in relation to a narrower category of disputes falling within this general field. Whether there is any competition in such circumstances will depend considerably upon the

[9] See 2001 Optional Rules for the Arbitration of Disputes Relating to Natural Resources and/or the Environment.

[10] The discussion that follows draws inspiration from the categorisation suggested by Lowe (A. Vaughan Lowe, 'Overlapping Jurisdiction in International Tribunals (1999) 20 *AustYBIL* 191, 192–3) and, to a lesser extent, by Shany (Yuval Shany, *The Competing Jurisdictions of International Courts and Tribunals* (2003) 29–74) and Vigni (Patrizia Vigni, 'The Overlapping of Dispute Settlement Regimes: An Emerging Issue of International Law' (2003) XI *ItalYBIL* 139). See also J. G. Merrills, 'The Mosaic of International Dispute Settlement Procedures: Complementary or Contradictory' (2007) 54 *NILR* 361, 371–89.

characterisation of a dispute. Dispute settlement procedures typically provide that they only apply to cases concerning the interpretation and application of the instrument by which they are established.[11] Hence a dispute relating solely to one treaty will only enliven the dispute settlement mechanisms of that instrument, and there will be no competition with other dispute settlement systems. Increasingly, however, the interaction between environmental and other agreements renders such compartmentalisation of disputes impossible.

This problem of isolating the gist of a dispute implicating multiple environmental instruments has been encountered in two prominent environmental cases: the *Southern Bluefin Tuna* dispute,[12] which raised questions concerning the conservation of a threatened fishery, and the *MOX Plant* dispute,[13] which related to the commissioning of a nuclear processing plant in the United Kingdom. In the *Southern Bluefin Tuna* dispute the jurisdictional competition involved the mandatory and binding dispute settlement provisions of the LOS Convention on the one hand, and the optional and non-binding procedures of the CCSBT[14] on the other. The *MOX Plant* dispute raised even more acute difficulties of jurisdictional competition, as the dispute settlement systems of the LOS Convention, the OSPAR Convention and the EC Treaty[15] were all activated to deal with aspects of the controversy.

There is a third category of jurisdictional competition which may occur when a common set of facts gives rise to litigation under two dispute settlement systems, each with specialised subject matter jurisdiction. The paradigmatic example of such competition is the concurrent operation of trade and environment regimes. For instance states

[11] This formulation is near universal, and reflects the accepted treaty practice of seeking to confine the application of treaty provisions, including their dispute settlement procedures, to the subject matter of the treaty concerned. Only general arbitration agreements, or procedures such as the optional clause system under art. 36(2) of the Statute of the ICJ, purport to apply to all disputes.

[12] *Southern Bluefin Tuna*: cases *New Zealand* v. *Japan; Australia* v. *Japan* (provisional measures) (1999) 38 ILM 1624 (*Southern Bluefin Tuna* order); *Australia and New Zealand* v. *Japan* (award on jurisdiction and admissibility) (2000) 39 ILM 1359 (*Southern Bluefin Tuna* award).

[13] *MOX Plant* case: *Ireland* v. *United Kingdom* (provisional measures) (2002) 41 ILM 405 (*MOX Plant* order); *Ireland* v. *United Kingdom* (suspension of proceedings on jurisdiction and merits and request for further provisional measures) (order 3, of 24 June 2003) (2003) 42 ILM 1187 (order 4, of 14 November 2003) (available at www.pca-cpa.org) (order 5, of 22 January 2007) (*MOX Plant* award).

[14] See CCSBT, art. 16.

[15] 2002 Consolidated Version of the Treaty Establishing the European Community.

may seek, or may be required, to impose trade restrictive measures in order to achieve the objectives of an environmental regime, yet this may prompt complaints from other governments under the dispute settlement system of the WTO. There is no true overlap in these cases as the specialisation of the two regimes means that they have competence to deal only with juridically separate issues. Use of the geometric metaphor of 'parallelism'[16] to describe such competition is therefore appropriate; however, this does not mean that this type of competition is free from practical difficulties, as will now be seen.

9.2 Resultant difficulties

Potentially three main problematic scenarios can arise from jurisdictional competition, namely forum shopping, simultaneous proceedings in multiple fora, and successive proceedings in different tribunals. This section considers each of these in turn.

9.2.1 *Forum shopping*

The phenomenon of forum shopping is familiar in domestic and transnational litigation and is encountered when litigants 'shop' for the court or tribunal offering the greatest procedural and substantive advantages.[17] The practice ordinarily carries pejorative connotations in these contexts,[18] although there is ongoing debate as to whether it is always undesirable.[19] It is sometimes said that forum shopping undermines the rule of law by denying a defendant forewarning of the substantive law to apply to its conduct or of the court that will evaluate its compliance with the law.[20] Moreover in selecting the most expedient forum, and not the tribunal with the closest connection to the dispute, a plaintiff may initiate litigation that is costly and inconvenient both for the defendant and for the forum. In response to these perceived problems

16 The term is used here in a different sense from that suggested in the *Southern Bluefin Tuna* award (2000) 39 ILM 1359 (at [52]). In the dispute the two instruments in question effectively overlapped rather than operated in parallel in that the CCSBT was a specific agreement designed to implement the marine living resource conservation provisions of the LOS Convention.

17 See generally Andrew S. Bell, 'The Why and Wherefore of Transnational Forum Shopping' (1995) 69 *ALJ* 124.

18 Shany, above n. 10, 131–8.

19 Friedrich K. Juenger, 'What's Wrong with Forum Shopping?' (1994) 16 *SLR* 5; Brian Opeskin, 'The Price of Forum Shopping: A Reply to Juenger' (1994) 16 *SLR* 14.

20 Shany, above n. 10, 131.

various strategies have been developed in private international law to limit the opportunities to engage in forum shopping, such as the *forum non conveniens* doctrine, and the use of anti-suit injunctions.[21]

Forum shopping is now a feature in some fields of public international law, including human rights,[22] the law of the sea,[23] and international environmental law. Concerns arising from forum shopping in dispute settlement bodies represents part of a broader anxiety regarding the interaction between international organisations that have overlapping competence and areas of interest.[24] In international law the practice presents several challenges, some of which reflect the negative experiences encountered in domestic legal systems. One of these is the increasing unpredictability of international environmental litigation. Where there is a range of fora, states may find themselves brought before dispute settlement procedures they had not expected would be invoked. This is effectively what Japan asserted had occurred in the *Southern Bluefin Tuna* dispute, and Japan was ultimately successful in its argument that the dispute should be resolved under the rubric of the CCSBT's dispute settlement procedures rather than those of the LOS Convention. From the perspective of the applicants, Australia and New Zealand, the case generated a different type of unpredictability, as the CCSBT dispute settlement procedures were referred to, rather unexpectedly, to justify the non-applicability of the far more effective and robust settlement mechanisms of the LOS Convention.

21 The doctrine of *forum non conveniens*, which allows a court to refuse to hear a case where the forum court is either 'clearly inappropriate' or an alternative jurisdiction is 'more appropriate' has sometimes been an impediment to transnational environmental litigation: Philippa Webb, 'The Inconvenience of Liability: The Doctrine of *Forum Non Conveniens* in International Environmental Litigation' (2001) 6 *APJEL* 377. But see Peter Prince, 'Bhopal, Bougainville and Ok Tedi: Why Australia's *Forum non Conveniens* Approach is Better' (1998) 47 *ICLQ* 573.

22 Laurence R. Helfer, 'Forum Shopping for Human Rights' (1999) 148 *UPaLR* 285. Helfer identifies three types of forum shopping in the human rights context: (1) choice of tribunal forum shopping; (2) simultaneous complaint forum shopping; and (3) successive complaint forum shopping.

23 Donald R. Rothwell, 'Oceans Management and the Law of the Sea in the Twenty-First Century' in Alex G. Oude Elferink and Donald R. Rothwell (eds.), *Oceans Management in the 21st Century: Institutional Frameworks and Responses* (2004) 329, 352 (pointing to the variety of dispute settlement options available for law of the sea disputes, and the attendant problem of forum shopping).

24 One example of this is the competition between various international organisations addressing the issue of cetacean conservation: Alexander Gillespie, 'Forum Shopping in International Environmental Law: The IWC, CITES and the Management of Cetaceans' (2002) 33 *ODIL* 17.

Forum shopping in international environmental law raises a further concern, namely that proceedings may be commenced in tribunals not equipped with the necessary expertise or specialised procedures for determining disputes involving complex questions of environmental law and policy. Some features of an adjudicative body may render it more or less appropriate than others for resolving environmental controversies. For instance, permanent bodies are generally to be preferred over ad hoc arbitral panels for several functional and substantive reasons. One key reason is that standing courts and tribunals are better suited for dealing with international environmental disputes involving issues in which the international community as a whole has an interest. In addressing these essentially public disputes, permanent courts can therefore perform an important community function as opposed to the merely private task of adjusting rights and obligations *inter partes*.[25]

Inappropriate forum selection can effectively undermine the operation and regulatory purpose of environmental regimes if procedures outside that regime are utilised in preference to those established specifically to deal with such disputes.[26] In this regard several commentators have argued that the dispute settlement system of the WTO is completely unsuited for determining environmental disputes.[27] Some members of the WTO have been alive to these criticisms, and aware of the WTO's limitations in this respect and for this reason the WTO Committee on Trade and Environment (CTE), established with the WTO in 1994, was given the mandate of exploring 'the relationship between the dispute

[25] A. Neil Craik, 'Recalcitrant Reality and Chosen Ideals: The Public Function of Dispute Settlement in International Environmental Law' (1998) 10 *GeoIELR* 551, 562.

[26] Such a problem can arise even as between the dispute settlement systems of the one regime. Oxman has argued that the divergent conclusions regarding jurisdiction reached by ITLOS and the subsequent annex VII tribunal in the *Southern Bluefin Tuna* dispute may be because judges of ITLOS regarded themselves as part of the system created by the LOS Convention, while the majority of the annex VII tribunal saw themselves as 'outsiders looking in': Bernard H. Oxman, 'Complementary Agreements and Compulsory Jurisdiction' (2001) 95 *AJIL* 277, 288.

[27] Richard J. McLaughlin, 'Settling Trade-Related Disputes Over the Protection of Marine Living Resources: UNCLOS or WTO?' (1997) 9 *GeoIELR* 29; Lakshman D. Guruswamy, 'Environment and Trade: Competing Paradigms in International Law' in Antony Anghie and Garry Sturgess (eds.), *Legal Visions of the 21st Century: Essays in Honour of Judge Christopher Weeramantry* (1998) 574, 575 (arguing that

> '[i]t is unfair and unjust to allow a court created by the DSB of GATT/WTO which recognizes only trade law, to adjudicate conflicts between the trade laws that the tribunal is established to advance, and environmental laws based on different and contradictory goals.

settlement mechanisms in the multilateral trading system and those found in multilateral environmental agreements'.[28] In 1996 the CTE recommended that WTO parties involved in a dispute principally arising out of a multilateral environmental agreement should consider trying to resolve it through that agreement's dispute settlement mechanisms.[29] Skeen explains that this recommendation was partly born out of concerns relating to forum shopping, as the '[t]he Committee feared that the exclusive jurisdiction and binding nature of the WTO dispute settlement system might attract environmentally related suits that were not the province of the WTO dispute settlement panel'.[30]

While forum shopping may therefore have several undesirable consequences for international environmental litigation, it must also be acknowledged that benefits can flow from litigant autonomy. It may act as an incentive for existing courts and tribunals to improve their capacity to deal with environmental questions, and encourage courts to provide the best 'service'[31] which in turn can mean greater resort to judicial modes of environmental dispute settlement. The attempts by the ICJ, the PCA, and ITLOS to adopt environment-specific procedures may be viewed from this perspective. Moreover, some degree of forum shopping may be an inevitable price for an expansion in the range of jurisdictions applicable to environmental disputes. In relation to the LOS Convention, for example, the creation of multiple procedures was a prerequisite for agreement on a compulsory dispute settlement regime, and on the convention as a whole.[32] Rather than relying exclusively on a single body such as the ICJ, part XV of the LOS Convention presents states with a 'cafeteria'[33] or 'smorgasbord'[34] of options for resolving

[28] Trade and Environment (14 April 1994) (1994) 33 ILM 1267 (GATT Ministerial Decision).

[29] Report of the WTO Committee on Trade and Environment, [178], WTO Doc. WT/CTE/1 (1996).

[30] Richard Skeen, 'Will the WTO Turn Green? The Implications of Injecting Environmental Issues Into the Multilateral Trading System' (2004) 17 *GeoIELR* 161, 173. See also Joost Pauwelyn, *Conflict of Norms in Public International Law* (2003) 452–3 (arguing that in certain circumstances involving both WTO rules and other regimes, it is possible for a WTO panel to decide that it does not have jurisdiction, or if it does have jurisdiction that it would be inappropriate for the proceedings to continue).

[31] Jonathan I. Charney, 'The Implications of Expanding International Dispute Settlement Systems: The 1982 Convention on the Law of the Sea' (1996) 90 *AJIL* 69, 71; Shany, above n. 10, 122–3.

[32] Natalie Klein, *Dispute Settlement in the UN Convention on the Law of the Sea* (2005) 54.

[33] Alan E. Boyle, 'Dispute Settlement and the Law of the Sea Convention: Problems of Fragmentation and Jurisdiction' (1997) 46 *ICLQ* 37, 40.

[34] Charney, above n. 31, 71.

marine environmental disputes which comprises the ICJ, ITLOS, and two arbitral tribunals. In this way the LOS Convention 'sought to balance flexibility with the goal of compulsory settlement'.[35] This type of adaptable system may encourage the increased use of judicial bodies in environmental cases, and to the extent that these bodies give effect to rules and principles of international environmental law then this may be regarded as a beneficial outcome that generally outweighs any potential problems stemming from forum shopping.

9.2.2 Simultaneous proceedings

A second potential challenge posed by jurisdictional competition is the possibility of litispendence, that is proceedings being pursued simultaneously in two or more courts. Such situations may arise not only from multiple suits commenced by an applicant state, but could also occur where a respondent seeks to utilise a different forum to pursue what is effectively a counterclaim.[36] The availability of multiple dispute settlement procedures that can address aspects of the same dispute can therefore encourage 'claim splitting', with all the implications this carries for complicating dispute settlement and increasing its costs.[37]

A situation in which an identical dispute is litigated in two tribunals is highly unlikely to be permitted to continue. Indeed, some environmental instruments expressly seek to prevent such a situation: the NAAEC exists alongside NAFTA, and under it the secretariat of the Commission on Environmental Cooperation may not consider a complaint that a NAFTA party is not complying with its environmental obligations if this question is already before investment arbitration under chapter 11 of NAFTA.[38] In the absence of such treaty-based regulation

[35] Shirley V. Scott, 'The Contribution of the LOS Convention's Organisations to its Harmonious Implementation' in Alex G. Oude Elferink and Donald R. Rothwell (eds.), *Oceans Management in the 21st Century: Institutional Frameworks and Responses* (2004) 313, 321.

[36] In domestic law a counterclaim may be defined as a 'claim or a cross-claim capable of supporting an independent action but which is pleaded in the existing action for the sake of convenience': *Butterworths Australian Legal Dictionary* (1997) 292.

[37] Yuval Shany, 'The First *MOX Plant* Award: The Need to Harmonize Competing Environmental Regimes and Dispute Settlement Procedures' (2004) 17 *LJIL* 815, 825.

[38] NAAEC, art. 14(3)(a). Just such a situation was encountered in 1999 when a Canadian company lodged a complaint with the NAAEC secretariat alleging that the United States had failed to enforce environmental regulations in the state of California. See *Methanex* Submission, SEM-99-001, 18 October 1999 (available at www.cec.org/citizen/).

of litispendence, it is possible to turn to rules of a more general character such as the *lis alibi pendens*[39] and *res judicata*[40] doctrines.

9.2.2.1 *MOX Plant* dispute

In practice, however, situations of parallel environmental proceedings have not been amenable to resolution in a straightforward fashion, as is seen in the environmentally important, but unresolved, *MOX Plant* dispute. The dispute between Ireland and the United Kingdom in the *MOX Plant* dispute relates to the establishment of a MOX nuclear fuel plant at the Sellafield nuclear processing facility located on the Irish Sea, in north-west England.[41] Ireland has made a number of claims concerning the non-performance by the United Kingdom of its environmental obligations under the LOS Convention, the EC Treaty, and the OSPAR Convention. The dispute has now led to litigation under four regimes,[42] in four different tribunals,[43] and offers a paradigmatic example of difficulties encountered in contemporary international environmental law as a result of jurisdictional competition.

The litigation first began in June 2001, when Ireland requested the establishment of an arbitral tribunal under article 32 of the OSPAR Convention to determine a dispute with the United Kingdom concerning the release of information relating to the commissioning of the MOX plant.[44] Subsequently, in October 2001, Ireland began proceedings against the United Kingdom under part XV of the LOS Convention, alleging

[39] 'A suit pending elsewhere': see Lowe, above n. 10, 202. See also *Certain German Interests in Polish Upper Silesia* (*Germany* v. *Poland*) (jurisdiction) [1925] PCIJ (ser. A) no. 6, 20 in which the PCIJ noted that '[i]t is a much disputed question … whether the doctrine of *litispendence*, the object of which is to prevent the possibility of conflicting judgments, can be invoked in international relations'. However, the Court went on to conclude that it was not necessary to consider the doctrine as it only applied where there were 'two identical actions'.

[40] The *res judicata* ('thing decided') doctrine may be regarded as a general principle of law. See Iain Scobbie, '*Res Judicata*, Precedent and the International Court: A Preliminary Sketch' (1999) 20 *AustYBIL* 299, 299; Chester Brown, *A Common Law of International Adjudication* (2007) 153–6.

[41] See ch. 7.

[42] OSPAR Convention; LOS Convention; EC Treaty; and the 1957 Treaty Establishing the European Atomic Energy Authority (Euratom Treaty).

[43] ITLOS, an annex VII tribunal (convened pursuant to the LOS Convention under PCA auspices), an OSPAR arbitral tribunal (also under PCA auspices), and the ECJ.

[44] *OSPAR Arbitration* (*Ireland* v. *United Kingdom*) (final award) (2003) 42 ILM 1118. See generally Shany, above n. 37; Malgosia A. Fitzmaurice, 'Dispute Concerning Access to Information Under Article 9 of the OSPAR Convention (*Ireland v United Kingdom*)' (2003) 18 *IJMCL* 541.

violations of the marine environmental protection provisions of that instrument. Ireland also indicated an intention to commence a case in the ECJ in relation to alleged breaches of the EC Treaty and the Euratom Treaty.[45] However, before it was able to do so the European Commission itself initiated action against Ireland in the ECJ,[46] on the grounds that by bringing the case under part XV of the LOS Convention, Ireland had violated the exclusive jurisdiction of the ECJ.[47] These proceedings effectively brought to a halt the proceedings under the LOS Convention. While Ireland was successful in obtaining an order of provisional measures in ITLOS (the *MOX Plant* order), the annex VII arbitral tribunal empanelled to determine the merits of the case suspended proceedings pending the conclusion of the ECJ case (the *MOX Plant* award).[48]

In the *MOX Plant* award, the annex VII tribunal refrained from attempting a definitive resolution of the jurisdictional issues that complicated the *MOX Plant* dispute. Instead, the tribunal adopted a compromise approach of affirming its prima facie jurisdiction, which was necessary to support its provisional measures order, while at the same time suspending the hearing of the merits of the case until its competence could be clearly determined. From a technical perspective this approach appeared entirely appropriate in the context of a complex dispute involving several competing regimes;[49] however, it also meant that an important environmental dispute continued to languish unresolved. The tribunal revealed some awareness of this situation in seeking to fashion interim orders, based on those prescribed by ITLOS in the *MOX Plant* order, that would ensure that the interests of the parties were preserved, and the dispute was not further inflamed. However, given the seriousness of the environmental questions raised before ITLOS and the annex VII tribunal it was unfortunate that the substantive issues concerning nuclear pollution of the Irish Sea were left unanswered. The fact that they were confirms that environmental regimes can be substantially weakened if the institutions designed to supervise their implementation are paralysed by jurisdictional competition.

[45] *MOX Plant* order (2002) 41 ILM 405, [42].

[46] *Commission of the European Communities* v. *Ireland* (2006) 45 ILM 1051.

[47] See EC Treaty, art. 292, which provides that 'Member States undertake not to submit a dispute concerning the interpretation or application of [the *EC Treaty*] to any method of settlement other than those provided for therein'. Art. 193 of the Euratom Treaty is in similar terms.

[48] *MOX Plant* award (order 3, of 24 June 2003) (2003) 42 ILM 1187.

[49] But see Klein who argues that the decision might be criticised for being 'overly cautious and premature': Klein, above n. 32, 51.

9.2.2.2 *Swordfish Stocks* case

A somewhat different example of concurrent proceedings was witnessed in the *Conservation and Sustainable Exploitation of Swordfish Stocks in the South-Eastern Pacific Ocean case*,[50] a dispute between Chile and the EC that raised not only environmental issues relevant to the LOS Convention, but also trade issues under the WTO. Issues of international economic law were implicated because Chile sought to protect an overexploited straddling fishery by a trade measure, in the form of port bans imposed upon Spanish fishing vessels targeting swordfish near the Chilean EEZ.[51]

In August 2000, in response to these bans, the EC initiated consultations in the WTO[52] and subsequently, in November 2000, requested the establishment of a panel[53] to resolve the dispute. For its part Chile responded by commencing what were effectively counterclaim proceedings under part XV of the LOS Convention.[54] Chile claimed that the EC had violated several provisions of the LOS Convention relating to the conservation of high seas fisheries,[55] and also argued that the dispute was in essence an environmental one and therefore that the dispute settlement procedures of the LOS Convention should prevail over those of the WTO. The dispute was eventually resolved by negotiation before a hearing took place either in ITLOS or in a WTO panel, although the *Swordfish Stocks* case technically remains on foot as the only case currently in the ITLOS docket. It would seem that one

[50] *Conservation and Sustainable Exploitation of Swordfish Stocks in the South-Eastern Pacific Ocean (Chile/European Community)* (proceedings suspended) (15 March 2001 and 16 December 2003) (available at www.itlos.org). See ch. 7.

[51] See John Shamsey, 'ITLOS vs Goliath: The International Tribunal for the Law of the Sea Stands Tall with the Appellate Body in the Chilean-EU Swordfish Dispute' (2002) 12 *TransL&CP* 513. This dispute raised similar questions to those addressed in *United States – Restrictions on Imports of Tuna*, GATT Doc. DS21/R (1991) (*Tuna-Dolphin I*); *United States – Restrictions on Imports of Tuna*, GATT Doc. DS29/R (1994) (*Tuna-Dolphin II*); *United States – Import Prohibition of Certain Shrimp and Shrimp Products*, WTO Doc. WT/DS58/R (1998) (report of the panel), WTO Doc. WT/DS58/AB/R (1998) (report of the Appellate Body) (*Shrimp–Turtle I*); and *United States – Import Prohibition of Certain Shrimp and Shrimp Products* (*Shrimp–Turtle II*), WTO Doc. WT/DS58/RW (2001) (report of the panel), WTO Doc. WT/DS58/AB/RW (2001) (report of the Appellate Body) (*Shrimp–Turtle II*).

[52] *Chile – Measures Affecting the Transit and Importation of Swordfish*, WTO Doc. WT/DS193/1 (2000) (request for consultations by the European Communities).

[53] *Chile – Measures Affecting the Transit and Importation of Swordfish*, WTO Doc WT/DS193/2 (2000) (request for the establishment of a panel by the European Communities).

[54] *Swordfish Stocks* case (15 March 2001 and 16 December 2003) (available at www.itlos.org).

[55] In particular LOS Convention, arts. 116 and 119.

important factor encouraging the parties to settle was the prospect that Chile might lose in any proceedings in the WTO, while the EC might similarly be the subject of an adverse result in ITLOS.[56]

Serdy has argued that the trade/environment dichotomy invoked by Chile was a false one,[57] and that it would be 'perverse'[58] to conclude that simply because one forum could hear claims under one treaty that this must preclude another forum from hearing claims in the same dispute under a second treaty. Lowe has similarly contended that in circumstances such as these there is no real concurrent or conflicting jurisdiction, and therefore that the dispute could be determined by the two institutions in parallel.[59] Although this analysis may well be correct,[60] the parallel determination of disputes under these distinctive treaty regimes is none the less problematic. Had the proceedings continued it would have been for ITLOS to consider the law of the sea questions, while a WTO panel, and perhaps ultimately the WTO Appellate Body, would have been required to determine whether Chile's trade measure was WTO-consistent. Neither ITLOS nor the WTO dispute settlement system had general competence to consider all of the legal questions involved. However, this does not mean that in deciding the specific segments of this dispute there would not have been a considerable intersection between the two processes.[61]

There was the real possibility that these two dispute settlement systems might have reached divergent conclusions of fact, a clearly undesirable result that may well have hindered rather than helped in resolving the dispute. Boyle has also noted that either ITLOS or a WTO panel might 'incidentally determine questions arising under other treaties where it [was] necessary to do so in order to determine the

[56] Shamsey, above n. 51, 538.

[57] Andrew Serdy, 'See You in Port: Australia and New Zealand as Third Parties in the Dispute Between Chile and the European Community Over Chile's Denial of Port Access to Spanish Vessels Fishing for Swordfish on the High Seas' (2002) 3 *MJIL* 79, 90.

[58] *Ibid.*

[59] Lowe, above n. 10, 203. See also Vigni, above n. 10, 155: 'Formally speaking, such disputes cannot be considered "the same" even though they may concern the same set of facts.'

[60] But see Pauwelyn, above n. 30, 450 (noting that it can also be argued that the underlying basis of the dispute did not relate to trade at all, but rather the sustainable use of high seas fisheries resource).

[61] For a discussion of possible interactions between ITLOS and the WTO's dispute settlement system see John E. Noyes, 'The International Tribunal for the Law of the Sea' (1999) 32 *CornellILJ* 109, 179–80.

dispute that [was] properly before it'.[62] It was also possible for the LOS Convention to have been invoked before a WTO panel or the Appellate Body to justify what would otherwise be a violation of WTO rules. In such circumstances the WTO would have been called upon to interpret the provisions of the LOS Convention relating to coastal state responsibilities for fisheries conservation, a task that might lead to conclusions differing from those of ITLOS when confronted with the same question in the parallel proceeding.[63] Moreover if the two cases produced different overall outcomes, there was also the potential for the parties to be bound by conflicting orders, a consequence which would surely have undermined confidence in the administration of justice by international courts, and may well have forestalled effective conservation measures to protect a threatened fishery.

Cases such as *Swordfish Stocks* also invoke the spectre of parallel proceedings being utilised for purely tactical reasons in order to affect the outcome of environmental litigation. To vary somewhat the scenario presented in that case, it is possible that in a dispute involving both trade and marine environmental issues a respondent to an application brought under part XV of the LOS Convention might attempt to use parallel WTO dispute settlement procedures in order to force a negotiated rather than adjudicated outcome. If successful this could have the consequence that serious breaches of obligations to protect and preserve the marine environment were not brought before an independent forum, and therefore made subject to public scrutiny. In this type of situation it may be possible to apply the doctrine of abuse of rights to prevent the misuse of legal process.[64] However, in so doing it would seem essential that the second set of proceedings be shown to

[62] Alan E. Boyle, 'The World Trade Organization and the Marine Environment' in Myron H. Nordquist, John Norton Moore, and Said Mahmoudi (eds.), *The Stockholm Declaration and the Law of the Marine Environment* (2003) 109, 116.

[63] Marcos A. Orellana, 'The Swordfish Dispute between the EU and Chile at the ITLOS and the WTO' (2002) 71 *NordicJIL* 55, 65: 'The parallel proceedings at the WTO and before the ITLOS Chamber carry the risk of rendering contradictory and incompatible judgments, as both adjudicative bodies retain jurisdiction to rule upon the issue of port access to fishing vessels.'

[64] Shany argues that the doctrine of abuse of rights now forms part of customary international law: Shany, above n. 10, 255–60. Lowe refers more specifically to the doctrine of 'abuse of process': Lowe, above n. 10, 204. Support for the theory that courts may decline jurisdiction where an applicant has commenced malicious proceedings, or has made an application having a tenuous or artificial connection with the facts of the dispute, can be found in general principles of law and in treaty practice, including LOS Convention, art. 294(1) which relevantly provides that

be colourable (i.e. possessing no substance and no real connection with the dispute) and this could be a difficult hurdle to surmount.

9.2.3 *Successive proceedings*

The third, and less serious, problem flowing from jurisdictional competition in contemporary international environmental law is the risk of successive proceedings addressing the same or similar dispute. Serial litigation, in which claimant or respondent states seek to contest the same or similar legal claims, is inimical to the orderly administration of international justice. In addition to excessive costs and delay in the resolution of a dispute, there is also the possibility that such decisions could differ. As there is no rule of *stare decisis* in international law, such jurisprudential divergence can only be avoided to the extent that the *res judicata* doctrine is applicable. However, the latter doctrine, as with the *lis alibi pendens* rule applicable in relation to parallel proceedings, is only enlivened when the situation involves an identical dispute. As ITLOS explained in the *MOX Plant* order, it is often difficult to characterise a dispute raised before multiple fora as involving a single *lis* or controversy. Indeed the tribunal found that disputes arising out of several instruments possessing provisions that were in similar, or even identical terms, retained a separate existence.

There has not yet been an instance in international environmental law of successive proceedings seeking to ventilate essentially the same, or a similar, complaint. Ireland's claims in the *MOX Plant* dispute under the OSPAR Convention and the LOS Convention were different, with the former relating mainly to issues concerning access to environmental information, while the latter concerned substantive questions of marine environmental protection. The *Southern Bluefin Tuna* dispute involved sequential stages of the one proceeding, pursued under a single dispute settlement system, namely part XV of the LOS Convention. None the less, the dispute did involve distinct fora in the sense that the *Southern Bluefin Tuna* order was rendered by ITLOS, while the subsequent decision on jurisdiction and admissibility in the *Southern Bluefin Tuna* award was handed down by an ad hoc arbitral tribunal formed pursuant to annex VII of the LOS Convention. The major differences between the *Southern Bluefin Tuna* order and the award on the issue of

'[i]f the court or tribunal determines that the claim constitutes an abuse of legal process or is *prima facie* unfounded, it shall take no further action in the case'.

jurisdiction can therefore be cited as some illustration of the potential problems that can arise from successive proceedings.[65]

9.3 Jurisdictional coordination

The previous section examined some of the practical problems that have been faced in international environmental law as multiple dispute settlement bodies operate side by side. These problems of coordination could only be completely resolved by the wholesale rationalisation of the jurisdiction of these bodies. This appears a remote prospect. Not only is the establishment of a system or hierarchy of international courts a practical and political impossibility, but it would run counter to the desire of the international community for diverse fora with distinctive features tailored to meet particular needs.[66] It would also be contrary to the trend of international environmental law to develop sectoral and regional regimes in response to environmental problems.[67]

In the absence of systematic coordination it is inevitable that interactions between the patchwork of jurisdictions will continue. The purpose of this section is to consider the strategies currently available for addressing this interaction, and to assess how they have operated in practice. In broad terms there are two basic approaches, reflecting the sources of the applicable rules. The first comprises treaty provisions,

[65] Donald L. Morgan, 'Implications of the Proliferation of International Legal Fora: The Example of the *Southern Bluefin Tuna Cases*' (2002) 43 *HarvILJ* 541, 541 (the case is evidence of the many problems associated with the growth of international courts including 'fragmentation of international law, forum-shopping by litigants, rivalry among judiciaries with overlapping, and conflicting applications and interpretations of customary international law').

[66] Fragmentation of International Law: Difficulties Arising from the Diversification and Expansion of International Law: Report of the Study Group of the International Law Commission, Finalised by Chairman M Koskenniemi ILC, UN Doc. A/CN.4/L.682 [1]-[15] (in its study the ILC study group left the institutional question as to the relationship between international courts to one side, as a matter best addressed by the institutions themselves, and instead focused on the problem of fragmentation of substantive international law); Jonathan I. Charney, 'The Impact on the International Legal System of the Growth of International Courts and Tribunals' (1998–9) 31 *NYUJILP* 697, 698.

[67] For a discussion of this trend see Ben Boer, Ross Ramsay, and Donald R. Rothwell, *International Environmental Law in the Asia Pacific* (1998) 18–20; Martin List and Volker Rittberger, 'Regime Theory and International Environmental Management' in Andrew Hurrell and Benedict Kingsbury (eds.), *The International Politics of the Environment* (1991) 85, 109 (states often prefer regional rather than global approaches for managing environmental issues).

found in the constitutive instruments of international dispute settlement bodies, which seek to regulate how those bodies interact with other institutions. In addition to such treaty-based jurisdiction regulating rules there are also general norms, being either rules of custom or 'general principles of law recognised by civilised nations',[68] which may be called upon to deal with situations of jurisdictional competition when treaty-based rules are non-existent or unclear.

Alone, and in combination, both sets of rules are fairly rudimentary. Rosenne notes that even the most elemental procedures, such as the capacity to transfer cases from one jurisdiction to another, are generally absent.[69] One consequence of their nascent and developing character is that there is some degree of flexibility in their application. This means that precisely how they are deployed depends considerably upon the objective which is sought to be achieved.[70] For instance, in a situation of litispendence a desire to reduce inconvenience to the litigants might suggest a rather different outcome from a broader objective which seeks to ensure that an environmental dispute is resolved by the tribunal best equipped to deal with it. It might also differ from an objective to maintain the effectiveness of an environmental regime by ensuring, wherever possible, that an overlap between consensual and compulsory mechanisms of dispute settlement is resolved in favour of the latter.[71] This means that the central challenge in devising and applying appropriate jurisdiction regulating rules in the context of international environmental litigation is paying appropriate regard to the role of adjudication not only in resolving disputes amicably, but also in determining cases in a manner which best promotes the substantive objectives of the applicable environmental norms.

9.3.1 *Applying jurisdiction-regulating rules*

Environmental regimes seek to regulate or synchronise jurisdiction in several ways, mirroring the practice in international dispute settlement more generally. However, as yet no environmental dispute settlement

[68] Statute of the ICJ, art. 38(1)(c).

[69] Shabtai Rosenne, *The Perplexities of Modern International Law* (2004) 65.

[70] Vigni, above n. 10, 146 (emphasising that neither general principles nor rules of treaty law provide a definitive resolution of problems of jurisdictional overlap, and arguing that there is a need for 'contextual and teleological interpretation' of those norms in order 'to determine which regime must deal with a particular matter or dispute').

[71] *Ibid*. 147.

procedure has adopted the approach of some regional or issue-specific tribunals, such as the ECJ and the WTO, which possess exclusive jurisdiction over disputes concerning the interpretation or application of their respective constituent instruments.[72] Such provisions are designed to be protective of self-contained regimes, by ensuring consistency in the interpretation of regime rules, and are motivated by a concern that the involvement of external dispute-settlers may generate decisions that do not adequately address the needs of the regime.[73]

An example of such an approach, which has implications for environmental dispute settlement, is found in NAFTA. Under that regime the parties may rely upon only a limited number of multilateral environmental agreements to justify trade measures designed to protect human health and/or the environment that would otherwise be in conflict with NAFTA.[74] In order to prevent parties from commencing trade cases involving such environmental exceptions outside the NAFTA dispute settlement system, when a responding party seeks to rely on the specified environmental agreements a complainant may *only* resort to NAFTA for resolution of that dispute.[75] A similar approach is taken under EC law, with article 292 of the EC Treaty conferring exclusive jurisdiction on the ECJ to consider disputes involving EC Treaty matters.

Dedicated environmental regimes by contrast adopt a mostly deferential approach, allowing virtually any alternative procedure to be used to settle disputes concerning the regime. A typical provision in this respect is found in the Madrid Protocol, which establishes a system for the compulsory adjudication of disputes, either by the ICJ or an ad hoc arbitral tribunal.[76] The Madrid Protocol does not prevent the parties from seeking to utilise other mechanisms, including diplomatic means of settlement, and to this end article 18 provides that the parties to a dispute 'concerning the interpretation or application of this Protocol' shall

[72] EC Treaty, art. 292; 1994 Marrakesh Agreement Establishing the World Trade Organisation annex 2 (Understanding on Rules and Procedures Governing the Settlement of Disputes), art. 23.

[73] Shany, above n. 10, 182. [74] NAFTA, art 104. [75] *Ibid*. art. 2005(3).

[76] Madrid Protocol, art 19. Parties to the Madrid Protocol may declare that they accept the jurisdiction of the ICJ or of an arbitral tribunal constituted in conformity with the schedule to the protocol (art. 19(1)). A party which has not made a declaration is deemed to have accepted the competence of the arbitral tribunal (art. 19(3)), and in a case of differing preferences the dispute may be submitted only to the arbitral tribunal, unless the parties otherwise agree (art. 19(5)).

consult among themselves as soon as possible with a view to having the dispute resolved by negotiation, inquiry, mediation, conciliation, arbitration, judicial settlement or other peaceful means to which the parties to the dispute agree.

This flexibility built into the Madrid Protocol provides the parties with the widest range of options for resolving disputes, but also ensures that where no agreement between them is forthcoming that arbitration or judicial settlement applies by default.

The type of jurisdiction-regulating rule expressed in the Madrid Protocol is beginning to be considered in international litigation. It might be thought that the operation of such a rule would be relatively clear cut. However, this has not been the experience to date. Difficulties have been encountered in determining what constitutes an agreement to utilise an alternative means of peaceful settlement, and ascertaining whether it should override the procedure that has been invoked in the absence of express words to this effect. This was the quandary faced in both the *Southern Bluefin Tuna* dispute and the *MOX Plant* dispute, in which ITLOS and annex VII arbitral tribunals were asked to interpret provisions of the LOS Convention that are similar to article 18 of the Madrid Protocol, but go somewhat further in allowing the use of alternative dispute settlement mechanisms only insofar as this does not detract from the convention's own binding system. How these provisions have operated in practice provide a range of insights into the extent to which jurisdictional competition is problematic in the environmental context, and how the difficulties that do arise can be addressed.

9.3.1.1 Jurisdiction regulation under the LOS Convention

Jurisdiction-regulating norms are an essential feature of part XV of the LOS Convention, which establishes a compulsory system for the adjudication of disputes relating to the interpretation or application of the convention. The drafters were aware of the potential interaction between part XV and other mechanisms for resolving law of the sea disputes, and hence included several jurisdictional prerequisites in section 1 of part XV. These inject flexibility into the system, permitting states to agree upon alternative dispute settlement procedures. Article 280 emphasises that nothing in the LOS Convention prevents states from resolving disputes concerning the interpretation or application of the convention through peaceful means of their choosing. Article 281(1) goes on to provide that the compulsory dispute settlement mechanisms contained in section 2 of part XV will only operate where the parties to a dispute have not reached a settlement by their agreed means and that agreement does not exclude any further procedure. In addition, and recognising that parties to a dispute concerning the LOS Convention may also be parties to other agreements providing for the binding settlement of such disputes, article 282 provides that those procedures will apply in lieu of part XV. Hence while the parties retain the freedom to select another form of dispute settlement, they are not permitted to avoid the general obligation to submit convention-related disputes, such as those concerning the marine environment, to binding settlement.[77]

9.3.1.2 Southern Bluefin Tuna *dispute*

It was the effect of article 281 of the LOS Convention that emerged as the central jurisdictional issue in the *Southern Bluefin Tuna* dispute.[78]

Southern Bluefin Tuna *order*

In July 1999 Australia and New Zealand requested the establishment of an arbitral tribunal under annex VII of the LOS Convention to hear the merits of the dispute which related to a Japanese experimental fishing programme for an endangered fishery, southern bluefin tuna.[79] Pending the establishment of the tribunal, Australia and New Zealand successfully sought provisional measures in ITLOS to halt Japan's unilateral programme. In August 1999 ITLOS unanimously found that the annex VII tribunal to be established would prima facie have jurisdiction over the dispute between the parties.[80] ITLOS went on to order that the parties maintain their catches of southern bluefin tuna at previously agreed levels, and that none of the litigants engage in a unilateral programme.[81]

In what was akin to a claim that Australia and New Zealand were shopping for a forum that offered them particular advantages, Japan argued before ITLOS that the dispute between the parties concerned only the CCSBT, and not the LOS Convention, and therefore that the non-binding dispute settlement provisions of the CCSBT should prevail.

[77] Vigni, above n. 10, 154. [78] See also the discussion in ch. 7.

[79] As neither Australia, New Zealand, nor Japan had made a declaration under the LOS Convention, art. 287 electing a procedure, annex VII arbitration applied by default. The parties requested the World Bank's International Centre for Settlement of Investment Disputes to administer the arbitration.

[80] *Southern Bluefin Tuna* order (1999) 38 ILM 1624, [62].

[81] *Ibid.* [90(c)] and [90(d)].

However, ITLOS concluded that the fact that the CCSBT applied did not exclude the right of Australia and New Zealand to invoke the provisions of the LOS Convention relating to the conservation and management of southern bluefin tuna,[82] nor did it preclude recourse to the procedures in part XV.[83] ITLOS also accepted that there was in existence a dispute between the parties concerning the interpretation and application of the LOS Convention.[84] Accordingly ITLOS found that the annex VII tribunal to be established would prima facie have jurisdiction over the dispute.[85]

Southern Bluefin Tuna *award*

In August 2000 the annex VII arbitral tribunal handed down its award on jurisdiction and admissibility in which it reached a conclusion that was diametrically opposed to that of ITLOS. It found that it was not in fact competent to hear the dispute, and unanimously discharged the provisional measures prescribed by ITLOS. The main conclusion in the *Southern Bluefin Tuna* award was that, by operation of article 281 of the LOS Convention, the non-compulsory dispute resolution provisions of the CCSBT contained in article 16[86] excluded the operation of

[82] *Ibid.* [51]. [83] *Ibid.* [84] *Ibid.* [44]–[48].

[85] *Ibid.* [62]. Judge ad hoc Shearer argued in the *Southern Bluefin Tuna* order that ITLOS should have held that the jurisdiction of the annex VII tribunal was clearly manifest. Lowe acknowledges the reasonableness of such an approach ('it is understandable that the ITLOS, and its individual judges, should seek to exercise some benevolent oversight of the UNCLOS dispute settlement system'), but argues that the majority correctly refrained from stepping beyond the terms of their remit and pronouncing upon a jurisdictional issue properly the province of the tribunal constituted to determine the merits of the proceeding: A. Vaughan Lowe, 'Advocating Judicial Activism: The ITLOS Opinions of Judge Ivan Shearer' (2005) 24 *AustYBIL* 145, 152.

[86] Art. 16 provides:

> 1. If any dispute arises between two or more of the Parties concerning the interpretation or implementation of this Convention, those Parties shall consult among themselves with a view to having the dispute resolved by negotiation, inquiry, mediation, conciliation, arbitration, judicial settlement or other peaceful means of their own choice.
> 2. Any dispute of this character not so resolved shall, with the consent in each case of all parties to the dispute, be referred for settlement to the International Court of Justice or to arbitration; but failure to reach agreement on reference to the International Court of Justice or to arbitration shall not absolve parties to the dispute from the responsibility of continuing to seek to resolve it by any of the various peaceful means referred to in paragraph 1 above.
> 3. In cases where the dispute is referred to arbitration, the arbitral tribunal shall be constituted as provided in the Annex to this Convention. The Annex forms an integral part of this Convention.

the compulsory procedures contained in part XV of the LOS Convention. As a consequence of this controversial conclusion, the decision has given rise to voluminous, and mostly critical, commentary.[87]

The tribunal rejected Japan's submission that the CCSBT was a *lex specialis* which displaced the relevant conservation and management provisions of the LOS Convention. It found that an implementing convention such as the CCSBT does not necessarily vacate the obligations imposed by the LOS Convention, or other framework convention.[88] The tribunal concluded that while the dispute was centred on the CCSBT, it also arose under the LOS Convention:[89]

> [T]here is no reason why a given act of a State may not violate its obligations under more than one treaty. There is frequently a parallelism of treaties, both in their substantive content and in their provisions for settlement of disputes arising thereunder.[90]

However, the tribunal was not content simply to find that a 'parallelism' existed; instead it went further, finding that in this case there was in fact 'a *single dispute* arising under both Conventions'.[91] This was an essential step in its reasoning which ultimately led it to conclude that part XV was inapplicable, because it allowed the tribunal to conclude that the CCSBT constituted an agreement for the settlement of a dispute concerning the LOS Convention.

[87] For critical analysis of the decision see D. A. Colson and P. Hoyle, 'Satisfying the Procedural Prerequisites to the Compulsory Dispute Settlement Mechanisms of the 1982 Law of the Sea Convention: Did the *Southern Bluefin Tuna* Tribunal Get it Right?' (2003) 34 *ODIL* 59; Jacqueline Peel, 'A Paper Umbrella Which Dissolves in the Rain? The Future for Resolving Fisheries Disputes Under UNCLOS in the Aftermath of the Southern Bluefin Tuna Arbitration' (2002) 3 *MJIL* 53; Cesare P. R. Romano, 'The *Southern Bluefin Tuna* Dispute: Hints of a World to Come … Like it or Not' (2001) 32 *ODIL* 313; Tim Stephens, 'A Paper Umbrella Which Dissolves in the Rain? Implications of the *Southern Bluefin Tuna Case* for the Compulsory Resolution of Disputes Concerning the Marine Environment under the 1982 LOS convention' (2001) 6 *APJEL* 297; Leah Sturtz, '*Southern Bluefin Tuna Case*: Australia and New Zealand v. Japan' (2001) 28 *ELQ* 455; Deborah Horowitz, 'The Catch of Poseidon's Trident: The Fate of High Seas Fisheries in the *Southern Bluefin Tuna* Case' (2001) 25 *MULR* 810. For a more sympathetic appraisal of the decision see Barbara Kwiatkowska, 'The Southern Bluefin Tuna Arbitral Tribunal Did Get It Right: A Commentary and Reply to the Article by David A. Colson and Dr Peggy Hoyle' (2003) 34 *ODIL* 369; Barbara Kwiatkowska, 'The Australia and New Zealand Southern Bluefin Tuna (Jurisdiction and Admissibility) Award of the First Law of the Sea Convention Annex VII Arbitral Tribunal' (2001) 16 *IJMCL* 239 and Barbara Kwiatkowska, 'Southern Bluefin Tuna' (2001) 95 *AJIL* 162.

[88] *Southern Bluefin Tuna* award (2000) 39 ILM 1359, [52]. [89] *Ibid.* [90] *Ibid.*

[91] *Ibid.* [54] (emphasis added).

The tribunal noted that the first requirement of article 281 had been met because there had been serious and prolonged negotiations under the CCSBT which had produced no settlement.[92] In relation to the second requirement of article 281, the tribunal held that article 16 of the CCSBT 'exclude[d] any further procedure' and therefore rendered part XV inoperative.[93] The reasoning on this second aspect of article 281 had two main aspects.[94] First, the tribunal found that the CCSBT intended to exclude the compulsory dispute settlement mechanisms contained in part XV. This was despite the fact that article 16 of the CCSBT does not expressly purport to exclude part XV. Second, the tribunal interpreted article 281 broadly to support its conclusion that part XV procedures were displaced by an agreement that disclosed no clear intention to apply in its place. This conclusion also appears problematic, as the tribunal's expansive reading of article 281 would seem to catch all dispute resolution provisions in parallel instruments rather than being limited to specific agreements to seek a settlement of LOS Convention disputes outside the framework of part XV.

Various factors were said by the tribunal to support these contentious conclusions. First, the express obligation in article 16 of the CCSBT to continue to seek resolution by the means listed in that article stressed the consensual nature of the reference of any dispute to judicial settlement and indicated that the intent of article 16 was to remove proceedings from the reach of compulsory procedures.[95] Second, the tribunal found that article 16 of the CCSBT, like article XI of the 1959 Antarctic Treaty on which it was modelled, was obviously intended to exclude compulsory jurisdiction.[96] Third it was considered that, in light of the express exceptions from the part XV regime, the LOS Convention fell 'significantly short of establishing a truly comprehensive regime of compulsory jurisdiction entailing binding decisions'.[97] Finally it was said that many other agreements entered into after the LOS Convention excluded compulsory jurisdiction to varying degrees.

The reasoning of the *Southern Bluefin Tuna* award was challenged on a number of grounds by the lone dissentient, Sir Kenneth Keith. Sir Kenneth considered that clear wording was needed to exclude the obligations of states to submit to binding procedures under the LOS Convention and that article 16 of the CCSBT did not supply the necessary words.[98] Colson and Hoyle have similarly mounted a strong critique

[92] *Ibid.* [55]. [93] *Ibid.* [59]. [94] Colson and Hoyle, above n. 87, 67.

[95] *Southern Bluefin Tuna* award (2000) 39 ILM 1359, [57]. [96] *Ibid.* [58]. [97] *Ibid.* [62].

[98] *Ibid.* (2000) 39 ILM 1359, separate opinion of Judge Sir Kenneth Keith, [19].

of this aspect of the award, observing that 'the more compelling interpretation [of article 281] ... is that [part XV] would only be precluded if there were a *specific agreement* to do so in relation to a *specific process* being used to address a *specific dispute*'.[99]

If it is followed, the *Southern Bluefin Tina* award may have significant implications for the settlement of disputes that arise simultaneously under the LOS Convention and a specific implementing instrument, such as the CCSBT. It suggests that the dispute settlement system of the LOS Convention is highly vulnerable to displacement, and therefore that its effectiveness as a regime may be substantially weakened. The reasoning of the tribunal would also appear to be applicable to other situations of jurisdictional competition in which one instrument incorporates a jurisdiction-regulating provision in similar terms to article 281 of the LOS Convention. In such situations a mere agreement to negotiate, such as article 16 of the CCSBT, which adds little to the requirement under articles 2 and 33 of the UN Charter that states settle their disputes peacefully, may take precedence over compulsory procedures.

As far as high seas fisheries disputes are concerned, in the ultimate paragraph of its reasons the annex VII tribunal referred to a comprehensive solution to what the tribunal euphemistically described as the 'procedural problems' raised by the *Southern Bluefin Tuna* dispute.[100] The tribunal specifically discussed the Straddling Stocks Agreement[101] which, it was noted, was not only more detailed and expansive than the relevant provisions of the LOS Convention or CCSBT, but contains provisions that apply part XV of the LOS Convention mutatis mutandis to any dispute between the states parties concerning the agreement or a subregional, regional, or global fisheries agreement.[102]

Oxman has argued that the *Southern Bluefin Tuna* award confirmed that jurisdiction regulating norms are not necessarily capable of straightforward application, and that there may be a need to turn to presumptions

[99] Colson and Hoyle, above n. 87, 69.

[100] *Southern Bluefin Tuna* award (2000) 39 ILM 1359, [71].

[101] See Tullio Treves, 'The Settlement of Disputes According to the Straddling Stocks Agreement of 1995' in Alan E. Boyle and David Freestone (eds.), *International Law and Sustainable Development: Past Achievements and Future Challenges* (1999), 253, 269 (noting that unlike the 'usual approach of conventions for the protection of the environment, which stresses more the prevention and management of disputes than their solution by binding decisions' the Straddling Stocks Agreement relies heavily on compulsory dispute settlement as a compliance mechanism).

[102] *Southern Bluefin Tuna* award (2000) 39 ILM 1359, [71].

to resolve the interactions between competing procedures.[103] He asks whether, when there is competition between non-compulsory and compulsory procedures, there is a presumption against any restriction on state sovereignty and therefore that express consent will be required to maintain the mandatory system. Or instead is there a presumption in favour of what Oxman calls a 'regime-building conception' which only permits states to derogate from compulsory procedures where they have expressly sought to do so? The tribunal in the *Southern Bluefin Tuna* award appeared to adopt the former framework of analysis, the effect of which was to prevent a dispute concerning a threatened fishery from being considered in a forum that could offer authoritative guidance on the marine environmental provisions of the LOS Convention. While there is no doubt that the litigation in the *Southern Bluefin Tuna* dispute assisted the parties in resolving their dispute,[104] it must be questioned whether it also had the effect of leaving the parties with no precise legal guidance as to their marine environmental protection obligations.

9.3.1.3 *MOX Plant* dispute

The *MOX Plant* dispute also involved a consideration of the jurisdiction-regulating norms of the LOS Convention, this time article 282, a companion provision to article 281. Unlike the *Southern Bluefin Tuna* dispute, the *MOX Plant* dispute has not produced a determination that has clearly weakened the LOS Convention's dispute settlement regime. None the less, the practical result of the litigation has been to prevent the environmental dispute from being resolved (although proceedings by Ireland or the European Commission against the United Kingdom in the ECJ remain a possibility).

MOX Plant *order*

In the provisional measures phase ITLOS had an opportunity to consider some of the issues arising out of the interaction between the LOS Convention and other legal regimes applicable to the dispute. The United Kingdom had objected to the jurisdiction of ITLOS to order provisional measures on several grounds, including that article 282 of the LOS Convention prevented proceedings from continuing because

[103] Oxman, above n. 26, 277.

[104] See Bill Mansfield, 'Letter to the Editor: The Southern Bluefin Tuna Arbitration: Comments on Professor Barbara Kwiatkowska's Article' (2001) 16 *IJMCL* 361.

the parties had agreed to alternative binding procedures.[105] In this regard the United Kingdom pointed to the OSPAR Convention, the EC Treaty and the Euratom Treaty and the compulsory dispute settlement procedures of those three agreements.[106] For its part Ireland responded that the gist of the dispute with the United Kingdom concerned the interpretation and application of various provisions of the LOS Convention relating to marine environmental protection,[107] and not any other instrument.[108] Moreover it was contended that tribunals operating under the competing regimes would not have jurisdiction that extended to all the matters in dispute before ITLOS.[109] In characterising the case, Ireland suggested that the rights and duties under the range of instruments applicable to the dispute were cumulative, and therefore it could rely on any, or all of them, as it chose.[110]

ITLOS rejected the United Kingdom's objections based on article 282 for two closely related reasons. First, it held that the general, regional, or bilateral agreements to which article 282 refers will only apply in place of the LOS Convention dispute settlement system if they provide for the settlement of disputes concerning the interpretation or application of the LOS Convention itself.[111] The settlement mechanisms under the OSPAR Convention, the EC Treaty and the Euratom Treaty were said by ITLOS to concern 'the interpretation or application of those agreements, and not with disputes arising under the LOS Convention'.[112] Second, the Tribunal sought to distinguish disputes arising under the LOS Convention from those arising under the OSPAR Convention, EC Treaty and Euratom Treaty. The Tribunal held that:

> [E]ven if the OSPAR Convention, the EC Treaty and the Euratom Treaty contain rights or obligations similar to or identical with the rights or obligations set out in the Convention, the rights and obligations under those agreements have a separate existence from those under the Convention.[113]

In support of this conclusion ITLOS observed that even where treaty provisions were identical they might be construed differently having

[105] *MOX Plant* order (2002) 41 ILM 405 [38]. [106] *Ibid.* [43]. [107] *Ibid.* [36]

[108] *Ibid.* [45]. [109] *Ibid.* [46]. [110] *Ibid.* [47].

[111] *Ibid.* [48]. Note also the separate opinion of Judge Wolfrum in which he observed that taking into account the purpose of part XV, which is to give primary jurisdiction to art. 287 courts and tribunals unless the parties to a dispute have agreed otherwise, 'an intention to entrust the settlement of disputes concerning the interpretation and application of the [LOS Convention] to other institutions must be expressed explicitly in [those other] agreements'.

[112] *MOX Plant* order (2002) 41 ILM 405 [49]. [113] *Ibid.* [50].

regard to the objects and purposes of the treaty regimes of which they formed part.[114] Judge Wolfrum further explained this line of reasoning in his separate opinion:

> It is well known in international law and practice that more than one treaty may bear upon a particular dispute. The development of a plurality of international norms covering the same topic or right is a reality. There is frequently a parallelism of treaties, both in substantive content and in their provisions for settlement of disputes thereunder. However, a dispute under one agreement, such as the OSPAR Convention does not become a dispute under the LOS Convention by the mere fact that both instruments cover the [same] issue. If the OSPAR Convention, the Euratom Treaty or the EC Treaty were to set out rights and obligations similar or even identical to those of the LOS Convention, these still arise from rules having a separate existence from the ones of the LOS Convention.[115]

Both the ITLOS order and Judge Wolfrum's separate opinion usefully explain how a dispute implicating multiple instruments which seems on its face to be an indivisible case can in fact be separated into individual components. However, somewhat regrettably, there was no further engagement with the question that was subsequently faced in the *MOX Plant* award, namely how the interaction between the LOS Convention and the 'self-contained regime'[116] established by the EC Treaty was to be resolved. Specifically, which institution is to be the ultimate arbiter as to whether a dispute concerns only the LOS Convention, or in fact several instruments including the EC Treaty?

Having dismissed the United Kingdom's arguments regarding article 282, the Tribunal concluded that it did have jurisdiction, stating that since the dispute 'concerns the interpretation or application of the Convention and no other agreement, only the dispute settlement procedures under the Convention are relevant to that dispute'.[117] Judge

[114] *Ibid.* [51]. [115] *Ibid.* separate opinion of Judge Wolfrum, 2.

[116] Bruno Simma, 'Self-Contained Regimes' (1985) 16 *NethYBIL* 111, 123–9 (arguing that the EC Treaty constitutes a self-contained regime and that consequences of violations of the treaty must first be pursued within the regime itself before looking for procedures beyond the regime).

[117] *MOX Plant* order (2002) 41 ILM 405, [52]. In his separate opinion, Judge Nelson expressed doubts as to the breadth of the reasoning adopted by the majority, suggesting that it may render arts. 281 and 282 ineffective. Judge Anderson also questioned this aspect of the Tribunal's order, but did not explain the basis of his doubts as to the correctness of paragraph 52. Judge Jesus similarly doubted the Tribunal's interpretation of art. 282, and accepted the reasoning in the *Southern Bluefin Tuna* award (2000) 39 ILM 1359 that had the dispute in this case been amenable to characterisation as a single dispute arising under multiple instruments then part XV would be inapplicable. But see *contra* Judge Wolfrum,

Treves noted that had the United Kingdom's jurisdictional arguments been accepted, this law of the sea dispute would had to have been considered in separate parts by different courts and tribunals and been taken away from the only mechanism competent to consider it in its entirety.[118] The majority's approach is evidently a strong affirmation of the centrality of part XV of the LOS Convention for the resolution of marine environmental disputes.

MOX Plant *award*

The annex VII arbitral tribunal's order of 24 June 2003 in which it suspended proceedings did not greatly clarify the scope of article 282, although the decision did implicitly affirm aspects of the *MOX Plant* order. The tribunal concurred with the finding as to prima facie jurisdiction on the grounds that the dispute clearly concerned the interpretation and application of the LOS Convention.[119] However, the tribunal noted that although this was sufficient to support an order of interim measures, it had to be definitely satisfied as to its jurisdiction in order to pronounce on the merits.[120]

The United Kingdom once again argued that the jurisdiction of the LOS Convention's dispute settlement system was ousted by the OSPAR Convention and the EC Treaty. The tribunal was not swayed by the argument relating to the OSPAR Convention. It agreed with ITLOS that while the OSPAR Convention was relevant to some of the questions in issue, this fact did not alter 'the character of the dispute as one essentially involving the interpretation and application' of the LOS Convention.[121] Additionally the tribunal was not convinced that the OSPAR Convention substantially 'cover[ed] the field' of the dispute so as to activate article 282 of the LOS Convention.

However, the interaction between the LOS Convention and the EC Treaty raised far more difficult questions. Not only had Ireland and the United Kingdom transferred competence over law of the sea matters to the EC,[122] but the ECJ possessed exclusive jurisdiction over matters

who maintained that the interpretation of art. 282 offered by ITLOS did not leave the provision devoid of substance.

[118] *MOX Plant* order (2002) 41 ILM 405, separate opinion of Judge Treves, [6].

[119] *MOX Plant* award (order 3, of 24 June 2003) (2003) 42 ILM 1187 [14].

[120] *Ibid.* [15]. [121] *Ibid.* [18].

[122] By operation of LOS Convention, annex IX, an international organisation may become a party to the convention. Under annex IX, art. 5(1) the instrument of formal confirmation or accession 'shall contain a declaration specifying the matters governed by this Convention in respect of which competence has been

of EC law.[123] In June 2003, at the time of the initial annex VII tribunal order, there was a real possibility that the European Commission would institute proceedings against Ireland, and that the ECJ would find that Ireland had failed to respect the exclusive jurisdiction of the ECJ to interpret and apply the LOS Convention as part of EC law.[124] (Indeed this came to pass, with ECJ proceedings commenced in October 2003, and the ECJ finding against Ireland in its judgment of May 2006.)

Neither Ireland nor the United Kingdom argued that the interpretation and application of the LOS Convention fell entirely within the exclusive jurisdiction of the ECJ; however, the tribunal observed that the ECJ might well reach such a conclusion and, if it did, then part XV would be inapplicable by operation of article 282 of the LOS Convention.[125] It was of course a matter for the annex VII tribunal to determine the limits of its own jurisdiction,[126] and the tribunal observed that it could seek to identify those provisions of the LOS Convention not falling within the exclusive jurisdiction and competence of the EC. However, the tribunal stated that this would be inappropriate, not only because there was some lack of clarity as to which provisions of the LOS Convention were affected, but also because under EC law

transferred to the organisation by its members States which are Parties to this Convention'. Under art. 5(2), a member state of an international organisation shall, when ratifying or acceding, 'make a declaration specifying the matters governed by this Convention in respect of which it has transferred competence to the organisation'. Both Ireland (upon ratification on 21 June 1996) and the United Kingdom (upon accession on 25 July 1997) made declarations observing that competence in relation to certain matters had been transferred to the EC. In its declaration upon formal confirmation (1 April 1998) the EC stated that it had exclusive competence over various marine environmental matters, including fisheries issues and also marine pollution to the extent that 'such provisions of the Convention or legal instruments adopted in implementation thereof affect common rules established by the Community'.

123 *MOX Plant* award (order 3, of 24 June 2003) (2003) 42 ILM 1187, [20]. The ECJ has held that international agreements to which the EC is a party (either alone or side-by-side with member states) are an integral part of the Community's legal system (*Haegeman v. Belgium* [1974] ECR 499, [4]–[6]). The ECJ has the task of ensuring that EC law is observed (EC Treaty, art. 164). See generally Ellen Hey, 'The European Community's Courts and International Environmental Agreements' (1998) 7 *RECIEL* 4.

124 *MOX Plant* award (order 3, of 24 June 2003) (2003) 42 ILM 1187 [21].

125 *Ibid.* [22].

126 It is generally accepted that international courts possess jurisdiction to decide the limits of their own jurisdiction (the so-called *la compétence de la compétence* or *Kompetenz-Kompetenz*) as a necessary incident of the judicial function. See generally I. Shihata, *The Power of the International Court to Determine Its Own Jurisdiction: Competence de la Competence* (1965).

this was a matter ultimately to be decided by the ECJ.[127] It was also of relevance that had both the tribunal and the ECJ proceeded to a determination on jurisdiction, each decision would be equally binding upon the parties.[128] For these reasons, 'and bearing in mind considerations of mutual respect and comity which should prevail between judicial institutions both of which may be called upon to determine rights and obligations as between two States',[129] the tribunal suspended hearings on the merits pending a resolution of EC law issues.[130]

ECJ decision

It is highly unlikely that proceedings before the annex VII tribunal will resume given the ECJ's ruling that Ireland had violated EC law by turning to part XV of the LOS Convention in relation to the case.[131] In its May 2006 judgment the ECJ noted that the LOS Convention was a 'mixed agreement' to which the EC and its members were parties and in relation to which the EC and its members had shared competence over marine environmental matters. The declaration made by the EC when ratifying the LOS Convention made this clear in stating that with respect to provisions of the convention relating to the marine environment 'the Community has exclusive competence only to the extent that such provisions ... affect common rules established by the Community'.[132]

The central issue for the ECJ was whether there had been a transfer to the Community of these areas of shared competence, and this turned on the existence of Community rules, regardless of their scope and nature.[133] The ECJ held that

> the Convention provisions on the prevention of marine pollution relied on by Ireland, which clearly cover a significant part of the dispute relating to the MOX plant, come within the scope of Community competence which the Community has elected to exercise by becoming a party to the Convention.[134]

[127] *MOX Plant* award (order 3, of 24 June 2003) (2003) 42 ILM 1187, [26].

[128] *Ibid.* [27]. [129] *Ibid.* [28].

[130] *MOX Plant* award (order 4, of 14 November 2003) (available at www.pca-cpa.org) and see also order 5, of 22 January 2007 suspending periodic reporting by the parties.

[131] *Commission of the European Communities* v. *Ireland* (2006) 45 ILM 1051. For commentary see Cesare P. R. Romano, 'Commission of the European Communities v. Ireland' (2007) 101 *AJIL* 171; Paul James Cardwell and Duncan French, 'Who Decides? The ECJ's Judgment on Jurisdiction in the *MOX Plant* Dispute' (2007) 19 *JEL* 121; Nikolas Lavranos, 'The *MOX Plant* Judgment of the ECJ: How Exclusive is the Jurisdiction of the ECJ?' (2006) 15 *EELR* 291.

[132] *Commission of the European Communities* v. *Ireland* (2006) 45 ILM 1051, [8].

[133] *Ibid.* [108]. [134] *Ibid.* [120].

The provisions of the convention 'form an integral part of the Community legal order'.[135] Once it had determined the extent of Community competence the ECJ turned to consider the extent and operation of its jurisdiction. In this respect it was found that it was a matter for EC law alone to determine the 'autonomy of the Community legal system',[136] and that article 292 of the EC Treaty made it clear that the ECJ had exclusive jurisdiction over matters of Community law. The Court also noted that the violation of article 292 could have been avoided because of the operation of article 282 of the LOS Convention, which specifically provides that proceedings under the ECJ can take precedence over those under part XV of the LOS Convention. In further findings the Court determined that Ireland breached article 292 by referring and relying upon provisions of the EC Treaty in the LOS Convention proceedings,[137] and also fell foul of the duty of cooperation under article 10 of the EC Treaty by bringing proceedings without communicating and informing Community institutions.[138]

Now that proceedings in the *MOX Plant* dispute appear to be reaching a conclusion it is possible to reflect on their relevance to jurisdictional competition in international environmental litigation more generally. The decision in *Commission* v. *Ireland* is generally to be welcomed as it has clarified the interaction between the ECJ and other adjudicative bodies in disputes touching upon the environmental competence of the EC. None the less it is of some concern insofar as it suggests that the Community has exclusive competence over a mixed environmental agreement in a subject area in which it has taken action, even though the standards it sets are not as extensive as the environmental regime itself.[139] And while it has illuminated EC law in relation to environmental competence, the decision cannot determine how judicial institutions outside the Community may deal with this or similar cases. The annex VII tribunal has been extremely deferential towards the ECJ in the *MOX Plant* award, and proceedings are now likely to be terminated. However, the more assertive approach of ITLOS in the provisional measures proceedings suggests that this area of jurisdictional contestation has not been laid to rest. ITLOS, or an annex VII tribunal, in a future dispute involving Community law may well take the view adopted by ITLOS and explained by Judge Wolfrum that article 282 does not operate automatically to shift competence to the ECJ over marine

[135] *Ibid.* [126]. [136] *Ibid.* [123].
[137] *Ibid.* [146]–[157]. [138] *Ibid.* [168]–[182]. [139] Romano, above n. 131, 176.

environmental disputes and that LOS Convention institutions have a duty to determine a dispute raising provisions of the LOS Convention in order to uphold it as a legal framework.[140]

This means that in practice much will hinge on international environmental diplomacy rather than international environmental law, with states having to make decisions about which forum they will use, and the European Commission to make decisions how aggressively it will protect the autonomy of the EC and the jurisdiction of the ECJ. In this respect the Commission has sent ambiguous messages about when it will intervene to uphold the ECJ's exclusive jurisdiction. In the *Iron Rhine Railway* arbitration[141] between Belgium and the Netherlands submitted by the parties consensually under the auspices of the PCA, the Commission signalled no interest in taking the parties before the ECJ, notwithstanding that the arbitration concerned matters of environmental law within the EC's competence. A further matter now facing the Commission and the ECJ is how to deal with environmental compliance more generally. By making clear that it regards its competence over environmental matters to be supreme *vis-à-vis* EC members, the Commission bears a heavy responsibility to protect the environment and uphold international environmental agreements to which the Community and its members are parties.[142]

9.4 Conclusion

The varied dispute settlement procedures now operating in the environmental field, including the many international courts and tribunals, present a suite of options for resolving disputes and promoting compliance with environmental rules and standards. While benefits flow from this wide choice of litigation options, in that the opportunities for judicial determination of environmental disputes has never been greater, disadvantages derive from practical difficulties in the interaction between these mechanisms. As a consequence international environmental litigation has become more complex, lengthy, and costly, with some proceedings paralysed by procedural manoeuvring. This has attendant implications for the continued efficacy of international

[140] *Ibid.* 178.

[141] *Iron Rhine ('Ijzeren Rijn') Railway (Belgium/Netherlands)* arbitration (24 May 2005) (available at www.pca-cpa.org/showfile.asp?fil_id=377).

[142] Cardwell and French, above n. 131, 128.

courts and tribunals in dealing with environmental threats, as disputes involving such matters should be resolved promptly if the underlying environmental problem is to be addressed. There are also potentially more serious and long-term problems, which relate to determining an appropriate priority between competing dispute settlement procedures in dealing with environmental questions, and to the undermining of substantive environmental norms by preventing dispute settlement bodies from operating to ensure that these rules are effectively implemented.

It is unlikely that this interaction, conflict, and competition between dispute settlement procedures will lead to anomy in international environmental law and diplomacy, and it is unrealistic to expect complete eunomy through a systematic legal and institutional framework for dealing with all international environmental disputes. Arguably the most that might reasonably be expected is a basic level of harmony in the operation of potentially competing jurisdictions. This can only be achieved through greater formal and informal measures of coordination, and is essential as jurisdictional disputes are becoming an inevitable part of complex environmental litigation, which is severely slowing progress in addressing the legal aspects of environmental disputes. This chapter has identified several coordination strategies; however, these are in a state of flux and development and leave much room for interpretation in their application. In environmental cases it is important that they be applied having regard not only to the convenience of the parties or the judicial body, but also to broader considerations of environmental governance such as whether the matter can be resolved promptly and in a way that prevents, minimises, or compensates for the environmental threat or damage at the root of the dispute.

10 Fragmentation of international environmental law

International environmental litigation is now played out in an array of adjudicative institutions including permanent courts, ad hoc arbitral tribunals, regional courts, and judicial bodies with highly specialised subject matter jurisdiction. The preceding chapter examined the practical difficulties this presents for resolving environmental disputes. This chapter is concerned with the related but distinct question of whether international environmental law is being fragmented as a result of the patchwork character of contemporary environmental dispute settlement. Specifically by reference to human rights courts and complaints bodies and the dispute settlement system of the WTO, it assesses whether some judicial and quasi-judicial bodies are destabilising organising rules and principles of international environmental law by adopting parochial approaches to environmental norms that suit the specific purposes of non-environmental regimes. Such analysis is now desirable having regard to the recent expansion in the body of international case law on environmental issues,[1] particularly in the human rights and trade fields.

10.1 Fragmentation of international law

International law has always comprised general norms and rules of a more specific character. However, an important feature of the contemporary international legal order is its pluralism as reflected in an

[1] As Sands observed in 1999 'a few years from now the body of case law will probably require us to address how to maintain coherence among the various fora at which international environmental issues are litigated': Philippe Sands, 'International Environmental Litigation and Its Future' (1999) 32 *URichLR* 1619, 1641.

increasing number of specialised regimes, rules, and institutions.[2] While some commentators have argued that the development of quasi-autonomous legal orders unhelpfully compartmentalises international law,[3] others have observed that decentralisation can advance community objectives not attained through general rules.[4] The process of specialisation has been particularly evident in the environmental context, with detailed regulatory regimes devised at regional and global scales to address matters that could not be managed effectively by general international law. However, in the horizontal international legal order an inevitable byproduct of decentralisation has been divergence or fragmentation in legal standards, a phenomenon that in turn raises the possibility of conflict between legal norms applicable to the same state behaviour. International environmental law must confront two particular challenges as a result of fragmentation – internal conflicts (between different environmental regimes)[5] and external conflicts (between environmental and non-environmental regimes).

10.1.1 *International courts and fragmentation*

The debate concerning the nature and threat of the fragmentation phenomenon has acquired particular prominence as a result of the proliferation of international courts and tribunals and their increasing influence upon public international law. The judicialisation of several areas of international law appears to exacerbate the potential for international law to be compartmentalised as a result of the jurisprudence of issue-specific tribunals. It raises the prospect that new courts might coopt general norms for the narrow purposes of specialised regimes, and thereby undermine their universal applicability.[6] This seems more

[2] Joost Pauwelyn, *Conflict of Norms in Public International Law* (2003) 9.

[3] Ian Brownlie, 'The Rights of Peoples in Modern International Law' in James Crawford (ed.), *The Rights of Peoples* (1988) 1, 15.

[4] Karel C. Wellens, 'Diversity in Secondary Rules and the Unity of International Law: Some Reflections on Current Trends' in L. A. N. M. Barnhoorn and K. C. Wellens (eds.), *Diversity in Secondary Rules and the Unity of International Law* (1995) 3, 28: '[T]he relative autonomy of special fields...[has] promoted and guaranteed the growing effectiveness of their own particular set of primary rules, without putting in jeopardy the unity of coherence of the international legal order'; Thomas Franck, *Fairness in International Law and Institutions* (1995) 4 ('Specialization is a tribute which the profession pays to the maturity of the legal system').

[5] On this see Rüdiger Wolfrum and Nele Matz, *Conflicts in International Environmental Law* (2003).

[6] See Matthew Craven, 'Unity, Diversity and the Fragmentation of International Law' (2003) 14 *FinnYBIL* 3, 32.

than merely an abstract concern, as the legitimacy and authority of rules of public international law depend substantially upon their predictability, consistency, and universality.

Current and former members of the ICJ have been among the most prominent participants in the fragmentation debate, both as harbingers of calamity,[7] and as more sanguine commentators upon the expansion in the international adjudicative system.[8] Indeed the critique of the proliferation of international courts gained significant momentum after it was taken up by successive presidents of the ICJ, who issued dire warnings about the potential for forum shopping and inconsistent jurisprudence.[9] Particular anxiety was expressed for the future of the ICJ as the pre-eminent international court, and it was suggested that its caseload would decline and its decisions would become less influential. However, for many commentators such prognoses were too premature and pessimistic, it being argued that the growth of international courts and tribunals is a benign and often beneficial consequence of the expansion of international law into a wider range of activities. Such optimistic views range from bold claims that the proliferation of courts is indicative of 'the construction of coherent international order based on justice',[10] to the more tempered view that international law is acquiring greater maturity,[11] and is developing into a 'legal system'

[7] Robert Jennings, 'The Role of the International Court of Justice' (1997) 68 *BYBIL* 58; Robert Jennings, 'The Judiciary, International and National, and the Development of International Law' (1996) 45 *ICLQ* 1; Gilbert Guillaume, 'The Future of International Judicial Institutions' (1995) 44 *ICLQ* 848; Shigeru Oda, 'Dispute Settlement Prospects in the Law of the Sea' (1995) 44 *ICLQ* 863.

[8] Rosalyn Higgins, 'Respecting the Sovereignty of States and Running a Tight Courtroom' (2001) 50 *ICLQ* 121, 122: ('this is an inevitable consequence of the busy and complex world in which we live and is not a cause of regret'.

[9] Judge Stephen M. Schwebel, 'Address to the Plenary Session of the General Assembly of the United Nations' (speech delivered to the General Assembly of the United Nations, New York, 26 October 1999) [19] (available at www.icj-cij.org/icjwww/ipresscom/SPEECHES/iSpeechPresidentGA54_19991026.htm); Judge Gilbert Guillaume, 'Address to the General Assembly of the United Nations' (speech delivered to the General Assembly of the United Nations, 26 October 2000); Judge Gilbert Guillaume, 'Address to the Sixth Committee of the General Assembly of the United Nations' (speech delivered to the Sixth Committee of the General Assembly of the United Nations, 27 October 2000) (available at www.icj-cij.org/icjwww/ipresscom/SPEECHES/SpeechPresident_Guillaume_SixthCommittee_20001027.htm).

[10] Cesare P. R. Romano, 'The Proliferation of International Judicial Bodies: The Pieces of the Puzzle' (1999) 31 *NYUJILP* 709, 751.

[11] Pemmarajau S. Rao, 'Multiple International Judicial Forums: A Reflection of the Growing Strength of International Law or its Fragmentation?' (2004) 25 *MichJIL* 929, 960.

in the Hartian sense.[12] It has also been suggested that major points of jurisprudential difference can be reconciled through stronger and deeper informal links between international courts, which can thereby engage in a 'transjudicial' dialogue on issues of critical concern.[13]

In its recent study on the fragmentation of international law, a study group established by the ILC also found reason to be hopeful that the systemic integrity of international law could be maintained despite the emergence of multiple courts serving 'specialized and relatively autonomous spheres of social action and structure'.[14] The ILC study group was mandated only to consider substantive problems of normative interaction among regimes, rather than the broader institutional issues concerning 'the competence of various institutions applying international legal rules and their hierarchical relations *inter se*',[15] because the ILC took the view that procedural matters were best resolved by the institutions themselves. In relation to substantive fragmentation, the ILC study group concluded that an acceptable level of normative consistency could be achieved through the framework of existing rules, including the *lex specialis* maxim, the operation of 'self-contained regimes', principles of treaty interpretation, the doctrine *lex posterior derogat legi priori*, and the hierarchical relations between international legal norms. The ILC study group did not specifically address the challenges facing international environmental law in an age of 'specialized and (relatively) autonomous rules of rule-complexes, legal institutions and spheres of legal practice'[16] but it did recognise that international environmental law has emerged in 'response to growing concern over the state of the international environment'[17] and that the discipline advances policy imperatives that differ from other specialised areas, such as trade law.[18]

10.1.2 *Institutional imbalances*

Underlying the ILC study group's work was an appreciation that international law and its institutions function in an inescapably political context. While the ILC study group stressed that major difficulties of

[12] H. L. A. Hart, *The Concept of Law* (2nd edn 1994). See also Craven, above n. 6, 6–15.

[13] William W. Burke-White, 'International Legal Pluralism' (2004) 25 *MichJIL* 963, 977.

[14] Fragmentation of International Law: Difficulties Arising from the Diversification and Expansion of International Law: Report of the Study Group of the International Law Commission, Finalised by Chairman M Koskenniemi ILC, UN Doc. A/CN.4/L.682 [7].

[15] *Ibid.* [13]. [16] *Ibid.* [8]. [17] *Ibid.* [15]. [18] *Ibid.* [24].

normative conflict could be resolved on a case-by-case basis by resort to established techniques of legal reasoning, it recognised that the 'law cannot resolve in an abstract way any possible conflict that may arise between economic and environmental regimes'.[19] In this respect it was observed that '[e]ach [regime] has its experts and its ethos, its priorities and preferences, its structural bias' and that '[s]uch regimes are institutionally "programmed" to prioritize particular concerns over others'.[20] Viewed in this way the establishment of new courts and tribunals, and their subsequent efforts to develop a distinctive jurisprudence, are the result of underlying political forces.[21] It is therefore to be expected that in performing their mandate specialised courts and tribunals will adhere to interpretations of rules of international law that meet the regulatory needs of the regimes in which they operate.[22] Koskenniemi and Leino have described this process as one of 'hegemonic struggle' in which each court or tribunal seeks to have its own particular perspective regarded as the preferable general approach.[23]

The difficulty that international environmental law confronts in this context stems from the absence of dedicated environmental jurisdictions that can act as counterweights to powerful international organisations driving normative change in non-environmental arenas. It is certainly the case that efforts have been made to improve the environmental specialisation of existing bodies with general jurisdiction such as the PCA and the ICJ.[24] And it must be acknowledged that quasi-judicial bodies such as NCPs have been established within a growing number of environmental regimes. However, in areas of particular contention it is the dispute settlement bodies of non-environmental

[19] *Ibid.* [488]. [20] *Ibid.*

[21] Martti Koskenniemi and Päivi Leino, 'Fragmentation of International Law? Postmodern Anxieties' (2002) 15 *LJIL* 553, 561: '[T]he fact is that proliferating tribunals, overlapping jurisdictions and "fragmenting" normative orders . . . arise as effects of politics and not as technical mistakes or unfortunate side-effects of some global logic.' See also M. C. W. Pinto, 'Judicial Settlement of International Disputes: One Forum or Many' in Antony Anghie and Garry Sturgess (eds.), *Legal Visions of the 21st Century: Essays in Honour of Judge Christopher Weeramantry* (1998) 465, 467.

[22] Guillaume, 'Address to the General Assembly of the United Nations', above n. 9 ('specialised courts . . . are inclined to favour their own disciplines').

[23] Koskenniemi and Leino, above n. 21, 562. See also Martti Koskenniemi, 'What is International Law For?' in Malcolm D. Evans (ed.), *International Law* (2003) 89, 110; Martti Koskenniemi, 'International Legislation Today: Limits and Possibilities' (2005) 23 *WisILJ* 61, 78.

[24] See the discussion in ch. 2.

regimes that often possess the greater institutional potency.[25] As Eckersley has noted in relation to international trade law, the 'dispute resolution process of the WTO still remains the more powerful mechanism for the resolution of trade and environmental conflicts (when compared to the enforcement provisions of MEAs [multilateral environmental agreements])' and 'the [Appellate Body] thus stands as the final arbiter of the meaning of the relevant MEA obligations'.[26]

For the ILC study group such institutional imbalances need not be problematic, so long as judicial bodies take a common approach to the tasks of norm interpretation and application. On this view, the reality that much contemporary environmental litigation is channelled through non-environmental institutions presents an opportunity for international environmental law to be integrated within the decisions of specialised tribunals, and therefore within the specialised areas of law administered by those bodies. However, the reality is more complex and problematic because international environmental law is substantially made up of soft-law principles having a degree of normativity, but often falling short of binding legal status, which exert a profound influence upon environmental law and policy at national and international levels.[27] In a direct contest with a hard norm of treaty or custom, an international court or tribunal would have no choice but to give priority to the binding norm over the more general and indicative standard.[28] However, precisely because of their soft-law character the question is seldom whether environmental norms should take priority over other, harder, norms, but rather to what extent they are relevant for the purposes of interpreting treaty provisions or customary rules. It is here that the use of non-environmental courts and tribunals to

[25] Alexander Gillespie, *The Illusion of Progress: Unsustainable Development in International Law and Policy* (2001) 138. See also Daniel Esty, 'The World Trade Organization's Legitimacy Crisis' (2002) 1 *WTR* 7; Frank Biermann, 'The Emerging Debate on the Need for a World Environment Organization: A Commentary' (2001) 1 *GEP* 45; Fiona MacMillan, *WTO and the Environment* (2001) 272; Steve Charnovitz, 'A World Environment Organization' (2000) 27 *ColumJEL* 323.

[26] Robyn Eckersley, 'The Big Chill: The WTO and Multilateral Environmental Agreements' (2004) 4 *GEP* 24, 36–7.

[27] For a wide-ranging cross-disciplinary account of the discursive influence of environmental principles see Sharon Beder, *Environmental Principles and Politics: An Interdisciplinary Approach* (2006).

[28] The ILC study group did not specifically consider how conflicts between soft-law and hard-law norms could be addressed, although it was noted that the *lex specialis derogare lege generali* principle provided a conceptual framework for dealing with such inconsistencies: ILC study group report, above n. 14, [490].

address environmental disputes poses significant danger for the integrity of international environmental law. As environmental principles are relatively open-textured and flexible they are amenable to interpretation and change, and it is possible that non-environmental bodies will appropriate soft-law norms in to their decision-making in a way that challenges their original objects and purposes. In so doing they may undermine consensus that emerges as to their meaning, and thereby weaken their relevance for advancing global action to address environmental problems.

10.2 International environmental law in specialised courts and tribunals

Against this background, the following sections consider how judicial and quasi-judicial institutions of non-environmental regimes have considered relevant rules and principles of international law.

10.2.1 Human rights bodies

10.2.1.1 Human rights and environmental protection

The relationship between international environmental norms and human rights has generated considerable tension and ongoing uncertainty. Although there have been repeated calls for greater integration of the two fields of law,[29] a right to a clean, healthy, and safe environment has not been included in global or regional human rights instruments.[30] Nor have such substantive environmental rights been codified in international environmental agreements.[31] Both of these

[29] See in particular the UN Commission on Human Rights, Sub-Commission on Prevention of Discrimination and Protection of Minorities, *Human Rights and the Environment*, Final Report of the Special Rapporteur, UN Doc. E/CN.4/Sub.2/1994/9 (1994).

[30] Robin R. Churchill, 'Environmental Rights in Existing Human Rights Treaties' in Alan E. Boyle and Michael R. Anderson (eds.), *Human Rights Approaches to Environmental Protection* (1996) 89. However, Churchill notes that such rights have been included in some regional regimes: 1981 African Charter on Human and Peoples' Rights, 1988 Additional Protocol to the American Convention on Human Rights in the Area of Economic, Social and Cultural Rights and 1989 Convention on the Rights of the Child.

[31] But note the Aarhus Convention which, although concerned with procedural rights, declares in art. 1 that the convention's objective is to serve 'the protection of the right of every person of present and future generations to live in an environment adequate to his or her health and well-being'.

developments have been resisted on the grounds that human rights approaches to environmental protection are essentially anthropocentric, and cannot accommodate the notion that animals and nature possess intrinsic and not merely instrumental value.[32] Reflecting the reluctance to adopt a human rights approach to environmental protection, the Rio Declaration conspicuously avoided any reference to a right to a healthy environment.[33] This was in contrast to the Stockholm Declaration, which had declared in principle 1 that 'Man has the fundamental right to freedom, equality and adequate conditions of life in an environment of a quality that permits a life of dignity and well-being.'[34]

10.2.1.2 Environmental jurisprudence

Human rights and environmental regimes have therefore existed somewhat in isolation from one another. However, there have been increasing points of interaction, especially in cases before human rights complaints procedures operating within and outside the United Nations system. Despite the absence of express environmental rights from human rights texts, global, and regional human rights bodies including the Human Rights Committee, the ECtHR, and the Inter-American Commission on Human Rights (IAComHR) are confronting a growing number of environmental cases and interpreting human rights instruments to accommodate environmental issues.[35] This is mainly because these bodies hold out the only international procedures for individuals to challenge governmental action or inaction in relation to environmental matters.[36] And as a result these bodies have begun to develop an important body of environment-related human rights jurisprudence in relation to procedural rights (to information,

[32] Catherine Redgwell, 'Life, The Universe And Everything: A Critique of Anthropocentric Rights' in Alan E. Boyle and Michael R. Anderson (eds.), *Human Rights Approaches to Environmental Protection* (1996) 72, 72.

[33] See Dinah Shelton, 'What Happened in Rio to Human Rights' (1992) *YIEL* 75.

[34] UN Doc. A/CONF.48/14/Rev.1 (1973).

[35] Mariana T. Acevedo, 'The Intersection of Human Rights and Environmental Protection in the European Court of Human Rights' (2000) 8 *NYUELJ* 437, 439.

[36] Dinah Shelton, 'The Environmental Jurisprudence of International Human Rights Tribunals' in Romina Picolotti and Jorge Daniel Taillant (eds.), *Linking Human Rights and the Environment* (2003) 1, 2. See also Caroline Dommen, 'Claiming Environmental Rights: Some Possibilities Offered by the United Nations' Human Rights Mechanisms' (1998) 11 *GeoIELR* 1.

participation, and legal redress) and substantial guarantees (to life, health, and enjoyment of property).

10.2.1.3 Procedural human rights

While attempts to advance the cause of environmental protection through substantive human rights (such as a right to an 'adequate', 'decent', or 'healthy' environment) have met strong resistance, the same hurdles have not impeded the recognition of environmental rights of a procedural character. This is because procedural rights are concerned with enhancing the level of public participation in environmental decision-making, and both environmental and human rights texts recognise this as an important objective.

Environmental agreements and human rights instruments refer to three specific procedural guarantees: a right to obtain information, to participate in decision-making, and to be an effective remedy for breaches of the law. These are encapsulated in principle 10 of the Rio Declaration which provides that 'environmental issues are best handled with the participation of all concerned citizens', that each individual 'shall have appropriate access to information concerning the environment', and that there be 'effective access to judicial and administrative proceedings, including redress and remedy'. The most expansive statement of these procedural rights is now found in the Aarhus Convention, the first treaty to guarantee such rights in a legally binding instrument. It requires not only that states implement these rights at a national level,[37] but also that they promote their application in international environmental decision-making processes.[38] Expressed in more general terms, such civil and political rights also form an important part of human rights instruments, and their operation in relation to environmental matters has been considered in a growing collection of cases.

The right to environmental information has generally been construed narrowly by human rights bodies. In *Guerra and Others* v. *Italy*[39] the ECtHR considered the operation of article 10 of the 1950 Convention for the Protection of Human Rights and Fundamental Freedoms (ECHR), which guarantees 'the freedom to receive information'. The applicants asserted that the Italian government had violated the provision by failing to provide the public with information concerning risks from

[37] Aarhus Convention, art. 3(1). [38] *Ibid*. art. 3(7).

[39] *Guerra and Others* v. *Italy* (1998) 26 EHRR 357.

a chemical facility near the town of Manfredonia. Concluding that there was no breach in this instance, the Court held that article 10 did not impose a positive obligation to collect and disseminate information, but instead only prohibited governments from interfering with the freedom to receive information that others are willing to impart.[40] Just such a prohibited interference was found to have taken place in *Bladet Tromsø and Stensaas* v. *Norway*[41] after Norwegian defamation law prevented the publication of a newspaper report claiming that the government was aware of inhumane seal hunting practices.

In some environmental regimes a similarly restrictive approach to informational rights has been taken. The PCA held in the *OSPAR Arbitration* that the OSPAR Convention did not establish a general freedom of information scheme in relation to marine pollution.[42] By contrast, a far broader approach is adopted in the Aarhus Convention which applies beyond specific sectors of environmental management to environmental decision-making generally and imposes, in articles 4 and 5, wide-ranging obligations upon parties to provide access to environmental information, including an obligation to collect and disseminate all relevant information.

Turning to participatory rights, it is striking that human rights and environmental texts refer to the similar basic requirement that individuals have an opportunity to participate meaningfully in government.[43] The IAComHR has recognised that participatory rights contained in the 1969 American Convention on Human Rights (ACHR) extend to include involvement in decision-making on environmental matters. In its report on the human rights situation of indigenous peoples in Ecuador affected by rapid development, the IAComHR observed that article 23 of the ACHR, which provides that all persons enjoy a right 'to take part in the conduct of public affairs', implied a right 'to

[40] *Guerra* (1998) 26 EHRR 357, [53], following *Leander* v. *Sweden* (1987) 9 EHRR 433, [74].

[41] *Bladet Tromsø and Stensaas* v. *Norway* (2000) 29 EHRR 125.

[42] *OSPAR Arbitration (Ireland* v. *United Kingdom)* (final award) (2003) 42 ILM 1118. See generally Ted L. McDorman 'Access to Information under Article 9 of the OSPAR Convention (Ireland v. United Kingdom)' (2004) 98 *AJIL* 330; Malgosia A. Fitzmaurice, 'Dispute Concerning Access to Information Under Article 9 of the OSPAR Convention (*Ireland v. United Kingdom*)' (2003) 18 *IJMCL* 541.

[43] Human rights instruments referring to a right to participate in government include the Universal Declaration of Human Rights, GA Res. 217A(III) (10 December 1948) and the 1966 International Covenant on Civil and Political Rights. In the environmental context see the Rio Declaration, principle 10 and the Aarhus Convention, arts. 6, 7 and 8.

participate, individually and jointly, in the formulation of decisions which directly concern their environment'.[44] The Commission concluded that '[t]he quest to guard against environmental conditions which threaten human health requires that individuals have access to: information, participation in relevant decision-making processes, and judicial recourse'.[45] Ecuador was encouraged to take additional steps to ensure that these rights could be enjoyed. Although applicable only to participatory rights in relation to a human rights treaty, the Commission's conclusion would appear entirely consistent with the approach taken in environmental texts, including the Aarhus Convention.

A civil right that has often engaged the attention of human rights bodies in cases involving environmental issues is the guarantee of effective administrative or judicial remedies. The 1966 International Covenant on Civil and Political Rights (ICCPR) requires states to ensure that persons whose rights are violated have access to an effective remedy, to be determined by competent judicial, administrative or legislative authorities.[46] Article 6 of the ECHR is more limited, and provides only that in the determination of civil rights or criminal charges individuals are entitled to a fair and public hearing. However, it has frequently been relied upon by applicants asserting a failure to provide an adequate judicial hearing of disputes concerning matters such as the granting of permits to carry out activities affecting the environment. And the ECtHR has repeatedly referred to international instruments that support these procedural rights, including principle 10 of the Rio Declaration[47] and the Aarhus Convention.[48]

It has been made clear that article 6 can only have an application where an interest of the applicants has, or may be, directly affected. In *Balmer-Schafroth* v. *Switzerland*[49] the applicants who lived near a nuclear power station complained that they had been denied a hearing in relation to the renewal of an operating permit for the plant. The ECtHR accepted that there was a genuine and serious dispute between the applicants and the Swiss government over a right recognised under domestic law, that of 'physical integrity'. However, the complaint was ultimately rejected on the grounds that the applicants had failed 'to

[44] Inter-American Commission on Human Rights, *Report on the Situation of Human Rights in Ecuador*, OEA/Ser.L/V/II.96 Doc. 10 Rev. 1 (1997) 93.

[45] *Ibid.* 92. [46] ICCPR, art. 2(3). [47] See e.g. *Okyay* v. *Turkey* [2005] ECHR 476, [51]–[52].

[48] See e.g. *Taskin* v. *Turkey* [2004] ECHR 621, [99].

[49] *Balmer-Schafroth and Others v. Switzerland* (1998) 25 EHRR 598.

establish a direct link between the operating conditions of the power station…and their right to protection of their physical integrity'.[50] According to the majority, the applicants had not shown that the power plant exposed them to danger that was serious, specific, and, above all, imminent.[51] In the absence of such a finding 'neither the dangers nor the remedies were established with a degree of probability that made the outcome of the proceedings directly decisive'.[52] In a dissenting opinion, seven judges criticised this conclusion on the grounds that it ran counter to rules and principles of international environmental law including the precautionary principle, although it was not explained how these principles mandated a different result.[53] This opinion highlighted the careful way in which the majority had framed the dispute so that it could be resolved solely on the basis of procedural rights contained in the ECHR, rather than requiring the application of substantive norms of international environmental law.

10.2.1.4 Substantive human rights

Complainants to human rights bodies have made a range of innovative arguments in an effort to pursue remedies for environmental damage by reference to established rights including the right to life, the right to health, the right to respect for private life and home, and the right to peaceful enjoyment of possessions.

Although the right to life has been invoked in a number of petitions, most of these have been found to be inadmissible on the grounds that the applicants had not pointed to a real and imminent threat to life.[54]

[50] *Ibid.* [40]. [51] *Ibid.* [52] *Ibid.*

[53] *Ibid.* dissenting opinion of Judge Pettiti, joined by Judges Gölcüklü, Walsh, Russo, Valticos, Lopes Rocha, and Jambrek.

[54] See e.g. *Nöel Narvii Tauira and Eighteen Others* v. *France* (1995) 83-B Eur Comm HR 112. The applicants in this case were residents of French Polynesia who claimed that the decision of the French government to resume nuclear testing in the South Pacific in 1995 posed a real, substantial, and immediate risk to life. The European Commission on Human Rights rejected the application, noting that it was only in highly exceptional circumstances that an applicant could claim to be a victim of a violation of the Convention on the basis of a possible future violation, and that in such circumstances reasonable and convincing evidence must be presented. Similar reasons were given for the rejection of a parallel petition in the Human Rights Committee in *Bordes, Tauira and Temeharo* v. *France*, UN Doc. CCPR/C/57/D/645/1995 (1995). None the less, although not satisfied that the authors were victims of a rights violation, the committee reiterated the view it expressed in General Comment no. 14 (UN Doc. E/C.12/2000/4 (2000)) that 'the designing, testing, manufacture, possession and deployment of nuclear weapons are among the greatest threats to the right to life which confronts mankind today' (at [5.9]).

The Human Rights Committee has emphasised in this regard that there is no *actio popularis* in international human rights law that would allow individuals to commence proceedings to protect human health and the environment in the abstract.[55] However, there are a number of cases where environmental harm has been found to have violated the right to life, such as *Yanomami* v. *Brazil*[56] where the IAComHR held that Brazil violated the rights to life and health of a group of indigenous people. These violations resulted from a variety of factors, including the construction of a highway through indigenous lands, the failure to establish a promised Yanomami park, the authorisation of resource exploitation, and allowing outsiders carrying contagious diseases to penetrate Yanomami territory.

Another stark violation of the right to life as a result of environmental mismanagement was considered by the ECtHR in *Öneryildiz* v. *Turkey*.[57] Nine members of the applicant's family had perished when their home in a slum quarter of Istanbul was buried by a landslide of refuse from a nearby rubbish tip. Civil and criminal proceedings were instigated against local government officials who had failed to take preventive measures; however, no criminal sanctions were ultimately imposed, and the civil proceedings resulted in a modest damages pay-out. In these circumstances the ECtHR held that there had been a violation of the right to life, and developed its reasons by reference to European and international environmental law relating to civil and criminal liability including the 1993 Convention on Civil Liability for Damage Resulting from Activities Dangerous to the Environment. It concluded that article 2(1) of the ECHR

> enjoins the State not only to refrain from the intentional and unlawful taking of life, but also guarantees the right to life in general terms and, in certain well-defined circumstances, imposes an obligation on States to take appropriate steps to safeguard the lives of those within their jurisdiction.[58]

The Court noted that it was clear that a violation of the right to life 'can be envisaged in relation to environmental issues'.[59]

In the European human rights system the substantive right that has offered the most promising avenue for environment-focused human rights litigation is article 8(1) of the ECHR, which provides that

[55] *Brun* v. *France* CCPR/C/88/D/1453/2006 [2006] UNHRC 72 [6.3].
[56] *Yanomami* v. *Brazil*, case 7615 (Brazil) OAE/Ser.L/VII.66 Doc.10 rev.1 (1985).
[57] *Öneryildiz* v. *Turkey* (48939/99) [2002] ECHR 491.
[58] *Ibid.* [62]. [59] *Ibid.* [64].

'[e]veryone has the right to respect for his private and family life, his home and his correspondence'. This has only provided a basis for a claim where there has been direct interference with an applicant's home, family or private life, as the ECtHR has confirmed on several occasions that 'no right to nature preservation is as such included' in the ECHR.[60] The guarantee is also subject to several important qualifications set out in article 8(2), which permits interference with the exercise of this right if in the interests, among other things, of 'the economic well-being of the country'. The right has often been relied upon in tandem with article 1 of the 1963 Protocol to the Convention for the Protection of Human Rights and Fundamental Freedoms, which states that 'every natural or legal person is entitled to the peaceful enjoyment of his possessions'.[61] Cases brought in reliance on these two provisions are in many respects akin to common law private nuisance claims. Much as common law nuisance seeks to balance conflicting private property interests,[62] these human rights cases have often attempted to reconcile the interests of individuals in the quiet enjoyment of their property with broader community interests, such as economic development. None the less in finding for complainants affected by noise and other forms of pollution they have, in some cases, promoted a degree of incidental environmental protection.[63]

Most cases involving article 8 of the ECHR have related to noise pollution. In *Powell and Rayner* v. *United Kingdom*[64] the ECtHR concluded that although the applicants' properties were adversely affected by noise emanating from aircraft arriving or departing from London's

[60] See e.g. *Fadeyeva* v. *Russia* [2005] ECHR 376, [68], citing *Kyrtatos* v. *Greece* [2003] ECHR 242 ('the Court cannot accept that the interference with the conditions of animal life in the swamp constitutes an attack on the private or family life of the applicants').

[61] In one case with environmental aspects art. 1 was relied upon alone: *Chassagnou* v. *France* [1999] ECHR 22 (holding that compulsory transfer of hunting rights to a hunting association violated right to property of farmers opposed to hunting on ethical grounds).

[62] Sean Coyle and Karen Morrow, *The Philosophical Foundations of Environmental Law: Property, Rights and Nature* (2003) 111–12.

[63] However, this is not always the case. In *Fadeyeva* v. *Russia* [2005] ECHR 376 it was held that by failing to resettle the applicant from her residence near a highly polluting steel plant Russia had breached art. 8 of the ECHR. However as Judge Kovler noted in a concurring opinion, resettlement was 'not the best one: had the authorities been stricter…in applying domestic environmental regulations, the problem would have been resolved without any need to resettle…and with a positive impact on the environmental situation in general'.

[64] *Powell and Rayner* v. *United Kingdom* (1990) 12 EHRR 355.

Heathrow airport, there was no violation of article 8. The Court observed that 'regard must be had to the fair balance that has to be struck between the competing interests of the individual and of the community as a whole'[65] and that the United Kingdom 'enjoys a certain margin of appreciation in determining the steps to be taken to ensure compliance with the Convention'.[66] Highly relevant here was the importance of Heathrow airport to the United Kingdom economy.[67] A different result was reached in *Gomez* v. *Spain*,[68] a case involving the long-standing failure of local government authorities to control noise pollution from nightclubs in Valencia, in which the Court found that the severe effects on the applicant's enjoyment of her home life could not be justified by reference to the interests of the community.

Lopez-Ostra v. *Spain*[69] is arguably the most important decision of the ECtHR relating to environmental harm violating the right to private life and the home. In this case the applicant had brought a petition before the Court after suffering serious health effects from fumes emitted from a tannery waste-treatment plant located only 12 metres from her home. The start-up of the plant had emitted noxious fumes causing health problems for a number of local residents, and as a result the town council evacuated those affected, including the applicant, and rehoused them free of charge in the town centre. The authorities also ordered a partial closure of the plant, but permitted certain waste-treatment activities to continue. The applicant's claim in the ECtHR related to the failure of the municipality to respond adequately to the pollution emanating from the plant. The Court observed that:

> [S]evere environmental pollution may affect individuals' well-being and prevent them from enjoying their homes in such a way as to affect their private and family life adversely, without, however, seriously endangering their health.
>
> [In determining whether there has been compliance with Article 8] regard must be had to the fair balance that has to be struck between the competing

[65] *Ibid.* [41]. [66] *Ibid.*

[67] See also *Hatton and Others* v. *United Kingdom* [2003] ECHR 338 where a similar decision was reached. In this case the Grand Chamber of the ECtHR overturned an earlier chamber decision that had found a violation of art. 8 as a result of a substantial increase in night-time aircraft movements at London's Heathrow airport. The original chamber had observed that 'in the particularly sensitive field of environmental protection, mere reference to the economic well-being of the country is not sufficient to outweigh the rights of others': *Hatton and Others* v. *United Kingdom* [2001] ECHR 561.

[68] *Gomez* v. *Spain* [2004] ECHR 633. [69] *Lopez-Ostra* v. *Spain* (1995) 20 EHRR 277.

interests of the individual and of the community as a whole, and in any case the State enjoys a certain margin of appreciation. [70]

Having regard to the limited efforts by the authorities to mitigate the pollution problem, and despite the margin of appreciation open to them, Spain had not succeeded in striking a fair balance between the interest of the town's economic well-being and the applicant's effective enjoyment of her right to respect for her home and family life.[71]

A similar conclusion was arrived at by the Court in *Guerra* in which the ECtHR reiterated that environmental pollution may violate article 8 by affecting the well-being of individuals and preventing them from enjoying their homes. The ECtHR observed that article 8 did not merely prohibit member states from arbitrarily interfering with a person's private or family life, it also imposed a positive obligation that was inherent in effective respect for private or family life.[72] In this case involving pollution from a chemical factory, the Court found a violation of article 8 on the basis that local authorities took inadequate steps to protect the applicants' right to respect for their private and family life, and awarded compensation. However, the compensation that the applicants sought for biological damage was refused, a result that confirms that existing human rights, focused as they are on human well-being, can only offer indirect protection for strictly environmental interests.

These limits to how far the rights in article 8 can be pressed in environmental cases were also seen in *Kyrtatos* v. *Greece*,[73] which concerned a tourist development on a wetland in Ayios which was an important natural habitat for several protected species. The applicants, nearby property owners, complained that the destruction of a scenically beautiful and ecologically significant wetland adversely affected their lives, even though it posed no danger to health. The Court rejected the claim, finding that there was no impact upon the well-being of the applicants and that ECHR was '[not] specifically designed to provide general protection of the environment as such; to that effect, other international instruments and domestic legislation are more pertinent'.[74]

[70] *Ibid.* [51]. [71] *Ibid.* [58]. [72] *Guerra* (1998) 26 EHRR 357, [58].
[73] *Kyrtatos* v. *Greece* [2003] ECHR 242.
[74] *Ibid.* [52]. See also *Fadeyeva* v. *Russia* [2005] ECHR 376.

10.2.1.5 Evaluation

This overview of the developing environmental jurisprudence of human rights bodies suggests no collision or conflict with mainstream environmental jurisprudence, or any challenge to conventional understandings of rules and principles of international environmental law. In the majority of cases there has been no detailed consideration or application of environmental norms, and when international environmental law has been referred to it has been in broad and uncontroversial terms. Therefore, in addressing environmental questions through the terminology of international human rights law it would seem that the case law of human rights bodies has as yet posed no threat to the integrity of international environmental law. Indeed, given the synergies between procedural rights in human rights and environmental contexts, determinations on issues such as access to information, participation in decision-making, and right to legal redress for injury, form an important body of precedent for the implementation of similar rights recognised in environmental law. These decisions will be of considerable assistance in understanding and applying the more detailed provisions of the Aarhus Convention.

It should not be thought, however, that the relationship between human rights guarantees and international environmental law is necessarily unproblematic. The absence of conflict to date is largely reflective of the nature of the complaints that have been brought. Complainants have pointed to substantive human rights that assist them in addressing underlying environmental interests, and human rights bodies have tended to emphasise the importance of integrating human rights and environmental concerns.[75] However, it is possible to envisage conflicting scenarios in which the recognition of economic, cultural, or social rights may involve collision with norms requiring the protection of environments, ecosystems, or species. For instance, a state policy to impose restrictions upon activities in a protected area to preserve its biodiversity or other environmental values may well attract opposition by a local community on the grounds that such limitations constituted an infringement of 'cultural rights', or perhaps even the

[75] See e.g. *Belize* – Case 12/053 – *Maya Indigenous Community* – Report no. 40/04 (Inter-American Commission on Human Rights) [2004] IACommHR 34, [150]: 'development activities must be accompanied by appropriate and effective measures to ensure that they do not proceed at the expense of the fundamental rights of persons who may be…affected, including indigenous communities and the environment upon which they depend for their physical, cultural and spiritual well-being'.

'right to development'.[76] In the *Gabčíkovo-Nagymaros Project* case Judge Weeramantry suggested that the concept of 'sustainable development' had achieved a reconciliation between 'the right to development' and the 'right to environment'.[77] However, it is by no means clear that in concrete cases these twin goals can be convincingly resolved as priorities will need to be set and trade-offs made, and such a process may pose some risk of normative fragmentation.

10.3 WTO

Whereas discussion of the relationship between human rights and environmental protection has often emphasised important synergies, assessments of the interaction between international trade and environmental regimes have instead often highlighted problems of underlying tension and conflict.

10.3.1 *Trade law and environmental protection*

By virtue of the breadth, depth, and institutional sophistication, international trade law has far-reaching implications for environmental governance at domestic and international levels. The increase in global trade, a key dimension of economic globalisation, has inevitably meant that some domestic and international measures to protect human health or the natural environment have ramifications for international trade law. The most fundamental issue is whether trade and environmental policies are mutually supportive,[78] or whether the liberalisation of trade is inimical to environmental conservation and protection.[79] The evidence in this respect is mixed. Trade liberalisation may have negative environmental effects by, among other things,

[76] Principle 3 of the Rio Declaration stipulates that 'The *right to development* must be fulfilled so as to equitably meet developmental and environmental needs of present and future generations' (emphasis added). The UN General Assembly subsequently adopted a Declaration on the Right to Development in 1986, UN Doc. A/41/53 (1986). See also the 1966 International Covenant on Economic, Social and Cultural Rights, art. 1(2).

[77] *Gabčíkovo-Nagymaros Project* case [1997] ICJ Rep 7, separate opinion of Vice-President Weeramantry, 110ff.

[78] Doha Declaration, Doha Agenda Ministerial WT/MIN(01)/DEC/1 (2002) 41 ILM 746, [6]: 'We are convinced that the aims of upholding and safeguarding an open and non-discriminatory multilateral trading system, and acting for the protection of the environment and the promotion of sustainable development can and must be mutually supportive.'

[79] Mitsuo Matsushita, Thomas J. Schoenbaum, and Petros C. Mavroidis, *The World Trade Organization: Law, Practice and Policy* (2003) 444–7.

creating incentives for industry to move production to states with poor environmental standards (the so-called 'race to the bottom'),[80] or promoting practices that carry negative environmental impacts such as carbon intensive shipping or air freighting products across the globe. However, it can also have positive consequences if it eliminates tariffs or subsidies that promote ecologically unsustainable agricultural or fisheries industries.[81]

The debate concerning the compatibility of the trade and environment agendas has been particularly prominent in international law. Notwithstanding the attempt to integrate the agendas through the principle of sustainable development,[82] a range of questions continue to be raised concerning the extent to which there is conflict or congruence between trade law and environmental law. These issues have been elevated to particular prominence in the operation of dispute settlement bodies established by trade regimes including NAFTA and the WTO. As Notaro observes, 'the judiciary has been charged with the task of finding a way out of the trade and environment impasse, in part due to the contentious character of the disputes at issue and in part due to the absence of practicable alternatives'.[83] However, a recurrent criticism has been that in seeking to address this 'impasse' the dispute settlement bodies of trade regimes have exhibited a strong bias towards trade liberalisation at the expense of sound environmental management.[84] This is a concern from the perspective of fragmentation, because the WTO in particular is the source of 'a rapidly developing jurisprudence that is unequalled in other international regimes'.[85]

[80] Daniel C. Esty, 'Bridging the Trade–Environment Divide' (2001) 15 *Journal of Economic Perspectives* 113, 121.

[81] Håkan Nordström and Scott Vaughan, *Trade and Environment* (1999) 26.

[82] 1984 Marrakesh Agreement Establishing the World Trade Organization, preamble, 1st recital ('relations in the field of trade and economic endeavour should be conducted with a view to raising standards of living... while allowing for the optimal use of the world's resources in accordance with the objective of sustainable development'); Rio Declaration, principle 12 ('States should cooperate to promote a supportive and open international economic system that would lead to economic growth and sustainable development in all countries, to better address the problems of environmental degradation').

[83] Nicola Notaro, *Judicial Approaches to Trade and Environment: The EC and the WTO* (2003) 31. See also John H. Knox, 'The Judicial Resolution of Conflicts Between Trade and the Environment' (2004) 28 *HarvELR* 1, 70–4.

[84] J. L. Dunoff, 'Institutional Misfits: The GATT, the ICJ and Trade-Environment Disputes' (1994) 15 *MichJIL* 1043.

[85] Eckersley, above n. 26, 24.

10.3.2 *Environmental jurisprudence*

The WTO was established in 1995,[86] providing an institutional superstructure for the international trade rules that had developed out of GATT[87] agreed at the end of the Second World War.[88] Integral to the WTO is a compulsory and binding system of dispute settlement established by the DSU which affords broad rights of standing to WTO members to challenge the legality of actions by other members.[89] Under this procedure members may initiate consultations and, should they fail, request the establishment of a panel.[90] Appeals against Panel reports may thereafter be brought before a standing Appellate Body.[91] Unlike the previous ad hoc GATT panel system, the decisions of WTO panels and the Appellate Body are adopted automatically and are therefore binding unless the WTO DSB decides against adoption by consensus.[92]

Since it commenced operation in 1995, over 356 complaints have been notified to the WTO, with almost 200 panel and Appellate Body reports adopted.[93] By any measure the WTO dispute settlement system is highly active, and is vital to the development, consolidation, and constitutionalisation of the WTO regime.[94] The system has also encountered environmental issues, with a number of disputes involving essentially environmental questions being brought before GATT panels and the WTO. This has in turn implicated environmental rules and standards. While the WTO dispute system may only be used to resolve disputes relating to WTO

[86] 1994 Marrakesh Agreement Establishing the World Trade Organization.

[87] 1947 General Agreement on Tariffs and Trade. See now the 1994 Marrakesh Agreement, annex 1A (GATT 1994).

[88] See generally Gavin Goh and Trudy Witbreuk, 'An Introduction to the WTO Dispute Settlement System' (2001) 30 *WALR* 51, 52. Unlike GATT, which was originally intended as a temporary mechanism, the WTO possesses international legal personality and administers the WTO rules found in the updated GATT (GATT 1994) and the other multilateral trade agreements annexed to the 1994 Marrakesh Agreement, above n. 86.

[89] 1994 Marrekesh Agreement, annex 2 (DSU). [90] *Ibid.* arts. 4(7) and 5(4).

[91] *Ibid.* art. 17. [92] *Ibid.* arts. 16(4) and 17(14).

[93] Kara Leitner and Simon Lester, 'WTO Dispute Settlement from 1995 to 2006. A Statistical Analysis' (2007) 10 *JIEL* 165. By comparison only 196 cases had been commenced under GATT dispute settlement procedures throughout its forty-five years of existence.

[94] See Deborah Cass, 'The "Constitutionalization" of International Trade Law: Judicial Norm-Generation as the Engine of Constitutional Development in International Trade' (2001) 12 *EJIL* 39.

rules,[95] WTO panels and the Appellate Body are required by article 3(2) of the DSU to interpret the covered agreements by reference to 'customary rules of interpretation of public international law'. In *United States – Standards for Reformulated and Conventional Gasoline*[96] the Appellate Body stated that this meant that WTO agreements could not be read 'in clinical isolation from public international law'.[97] However, as will now be seen, debate continues to surround the extent to which international environmental law can inform decision-making under the DSU. Particularly contentious has been the question whether panels or the Appellate Body may directly apply rules and principles of international law, including international environmental law.

10.3.3 Cases concerning GATT environmental exemptions

The starting point for any analysis of the impact of WTO jurisprudence upon international environmental law is the substantial case law on the so-called 'environmental exemptions' to GATT. The key organising principles of the WTO system are the most-favoured nation principle,[98] and the national treatment principle.[99] Together they limit the circumstances in which states may impose trade restrictive measures. However, they are subject to article XX of GATT, which sets out certain limited exceptions for health and environmental measures:

> Subject to the requirement that such measures are not applied in a manner which would constitute a means of arbitrary or unjustifiable discrimination between countries where the same conditions prevail, or a disguised restriction on international trade, nothing in this Agreement shall be construed to prevent the adoption or enforcement by any contracting party of measures:
>
> ...
>
> (b) necessary to protect human, animal or plant life or health;
>
> ...

[95] DSU, arts. 1(1) and 3(2).

[96] *United States – Standards for Reformulated and Conventional Gasoline*, WTO Doc. WT/DS2/AB/R (1996).

[97] *Ibid.* 16.

[98] GATT 1994, art. I requires equality of treatment for like products, and therefore members of the WTO may not discriminate between like products of other members.

[99] *Ibid.* art. III stipulates that domestic and imported products should be treated equally in terms of the application of internal regulations and policies.

(g) relating to the conservation of exhaustible natural resources if such measures are made effective in conjunction with restrictions on domestic production or consumption.[100]

10.3.4 Tuna–Dolphin *cases*

United States: Restrictions on Imports of Tuna[101] (*Tuna–Dolphin I*) and *United States: Restrictions on Imports of Tuna*[102] (*Tuna–Dolphin II*) were important early cases that considered the scope of these exemptions. They were brought under the GATT panel system in response to restrictions imposed by the United States on imports of yellowfin tuna (*Thunnus albacares*) harvested in a manner that resulted in excessive by-catch of dolphins in the eastern tropical Pacific Ocean. Under the Marine Mammal Protection Act 1972 (US) (MMPA) tuna imports were prohibited unless the harvesting states maintained a programme to reduce incidental taking of marine mammals comparable with that of the United States, and unless the average rate of such incidental taking was similar to that for United States-flagged vessels engaged in tuna fishing. Imports were also prohibited from intermediary nations that processed tuna that had not been caught in conformity with MMPA standards.

In both *Tuna–Dolphin I* and *Tuna–Dolphin II*, GATT panels rejected the arguments of the United States that the import bans were justified under article XX(b) of GATT as measures necessary to protect animal life. The decisions attracted strong criticism on the grounds that they privileged trade considerations over legitimate efforts to achieve the protection of marine wildlife.[103] The panels had adopted a narrow interpretation of article XX and had decisively rejected the legality of using domestic measures for an extraterritorial purpose, namely to affect the environmental policies of other states. However, when considering the impact of these decisions upon international environmental law it must be noted that in neither case did the United States seek to make arguments beyond the terms of the GATT itself. Beyond

[100] Given the relatively recent emergence of environmental concerns in international law it is unsurprising that the only reference of GATT is to 'natural resources' rather than the environment more broadly: Mark Harris, 'Beyond Doha: Clarifying the Role of the WTO in Determining Trade–Environment Disputes' (2003) 21 *Law in Context* 307, 309.

[101] *United States – Restrictions on Imports of Tuna*, GATT Doc. DS21/R (1991).

[102] *United States – Restrictions on Imports of Tuna*, GATT Doc. DS29/R (1994).

[103] Daniel C. Esty, *Greening the GATT: Trade, Environment and the Future* (1994) 114–30.

suggesting that trade measures pursuant to a multilateral agreement to protect cetaceans would be GATT consistent[104] the panels made no reference to environmental instruments potentially having a bearing on the cases.[105]

10.3.5 *Shrimp–Turtle cases*

The environmental case law of the WTO was inaugurated in *Gasoline* but again it was not deemed necessary to address issues of international environmental law when rejecting the WTO consistency of United States gasoline standards designed to improve air quality. A markedly different approach was taken in *United States – Import Prohibition of Certain Shrimp and Shrimp Products* (*Shrimp–Turtle I*),[106] a decision that has been widely regarded as evidencing the greening of GATT/WTO jurisprudence.[107]

The issue in *Shrimp–Turtle I* was similar to that confronted in the *Tuna–Dolphin* cases. As required by the Endangered Species Act 1973 (US), the United States government imposed a prohibition on the import of shrimp harvested using methods that involved high rates of mortality for species of sea turtle protected by CITES. The ban applied to all imports of shrimp unless from certified nations, and certification was only forthcoming for nations harvesting shrimp in sea turtle habitats where it was established that turtle excluder devices or other preventative measures were used. The United States trade measure was challenged by India, Malaysia, Pakistan, and Thailand on the basis that it was inconsistent with articles I, XI, and XIII of GATT and not justified

[104] See now the 1998 Agreement on the International Dolphin Conservation Program.

[105] None of the other environmental cases decided under the GATT system addressed such questions either. See for instance *Canada – Measures Affecting Exports of Unprocessed Herring and Salmon*, GATT Doc. L/6268 (1988) (export restrictions as part of system of fishery resource management not justified under art. XX(g)); *Thailand – Restrictions on Importation of and Internal Taxes on Cigarettes*, GATT Doc. LDS10/R (prohibition on importation of cigarettes purportedly for reasons of public health not justified under art. XX(b)); *United States – Taxes on Automobiles*, GATT Doc. DS31/R (1994) (regulation regarding minimum fuel economy of imported cars not justified under art. XX(g)).

[106] *United States – Import Prohibition of Certain Shrimp and Shrimp Products*, WTO Doc. WT/DS58/R (1998) (report of the panel), WTO Doc. WT/DS58/AB/R (1998) (report of the Appellate Body), (*Shrimp–Turtle I* Appellate Body report). See A. H. Qureshi, 'Extraterritorial Shrimps, NGOs and the WTO Appellate Body' (1999) 48 *ICLQ* 199.

[107] Sam Blay, 'The WTO and the Greening of World Trade: A Look at WTO Jurisprudence' (2004) 21 *EPLJ* 27, 32; Gillian Triggs, 'World Trade Organization: Dispute Settlement and the Environment' (2002) 7 *APJEL* 43, 59–61.

as a permissible measure to protect animal life under article XX. The complainants were ultimately successful, with a panel finding that the import ban was inconsistent with WTO rules and that article XX did not apply. On appeal, the Appellate Body also upheld the earlier result. However, it effectively reversed the rationale for this conclusion, thereby opening the door for unilateral environmental measures in certain circumstances.

There is much that is significant about the Appellate Body report in *Shrimp–Turtle I* for national and transnational environmental management.[108] Not only did the Appellate Body find that *amicus curiae* submissions from environmental groups could be considered in the WTO dispute settlement process, it also developed a more flexible interpretation of article XX environmental exemptions having regard to developments in international environmental law. The Appellate Body adopted a two-stage test for determining whether the measures adopted by the United States were justified under article XX. In the first place it asked whether the measure fitted specifically within article XX(g) by relating to the 'conservation of exhaustible natural resources'. If so, the second stage involved determining whether the measure met the requirements of the article XX chapeau in not being applied in a manner that would constitute unjustifiable discrimination or a disguised restriction on international trade.[109] In applying both stages of this test the Appellate Body referred to international environmental law.

International environmental law was also relevant to a threshold question for the Appellate Body, namely whether sea turtles could be considered 'exhaustible natural resources' within the meaning of article XX(g) of GATT. Having regard to the need to interpret the GATT 'in light of contemporary concerns of the community of nations about the protection and conservation of the environment'[110] the Appellate Body held that sea turtles were indeed 'exhaustible natural resources' just as much as any non-living 'resource'.[111] The Appellate Body reached

[108] Notaro, above n. 83, 197–200; Philippe Sands, 'International Courts and the Application of the Concept of "Sustainable Development"' in John Hatchard and Amanda Perry-Kessaris (eds.), *Law and Development: Facing Complexity in the 21st Century* (2003) 147, 151–5; Robert Howse, 'The Appellate Body Rulings in the Shrimp/Turtle Case: A New Legal Baseline for the Trade and Environment Debate' (2002) 27 *ColumJEL* 491, 499–516.

[109] *Shrimp–Turtle I* Appellate Body report, WTO Doc. WT/DS58/AB/R (1998) [118]–[119].

[110] *Ibid.* [129]. [111] *Ibid.* [134].

this conclusion by reference to the concept of sustainable development included in the first recital of the preamble to the 1994 Marrakesh Agreement.[112] Also considered relevant to a contemporary interpretation of the term 'natural resources' were references to 'living natural resources' in the LOS Convention, the Biodiversity Convention, Agenda 21, and the 1980 Convention on the Conservation of Migratory Species of Wild Animals. For the Appellate Body all of these instruments confirmed that 'it was too late in the day to suppose that article XX(g) of the GATT may be read as referring only to the conservation of exhaustible mineral or other non-living natural resources'.[113] The Appellate Body also found that as all species of sea turtles were listed as endangered under CITES, they must therefore be considered 'exhaustible' under article XX(g) of GATT.[114]

After determining this initial issue it was then evident that the United States' trade measure was one 'relating to' the conservation of sea turtles,[115] and the Appellate Body turned to consider whether the 'provisionally justified' import ban was consistent with the requirements of the chapeau to article XX. The Appellate Body found against the United States on this point, concluding that the measure was 'a means of arbitrary or unjustifiable discrimination' within the meaning of the chapeau. In reaching this conclusion the principle of sustainable development was cited yet again, in order to give 'colour, texture and shading' to an interpretation of article XX. Precisely how the concept had relevance here was not explained, but there appeared to be nothing controversial about the Appellate Body's interpretation of the principle, which it achieved by reference to the Rio Declaration and Agenda 21.

According to the Appellate Body it was not acceptable for the United States to have adopted measures that prohibited imports from some countries where shrimp were caught using the same turtle-friendly methods employed in the United States simply because those countries had not been certified.[116] Moreover, the United States had failed to engage members exporting shrimp to the United States 'in serious, across-the-board negotiations with the objective of concluding bilateral or multilateral agreements for the protection and conservation of sea turtles, before enforcing the import prohibition'.[117] The Appellate

[112] *Ibid.* [130].
[113] *Shrimp–Turtle I* Appellate Body report, WTO Doc. WT/DS58/AB/R (1998) [131].
[114] *Ibid.* [132]. [115] *Ibid.* [142].
[116] *Ibid.* [165]. [117] *Ibid.* [166].

Body observed that 'the protection and conservation of highly migratory species of sea turtles ... demands concerted and cooperative efforts on the part of the many countries whose waters are traversed in the course of recurrent sea turtle migrations'[118] and to this end referred to the Rio Declaration, Agenda 21 and the 1992 Biodiversity Convention all of which declare that unilateral actions to protect the environment should generally be avoided, and that multilateral environmental measures should, as far as possible, be preferred.[119] The Appellate Body therefore emphasised the need for states to attempt a cooperative, multilateral, solution to environmental problems, an emphasis that is consistent with the notion of cooperation, which underpins many aspects of international environmental law.[120] In this case the United States had led negotiations on a regional agreement for the protection and conservation of sea turtles, a fact that demonstrated that an alternative course of action was reasonably open to the United States to secure the legitimate objective of sea turtle conservation.[121] However, while the United States had negotiated seriously with some members, it had not done the same with others, and according to the Appellate Body the effect was therefore plainly discriminatory and unjustifiable.

The follow-up case of *United States – Import Prohibition of Certain Shrimp and Shrimp Products (Shrimp–Turtle II)*[122] was brought by Malaysia, one of the original complainants in *Shrimp–Turtle I*, under article 21.5 of the DSU.[123] Malaysia argued that the United States had not taken WTO-consistent measures to implement the Appellate Body report in *Shrimp–Turtle I*; however, a panel and the Appellate Body disagreed. The main significance of this case is the ultimate finding that temporary measures imposed by the United States were permissible pending international agreement on sea turtle conservation. To justify

[118] *Ibid.* [168].

[119] Rio Declaration, principle 12; Agenda 21, [2.22(i)]; Biodiversity Convention, art. 5.

[120] Robyn Briese, 'Precaution and Cooperation in the World Trade Organization: An Environmental Perspective' (2002) 22 *AustYBIL* 113, 156.

[121] *Shrimp–Turtle I* Appellate Body report, WTO Doc. WT/DS58/AB/R (1998) [171].

[122] *United States – Import Prohibition of Certain Shrimp and Shrimp Products*, WTO Doc. WT/DS58/RW (2001) (report of the panel), WTO Doc. WT/DS58/AB/RW (2001) (report of the Appellate Body).

[123] DSU, art. 21.5 provides that '[w]here there is disagreement as to the existence or consistency with a covered agreement of measures taken to comply with the recommendations and rulings such disputes shall be decided through recourse to these dispute settlement procedures'.

this conclusion the Appellate Body referred to principle 12 of the Rio Declaration, which states that environmental measures should only be based upon consensus and cooperation as far as this is possible. The United States was therefore permitted to apply a unilateral measure, so long as it continued to negotiate an internationally agreed action plan to enhance the protection of endangered sea turtles.

The Appellate Body's use of international environmental law in *Shrimp–Turtle I* and *Shrimp–Turtle II* has not gone without criticism, although this has not involved critique of the Appellate Body's interpretation of international environmental law so much as its use in supposed derogation of WTO rules. For instance Triggs is critical of the 'judicial creativity' of the Appellate Body and notes that '[f]or the developing nations of Asia... the outcomes of the *Shrimp Case* may prove to be the harbinger of new interpretations of WTO rules that could be to their economic disadvantage'.[124] However, a close examination of the Appellate Body's reasons suggests that it turned to international environmental law to make sense of GATT in light of the concern of many states, including the complainants, that a threatened species of marine wildlife should receive appropriate and effective international legal protection.[125]

No article XX case before or after the *Shrimp–Turtle* cases has engaged in the same detailed consideration as to the relevance of international environmental law to the interpretation and application of GATT.[126] Nor has any other article XX case involved reliance by a respondent state upon a multilateral environmental agreement. The only dispute in which the prospect of such reliance has so far emerged was

[124] Triggs, above n. 107, 60–1. [125] ILC study group report, above n. 14, [443].

[126] See for instance the art. XX decision in *European Communities – Measures Affecting Asbestos and Products Containing Asbestos*, WTO Doc. WT/DS135/R (2000) (Report of the panel), WTO Doc. WT/DS135/AB/R (2001) (report of the Appellate Body) in which a panel and the Appellate Body found that French prohibitions on the import of asbestos were allowable under art. XX(g) as they addressed a legitimate human health risk. Neither the panel nor the Appellate Body referred to international environmental law in reaching this decision but see Marie-Claire Cordonier Segger and Markus W. Gehring, 'The WTO and Precaution: Sustainable Development Implications of the WTO Asbestos Dispute' (2003) 15 *JEL* 289 (arguing that the Appellate Body's decision was 'inspired by' precaution and sustainable development). See also Mary Footer and Saman Zia-Zarifi, 'European Communities – Measures Affecting Asbestos and Asbestos-Containing Products: The World Trade Organization on Trial for its Handling of Occupational Health and Safety Issues' (2002) 3 *MJIL* 120.

Chile – Measures Affecting the Transit and Importation of Swordfish[127] in which Chile justified closing its ports to Spanish vessels on the basis of the LOS Convention, which it was said required it to take measures to protect a straddling fishery under threat of collapse. The dispute, which also involved the commencement of parallel proceedings under the part XV dispute settlement system, was ultimately settled.[128]

10.3.6 Sanitary and phytosanitary measures

The second main category of trade/environment disputes in the WTO are those under the rubric of the Sanitary and Phytosanitary Agreement[129] (SPS Agreement), which regulates the extent to which states may impose quarantine restrictions and other measures to safeguard animal and plant health.[130] The SPS Agreement is arguably the WTO agreement most closely situated at the intersection between free trade and environmental protection agendas, and in respect of sanitary and phytosanitary (SPS) measures it elucidates upon the general environmental exemption contained in article XX(b) of GATT.[131] Member states are permitted to take their own decisions concerning SPS measures,[132] however, if these restrict imports they are only permissible if supported by scientific investigation[133] and a rigorous risk assessment. Under no circumstances may they be disguised attempts at protectionism or discrimination.

Disputes over the interpretation and application of these provisions are a burgeoning area of environment-related litigation in the WTO and there is the potential for a range of issues of international environmental law to be implicated in their resolution. Most obvious is the specific question as to whether the precautionary principle may be relied upon to justify quarantine and other health-related trade measures, or whether the SPS Agreement establishes a *sui generis* system for the evaluation of scientific uncertainty and risk. This question

[127] WTO Doc. WT/DS193/2 (2000) (request for consultations).

[128] *Conservation and Sustainable Exploitation of Swordfish Stocks in the South-Eastern Pacific Ocean (Chile/European Community)* (available at www.itlos.org).

[129] 1994 Marrakesh Agreement, annex 1A (SPS Agreement).

[130] See Steve Charnovitz, 'The Supervision of Health and Biosafety Regulation by World Trade Rules' (1999–2000) 13 *TulELJ* 271. Sanitary measures are those designed to protect the health of animals, including human beings, while phytosanitary measures are those that seek to protect the health of plants (from the Greek *phyton* meaning 'plant').

[131] Andreas F. Lowenfeld, *International Economic Law* (2002) 324.

[132] SPS Agreement, art. 2(1).

[133] *Ibid.* art. 2(2).

has now arisen in two SPS disputes, and in both it has been concluded that the WTO is in effect a self-contained regime in relation to such issues.

The first dispute was *European Communities – Measures Concerning Meat and Meat Products (Beef Hormones)*,[134] which related to import bans imposed by the EC on hormone-fed livestock and meat in 1997.[135] European regulators had concerns that certain hormones administered to livestock could have a carcinogenic effect upon consumers and after consultations with the United States and Canada failed, panels were established to determine the disputes in which the complainants contended that the EC measures were inconsistent both with GATT and with the SPS Agreement.

To defend its actions the EC relied on the precautionary principle, arguing that it was a binding rule of customary international law. For their part the United States and Canada argued that it was only an emerging norm that might eventually crystallise into a general principle of law recognised by civilised nations. Each of the panels found that to the extent that the principle could be considered as part of customary international law it could be used to interpret articles 5.1 and 5.2. However, the principle could not override the express wording of these articles, because the precautionary principle had been incorporated and given a specific meaning in article 5.7.[136] For these and other reasons the panels ultimately held that the EC had acted inconsistently with the SPS Agreement.

The Appellate Body reached the same conclusion, but for somewhat different reasons. On the issue of the precautionary principle the Appellate Body avoided answering the question as to its character. It considered that regardless of its status 'under international environmental law'[137] the principle did not need to be applied because the relevant rules governing the assessment of risk were set out in the SPS Agreement. Articles 5.1 and 5.2 specify the need for a risk assessment,

[134] *European Communities – Measures Concerning Meat and Meat Products*, WTO Doc. WT/DS26/R/USA (1997) (complaint by the United States – report of the panel), WTO Doc. WT/DS48/4/CAN (1997), (complaint by Canada – report of the panel), WTO Doc. WT/DS26/AB/R, WT/DS48/AB/R (1998) (report of the Appellate Body).

[135] EC Directive 96/22/EC (which repealed and replaced similar directives going back to 1981, including 91/602/EEC).

[136] *Beef Hormones*, WTO Doc. WT/DS26/R/USA (1997) (complaint by the United States – report of the panel) [8.157].

[137] *Beef Hormones*, WTO Doc. WT/DS26/AB/R, WT/DS48/AB/R (1998) (report of the Appellate Body), [125].

and for that assessment to be based upon scientific evidence. In addition, because the import bans had been in place for over a decade, the EC had not sought to rely on article 5.7, which allows provisional measures to be implemented pending a more complete assessment of the risk. The Appellate Body explained that:

> It is unnecessary, and probably imprudent, for the Appellate Body in this appeal to take a position on this important but abstract question. We note that the Panel itself did not make any definitive finding with regard to the status of the precautionary principle and that the precautionary principle, at least outside the field of international environmental law, still awaits authoritative formulation.[138]

Nevertheless, the Appellate Body noted 'some aspects of the relationship of the precautionary principle to the SPS Agreement', observing that:

> A panel charged with determining...whether sufficient scientific evidence exists to warrant the maintenance by a member of a particular SPS measure may, of course, and should, bear in mind that responsible, representative governments commonly act from perspectives of prudence and precaution where risks of irreversible, e.g. life-terminating, damage to human health are concerned.[139]

In summary, the Appellate Body considered that the SPS Agreement itself permitted the taking of precautionary measures, where prudence and precaution demanded them.[140]

In *Beef Hormones* the Appellate Body approached the precautionary principle from the perspective of interpreting WTO law, and did not consider whether the principle could modify the obligations of the parties, if it were found to be part of customary international law. In this respect Pauwelyn has criticised the Appellate Body's approach,[141] on the basis that 'there was no need for the SPS Agreement to refer explicitly to the precautionary principle for this principle to be a possible defence in WTO dispute settlement'.[142] This is because the principle could have been applied if it was concluded that it was a rule of customary international law that arose later in time and which was in conflict with an earlier WTO rule. Pauwelyn therefore considers the

138 *Ibid.* [123]. 139 *Ibid.* [124].

140 Jacqueline Peel, 'Precaution: A Matter of Principle, Approach or Process?' (2004) 5 *MJIL* 438, 493.

141 Pauwelyn, above n. 2, 482. 142 *Ibid.*

Appellate Body's decision to have been far too categorical, ignoring critical questions as to the meaning of the precautionary principle and its normative value.[143]

In relation to the precautionary principle the approach in *Beef Hormones* was essentially followed in *European Communities – Measures Affecting the Approval and Marketing of Biotech Products*.[144] However, the panel engaged in substantially wider analysis of the relevance of this principle, and other aspects of international environmental law to WTO dispute settlement.

In *Biotech Products*, Argentina, Canada, and the United States[145] pursued a complaint in relation to delays in the approval by the EC of genetically modified (GM) crops within Europe.[146] The target of the complaint was a *de facto* moratorium imposed on approvals of GM products in Europe in 1998. Since the early 1990s the EC has adopted a precautionary stance towards the importation and approval of genetically modified organisms (GMOs). In 1996, under Council Directive 90/220/EEC,[147] the importation of GM soybeans from the United States was permitted and generated widespread public opposition. This led to the EC blocking further authorisations of GM products pending a strengthening of Council Directive 90/220/EEC to deal with several issues, including product labelling and traceability. The regulatory framework was thereafter substantially reformed through the adoption of Council Directive 2001/18/EC[148] (which came into force in October 2002) and two new regulations, which entered into force in April 2004. These replaced the earlier directive, and under this new regime a number of applications for GMOs were resubmitted for approval. The dispute in *Biotech Products* revolved around the delays experienced from 1998 under the previous regime, rather than the new approvals system.

The complainants and respondent took radically different approaches both to the issues of risk management involved in the dispute and the

[143] *Ibid.*

[144] *European Communities – Measures Affecting the Approval and Marketing of Biotech Products*, WTO Docs. WT/DS291/R, WT/DS292/R, WT/DS293/R (2006) (report of the panel).

[145] Australia and several other states also joined the litigation in support of the complainants.

[146] Genetic modification involves the use of techniques of molecular biology to add or remove genes within an organism, such as the transfer of genes from one species of cropping plant to another.

[147] [1990] OJ L 117/15. [148] [2001] OJ L 106/1.

applicability of international environmental law.[149] All three complainants asserted that the moratorium on approvals of agricultural biotech products was inconsistent with the SPS Agreement. It was argued that as a result of several violations there was a disguised restriction on international trade within the meaning of articles 2.3 and 5.5 of the SPS Agreement. Much of the argument in this respect turned on the alleged failure of the EC to undertake a risk assessment in accordance with article 5.1 or to provide scientific justification in accordance with article 2.2. The centre of the dispute was the meaning and practice of 'risk management'. Could this process, as the United States suggested, be conceived as one that was entirely objective, based on impartial scientific investigation? Or conversely, and having regard to the way in which other states approach questions of risk, is the very process of risk assessment one that depends upon values and policy judgments?[150] As Peel, Nelson, and Godden explain, there was here a clash between the complainants' 'science-based model' and the European 'precaution-based model':[151]

> The science-based model embodies the idea that risk regulation, including the way in which it deals with scientific uncertainty, should be founded on scientific methods and risk assessment techniques. Under a precaution-based approach, risks that are subject to uncertainty are treated as complex problems best resolved by an inclusive and deliberative decision-making process.

On issues of international environmental law the complainants' submissions were a model of simplicity and economy. Relying exclusively upon WTO rules, in particular the SPS Agreement, they rejected any suggestion that the precautionary principle, Biodiversity Convention or 2000 Cartagena Protocol on Biosafety to the Convention on Biological Diversity could aid the resolution of the dispute. In contrast the EC adopted a more complex line of argument. It was contended that WTO agreements must be interpreted and applied having regard to other norms of international law.[152] In particular, the argument went, the

[149] For comprehensive analysis of the submissions of the parties and the *amici curiae* see Jacqueline Peel, Rebecca Nelson, and Lee Godden, 'GMO Trade Wars: The Submissions in the *EC–GMO* Dispute in the WTO' (2005) 6 *MJIL* 141.

[150] This dialectic is raised and considered in depth in David Winickoff *et al.* 'Adjudicating the GM Food Wars: Science, Risk, and Democracy in World Trade Law' (2005) 30 *YaleJIL* 81.

[151] Peel *et al.*, above n. 149, 157.

[152] *Biotech Products*, WTO Doc. WT/DS291, WT/DS292, WT/DS293 (2004) [456] (first written submission of the European Communities).

Cartagena Protocol was 'the international agreement which is most directly relevant to the matters raised by the present proceedings'[153] and that:

> [T]here is ample authority to support the proposition that the [Cartagena] Protocol and the SPS Agreement (as well as the TBT Agreement and GATT 1994) are so closely connected that they should be interpreted and applied consistently with each other, to the extent that is possible (as is the case in this dispute).[154]

Hence for the EC it was not an issue of a normative hierarchy; rather the SPS Agreement and the Cartagena Protocol were complementary instruments. And this also meant that the precautionary principle as stated in the Cartagena Protocol could be applied to the dispute.[155] However, the difficulty with any reference to this agreement is that it was not in force, and as among the disputants only the EC was a party.[156] Argentina and Canada had signed but not ratified the protocol,[157] while the United States and third party states had not even taken this step. Finally, as regards the process of interpreting WTO rules, the Cartagena Protocol includes somewhat ambiguous language in its preamble concerning its relationship with other regimes. It emphasises on the one hand that the protocol 'shall not be interpreted as implying a change in the rights and obligations of a Party under any existing international agreement' while at the same time stating

[153] *Ibid.* [457]. [154] *Ibid.*

[155] See especially the Preamble, and art. 1, which provides that

> [i]n accordance with the precautionary approach contained in principle 15 of the Rio Declaration on Environment and Development, the objective of this Protocol is to contribute to ensuring an adequate level of protection in the field of the safe transfer, handling and use of living modified organisms resulting from modern biotechnology that may have adverse effects on the conservation and sustainable use of biological diversity, taking also into account risks to human health, and specifically focusing on transboundary movements.

See also Ruth Mackenzie and Philippe Sands, 'Prospects for International Environmental Law' in Christoph Bail, Robert Falkner, and Helen Marquard (eds.), *The Cartagena Protocol on Biosafety: Reconciling Trade in Biotechnology with Environment and Development?* (2002) 458, 462: '[r]ather than setting out precaution as a general principle, the protocol sets out a specific framework and some operational guidance for its implementation'.

[156] The EC signed the protocol on 24 May 2000, and ratification followed on 27 August 2003.

[157] Argentina and Canada signed the protocol on 24 May 2000 and 19 April 2001 respectively.

that this 'recital is not intended to subordinate this Protocol to other international agreements'.

These three issues were identified by the United States in its rebuttal.[158] It argued that the Cartagena Protocol, along with any asserted rule of precaution, could only be pertinent if under article 3.2 of the DSU it could help clarify provisions of the SPS Agreement or other WTO agreements.[159] However, the EC submissions did not explain precisely how these norms could so assist. Even if they did, said the United States, they could only help interpret particular treaty terms, and could not override any provision of the SPS Agreement. Above all, the United States entreated the panel to take the same approach as the Appellate Body in the *Beef Hormones* case:

> Just as the Appellate Body found it unnecessary and imprudent to make a finding on the status of the precautionary principle in international law, this Panel also should have no need to address this theoretical issue. Nonetheless, the United States notes that it strongly disagrees that 'precaution' has become a rule of international law. In particular, the 'precautionary principle' cannot be considered a general principle or norm of international law because it does not have a single, agreed formulation. In fact, quite the opposite is true: the concept of precaution has many permutations across a number of different factors. Thus, the United States considers precaution to be an 'approach', rather than a 'principle' of international law.[160]

The panel dealt with these issues remarkably briefly (in 14 of the report's 2400 pages) in reaching the conclusion that the EC had implemented a *de facto* moratorium that led to 'undue delay', contrary to procedural obligations set out in the SPS Agreement.[161] The EC did not assert that norms of international environmental law were directly applicable to the dispute, and accordingly the panel did not have to grapple with the contentious issue of whether the DSU permitted it to apply law extrinsic to the covered agreements.[162] Instead the question was solely what use the precautionary principle, the Biodiversity

[158] *Biotech Products*, WTO Doc. WT/DS291, WT/DS292, WT/DS293 (2004) [456] (executive summary of the rebuttal submission of the United States).

[159] *Ibid.* [13]. [160] *Ibid.* [15].

[161] Art. 8 and Annex C(1)(a). See *Biotech Products*, WTO Docs. WT/DS291/R, WT/DS292/R, WT/DS293/R (2006) (report of the panel) [7.1567]ff.

[162] Margaret Young, 'The WTO's Use of Relevant Rules of International Law: An Analysis of the *Biotech* Case' (2007) 56 *ICLQ* 907, 912. However Young (at 913) points to a somewhat ambiguous passage in the report ([7.72]) which appears to leave open the possibility that a rule of international environmental law binding on all the parties could be found to be applicable in future disputes.

Convention, and the Cartagena Protocol could be put in the process of interpreting WTO agreements under the operation of article 3.2 of the DSU which requires WTO agreements to be interpreted 'in accordance with customary rules of interpretation of public international law'. Here the panel considered that the VCLT reflected customary rules and gave rise to two separate ways in which international environmental law could have interpretive relevance. First, was the application of Article 31(3)(c) which states that in interpreting a treaty '[t]here shall be taken into account…any relevant rules of international law applicable in the relations between the parties'. Here the panel took the view that the environmental rules cited by the EC could be used to interpret WTO agreements if they were 'applicable in the relations between the parties'.[163]

This is an important conclusion, because it means that in WTO disputes it is permissible to read WTO agreements in light of accepted rules of international law, whatever their source. However, in this case the panel followed the Appellate Body's approach in *Beef Hormones* eight years previously, in finding that 'the legal status of the precautionary principle remains unsettled' and that 'prudence suggests that we not attempt to resolve this complex issue, particularly if it is not necessary to do so'.[164] To reinforce this conclusion the panel referred to various statements of the precautionary principle in national laws, soft-law texts, binding environmental treaties, and international judicial decisions. The panel arguably overplayed the divergences that exist over the core meaning of the principle, and also took a dismissive approach to its general applicability by finding that its adoption had 'for the most part [been limited] to environmental conventions and declarations'[165] or domestic environmental law.[166]

The Biodiversity Convention and the Cartagena Protocol were of far clearer normative status, but because of the interpretation that the panel took of article 31(3)(c) of the VCLT it concluded that it was not required to take them into account. The panel found that the VCLT should be read 'as requiring consideration of those rules of international law which are applicable in the relations between all parties to the treaty which is being interpreted'.[167] In this respect the panel noted that this rule 'contributes to avoiding conflicts between the relevant

[163] *Biotech Products*, WTO Docs. WT/DS291/R, WT/DS292/R, WT/DS293/R (2006) (report of the panel), [7.67].

[164] *Ibid.* [7.89]. [165] *Ibid.* [7.88]. [166] *Ibid.* [7.88]. [167] *Ibid.* [7.70].

rules'.[168] However, it was not applicable here for two reasons. First, because not all members of the WTO were parties to the Biodiversity Convention and Cartagena Protocol, and second because not all litigants in *Biotech Products* were parties to these agreements. The United States was alone among the disputants in not having ratified the Biodiversity Convention (although it had signed the treaty), while the Cartegena Protocol had been signed but not ratified by Argentina and Canada, and had not been signed by the United States. Although it may be argued that the panel's approach here was doctrinally correct,[169] the ILC study group on fragmentation observed that the result of such a restrictive approach to article 31(3)(c) 'would be the isolation of multilateral agreements as "islands" permitting no references *inter se* in their application' and would be 'contrary to the legislative ethos behind most of multilateral treaty-making'.[170]

The panel's interpretation of article 31(3)(c) of the VCLT effectively cuts the WTO regime off from other fields of international law, including international environmental law, with the implication that international environmental rules are perhaps now less likely to come within the gaze of WTO dispute settlement. For those concerned about the cooption of environmental norms in WTO cases this might be seen to be a good thing. However, it can also be viewed as 'a missed opportunity to enhance the compatibility of, and minimise the conflict between, these different spheres of international law'.[171] It thereby further highlights the need for political agreement on the interaction between international trade law and international environmental law. This is especially the case given that in *Biotech Products* the panel interpreted the SPS Agreement in such a way as to substantially extend its reach and as a consequence the potential for conflict with environmental treaties.[172]

Juxtaposed against the panel's restrictive approach to article 31(3)(c) of the VCLT which left little room for international environmental law, was an expansive approach to the companion provision article 31(1) which provided considerable space for international environmental law to have an influence. Article 31(1) requires the terms of a treaty to

[168] *Ibid.* [169] Young, above n. 162, 918.

[170] ILC study group report, above n. 14, [740].

[171] Jan McDonald, 'Look While You Leap: The WTO Biotech Dispute Panel Report' (2006) 23 *EPLJ* 417, 420.

[172] Jacqueline Peel, 'A GMO by Any Other Name...Might Be an SPS Risk!' (2006) 17 *EJIL* 1009, 1028–9.

be interpreted in accordance with the 'ordinary meaning' to be given to those terms in their context, and in light of their object and purpose. The panel held that in determining 'ordinary meaning' it was appropriate to refer to dictionaries, and that by the same logic 'other relevant rules of international law may…aid a treaty interpreter'.[173] So they would be considered not because they were legal rules, but rather because of their 'informative character'.[174] This was said to be the approach taken in *Shrimp–Turtle I* where the Appellate Body, as we have seen, construed the term 'exhaustible natural resources' in article XX(g) of GATT by reference to international environmental instruments. However, while opening the door for international environmental law to have an influence in this way, the panel abruptly closed it by a cursory statement that the EC had not explained how provisions of the Biodiversity Convention or Cartagena Protocol were relevant to interpreting WTO agreements, and after 'carefully' assessing the provisions it was 'not…necessary or appropriate to rely on these particular provisions in interpreting the WTO agreements at issue'.[175]

10.3.7 Evaluation

Although trade liberalisation and environmental regimes reflect substantially different objectives, which are pursued through distinctive institutions, the foregoing review of relevant WTO jurisprudence has identified no evidence to suggest that the WTO has adopted parochial interpretations of international environmental law in conflict with prevailing understandings. Instead, in key cases WTO panels and the Appellate Body have sought to integrate accepted environmental rules and concepts within the WTO regime. This conclusion that the WTO has demonstrated 'integrative' rather than 'disintegrative' tendencies is in line with an early assessment of the place of treaty law and other basic principles of public international law within WTO jurisprudence.[176]

In the *Shrimp–Turtle* cases the Appellate Body referred to a range of international environmental instruments to justify its decision on several questions relating to the interpretation of GATT. In essence GATT

[173] *Biotech Products*, WTO Docs. WT/DS291/R, WT/DS292/R, WT/DS293/R (2006) (report of the panel), [7.92].

[174] *Ibid.* [175] *Ibid.* [7.95].

[176] Jonathan I. Charney, 'International Law and Multiple International Tribunals' (1998) 271 *RDC* 101, 153.

was updated to reflect contemporary environmental standards,[177] and in no respect did the Appellate Body appear to prefer 'trade-friendly' interpretations of environmental rules. Quite to the contrary, it may be argued that by faithfully reciting the principle of sustainable development, and drawing upon environmental instruments, the Appellate Body was anxious to address the criticism that the WTO was indifferent or hostile to environmental concerns.[178] Indeed one commentator has suggested that the Appellate Body has displayed a greater willingness to integrate environmental concerns in trade law than the political organs of the WTO, giving rise to a 'hiatus between the rule-making and rule-adjudicating arms of the WTO'.[179]

The *Beef Hormones* case is essentially neutral as regards its influence upon international environmental law as the Appellate Body found it unnecessary to enter into an evaluation of the precautionary principle. None the less, the decision is controversial in the sense that the Appellate Body adopted a curious approach to relating this asserted rule of customary international law to WTO rules. If the Appellate Body's reasoning is followed it will reinforce the view of some commentators that the WTO regime is closed except in so far as other rules of international law are relevant for the limited purpose of interpreting GATT and other covered agreements.[180] Admittedly, WTO panels and the Appellate Body can only determine disputes arising out of or relating to WTO rules. None the less, in dealing with these disputes they may be called upon to apply all relevant rules of international law, including those set out in environmental agreements, which are binding on the disputing parties.[181] This will include not only those rules articulated in international environmental agreements, but also relevant norms of customary international law having a bearing upon questions of environmental protection, should such questions be implicated in the controversy.

177 Alan E. Boyle, 'The World Trade Organization and the Marine Environment' in M. H. Nordquist, J. N. Moore, and S. Mahmoudi (eds.), *The Stockholm Declaration and Law of the Marine Environment* (2003) 109, 110.

178 Lowenfeld, above n. 131, 322.

179 Eckersley, above n. 26, 29. See also at 37 ('WTO politics lags well behind WTO jurisprudence').

180 Philippe Sands, 'Treaty, Custom and the Cross-Fertilization of International Law' (1998) 10 *YaleHR&DevLJ* 3, 12; Lakshman D. Guruswamy, 'Should UNCLOS or GATT/WTO Decide Trade and Environment Disputes?' (1998) 7 *MinnJGT* 287, 311.

181 Joost Pauwelyn, 'Recent Books on Trade and Environment: GATT Phantoms Still Haunt the WTO' (2004) 15 *EJIL* 575, 588–9.

The *Biotech Products* case was also problematic from this perspective, further isolating trade law from international environmental law in substantive terms as seen in the view taken on the relevance of environmental norms to the interpretation of WTO rules. At the same time the case occasioned an increase in the institutional potency of the WTO system, such that the SPS Agreement has been given a wider scope of operation. This indicates that silence itself is enormously significant – by applying international trade law in isolation from international environmental law the WTO has effectively marginalised the operation of environmental norms and principles. No explicit damage is done to the content of international environmental law in this process, but violence is occasioned to its general scope and import by the implicit suggestion that it is of lesser relevance than international trade law even though it is prima facie applicable.

It is precisely because of the privileged institutional position of the WTO that the question of fragmentation of international environmental law remains a live one. In this respect Charnovitz has also noted that while the first decade of the WTO dispute settlement system has been largely positive from the perspective of environmental law, there are challenges looming on the horizon including 'government-created marketable rights to address climate change, biofuels production of deforested land, and genetically modified agriculture'.[182] The apparent 'greening' of world trade rules achieved in the *Shrimp–Turtle* cases should not be regarded as an irreversible process. Just as the Appellate Body sought in that dispute to meet the expectations of many WTO members that environmental considerations be given a more prominent place in international trade law, it is entirely possible that future decision-makers may be more sympathetic to the views of some WTO members from the global south that the WTO regime should not privilege environmental interests at the expense of trade-led developmental policies.

10.4 Conclusion

This chapter has examined the expanding body of environmental jurisprudence emanating from some of the most active international adjudicative institutions that are not environmentally focused in their subject matter jurisdiction. This review has not sought to argue that

[182] Steve Charnovitz, 'The WTO's Environmental Progress' (2007) 10 *JIEconL* 685, 706.

these bodies have rendered decisions that have always appropriately recognised environmental considerations. Indeed failings of this type are to a large degree unavoidable given the particular institutional perspectives adopted by design or acculturation. What has been suggested, however, is that to date there is no indication that these institutions have preferred 'skewed' interpretations of environmental rules and principles in order to uphold the policy objectives of the issue-specific regimes that they operate within.

The main reasons for this conclusion in relation to human rights bodies were seen to be twofold. In the first place, in relation to substantive human rights, the attempts to seek redress for environmental damage have been pursued predominantly through the language of human rights, including the right to life, relieving the relevant bodies of any need to examine potentially relevant environmental norms. None the less, the point was also made that future petitions involving human rights and environmental issues may not be so unproblematic from the perspective of international environmental law. There are distinct possibilities of normative conflict if complaints are made concerning state environmental policies that, among other things, interfere with social, economic, or cultural rights, including a right to development. Second, in relation to procedural rights, the potential for fragmentation has been lessened by the almost complete overlap between the human rights and environmental agendas to improve access to information, to enhance public participation, and to provide effective remedies for rights infringements. Indeed it was suggested that the human rights jurisprudence on such matters is likely to be of considerable value as procedural environmental rights receive greater recognition in international environmental law.

The resolution of disputes involving environmental issues in the WTO system involves substantially greater opportunities for environmental norms to be considered in a problematic manner. This is because such norms may be pertinent in interpreting several WTO rules relating to natural resources and environmental risk, and also because environmental prescriptions may be relied upon to justify what would otherwise constitute violations of WTO disciplines. However, and despite dire predictions to the contrary, the WTO's judicial bodies have so far evinced a willingness to consider international environmental law faithfully, on its own terms. This reflects both the nature of the disputes that have been litigated, and the careful way in which they have been framed by panels and the Appellate Body to avoid straying beyond narrow questions of international trade law. However, it is also indicative of the sensitivity of these bodies to the concern that trade liberalisation and environmental protection agendas are irreconcilable. None the less it is too early to draw definitive conclusions. The WTO dispute settlement system has not been fully tested as no case has yet arisen where a state has sought to rely upon environmental rules in express derogation from WTO commitments. Such a situation would pose most acutely the potential problem of 'fragmentation' as it affects international environmental law, as WTO dispute settlement bodies will no doubt be called upon by one or more disputing parties to prefer interpretations of applicable environmental norms that have the least trade restrictive effects. Such a dispute would doubtless set the scene for a further outpouring of anxiety over the channelling of key concepts of international environmental law away from their central rationale.

11 The future of international environmental litigation

11.1 The flourishing of international environmental litigation

In concluding this book it must be asked what the future holds in store for international environmental dispute settlement. It certainly could not have been imagined at the Stockholm or Rio conferences, the two key 'constitutional moments' for international environmental law, that within decades international litigation on environmental matters would become a relatively routine occurrence in international relations. By 1972 only a handful of environmentally significant cases had been decided, the most important being the arbitral awards in the *Bering Sea Fur Seals*,[1] *Trail Smelter*,[2] and *Lake Lanoux* cases.[3] No environmental case had yet been determined by the ICJ, although the *Fisheries Jurisdiction* cases[4] were commenced just prior to the Stockholm Conference.[5]

There were some important additions in the years leading up to the Rio Conference, beginning with the *Nuclear Tests* cases,[6] which marked a new era in international environmental litigation in which ecological threats were identified clearly and directly, and claims began to be asserted on the basis of a growing collection of applicable rules and

[1] *Bering Sea Fur Seals* case (*Great Britain/United States of America*) (1893) 1 Moore 827.

[2] *Trail Smelter* case (*Canada/United States of America*) (1938 and 1941) 3 RIAA 1911.

[3] *Lake Lanoux* case (*France/Spain*) (1957) 12 RIAA 285.

[4] *Fisheries Jurisdiction* cases: *United Kingdom* v. *Iceland* (jurisdiction) [1973] ICJ Rep 3, (merits) [1974] ICJ Rep 3; (*Germany* v. *Iceland*) (jurisdiction) [1973] ICJ Rep 49, (merits) [1974] ICJ Rep 175.

[5] The United Kingdom formally instituted proceedings against Iceland on 14 April 1972, while the Federal Republic of Germany followed on 5 June 1972, the day the Stockholm Conference opened.

[6] *Nuclear Tests* cases: (*Australia* v. *France*) (interim measures) [1973] ICJ Rep 99, (merits) [1974] ICJ Rep 253; (*New Zealand* v. *France*) (interim measures) [1973] ICJ Rep 135, (merits) [1974] ICJ Rep 457.

standards. Similarly, Nauru's application in the *Certain Phosphate Lands in Nauru*,[7] which began in 1989, was built upon evidence of massive environmental degradation suffered while the Pacific microstate was under the administration of Australia, New Zealand, and the United Kingdom.[8] Since the Rio Conference there has been a tremendous intensification and diversification in the practice of environmental dispute settlement. States have shown an ever greater willingness to establish and utilise dispute settlement procedures, including judicial and quasi-judicial bodies. There has also been an expansion in the range of actors participating in these institutions, as international organisations, NGOs, and individuals begin to gain access either as litigants in their own right, or as *amici curiae*.

Arriving at a definitive total of environmental cases commenced and concluded in these bodies is difficult, given that any precise categorisation of an 'environmental case' is contentious.[9] Taking an expansive definition, so that all those disputes involving at least one issue of environmental protection or management are captured, the extent of the litigation is indeed impressive. By December 2007, ten cases directly or indirectly involving environmental questions had been (or were currently being) litigated in the ICJ,[10] panels established under the auspices of the PCA had considered five environmental cases,[11]

[7] *Certain Phosphate Lands in Nauru* (*Nauru* v. *Australia*) [1992] ICJ Rep 240.

[8] The case was subsequently settled in 1993. See the 1993 Settlement of the Case in the ICJ Concerning Certain Phosphate Lands in Nauru.

[9] See Richard B. Bilder, 'The Settlement of Disputes in the Field of the International Law of the Environment' (1975) 144 *RDC* 139, 153 (defining such disputes as 'any disagreement or conflict of views or interests between States relating to the alteration, through human intervention, of natural environmental systems').

[10] *Fisheries Jurisdiction* cases [1974] ICJ Rep 3; [1974] ICJ Rep 175; *Nuclear Tests* cases [1974] ICJ Rep 253; [1974] ICJ Rep 457; *Delimitation of the Maritime Boundary in the Gulf of Maine Area* (*Canada/United States of America*) [1984] ICJ Rep 246; *Nauru* case [1992] ICJ Rep 240; *Maritime Delimitation in the Area Between Greenland and Jan Mayen* (*Denmark* v. *Norway*) [1993] ICJ Rep 38; *Request for an Examination of the Situation in Accordance with Paragraph 63 of the Court's Judgment of 20 December 1974 in the Nuclear Tests* (*New Zealand* v. *France*) case [1995] ICJ Rep 288 (1995 *Nuclear Tests* case); *Legality of the Threat or Use of Nuclear Weapons* [1996] ICJ Rep 226; *Gabčíkovo-Nagymaros Project* case (*Hungary/Slovakia*) [1997] ICJ Rep 7; *Fisheries Jurisdiction* case (*Spain* v. *Canada*) (jurisdiction and admissibility) [1998] ICJ Rep 431 (*Estai* case); *Pulp Mills on the River Uruguay* (*Argentina v. Uruguay*) (request for provisional measures by Argentina) (2006) 45 ILM 1025 (request for provisional measures by Uruguay) (2007) (available at www.icj-cij.org/docket/files/135/13615.pdf).

[11] *North Atlantic Coast Fisheries* case (*Great Britain/United States of America*) (1910) 11 RIAA 167; *MOX Plant* award (order 3, of 24 June 2003) (2003) 42 ILM 1187 (order 4, of 14 November 2003) (order 5, of 22 January 2007) (available at www.pca-cpa.org); *OSPAR*

and ITLOS had been activated in eight disputes raising environmental issues.[12] The activity of other judicial bodies has also been substantial, including the dispute settlement system of the WTO, which is increasingly engaging with disputes possessing important environmental dimensions.[13] Other specialised judicial and quasi-judicial procedures, including human rights tribunals and complaints bodies, have also heard essentially environmental complaints.[14] Finally it should be noted that any aggregate of environmental cases is increased by an order of magnitude if all such decisions of the ECJ are included.[15]

This flourishing of international environmental litigation appears remarkable when one reflects upon the genesis of international environmental law. As the discipline largely emerged from soft-law instruments, incorporating informal and non-binding principles, it appeared that it was effectively non-adjudicable, and therefore essentially unenforceable.[16] However, in recent decades several areas of international environmental law have acquired precise and technical legal content,

Arbitration (Ireland v. *United Kingdom)* (final award) (2003) 42 ILM 1118; *Protection of the Rhine Against Pollution by Chlorides, Arbitration in Application of the Convention of 3 December 1976 and the Additional Protocol of 25 September 1991* (12 March 2004) (Pt I available at www.pca_cpa.org/ENGLISH/RPC/PBF/Sentence%20I.pdf and Pt II available at www.pca_cpa.org/ENGLISH/RPC/PBF/Sentence%20II.pdf); *Iron Rhine ('Ijzeren Rijn') Railway (Belgium/Netherlands)* arbitration (24 May 2005) (available at www.pca-cpa.org/showfile.asp?fil_id=377).

12 *Southern Bluefin Tuna* cases (*New Zealand* v. *Japan; Australia* v. *Japan*) (provisional measures) (1999) 117 ILR 148, (1999) 38 ILM 1624 (*Southern Bluefin Tuna* order); *Camouco* case (*Panama* v. *France*) (prompt release) (2000) 125 ILR 151, (2000) 39 ILM 666; *Monte Confurco* case (*Seychelles* v. *France*) (prompt release) (2000) 125 ILR 203; *Conservation and Sustainable Exploitation of Swordfish Stocks in the South-Eastern Pacific Ocean (Chile/European Community)* (proceedings suspended 15 March 2001 and 16 December 2003) (available at www.itlos.org); *MOX Plant* case (*Ireland* v. *United Kingdom*) (provisional measures) (2002) 41 ILM 405 (*MOX Plant* order); *Volga* case (*Russian Federation* v. *Australia*) (prompt release) (2003) 42 ILM 159 (*MOX Plant* order); *Land Reclamation by Singapore in and Around the Straits of Johor* (*Malaysia* v. *Singapore*) (provisional measures) (2003) (available at www.itlos.org); *Juno Trader* case (*St Vincent and the Grenadines* v. *Bissau*) (prompt release) (2004) (available at www.itlos.org).

13 See ch. 10. 14 See ch. 10.

15 However, some of this sizeable body of case law is clearly more important for European environmental law than others. The European Commission includes fifty cases in its list of the leading cases and judgments of the ECJ on environmental matters: see ec.europa.eu/environment/law/cases_judgements.htm.

16 Douglas M. Johnston and David L. VanderZwaag, 'The Ocean and International Environmental Law: Swimming, Sinking, and Treading Water at the Millennium' (2000) 43 *OCM* 141, 145 (noting the 'preponderance of soft, informal, non-binding, ostensibly non-adjudicable (or even unenforceable) commitments generated by [environmental] diplomacy').

readily permitting the deployment of legal methods of dispute settlement in addition to negotiatory procedures. Moreover, it has become clear that even soft-law principles of somewhat amorphous content, and even more uncertain normative status, can be given concrete effect by international courts. For, example, the ICJ gave practical meaning and import to the principle of sustainable development in the *Gabčíkovo-Nagymaros Project* case without recognising the principle as a binding rule of law. In a somewhat similar fashion ITLOS has attempted to implement the precautionary principle in several of its provisional measures orders while side-stepping difficult questions as to the content of the principle, and whether it has entered the pantheon of customary norms relating to environmental protection.[17]

11.2 Judicial development of international environmental law

11.2.1 Origins and development

The origins and early development of international environmental law in the core areas of wildlife protection and responsibility for transboundary environmental harm owe much to several judicial decisions. The *Bering Sea Fur Seal* case did not conclude that states were under a general obligation to protect faunal species under the threat of extinction, but it did set out a detailed and practical management regime to prevent this fate befalling the Alaskan fur seal, and this ultimately led to improved regional cooperation to protect the species. The regulations adopted by the tribunal also provided a model for managing other marine wildlife, particularly fisheries. Some forty years later the *Trail Smelter* case articulated what is widely regarded as a keystone of international law in the field of environmental protection by concluding that states have a duty to ensure that activities within their control do not cause damage in the territory of other states.

Admittedly these were somewhat embryonic developments, and provided no more than the most general normative guidance. International environmental law only began to emerge as a fully fledged and coherent field of law much later in the twentieth century when the seriousness of global environmental threats could no longer be ignored, and when popular environmental movements began to exert political influence, particularly in northern states. These developments resulted in

[17] *Southern Bluefin Tuna* order (1999) 117 ILR 148, (1999) 38 ILM 1624; *MOX Plant* order (2002) 41 ILM 405; *Straits of Johor* case (available at www.itlos.org).

agreement on two types of international legal measure to address various environmental challenges such as habitat protection and marine pollution. The first of these comprised a raft of soft-law instruments. Although states have a long history of agreeing upon essentially diplomatic and non-binding resolutions, declarations, guidelines, codes, standards, and the like, such instruments were especially important for the consolidation of international environmental law. They allowed agreement upon important goals that would otherwise not have been forthcoming, and also provided a principled framework within which states could settle their ongoing disputes over contentious environmental issues such as the equitable and sustainable use of shared resources.[18] The second way in which an emerging international consensus on the need to address environmental problems found legal manifestation was in regulatory agreements. Building upon the general principles found in soft-law texts, these hard-law treaties and conventions seek to advance the objective of ecologically sustainable development by requiring states to regulate, with varying degrees of specificity, environmentally damaging activities taking place within their territory, or otherwise within their jurisdiction and control.

In the context of such important and extensive legislative developments, the judicial contribution to international environmental law has mostly been to provide general direction rather than to articulate precise rules. International environmental litigation has also illustrated, often starkly, situations where legal principles concerning environmental protection have been lacking and are in need of development. However, in both respects the judicial influence has been felt within specific topic areas rather than across the whole spectrum of issues of relevance to global environmental governance. Most decisions of international courts directly and substantially considering environmental questions have fallen within three categories: transboundary harm, the sustainable utilisation of freshwater resources, or the protection of the marine environment.[19]

The body of jurisprudence in the first category is compact.[20] The *Trail Smelter* case remains the only example of an intergovernmental dispute

[18] Patricia W. Birnie, 'Legal Techniques of Settling Disputes: The "Soft" Settlement Approach' in William E. Butler (ed.), *Perestroika and International Law* (1990) 177.

[19] Inevitably there has been some overlap in these cases. Note for instance the issues of transboundary damage raised by Hungary in the *Gabčíkovo-Nagymaros Project* case [1997] ICJ Rep 7. See chs. 5 and 6.

[20] See ch. 5.

in which claims concerning transboundary environmental damage have been successfully litigated to conclusion. Instead states have normally resolved such problems directly through negotiation, or through regional regulatory regimes. Moreover, although seminal, the significance of the principle stated in the *Trail Smelter* case regarding state responsibility for transboundary damage should not be exaggerated as it constitutes no more than a translation of general concepts concerning state sovereignty and territorial integrity into a form that can be applied to a situation of transboundary pollution. Some of the limitations of the *Trail Smelter* case dictum emerged with clarity in the *Nuclear Tests* cases. France's impugned atmospheric nuclear tests involved complex environmental threats not only to the applicants, Australia and New Zealand, and many other South Pacific states, but also to marine ecosystems beyond national jurisdiction. While Australia and New Zealand could point to sovereignty concerns as regards the impact of this testing upon their own territories and populations, they also made a host of innovative arguments regarding a general duty to protect the environment, submissions that could not have been advanced within the narrow conceptual rubric offered by the *Trail Smelter* case. These submissions were well ahead of their time and hence the main contribution of the litigation was in pinpointing several deficiencies in international environmental law, notwithstanding the milestones that had already been reached at the Stockholm Conference. By the time New Zealand unsuccessfully sought to re-open the litigation in 1995,[21] in response to a new round of nuclear tests, it was evident that many of these gaps in the legal framework had been filled, but several issues still required further clarification, including the extent to which there existed environmental obligations of an *erga omnes* character, the breach of which any state may invoke in international judicial proceedings.

The second field where judicial decisions have been prominent in international environmental law has been in the context of shared freshwater systems.[22] For almost all of its history international water law has had a very strong resource focus. Its traditional concern has been to promote the rational and equitable utilisation of international rivers and other freshwater basins, and only indirectly to address the ecological problems that are implicated in any fragmentation of hydrographic systems occasioned by dams and other projects. However, since

[21] *1995 Nuclear Tests* case [1995] ICJ Rep 288. [22] See ch. 6.

the *Territorial Jurisdiction of the International Commission of the River Oder* case,[23] successive decisions have helped to provide this area of law with a conceptual structure in which environmental considerations have progressively been given a more prominent place. The absolute notion that upstream states have complete autonomy in exploiting river systems was rejected in the *Lake Lanoux* case in favour of an approach that affirmed the limited sovereignty of upstream users. The latter are thereby required to have due regard to downstream states, and to enter into meaningful consultation to ascertain and respond to their interests. A further important step was taken in the *Gabčíkovo-Nagymaros Project* case where the concept of limited sovereignty was displaced by the community of interest theory enunciated in the *River Oder* case, this time being applied in a non-navigational context. The idea of a perfect equality of users, forming a community of states equally interested in the sustainable utilisation of freshwater resources, is a major advance on earlier legal conceptions of international river management. However, it remains to be seen how far the concept can be taken, and whether it can ever be used as a basis for asserting that all stretches of an international river or other freshwater basin constitute a 'commons space' or 'common heritage', the ecological integrity of which is a shared concern of all riparian states.

The third main body of international environmental case law concerns the protection of the marine environment and the sustainable exploitation of marine wildlife.[24] The vast majority of marine environmental cases have concerned marine 'living resources'.[25] Commencing with the *Bering Sea Fur Seals* case, adjudicators have sought to grapple with fundamental issues of resource management and ecosystem protection in the complex marine environment where the ecological artificiality of political boundaries is readily apparent. One of the notable features of this area of law was its early malleability, and the accompanying potential for judicial decisions to have a major influence upon its development. Arguably it was open to the tribunal in the *Bering Sea*

[23] *Territorial Jurisdiction of the International Commission of the River Oder (Czechoslovakia, Denmark, France, Germany, Great Britain, Sweden/Poland)* [1929] PCIJ (ser. A) no. 23, 5.

[24] See ch. 7.

[25] Only a few cases have raised issues such as marine pollution, or other human alteration of the marine environment, and none of these has yet led to a decision on the merits. See the *MOX Plant* order (2002) 41 ILM 405 and *MOX Plant* award (order 3, of 24 June 2003) (2003) 42 ILM 1187 and the *Straits of Johor* case (available at www.itlos.org).

Fur Seals case to accept the submissions of the United States regarding asserted patrimonial rights to conserve a threatened species of marine wildlife. The connections with the Alaskan fur seals, which were begotten, born, and reared on United States territory, were equally as strong as Iceland's historic interest in adjacent cod and other high seas fisheries considered in the *Fisheries Jurisdiction* cases. Yet while the United States' arguments were summarily rejected in the *Bering Sea Fur Seals* case, in favour of the *mare liberum* doctrine, in the *Fisheries Jurisdiction* case the ICJ developed the 'preferential fishing rights' doctrine which accorded priority to Iceland in the management and exploitation of high seas fisheries on the Icelandic continental shelf. Admittedly the ICJ did not incorporate environmental considerations within the preferential rights concept, but the case none the less demonstrated the potential for the law to be transformed by judicial exegesis to reflect conservationist objectives.

With the conclusion of the LOS Convention contentious questions regarding coastal resource management were addressed by arrogating to coastal states extensive rights to manage the marine wildlife found in their EEZs.[26] An important effect of this innovation has been to move the area of contestation over marine living resources seawards, that is to the margins of the EEZ and to the high seas. Hence in the *Estai* case the disputants were concerned to resolve ongoing uncertainties as to the capacity of coastal states to manage straddling and highly migratory fisheries consistent with the LOS Convention. This dispute between Canada and Spain over the arrest of a Spanish-flagged fishing vessel was never decided on its merits, but it was an important catalyst for agreement on the Straddling Stocks Agreement[27] which is designed to bring greater clarity to the law of the sea as regards the exploitation and conservation of fisheries that move between high seas and EEZ areas. Finally, in the *Southern Bluefin Tuna* order, which also involved a highly migratory fishery, the dispute was argued by the applicants as one involving the duty of Japan to respect the provisions of the LOS Convention relating to marine resource conservation on the high seas. This led to the prescription of important provisional measures by ITLOS, in which the Tribunal recognised that 'the conservation of the

[26] See LOS Convention, art. 56.

[27] 1995 Agreement for the Implementation of the Provisions of the United Nations Convention on the Law of the Sea of 10 December 1982 Relating to the Conservation and Management of Straddling Fish Stocks and Highly Migratory Fish Stocks.

living resources of the sea is an element in the protection and preservation of the marine environment'.[28]

11.2.2 *New fields for judicial development*

Cases concerning transboundary environmental damage, the sustainable use of freshwater resources, and the protection of riverine ecosystems, are restricted in number and in scope largely because states have increasingly addressed such environmental disputes by means other than international litigation. Through regulatory regimes and international institutions such as civil liability regimes and river commissions, it has been possible to develop a range of necessary environmental standards and to resolve disputes concerning their implementation. There is accordingly little reason to expect that the jurisprudence on these issues will expand to any substantial extent in the twenty-first century, and the existing case law will become progressively less germane as it is further separated in time from contemporary practice.

By contrast there is considerable judicial activity in the field of marine environmental protection, thanks largely to the operation of the dispute settlement system of the LOS Convention. The important environmental protection provisions of the LOS Convention were negotiated several decades ago and will doubtless require ongoing interpretation and clarification if they are to remain relevant to contemporary conditions. The residual compulsory jurisdiction of ITLOS to issue provisional measures orders,[29] together with its competence in prompt release cases,[30] has ensured this relatively new tribunal an important function in this regard. As it develops a body of practice and precedent it may also attract greater interest from states as their judicial body of choice for dealing with all law of the sea disputes.[31] The role of ad hoc arbitral tribunals operating under the auspices of the LOS Convention seems less certain, as there have been several false starts in environmental cases brought before such bodies.[32] Notwithstanding these teething problems, a sizeable body of jurisprudence may well emerge,

[28] *Southern Bluefin Tuna* order (1999) 38 ILM 1624, [70].

[29] LOS Convention, art. 290.

[30] *Ibid.* art. 292.

[31] Only 25 states (from a total of 155 states parties to the LOS Convention) have nominated ITLOS, under art. 287, as their first preference for resolving disputes arising from the Convention. See ch. 2, table 2.2.

[32] See the *MOX Plant* award (order 3, of 24 June 2003) (2003) 42 ILM 1187 and the *Southern Bluefin Tuna* case (*Australia and New Zealand* v. *Japan*) (award on jurisdiction and admissibility) 39 ILM 1359 (2000).

given that arbitration remains the default procedure for the resolution of most marine environmental disputes under the LOS Convention.

In what other contexts is judicial involvement in the development of international environmental law likely? Many environmental agreements permit states to consent in advance to the adjudication of their disputes; however, few states have taken up these opportunities. Unless states agree on a case-by-case basis to submit their disputes to such procedures, it is likely that compulsory procedures in environmental regimes will provide the greatest opportunity for litigation. Most of these are concerned, however, with marine environmental issues,[33] and only one has been used to date, namely the arbitral procedure established by the OSPAR Convention. There are only a few examples of such procedures beyond the maritime context, such as the Madrid Protocol.[34] However, in all likelihood the latter procedure will remain unused while states seek to deal with questions of regime compliance and the settlement of disputes through the alternative mechanisms operating under the Antarctic Treaty System.

There are other important fields for judicial involvement in the development of international environmental law. One of the most intriguing is in the context of trade regimes. As the volume of international trade increases the international community has sought to establish bilateral, regional, and global legal frameworks to facilitate the free movement of goods and services, and to promote foreign investment. The globalisation of trade has many environmental effects, yet international trade law generally limits the extent to which states may implement environmental policies that affect trade flows. The dispute settlement systems forming part of trade regimes at regional and global levels have been used ever more frequently to deal with controversies arising from this intersection between the agendas of trade liberalisation and environmental protection. Important regional examples in this respect include NAFTA, and the much more established regime for European economic integration. Globally, the

[33] See for instance the Straddling Stocks Agreement, the 2000 Convention on the Conservation and Management of Highly Migratory Fish Stocks in the Western and Central Pacific Ocean and the 2001 Convention on the Conservation and Management of Fishery Resources in the South-East Atlantic Ocean, all of which incorporate by reference the dispute settlement system of the LOS Convention. See also the 1973 International Convention for the Prevention of Pollution from Ships (as amended and given effect by the Protocol of 1978 Relating to the International Convention for the Prevention of Pollution from Ships) art. 10.

[34] Arts. 18–20.

WTO dispute settlement system will continue to be a site for vigorous contests concerning the interaction between WTO trade rules and environmental norms and principles, although over time the emergence of bilateral and regional free trade agreements may lead to a reduction in WTO disputation and the use of alternative mechanisms under sub-global arrangements.

Another avenue for judicial contribution to international environmental law is the operation of human rights tribunals and complaints procedures. Much controversy continues to surround the notion of substantive environmental rights; no such rights are currently recognised in the leading human rights texts, and they have not been taken up to any serious extent in international environmental instruments. None the less, essentially environmental claims will continue to be raised within human rights bodies for the simple reason that they provide a means of redress to individuals otherwise excluded from international processes of review. As this practice develops it would seem inevitable that there will be some cross-pollination in jurisprudence, with human rights courts, commissions, and complaints procedures calling upon environmental rules and principles when interpreting and giving effect to several human rights, including the right to life.

In the coming decades international environmental litigation therefore appears likely to be played out more routinely in a variegated system in which courts and tribunals with a non-environmental focus are particularly prominent. This necessitates some consideration being given to the practical and normative impacts of this development. The practical challenges are real and immediate ones, as illustrated in the *Southern Bluefin Tuna* and the *MOX Plant* disputes in which important environmental cases were effectively stymied because of problematic interactions between the LOS Convention dispute settlement system and other regimes.[35] The consequences for the normative structure of international environmental law are more subtle, and will be evident only in the longer term.[36] On the one hand there appears to be a welcome opportunity for the mainstreaming of environmental concerns within the decisions of specialised tribunals, and therefore within those specific areas of law. However, at the same time these bodies may develop problematic and inconsistent approaches to rules and principles of international environmental law. For instance, the WTO

[35] See ch. 9. [36] See ch. 10.

Appellate Body could pronounce upon the precautionary principle or the concept of sustainable development in a way that may be seen to strip them of their environmental content, particularly as these principles remain in a state of flux and development.[37] Thankfully the available evidence does not suggest that this has yet occurred, but it may only be a matter of time before difficult interpretative decisions can no longer be avoided.

11.2.3 Assessment

The review of international environmental jurisprudence undertaken in this study suggests that international courts and tribunals have made a somewhat variable contribution to the development of international environmental law. While in some areas the 'greening' of international law may partly be attributed to the influence of judicial decisions, in others the case law may actually have impeded the recognition of environmental objectives.

Sands has observed that there are three key questions that should be asked when assessing the extent to which environmental considerations have been appropriately integrated in judicial decisions.[38] The first of these is whether courts have recognised the importance of environmental objectives among other goals being pursued in the international legal system. Second, it may be asked whether they have been willing to give precedence to environmental over non-environmental (principally developmental) values. A third question is whether judicial bodies have evinced an awareness and appreciation

[37] E.g., for an attempt to circumscribe the precautionary principle, which also recognises that the principle has an inherent vagueness conducive to its application to various factual situations, see Arie Trouwborst, 'The Precautionary Principle in General International Law: Combating the Babylonian Confusion' (2007) 16 *RECIEL* 185.

[38] Philippe Sands, 'The International Court of Justice and the European Court of Justice' in Jacob Werksman (ed.), *Greening International Institutions* (1996) 219; Philippe Sands, 'International Environmental Litigation and Its Future' (1999) 32 *URichLR* 1619, 1625. Sands considered these issues in relation to the ICJ and the ECJ; however, they appear equally applicable to other international courts and tribunals. He concluded that while the ICJ has refrained from engaging fully with issues of environmental law and policy in its decisions, the ECJ has been at the forefront of European environmental governance. See also Malgosia A. Fitzmaurice, 'Equipping the ICJ to Deal with Environmental Law' in Connie Peck and Roy S. Lee (eds.), *Increasing the Effectiveness of the International Court of Justice* (1997) 398, 402 (noting that the ICJ 'cannot, so far, be said to have grasped the nettle' in terms of contributing to the development of international environmental law).

of the unique policy and science considerations involved in environmental disputes.

There have undoubtedly been some promising signals in the case law in respect of all three of these issues. This study has traced the discernible shift from judicial ignorance of, and indifference to, environmental issues, to an increased awareness of problems of resource management and ecosystem protection, and greater fluency in the understanding and use of concepts of environmental science, policy, and law. It should also be emphasised that a fair assessment of environmental cases to date must pay appropriate regard to the context in which they were decided, including the degree to which environmental rules and principles were fully formed and expressed at the time of the litigation, whether and to what extent environmental issues were raised by the parties, and also wider issues including the general level of environmental awareness within the international community.[39] Despite the progress that has been made, and after appropriate allowance is made for contextual considerations, it is difficult to escape the conclusion that the judicial treatment of environmental disputes has often been unsatisfactory. The notion that a decision represents a 'missed opportunity' is a cliché repeated in countless case notes, but it bears repeating that the paths presented for developing a jurisprudence that addresses issues of ecological sustainability have often not been taken, or have been avoided.

What accounts for these missed opportunities, and the limited conceptual and ethical framework often adopted by courts in considering environmental issues? The main answer appears to be that courts and tribunals have generally sought to do no more than is necessary to resolve those disputes placed before them. Whether this is considered an appropriate approach evokes age-old jurisprudential debates concerning the proper function of the judiciary in the process of legal development.[40] From one perspective it might be suggested that courts ought to take a programmatic, or 'activist' stance, to address problems and issues that have not been adequately dealt with through legislative developments. At the opposite end of the spectrum a 'formalist'

[39] Without an appreciation of these and other background considerations it is tempting to be overly critical of much of the case law. Equally, without understanding the precise economic, social and other considerations in which a case was decided it is possible to rely excessively or inappropriately upon decisions that now have limited usefulness in contemporary law and practice.

[40] Sands, above n. 38, 1637.

approach may be preferred, on the basis that courts should do no more than is required to bring disputes to a close, and to this end must apply the law strictly as it is found, even if it is possible to adopt an interpretation or application of the law that more effectively advances environmental objectives.

There are many reasons why charting a course between these two approaches is challenging for courts in the resolution of international environmental disputes. One of these stems from the way in which some dispute settlement bodies relate to environmental agreements. Judicial and other procedures for dispute settlement are sometimes established without appropriate attention being given to the resolution of underlying normative issues. Indeed fundamental disagreements relating to appropriate levels of conservation of natural resources and other environmental issues may be deliberately deferred when concluding environmental agreements in the hope that they may be resolved by subsequent state practice, including through the use of dispute settlement procedures. Some have suggested that these situations involve an implicit delegation of law-making authority, so that international adjudicators are empowered to develop the law and thereby reduce transaction costs in negotiating treaty rules.[41] However, in the absence of an unambiguous normative framework, courts or other bodies seised of disputes under environmental agreements may simply encourage the parties to resolve their dispute as between themselves, rather than articulating legal rules that may be applied to reach a definitive conclusion in the instant and future cases.

The main reason for this judicial reticence is that international courts are creatures of consent, operating in a demanding political setting in which they necessarily behave strategically. Should they seek to adopt too innovative or creative an approach there is every possibility that their standing may be diminished, with attendant implications for the authority of their decisions, and the health of their dockets. Brownlie has argued along these lines that to prevent states from becoming wary of accepting jurisdiction in relation to environmental and other matters, international courts must not be 'seduced by academic fashion'[42] to develop the law, and must instead remain focused

[41] Tom Ginsburg, 'Bounded Discretion in International Judicial Lawmaking' (2005) 45 *VaJIL* 631, 644.

[42] Ian Brownlie, 'Some Questions Concerning the Applicable Law in International Tribunals' in Jerzy Makarczyk (ed.), *Theory of International Law at the Threshold of the 21st Century: Essays in Honour of Krzysztof Skubiszewski* (1996) 761, 764.

upon the actual practice of states. The pressure upon courts to be alive to the political context in which they operate is pronounced in most arbitral settings. However, it is also a factor in the operation of judicial bodies such as the ICJ which assume jurisdiction only occasionally, and then normally on the basis of special agreement.

Those judicial bodies best able to forge a distinctive approach to environmental issues are those institutions at the greatest distance from pressures of this character. Arguably this is one of the main reasons why the ECJ has been able to develop an innovative approach to environmental questions, while the ICJ has been far more circumspect. However, there is also evidence that adjudicative institutions can acquire greater independence over time. In some respects ITLOS has taken a cautious approach to environmental questions since it began operating in 1996, no doubt in response to the strident criticism that the Tribunal's creation attracted in some quarters.[43] However, the practice in ITLOS also indicates how important gains can be made incrementally as it shook off initial doubts and acquired international recognition. This process is evident in the successive prompt release cases arising from the arrest of fishing vessels.[44] While in none of its earlier decisions did the Tribunal expressly recognise the seriousness of the environmental problem of IUU fishing, in the *Volga* case it stated that it understood 'the international concerns about [IUU] fishing' and 'appreciate[d]' the measures taken by states to address the problem.[45] This was no doubt important in leading the Tribunal to set the very substantial bond that it did for the release of the *Volga*.

11.3 International courts and international environmental governance

11.3.1 General adjudicative machinery

In addition to considering the relevance of judicial decisions to the development of international environmental law, this study has also explored the functional importance of international courts and

[43] See especially Shigeru Oda, 'Dispute Settlement Prospects in the Law of the Sea' (1995) 44 *ICLQ* 863, 866–7.

[44] See the *Camouco* case (2000) 125 ILR 151; *Monte Confurco* case (2000) 125 ILR 203; *Grand Prince* case (*Belize* v. *France*) (prompt release) (2001) 125 ILR 251; *Volga* case (2003) 42 ILM 159.

[45] *Volga* case (2003) 42 ILM 159, [68].

tribunals for settling environmental disputes and promoting compliance with international environmental law. It has been seen that much commentary upon the practice of environmental dispute settlement has focused upon the problems encountered when using the basic architecture of international law for dealing with environmental controversies. It now seems self-evident that the general institutions of public international law are not adequately responsive to the particular demands of international environmental governance. There are relatively few customary norms of international law with strong environmental content. There are also doubts as to the extent to which the responsibility of states may be invoked effectively in response to breaches of these norms, or in respect of other internationally wrongful acts resulting in environmental damage. This is not least because of the requirement to establish a requisite legal interest or injury, a hurdle which may be insurmountable in a number of cases, including those relating to damage to the global commons. Moreover, these basic primary and secondary rules are not supported by dedicated environmental institutions of a universal character that can supervise their implementation. The UN Charter makes no reference to environmental matters, and establishes no specialised environmental organ. Additionally the ICJ, the principal judicial organ of the United Nations, has been granted compulsory jurisdiction by only sixty-five states, six of which have included reservations in relation to environmental matters.[46]

It can also be argued that when such general mechanisms are relied upon they may produce unsatisfactory results. Notwithstanding the remarkable proliferation in multilateral environmental agreements, states have shown little propensity for utilising the ICJ to bring other governments to account for environmentally damaging activities, and in no environmental case where the Court's contentious jurisdiction has been invoked unilaterally has the Court produced a satisfactory decision, or an acceptable solution to an environmental dispute.[47] Paradigmatic examples of the problems that may be encountered in this respect are found in the *Fisheries Jurisdiction* cases and the *Nuclear*

[46] See ch. 2. This is despite repeated calls for greater acceptance of the Court's compulsory jurisdiction in order to promote the rule of law at the international level. See e.g., 2005 World Summit Outcome, [134(f)], UN Doc. A/60/L.1 (2005).

[47] Arguably the most important decision of the ICJ on environmental matters was the *Gabčíkovo-Nagymaros Project* case [1997] ICJ Rep 7 and this dispute was submitted by special agreement.

Tests cases in which the respondents refused to accept the jurisdiction of the Court, and did not participate in the proceedings.

Pointing to these disappointing results in the ICJ, Romano has argued that ad hoc arbitration, another 'classical' adjudicative institution of international law, has been far more effective as a tool of environmental dispute settlement.[48] However, effectiveness in this context is in the eye of the beholder as it depends on the purpose that dispute settlement mechanisms are thought to serve. There can be no doubt that ad hoc arbitral panels have helped to resolve a number of fractious environmental controversies. The *Bering Sea Fur Seals, Trail Smelter* and *Lake Lanoux* cases all brought about the conclusion to difficult and long-standing environmental disputes. In each of these cases the arbitral tribunals were able to reach a determination acceptable to the parties precisely because the disputants had delegated ample authority to these bodies to address most, if not all, of the highly contentious political issues implicated in each dispute. Therefore, when measured solely against the objective of peaceful dispute settlement these environmental arbitrations appear highly successful. This is no small achievement and the importance of furthering this goal is likely to become even more pronounced as resource scarcity, and other threats to global environmental security, generate increased political tensions. Indeed in recognition of such challenges principle 26 of the Rio Declaration called upon all states 'to resolve all their environmental disputes peacefully, by appropriate means and in accordance with the Charter of the United Nations'. However, as has been emphasised throughout this work, when considering the effectiveness of any process for resolving environmental disputes it is also important to look at other considerations of a community character, beyond the legitimate interest in ensuring that environmental disputes are resolved in a peaceful manner in accordance with the UN Charter. These include the extent to which the adjudicative or other procedure can uphold the relevant rules of international environmental law, and can promote tangible outcomes of sustainable resource management and ecosystem protection.

There have been substantial efforts to address some of the deficiencies manifest in general international law as it applies to environmental issues. In the Articles on Responsibility of States for Internationally

[48] Cesare P. R. Romano, *The Peaceful Settlement of International Environmental Disputes: A Pragmatic Approach* (2000) 324–31.

Wrongful Acts[49] the ILC fulfilled its mandate to contribute to the progressive development of international law by providing for the possibility of an *actio popularis* in relation to environmental obligations of an *erga omnes* character.[50] The ICJ has also established a permanent Chamber for Environmental Matters, while the PCA has adopted impressive rules for arbitration and conciliation of environmental disputes.[51] However, none of this machinery has been used, a fate that is likely also to confront any general international court for the environment, should such an institution be established.[52] Notwithstanding the good intentions of proponents of such a body, in the form that it is most commonly proposed it would be no more than a general institution established in the hope that states may in time come to support it. That appears a remote prospect, and states are likely to stay away from its doors, for the same reasons they have generally avoided turning to the ICJ.

11.3.2 *Distinctive approach of international environmental law*

It is not to institutions of a general character that international environmental law is increasingly looking to perform the indispensable governance tasks of dispute settlement and enforcement. Rather these objectives have been more profitably pursued through dedicated environmental regimes, together with supervisory institutions specifically designed to uphold their provisions. Such treaty-based bodies build upon procedural obligations that have been used in international agreements for many years. Inspection procedures, reporting obligations, and other measures designed to identify situations of non-compliance or breach, are thereby united with treaty bureaucracies including scientific committees, environment committees, and regular meetings of the parties in plenary.

One of the most important institutional innovations in this respect was the emergence of NCPs, the first of which was established in 1992 under the Montreal Protocol. This was followed by the establishment of

[49] Articles on Responsibility of States for Internationally Wrongful Acts, Report of the International Law Commission, 53rd Session, 43–59, UN Doc. A/56/10 (2001).

[50] *Ibid.* art. 48.

[51] 2001 Optional Rules for the Arbitration of Disputes Relating to Natural Resources and/or the Environment; 2002 Optional Rules for Conciliation of Disputes Relating to Natural Resources and/or the Environment.

[52] See ch. 2.

further NCPs for global[53] and regional[54] environmental regimes. NCPs share similar characteristics with some judicial or quasi-judicial procedures in allowing states to raise complaints concerning another state's performance of its environmental obligations, thereby raising the political profile of a particular environmental problem. This may in turn lead to greater compliance. However, whereas adjudication is an essentially confrontational and adversarial process, ultimately concerned to ascertain whether there has been a breach of legal obligation, NCPs are a softer form of dispute settlement more focused upon promoting the overall objectives of the regime, and to this end can involve the provision of practical assistance to defaulting states to ensure that they meet their regime commitments.

In most major and regional environmental regimes the preference is clearly for such new and softer forms of compliance control. Many global regimes for dealing with the most serious and pressing problems of international environmental management, such as stratospheric ozone depletion[55] and global warming,[56] have shunned adjudication in preference for NCPs and other techniques of compliance management. The effect of this has been to isolate large fields of international environmental law from any routine use of judicial procedures for resolving disputes concerning their implementation. Comprehensive amendment of these regimes to provide participants

[53] See e.g., Decision V/16, Report of the Fifth Meeting of the Conference of the Parties to the Basel Convention, UN Doc. UNEP/CH.5/29 (1999); decision 24/CP.7, of the Conference of the Parties on its Seventh Session, Report of the Conference of the Parties on its Seventh Session, UN Doc. FCCC/CP/2001/13/Add.3 (2002); decision BS-I/7, Report of the First Meeting of the Conference of the Parties of the Convention Serving as the Meeting of the Parties to the Protocol, UN Doc. UNEP/CBD/BS/COP-MOP/1/15 (2004).

[54] See e.g. decision 1997/2, Report of the Fifteenth Session of the Executive Body for the Convention on Long-Range Transboundary Air Pollution, UN Doc. ECE/EB.AIR/53 (1998); decision II/4, of the Second Meeting of the Parties of the Convention on Environmental Impact Assessment in a Transboundary Context, Report of the Second Meeting of the Parties, UN Doc. ECE/MP/EIA/4 (2001); decision 1/7, Report of the First Meeting of the Parties to the Convention on Access to Information, Public Participation in Decision-Making and Access to Justice in Environmental Matters, UN Doc. ECE/MP.PP/2/Add.8 (2002); decision VII/4 of the Seventh Meeting of the Parties of the Convention on the Protection of the Alps (2002) (available at www.convenzionedellealpi.org).

[55] See the 1985 Vienna Convention on the Protection of the Ozone Layer and the Montreal Protocol.

[56] See the 1992 United Nations Framework Convention on Climate Change and the 1997 Kyoto Protocol.

with an additional, adjudicative, framework for eliciting compliance is highly unlikely. Nor indeed is the general trend in favour of non-adjudicative mechanisms of compliance control likely to be reversed as new multilateral environmental agreements are concluded. Quite to the contrary, NCPs are under consideration in respect of existing environmental regimes.[57]

At the same time it must also be emphasised that state preference for these alternative mechanisms is not universal and does not in itself disprove the utility of adjudication. Courts and tribunals can perform important enforcement and dispute settlement functions within environmental regimes, as is evident in the operation of the LOS Convention's dispute settlement system. Unlike NCPs, judicial bodies are also more authoritative sites for independent decision-making, and therefore are potentially more useful for assisting in the principled development of the law. However, their utility ultimately depends upon a complex of factors relating among other things to the environmental problem addressed by the environmental regime in question, and the extent to which the court or tribunal is incorporated into the regime as part of its operational structure.

Beyond the LOS Convention, few institutions meet such criteria. However, there is some developing practice which may suggest a resurgence in interest for judicial or quasi-judicial procedures operating in environmental regimes. The citizen submissions procedure of the NAAEC was cited in chapter 4 as an imaginative and exciting example in this respect, which draws upon the successful use of supranational adjudication in other contexts and transposes it to an environmental regime. One of the major innovations of the NAAEC is that the regime melds both supervisory and adjudicatory functions. Among other things this suggests a possible reconciliation between the more confrontational approach to compliance issues preferred in some regimes such as the LOS Convention and the cooperative and supervisory strategy adopted in most other major environmental agreements. Another important feature of the NAAEC citizen submission procedure is its openness to private actor participation. Such demands for greater civil society involvement in international environmental litigation are also

[57] Such as the 1994 United Nations Convention to Combat Desertification in Countries Experiencing Serious Drought and/or Desertification, Particularly in Africa (see UN Doc. ICCD/COP(6)/7 (2003)) and the 1998 Rotterdam Convention on the Prior Informed Consent Procedure for Certain Hazardous Chemicals and Pesticides in International Trade (see UN Doc. UNEP/FAO/PIC/INC.10/20 (2003)).

being made of existing judicial bodies. Despite the dramatic opening of many areas of international environmental diplomacy to public participation, most international courts and tribunals remain bastions of statism, in which individuals and other non-state actors have limited opportunities to have their voices heard. This situation is also under challenge, and the way in which existing bodies respond to persistent demands for greater public accountability and transparency promises to be one of the most important areas for future developments in the way in which international courts and tribunals address international environmental disputes.

11.4 Conclusion

Quick to defend the discipline against the charge that it is not in fact 'law', international lawyers have been transfixed by questions of enforcement and compliance and have increasingly drawn upon international relations scholarship to explain the ways in which international legal regimes may be made more effective. This work has entered into these debates in the specific context of environmental regimes, and by examining the actual and potential function of international courts and tribunals it has sought to explain the circumstances in which international environmental litigation may make a positive contribution to the successful implementation of international environmental law. Perhaps the most important lesson from this analysis is that there can be no general and universal approach to regulating environmental challenges. Individual environmental regimes must be tailored in response to the particular nature of the environmental problem that is being regulated. And as norms and processes must vary according to the topic being addressed, so must those institutional structures that are designed to promote compliance. For these reasons international adjudication cannot be advocated as an institutional panacea; however, nor can its potential contribution in the effective functioning of international environmental law be dismissed.

Bibliography

A-Khavari, Afshin and Rothwell, Donald R., 'The ICJ and the Danube Dam Case: A Missed Opportunity for International Environmental Law?' (1998) 22 *MULR* 507

Abbott, Kenneth W. *et al.*, 'The Concept of Legalization' (2000) 54 *IntOrg* 401

Acevedo, Mariana T., 'The Intersection of Human Rights and Environmental Protection in the European Court of Human Rights' (2000) 8 *NYUELJ* 437

Adams, W. M., *Green Development: Environment and Sustainability in the Third World* (2nd edn 2001)

Adede, Andronico O., 'Management of Environmental Disputes: Avoidance Versus Settlement' in Laing, Winfried (ed.), *Sustainable Development and International Law* (1995) 115

Akehurst, Michael, 'International Liability for Injurious Consequences Arising out of Acts Not Prohibited by International Law' (1985) 16 *NethYBIL* 3

Al-Qahtani, Mutlaq, 'The Role of the International Court of Justice in the Enforcement of its Judicial Decisions' (2002) 15 *LJIL* 781

Alexandrov, Stanimir A., 'Accepting the Compulsory Jurisdiction of the International Court of Justice with Reservations: An Overview of Practice with a Focus on Recent Trends and Cases' (2001) 14 *LJIL* 89

Allott, Philip, 'The International Court and the Voice of Justice' in Lowe, A. Vaughan and Fitzmaurice, Malgosia A. (eds.), *Fifty Years of the International Court of Justice* (1996) 17

The Health of Nations: Society and Law Beyond the State (2002)

Almqvist, Jessica Maria, 'The Accessibility of European Integration Courts from an NGO Perspective' in Treves, Tullio *et al.* (eds.), *Civil Society, International Courts and Compliance Bodies* (2005) 271

Alter, Karen J., 'Do International Courts Enhance Compliance with International Law?' (2003) 25 *RevAPS* 51

'Delegating to International Courts: Self-Binding vs Other-Binding Delegation' (2007) *Law and Contemporary Problems* (forthcoming 2008)

Alvarez, José E., 'Do Liberal States Behave Better? A Critique of Slaughter's Liberal Theory' (2001) 12 *EJIL* 183

'The New Dispute Settlers: (Half) Truths and Consequences' (2003) 38 *TexILJ* 405

International Organizations as Law-Makers (2005) 460

Anderson, Michael R., 'Human Rights Approaches to Environmental Protection: An Overview' in Boyle, Alan E. and Anderson, Michael R. (eds.), *Human Rights Approaches to Environmental Protection* (1996) 8

Anderson, Steinar, 'The Convention for the Conservation of Antarctic Marine Living Resources: Improving Procedures but Lacking Results' in Miles, Edward L. *et al.* (eds.), *Environmental Regime Effectiveness: Confronting Theory with Evidence* (2002) 405

Anton, Donald K. *et al.*, 'Memorandum on the Legality of the Planned Resumption of Nuclear Testing by France' (1995) 12 *EPLJ* 300

Baldock, Julia, 'Determining the Fate of Southern Bluefin Tuna: International Tribunal for the Law of the Sea (1999) New Zealand v. Japan; Australia v. Japan' (2000) 17 *EPLJ* 157

Barboza, Julio, 'The ILC and Environmental Damage' in Wetterstein, Peter (ed.), *Harm to the Environment: The Right to Compensation and the Assessment of Damages* (1997) 76

Barker, Michael, 'Standing to Sue in Public Interest Environmental Litigation: From ACF v. Commonwealth to Tasmanian Conservation Trust v. Minster for Resources' (1996) 13 *EPLJ* 186

Barnhoorn, L. A. N. M. and Wellens, Karel C. (eds.), *Diversity in Secondary Rules and the Unity of International Law* (1995)

Bates, Gerry, *Environmental Law in Australia* (5th edn 2002; 6th edn 2006)

Beaulac, Stéphane, 'The Social Power of Bodin's "Sovereignty" and International Law' (2003) 4 *MJIL* 1

Beder, Sharon, *Environmental Principles and Politics: An Interdisciplinary Approach* (2006)

Bederman, David J., *International Law in Antiquity* (2001)

The Spirit of International Law (2002)

Bekker, Peter H.-F., '*Gabcikovo-Nagymaros Project*' (1998) 92 *AJIL* 273

Bell, Andrew S., 'The Why and Wherefore of Transnational Forum Shopping' (1995) 69 *ALJ* 124

Benzing, Markus, 'Community Interests in the Procedure of International Courts and Tribunals' (2006) 5 *LPICT* 369

Berber, F. J., *Rivers in International Law* (1959)

Bergin, A. and Haward, M., 'Southern Bluefin Tuna Fishery: Recent Developments in International Management' (1994) 18 *Marine Policy* 263

Beyer, Peter *et al.*, 'The Draft Constitution for Europe and the Environment' (2004) 13 *EELR* 218

Bialek, Dean 'Sink or Swim: Measures Under International Law for the Conservation of the Patagonian Toothfish in the Southern Ocean' (2003) 34 *ODIL* 105

Bierman, Frank, 'The Emerging Debate on the Need for a World Environment Organization: A Commentary' (2001) 1 *GEP* 45

Bilder, Richard B., 'The Anglo-Icelandic Fisheries Dispute' (1973) 37 *WisLR* 37
'The Settlement of Disputes in the Field of the International Law of the Environment' (1975) 144 *RDC* 139
'Some Limitations of Adjudication as an International Dispute Settlement Technique' (1982) 23 *VaJIL* 1
Birnie, Patricia W., 'Legal Techniques of Settling Disputes: The "Soft" Settlement Approach' in Butler, William E. (ed.), *Perestroika and International Law* (1990)
'The Role of International Law in Solving Certain Environmental Conflicts' in Carroll, John E. (ed.), *International Environmental Diplomacy: The Management and Resolution of Transfrontier Environmental Problems* (1988) 95
'International Environmental Law: Its Adequacy for Present and Future Needs' in Hurrell, Andrew and Kingsbury, Benedict (eds.), *The International Politics of the Environment: Actors, Interests, and Institutions* (1991) 51
Birnie, Patricia W. and Boyle, Alan E., *International Law and the Environment* (2nd edn 2002)
Blay, Sam, 'New Trends in the Protection of the Antarctic Environment: The 1991 Madrid Protocol' (1992) 86 *AJIL* 377
'The WTO and the Greening of World Trade: A Look at WTO Jurisprudence' (2004) 21 *EPLJ* 27
Bodansky, Daniel, 'Customary (and Not so Customary) International Environmental Law' (1995) 3 *IndJGLS* 105
'The Legitimacy of International Governance: A Coming Challenge for International Environmental Law?' (1999) 93 *AJIL* 596
'What's So Bad about Unilateral Action to Protect the Environment?' (2000) 11 *EJIL* 339
Bodansky, Daniel and Brunnée, Jutta, 'The Role of National Courts in the Field of International Environmental Law' (1998) 7 *RECIEL* 11
Bodansky, Daniel, Brunnée, Jutta, and Hey, Ellen, 'International Environmental Law: Mapping the Field' in Bodansky, Daniel, Brunnée, Jutta, and Hey, Ellen (eds.), *The Oxford Handbook of International Environmental Law* (2007) 1
Bodin, Jean, *On Sovereignty* [1583] (1992)
Boer, Ben, 'The Globalisation of Environmental Law: The Role of the United Nations' (1995) 20 *MJIL* 101
Boer, Ben, Ramsay, Ross, and Rothwell, Donald R., *International Environmental Law in the Asia Pacific* (1998)
Boos-Hersberger, Astrid, 'Transboundary Water Pollution and State Responsibility: The Sandoz Spill' (1997) 4 *AnnSICL* 103
Bosselmann, Klaus, 'Environmental Governance: A New Approach to Territorial Sovereignty' in Goldstein, Robert J. (ed.), *Environmental Ethics and Law* (2004) 293
Botchway, Francis N., 'The International Adjudicatory Process and Trans-Boundary Resource Disputes' [2001] *AILJ* 143

Boyle, Alan E., 'Nuclear Energy and International Law: An Environmental Perspective' (1989) 60 *BYBIL* 257

'State Responsibility and International Liability for Injurious Consequences of Acts Not Prohibited by International Law: A Necessary Distinction?' (1990) 39 *ICLQ* 1

'International Law and the Protection of the Global Atmosphere: Concepts, Categories and Principles' in Churchill, Robin R. and Freestone, David (eds.), *International Law and Global Climate Change* (1991) 7

'Saving the World? Implementation and Enforcement of International Environmental Law Through International Institutions' (1991) 3 *JEL* 229

'The Principle of Co-operation: The Environment' in Lowe, A. Vaughan and Warbrick, Colin (eds.), *The United Nations and the Principles of International Law: Essays in Honour of Michael Akehurst* (1994) 120

'The Role of International Human Rights Law in the Protection of the Environment' in Boyle, Alan E. and Anderson, Michael R. (eds.), *Human Rights Approaches to Environmental Protection* (1996) 43

'Dispute Settlement and the Law of the Sea Convention: Problems of Fragmentation and Jurisdiction' (1997) 46 *ICLQ* 37

'Remedying Harm to International Common Spaces and Resources: Compensation and Other Approaches' in Wetterstein, Peter (ed.), *Harm to the Environment: The Right to Compensation and the Assessment of Damages* (1997) 83

'The *Gabcikovo-Nagymaros* Case: New Law in Old Bottles' (1997) 8 *YIEL* 13

'Codification of International Environmental Law and the International Law Commission: Injurious Consequences Revisited' in Boyle, Alan E. and Freestone, David (eds.), *International Law and Sustainable Development: Past Achievements and Future Challenges* (1999) 61

'Reparation for Environmental Damage in International Law: Some Preliminary Problems' in Bowman, Michael R. and Boyle, Alan E. (eds.), *Environmental Damage in International and Comparative Law: Problems of Definition and Valuation* (2002) 17

'The World Trade Organization and the Marine Environment' in Nordquist, Myron H., Moore, John Norton, and Mahmoudi, Said (eds.), *The Stockholm Declaration and the Law of the Marine Environment* (2003) 109

'Globalising Environmental Liability: The Interplay of National and International Law' (2005) 17 *JEL* 3

Bratspies, Rebecca M. and Miller, Russell A., *Transboundary Harm in International Law: Lessons from the Smelter Arbitration* (2006)

Briese, Robyn, 'Precaution and Cooperation in the World Trade Organization: An Environmental Perspective' (2002) 22 *AustYBIL* 113

Brown, Chester 'Provisional Measures Before the ITLOS: The MOX Plant Case' (2002) 17 *IJMCL* 267

'The Proliferation of International Courts and Tribunals: Finding Your Way Through the Maze' (2002) 3 *MJIL* 453

"Reasonableness" in the Law of the Sea: The Prompt Release of the *Volga*' (2003) 16 *LJIL* 621

A Common Law of International Adjudication (2007)

Brown, E. D., 'The Lessons of the Torrey-Canyon: International Law Aspects' (1968) 21 *Current Legal Problems* 113

Brown Weiss, Edith, *In Fairness to Future Generations: International Law, Common Patrimony and Intergenerational Equity* (1989)

'Our Rights and Obligations to Future Generations for the Environment' (1990) 84 *AJIL* 198

'Opening the Door to the Environment and to Future Generations' in Boisson de Chazournes, Laurence and Sands, Philippe (eds.), *International Law, The International Court of Justice and Nuclear Weapons* (1999) 338

'Understanding Compliance with International Environmental Agreements: The Baker's Dozen Myths' (1999) 32 *URichLR* 1555

'Invoking State Responsibility in the Twenty-first Century' (2002) 96 *AJIL* 798

Brown Weiss, Edith and Jacobson, Harold K. (eds.), *Engaging Countries: Strengthening Compliance with International Environmental Accords* (1998)

Brownlie, Ian, 'A Survey of International Customary Rules of Environmental Protection' (1973) 13 *NatResJ* 179

'A Survey of International Customary Rules of Environmental Protection' in Teclaff, L. A. and Utton, A. E. (eds.), *International Environmental Law* (1974) 1

State Responsibility (Pt I) (1983)

'Arbitration and Judicial Settlement: Comments on a Paper by Judge Lachs' in Soons, Alfred H. A. (ed.), *International Arbitration: Past and Prospects* (1990) 60

'State Responsibility and International Pollution: A Practical Perspective', in Magraw, Daniel Barstow (ed.), *International Law and Pollution* (1991) 120

'Some Questions Concerning the Applicable Law in International Tribunals' in Makarczyk, Jerzy, *Theory of International Law at the Threshold of the 21st Century: Essays in Honour of Krzysztof Skubiszewski* (1996) 761

Principles of Public International Law (6th edn 2003)

Brunnée, Jutta, 'The United States and International Environmental Law: Living with an Elephant' (2004) 15 *EJIL* 617

Brus, Marcel T. A., *Third Party Dispute Settlement in an Interdependent World: Developing a Theoretical Framework* (1995) 191

Buergenthal, T., 'Proliferation of International Courts and Tribunals: Is It Good or Bad?' (2001) 14 *LJIL* 267

Burke, William T., *The New International Law of Fisheries: UNCLOS 1982 and Beyond* (1994)

Burke-White, William W., 'International Legal Pluralism' (2004) 25 *MichJIL* 963

Byers, Michael, 'Abuse of Rights: An Old Principle, A New Age' (2002) 47 *McGillLJ* 389

Caflisch, L., 'Judicial Means for Settling Water Disputes' in International Bureau of the Permanent Court of Arbitration (ed.), *Permanent Court of Arbitration Peace Palace Papers: Resolution of International Water Disputes* (2003) 235

Caldwell, Lynton Keith, 'Concepts in Development of International Environmental Policies' (1973) 13 *NatResJ* 190

International Environmental Policy: From the Twentieth to the Twenty-First Century (3rd edn 1996)

Cameron, James, 'Compliance, Citizens and NGOs' in Cameron, James, Werksman, Jacob, and Roderick, Peter (eds.), *Improving Compliance with International Environmental Law* (1996) 29

Cameron, James and Mackenzie, Ruth, 'Access to Environmental Justice and Procedural Rights in International Institutions' in Boyle, Alan E. and Anderson, Michael R. (eds.), *Human Rights Approaches to Environmental Protection* (1996) 129

Cardwell, Paul James, and French, Duncan, 'Who Decides? The ECJ's Judgment on Jurisdiction in the *MOX Plant* Dispute' (2007) 19 *JEL* 121

Carnwath, Lord Justice, 'Judicial Protection of the Environment: At Home and Abroad' (2004) 16 *JEL* 315

Caron, David D., 'War and International Adjudication: Reflections on the 1899 Peace Conference' (2000) 94 *AJIL* 4

Carroll, John E., 'The Acid Rain Issue in Canadian-American Relations: A Commentary' in Carroll, John E. (ed.), *International Environmental Diplomacy: The Management and Resolution of Transfrontier Environmental Problems* (1988) 141

Cass, Deborah, 'The "Constitutionalization" of International Trade Law: Judicial Norm-Generation as the Engine of Constitutional Development in International Trade' (2001) 12 *EJIL* 39

Charlesworth, Hilary and Chinkin, Christine M., *The Boundaries of International Law: A Feminist Analysis* (2000)

Charney, Jonathan I., 'Compromissory Clauses and the Jurisdiction of the International Court of Justice' (1987) 81 *AJIL* 855

'The Marine Environment and the 1982 United Nations Convention on the Law of the Sea' (1994) 28 *International Lawyer* 879

'The Implications of Expanding Dispute Settlement Systems: The 1982 Convention on the Law of the Sea' (1996) 90 *AJIL* 69

'International Law and Multiple International Tribunals' (1998) 271 *RDC* 115

'The Impact on the International Legal System of the Growth of International Courts and Tribunals' (1999) 31 *NYUJILP* 697

Charnovitch, Steve, 'Participation of Nongovernmental Organizations in the World Trade Organization' (1996) 17 *UPaJIEconL* 331

'The Supervision of Health and Biosafety Regulation by World Trade Rules' (1999–2000) 13 *TulELJ* 271

'A World Environment Organization' (2000) 27 *ColumJEL* 323

Charnovitch, Steve, 'WTO Dispute Settlement as a Model for International Governance' in Kiss, Alexandre, Shelton, Dinah, and Ishibashi, Kanami (eds.), *Economic Globalization and Compliance with International Environmental Agreements* (2003) 245

'The WTO's Environmental Progress' (2007) 10 *JIEconL* 685

Chauhan, B. R., *Settlement of International Water Law Disputes in International Drainage Basins* (1981)

Chayes, Abram and Chayes, Antonia Handler, *The New Sovereignty: Compliance with International Regulatory Agreements* (1995)

Chayes, Abram, Chayes, Antonia Handler, and Mitchell, Ronald B., 'Managing Compliance: A Comparative Perspective' in Brown Weiss, Edith and Jacobson, Harold K. (eds.), *Engaging Countries: Strengthening Compliance with International Environmental Accords* (1998) 39

Chayes, Antonia Handler, Chayes, Abram and Mitchell, Ronald B., 'Active Compliance Management in Environmental Treaties' in Lang, Winfried (ed.), *Sustainable Development and International Law* (1995) 75

Chinkin, Christine M., *Third Parties in International Law* (1993)

'The Peaceful Settlement of Disputes: New Grounds for Optimism?' in Macdonald, Ronald St John (ed.), *Essays in Honour of Wang Tieya* (1993) 165

'Dispute Resolution and the Law of the Sea: Regional Problems and Prospects' in Crawford, James and Rothwell, Donald R. (eds.) *The Law of the Sea in the Asian Pacific Region: Developments and Prospects* (1995) 237

'Alternative Dispute Resolution under International Law' in Evans, Malcolm D. (ed.), *Remedies in International Law: The Institutional Dilemma* (1998) 123

Chinkin, Christine M. and Mackenzie, Ruth, 'Intergovernmental Organizations as "Friends of the Court"' in Boisson de Chazournes, Laurence, Romano, Cesare P. R., and Mackenzie, Ruth (eds.), *International Organizations and International Dispute Settlement: Trends and Prospects* (2002) 135

Chinkin, Christine M. and Sadurska, Romana, 'The Anatomy of International Dispute Resolution' (1991) 7 *OhioStJDR* 39

Chircop, A., VanderZwaag, D., and Mushkat, P., 'The Gulf of Maine Agreement and Action Plan: A Novel but Nascent Approach to Transboundary Marine Environmental Protection' (1995) 19 *Marine Policy* 317

Churchill, Robin R., 'The Fisheries Jurisdiction Cases: The Contribution of the International Court of Justice to the Debate on Coastal States' Fishing Rights' (1975) 24 *ICLQ* 82

'Environmental Rights in Existing Human Rights Treaties' in Boyle, Alan E. and Anderson, Michael R. (eds.), *Human Rights Approaches to Environmental Protection* (1996) 89

'Fisheries Jurisdiction Case (Spain v. Canada)' (1999) 12 *LJIL* 597

Churchill, Robin R. and Lowe, A. Vaughan, *The Law of the Sea* (3rd edn 1999)

'The International Tribunal for the Law of the Sea: Survey for 2000' (2003) 18 *IJMCL* 447

Churchill, Robin, and Scott, Joanne, 'The MOX Plant Litigation: The First Half-life' (2004) 53 *ICLQ* 643

Collier, John and Lowe, A. Vaughan, *The Settlement of Disputes in International Law: Institutions and Procedures* (1999)

Collins, L., 'Provisional and Protective Measures in International Litigation' (1992) 234 *RDC* 9

Colson, D. A. and Hoyle, P., 'Satisfying the Procedural Prerequisites to the Compulsory Dispute Settlement Mechanisms of the 1982 Law of the Sea Convention: Did the Southern Bluefin Tuna Tribunal Get it Right?' (2003) 34 *ODIL* 59

Conforti, Benedetto, 'Do States Really Accept Responsibility for Environmental Damage?' in Francioni, Francesco and Scovazzi, Tullio (eds.), *International Responsibility for Environmental Harm* (1991) 179

Contini, Paolo and Sand, Peter H., 'Methods to Expedite Environment Protection: International Ecostandards' (1972) 66 *AJIL* 37

Cooney, Rosie, *The Precautionary Principle in Biodiversity Conservation and Natural Resource Management* (2004)

Coyle, Sean and Morrow, Karen, *The Philosophical Foundations of Environmental Law: Property, Rights and Nature* (2003)

Craik, A. Neil, 'Recalcitrant Reality and Chosen Ideals: The Public Function of Dispute Settlement in International Environmental Law' (1998) 10 *GeoIELR* 551

Craven, Matthew, 'New Zealand's Request for an Examination of the Situation in Accordance with Paragraph 63 of the Court's Judgment of 20 December 1974 in the Nuclear Tests Case' (1996) 45 *ICLQ* 725

'Unity, Diversity and the Fragmentation of International Law' (2003) 14 *FinnYBIL* 3

Crawford, James, *The International Law Commission's Articles on State Responsibility* (2002)

International Law as an Open System (2002)

Davidson, James, 'Resolution of Transboundary Pollution Disputes: The Great Lakes Experience' (1998) 3 *APJEL* 233

Davies, Peter G. G., *European Union Environmental Law* (2004)

de Castro, Paulo Canelas 'The Judgment in the *Case Concerning the Gabcikovo-Nagymaros Project:* Positive Signs for the Evolution of International Water Law' (1997) 8 *YIEL* 21

De La Fayette, Louise, 'The Fisheries Jurisdiction Case (Spain v. Canada), Judgment on Jurisdiction of 4 December 1998' (1999) 48 *ICLQ* 664

de Sadeleer, Nicolas, *Environmental Principles: From Political Slogans to Legal Rules* (Susan Leubusher trans. 2002)

DeGarno, Denise K., *International Environmental Treaties and State Behavior: Factors Influencing Cooperation* (2005)

Dehan, Audra E., 'An International Environmental Court: Should There Be One?' (1992) 3 *TouroJTL* 31

Dinwoodie, D. H., 'The Politics of International Pollution Control: The Trail Smelter Case' (1971–2) 27 *International Journal* 219

Dobos, Daniel, 'The Necessity of Precaution: The Future of Ecological Necessity and the Precautionary Principle' (2002) 13 *FordhamELJ* 375

Dommen, Caroline, 'Claiming Environmental Rights: Some Possibilities Offered by the United Nations' Human Rights Mechanisms' (1998) 11 *GeoIELR* 1

Donnelly, Jack, *Realism and International Relations* (2000)

Downs, George W., Danish, Jyle W., and Barsoom, Peter N., 'The Transformational Model of International Regime Design: Triumph of Hope or Experience?' (2000) 38 *ColumJTL* 465

Dugard, John, 'The Nuclear Tests Cases and the South West Africa Cases: Some Realism About the International Judicial Decision' (1975–6) 16 *VaJIL* 463

Dunoff, Jeffrey L., 'Institutional Misfits: The GATT, the ICJ and Trade-Environment Disputes' (1994) 15 *MichJIL* 1043

'The Misguided Debate over NGO Participation at the WTO' (1998) *JIEconL* 433

Dupuy, Pierre-Marie, 'Le concept de société civil internationale, identification et genèse' in Gherari, H., and Szurek, S. (eds.), *L'émergence de la société civile internationale vers la privatisation du droit international?* (2003) 5

Dworkin, Ronald, *Taking Rights Seriously* (3rd edn 1981)

Eckersley, Robyn, *Environmentalism and Political Theory: Toward an Ecocentric Approach* (1992)

'The Big Chill: The WTO and Multilateral Environmental Agreements' (2004) 4 *GEP* 24

Ehrmann, Markus, 'Procedures of Compliance Control in International Environmental Treaties' (2002) 13 *ColoJELP* 377

Eiriksson, Gudmundur, *The International Tribunal for the Law of the Sea* (2000)

Elkind, Jerome B., 'French Nuclear Testing and Article 41: Another Blow to the Authority of the Court?' (1974) 8 *VandJTL* 39

Ellis, Jaye, 'Overexploitation of a Valuable Resource? New Literature on the Precautionary Principle' (2006) 17 *EJIL* 445

Esty, Daniel C., *Greening the GATT: Trade, Environment and the Future* (1994)

'The World Trade Organization's Legitimacy Crisis' (2002) 1 *WTR* 7

Fabra, Adriana, 'The LOSC and the Implementation of the Precautionary Principle' (1999) 10 *YIEL* 15

Fitzmaurice, Malgosia A., 'International Environmental Law as a Special Field' in Barnhoorn, L. A. N. M. and Wellens, K. C. (eds.), *Diversity in Secondary Rules and the Unity of International Law* (1995) 181

'Environmental Protection and the International Court of Justice' in Lowe, A. Vaughan and Fitzmaurice, Malgosia A. (eds.), *Fifty Years of the International Court of Justice: Essays in Honour of Sir Robert Jennings* (1996) 293

'Equipping the ICJ to Deal with Environmental Law' in Peck, Connie and Lee, Roy S. (eds.), *Increasing the Effectiveness of the International Court of Justice* (1997) 398

'The Optional Clause System and the Law of Treaties: Issues of Interpretation in Recent Jurisprudence of the International Court of Justice' (1999) 20 *AustYBIL* 127
'International Protection of the Environment' (2001) 293 *RDC* 9
'Dispute Concerning Access to Information Under Article 9 of the OSPAR Convention (*Ireland v. United Kingdom*)' (2003) 18 *IJMCL* 541
'Public Participation in the North American Agreement on Environmental Cooperation' (2003) 52 *ICLQ* 333
'The Kyoto Protocol Compliance Regime and Treaty Law' (2004) 8 *SingYBIL* 23
Fitzmaurice, Malgosia A. and Redgwell, Catherine, 'Environmental Non-Compliance Procedures and International Law' (2000) 31 *NethYBIL* 35
Fleming, John G., *The Law of Torts* (9th edn 1998)
Footer, Mary and Zia-Zarifi, Salman, 'European Communities – Measures Affecting Asbestos and Asbestos-Containing Products: The World Trade Organization on Trial for its Handling of Occupational Health and Safety Issues' (2002) 3 *MJIL* 120
Forster, Malcolm, 'The *Mox Plant* Case: Provisional Measures in the International Tribunal for the Law of the Sea' (2003) 16 *LJIL* 611
Francioni, Francesco, 'Dispute Avoidance in International Environmental Law' in Kiss, Alexandre, Shelton, Dinah, and Ishibashi, Kanami (eds.), *Economic Globalization and Compliance with International Environmental Agreements* (2003) 229
Franck, Thomas M., 'Word Made Law: The Decision of the ICJ in the Nuclear Tests Cases' (1975) 69 *AJIL* 612
The Power of Legitimacy Among Nations (1990)
'The Emerging Right to Democratic Governance' (1992) 86 *AJIL* 46
Fairness in International Law and Institutions (1995)
'Fairness and the General Assembly Advisory Opinion' in Boisson de Chazournes, Laurence and Sands, Philippe (eds.), *International Law, The International Court of Justice and Nuclear Weapons* (1999) 511
Frankel, Kathie D., 'The Nuclear Tests Cases' (1974) 7 *NYUJILP* 163
Freedman, Joseph, 'Implications of the NAFTA Investment Chapter for Environmental Regulation' in Kiss, Alexandre, Shelton, Dinah, and Ishibashi, Kanami (eds.), *Economic Globalization and Compliance with International Environmental Agreements* (2003) 89
Freestone, David, 'The Precautionary Principle' in Churchill, Robin R. and Freestone, David (eds.), *International Law and Global Climate Change* (1991) 21
'Caution or Precaution: "A Rose By Any Other Name…?"' (1999) 10 *YIEL* 15
French, Duncan, *International Law and Policy on Sustainable Development* (2005)
Fuller, Lon L., 'The Forms and Limits of Adjudication' (1978) 92 *HarvLR* 353
Gautier, Philippe, 'The International Tribunal for the Law of the Sea: Activities in 2002' (2003) 2 *ChineseJIL* 341
'NGOs and Law of the Sea Disputes' in Treves, Tullio *et al.* (eds.), *Civil Society, International Courts and Compliance Bodies* (2005) 233

Gehring, Thomas, 'International Environmental Regimes: Dynamic Sectoral Legal Systems' (1990) 1 *YIEL* 35

Gillespie, Alexander, *International Environmental Law Policy and Ethics* (1997)

The Illusion of Progress: Unsustainable Development in International Law and Policy (2001)

'Forum Shopping in International Environmental Law: The IWC, CITES and the Management of Cetaceans' (2002) 33 *ODIL* 17

Ginsburg, Tom, 'Bounded Discretion in International Judicial Lawmaking' (2005) 45 *VaJIL* 631

Giraud, Catherine, 'French Nuclear Testing in the Pacific and the 1995 International Court of Justice Decision' (1996) 1 *APJEL* 125

Giustini, A., 'Compulsory Adjudication in International Law: The Past, The Present, and Prospects for the Future' (1986) 9 *FordhamILJ* 213

Goh, Gavin and Witbreuk, Trudy, 'An Introduction to the WTO Dispute Settlement System' (2001) 30 *WALR* 51

Golder Associates Ltd, *Analysis of the Effects of Smelter Emissions on Vegetation within the Trail Regional Area* (2004) (available at www.teckcominco.com/articles/tr-ecorisk/techreports/2004/2004-05-veganalysis.pdf)

Goldie, L. F. E., 'Liability for Damage and the Progressive Development of International Law' (1965) 14 *ICLQ* 1189

Gray, Christine, *Judicial Remedies in International Law* (1987)

Gray, Christine and Kingsbury, Benedict, 'Inter-State Arbitration since 1945: Overview and Evaluation' in Janis, M. W. (ed.), *International Courts for the Twenty-First Century* (1992) 55

Grewe, E., *The Epochs of International Law* (Michael Byers trans. 2000)

Grieves, Forest L., *Supranationalism and International Adjudication* (1969)

Gross, Leo (ed.), *The Future of the International Court of Justice*, vol. I (1976)

Grotius, Hugo, *The Freedom of the Seas: or the Right Which Belongs to the Dutch to Take Part in the East Indian Trade* [1609] (Ralph van Deman Magoffin trans. 1916)

Guillaume, Gilbert, 'The Future of International Judicial Institutions' (1995) 44 *ICLQ* 848

'Address to the General Assembly of the United Nations' (speech delivered to the General Assembly of the United Nations, 26 October 2000) (available www.icj-cij.org/icjwww/ipresscom/SPEECHES/SpeechPresident_Guillaume_GA55_20001026.htm)

'Address to the Sixth Committee of the General Assembly of the United Nations' (speech delivered to the Sixth Committee of the General Assembly of the United Nations, 27 October 2000) (available at www.icj-cij.org/icjwww/ipresscom/SPEECHES/SpeechPresident_Guillaume_SixthCommittee_20001027.htm)

Guruswamy, Lakshman D., 'Environment and Trade: Competing Paradigms in International Law' in Anghie, Antony and Sturgess, Garry (eds.), *Legal Visions of the 21st Century: Essays in Honour of Judge Christopher Weeramantry* (1998) 574

'Should UNCLOS or GATT/WTO Decide Trade and Environment Disputes?' (1998) 7 *MinnJGT* 287

Haas, Peter M., 'Banning Chlorofluorocarbons: Epistemic Community Efforts to Protect Stratospheric Ozone' (1992) 46 *IntOrg* 187

'Introduction: Epistemic Communities and International Policy Coordination' (1992) 46 *IntOrg* 1

Haas, Peter M., Keohane, Robert O., and Levy, Marc A. (eds.), *Institutions for Earth: Sources of Effective International Environmental Protection* (1993)

Hafner, Gerhard, 'Should One Fear the Proliferation of Mechanisms for the Peaceful Settlement of Disputes?' in Caflisch, L. (ed.), *The Settlement of Disputes Between States: Universal and European Perspectives* (1998) 25

'Pros and Cons Ensuing from Fragmentation of International Law' (2004) 25 *MichJIL* 849

Hahn, R. W. and Richards, K. R., 'The Internationalization of Environmental Regulation' (1989) 30 *HarvILJ* 421

Hallum, Victoria, 'International Tribunal for the Law of the Sea: The MOX Nuclear Plant Case' (2002) 11 *RECIEL* 372

Hambro, E., 'The Reasons Behind the Decisions of the International Court of Justice' (1954) 7 *Current Legal Problems* 212

Handl, Günther, 'Balancing of Interests and International Liability for the Pollution of International Watercourses: Customary Principles of Law Revisited' (1975) 3 *CanYBIL* 156

'Territorial Sovereignty and the Problem of Transnational Pollution' (1975) 69 *AJIL* 50

'Compliance Control Mechanisms and International Environmental Obligations' (1997) 5 *TulJICL* 29

Hannam, Ian and Boer, Ben, *Drafting Legislation for Sustainable Soils: A Guide* (2004)

Hardcastle, Rohan, 'Environmental Trade Measures Under Siege: The WTO US Shrimp Case' (1998) 3 *APJEL* 157

Harris, Mark, 'Beyond Doha: Clarifying the Role of the WTO in Determining Trade-Environment Disputes' (2003) 21 *Law in Context* 307

Hart, H. L. A., *The Concept of Law* (2nd edn 1994)

Helfer, Laurence R., 'Forum Shopping for Human Rights' (1999) 148 *UPaLR* 285

Helfer, Laurence R. and Slaughter, Anne-Marie, 'Toward a Theory of Effective Supranational Adjudication' (1997) 107 *YaleLJ* 273

'Why States Create International Tribunals: A Response to Professors Posner and Yoo' (2005) 93 *CalLR* 901

Henkin, L., *How Nations Behave* (1961)

Herr, Richard, 'The International Regulation of Patagonian Toothfish: CCAMLR and High Seas Fisheries Management' in Stokke, Olav Schram (ed.), *Governing High Seas Fisheries: The Interplay of Global and Regional Regimes* (2001) 303

Hewison, Grant J., 'The Precautionary Approach to Fisheries Management: An Environmental Perspective' (1996) 11 *IJMCL* 301

Hey, Ellen, *The Regime for the Exploitation of Transboundary Marine Fisheries Resources* (1989)
'The European Community's Courts and International Environmental Agreements' (1998) 7 *RECIEL* 4
'The Fisheries Provisions of the LOS Convention' in Hey, Ellen (ed.), *Developments in International Fisheries Law* (1999) 13
Reflections on an International Environmental Court (2000)
Hicks, Bethany Lukitsch, 'Treaty Congestion in International Environmental Law: The Need for Greater International Coordination' (1999) 32 *URichLR* 1643
Higgins, Rosalyn, 'Policy Considerations and the International Judicial Process' (1968) 17 *ICLQ* 58
Problems and Process: International Law and How We Use It (1994)
'Natural Resources in the Case Law of the International Court' in Boyle, Alan E. and Freestone, David (eds.), *International Law and Sustainable Development: Past Achievements and Future Challenges* (1999) 87
'Respecting the Sovereignty of States and Running a Tight Courtroom' (2001) 50 *ICLQ* 121
Highes, Layla, 'Limiting the Jurisdiction of Dispute Settlement Panels: The WTO Appellate Body Beef Hormone Decision' (1998) 10 *GeoIELR* 915
Hinde, Susan M., 'The International Environmental Court: Its Broad Jurisdiction as a Possible Flaw' (2003) 32 *HosfraLR* 727
Hollis, D. B., 'Private Actors in Public International Law: *Amicus Curiae* and the Case for the Retention of State Sovereignty' (2002) 25 *BCICLR* 235
Horbach, Nathalie L. J. T. and Bekker, Pieter H. F., 'State Responsibility for Injurious Transboundary Activity in Retrospect' (2003) 50 *NILR* 327
Horn, Laura, 'The Role of the Mediator in International Environmental Law' (1993) 4 *AustDRJ* 16
'Emerging Trends in Sustainable Development: The International Initiatives' [2002] *AILJ* 24
Horowitz, Deborah, 'The Catch of Poseidon's Trident: The Fate of High Seas Fisheries in the *Southern Bluefin Tuna* Case' (2001) 25 *MULR* 810
Howse, Robert, 'The Appellate Body Rulings in the Shrimp/Turtle Case: A New Legal Baseline for the Trade and Environment Debate' (2002) 27 *ColumJEL* 491
Hudson, Manley O., *By Pacific Means: The Implementation of Article Two of the Pact of Paris* (1935)
Hyvarinen, Joy, 'The 2005 World Summit: UN Reform, Security, Environment and Development' (2006) 15 *RECIEL* 1
Independent World Commission on the Oceans, *The Ocean Our Future* (1998)
International Bureau of the Permanent Court of Arbitration (ed.), *International Investments and Protection of the Environment* (2001)
International Law Association, 'Searching for the Contours of International Law in the Field of Sustainable Development' in Ku, C. and Diehl, P. F. (eds.), *International Law: Classic and Contemporary Readings* (2003) 397

International Law Association, *Report of the 52nd Conference* (1966)
Jackson, J. H., *The Jurisprudence of GATT and the WTO* (2000)
Jahnke, Marlene, 'UNCED: Rio Conference on Environment and Development' (1992) 22 *EPL* 204
Jansky, Libor, Murakami, Masahiro, and Pachova, Nevelina I., *The Danube: Environmental Monitoring of an International River* (2004)
Jennings, Robert Y., 'Need for an Environmental Court?' (1992) 20 *EPL* 312
'The Judicial Enforcement of International Obligations' (1987) 47 *Zeitschrift für ausländisches öffentliches Recht und Völkerrecht* 3
'The Judiciary, International and National, and the Development of International Law' (1996) 45 *ICLQ* 1
'The Role of the International Court of Justice' (1997) 68 *BYBIL* 58
Jessup, Philip C., 'Do New Problems Need New Courts?' (1971) 65 *ProcASIL* 261
Johnson, Lise and Tuerk, Elisabeth, 'CIEL's Experience in WTO Dispute Settlement: Challenges and Complexities from a Practical Point of View' in Treves, Tullio *et al.* (eds.), *Civil Society, International Courts and Compliance Bodies* (2005) 243
Johnston, Douglas M., *The International Law of Fisheries: A Framework for Policy-Oriented Inquiries* (1985)
'Fishery Diplomacy and Science and the Judicial Function' (1999) 10 *YIEL* 33
Johnston, Douglas, M., and VanderZwaag, David, L., 'The Ocean and International Environmental Law: Swimming, Sinking, and Treading Water at the Millennium' (2000) 43 *OCM* 141
Joint Group of Experts on the Scientific Aspects of Marine Environmental Protection, *A Sea of Troubles:* Report no. 70 (2001) 12
Joyner, Christopher C., 'On the Borderline? Canadian Activism in the Grand Banks' in Stokke, Olav Schram (ed.), *Governing High Seas Fisheries: The Interplay of Global and Regional Regimes* (2001) 207
Joyner, Christopher C. and von Gustedt, Alejandro Alvarez, 'The Turbot War of 1995: Lessons for the Law of the Sea' (1996) 11 *IJMCL* 425
Juda, Lawrence, *International Law and Ocean Use Management: The Evolution of Ocean Governance* (1996)
Juenger, Friedrich K., 'What's Wrong with Forum Shopping?' (1994) 16 *SLR* 5
Justinian, *Institutiones* (trans. Peter Birks and Grant McLeod, 1987)
Kalas, Peggy Rogers, 'International Environmental Dispute Resolution and the Need for Access by Non-State Entities' (2001) 12 *ColoJIELP* 191
Kalas, Peggy Rogers and Herwig, Alexia, 'Dispute Resolution Under the Kyoto Protocol' (2000) 27 *ELQ* 53
Kanie, Norichika and Haas, Peter M., (eds.), *Emerging Forces in Environmental Governance* (2004)
Keohane, Robert O., Haas, Peter M., and Levy, Marc A., 'The Effectiveness of International Environmental Institutions' in Keohane, Robert O., Haas, Peter M., and Levy, Marc A. (eds.), *Institutions for the Earth: Sources of Effective International Environmental Protection* (1993) 3

Keohane, Robert O., Moravcsik, Andrew, and Slaughter, Anne-Marie, 'Legalized Dispute Resolution: Interstate and Transnational' (2000) 54 *IntOrg* 457

Kindt, J. W., 'Dispute Settlement in International Environmental Issues: The Model Provided by the 1982 Convention on the Law of the Sea' (1989) 22 *VandJTL* 1097

Kingsbury, Benedict, 'The Concept of Compliance as a Function of Competing Conceptions of International Law' (1997–8) 19 *MichJIL* 345

Kiss, Alexandre, 'Le règlement des différends dans les conventions multilaterals relatives à la protection de l'environnement' in Dupuy, R.J. (ed.), *The Settlement of Disputes on the New Natural Resources* (1983) 119

'Environmental Information and Public Participation in Decision-Making' in Kiss, Alexandre, Shelton, Dinah, and Ishibashi, Kanami (eds.), *Economic Globalization and Compliance with International Environmental Agreements* (2003) 193

Kiss, Alexandre and Shelton, Dinah, *International Environmental Law* (2000)

Klabbers, Jan, 'Compliance Procedures' in Bodansky, Daniel, Brunneé, Jutta, and Hey, Ellen (eds.), *The Oxford Handbook of International Environmental Law* (2007) 995

Klein, Natalie, *Dispute Settlement in the UN Convention on the Law of the Sea* (2005)

Knecht, G. Bruce, *Hooked: A True Story of Pirates, Poaching and the Perfect Fish* (2006)

Knox, John H., 'A New Approach to Compliance with International Environmental Law: The Submissions Procedure of the NAFTA Environmental Commission' (2001) 28 *ELQ* 1

'The Myth and Reality of Transboundary Environmental Impact Assessment' (2002) 96 *AJIL* 291

'The Judicial Resolution of Conflicts Between Trade and the Environment' (2004) 28 *HarvELR* 1

'The Flawed Trail Smelter Procedure: The Wrong Tribunal, the Wrong Parties, and the Wrong Law' in Bratspies, Rebecca and Miller, Russell (eds.), *Transboundary Harms in International Law: Lessons from the Trail Smelter Arbitration* (2006) 66

Knox, John H., and Markell, David L., 'The Innovative North American Commission for Environmental Cooperation' in Markell, David L. and Knox, John H. (eds.), *Greening NAFTA: The North American Commission for Environmental Cooperation* (2003) 1

Koester, Veit, 'The Compliance Committee of the Aarhus Convention: An Overview of Procedures and Jurisprudence' (2007) 37 *EPL* 83

Koremenos, Barbara, 'If Only Half of International Agreements Have Dispute Resolution Provisions, Which Half Needs Explaining?' (2007) 36 *JLS* 189

Kós, J. S., 'Interim Relief in the International Court: New Zealand and the Nuclear Tests Cases' (1984) 14 *VUWLR* 357

Koskenniemi, Martti, 'The Future of Statehood' (1991) 32 *HarvILJ* 397

'Peaceful Settlement of Environmental Disputes' (1991) 60 *NordicJIL* 73

'Breach of Treaty or Non-Compliance? Reflections on the Enforcement of the Montreal Protocol' (1992) 3 *YIEL* 123

'Comment on the Paper by Antonia Handler Chayes, Abram Chayes, and Ronald B. Mitchell' in Lang, Winfried (ed.), *Sustainable Development and International Law* (1995) 9

'New Institutions and Procedures for Implementation Control and Reaction' in Werksman, Jacob, (ed.), *Greening International Institutions* (1996) 236

'International Law in a Post-Realist Era' (1997) 16 *AustYBIL* 1

'The Silence of Law/The Voice of Justice' in Boisson de Chazournes, Laurence and Sands, Philippe (eds.), *International Law, The International Court of Justice and Nuclear Weapons* (1999) 488

From Apology to Utopia: The Structure of International Legal Argument (reissue, 2005)

'International Legislation Today: Limits and Possibilities' (2005) 23 *WisILJ* 61

Koskenniemi, Martti and Päivi, Leino, 'Fragmentation of International Law? Postmodern Anxieties' (2002) 15 *LJIL* 553

Krämer, Ludwig, 'The Implementation of Environmental Laws by the European Economic Communities' (1991) 34 *GerYBIL* 1

'Public Interest Litigation in Environmental Matters Before European Courts' (1996) 8 *JEL* 1

Kravchenko, Svitlana, 'The Aarhus Convention and Innovations in Compliance with MEAs' (2007) 18 *ColoJIELP* 1

Kuhn, Thomas, *The Structure of Scientific Revolutions* (1962)

Kuokkanen, Tuomas, *International Law and the Environment: Variations on a Theme* (2002)

Kwiatkowska, Barbara, '*New Zealand v. France Nuclear Tests Cases:* The "Little" Big Order of the International Court of Justice' [1995] *FinnYBIL* 1

'The Southern Bluefin Tuna (New Zealand v. Japan; Australian v. Japan) Cases' (2000) 15 *IJMCL* 1

'The Australia and New Zealand Southern Bluefin Tuna (Jurisdiction and Admissibility) Award of the First Law of the Sea Convention Annex VII Arbitral Tribunal' (2001) 16 *IJMCL* 239

'Southern Bluefin Tuna' (2001) 95 *AJIL* 162

'The *Ireland v. United Kingdom (MOX Plant)* Case: Applying the Doctrine of Treaty Parallelism' (2003) 18 *IJMCL* 1

'The Southern Bluefin Tuna Arbitral Tribunal Did Get It Right: A Commentary and Reply to the Article by David A. Colson and Dr Peggy Hoyle' (2003) 34 *ODIL* 369

Lagoni, R., Heinrich-Noll, H., and Vogel, H., 'The International Tribunal for the Law of the Sea: Establishment and "Prompt Release" Procedures' (1996) 11 *IJMCL* 137

Lammers, Johan G., *Pollution of International Watercourses: A Search for Substantive Rules and Principles of Law* (1984)

Lammers, Johan G., 'The Present State of Research Carried out by the English-Speaking Section of the Centre for Studies and Research' in Académie de Droit International de la Haye, *La Pollution Transfrontière* (1985) 90

'The Gabcikovo-Nagymaros Case Seen in Particular from the Perspective of the Law of International Watercourses and the Protection of the Environment' (1998) 11 *LJIL* 287

Lauterpacht, Elihu, *Aspects of the Administration of International Justice* (1991).

Lavranos, Nikolas, 'The *MOX Plant* Judgment of the ECJ: How Exclusive is the Jurisdiction of the ECJ?' (2006) 15 *EELR* 291

Laylin, J. G. and Biancho, R. L., 'The Role of Adjudication in International River Disputes' (1959) 53 *AJIL* 30

Lefeber, René, *Transboundary Environmental Interference and the Origin of State Liability* (1996)

Leigh, Kathy, 'Liability for Damage to the Global Commons' (1992) 14 *AustYBIL* 129

Leither, Kara and Lester, Simon, 'WTO Dispute Settlement from 1955 to 2006: A Statistical Analysis' (2007) 10 *JIEL* 165

List, Martin and Rittberger, Volker, 'Regime Theory and International Environmental Management' in Hurrell, Andrew and Kingsbury, Benedict (eds.), *The International Politics of the Environment* (1991) 85

Louka, Elli, 'Cutting the Gordian Knot: Why International Environmental Law is Not Only About the Protection of the Environment' (1996) 10 *TempICLJ* 80

International Environmental Law: Fairness, Effectiveness and World Order (2006)

Lowe, A. Vaughan, 'Overlapping Jurisdiction in International Tribunals' (1999) 20 *AustYBIL* 191

'Sustainable Development and Unsustainable Arguments' in Boyle, Alan E. and Freestone, David (eds.), *International Law and Sustainable Development: Past Achievements and Future Challenges* (1999) 19

'The Politics of Law-Making: Are the Method and Character of Norm-Creation Changing?' in Byers, Michael (ed.), *The Role of Law in International Politics* (2000) 19

'Advocating Judicial Activism: The ITLOS Opinions of Judge Ivan Shearer' (2005) 24 *AustYBIL* 145

Lowenfeld, Andreas F., *International Economic Law* (2002)

Lyster, Simon, *International Wildlife Law* (1985)

Macdonald, John M., 'Appreciating the Precautionary Principle as an Ethical Evolution in Ocean Management' (1995) 26 *ODIL* 255

MacKay, Don, 'Nuclear Testing: New Zealand and France in the International Court of Justice' (1995–6) 19 *FordhamILJ* 1857

Mackenzie, Ruth, 'The *Amicus Curiae* in International Courts: Towards Common Procedural Approaches?' in Treves, Tullio *et al.* (eds.), *Civil Society, International Courts and Compliance Bodies* (2005) 29

Mackenzie, Ruth and Sands, Philippe, 'Prospects for International Environmental Law' in Bail, Christoph, Falkner, Robert and

Marquard, Helen (eds.), *The Cartagena Protocol on Biosafety: Reconciling Trade in Biotechnology wuth Environment and Development?* (2002) 458.
MacMillan, Fiona, *WTO and the Environment* (2001)
Maine, Henry Sumner, *International Law: A Series of Lectures Delivered Before the University of Cambridge 1887* (1888)
Malone, Linda A. and Pasternack, Scott, *Defending the Environment: Civil Society Strategies to Enforce International Environmental Law* (2004)
Mann, Howard, 'Opening the Doors, At Least a Little: Comment on the Amicus Decision in Methanex v United States' (2002) 10 *RECIEL* 241
Mansfield, Bill, 'Letter to the Editor: The Southern Bluefin Tuna Arbitration: Comments on Professor Barbara Kwiatkowska's Article' (2001) 16 *IJMCL* 361
'Compulsory Dispute Settlement after the Southern Bluefin Tuna Award' in Oude Elferink, Alex G. and Rothwell, Donald R. (eds.), *Oceans Management in the 21st Century: Institutional Frameworks and Responses* (2004) 255
Markell, David L., 'The Commission for Environmental Cooperation's Citizen Submission Process' (2000) 12 *GeoIELR* 545
'The CEC Citizen Submissions Process: On or Off Course?' in Markell, David L. and Knox, John H., (eds.), *Greening NAFTA: The North American Commission for Environmental Cooperation* (2003) 274
Marr, Simon, 'The Southern Bluefin Tuna Cases: The Precautionary Approach and Conservation and Management of Fish Resources' (2000) 11 *EJIL* 815
Matheson, Michael J. and Bickler, Sara, 'The Fifty-Fifth Session of the International Law Commission' (2004) 98 *AJIL* 317
Matsushita, Mitsuo, Schoenbaum, Thomas J., and Mavroidis, Petros C., *The World Trade Organization: Law, Practice and Policy* (2003)
McCaffrey, Stephen C., 'Water Scarcity: Institutional and Legal Responses' in Brans, Edward H.P. *et al.* (eds.), *The Scarcity of Water: Emerging Legal and Policy Responses* (1997) 52
'Water, Water Everywhere, But Too Few Drops to Drink: The Coming Freshwater Crisis and International Environmental Law' (2000) 28 *DenJILP* 325
The Law of International Watercourses: Non-Navigational Uses (2001) 435
McCallion, Kenneth F., 'International Environmental Justice: Rights and Remedies' (2002–3) 26 *HastingsICLR* 427
McCallion, Kenneth F. and Sharma, H. Rajan, 'Environmental Justice Without Borders: The Need for an International Court of the Environment To Protect Fundamental Human Rights' (2000) 32 *GeoWashJILEcon* 351
McCallum, R., 'Evaluating the Citizens Submissions Procedure Under the North American Agreement on Environmental Cooperation' (1997) 8 *ColoJELP* 395
McDonald, Jan, 'Look While you Leap: The WTO Biotech Dispute Panel Report' (2006) 23 *EPLJ* 417
McDorman, Ted L., 'Fisheries Conservation and Management and International Trade Law' in Hey, Ellen (ed.), *Developments in International Fisheries Law* (1999) 501

McDorman, Ted L., 'Global Ocean Governance and International Adjudicative Dispute Resolution' (2000) 43 *OCM* 255

'International Tribunal for the Law of the Sea' (2001) 12 *YIEL* 589

'Access to Information under Article 9 of the OSPAR Convention (Ireland v. United Kingdom' (2004) 98 *AJIL* 330

McIntyre, Owen and Mosedale, Thomas, 'The Precautionary Principle as a Norm of Customary International Law' (1997) 9 *JEL* 221

McLaughlin, Richard J., 'Settling Trade-Related Disputes Over the Protection of Marine Living Resources: UNCLOS or WTO?' (1997) 9 *GeoIELR* 29

McWhinney, Edward, 'International Law-Making and the Judicial Process: The World Court and the French Nuclear Tests Case' (1975) 3 *SyracuseJIL&Com* 9

Mensah, Chris, 'The United Nations Commission on Sustainable Development' in Werksman, Jacob (ed.), *Greening International Institutions* (1996) 21

Mensah, Thomas A., 'The International Legal Regime for the Protection and Preservation of the Marine Environment from Land-Based Sources of Pollution' in Boyle, Alan E. and Freestone, David (eds.), *International Law and Sustainable Development: Past Achievements and Future Challenges* (1999) 297

'The International Tribunal for the Law of the Sea and the Protection and Preservation of the Marine Environment' (1999) 8 *RECIEL* 1

Merrills, J. G., 'The Role and Limits of International Adjudication' (1987) 24 *Coexistence* 169

International Dispute Settlement (3rd edn 1998)

'The Mosaic of International Dispute Settlement Procedures: Complementary or Contradictory' (2007) 54 *NILR* 361

Mickelson, Karin, 'Rereading *Trail Smelter*' (1993) 31 *CanYBIL* 219

Miles, Edward L. *et al.* (eds.), *Environmental Regime Effectiveness: Confronting Theory With Evidence* (2002)

Millennium Ecosystem Assessment, *Ecosystems and Human Well-being: Synthesis* (2005)

Miller, C., 'The European Convention on Human Rights: Another Weapon in the Environmentalist's Armory' (1999) 11 *JEL* 157

Miller, Nathan, 'An International Jurisprudence? The Operation of "Precedent" Across International Tribunals' (2002) 15 *LJIL* 483

Mills, Alex and Stephens, Tim, 'Challenging the Role of Judges in Slaughter's Liberal Theory of International Law' (2005) 18 *LJIL* 1

Mitchell, Ronald B., 'Compliance Theory: An Overview' in Cameron, James, Werksman, Jacob, and Roderick, Peter (eds.), *Improving Compliance with International Environmental Law* (1996) 3

'International Environmental Agreements: A Survey of Their Features, Formation, and Effects' (2003) 28 *AnnRevEnvRes* 429

'Problem Structure, Institutional Design, and the Relative Effectiveness of International Environmental Agreements' (2006) 6 *GEP* 72

Molenaar, Erik J., 'Multilateral Hot Pursuit and Illegal Fishing in the Southern Ocean: the Pursuits of the *Viarsa 1* and the *South Tomi*' (2004) 19 *IJMCL* 19

Monbiot, George, *Heat: How to Stop the Planet Burning* (2006)

Montini, Massimiliano, 'Improving Compliance with Multilateral Environmental Agreements through Positive Measures: The Case of the Kyoto Protocol on Climate Change' in Kiss, Alexandre, Shelton, Dinah, and Ishibashi, Kanami (eds.), *Economic Globalization and Compliance with International Environmental Agreements* (2003) 157

Morgan, Donald L., 'Implications of the Proliferation of International Legal Fora: The Example of the *Southern Bluefin Tuna Cases*' (2002) 43 *HarvILJ* 541

Morgera, Elisa, 'An Update on the Aarhus Convention' (2005) 14(2) *RECIEL* 138

Mosler, Hermann, 'Judgments of International Courts and Tribunals' in Bernhardt, Rudolph (ed.), *Encyclopaedia of Public International Law*, vol. III (1992) 31

Murphy, Sean D., 'Does the World Need a New International Environmental Court?' (2000) 32 *GeoWashJILEcon* 333

Nelson, L. D. M., 'The Development of the Legal Regime of High Seas Fisheries' in Boyle, Alan E. and Freestone, David (eds.), *International Law and Sustainable Development: Past Achievements and Future Challenges* (1999) 113

Nicols, Phillip M., 'Extension of Standing in the World Trade Organization Disputes to Nongovernmental Parties' (1996) 17 *UPaJIEcon* 295

Nordström, Håkan and Vaughan, Scott, *Trade and Environment* (1999)

Notaro, Nicola, *Judicial Approaches to Trade and Environment: The EC and the WTO* (2003)

Noyes, John E., 'The International Tribunal for the Law of the Sea' (1998) 32 *CornellILJ* 109

Nygh, Pele E. and Davies, Martin, *Conflict of Laws in Australia* (7th edn 2002)

O'Connell, Mary Ellen, 'Enforcing the New International Law of the Environment' (1992) 35 *GerYBIL* 293

'Enforcement and the Success of International Environmental Law' (1995–6) 3 *IndJGLS* 47

Oda, Shigeru, 'Fisheries under the United Nations Convention on the Law of the Sea' (1983) 77 *AJIL* 739

International Control of Sea Resources (2nd edn 1988)

'The ICJ Viewed From the Bench' (1993) 244 *RDC* 139

'Dispute Settlement Prospects in the Law of the Sea' (1995) 44 *ICLQ* 863

Okowa, Phoebe N., 'Procedural Obligations in International Environmental Agreements' (1996) 67 *BYBIL* 275

'Environmental Dispute Settlement: Some Reflections on Recent Developments' in Evans, Malcolm D. (ed.), *Remedies in International Law: The Institutional Dilemma* (1998) 157

State Responsibility for Transboundary Air Pollution in International Law (2000)

Opeskin, Brian, 'The Price of Forum Shopping: A Reply to Juenger' (1994) 16 *SLR* 14

Orellana, Marcos A., 'The Swordfish Dispute between the EU and Chile at the ITLOS and the WTO' (2002) 71 *NordicJIL* 55

Oxman, Bernard H., 'Complementary Agreements and Compulsory Jurisdiction' (2001) 95 *AJIL* 277

Pallemaerts, Marc, 'International Environmental Law from Stockholm to Rio: Back to the Future' (1992) 1 *RECIEL* 254

Palmer, Geoffrey, 'New Ways to Make International Environmental Law' (1996) 86 *AJIL* 259

Panjabi, Ranee Khooshie Lal, 'From Stockholm to Rio: A Comparison of the Declaratory Principles of International Environmental Law' (1993) 21 *DenJILP* 215

Parrish, Austen L., '*Trail Smelter* Déjà Vu: Extraterritoriality, International Environmental Law, and the Search for Solutions to Canadian-US Transboundary Water Pollution Disputes' (2005) 85 *BULR* 363

Parson, Edward A., 'Protecting the Ozone Layer' in Haas, Peter M., Keohane, Robert O., and Levy, Marc A. (eds.), *Institutions for the Earth: Sources of Effective International Environmental Protection* (1993) 27

Paulson, Colter, 'Compliance with Final Judgments of the International Court of Justice Since 1987' (2004) 98 *AJIL* 434

Paulus, Andreas L., 'Dispute Resolution' in Ulfstein, Geir (ed.), *Making Treaties Work: Human Rights, Environment and Arms Control* (2007) 351

Pauwelyn, Joost, *Conflict of Norms in Public International Law* (2003)

'Recent Books on Trade and Environment: GATT Phantoms Still Haunt the WTO' (2004) 15 *EJIL* 575

Peel, Jacqueline, 'A Paper Umbrella Which Dissolves in the Rain? The Future for Resolving Fisheries Disputes Under UNCLOS in the Aftermath of the Southern Bluefin Tuna Arbitration' (2002) 3 *MJIL* 53

'Giving the Public a Voice in the Protection of the Global Environment: Avenues for Participation by NGOs in Dispute Resolution at the European Court of Justice and World Trade Organization' (2001) 12 *ColoJIELP* 47

'Precaution: A Matter of Principle, Approach or Process?' (2004) 5 *MJIL* 483

The Precautionary Principle in Practice: Environmental Decision-Making and Scientific Uncertainty (2005)

Peel, Jacqueline, Nelson, Rebecca, and Godden, Lee, 'GMO Trade Wars: The Submissions in the EC–GMO Dispute in the WTO' (2005) 6 *MJIL* 141

Perez, Oren, *Ecological Sensitivity and Global Legal Pluralism: Rethinking the Trade and Environment Conflict* (2004)

Picolotti, Romina and Bordenave, Sofia, 'The Enforcement of Environmental Law from a Human Rights Perspective' (2003) 3 *SDL&P* 11

Pinto, M. C. W., 'Judicial Settlement of International Disputes: One Forum or Many' in Anghie, Antony and Sturgess, Garry (eds.), *Legal Visions of the 21st Century: Essays in Honour of Judge Christopher Weeramantry* (1998) 465

Pitea, Cesare, 'NGOs in Non-Compliance Mechanisms under Multilateral Environmental Agreements: From Tolerance to Recognition?' in Treves,

Tullio *et al.* (eds.), *Civil Society, International Courts and Compliance Bodies* (2005) 205
Plant, Glen, 'The EC/Canadian Fisheries Dispute in the Northwest Atlantic' (1995) 44 *ICLQ* 927
Porras, Illeana, M., 'The Rio Declaration: A New Basis for International Cooperation' in Sands, Philippe (ed.), *Greening International Law* (1994) 20
Postiglione, Amedeo, 'A More Efficient International Law on the Environment and Setting Up an International Court for the Environment Within the United Nations' (1990) 20 *Environmental Law* 321
The Global Environmental Crisis: The Need for an International Court of the Environment (1996)
Preston, Brian J., 'Role of Public Interest Environmental Litigation' (2006) 23 *EPLJ* 337
Prince, Peter, 'Bhopal, Bougainville and Ok Tedi: Why Australia's *Forum non Conveniens* Approach is Better' (1998) 47 *ICLQ* 573
Prott, Lyndel V., 'Avoiding a Decision on the Merits in the International Court of Justice' (1976) 7 *SLR* 433
Qureshi, A. H., 'Extraterritorial Shrimps, NGOs and the WTO Appellate Body' (1999) 48 *ICLQ* 199
Ralston, John, *The Law and Procedure of International Tribunals* (1926)
Ranjeva, Raymond, 'Jurisdiction International Arbitrage: L'énvironnement, Le Court International de la Justice et sa Chamber spéciale pour les questions d'énvironnement' (1994) *XL AnnFDDI* 433
Rao, Pemmarajau S., 'Multiple International Judicial Forums: A Reflection of the Growing Strength of International Law or its Fragmentation?' (2004) 25 *MichJIL* 929
Ratliff, D. P., 'The PCA Optional Rules for Arbitration of Disputes Relating to Natural Resources and/or The Environment' (2001) 14 *LJIL* 887
Raustiala, Kal, 'The "Participatory Revolution" in International Environmental Law' (1997) 21 *HarvELR* 537
'Citizen Submissions and Treaty Review in the NAAEC' in Markell, David L. and Knox, John H. (eds.), *Greening NAFTA: The North American Commission for Environmental Cooperation* (2003) 256
Rayfuse, Rosemary, 'International Environmental Law' in Blay, Sam, Piotrowicz, Ryszard, and Tsamenyi, B. Martin (eds.), *Public International Law: An Australian Perspective* (1997) 355
'Canada and Regional Fisheries Organizations: Implementing the UN Fish Stocks Agreement' (2003) 34 *ODIL* 209
Read, John E., 'The Trail Smelter Dispute' (1963) 1 *CanYBIL* 213
Redgwell, Catherine, 'Environmental Protection in Antarctica: The 1991 Protocol' (1994) 43 *ICLQ* 599
'Life, the Universe and Everything: A Critique of Anthropocentric Rights' in Boyle, Alan E. and Anderson, Michael R. (eds.), *Human Rights Approaches to Environmental Protection* (1996) 72

Redgwell, Catherine, 'International Environmental Law' in Evans, Malcolm D. (ed.), *International Law* (2003) 657

Rehbinder, Eckard and Loperena, Demetrio, 'Legal Protection of Environmental Rights: The Role and Experience of the International Court of Environmental Arbitration and Conciliation' (2001) 31 *EPL* 282

Rest, Alfred, 'Need for an International Court for the Environment?' (1994) 24 *EPL* 173

'The Indispensability of an International Environmental Court' (1998) 7 *RECIEL* 63

'Enhanced Implementation of the Biological Diversity Convention by Judicial Control' (1999) 29 *EPL* 32

'An International Court for the Environment: The Role of the Permanent Court of Arbitration' (1999) 4 *APJEL* 107

Reus-Smit, Christian, 'The Politics of International Law' in Reus-Smit, Christian (ed.), *The Politics of International Law* (2004) 14

Rieu-Clarke, Alistair, *International Law and Sustainable Development: Lessons From the Law of International Watercourses* (2005)

Röben, Volker, 'The Order of the UNCLOS Annex VII Arbitral Tribunal to Suspend Proceedings in the Case of the MOX Plant at Sellafield: How Much Jurisdictional Subsidiarity?' (2004) 73 *NordicJIL* 223

Roch, Philippe and Perrez, Franz Xaver, 'International Environmental Governance: The Strive Towards a Comprehensive, Coherent, Effective and Efficient International Environmental Regime' (2005) 16 *ColoJIELP* 1

Romano, Cesare P.R., 'The Proliferation of International Judicial Bodies: The Pieces of the Puzzle' (1999) 31 *NYUJILP* 709

The Peaceful Settlement of International Environmental Disputes: A Pragmatic Approach (2000)

'The *Southern Bluefin Tuna* Dispute: Hints of a World to Come...Like it or Not' (2001) 32 *ODIL* 313

'International Justice and Developing Countries: A Quantitative Analysis' (2002) 1 *LPICT* 367

'Commission of the European Communities v. Ireland' (2007) 101 *AJIL* 171

'International Dispute Settlement' in Bodansky, Daniel, Brunnée, Jutta, and Hey, Ellen (eds.), *The Oxford Handbook of International Environmental Law* (2007) 1036

Rose, Gregory, 'A Compliance System for the Kyoto Protocol' (2001) 24 *UNSWLJ* 588

Rosenne, Shabtai, 'Some Reflections *Erga Omnes*' in Anghie, Antony and Sturgess, Garry (eds.), *Legal Visions of the 21st Century: Essays in Honour of Judge Christopher Weeramantry* (1998) 509

Rosenne, Shabtai and Sohn, L.B. (eds.), *United Nations Convention on the Law of the Sea: A Commentary*, vol. V (1989)

The Perplexities of Modern International Law (2004)

Provisional Measures in International Law: The International Court of Justice and the International Law of the Sea (2005)

Rothwell, Donald R., 'A Maritime Analysis of the Conflicting International Law Regimes in Antarctic and the Southern Ocean' (1994) 15 *AustYBIL* 155
The Polar Regions and the Development of International Law (1996)
'Reassessing International Environmental Dispute Resolution' (2001) 6 *APJEL* 201
'Oceans Management and the Law of the Sea in the Twenty-First Century' in Elferink, Alex G. and Rothwell, Donald R. (eds.), *Oceans Management in the 21st Century: Institutional Frameworks and Responses* (2004) 329
Rothwell, Donald R. and Stephens, Tim, 'Dispute Resolution and the Law of the Sea: Reconciling the Interaction Between the LOS Convention and Other Environmental Instruments' in Oude Elferink, Alex G. and Rothwell, Donald R. (eds.), *Oceans Management in the 21st Century: Institutional Frameworks and Responses* (2004) 209
'Illegal Southern Ocean Fishing and Prompt Release: Balancing Coastal and Flag State Rights and Interests' (2004) 53 *ICLQ* 171
Rubin, Alfred P., 'Pollution by Analogy: the Trail Smelter Arbitration' (1971) 50 *OrLR* 259
Sachariew, K., 'Promoting Compliance with International Environmental Standards: Reflections on Monitoring and Reporting Mechanisms' (1991) 2 *YIEL* 31
Saeijs, H. L. F. and van Berkel, M. V., 'The Global Water Crisis: The Major Issue of the 21st Century' in Brans, Edward H. P. *et al.* (eds.), *The Scarcity of Water: Emerging Legal and Policy Responses* (1997) 3
Sagoff, Mark, *The Economy of the Earth* (1988)
Sand, Peter H., *Transnational Environmental Law: Lessons in Global Change* (1999)
Sandholtz, Wayne and Stone Sweet, Alec, 'Law, Politics and International Governance' in Reus-Smit, Christian (ed.), *The Politics of International Law* (2004) 238
Sands, Philippe, *Chernobyl: Law and Communication* (1988)
'The Environment, Community and International Law' (1989) 30 *HarvILJ* 393
'International Law in the Field of Sustainable Development: Emerging Legal Principles' in Lang, Winfried (ed.), *Sustainable Development and International Law* (1995) 53
'The International Court of Justice and the European Court of Justice' in Werksman, Jacob (ed.), *Greening International Institutions* (1996)
'International Environmental Litigation: What Future?' (1998) 7 *RECIEL* 1
'Pleadings and the Pursuit of International Law: Nuclear Tests II (*New Zealand v. France*)' in Anghie, Antony and Sturgess, Garry (eds.), *Legal Visions of the 21st Century: Essays in Honour of Judge Christopher Weeramantry* (1998) 601
'Treaty, Custom and the Cross-Fertilization of International Law' (1998) 10 *YaleHR&DevLJ* 3
'International Courts and the Application of the Concept of "Sustainable Development"' (1999) 3 *MaxPlanckYBUNL* 404
'International Environmental Litigation and its Future' (1999) 32 *URichLR* 1619

Sands, Philippe, 'Turtles and Torturers: The Transformation of International Law' (2000) 33 *NYUJILP* 527

'"Unilateralism", Values and International Law' (2000) 11 *EJIL* 291

'International Courts and the Application of the Concept of 'Sustainable Development' in Hatchard, John and Perry-Kessaris, Amanda (eds.), *Law and Development: Facing Complexity in the 21st Century* (2003) 147

Lawless World (2005)

Principles of International Environmental Law (2nd edn 2003).

Sands, Philippe (ed.), *Greening International Law* (1994)

Sands, Philippe and Mackenzie, Ruth, 'Guidelines for Negotiating and Drafting Dispute Settlement Clauses for International Environmental Agreements' in International Bureau of the Permanent Court of Arbitration (ed.), *International Investments and Protection of the Environment* (2001) 305

Sands, Philippe, Mackenzie, Ruth and Shany, Yuval, *Manual on International Courts and Tribunals* (1999)

Sax, Joseph L., *Defending the Environment: A Handbook for Citizen Action* (1970)

Schachter, Oscar, 'The Enforcement of International Judicial and Arbitral Decisions' (1960) 54 *AJIL* 1

Schaefer, Andrew, 'Canada-Spain Fishing Dispute (The Turbot War)' (1996–7) 8 *GeoIELR* 437

Schiffman, H. S., 'UNCLOS and Marine Wildlife Disputes: Big Splash or Barely a Ripple?' (2001) 4 *JIWLP* 257

Schmitt, Michael N., 'Humanitarian Law and the Environment' (2002) 28 *DenJILP* 265

Schwebel, Stephen M., 'Ad Hoc Chambers of the International Court of Justice' (1987) 81 *AJIL* 831

'Address to the Plenary Session of the General Assembly of the United Nations' (speech delivered to the General Assembly of the United Nations, New York, 26 October 1999) (available at www.icj-cij.org/icjwww/ipresscom/SPEECHES/iSpeechPresidentGA54_19991026.htm)

'The Judgment of the International Court of Justice in the *Case Concerning the Gabčíkovo-Nagymoros Project (Hungary/Slovakia)*' in International Bureau of the Permanent Court of Arbitration (ed.), *Resolution of International Water Disputes* (2003) 247

Scobbie, Iain, '*Res Judicata*, Precedent and the International Court: A Preliminary Sketch' (1999) 20 *AustYBIL* 299

Scott, Shirley V., 'The Contribution of the LOS Convention's Organisations to its Harmonious Implementation' in Oude Elferink, Alex G. and Rothwell, Donald R. (eds.), *Oceans Management in the 21st Century: Institutional Frameworks and Responses* (2004) 313

Scovazzi, Tullio, 'State Responsibility for Environmental Harm' (2001) 12 *YIEL* 43

Segger, Marie-Claire Cordonier and Gehring, Markus W., 'The WTO and Precaution: Sustainable Development Implications of the WTO Asbestos Dispute' (2003) 15 *JEL* 289

Serdy, Andrew, 'See You in Port: Australia and New Zealand as Third Parties in the Dispute Between Chile and the European Community Over Chile's Denial of Port Access to Spanish Vessels Fishing for Swordfish on the High Seas' (2002) 3 *MJIL* 79

Serdy, Andrew and Bliss, Michael, 'Prompt Release of Fishing Vessels: State Practice in the Light of the Cases Before the International Tribunal for the Law of the Sea' in Oude Elferink, Alex G. and Rothwell, Donald R. (eds.), *Oceans Management in the 21st Century: Institutional Frameworks and Responses* (2004) 273

Shahabuddeen, Mohamed, *Precedent in the World Court* (1996)

Shamsey, John, 'ITLOS vs Goliath: The International Tribunal for the Law of the Sea Stands Tall with the Appellate Body in the Chilean-EU Swordfish Dispute' (2002) 12 *TransL&CP* 513

Shany, Yuval, *The Competing Jurisdictions of International Courts and Tribunals* (2003)

'The First *MOX Plant* Award: The Need to Harmonize Competing Environmental Regimes and Dispute Settlement Procedures' (2004) 17 *LJIL* 815

Shapiro, Martin and Stone Sweet, Alec, *On Law, Politics and Judicialization* (2002)

Sharp, Peter, 'Prospects for Environmental Liability in the International Criminal Court' (1999) 18 *VaELJ* 217

Shaw, Malcolm, *International Law* (5th edn 2003)

Shearer, I. A., *Starke's International Law* (11th edn 1994)

Shearer, Ivan, 'Oceans Management Challenges for the Law of the Sea in the First Decade of the 21st Century' in Oude Elferink, Alex G. and Rothwell, Donald R. (eds.), *Oceans Management in the 21st Century: Institutional Frameworks and Responses* (2004) 1

Shelton, Dinah, 'What Happened in Rio to Human Rights' (1992) *YIEL* 75

'The Participation of Non-Governmental Organizations in International Judicial Proceedings' (1994) 88 *AJIL* 611

'Legal Norms to Promote the Independence and Accountability of International Tribunals' (2003) 2 *LPICT* 27

'The Environmental Jurisprudence of International Human Rights Tribunals' in Picolotti, Romina and Taillant, Jorge Daniel (eds.), *Linking Human Rights and the Environment* (2003) 1

Remedies in International Human Rights Law (2nd edn 2005)

Shihata, I., *The Power of the International Court to Determine Its Own Jurisdiction: Compétence de la Compétence* (1965)

Shulte, Constanze, *Compliance with Decisions of the International Court of Justice* (2004)

Simma, Bruno, 'Self-Contained Regimes' (1985) 16 *NethYBIL* 111

'Counter-Measures and Dispute Settlement: A Plea for a Different Balance' (1994) 5 *EJIL* 102

'The Work of the International Law Commission at Its Fifty-Third Session' (2002) 71 *NordicJIL* 123

Simmons, Beth A., 'Compliance with International Agreements' in Ku, Charlotte and Diehl, Paul F. (eds.), *International Law: Classic and Contemporary Readings* (2003) 181

Skeen, Richard, 'Will the WTO Turn Green? The Implications of Injecting Environmental Issues into the Multilateral Trading System' (2004) 17 *GeoIELR* 161

Slaughter, Anne-Marie, 'International Law and International Relations Theory: A Dual Agenda' (1993) 87 *AJIL* 205

'International Law in a World of Liberal States' (1995) 6 *EJIL* 503

A New World Order (2004)

Sohn, Louis B., 'The Stockholm Declaration on the Human Environment' (1973) 14 *HarvILJ* 423

Somsen, Han, 'The Private Enforcement of Member State Compliance with EC Environmental Law: An Unfulfilled Promise?' (2000) 1 *YBEuroEL* 311

Spiro, Peter J., 'Non-Governmental Organisations' in Bodansky, Daniel, Brunnée, Jutta, and Hey, Ellen (eds.), *The Oxford Handbook of International Environmental Law* (2007) 771

Starr, J., 'Water Wars' (1991) 82 *Foreign Policy* 17

Stec, Stephen and Eckstein, Gabriel E., 'Of Solemn Oaths and Obligations: The Environmental Impact of the ICJ's Decision in the *Case Concerning the Gabcikovo-Nagymaros Project*' (1997) 8 *YIEL* 41

Stein, Paul L., 'A Specialist Environmental Court: An Australian Experience' in Robinson, David and Dunkley, John (eds.), *Public Interest Perspectives in Environmental Law* (1995) 256

'The Role of the New South Wales Land and Environment Court in the Emergence of Public Interest Environmental Law' (1996) 13 *EPLJ* 179

'Judges Active in Promoting Environmental Law Capacity Building' (2003) 33 *EPL* 56

Stephens, Tim, 'A Paper Umbrella Which Dissolves in the Rain? Implications of the *Southern Bluefin Tuna Case* for the Compulsory Resolution of Disputes Concerning the Marine Environment Under the 1982 LOS Convention' (2001) 6 *APJEL* 297

'Enforcing Australian Fisheries Laws: Testing the Limits of Hot Pursuit in Domestic and International Law: The Pursuits of the *Viarsa 1* and the *South Tomi*' (2004) 15 *PLR* 12

'International Criminal Law and the Response to International Terrorism' (2004) 27 *UNSWLJ* 454

'The Limits of International Adjudication in International Environmental Law: Another Perspective on the Southern Bluefin Tuna Case' (2004) 19 *IJMCL* 173

Stephens, Tim and Boer, Ben, 'Enforcement and Compliance in the Australian Antarctic Territory: Legal and Policy Dilemmas' in Kriwoken, Lorne K., Jabour, Julia, and Hemmings, Alan D., (eds.), *Looking South: Australia's Antarctic Agenda* (2007) 54

Stephens, Tim and Rothwell, Donald R., 'The 'Volga' Case (Russian Federation v. Australia)' (2004) 35 *JMLC* 283

Stern, Nicholas, *The Economics of Climate Change: The Stern Review* (2007)

Stone, Christopher D., 'Defending the Global Commons' in Sands, Philippe (ed.), *Greening International Law* (1994) 34

Stone, Christopher D., *Should Trees Have Standing? And Other Essays on Law, Morals, and the Environment* (1996)

Stone, Julius, 'Non Liquet and the Function of Law in the International Community' (1959) 35 *BYBIL* 124

Stone Sweet, Alec, 'Judicialization and the Construction of Governance' (1999) 32 *ComPPolStud* 147

Stone Sweet, Alec and Gehring, Markus, 'Environmental Protection' in Alec Stone Sweet, *The Judicial Construction of Europe* (2004) 199

Sturtz, Leah, '*Southern Bluefin Tuna Case*: Australia and New Zealand v. Japan' (2001) 28 *ELQ* 455

Sunstein, Cass R., 'Of Montreal and Kyoto: A Tale of Two Protocols' (2007) 31 *HarvELR* 1

Sureda, Andrés Rigo, 'Process Integrity and Institutional Independence in International Organisations: The Inspection Panel and the Sanctions Committee of the World Bank' in Boisson de Chazournes, Laurence, Romano, Cesare P.R., and Mackenzie, Ruth (eds.), *International Organisations and International Dispute Settlement: Trends and Prospects* (2002) 165

Sydnes, Are K., 'Establishing a Reginal Fisheries Management Organisation for the Western and Central Pacific Tuna Fisheries' (2001) 44 *OCM* 787

Széll, Patrick, 'The Development of Multilateral Mechanisms for Monitoring Compliance' in Lang, Winfried (ed.), *Sustainable Development and International Law* (1995) 97

Tams, Christian J., 'Enforcement' in Ulfstein, Geir (ed.), *Making Treaties Work: Human Rights, Environment and Arms Control* (2007) 391

Tan, Alan Khee-Jin, 'Forest Fires or Indonesia: State Responsibility and International Liability' (1999) 48 *ICLQ* 826

Tanaka, Maki, 'Bridging the Gap Between Northern NGOs and Southern Sovereigns in the Trade-Environment Debate: The Pursuit of Democratic Dispute Settlements in the WTO Under the Rio Principles' (2003) 30 *ELQ* 113

Tanaka, Yoshifumi, 'Prompt Release in the United Nations Convention on the Law of the Sea: Some Reflections on the ITLOS Jurisprudence' (2004) 51 *NILR* 237

Tansley, Arthur G., 'The Use and Abuse of Vegetational Concepts and Terms' (1935) 16 *Ecology* 284

Tanzi, Attila and Pitea, Cesare, 'Emerging Trends in the Role of Non-State Actors in International Water Disputes' in International Bureau of the Permanent Court of Arbitration (ed.), *Resolution of International Water Disputes* (2003) 259

Teck Cominco Metals Ltd, *Living Summary: Trail Ecological Risk Assessment* (2004) (available at www.teckcominco.com/articles/tr-ecorisk/eranews/2004-09-living.pdf)

Thacher, Peter S., 'The Role of the United Nations' in Hurrell, Andrew and Kingsbury, Benedict (eds.), *The International Politics of the Environment* (1991) 183

Thirlway, Hugh, 'The Indication of Provisional Measures by the International Court of Justice' in Bernhardt, R. (ed.), *Interim Measures Indicated by International Courts* (1994) 1

Tienhaara, Kyla, 'Third Party Participation in Investment-Environment Disputes: Recent Developments' (2007) 16 *RECIEL* 230

Timoshenko, Alexandre S., 'From Stockholm to Rio: The Institutionalisation of Sustainable Development' in Lang, Winfried (ed.), *Sustainable Development and International Law* (1995) 143

Tod, M. N., *International Arbitration Amongst the Greeks* (1913)

Tomasevich, Jozo, *International Agreements on Conservation of Marine Resources* [1943] (1971)

Torrens, Diana L., '*Locus Standi* for Environmental Associations under EC Law – *Greenpeace* – A Missed Opportunity for the ECJ' (1999) 8 *RECIEL* 336

Treves, Tullio, 'Compulsory Settlement of Disputes: A New Element in the Antarctic System' in Francioni, Francesco and Treves, Tullio (eds.), *International Law for Antarctica* (1996) 603

'Conflicts Between the International Tribunal for the Law of the Sea and the International Court of Justice' (1999) 31 *NYUJILP* 809

'Dispute Settlement Clauses in the Law of the Sea Convention and their Impact on the Protection of the Marine Environment: Some Observations' (1999) 8 *RECIEL* 6

'The Settlement of Disputes According to the Straddling Stocks Agreement of 1995' in Boyle, Alan E. and Freestone, David (eds.), *International Law and Sustainable Development: Past Achievements and Future Challenges* (1999) 253

Le Controversie Internazionali. Nuovi Tendenze, Nuovi Tribunali (1999)

'The Role of Dispute Settlement Mechanisms in the Protection of the Marine Environment in Cases Concerning Economic Activities in the Sea and Seabed' in International Bureau of the Permanent Court of Arbitration (ed.), *International Investments and Protection of the Environment* (2001) 113

'Introduction' in Treves, Tullio *et al.* (eds.), *Civil Society, International Courts and Compliance Bodies* (2005) 1

Triggs, Gillian, 'World Trade Organization: Dispute Resolution and the Environment' (2002) 7 *APJEL* 43

'Implementation of the Rome Statute for the International Criminal Court: A Quiet Revolution in Australian Law' (2003) 25 *SLR* 507

Trouwborst, Arie, 'The Precautionary Principle in General International Law: Combating the Babylonian Confusion' (2007) 16 *RECIEL* 185

Tunkin, Grigorii I., *Theory of International Law* (1974)

Ulfstein, Geir, 'Dispute Resolution, Compliance Control and Enforcement in International Environmental Law' in Ulfstein, Geir (ed.), *Making Treaties Work: Human Rights, Environment and Arms Control* (2007) 115

Umbricht, Georg C., 'An "Amicus Curiae Brief" on Amicus Curiae Briefs at the WTO' (2001) *JIEconL* 773

Unger, R., 'Brandishing the Precautionary Principle Through the Alien Torts Claim Act' (2001) 9 *NYUELJ* 638

United Nations Environment Programme, *Global Environment Outlook 3* (2002)

United Nations Food and Agriculture Organisation, *The State of the World Fisheries and Aquaculture* (2006)

Van Alstyne, W. W., 'The Justiciability of International River Disputes: A Study in the Case Method' [1964] *DukeLJ* 307

van der Mei, Anne Pieter, 'The New African Court on Human and Peoples' Rights: Toward an Effective Human Rights Protection Mechanism for Africa?' (2005) 18 *LJIL* 113

van Woudenberg, Nout, 'Compliance Mechanisms: A Useful Instrument' (2004) 34 *EPL* 185

VanderZwaag, David, 'The Precautionary Principle and Marine Environmental Protection: Slippery Shores, Rough Seas, and Rising Normative Tides' (2002) 33 *ODIL* 165

Varuhas, Jason N. E., 'One Person Can Make a Difference: An Individual Petition System for International Environmental Law' (2005) 3 *NZJPIL* 329

Verheyen, Roda, *Climate Change Damage and International Law: Prevention Duties and State Responsibility* (2005)

Vespa, M., 'An Alternative to an International Environmental Court? The PCA's Optional Arbitration Rules for Natural Resources and/or the Environment' (2003) 2 *LPICT* 295

Victor, David G., 'Toward Effective International Cooperation on Climate Change: Numbers, Interests and Institutions' (2006) 6 *GEP* 90

Victor, David G., House, Joshua C., and Joy, Sarah, 'A Madisonian Approach to Climate Policy' (2005) 309 *Science* 1820

Victor, David G., Raustiala, Kal, and Skolnikoff, Eugene B. (eds.), *The Implementation and Effectiveness of International Environmental Commitments: Theory and Practice* (1998)

Vicuña, Francisco Orrego, *The Changing International Law of High Seas Fisheries* (1999)

'The International Law of High Seas Fisheries: From Freedom of Fishing to Sustainable Use' in Stokke, Olav Schram (ed.), *Governing High Seas Fisheries: The Interplay of Global and Regional Regimes* (2001) 23

International Dispute Settlement in an Evolving Global Society (2004)

Vigni, Patrizia, 'The Overlapping of Dispute Settlement Regimes: An Emerging Issue of International Law' (2001) XI *ItalYBIL* 139

Visek, Richard C., 'Implementation and Enforcement of EC Environmental Law' (1995) 7 *GeoIELR* 377

Voeffray, François, *L'actio popularis, ou la défense de l'intérêt collectif devant les jurisdictions internationals* (2004)

Wates, Jeremy, 'NGOs and the Aarhus Convention' in Treves, Tullio *et al.* (eds.), *Civil Society, International Courts and Compliance Bodies* (2005) 167

Webb, Philippa, 'The Inconvenience of Liability: The Doctrine of *Forum Non Conveniens* in International Environmental Litigation' (2001) 6 *APJEL* 377

Wellens, Karel C., 'Diversity in Secondary Rules and the Unity of International Law: Some Reflections on Current Trends' in Barnhoorn, L. A. N. M. and Wellens, K. C. (eds.), *Diversity in Secondary Rules and the Unity of International Law* (1995) 3

Werksman, Jacob, 'Designing a Compliance System for the UN Framework Convention on Climate Change' in Cameron, James, Werksman, Jacob, and Roderick, Peter (eds.), *Improving Compliance with International Environmental Law* (1996) 86

Greening International Institutions (1996)

Wettestad, Jørgen, 'The Vienna Convention and the Montreal Protocol on Ozone-Layer Depletion' in Miles, L. Edward *et al.* (eds.), *Environmental Regime Effectiveness: Confronting Theory with Evidence* (2002)

Williams, P., 'International Environmental Dispute Resolution: The Dispute Between Slovakia and Hungary Concerning Construction of the Gabcikovo and Nagymaros Dams' (1994) 19 *ColumJEL* 1

Williams, Paul R., *International Law and the Resolution of Central and East Asian Tranboundary Environmental Disputes* (2000)

Williams, R., 'The European Commission and the Enforcement of Environmental Law: An Invidious Position' (1995) 14 *YBEuroL* 351

Williams, William, 'Reminiscences of the Bering Sea Arbitration' (1943) 37 *AJIL* 562

Winickoff, David, Jasanoff, Sheila, Busch, Lawerence, Grove-White, Robin, and Wynne, Brian, 'Adjudicating the GM Food Wars: Science, Risk, and Democracy in World Trade Law' (2005) 30 *YaleJIL* 81

Wirth, David A., 'Reexamining Decision Making Processes in International Environmental Law' (1994) 79 *IowaLR* 769

'The Rio Declaration on Environment and Development: Two Steps Forward and One Back or Vice Versa?' (1995) 29 *GaLR* 599

Wirth, John D., *Smelter Smoke in North America: The Politics of Transborder Pollution* (2000)

Wolfrum, Rüdiger, 'Means of Ensuring Compliance with and Enforcement of International Environmental Law' (1998) 272 *RDC* 9

'The Role of the International Tribunal for the Law of the Sea' in Nordquist, Myron H. and Moore, John N. (eds.), *Current Fisheries Issues and the Food and Agriculture Organization of the United Nations* (2000) 369

Wolfrum, Rüdiger and Matz, Nele, *Conflicts in International Environmental Law* (2003)

World Commission on Dams, *Dams and Development: A New Framework for Decision-Making* (2000)

World Commission on Environment and Development, *Our Common Future* (1987)

Wu, C. Q., 'A Unified Forum? The New Arbitration Rules for Environmental Disputes Under the Permanent Court of Arbitration' (2002) 3 *ChicJIL* 263

Yamin, Farhana, 'NGOs and International Environmental Law: A Critical Evaluation of their Roles and Responsibilities' (2001) 10 *RECIEL* 149

Yankov, Alexander, 'The Law of the Sea Convention and Agenda 21: Marine Environmental Implications' in Boyle, Alan E. and Freestone, David (eds.), *International Law and Sustainable Development: Past Achievements and Future Challenges* (1999) 27

Young, Oran R., *International Governance: Protecting the Environment in a Stateless Society* (1994)

The Institutional Dimensions of Environmental Change: Fit, Interplay, and Scale (2002)

Young, Oran R. (ed.), *The Effectiveness of International Environmental Regimes* (1999)

Index

Note: Names of cases appear in the index, in the form in which they are commonly referred to in the text, to denote detailed analysis or illumination of a significant legal issue. For full citations and a complete list of references refer to the table of cases.

CAMBRIDGE STUDIES IN INTERNATIONAL AND COMPARATIVE LAW

Books in the series

International Courts and Environmental Protection
Tim Stephens

Legal Principles in WTO Disputes
Andrew D. Mitchell

War Crimes in Internal Armed Conflicts
Eve La Haye

Humanitarian Occupation
Gregory H. Fox

The International Law of Environmental Impact Assessment: Process, Substance and Integration
Neil Craik

The Law and Practice of International Territorial Administration: Versailles, Iraq and Beyond
Carsten Stahn

Cultural Products and the World Trade Organization
Tania Voon

United Nations Sanctions and the Rule of Law
Jeremy Farrall

National Law in WTO Law: Effectiveness and Good Governance in the World Trading System
Sharif Bhuiyan

The Threat of Force in International Law
Nikolas Stürchler

Indigenous Rights and United Nations Standards
Alexandra Xanthaki

International Refugee Law and Socio-Economic Rights
Michelle Foster

The Protection of Cultural Property in Armed Conflict
Roger O'Keefe

Interpretation and Revision of International Boundary Decisions
Kaiyan Homi Kaikobad

Multinationals and Corporate Social Responsibility: Limitations and Opportunities in International Law
Jennifer A. Zerk

Judiciaries within Europe: A Comparative Review
John Bell

Law in Times of Crisis: Emergency Powers in Theory and Practice
Oren Gross and Fionnuala Ní Aoláin

Vessel-Source Marine Pollution: The Law and Politics of International Regulation
Alan Tan

Enforcing Obligations Erga Omnes in International Law:
Christian J. Tams

Non-Governmental Organisations in International Law
Anna-Karin Lindblom

Democracy, Minorities and International Law
Steven Wheatley

Prosecuting International Crimes: Selectivity and the International Law Regime
Robert Cryer

Compensation for Personal Injury in English, German and Italian Law: A Comparative Outline
Basil Markesinis, Michael Coester, Guido Alpa, Augustus Ullstein

Dispute Settlement in the UN Convention on the Law of the Sea
Natalie Klein

The International Protection of Internally Displaced Persons
Catherine Phuong

Imperialism, Sovereignty and the Making of International Law
Antony Anghie

Necessity, Proportionality and the Use of Force by States
Judith Gardam

International Legal Argument in the Permanent Court of International Justice: The Rise of the International Judiciary
Ole Spiermann

Great Powers and Outlaw States: Unequal Sovereigns in the International Legal Order
Gerry Simpson

Local Remedies in International Law
C. F. Amerasinghe

Reading Humanitarian Intervention: Human Rights and the Use of Force in International Law
Anne Orford

Conflict of Norms in Public International Law: How WTO Law Relates to Other Rules of Law
Joost Pauwelyn

Transboundary Damage in International Law
Hanqin Xue

European Criminal Procedures
Edited by Mireille Delmas-Marty and John Spencer

The Accountability of Armed Opposition Groups in International Law
Liesbeth Zegveld

Sharing Transboundary Resources: International Law and Optimal Resource Use
Eyal Benvenisti

International Human Rights and Humanitarian Law
René Provost

Remedies Against International Organisations
Karel Wellens

Diversity and Self-Determination in International Law
Karen Knop

The Law of Internal Armed Conflict
Lindsay Moir

International Commercial Arbitration and African States: Practice, Participation and Institutional Development
Amazu A. Asouzu

The Enforceability of Promises in European Contract Law
James Gordley

International Law in Antiquity
David J. Bederman

Money Laundering: A New International Law Enforcement Model
Guy Stessens

Good Faith in European Contract Law
Reinhard Zimmermann and Simon Whittaker

On Civil Procedure
J. A. Jolowicz

Trusts: A Comparative Study
Maurizio Lupoi

The Right to Property in Commonwealth Constitutions
Tom Allen

International Organizations Before National Courts
August Reinisch

The Changing International Law of High Seas Fisheries
Francisco Orrego Vicuña

Trade and the Environment: A Comparative Study of EC and US Law
Damien Geradin

Unjust Enrichment: A Study of Private Law and Public Values
Hanoch Dagan

Religious Liberty and International Law in Europe
Malcolm D. Evans

Ethics and Authority in International Law
Alfred P. Rubin

Sovereignty Over Natural Resources: Balancing Rights and Duties
Nico Schrijver

The Polar Regions and the Development of International Law
Donald R. Rothwell

Fragmentation and the International Relations of Micro-States: Self-determination and Statehood
Jorri Duursma

Principles of the Institutional Law of International Organizations
C. F. Amerasinghe